ORPHANS (The Aborted Ones)

...confront Jerusalem with her detestable practices:
...You were thrown out into the open field,
for on the day you were born you were despised.

Then I passed by and saw you kicking about in your blood,
and as you lay there in your blood
I said to you, "Live!"

But... you took your sons and daughters...
My children, and sacrificed them to the idols.

Ezekiel 16:1-6, 20-21.

BABYLON (The U.S.A.)

Fallen is Babylon the Great!
She has become a home for demons and a haunt for every evil spirit...
For all the nations have drunk the maddening wine of her adulteries...

Come out of her, my people, so that you will not share in her sins,
so that you will not receive any of her plagues;
for her sins are piled up to heaven, and God has remembered her crimes...

In her heart she boasts,
"I sit as queen; I am not a widow, and I will never mourn."
Therefore in one day her plagues will overtake her: death, mourning and famine.
She will be consumed by fire, for mighty is the Lord God who judges her:

"By your magic spell all the nations were led astray.
In you was found the blood of prophets and of the saints,
and of all who have been killed on the earth."

Revelation 18:2-5, 7-8, 23-24.

Take a "Sampler" approach to Previewing *Orphans in Babylon*

First, check out all pages and sections listed. Then go back to investigate more deeply the parts that spark your interest.

Index "Outline" (the last page)

The Nazi Holocaust, Parallel to Abortion (Title page, bottom)

This Book's "Thesis in One Page" (before Contents pages)

292. Timeline. Events and Developments from 1500 AD until Now

302. Twenty-One Bible Themes (364 Bible references)

82. The Biblical Case Against Abortion

39. Abortion Pretexts Touted by Pro-choicers

98-99. Biblical Prophets

102-106. Religious Zeal

114. World Precedents for Godly Obedience

138. The Abolition of Slavery

158. The Seeds of Moral Destruction

166. Pivotal Developments in the USA

187. Abortive Links

239-242. Legislation and Law Enforcement

269-275. Problems after Abortion is Prohibited

277. Victory as Defined by Various Prolifers

ORPHANS in BABYLON

Abortion in America.

Where are we now?

How did we get here?

Where should we be?

How can we get there?

Sixty years after the Nazi Era, we still ask,
"What were German Christians
***thinking* and *doing* during Hitler's Holocaust?"**

For the benefit of our great-grandchildren,
this book is intended to help answer the same questions
about the **Era of the American Abortion Holocaust**.
My goal is to leave a **lasting record**, giving voice
to every branch of the Prolife Movement, without censorship.
Faithful reporting should not be mistaken for endorsement.

Roger Domingo
Researcher, Author, Publisher
OrphBaby.Wixsite.com/book

Turnstyle Ministries
1511 West 100 South
Portland, Indiana 47371

ORPHANS IN BABYLON

Version 1.0

ISBN Number
0-9668541-0-1
Library of Congress Catalog Card Number
98-94109

*Special Thanks to Super-wife June Domingo,
editorial assistant Dave Domingo,
Omega Print of Temecula, California
and Whitehall Printing of Naples, Florida.*

The ORPHANS IN BABYLON THESIS in ONE PAGE

Part 1
The CONFLICT
CLASH OF CONVICTIONS

Abortion is anathema to God, dwarfing all other evils of our age. The Christian Church, long fragmented by prideful divisions has now become radically polarized into foreign camps. "Christians" who champion secular belief in accidental evolution, a good and perfectible human nature, the Bible as just a helpful resource, and preborn babies as disposable life are nothing less than enemies of all disciples of Christ who believe in a purposeful creation, sinful but redeemable human nature, the Bible as the authoritative Word of God, and preborn children as human persons created in the image of God.

Part 2
The PRETEXTS
ALLEGATIONS OF EXPENDABILITY

The vast majority of the nations of the world have embraced abortion, while the United States government has gone to bed with her. The substantial body of domestic and International Human Rights law – if applied to the preborn – would prohibit all but a fraction of one percent of current abortions, but most countries choose to ignore that truth.

The President of the United States twice vetoed the bill which would have outlawed partial birth abortions. Clinton's reelection landslide confirmed that the majority of those who vote do not object to sucking the brains out of a child on the day that should mark her birth. Prolife Christians are a minority in the U.S.A.

Part 3
Our MANDATE
SEEKING BIBLICAL GUIDANCE

Biblical discipleship concerns justice, obedience, discipline, holiness, risk, confrontation, and sanctification. Only repentant revival can reconcile the Bride to her Groom, and only they, together, can effectively stand against abortion and the idolatries which spawn it.

Part 4
The LEGACY
A HISTORY OF DEFINITIVE BATTLES

The Church has much to learn from the conquest of the Promised Land, Jesus' instructions to His disciples, the valor of the early Church, America's founding fathers, the abolition movement and Civil War, social crusades, the holocaust, civil rights, International Human Rights, apartheid and amnesty, and other relevant history.

Part 5
The DEATH WISH
LINKS IN THE ABORTIVE CHAIN

Recriminalization of the abortionists' trade would not solve the problem. The abortion holocaust is the result of a series of disasters: recreational sex, reproductive technology, the abortion industry, governmental action, social climate, religious confusion, and the personal will to abort. The pro-life movement must attack each link in the abortive chain simultaneously.

Part 6
The DILEMMA
STATE OF THE PRO-LIFE MOVEMENT

Beyond the horrific magnitude of the abortion holocaust, the Church's preoccupation with the trivial and its neglect of the cosmic is an even greater sacrilege. If America's *Constitution* miraculously gained a prolife amendment, and if the international community unanimously ratified a prolife convention, and if both were effectively implemented, the heavenly alleluias would be muffled by the fact that the Church neither championed nor publicly assented to either one.

Too often the Church and the prolife movement have slid backward – allowing concern over image to compromise witness, preoccupation with strategy to eclipse the leading of the Holy Spirit, and zeal for results to quench revival.

Part 7
Our DESTINY
FUTURE COURSE OF ACTION

Only valiant shepherds can stand as worthy watchmen and faithful lighthouse-keepers, under God. Local congregations need definitive labels. Penitent Christians must become bold witnesses against child-killing, and stand as citizens on-record for life.

This work proposes the promulgation of three simple tools – a proclamation, a declaration, and a banner – which could become as historically significant as the five smooth stones David held in the shadow of Goliath.

OUTLINE of CONTENTS

Orphaned by Choice 1

I. Clash of Convictions: Culture Wars in the U.S.A. Today 2

A. Polarizing Certainties in American Society 5
1. Creation vs. Accident 6
2. Design [for life] vs. Mechanism [spontaneous generation] 7
3. Commandments vs. Positivism 9
4. Justice vs. Pragmatism 12
5. Virtue vs. Pleasure 14
6. Universalism vs. Relativism 16
7. Accountability vs. Autonomy 18

B. World View Complicity in Polarizing Assumptions 21
1. Deism 22
2. Naturalism 23
3. Nihilism 24
4. Existentialism 25
5. Postmodernism 26
6. Eastern Pantheistic Monism 27
7. New Age 28
8. "Humanism" 29

C. Human Condition Convictions 31
1. Fallen & Sinful vs. Naturally Good 32
2. Redeemable vs. Perfectible 33
3. Sanctity of the Preborn vs. Potentiality 34
4. Right-to-Life of the Preborn vs. Expendability 35

D. Stewards vs. Masters: Our Polarized Culture 36

II. The Abortion Pretexts: Allegations of Expendability 39

A. Autonomy of the Mother 41
1. Fundamental Right of the Mother to Abort 41
2. Privacy of the Mother 43
3. Equality for Women Requires Freedom of Choice to Abort 44
4. Tolerance & Multiculturalism Support Freedom of Choice 46
5. Free Abortions are Every Woman's Right 49

B. Relativism and the Worth of the Preborn 50
1. Personhood of the Preborn Denied 51
2. Humanity of the Preborn Challenged 53

C. Mechanism, Gradualism: An Emerging Right to Life 57

D. Pleasure / Pain: 63
1. Personal Tragedy can be Diminished by Abortion 63
2. Burden Bearing should not be Required of a Woman 65
3. Anonymous Fetuses seem much different from Born Babies 65

E. Accident Justifies Abortion as a Remedy 66
1. Birth Control was used but it Failed 66
2. Incapacitated Woman (drunk / naive / retarded / in a coma) 66

F. Pragmatism and the Fate of the Unborn 66
1. Self Defense against a Tiny Attacker 66
2. Political Expediency 69
3. Social Benefits 74

G. Positivism & the Abortion Problem 77
1. The Politics of an Abortion Policy for the Nation 77
2. The "Futility" of Criminalizing Abortion 77

III. The Mandate: Seeking Biblical Guidance 79

A. Biblical Authority Relating to Abortion 79
1. Evidence from a Pro-Abortionist's Bible 79
2. Evidence from a Pro-Lifer's Bible 82

B. The Roles of a Biblical Disciple 93
1. Pilgrim & Alien [God's Creation] 93
2. Theologian [Divine Design and Image of God] 94
3. Pious Priest [Commandments] 95
4. Prophet [Justice] 98
5. Loving Neighbor [Virtue] 100
6. Zealot [Universal Truth] 102
7. Evangelist [Accountability] 107

IV. The Legacy: Stewards vs. Masters 109

A. Christian Tradition 109
1. Early Church 109
2. Reformation Era 111

B. World Precedents 114
1. Holocaust 115
2. Nuremberg 123
3. Geneva 124
4. United Nations & Human Rights 124
5. The Unborn Child's Human Rights 125
6. Global Norms Regarding Abortion 126
7. Apartheid: "Truth & Reconciliation" 128

OUTLINE of CONTENTS, Second Page

C. United States of America **135**
1. Independence **135**
2. Liberty & Rights **137**
3. Abolition of Slavery **138**
a. Pretexts for Retaining Slavery 139
b. Links in the Chains of Slavery 140
c. Discipleship and Slavery 143
d. Parallels between Slavery and Abortion 146
4. U.S. Women's Rites of Passage **147**
a. Protection & Rights Movements 148
(1) Abortion Outlawed in the Late Nineteenth Century... 148
(2) Anti-Prostitution Developments 152
(3) Employment for Women 152
(4) Voting Rights forWomen 152
(5) Alcohol's Impact on Women & Society 152
b. Anti-Family Developments and Margaret Sanger 154
(1) Motherhood as a Burden: Contraception 155
(2) Children as the Enemy: Abortion & Eugenics 155
(3) Women as Victims: All Sex as Exploitation by Men 156
c. Feminist Movements 156
(1) Women and Equal Opportunity: "Equity Feminism" 157
(2) Women and Equal Results: "Gender Feminism" 157
5. Seeds of Social Destruction **158**
a. Nietzsche: "God is Dead" 158
b. Malthus: "Population Bomb" 159
c. Darwin: "Godless Accidental Mechanism" 160
d. Marx: "Militant Materialistic Victims" 160
e. Freud: "Sex is Natural; Guilt is a Neurosis" 160
6. Between two World Wars **161**
a. Technology & Prosperity 162
b. Modernism: The Enlightenment Project [Naturalism] 163
c. Fundamentalism 164
d. Scopes "Monkey" Trial 165
e. Capone vs. Ness 165
7. Pivotal Developments **166**
a. Public Education, and *1984*'s "Big Brother is Watching You." 166
b. Market Crash: The Nation becomes Greatly Depressed 169
c. Television, Mastercard & Trump: Post-War Materialism 169
d. The NFL & MTV: Artificial Heroes and Glorified Physicality 170
e. McCarthy & Patty Hearst: Post-War Paranoia 171
f. Kinsey, Elvis & Madonna: The Sexier the Better 171
g. Bob Dylan & the Clinton Generation: Nihilism with a Happy Face 172
8. Civil Rights Movement **174**
9. Parental-Responsibility Statutes **177**
10. Humaneness in Our Culture **178**
a. Animal Rights 179
b. Endangered Species 181
c. Environmentalism 182
d. American Hospitality toward Aliens 183
e. Criminal Rights, and Capital Punishment 183
f. Children's Rights 184
V. The Death Wish: Links in the Abortive Chain **187**
A. Recreational (vs. Procreational) Sex **188**
B. Reproductive Technology **189**
C. Abortion Industry **206**
1. Problems: What's so bad about Abortion? **206**
2. Excuses for Inaction by Christians / Pro-lifers **208**
3. Goals of Intervention **212**
4. Types of Intervention **219**
5. Justifications Offered **223**
a Civil Disobedience 224
b. Necessity Defense and Justifiable Homicide 226
D. Governmental Action **228**
1. Involuntary Complicity: Taxes, Fines and Judgments **228**
2. Supreme Court **229**
3. Politics **232**
4. Legislation **235**
a. The Hyde Amendment 235
b. F.A.C.E.: The Freedom of Access to Clinic Entrances Law 235
c. Blood Money from Congress 235
d. Human Life Amendment 236
e. Partial-Birth Abortion (D&X) 236
f. The Value of a Child 237
5. Law Enforcement **239**
a. Bureaucratic Functioning – "Big Brother" does more than Watch 239
b. Police Practice 240
6. "Due Process" in Court for Pro-life Activists **241**
a. Injunctions and Restraining Orders 241
b. Prosecution Charges 241
c. The Necessity Defense 242
d. Jury Nullification 242
7. "Justice" and Consequences of Pro-life Activism **242**

OUTLINE of CONTENTS, Third Page

E. Social Climate **243**
1. Education **243**
2. Media **243**
a. World View of the Media 243
b. The Power of the Media 244
c. Bias of the Media 244
d. Christianity as Portrayed by the Media 245
e. Abortion as Portrayed by the Media 245
f. Crisis Pregnancy Centers (CPCs) as Portrayed by the Media 245
g. Rescue as Portrayed by the Media 246
h. The Elite Few who Control the Media 247
F. Religious Confusion **247**
1. Polarization of the Faithful **247**
a. Religious Pluralism 248
b. Reshuffled Priorities 248
c. Theological Shifts 249
d. Liberalized "Mainline" Denominations 250
e. Social Gospel 250
f. Crises of Leadership 251
2. Public Orthodoxy, its Rise and Fall **252**
a. The Religious Right 253
b. Neutralized from Within 254
c. Faithfulness Stigmatized and Marginalized 254
d. Revival Time? Are Christians also *Orphans in Babylon*? 255
3. Religious Controversy over Abortion **256**
a. Universality & The "Catholic" Position 256
b. Sanctity & Image of God 256
c. Personhood of the Preborn 257
d. Human Rights of the Preborn 257
e. Exceptions Justifying Abortion [Relativism] 257
f. Freedom to Choose [Autonomy] 258
g. Has the Church Failed? 258
G. Personal Decision to Abort **259**
1. Dissuade Abortion-Bound Women **259**
2. Last-Ditch Miracles **259**
3. Give Women Real Pro-life Choices **260**
VI. Dilemma: State of the Pro-Life Movement **261**
A. Magnitude of the Problem: the Situation Now **261**
1. The World Scene **261**
2. The Death Toll **261**
3. Who Aborts? **262**
4. Governmental Blunders **262**
5. Reduced Access to Surgical Abortion **263**
6. Who Cares about the Unborn, and How Much? **263**
B. Paradox of Restrained Outrage **264**
1. A Century of Martyrs **265**
2. Rhetoric & Reality **265**
3. Worth Any Cost? **266**
4. Righteous Intolerance **267**
C. Why all this Infighting? **268**
D. Nature of the Problem: What if "The Amendment" Came to Be? **269**
1. Fraud in the Medical Community **270**
2. Non-Enforcement **272**
3. Loopholes in the Law **272**
4. Defiance of the Law **273**
5. Opportunists **274**
6. Privatization **275**
7. Undetectability **275**
E. Victory as Defined by Various Pro-lifers **277**
1. Close Down the Abortion Clinics **277**
2. Reform Reproductive Technology **277**
3. Pass Pro-life Laws and a Human Life Amendment **277**
4. Reshape a Pro-life Society **277**
5. Promote Personal Pro-life Commitments **277**
6. Upgrade Personal Morality **277**
7. Ignite Religious Revival **277**
VII. Our Destiny: Future Course of Action **279**
A. We Must Answer the "Hell Objection" **279**
B. Repentance & Dedication: One Body, Many Parts **281**
C. Witness & Activism: Three Things we just 'Gotta Do' **282**
1. Proclamation by a Local Pro-life Congregation **282**
2. Banner: Personal Testimony of Grave National Emergency **283**
3. *Declaration of Dependence upon God* **284**
D. Final Word **284**
• Bibliography **287**
• Timeline **292**
• Bible Themes **302**
Overview for Quick Reference, with page numbers **312**

ORPHANS in BABYLON

Orphaned by Choice

The aborted ones are orphans

The child who is aborted is fatherless. The fathers don't know, or don't care, or they are denied the rights of fatherhood by the state, or they both will and demand the right to become childless. The preborns who are aborted are motherless. Their mothers don't know they have both engendered and destroyed their posterity, or they both know and "know not what they do,"[1] or they knowingly conspire to murder that which they – by divine design – should be cherishing.

Those who are being aborted are made orphans by the state, which – rather than guarding their right to live – chooses to legitimize their demise. The helpless, hapless ones are made orphans, eternally, by the church on whose doorstep they are placed, but which has not enough room for millions of them in its heart.

The United States of America has become Babylon

America's government, its public culture, and its foreseeable future have become not only godless, but the sworn enemies of both God and the godly. **"Where are we now?"** will be analyzed in Part One, "Clash of Convictions," and Part Two, "The Abortion Pretexts: Allegations of Expendability." **"How did we get here?"** will be shown in Part Four, "The Legacy... Endless Struggle," and Part Five, "The Death Wish: Links in the Abortive Chain." **"Where should we be?"** will be explored in Part Three, "The Mandate: Seeking Biblical Guidance." **"How can we get there?"** is the subject of Part Six, "The Dilemma: State of the Pro-Life Movement," and Part Seven, "Our Destiny: Future Course of Action."

Legalized abortion certifies that America is not now a "Christian nation," whether it ever was or could ever be. The conclusions of *Orphans in Babylon* are that: 1) We, the entire people of faith, must zealously and righteously promote anti-abortion legislation and judicial verdicts, and the passage of a Right to Life Amendment to the Constitution; 2) We must show God's love in every way to our neighbor, particularly to those who would otherwise be killed before birth, and to the mothers, fathers and families and society who have or who would have suffered such a loss; 3) We must, above all, rightly come to terms with the realities we face, and with the distinction between victory and virtue; 4) If the Church continues to ignore the struggle, and if the called-ones abandon it, even a miraculous elimination of abortion would be hollow, a monument to our great shame; 5) In fighting this fight we will proclaim our Lord's kingdom until he comes, even though countless innocents are certain to be lost in spite of our best efforts; 6) There are simple but essential steps which must be taken in order to remove abortion from the indictment against the Church and each of her members.

---

1. *Luke* 23: 34.
2. This format is employed to provide the reader with ready access to citations – author and page number – for both quotations and assertions in the text.
3. A complete bibliography of sources appears at the end of this volume.
4. The **"Scope and Focus"** outline is shown on each pair of pages (above) to identify where the reader IS in the overall scheme of presentation.
5. The Appendix contains a Timeline relating to "Discipleship Tests and Abortion," which the reader may find a helpful reference before, during and after the reading of the main text.
6. It is hoped that the format will facilitate both a quick reading of the overall thesis, and also a more careful study of each part.
7. Parenthetical references in quoted passages are enclosed in (parentheses) and the researcher's quips are [bracketed].
8. The researcher's prayer is that each reader will be guided by the Holy Spirit to gain fresh understandings and to embrace our common destiny as Stewards of the Gospel of our Creator, whose Image we are designed to reflect.
9. **"The opinions expressed by the writer of *Orphans in Babylon* are not necessarily those of God,"** ...although to know His thoughts and to gain His heart, humbly, have been the goals.

I. Clash of Convictions

The household of God has been engulfed by an avalanche "of suspicious origin"

"The global village... will ultimately require all traditional religions to be pushed to the fringe of society," writes Harold O.J. Brown.[1] Another writer says, "The Christian Right correctly observed that an increasingly secularized society was systematically attacking Christian values... The attack also took form directly against the Church."[2]

This is far from a new development. *America in the Twenties: A History* summarizes, "The new sexual freedom rolled forward... All the forces of modern life were behind it..."[3] The actual "throwing down of the gauntlet" may have occurred in 1927 with this declaration of war by the president of the Science League of America:

> In the United States today there exist, side by side, two opposing cultures, one or the other of which must eventually dominate our public institutions, political, legal, educational, and social. On the one side we see arrayed the forces of progress and enlightenment, on the other the forces of reaction, the apostles of traditionalism. There can be no compromise between these diametrically opposed armies.[4]

By 1960, the head of the United Nations saw polarization on a global scale, declaring, "The human world is today as never before split into two camps, each of which understands the other as the embodiment of falsehood and itself as the embodiment of truth."[5] His reference was to the Cold War's antagonists – atheistic communism and the "Christian" West – but as American government abandoned its historic faith, it retained its air of condescension toward those it opposed, both abroad and at home.

It was reflected in 1964 that "Social conflict is most potent in civil war, between brothers, or between emerging groups of once shared but now competitive orientations. Each such move or stress occasions some sort of territorial demarcation."[6] James Hunter, in *Culture Wars: The Struggle to Define America*, identifies the five major battlefields of that warfare as the family, education, the popular media, law, and politics.[7]

For the Church, the culture war is a crisis of faith

"When religious groups compromise their foundational beliefs in order to coexist with the late sensate culture rather than challenging it or standing against it, they in effect consent to their own liquidation," declares Brown.[8] John Whitehead says that we are "at an important crossroads in time and history."[9]

According to Hunter, the struggle sets "orthodoxy" – cultural conservatives and moral traditionalists – as defenders against the "progressivism" of cultural liberals.[10] But he goes on to clarify that the defenders are those who hold to traditional-evangelical and orthodox-Catholic and Jewish faiths, who are thrust together ideologically by their shared status as victims of liberal attack. These challenges are coming from their estranged brothers as well as from assorted outsiders.

When Choice Becomes God brings the conflict into focus: " ...although abortion undoubtedly is the toughest battle of all, our cultural war is bigger than the issue of abortion alone. We are engaged in a great conflict over our most basic assumptions about life and about the source of our moral values."[11] Paul Johnson says, "In the last generation, with public Christianity in headlong retreat, we have caught our first, distant view of a de-Christianized world, and it is not encouraging."[12]

1 Harold O.J. Brown, *The Sensate Culture*, 67.

2 Colonel V. Doner, *The Samaritan Strategy*, 14.

3 Geoffrey Perrett, 156: "...the growing economic and intellectual independence of women, the craving for excitement in a world becoming dull and standardized, the energy and loneliness of life in cities, the development of birth control, the sanction of science, the collapse of the old moral order, the rejection of puritanism."

4 James Hunter, *Culture Wars*, 137.

5 Dag Hammarskjold, in Trueblood, *New Man for Our Time*, 18.

6 Robert Lee, *Religion and Social Conflict*, 184.

7 James Hunter, 174.

8 Harold Brown, 67.

9 John Whitehead, *The Second American Revolution*, 145.

10 James Hunter, 44-6.

11 F. LaGard Smith, 270-1: "... It is a question of who will be God. Will individual *choice* become our God, or will the God of Creation be our God?"

12 Johnson, in Robert Bork, *Slouching Towards Gomorrah*, 295.

13 Harold Brown, 67.

14 Schaffer, in Hunter, 103: "...Unlike liberal ecumenism which is bound together by unbelief, this ecumenism is based upon what we agree to be the essence of Christian faith, including an orthodoxy of belief in social concerns and priorities."

15 B. & P. Berger, *War Over the Family*, 73-4: "...We would contend that this presents a problem of grave proportions and one that may not be easily solved by the mechanisms set up to 'contain' religious conflicts."

16 Bahm, 4-5: "Many believe that ethics consists mainly, if not entirely, of codes... Thus, unfortunately, ethics, which deals primarily with what is good and how to get it, comes to be misinterpreted as a set of evils... Ethical principles are assertions about oughts. But they state 'Why ought?' rather than 'ought' merely. Ethical principles explain rather than command."

SCOPE and FOCUS
I. CONVICTIONS
Polarizing Certainties
Creation vs. Accident
Design vs. Mechanism
Commandments vs. Positivism
Justice vs. Pragmatism
Virtue vs. Pleasure
Universalism vs. Relativism
Accountability vs. Autonomy
Worldview Confusion
Human Condition & Life
Stewards vs. Masters
II. PRETEXTS
III. MANDATE
IV. LEGACY
V. ABORTIVE LINKS
VI. DILEMMA
VII. DESTINY

Harold Brown says that the Church has only three options: abandon our religion, repudiate the culture, "or somehow find a way to live in a situation of constant tension."[13] Those of us who have attempted to live with the tension, by now have a taste of the rigors of hell. This work is an attempt to ascertain the direction of at least an effective "repudiation" of the culture – if not total cultural transformation. Franky Schaeffer in 1984 wrote:

> ...our backs are against the wall and we are facing an aggressively secularist society whose powerful elements are deliberately attempting to eradicate what little remains of orthodox influence in society. The majority of Christians are either asleep or simply do not care. The time has come for those who remain to band together in an ecumenism of orthodoxy.[14]

The enemy's agenda demands the radical redefinition of the moral authority undergirding our culture

In *The War Over the Family*, we are shown that "...the abortion issue reveals a highly significant rupture in the moral fabric... It discloses a phenomenon that may aptly be called 'moral pluralism.'"[15] To begin to answer the question, *Why Be Moral?*, Archie Bahm clarifies, in ethics, the "distinction between codes and principles" and says that "principles, not codes, constitute the foundations of both ethical theory and practice."[16]

Hunter tells us that people's deep-seated commitments and beliefs form the basis of their moral understanding and give them their sense of purpose, identity and relatedness to others. For this reason, people become passionate in the face of expressions of moral understanding which contradict their own, and "moral visions take expression as polarizing impulses or tendencies in American culture."[17] He makes it clear that world views derive from commitments to particular bases of moral authority. This helps to explain why we don't have "card-carrying" existentialists or postmodernists; world view labels identify certain sets of convictions one has come to hold. The world view does not convey particular tenets of faith, but the allegiances are given recognition by the world view label.

James Hunter later states the seriousness of these fundamentally different belief systems: "...As a consequence of this mutual moral estrangement, concessions on many policy matters become a virtual impossibility. The abortion debate exemplifies this most poignantly..."[18] He eventually follows this thought with a sobering truth: "What is ultimately at stake is the ability to define the rules by which moral conflict of this kind is to be resolved... Those who define how a contest is to be played out will have the advantage of shaping its final outcome."[19]

Leroy Augenstein identified in 1969 a conscious intellectual effort to bring the scientist and the humanist together, because "neither group alone can resolve our dilemmas... [We] must work carefully with the politicians who know how to set up a proper apparatus to make and carry out decisions."[20] Alfred North Whitehead described what he called "the cultural definition of rationality, the beginning of reason."[21]

In *Culture Wars,* we are told, "Whatever else may be involved, cultural conflict is about power – a struggle to achieve or maintain the power to define reality."[22]

17 James Hunter, *Culture Wars: The Struggle to Define America*, 43.

18 James Hunter, 128-9.

19 James Hunter, 271.

20 Leroy Augustein, *Come, Let Us Play God*, 15.

21 Whitehead, in Johnson, *Reason in the Balance*, 195-6: "In his classic work *Science and the Modern World* Whitehead wrote that to understand the philosophy of an age, the important things to concentrate on... are the presuppositions that practically everybody with any influence takes for granted, presuppositions that are rarely defended or even articulated because they seem so obviously true."

22 James Hunter, *Culture Wars*, 52.

"When religious groups compromise their foundational beliefs in order to coexist with the late sensate culture rather than challenging it or standing against it, they in effect consent to their own liquidation."[8] **– Harold O.J. Brown**

Abortion is the defining battle of our age

R.C. Sproul contends that "A single issue rarely divides the American people. But a few have, including slavery... civil rights... Vietnam. Now another issue has surfaced, an issue of such magnitude that our national solidarity is threatened. To many citizens, it is a matter of life and death and may be the most serious ethical dilemma ever faced by the United States. The issue is abortion."[1] Nigel Cameron says, "Bioethics is to be viewed as a central cultural phenomenon; a project whose subject matter – human beings at their most vulnerable and dependent – is of defining significance for the future of the culture."[2]

Robert Mnookin thinks that abortion has cut the American cultural pie into quarters, with two pieces – half of the population – ambivalent [which does not mean disinterested but, rather, conflicted and undecided], leaving two radically polarized fourths locked hopelessly and passionately in conflict over fundamentally opposite convictions, and seeking to win the support of the uncommitted.[3]

Our stake in the abortion struggle is not only major; it is paramount and eternal

In 1970, the California Medical Association explained the reason for the extensive revision of medical vocabulary necessary to sell abortion to the public: "Since the old ethic [perhaps Christianity?] has not yet been fully displaced it has been necessary to separate the idea of abortion from the idea of killing, which continues to be socially abhorrent. The result has been the curious avoidance of the scientific fact, which everyone really knows, that human life begins at conception... The very considerable semantic gymnastics... is necessary because while a new ethic [could this be, 'Do your own thing'?] is being accepted the old has not been rejected."[4]

Just how serious the abortion-centered battle is to the survival of the Church and of our culture is summed up in the words of a few key observers:

"How can the moral consensus of society be maintained if half the population views the other half as actual or potential murderers, and is in turn viewed by the other half as violating the fundamental rights of women?"[5]

"The choice to be made is between two diametrically opposed philosophies which cannot co-exist, for the adoption of one inevitably destroys the other."[6]

"Winning the war for America's soul will not come easily, cheaply, nor quickly. Childkilling is entrenched in our culture and the death forces will not be dethroned overnight, or without a serious fight... If we won't pay the price... America will lie in the ash heap of history, testifying against our cowardice and selfishness..."[7]

"I really believe that we are in a fierce battle for the very survival of our culture..."[8]

"There is no 'slippery slope:' ...The likes of Kevorkian; starving Nancy Beth Cruzan to death; homosexuals in the pulpit, [and abortion] are not an indication that our society is going into some dark hole. We are already there."[9]

"The contemporary culture war has become a contest that will determine not who is right but who is *left*."[10]

"That so few are willing to recognize the dilemma... is the most disturbing element in the whole debate."[11]

SCOPE and FOCUS
I. CONVICTIONS
Polarizing Certainties
Creation vs. Accident
Design vs. Mechanism
Commandments vs. Positivism
Justice vs. Pragmatism
Virtue vs. Pleasure
Universalism vs. Relativism
Accountability vs. Autonomy
Worldview Confusion
Human Condition & Life
Stewards vs. Masters
II. PRETEXTS
III. MANDATE
IV. LEGACY
V. ABORTIVE LINKS
VI. DILEMMA
VII. DESTINY

1 R.C. Sproul, *Abortion: A Rational Look at an Emotional Issue*, 13.

2 Cameron, in Kilner, et. al., *Bioethics and the Future of Medicine, A Christian Appraisal*, 5.

3 Robert Mnookin, *In the Interest of Children: Advocacy, Law, Reform, and Public Policy*, 155.

4 In Jean Garton, *Who Broke the Baby?*, 99.

5 B. & P. Berger, *War Over the Family*, 76.

6 Jean Garton, 94.

7 Randall Terry, in Foreman, 168-9.

8 Tim LaHaye, in Hunter, 103.

9 Cathy Ramey, in *Life Advocate*, 4/'94, 30.

10 James Hunter, 136.

11 Daniel Callahan, in J. Douglas Butler, *Abortion, Medicine and the Law*, 349.

12. In F. LaGard Smith, *When Choice Becomes God*, 10.

A. Polarizing Certainties in American Society

The abortion controversy is about the foundations of ethics

There is no way of knowing if Norman Geisler had the Supreme Court in mind, two years before *Roe v. Wade*, in saying, "When there are no objective moral standards which transcend the subjectivity of individuals and nations, then there is no objective way to declare an act morally good or bad."[13]

Disputes over the source of moral authority have pushed groups of Americans to opposite and incompatible conclusions.

An individual's personal ethics is a product of his world view. That world view emerges from a configuration of fundamental assumptions about reality. Those basic interpretations of reality are defined by answers to metaphysical questions: What made the universe the way it is? How did life in all its variations, including mankind, come to be as we know it today? Must we conform to divine Commandments, or is Man free to make up his own rules? Are there basic standards of justice, or do we measure actions as good and bad by their results? Is there such a thing as virtue, or are pain and pleasure the only yardstick of success? Are there universal norms of right action, or is each individual a judge unto himself? And are souls morally accountable in the eternal sense, or is each person autonomous, bounded only by flesh, matter and time?

The course and character of every individual's life are shaped by the answers to these questions. Whether the answering has been a conscious or an unconscious exercise, these deep seated assumptions constantly emanate from the base of one's soul. It is when these fundamental certainties collide against conflicting certitudes held by others that the battles of the "culture wars" erupt.

Seven sets of mutually exclusive convictions define the foundations of the schisms within our society

In the United States of America, orthodox believers – Catholic, Protestant and Jewish – base their religious practice on a firm belief in God's creation, His design and scriptural commandments, on the principles of justice and virtue, and on universal ethics and moral accountability. Each and all of these convictions are challenged and attacked by those – within the flock as well as without – who champion: accident and blind mechanism as the source of all life forms, including mankind; positivism and pragmatism in ethics; and self-gratification, relativism and personal autonomy in morals. When paired as opposites, these convictions can best be understood as clashes of conviction: creation vs. accident; design vs. mechanism; commandments vs. positivism; justice vs. pragmatism; virtue vs. pleasure; and accountability vs. autonomy. We will discuss each of these colliding pairs of certainties, then explore how the secular assumptions combine to drive popular world views. We will then see how these fundamental heresies impact a person's convictions relating to the human condition.

13 Geisler, *Ethics: Alternatives and Issues*, 13-4.

Geisler teamed up with J.P. Moreland in 1990 to write *The Life and Death Debate: Moral Issues of Our Time*. In the Introduction they write, "Ethics can be understood as the philosophical study of morality. Morality is concerned with our beliefs and judgments regarding right and wrong motives, attitudes and conduct" (viii).

Referring back to Geisler's *Alternatives*, if we can wade through terms like *teleological* and *deontological*, he seems to be explaining that systems of ethics can be divided into two basic approaches: those based on good actions or normative ethics (*deontological*), and those pursuing good purposes (*no norms*). He says that the "good acts" group has two divisions: the "obedience to universal laws" group [let's call them Absolutists], and the "only one rule (love, for instance)" group [we'll name them Situationalists]. Geisler subdivides the other main group, the "good purposes" folks, into two ideological factions: the "*teleological* standards" corps, who judge an act by its results [they'll be our Utilitarians], and the "no standards" bunch, who believe in freedom of choice for all [making them the Subjectivists].

All of this is to say that if our religious orthodoxy causes us to believe in God's Commandments, then in the ethical marketplace our Absolutists are going to be outnumbered three-to-one by Situationalists, Utilitarians and Subjectivists.

> **"...at the core of the revolution is choice: The right for us to decide for ourselves, and the right of others to decide for themselves. Being nonjudgmental about others seems to be our only guarantee of their being nonjudgmental about us."[12]**
>
> **– an unnamed abortion advocate**

1. Creation vs. Accident

Like Cain, science chose to become his brother's mortal enemy

"The issue of Creation versus Evolution is one of the fundamental reasons why there is such an impasse in the ongoing abortion debate."[1] One of the Church Fathers, Tertullian, expressed our faith well: "The object of our worship is the One God, He who by His commanding word, His arranging wisdom, His mighty power, brought forth from nothing this entire mass of our world, with all its array of elements, bodies, spirits, for the glory of His majesty..."[2]

Historian Kenneth Walker comments, "When we trace the history of theology and science... we find that they slowly diverged from each other and in the course of time became isolated departments of knowledge expressing contradictory views of the universe."[3]

Only Creation remains, once Accident self-destructs

Antony van Leeuwenhoek [who, with his home-made microscope, first discovered protozoa and bacteria, and sperm in 1677] opposed the theory of spontaneous generation of lower forms of life, and presented much evidence against it."[4] Huse tells us that Redi, Pasteur, and Spallanzani "proved that life can only come from pre-existing life."[5] The list of supporters is extended by Geisler: "Most of the famous people in the early years of modern science were creationists. They believed in the supernatural origin of the universe and of life. Included among them are: Kepler, Pascal, Newton, Faraday, Babbage, Mendel, Pasteur, Lister, Maxwell..."[6]

In his own words, Jean-Paul Sarte said, "I do not feel that I am a product of chance, a speck of dust in the universe, but someone who was expected, prefigured. In short, a being whom only a creator could put here; and this idea of a creating hand refers to God."[7] "In general, scientists before 1860 tended to be creationists. Sir Isaac Newton's statement about the origin of the universe is typical: 'This most beautiful system of the sun, planets, and comets, could only proceed from the counsel and dominion of an intelligent and powerful Being.'"[8]

Dr. George Wald, winner of the 1967 Nobel Prize in Science, has written: "When it comes to the origin of life on this earth, there are only two possibilities: creation or spontaneous generation (evolution). There is no third way. Spontaneous generation was disproved 100 years ago, but that leads us only to one other conclusion: that of supernatural creation. [But] we cannot accept that on philosophical grounds [personal reasons]; therefore, we choose to believe the impossible: that life arose spontaneously by chance."[9]

Illogical commitment to the accident theory bodes ill for all

"If our existence is the result of mere chance, then all fundamental human rights are at serious risk," says F.L. Smith,[10] who also asks a great question: "Are we to look proudly upon an 'American way' that teaches 12-year-olds about abortion as an option, but censors any teaching about Creation as an option?"[11] Will Durant has another. "The greatest question of our time is not communism versus individualism, not Europe versus America, not even the East versus the West; it is whether men can live without God."[12]

1 F.L. Smith, *When Choice Becomes God*, 97.

2 Roberts, *Ante-Nicene Fathers*, vol. III, 31.

3 In Kerby Anderson, 28.

4 Hart, *The 100: A Ranking of the Most Influential Persons in History*, 226-7.

5 Huse, *The Collapse of Evolution*, foreword.

6 Geisler, *Is Man the Measure?: An Evaluation of Contemporary Humanism*, 132-33.

7 In R.C. Sproul, 25.

8 In Geisler, *Is Man the Measure?*, 133.

9 In Huse, *The Collapse of Evolution*, 3.

10 F.L. Smith, *When Choice Becomes God*, 97.

In *God and Caesar*, John Eidsmoe adds insight: "Abortion, euthanasia, infanticide, geriatricide – all are inherent in the humanist view of man. For while humanists claim to glorify man as the supreme value in the universe, they in fact reduce man to an animal. For they remove that which separates man from animals – the conviction that man is created in the image of God. If man is nothing but a complex animal, his value and worth are relative. An individual human being may be sacrificed for the common good, just as one sheep may be sacrificed for the good of the flock. Hence, the unwanted child may be aborted because his or her birth would be inconvenient, expensive, or otherwise undesirable" (170).

11 F.L. Smith, *When Choice Becomes God*, 100.

12 Durant, in Colson, *Kingdoms in Conflict*, 225.

13. Newton in Carr, et.al., *Celebrate Life: Hope for a Culture Preoccupied with Death*, 116.

14 Anderson, *Living Ethically in the '90s*, 42.

He continues: "[God] is the ultimate whose character provides the absolute standard for morality...

(Continued next column)

"Atheism is so senseless. When I look at the solar system, I see the earth at the right distance from the sun to receive the proper amounts of heat and light. This did not happen by chance. The motions of the planets require a divine Arm to impress them."[13]

– Sir Isaac Newton

SCOPE and FOCUS
I. CONVICTIONS
Polarizing Certainties
Creation vs. Accident
Design vs. Mechanism
Commandments vs. Positivism
Justice vs. Pragmatism
Virtue vs. Pleasure
Universalism vs. Relativism
Accountability vs. Autonomy
Worldview Confusion
Human Condition & Life
Stewards vs. Masters
II. PRETEXTS

2. Design vs. Mechanism

Evolution offers a blind, mechanistic challenge to traditional belief that God designed Man in His image

Kerby Anderson has a good grasp of the Christian belief in God's design: "Theism proposes a personal beginning to the universe. Man is the product of an intelligent and personal ordering-agent rather than an impersonal and mindless cosmos."[14]

Newspapers consistently spew out the evolutionary line: "The vast majority of the country's scientists believe that life on Earth is the result of billions of years of evolution, an unsupervised, impersonal, unpredictable process of natural development."[15] Harvard paleontologist George Gaylord Simpson says the "meaning of evolution" is that "Man is the result of a purposeless and natural process that did not have him in mind."[16]

The author of a widely used evolutionary biology college textbook says, gently, "Some shrink from the conclusion that the human species was not designed, has no purpose, and is the product of mere mechanical mechanisms – but this seems to be the message of evolution."[17] A philosopher, Edward Carnell, says it more poetically: "Modern man appears to be but a grown-up germ, sitting on a gear of a vast cosmic machine which is some day destined to cease functioning because of lack of power."[18]

Oliver Wendell Holmes said that he saw "no reason for attributing to man a significance in kind different from that which belongs to a baboon or a grain of sand."[19]

The acceptance of evolution without question, is an amazing paradox of modern science.

Evolution has so saturated our culture that most who use the everyday expressions, "struggle for existence" and "survival of the fittest" do not connect them directly with the theory.[20] Geisler tells us that when "Huxley took up Morley's challenge to develop a scientific religion... he called it evolutionary humanism. One of the foundational tenets, as the name signifies, is the theory of evolution."[21]

The mechanistic component of evolution became the backbone of B.F. Skinner's radical behaviorism. Beginning with naturalism – the view that the material world is all that exists – and extending it through a matrix of purely physical causes and effects, Skinner concluded that what psychologists call "reinforcement" is the essence of morality: anything "rewarding" which makes a behavior more likely to be repeated is termed "good" with the implied assumption that neither the act itself, nor its motivation, nor even its consequences play any role in the moral equation.[22]

There will be a later examination of International Human Rights [in Part IV.B], but it should be noted here that evolutionary jargon is alive and well in the international arena; the very first article of the United Nations *Declaration on Race and Racial Prejudice* begins, "All human beings belong to a single species and are *descended* from a common stock."[23]

"Nature itself is not rational or moral, but its Creator is... God is not only transcendent; He is also immanent. Instead of being silent, He has communicated to man... Because of God's revelation to us, our concept of God need not be limited to a fabrication of our own minds."

15 *Press*, 10-25-96, A11.

16 Simpson, in Phillip Johnson, 8-9.

17 Douglas Futuyma, in Johnson, *Reason in the Balance: The Case against Naturalism in Science, Law & Education*, 9.

18 Carnell, in Sproul, *Abortion: A Rational Look at an Emotional Issue*, 29.

19 Holmes, in Sproul, 39.

20 Michael H. Hart, 121.

21 Geisler, *Is Man the Measure?*, 14.

22 Geisler, *Is Man the Measure?*, 21-27.

23 *Human Rights*, vol. I (First Part), 132-9.

24. Thielicke, *The Doctor as Judge of Who Shall Live and Who Shall Die*, 40.

"What I reject is the attempt to define man... as a variation of tadpoleness... I will have to ask about the end for which he was created and the destiny for which he was intended by a higher hand."[24]

–Helmut Thielicke

Secularists have capitalized on every opportunity to publicize religious support for evolution

The Lessons of History, the classic by historians Will and Ariel Durant, encapsulates the religious drift toward evolutionary mechanism: "...the 'death of God' ...required many causes besides the spread of science... First the Protestant Reformation, which originally defended private judgment. Then the multitude of Protestant sects and conflicting theologies, each appealing to both Scriptures and reason. Then the higher criticism of the Bible... as the imperfect work of fallible men. Then the deistic movement in England, reducing religion to a vague belief in a God hardly distinguishable from nature."[1] The Durants also underscore the part that scientific developments played in the shaking of faith: "The growing awareness of man's minuscule place in the cosmos has furthered the impairment of religious belief. In Christendom we may date the beginning of the decline from Copernicus (1543). The process was slow, but by 1611 John Donne was mourning that the earth had become a mere 'suburb' ...and Francis Bacon, while tipping his hat occasionally to the bishops, was proclaiming science as the religion of modern emancipated man. In that generation began the 'death of God' as an external deity."[2]

Special treatment will be given later to religious Fundamentalism and the Scopes trial [part IV.C.6.d], but George Grant gives us a snapshot of the progress of the decline in 1930, when the organization that was to become the National Council of Churches [then the Federal Council of Churches] endorsed the idea of "choice" regarding abortion: "When the Catholic Church [*criticized* that action], several leading Protestants from around the world offered a defense arguing that God 'is revealed in the endless sweep of evolution and His message is being slowly translated by science into the accents of the human tongue.'"[3]

Another verbal snapshot, this one from the newspaper late in 1996: "Fundamentalists object to any idea of coexistence between Darwinism and God. When Pope John Paul II issued a statement last week supporting physical evolution, the reaction among many Catholics, Jews and mainline Protestants was probably, 'so what.' ...John Haught, professor of theology at [Catholic] Georgetown University says: 'Catholic theology has for a long time considered that God can create the world through an evolutionary process... There's a difference between taking scriptures literally and taking them seriously.'"[4]

The current discussion brings us, a bit early, into one of the basic purposes of this work: identifying those convictions which will enable us to be both "wise and innocent"[5] as we draw lasting and far-reaching conclusions as to who is "with us" and who is "against us."[6] It is the researcher's contention that the members of the pro-life movement should stand as brethren, particularly in public, with all who will affirm the seven orthodox convictions currenly being examined. That unity derives from "where we are coming *from*" (Whom we serve), as contrasted with all of the variety of places He sends us, and especially what we do in good conscience – with God as our judge – when we get there!

As to the basics, where we are coming from, and the Creation and Design convictions in particular, it is proposed that a bold affirmation to "In the beginning God created"[7] and to "God created man in his own image"[8] be the *necessary and sufficient* test of solidarity in this matter. This threshold easily encompasses the Evangelicals and the traditional Catholics whose longstanding unity in pro-life activism is a celestial delight. It is hoped that it is also inclusive of orthodox Jews and Christian Fundamentalists.

1 Will and Ariel Durant, *The Lessons of History*, 47.

2 Durant, 46-7.

3 Grant, *Third Time Around: A History of the Pro-Life Movement from the First Century to the Present*, 125-6. The books by Grant are *must* reading for any pro-lifer. This one chronicles Christian pro-life activism in three epochs: under the Roman Empire in the early centuries of Christianity when, despite bloody persecution, Christians denounced the practices of abortion, infanticide and child abandonment, and when Christians regularly – and illegally – rescued discarded newborns from exposure; in the U.S. in the mid-to-late nineteenth century when Christians were one of several segments of society – journalists, pharmacists, doctors, and lawyers were others – which succeeded in enacting anti-abortion laws in every state; and, of course, the current holocaust, which rages on, unabated.

Most Christian writers paint Believers as the heroes in the nineteenth century victory in outlawing abortion. This work will examine [in part IV.A and C] all three historical examples of pro-lifeism from various angles. Viewing the crucial roles of other contributors will bring the "Christian" victory into better focus.

4 *Press*, 11-2-96, A13.

5 *Matthew* 10:16: "I am sending you out like sheep among wolves. Therefore be as wise as snakes and as innocent as doves."

6 *Matthew* 12:28-30: "...I drive out demons by the Spirit of God... He who is not with me is against me..." and *Mark* 9:35-40: "If anyone wants to be first, he must be the very last, and the servant of all... Whoever welcomes one of these little children in my name, welcomes me; whoever welcomes me does not welcome me but the one who sent me...

(Continued on 9)

SCOPE and FOCUS
I. CONVICTIONS
Polarizing Certainties
Creation vs. Accident
Design vs. Mechanism
Commandments vs. Positivism
Justice vs. Pragmatism
Virtue vs. Pleasure
Universalism vs. Relativism
Accountability vs. Autonomy
Worldview Confusion
Human Condition & Life
Stewards vs. Masters
II. PRETEXTS
III. MANDATE
IV. LEGACY
V. ABORTIVE LINKS
VI. DILEMMA
VII. DESTINY

The "missing link" is the skeleton that's *not* in the closet

The part of evolutionary theory that most flies in the face of biblical creation is the notion that all species of animal life, including man, evolved from a common ancestor. Hence, one driving force of archaeology has been to find evidence that that really happened. Amazingly – for evolutionists – the missing links, those supposed transitional stages, seem not to exist. Robert Bork asserts: "Freud and Marx are no longer taken as irrefutable by intellectuals, and now it appears to be Darwin's turn to undergo a devaluation. The fossil record is proving a major embarrassment to evolutionary theory. Though there is ample evidence of evolution and adaptation to environment within species, there is not evidence of the gradual change that is supposed to slowly change one species into another."[9]

There have even been spurious attempts to explain this away with subtheories such as "punctuated equilibrium," which holds that species act like we see them acting for very long stretches of time, and then mysteriously and quickly make the changes [that's the *punctuated* part], and then settle back, again, to behaving like species always seem to behave, for long periods of *equilibria*. Not very many scientists are able to talk about this theory with a straight face.

Michael Behe, a microbiologist, demonstrates that current scientific advances make evolution even harder to defend: "Scientists at the time of Darwin had no conception of the enormous complexity of bodies and their organs... For evolution to be the explanation of features such as the coagulation of blood and the human eye, too many unrelated mutations would have to occur simultaneously."[10]

Not all scientists are so polite in their criticism of Darwin. In the heartland of secular thought – Harvard University – the eminent paleontologist Stephen Jay Gould freely asserts that "Darwin's notion of predictable progressive evolution is so much claptrap."[11]

3. Commandments vs. Positivism

The U.S. was birthed amid controversy over the basis of law.

An associate justice of the Supreme Court in 1968 summed up the history of law into two phases: 1) getting mankind to accept laws as the degree of restraint necessary to permit communal life, and 2) securing freedoms for the individual within those restraints. He capped that concept with, "Conflict between the demands of ordered society and the desires and aspirations of the individual is the common theme of life's development."[12]

Metaphysical moralism and legal positivism are seen by Harold Brown as the two main options for the basis of law. He asks, "Which of the two fundamental approaches is ours...? 1. Metaphysical moralism. Do we look to God, to a divine order that is above us and that does not depend on our desires, fears, or prejudices? 2. Legal positivism. Do we believe that men and women can make laws and that the concept of an unjust law is a contradiction in terms because it is the law that defines justice?"[13]

Perhaps the shift from divine law to positivism began with the rejection of the theory of the divine right of kings. While King Louis XIV of France was asserting that right, his contemporary (1632-1704) John Locke was formulating his social contract theory – that governments get their authority from the consent of those governed.[14]

...[as to the one seen casting out devils in the name of Jesus, but not one of the disciples:] Do not stop him. No one who does a miracle in my name can in the next moment say anything bad about me, for whoever is not against us is for us."

7 *Genesis* 1:1.

8 *Genesis* 1:27.

9 Robert Bork, 294.

10 Bork regarding Behe's view, 294: "This may be read as the modern, scientific version of the argument from design to the existence of a designer."

11 F.L. Smith, *When Choice Becomes God*, 98.

12 Abe Fortas, *Concerning Dissent and Civil Disobedience*, 59.

13 Brown, *The Sensate Culture*, 80.

14 Michael Hart, 261-3.

15. Smith, *When Choice Becomes God*, 261.

"Who says we can't legislate morality? Legislation itself has *become* our morality!"[15]
—F. LaGard Smith

Once a people asserts that its will trumps God's will in the authority *of* government – witness the American and French revolutions – it follows naturally, *democratically*, that the will of the people should not only validate the law but determine it. Both the *Declaration of Independence* and the U.S. *Constitution* give evidence to the progress of this line of thinking: God has effectively been dethroned, and Natural Law is being invoked as sort of a silent regent who rubber-stamps the congressional will. Scores of compromises were made in the launching of America. Natural law "served as a convenient middle ground to satisfy religious as well as nonreligious people."[1] Natural law has accomplished that purpose so well that our contemporaries normally list it as one of three options for the moral basis of civil government: "human law, natural law, and divine law."[2]

Positivism, even under democracy, carries major side effects

Here is one big problem with positivism: "As long as a society believes that there is a divine Judge standing behind its laws, and as long as it assumes that every human judge knows himself answerable to the divine Judge, it can write its statutes in rather broad and general terms... [But] As this confidence in a divine Lawgiver wanes, human laws necessarily become more and more complex; the legislators seek to guarantee the outcome of any legal dispute, leaving nothing to the human judge."[3]

"As the state creates new rights for some, it necessarily diminishes some rights for others... Legisprudence," says John Whitehead, "does not seek what is just, but only what is legal."[4]

John Locke, in expressing virtually all of the major ideas that drove the American Revolution a hundred years later, also talked of the danger of what we would call today "the tyranny of the majority" crushing the rights of individuals.[5] Whitehead, in another book The *Stealing of America*, gives this dark warning: "The secular state will inevitably lead to authoritarian government in one form or another. Such a state has no absolute reference point. It is bound by no philosophy except one of its own making; it recognizes no right as absolute and no Creator as the father of rights, morality, or human dignity. With a relativistic philosophy, the secular state can do or declare anything and justify it on the basis that it is for the good of the people."[6]

Kerby Anderson believes that "...societies can pursue paths as evil as those followed by any individual."[7] According to R.C. Sproul: "In human societies, unjust laws may be passed... Thus, moral rights may be made illegal and immoral activities may become legal... The unspoken assumption is that if it is legal, it is therefore moral."[8] Brian Clowes says that "Our solid value system has been entirely displaced by an amorphous and indefinable 'anything goes as long as you can make it legal' mentality."[9]

1 R.C. Sproul, 21.

2 Geisler, in Ball, *In Search of a National Morality: A Manifesto for Evangelicals and Catholics* [1992], 112.

3 Harold Brown, 82.

4 John Whitehead, *The Second American Revolution*, 89.

5 Michael Hart, 261-3.

6 Whitehead, *Stealing of America*, 96.

7 Anderson, *Living Ethically in the '90s*, 40-1.

8 Sproul, 21, and 70: "I suspect that the greatest cause of the change of public opinion [in favor of abortion] is the Supreme Court decision in *Roe v. Wade*. There is a strong tendency among people of any nation to take their direction for what is ethically right from what the law allows or what the society condones."

9 Clowes, Brian, *Pro-Life Activist's Encyclopedia*, acknowledgments: "...a process that one would rather not see: the gradual and inexorable decomposition of a once-great Christian country... into a pagan nation where the most honored personal characteristics are nonjudgmentalism, tolerance, and diversity."

10. John Whitehead, *The Second American Revolution*, 88.

11 R.C. Sproul, 70.

12 Christopher Stone, *Should Trees Have Standing?*, 32.

13 Whitehead, *The Second American Revolution*, 88-9: "In the process of yielding to the 'will of the people' and creating new rights, the state inevitably enlarges itself and its bureaucracy. Each new right seems to demand a new agency to guarantee it, administer it, or deliver it."

"Legal positivism is the idea that law is established or recognized by state authority. The law sets the standard for justice. What is legal is by definition just. Once the law is enacted, it is obligatory. There is no higher or transcendent law by which to measure it because the state is the ultimate source of the law."[10]

–John Whitehead

*** REMEMBER ***
that every pair of pages contains this nifty OUTLINE, with the current topics underlined:

SCOPE and FOCUS
I. CONVICTIONS
Polarizing Certainties
Creation vs. Accident
Design vs. Mechanism
Commandments vs. Positivism
Justice vs. Pragmatism
Virtue vs. Pleasure
Universalism vs. Relativism
Accountability vs. Autonomy
Worldview Confusion
Human Condition & Life
Stewards vs. Masters
II. PRETEXTS
III. MANDATE
IV. LEGACY
V. ABORTIVE LINKS
VI. DILEMMA
VII. DESTINY

As a policy, positivism engenders a Rights orientation

One of the paramount results of positivism is that it undermines respect for the law. Citizens develop the attitude that it's illegal today but not yesterday or tomorrow. We become aware that a statute passed – or failed – by just *one* vote. "Our nation has reversed itself on slavery, prohibition, racial discrimination, conscientious objection to wars, capital punishment, and other issues of ethics and justice... Contemporary community standards become the highest court of appeal, the ultimate norm of justice and ethics."[11] Christopher Stone says, "What we are really doing is making implicit normative judgments [and] laying down rules as to what the society is going to value."[12]

"In recent years we have witnessed numerous marches on Washington in which one group or another has demanded new 'rights.' Frequently, such rights have not meant freedom from state control [the traditional concept of rights], but rather entitlements to state action, protection, or subsidy."[13]

As to abortion and the *Roe v. Wade* decision, Whitehead says, "...privacy is *not* a God-given, natural law on the same level as the right to life. But the Court in effect ignored the natural law argument and considered privacy a constitutional, man-made right."[14] He speaks his mind very clearly: "An illegitimate government is in the business of assuming the prerogative of granting so-called civil rights."[15]

John Whitehead has much to say about positivism. He traces the downward spiral that began when the social contract theory deposed the divine right of kings: "The eventual consequence of the loss of the higher law and the rise of a perverted, autonomous natural justice is that the state, developing as the expression of a manipulative elite, dictates law. This is legal positivism... Aleksandr Solzhenitsyn has said, with much insight, that if people give away the absolutes of right and wrong as found in the laws of God, there is nothing left but to manipulate one another."[16]

"The modern secular view holds that individuals have just such rights as the Constitution and other laws give them... Unless we succeed in clarifying what we mean by rights... we will neither be able to understand nor to influence what is going on in America today."[17]
–John Whitehead

Where man's law contravenes God's law, divinity should prevail

Henry David Thoreau was quite angry when John Brown was hanged after a failed raid at Harper's Ferry, Virginia. He railed, "Let lawyers decide *trivial* cases... If they were the interpreters of the everlasting laws which rightfully bind man, that would be another thing. A counterfeiting law factory, standing half in a slaveland and half in a free! What kind of laws for freemen can you expect from that?"[18]

Robert Downs tells us that Thoreau urged that those who opposed slavery "should at once effectively withdraw their support, both in person and property, from the government... and not wait until they constitute a majority of one, before they suffer the right to prevail through them. I think that it is enough if they have God on their side, without waiting for that other one. Moreover, any man more right than his neighbors constitutes a majority of one already."[19]

14 Whitehead, *Second*, 116.
15 Whitehead, *Second*, 89: "..the term *civil rights* is a contradiction in terms. *Civil* basically means government created. If something is government created, it cannot legitimately be a 'right' in the old sense but should only be an exercise of privilege. Freedom of worship is a right. Food stamps and social security benefits are privileges."
16 Whitehead, *Second*, 192.
17 Whitehead, *Second*, 116.
18 Michael Bray, 93.
19 Robert Downs, *Books that Changed the World*, 69.

Two days after the *Roe v. Wade* decision in 1973, the National Conference of Catholic Bishops publicly proclaimed it to be "a flagrant rejection of the unborn child's right to life... Although as a result of the court decision abortion may be legally permissible, it is still morally wrong, and no Court opinion can change the law of God prohibiting the taking of innocent human life."[1]

The justification for a clinic Rescue is made on the basis of "necessity" (e.g. breaking down someone's door to rescue their child from a housefire) and "higher laws." The latter holds that God's "Thou shalt not kill" Commandment trumps the positivist's "No trespassing" sign. Rescuer and pastor, Joseph Foreman says, "...to refuse to save a child whom we could have saved is to incur the guilt of innocent blood... Saving an innocent life is *not* breaking a law, no matter what the policemen and judges of this age might think. God, not man, still defines law."[2]

Cathy Ramey has said, "The reason that *every* Christian is obligated to stand against abortion... is because inherent in the decision to legalize the act of abortion was the decision to utterly reject God's Law. That's something that *every* Christian ought to take offense at, whether they have an abortionist in town or not."[3] From *The Second American Revolution*: "Government is not God, to create rights, but is God's minister to protect the rights God has given to man."[4] We Christians are more than citizens of the United States; we are adopted children of God, citizens in His eternal home, and we are His ambassadors to this planet. "The statute law of the moment... does not adequately take into account what many of us see as our responsibilities as trustees of the earth."[5]

Not only Christians have duties above the civil law. Gary DeMar tells us that "East German border guard Ingo Heinrich killed a man escaping East Berlin for the freedom of the West. He justified his action by saying, 'I was just following orders to shoot to kill.' In the eyes of his supervisors, Heinrich's actions were not only legal, they were commendable. But Heinrich now lives in a *new* Berlin, serving 3½ years in prison. Judge Theodore Seidel ruled that he was guilty of following the laws of his country rather than his conscience, stating that 'Not everything that is legal is right.'"[6]

4. Justice vs. Pragmatism

Because the progressives have so successfully remodeled American government to conform to Enlightenment specifications, installing positivism in place of God as the basis of law, the *rational* choice for a mode of arriving at *sensible* laws is *logically*: pragmatism.

Pragmatism begins with a detached, purely rational approach to problem solving

A prime example of pragmatism in action is evidenced in this newspaper report: "President Clinton delivered an emotional defense of his veto of last summer's late-term abortion legislation: 'This is not a pro-life, pro-choice issue. This is a practical problem.'"[7]

"Pragmatism is the idea that if something has utility (if it *works*) then it should be put into effect... Pragmatism means that there is no such thing as absolute truth. Pragmatism thus leads to relativism (there is no truth and there are no absolutes)," says Whitehead.[8]

SCOPE and FOCUS

I. CONVICTIONS

Polarizing Certainties

Creation vs. Accident

Design vs. Mechanism

Commandments vs. Positivism

Justice vs. Pragmatism

Virtue vs. Pleasure

Universalism vs. Relativism

Accountability vs. Autonomy

Worldview Confusion

Human Condition & Life

Stewards vs. Masters

II. PRETEXTS

1 Clowes, *Pro-Life Activist's Encyclopedia*, page 43.14.

2 Foreman, *Shattering the Darkness*, 19.

3 *Life Advocate*, 4/'94, 30.

4 Whitehead, *Second*, 89.

5 Garret Hardin, in Stone, foreword.

6 DeMar, in Foreman, xv.

7 *Press*, 12-14-96, A11.

8 Whitehead, *Stealing of America*, 13-14: "Essentially the philosophy of Kant and Hegel can be summarized in two terms: *pragmatism* and *collectivism*. Hitler added a third solidifying idea to this matrix: *social and political evolution*... Collectivism is the idea that the group (the collective) has primacy over the individual. In other words, the wishes of the majority are more important than the wishes of an individual, even if the effect is deprivation of that individual's freedom."

9 John Eidsmoe, *God and Caesar*, 170.

"The ultimate test of human worth in the humanist scheme of values is how useful is this person to society?"[9] –John Eidsmoe

John Dewey is called the father of public education. He was a pragmatist. The effects of Dewey's pragmatism, as of Hitler's, will be summarized later [parts IV.B.1+2; IV.C.7.a].[10] After writing millions of words to chronicle the history of mankind on this planet, Will and Ariel Durant placed all of their most profound conclusions in a slender volume called *The Lessons of History*. Their thoughts from that tome will be quoted repeatedly in this work. They epitomize, unfortunately, the loftiest wisdom of secular intellectuals. In these words they reveal the utter poverty of the pragmatic view of life: "We shall here define progress as the increasing control of the environment by life... Our problem is whether the average man has increased his ability to control the conditions of his life."[11]

Pragmatism as a government policy leads to disaster

"China's leadership has meticulously yet unwittingly laid the groundwork for today's youth to ask tomorrow's revolutionary question: Do you remember Tianenmen Square?"[12] Tianenmen Square was a pragmatic solution to the problem of thousands of citizens crying out for liberty. Another example of pragmatism is revealed in this Associated Press article: "House International Relations Committee members were most critical of the Clinton administration for maintaining normal trade relations with China and inviting its defense minister, Gen. Chi Haotian, who led the 1989 Tinanmen Square massacre, to visit the United States and the White House..."[13] On the same page, the chairman of that committee is quoted as saying, "The message we are sending to the world is that the government of the United States is committed to the protection of fundamental human rights only insofar as such a commitment does not threaten to interfere with anything else it wants to accomplish."[13]

Have Americans figured out that government policies are driven not by a commitment to justice but by pragmatism? Here are the results of a 1997 Scripps Howard News Service poll: 40% of Americans think the government deliberately set the fires at Waco; 48% think it is withholding proof of extraterrestrial intelligence; 51% believe that government agencies were responsible for the assassination of President Kennedy; 52% are convinced that government policy has included letting drug dealers sell cocaine to black kids; and 80% are certain that the government is covering up germ and nerve gas exposure during Desert Storm.[14] As public policy, the injustice of pragmatism simply stinks.

Some recommend pragmatism for solving ethical problems

When pragmatism gets dressed up and tries to look respectable, it is called Situation Ethics. "Joseph Fletcher is the principal spokesman for *situationalism*. He delineates three of its major facets: 1) A loving act is one done with loving intentions; 2) The end justifies the means; and 3) An act can be judged as loving or unloving because of the consequences."[15]

As will be shown later, pragmatism is one of many liberal maladies that infected the "mainline" denominations in this century. For now, this might be instructive. The Friends are perhaps best known by their nickname, Quakers, and for their pacifism, pietism and long prayerful silences awaiting unanimity in decision making. This last practice would not normally qualify for the label pragmatic, but here is what happened. Amid the social turmoil that preceded *Roe v. Wade*, the Friends issued this very pragmatic pronouncement: "On religious, moral and humanitarian grounds, we arrived at the view that it is far better to end an unwanted pregnancy than to encourage the evils resulting from forced pregnancy and childbirth. We therefore urge the repeal of all laws limiting either the circumstances under which a woman may have an abortion or the physician's freedom to use his or her best professional judgment in performing it."[16]

10 Geisler, *Is Man the Measure? An Evaluation of Contemporary Humanism*, 57: "Dewey's pragmatism is manifest on two important levels: truth and ethics. The pragmatic view of truth is that whatever works is true. This, however, is an insufficient view of truth. For many things that work very well (such as lies) are false... Pragmatism fares no better in the realm of ethics. Not everything that works [gets you the results you like] is right. Some things that work very well are simply evil. Cheating, deceiving, and even killing undesirables are only a few of man's successful but evil activities."

11 Durant, *Lessons*, 98.

12 Aeschliman, *Global Trends: Ten Changes Affecting Christians Everywhere*, 63: "...The horrifying sound of skulls being run over by tanks, the images of machine guns fired point-blank in the faces of thousands of unarmed civilians, the stories of lobotomies performed on student leaders, and the unabashed denial by the Chinese government that any such atrocities occurred..."

13 *Press*, 2-1-97, A11, [two quotes]

14 *Press*, 7-5-97, A11, A12.

15 Kerby Anderson, 11.

John Jefferson Davis, in *Abortion and the Christian: What Every Believer Should Know*, quotes Jospeh Fletcher: "There are in the end only two ways of deciding what is right. Either we will obey a rule (or a ruler) of conscience, which is the *a priori* [point of beginning, before analysis] or prejudiced approach, or we will look as reasonably as we can at the facts and calculate the consequences, the human costs and benefits – the pragmatic way. ...Most of us decide for or against things on the principle of proportionate good" (10).

16 Grant, *Third Time*, 127.

5. Virtue vs. Pleasure

Let's do an informal study to find out if the dictionaries are describing virtue as an "archaic" word yet. Robert Bork says that thirty years ago, Clinton's sexual antics would have been "absolutely disqualifying" for election to the White House, but amazingly, "none of this appears to affect his popularity."[1]

We really shouldn't be so surprised. We're the ones who know that mankind is sinful by nature. Leo Strauss, in *Natural Right and History*, tells us that, "...what induces man to deviate from the narrow path of ancestral custom or divine law appears to be the desire for pleasure and the aversion to pain. The natural good thus appears to be pleasure. Orientation by pleasure becomes the first substitute for the orientation by the ancestral."[2]

If so many are convinced that we were once a "Christian nation," how did we get so unbuttoned?

Strauss traces the preoccupation with pleasure all the way back to ancient Greece. He says that the Epicureans decided that the philosophical "good" was the same as what came naturally. The rest is history. Even the word hedonism began with the concept that defined the good as the maximum achievement of pleasure while minimizing the pain; the sex and alcohol connotations came later, but perhaps not much later.[3]

Narcissism also got its start with the Greeks, in a story about me-ism and self-infatuation. We'd like to think that Christianity got all of those things under control for a couple of thousand years until Ed Sullivan met Elvis, but the truth is probably a bit different from that.

Concerning this struggle between virtue and pleasure, the Reformation would be a good place to look for clues; we've mentioned already the Protestant emphasis on the individual. Also, the artists of the Renaissance were focusing much more on earthly than on heavenly delights. Paul deParrie tells us that even the meaning of the word, *love*, was being retailored from its virtuous and biblical form of commitment, duty and fidelity, to a more stylish and pleasure-focused orientation of *how I feel about you* and *how you make me feel*.[4]

Paul deParrie calls this development the Love Myth and he traces its influence all the way down to the present, not just among the pagans, but particularly in such forms as mainline denominational feel-good theology, everybody's seeker-friendly church atmosphere, and the preoccupation of contemporary Christian music with how good Jesus makes me *feel*.[5]

We are told that the effect of Kinsey's sex surveys was "to unshackle a generation from its repressive past."[6] Robert Bork says that, "The Sixties combined domestic disruption and violence with an explosion of drug use and sexual promiscuity; it was a decade of hedonism and narcissism... Nihilism was the order of the decade."[7]

The following summary seems to verify, conclusively, that a quest for spiritual virtue is not now a national preoccupation: "Recent sex surveys report that... since Kinsey... in an economy characterized by abundance and oriented toward the production of luxury items and consumer goods, sexual pleasure has become a means of recreation for all classes. Character structure and child rearing practices have shifted accordingly, away from an emphasis on autonomous self-control and toward the rational acceptance of pleasure, personal fulfillment, and happiness."[8]

1 Robert Bork, *Slouching Towards Gomorrah*, 341: "Something about our moral perceptions and reactions has changed profoundly. If that change is permanent, the implications for our future are bleak."

2 Leo Strauss, 109.

3 R.C. Sproul, 128.

4 Paul deParrie, *Romanced to Death: The Sexual Seduction of American Culture*, 14.

5 Paul deParrie, 171.

[Several influences relating to the ascendancy of the pleasure orientation over virtue will be given special treatment later, but they should be mentioned for their relevance here: various women's movements and the Margaret Sanger contraception-and-sex-and-abortion enterprise; Freud's synthesis of the what's-natural-is-good theme with the sex-is-natural-and-central and the religion-induced-sexual-repression-causes-mental-illness theories.]

6 Regina Markell Morantz, in Altherr, *Procreation or Pleasure?: Sexual Attitudes in American History*, 160.

7 Robert Bork, 50-1.

8 Regina Markell Morantz, in Altherr, 164.

9 Norman Geisler, *Is Man the Measure?*, 70-1.

10 Joseph Foreman, 164.

11 By Mark Crutcher, *Access: The Key to Pro-Life Victory*, 21.

12 Robert Bork, 82.

13 Emil Brunner, 83.

14 R.C. Sproul, *Abortion: A Rational Look at an Emotional Issue*, 128.

"While traditional Christians have defined the chief end of man as glorifying God and enjoying Him forever, Ayn Rand boldly proclaims that man's chief end is himself and his own happiness."[9]

SCOPE and FOCUS
I. CONVICTIONS
Polarizing Certainties
Creation vs. Accident
Design vs. Mechanism
Commandments vs. Positivism
Justice vs. Pragmatism
Virtue vs. Pleasure
Universalism vs. Relativism
Accountability vs. Autonomy
Worldview Confusion
Human Condition & Life
Stewards vs. Masters
II. PRETEXTS
III. MANDATE
IV. LEGACY
V. ABORTIVE LINKS
VI. DILEMMA
VII. DESTINY

"Suffering pain in order to do what is right is the mark of a virtuous person.

Doing what *feels* good is often easy. It's not so easy to do what *is* good.

Cultural mores reach the bottom when an ethic like *If it feels good, do it* is embraced.

Such slogans become the epitaphs of a corrupt society."[14]

–R.C. Sproul

The pleasure/pain principle is central to the abortion battle

Pleasure, pain and virtue – all three – are tightly woven into the fabric of the tragedy called abortion. It was desire for the pleasures of sex that produced this now unwanted child. It was the pain of a thousand fears that led to the awful decision. Some would argue that there is virtue in the willingness of the abortionist, staff and escorts to provide a desperately needed service in this woman's hour of need.

On the pro-life side there is virtue, although cynics would quip that a feeling of self-righteousness is the reward that makes every apparent act of altruism an egotistical charade. They're sure that pro-lifers sacrifice just enough so they stop feeling bad about not doing enough, and so they begin to feel good about what they've done. A wise professor was once heard to say that, because of our sin nature, "Even the righteous acts of redeemed believers are sinful." Thinking that thought, and believing it, can be painful too.

Rev. Joseph Foreman was one of many bright lights in the leadership of Operation Rescue. He wrote a book in 1992, *Shattering the Darkness: The Crisis of the Cross in the Church Today*. Surely this passage speaks volumes about pleasure, pain and virtue:

> Operation Rescue as a concept and as a movement was headed in the right direction, but still held too many presuppositions of the world... And we still long after earthly power... without stopping to earn the divine character to wield such power wisely. God's counter-offer is a cross... loving obedience at any cost. Only out of the standards of righteousness and the sacrifice of the Cross can politics become Christian, redemptive, and fruitful. All too easily the world proved that we were not willing to sacrifice to save a life... [and yet] we [all] ask the young mother to sacrifice for us: either her child through abortion, or her life-style by bearing the unwanted child.[10]

And the pain of the frantic, pregnant mother? For those who do not know, a pro-life feminist writer, Frederica Mathewes-Green, tells us, "Like an animal caught in a trap, trying to gnaw off its own leg, a woman who seeks abortion is trying to escape a desperate situation by an act of violence and self-loss. Abortion is not a sign that women are free, but a sign that they are desperate."[11]

Multiply that anguish times the twenty or thirty million American who have lived it. Then add the empathy of family members and friends who were close to them. The result will give you a glimpse of the political momentum in the direction of retaining "abortion rights." There are commitments born of action, just as there are actions demanded by convictions. It has been observed that the pro-abortion political block gains at least 2000 new voters every day – women who had been ambivalent about abortion but just found out they are pregnant. Sales trainers tell us that pleasure and pain are not just the best sources of motivation, they are the *only* motivators; and of the two, fear is by far the stronger.

Robert Bork says, "Democratic man, thinking that others are like himself, identifies with anyone who suffers. This compassion born of the passion for equality leads to the power of claiming victim status... [We have become] a nation of victims who stress their pain as a way of demanding special treatment from others... There is also power to be gained by the politician who assures us that 'I feel your pain.'"[12]

As members of the family of God who are called to take part in this battle – that is all of us, in one way or another – we must accept the mandate to live, by the grace of God, lives of virtue.

In *The Divine Imperative: A Study in Christian Ethics*, Emil Brunner says that, "In the Christian view, that alone is 'good' which is free from all caprice, which takes place in unconditional obedience. There is no Good save obedient behavior, save the obedient will... the Good consists in always doing what God wills at any particular moment."[13]

6. Universalism vs. Relativism

Only a universalist can say, "There *ought* to be a law!"

We have discussed Positivism's challenge to the divine Commandments of God. Leo Strauss, in a comprehensive study called *Natural Right and History*, reveals historical shifts in philosophical thought. From the ancient Greeks' contemplation of "the good" [which is akin to the Christian view of Virtue] to the later search for "modern natural right" [17th century] which degenerated into a fascination with all things "natural," and an eventual popularization of slogans like "If it feels good, do it." His prodigious work might be summed up as a contrasting of three types of law: divine, natural and civil.[1]

As we have seen, modern secularists have embraced civil law based on a positivism that utterly rejects any reference to divine law. For this reason, the exploration of the concepts of natural law and natural right hold the prospect of an avenue by which universal morality might be injected into debates where, otherwise, relativism will stand unopposed.[2]

Relativism is so widely practiced and so fervently defended, that its essential correctness seems to be held as a universal principle. [It is hoped that you notice the humor in this statement.] To be consistent and precise, a dyed-in-the-wool relativist should admit: *There are no absolute truths except this one which I am now declaring*. Kerby Anderson says that "all people tend to believe that some things are right and some things are wrong. Even for those who claim that there is really no such thing as what they would call right or wrong, every time they criticize, applaud, approve, or accuse, they implicitly appeal to some fixed standard of right and wrong."[3]

Everyone agrees that there are universals

Among sane and civilized people, it is universally accepted that it would be morally wrong to pour gasoline on a stray cat and light it on fire, whether there is a law against it or not. So all self-proclaimed moral relativists are universalists – their relativism is actually selective; it means that they object to the application of any external moral standard to themselves.

Behaviorists might argue that every human being begins as a moral and ethical "blank slate," that everything is learned, and that there is no such thing as natural law or an intuitive sense of justice. They are opposed, however, by a long history of belief in "natural law" of one kind or another, from the biblical "law written on their hearts,"[4] to the ancient philosophers' quest to understand "first things," those truths older than the ancestral wisdom. Leo Strauss tells us that the Classic Natural Right theory of Socrates and Plato included the belief that "Man's freedom is accompanied by a sacred awe, by a kind of divination that not everything is permitted... We may call this awe-inspired fear 'man's natural conscience.'"[5]

Geisler tells us that Thomas Aquinas "distinguished natural law, which is common to all rational creatures, from divine law, which is imposed only on believers."[6] He goes on to tell us that for John Calvin, "not only is the natural law clear but it is also specific. It includes a sense of justice "imprinted by nature in the hearts of men... by which they distinguish between justice and injustice, honesty and dishonesty."[7]

1 Leo Strauss, *Natural right and History*, 86.

2 In the words of Harold O.J. Brown, "The transformation of American society reveals two increasingly strong developments: a loss of fixed standards of moral value and an incredibly narcissistic fascination with ourselves... Nothing external matters, only, as Sorokin said, our own fancy or will" [in Ball, 60].

3 Kerby Anderson, *Living Ethically in the '90s*, 34.

4 Kilner, *Life on the Line*, 40, and *Jeremiah* 31:33.

5 Leo Strauss, 91-2, and 130, and Randy Alcorn, *Is Rescuing Right? Breaking the Law to Save the Unborn*, 69, and *Romans* 2:14-15.

Strauss teaches us that for the philosophers, "There are things which are admirable, or noble, by nature, intrinsically, [which] all point toward the well-ordered soul, incomparably the most admirable human phenomenon" [128].

6 +7 Norman Geisler, in William B. Ball, 116, [two quotes].

8 Wolterstorff, in Audi and Wolterstorff, *Religion in the Public Square: The Place of Religious Convictions in Political Debate*, 84-5.

9 Michael Hart, *The 100: A Ranking of the Most Influential Persons in History*, 261-3.

10 Leo Strauss, 141.

11 Leo Strauss, 118.

12 Leo Strauss, 83-4.

13 Leo Strauss, 102.

14 Leo Strauss, 106.

15 Robert Bork, *Slouching Towards Gomorrah*, 276.

16 Schaeffer, in Scheidler, *Closed: 99 Ways to Stop Abortion*, 11.

17 Anderson, *Living Ethically in the '90s*, 11.

18 Smith, *When Choice Becomes God*, 10

"There exist divine moral laws, not easy to apprehend, but operating upon all mankind... God, not man, is the measure of all things."[20]
–Plato

SCOPE and FOCUS
I. CONVICTIONS
Polarizing Certainties
Creation vs. Accident
Design vs. Mechanism
Commandments vs. Positivism
Justice vs. Pragmatism
Virtue vs. Pleasure
Universalism vs. Relativism
Accountability vs. Autonomy
Worldview Confusion
Human Condition & Life
Stewards vs. Masters
II. PRETEXTS
III. MANDATE
IV. LEGACY
V. ABORTIVE LINKS
VI. DILEMMA
VII. DESTINY

Relativism is great for Liberty but very bad for moral virtue

Wolterstorff tells us that John Locke believed, "We could arrive at a very substantial body" of natural law: "moral truths that are accessible to human reason, unaided by divine revelation."[8] Hart says that Locke adds this caution to his democratic ideals: "A majority must not violate the natural rights of men."[9]

Strauss clarifies the shift of emphasis that democracy and the social contract theory brought about. "The political problem consists in reconciling the requirement for wisdom [in civic leadership] with the requirement for consent [of 'the people']. But whereas, from the point of view of classic natural right [Socrates and Plato], wisdom takes precedence over consent, from the point of view of egalitarian natural right [social contract and democracy] consent takes precedence over wisdom."[10]

As popular consent of free and equal individuals became the standard of authority in government,[11] many other changes followed. Anything unpopular [whatever is not "the will of the people"] had to go. In France the guillotine ended the "divine right of kings" to rule. The Colonies won their independence from England. Traditional sources of authority were challenged in many ways.[12]

The concept of justice received a make-over. In place of nobility, virtue and obedience to divine commandments, the "common good" became the test of what was just,[13] and since "justice has no basis in nature [the] common good proved to be the selfish interest of a collective."[14]

Relativism is growing like a cancer in the United States

"Over the past 30 years, all the major philosophical as well as cultural trends began to repudiate secular rationalism in favor of an intellectual and moral relativism and/or nihilism."[15] Franky Schaeffer tells us that "As the last chapters of the twentieth century unfold, we Americans find ourselves being led in the 1990s by leaders who, for the most part, have abandoned belief in moral absolutes."[16]

We can get tuned-in by Kerby Anderson: "Situation ethics is everywhere in this generation: *That's just your belief. It's your decision. It may be wrong for you, but not for me.* It is making decisions believing that there are no universal moral principles, that only the situation determines what is moral or immoral. Its summary rule is: *Do the most loving thing.*"[17] "All choices are now thought to possess equal value or at least merit equal recognition under the canopy of being socially acceptable 'alternative lifestyles,'" says F. LaGard Smith in *When Choice Becomes God.*[18] Arthur Schlesinger said it well: "The American mind is by nature and tradition skeptical, irreverent, pluralistic and relativistic. ...Relativism is the American way."[19]

19 Schlesinger, in Hunter, 113.

Clowes quotes Lester A. Kirkendall: "...as the rigid [sexual conduct] code relaxed, new concepts evolved. At the same time vocabulary was altered [here is an example of the 'slippery slope' in action]: Perversions became abnormalities, abnormalities became deviancies, deviancies became variations, variations became options, options became preferences, preferences became choices, and choices became life-enhancing experiences" (page 15.5).

20 Plato, in Colson, *Kingdoms in Conflict*, 228.

21 Roche, *The Bewildered Society*, 323-4.

"Ours is the most complete secularization of culture the world has ever known... Lasting political cohesion demands common moral beliefs and attitudes... The political regime which cannot discover a universal definition of justice cannot govern justly – and soon cannot govern at all."[21] –George Charles Roche, III

Relativism has been enshrined and given civil sanction

Roe v. Wade in 1973 was a prime example of pragmatism, positivism [lawmaking done illicitly by the Supreme Court], and relativism, all functioning in concert: "...the Court in effect ignored the natural law argument and considered privacy a constitutional, man-made right."[1]

In 1992, William Bentley Ball quoted Paul C. Vitz, speaking about moral relativism: "The idea is now widespread that each individual has some kind of sovereign right to create, develop, and express whatever values he or she happens to prefer."[2]

If the idea was not already "widespread" enough, the Supreme Court almost immediately chiseled it in stone. In what is now termed the *mystery passage*, part of the *Casey* decision, the justices proclaimed, "At the heart of liberty is the right to define one's own concept of existence, of meaning, of the universe, and of the mystery of human life."[3]

In October of 1997, James Dobson revisited that passage: "With those words, the Court discarded its historic reliance on 'a law beyond the law,' or a transcendent standard [universalism]. The bottom line is... Everything is relative and subject to individual interpretation. For the U.S. Supreme Court to descend into this abyss of moral relativism is disastrous."[4]

Dr. Dobson is exactly right, although the mystery passage may have a silver lining. In court, with only the rarest exception, Rescuers have not even been permitted to introduce the "necessity" defense for their action to save a life. The judicial rationale was that in *Roe* the Court declared its inability to determine when human life begins, but it could assert that preborns are *not* 14th Amendment "persons;" therefore, you can't trespass to save a person if no *person* is in danger. But now, in *Casey*, the court has declared that every individual, including a Rescuer we would assume, has "the right to define one's own concept of existence... and of the mystery of human life."[3] From now on, Rescuers on trial do not have to plead insanity to declare that they were convinced that a live human baby was about to be killed! Relativism, in this one instance at least, might just be a great thing.

7. Accountability vs. Autonomy

The parishioner in the pew got a healthy dose of fire and brimstone when Jonathan Edwards preached about "Sinners in the hands of an angry God." Those things, sermons, have cooled down considerably: Fundamentalists still use hell as a trump card, Evangelicals concentrate on the *joys* of being in the kingdom, and Mainliners never talk about heaven at all except at funerals, where it seems like all dead people go to an eternal *reward*. The ignorance and ignore-ance of the reality and finality of each person's spiritual destiny is a disgrace, in our nation and in many congregations.

In politics, everybody is in favor of "freedom and justice." But Hunter, in *Culture Wars*, points out a curious difference between what political liberals ["progressivists"] and conservatives mean when they use these words.[5] He says that Freedom, to a conservative means economic Opportunity, but means Rights to a liberal – those rights that translate into social Autonomy and entitlements. Likewise, when a conservative speaks of Justice he means ethics and Accountability, while a liberal says Justice when she means social Equality. Perhaps we need a truth-in-labeling-law for political parties: "The Surging Generalist warns that if you buy Donkey brand 'Freedom and Justice' you will get Social Equality and Autonomy, but Elephant brand 'Freedom and Justice' will get you Opportunity with Accountability." Robert Bork says that "Liberalism itself (putting aside, for the moment, its egalitarian element) is nothing but an effort to struggle free of restraints on the individual."[6]

1 John Whitehead, *The Second American Revolution*, 116.

2 William B. Ball, *In Search of a National Morality: A Manifesto for Evangelicals and Catholics*, 43.

3 *Focus on the Family* newsletter, July 1997, 2.

4 *Family News From Dr. James Dobson*, October, 1997, 2.

Dobson's letter quotes John Leo: "This 'mystery passage' can be cited easily next time to justify suicide clinics, gay marriage, polygamy, inter-species marriage (such as marrying one's dog or cat) or whatever new individual right the court feels like inventing. We are moving firmly into the court's post-constitutional phase."

5 Hunter, 114-5.

Elsewhere Hunter explains that "Richard Merleman... has speculated that the strains in American culture are those that exist between the 'tight-bounded' and 'loose-bounded' moral communities within our society. Moral obligation with tight-bounded communities tends to be fixed and rigid, viewed by its members as a 'given' of social life. In opposition are the loose-bounded communities for whom moral commitment tends to be voluntary, contingent, and fluid – where the liberated individual, not the social group, becomes the final arbiter of moral judgment" (119-20).

6 Robert Bork, *Slouching Towards Gomorrah: Modern Liberalism and American Decline*, 57-8.

7 Kilner, *Life on the Line*, 58-9.

8 Michael Hart, *The 100: A Ranking of the Most Influential Persons in History*, 149-50.

9 Robert Bork, 273.

10 Robert Bork, 57-61 and 63-4.

11 Durant, *The Lessons of History*, 89-90.

SCOPE and FOCUS
I. CONVICTIONS
Polarizing Certainties
Creation vs. Accident
Design vs. Mechanism
Commandments vs. Positivism
Justice vs. Pragmatism
Virtue vs. Pleasure
Universalism vs. Relativism
Accountability vs. Autonomy
Worldview Confusion
Human Condition & Life
Stewards vs. Masters
II. PRETEXTS
III. MANDATE
IV. LEGACY
V. ABORTIVE LINKS
VI. DILEMMA
VII. DESTINY

In light of all that, let's try to guess John Kilner's political leanings from these words: "...freedom has a dual dimension of a particular kind. It involves freedom from restrictions, but not all restrictions. It is not autonomy... Autonomy by definition knows no law but the self, but God intends that even this law be replaced – and fulfilled – by love of God and neighbor. This restriction is less a restraint than it is an opportunity, for it is at the heart of the life in which people were created to flourish."[7]

Denying eternity makes you king/queen for a day

Luther was rejecting his accountability to the pope when he declared his right to beliefs guided only by the Bible and plain reason,[8] and Protestantism was built upon that attitude of individual [dare we say: autonomous] accountability to God alone. Bork tells us that Tocqueville, reflecting in 1840 on his travels through the United States, had observed "...the struggle of religion with that spirit of individual independence which is her most dangerous opponent... In a few pages Tocqueville not only recognized that [individualism/autonomy] was capable of changing the substance of religion but anticipated the ravages that radical individualism would inflict upon religion."[9]

Regarding personal liberty, someone has observed [discovered in Natural Law, for all we know] that "Your freedom to swing your fist stops where my nose begins." That seems to have been a major theme in *On Liberty*, published in 1859 by John Stuart Mill. According to Bork, Mill's contention was that the only limit to the individual's autonomy should be that required by the right of self-protection, either by a person or by the society collectively.[10]

As described by the Durants, Oswald Spengler – whose adulthood began in 1900 – surveyed the great civilizations of history and saw "...each with an independent life span and trajectory composed of four seasons but essentially two periods: one of centripetal organization unifying a culture in all its phases...; the other a period of centrifugal disorganization in which creed and culture decompose in division and criticism, and end in a chaos of individualism [and] skepticism..."[11]

To whatever degree we subscribe to Spengler's concept, it would be easy to trace America's "centripetal" ascent: from a *Declaration* and Revolution through a federation of independent "states," a Civil War to prove the *indivisibility* of that Union, and a great series of political solutions to social problems: slavery, abortion [the *first* time],[12] women's suffrage, child labor, and civil rights. A great irony can be found as we further apply Spengler's model: The very successes by which government consolidated and asserted its control over society [centripetal organization] were, in each instance we have cited, actions that also expanded the progressive brand of freedom and justice: individual rights and social equality. The very fruit of governmental power contained the seeds of [Spengler's] "division and individualism," and invited the "skepticism and criticism" which replaced individual Accountability with personal Autonomy.

Bork says that it was the American intellectual community that became infatuated with "expressive individualism" as early as the 1890s, and that by the 1920s they had made it their pet ideology. His view is that the explosion of that philosophy of personal autonomy which we experienced in the 1960s was delayed that long only because of the Great Depression and World War II.[13]

12 James C. Mohr, *Abortion in America: The Origins and Evolution of National Policy, 1800-1900*, 226. "When [Indiana] revised its state code in 1881, it added two new sections to its 1859 abortion law. The first made a consenting woman guilty of a crime punishable by fine and jailing" (277)... [Pro-abortionists have now claimed that the only motivation behind the nineteenth century anti-abortion movement was, not any belief in the humanity or rights of the preborn, but, only the need to protect women from what was then – but "is no longer" – frequently a danger to the woman's life. On the contrary: at least one state, Indiana, put teeth into the belief that it is *criminal* for a woman to consent to the murder of her unborn child.] "By 1900 abortion no longer seemed to be a threat to the native [already born] population" (245).

13 Robert Bork, 88.

14 Robert Bork, 54.

"The Sixties generation's fixation on equality has permeated our society and its institutions, much to our disadvantage. Their idea of liberty has now become license..."[14] –Robert H. Bork

"It is cultural suicide to demand all space and no walls."[9] –Robert H. Bork

Tee shirts today broadcast an up-dated hippie slogan: "No Rules!"

Documenting the radical rise of autonomy and rejection of accountability, William Bennet says: "During the past 30 years, we have witnessed a profound shift in public attitudes... We Americans now place less value on what we owe others as a matter of moral obligation; less value on sacrifice as a moral good, on social conformity, respectability, and observing the rules; less value on correctness and restraint in matters of physical pleasure and sexuality – and correlatively greater value on things like self-expression, individualism, self-realization, and personal choice."[1]

One of the *Lessons of History* asserted by Will and Ariel Durant glories in personal autonomy: "Our finest contemporary achievement is... the enlargement of man's understanding, control, embellishment, and enjoyment of life."[2] Regina Morantz celebrates the assertiveness of women: "If a sexual revolution has occurred, its base has been changes in female attitudes and behavior... while male trends shifted only minimally... It would seem that sexual liberation... presupposes and encourages the development of individuality and autonomy among women."[3] Psychology, too, has helped to give more social autonomy to the individual. As Rev. Jerry L. Propst summarizes: "For nearly a full generation now it has been popular to define people as victims, and in so doing remove from them responsibility for their actions."[4]

Many have seen throughout history the repetition of similar trends and progressions, likened unto "cycles" or the swinging of a pendulum. Roughly two hundred years ago, Comte de Saint-Simon was describing alternations of "organic" and "critical" phases in history. His point was that civilizations are built up (the organic phase) when citizens share [accountability] what we might call a common world view, and that such unity is lost because of widespread challenges to the core assumptions (the critical phase), and the culture breaks up into an "agglomeration of separate [autonomous and destructive] individuals." Therefore "...all community of thought, all communal action, all coordination have ceased."[5]

Most orthodox believers would sadly agree that we are experiencing such a "critical" phase in America today. Our Accountability to God has been thrown off, and Autonomy is cheered: "Every man... is an end in himself, he exists for his own sake, and the achievement of his own happiness is his highest moral purpose."[6] Some proudly declare: "Promises of immortal salvation or fear of eternal damnation are both illusory and harmful. They distract humans from present concerns, from self-actualization..."[7] and "The extralegal abortion rate [written in 1954] shows that mature women have already illegally assumed [autonomy over the decision to abort, and therefore:] It should be theirs legally."[8]

"Medical ethics authors discuss beneficence, nonmaleficence, and justice, but they never say whether an action is right or wrong."[10] –Loreen A. Herwaldt, MD

1 Bennett, in Bork, 65. [Bennett did not address this concept, but the researcher would challenge anyone to demonstrate that Bennett's description applies any less to the average Christian than it does to the average American.]

If we are inclined to pick up the thread of individualism that has been described within the Protestant Reformation, it might be traced through the theistic existentialism found in Kierkegaard and Barth (Sire, 116), and in the observation of George Grant that "Under the barrage of Darwinism and Malthusian [both will be described in part IV.C.5] prevarication, the bulk of the church began to confuse the *moral faculty* – the ability to make choices – with the *moral good.* Subjective whims and fashions were given the weight of objective authority and truth" [*Third Time Around*, 125].

2 Durant, 101.

3 Morantz, in Altherr, *Procreation or Pleasure? Sexual Attitudes in American History*, 165.

4 Propst, in *Life Advocate*, 4/'94, 26.

John Whitehead broadens that view: "Our country, as it has moved toward a post-Christian consensus, has adopted pragmatic relativism and collectivism as basic themes of American society... A consequence of these ideas has been the shift from individual responsibility to a societal responsibility for all acts of American society... Prevalent today is the idea that criminals are not responsible for their behavior. Society is to blame. As a result Criminal rights are minutely protected while a victim's rights are often ignored. There is also no-fault insurance and no-fault divorce. This philosophy is devastating because it shifts guilt to society (the collective) from the individual" [*Stealing of America*, 16].

5 Durant, 89.

6 Ayn Rand, quoted in Sproul, 97.

7 Summarized by Jorgenson, *Christianity and Humanism*, 57-8.

8 Rosen, *Abortion in America: Medical, Psychiatric, Legal, Anthropological, and Religious Considerations*, ©1954 and 1967, 320

9 Bork, 65

10 Herwaldt, in Kilner, *Bioethics...*, 30.

SCOPE and FOCUS
I. CONVICTIONS
Polarizing Certainties
Creation vs. Accident
Design vs. Mechanism
Commandments vs. Positivism
Justice vs. Pragmatism
Virtue vs. Pleasure
Universalism vs. Relativism
Accountability vs. Autonomy
Worldview Confusion
Deism
Naturalism
Nihilism
Existentialism
Postmodernism
Eastern pantheistic monism
New age
"Humanism"
Human Condition & Life
Stewards vs. Masters
II. PRETEXTS
III. MANDATE
IV. LEGACY
V. ABORTIVE LINKS
VI. DILEMMA
VII. DESTINY

B. World-View Complicity in Polarizing Assumptions

The goal of *Orphans in Babylon* is to address the fundamental questions of our day, questions the Church must ask and answer, and answers the world must hear and understand. Unless this task is accomplished, the Church may very well be *going* "unto all the world,"[11] but it will definitely *not* be fulfilling the charge to be His witnesses.[12] Biblically, if we are to be God's light, salt, watchmen and trumpeters, we *must* address these questions regarding abortion: Where are we now? How did we get here? Where should we be? and How can we get there?

In researching the answer to Where are we now?, these were the guiding perplexities: Why aren't more "prolife" pastors and Christians treating abortion like a life-and-death issue? Addressing the Pro-life Movement – although it is dedicated, focused and zealous – why isn't it treating abortion like an immediate life-and-death emergency? And Operation Rescue – since it professed to be "acting like abortion is murder" – why weren't its tactics of intervention "to save a human life" of a style that would lead to physical martyrdom? These questions are not issued as judgments, just as observations of apparent inconsistencies which we all must be addressing, together, in humility before God.

The answers – or much more accurately – *some clues* to put us on the track of the answers – to all of the above questions will be summed up in part VI, the sections on Paradox and on Victory.

This student has been fascinated by James W. Sire's *The Universe Next Door: A Basic Worldview Catalog*. That volume opened the door to an understanding of the sources of the passionate zeal of abortion advocates. We must figure out what makes them so adamant about the *rightness* of killing unborn children. But the hope of easy answers was quickly dashed: a sentence is expected to express a complete thought, but a statement like "He supports abortion because he is an existentialist" is not complete; the reader needs more precise information than that. This dilemma, plus much study and anguish, resulted in the identification of the seven clashing convictions which have been presented as the foundation of *Orphans in Babylon*. With those polarized beliefs in mind, it is much easier to comprehend how the assorted worldviews Mr. Sire catalogues contribute to the fervent support of "abortion rights."

Here is James Sire's definition: "A worldview is composed of a number of basic presuppositions... They are generally unquestioned by each of us... and only brought to mind when we are challenged by a foreigner from another ideological universe."[13]

James Hunter, in describing our *Culture Wars*, says: "The older agreements have unraveled. The divisions of political consequence today are not theological and ecclesiastical in character but the result of differing worldviews... Our most fundamental ideas about who we are as Americans are now at odds. Because this is a culture war, the nub of political disagreement today on the range of issues debated... can be traced ultimately and finally to the matter of moral authority. By moral authority I mean the basis by which people determine whether something is good or bad, right or wrong, acceptable or unacceptable."[14]

These world view names are in frequent use today, even though, in most minds, the specific presuppositions underlying the labels are probably pretty fuzzy. James Dobson gently informs his readers of what he means by the world views he mentions: "...the changing culture forced yet another reexamination of [the Focus on the Family] ministry in 1996. Secular humanism, the sexual revolution and the New Age movement had taken their toll... [Our] society was rapidly forgetting its Christian underpinnings."[15]

11 *Matthew* 28: 19-20. "Therefore go and make disciples of all nations, baptizing them in the name of the Father and of the Son and of the Holy Spirit, and teaching them to obey everything I have commanded you."
Acts 1:8, "But you will receive power when the Holy Spirit comes on you; and you will be my witnesses in Jerusalem, and in all Judea and Samaria, and to the ends of the earth."

12 *Mark* 14: 54. "Peter followed Him at a distance, right into the courtyard of the high priest. There he sat with the guards and warmed himself at the fire."

13 Sire, 17.

14 Hunter, *Culture Wars: The Struggle to Define America*, 42.

15 *Family News From Dr. James Dobson*, 2/'98, 1.

Kerby Anderson, teaching about *Living Ethically in the '90s*, helps his readers identify foundations underlying the worldviews: "It is evident that the views of skepticism, naturalism, humanism and pantheism all fall short of providing man with an adequate basis for moral values... Because of their relativism, these systems are unable to offer a valid answer to the question, Why is murder wrong?"[1]

Before we examine the contours of particular modern world views, we need to imagine the situation in that part of the Middle Ages in Europe when the Catholic Church faced virtually no intellectual opposition and the Christian world view was almost universally taken for granted. Into that scene galloped two brazen knights, the Protestant Reformation and the Enlightenment, whose combined effect was to challenge the authority of the pope, and ultimately, of God. The Reformation, as champion of the spiritual independence of the individual, launched a convoluted crusade which has ultimately resulted in the enshrinement of Autonomy and Relativism. And the Enlightenment, as champion of human reason's battle against blind faith, has led mankind not only to the ultra-rational conclusion that God never existed but to the belief that humans are either god-like or wretched, or both. The certainties which drive modern world views are merely variations on these themes.

1. Deism

We have previewed Deism in our look at the theological compromises which were necessary in order for our forefathers to formally justify their *Declaration of Independence* from England and officially Constitute their new government. James Sire explains that Deism "sees God only in 'Nature' by which was meant the *system* of the universe. And since the system of the universe is seen as a giant clockwork, God is seen as the clock maker."[2]

What may have been the most profound feature of deism is that it was embraced by many as an act of Pragmatism.[3] The founding Fathers who were Christians, being *reasonable* men, agreed not to offend the sensitivities of any agnostics or atheists who might be among them, and agreed to various deistic compromises ["...the Laws of Nature and of Nature's God," in the *Declaration*, etc.]. That these compromises may have been necessary for the progress of democracy – undoubtedly a very good thing – does not change the fact that they were incremental steps of Relativism to the degree that believers were acknowledging the legitimacy of others' beliefs which contradicted their own.

In Deism, itself, there was the strong allegiance to the Creator God of the Bible. As bearers of bright Enlightenment brains, the Deists marveled in each new scientific discovery as another evidence of the wonder of the Creator's universal Design. The key is, however, a subtle shift of emphasis away from the Designer to the Mechanism itself. It was soon clear that the Great Clockmaker was presumed to have built the universe, to have wound up its giant spring-mechanism to set it in motion, and then put Himself on the shelf! Deists came to believe in the God who doesn't want to get involved with his creation. From this notion flowed all sorts of heresies: denial of divine inspiration of scripture, of miracles in any form, of the Messiah and of eternal life.

In short, a deist was a humanist with one quirky belief: that there once was a creative God who suddenly vanished without a trace. To sum up where deism falls within our seven polarizations: The only orthodox belief retained by a deist was in God the Creator; Deists waffled on Design which boosted Mechanism. They rejected Commandments and Accountability, giving credence to Positivism and Autonomy. For a deist, what may have appeared to be fidelity to Universalism, Justice and Virtue turned out to be defection from God's Law to the camp of Natural Law.[4]

1 Kerby Anderson, 42.

2 James Sire, 43.

3 The reader will notice that we capitalize some words as a means of emphasis, in this case the name of one of the seven paired convictions we are currently examining. This will hopefully cause little distress, except among English teachers who must be holding a red pen in order to read, and to those theological purists who may accuse us of deifying the profane!

4 John Whitehead, *The Second American Revolution*, 116.

5 James Sire, 53.

"Deism is the isthmus between two great continents – theism and naturalism.

To get from the first to the second, deism is the natural route... only a passing phase."[5]

–James Sire

SCOPE and FOCUS
I. CONVICTIONS
Polarizing Certainties
Worldview Confusion
Deism
Naturalism
Nihilism
Existentialism
Postmodernism
Eastern pantheistic monism
New age
"Humanism"
Human Condition & Life
Stewards vs. Masters
II. PRETEXTS
III. MANDATE
IV. LEGACY
V. ABORTIVE LINKS
VI. DILEMMA
VII. DESTINY

2. Naturalism

Naturalism as a world view is the adult child of the Enlightenment Project – the exaltation of human reason. It is atheism with a happy face: Since all supernaturalism is simply bunk, the naturalist totally ignores the god-who-never-was and states flatly, Nature is all there is.

In the 1600s, Rene Descartes inspired others to share his wonderment at the fantastic potential of the human mind, and John Locke asserted that human reason was the tool with which an individual could judge the truth within the Bible,[6] while Baruch Spinoza declared that every event seeming to be miraculous was really a natural occurrence not yet understood.[7]

Robert Bork explains the intellectual seductiveness of science as its "increasing ability to predict and explain much that had previously been mysterious, and also to continually improve the material conditions of life."[8] Phillip Johnson sums it up: "Science, reason and knowledge easily trump religion, faith and belief."[9]

Sire tells us that there are six basic tenets of Naturalism: 1) God does not exist, so Matter is all there is; 2) "The cosmos exists as a uniformity of cause and effect in a closed system"; 3) Human beings are complex machines: physical and chemical; 4) Death is extinction; 5) "History is a linear stream of events linked by cause and effect but without an overarching purpose"; 6) Ethics is man-made and is only concerned with man.[10]

As it turns out, Naturalism entails the total repudiation of nearly every basic conviction of Christian theism. For starters, it rejects both the Creator and divine Design. The royal reception Darwin's *Origin of Species* received in the mid 1800s gives evidence to how hungry Naturalists were for an intellectual theory – any theory – they could hold up as refuting Creation. In Sire's listing of the Naturalistic doctrines, above, Accident and Mechanism stand out prominently, as does Autonomy [in the rejection of spiritual Accountability], and there is more than a hint of Positivism.

Kerby Anderson seems to be pointing to Pragmatism and Positivism when he says, "Naturalism has no place for a personal or supernatural agent... so the naturalist looks to utility, to instinct, or to reason as his source for moral values."[11] Paul deParrie finds the Pleasure principle hard at work: "The conclusions of naturalism laid the foundations for the later acceptance of premarital sex and hedonism."[12] And Carl F.H. Henry finds in the naturalism of the Enlightenment an Autonomy of human reason over faith and traditional authority.[13]

It appears that the one exception that keeps Naturalism from embracing every anti-Christian conviction on our list is that, in its certainty that science can produce all of the answers, it won't subscribe to Relativism!

One of the most sobering aspects of the strangle-hold Naturalism has gained over American intellectual and political life is that Christian faith has been utterly vanquished from the marketplace of ideas. According to Carl Henry: "[In a] ...society such as ours, any confident statement of ultimate belief, any claim to announce the truth about God and his purpose for the world, is liable to be dismissed as ignorant, arrogant, dogmatic."[14]

6 James Sire, 53-4.

7 Paul deParrie, *Romanced to Death: The Sexual Seduction of American Culture*, 70.

8 Robert H. Bork, 281.

9 Johnson, *Reason in the Balance, The Case Against Naturalism in Science, Law and Education*, 10.

10 James W. Sire, 54-64.

11 Kerby Anderson, 38.

12 Paul deParrie, *Romanced to Death: The Sexual Seduction of American Culture*, 65.

13 Henry, in Ball, *In Search of a National Morality*, 18.

14 Henry, in Ball, 19.

15 Henry, in Ball, 17.

"The diffusion of cultural naturalism... has precipitated a crisis in religion and culture of unprecedented dimensions. Our society is the first in the history of humanity that, while forsaking the supernatural and discarding fixed truth and the good, expects nonetheless to preserve civilization."[15]

–Carl F. H. Henry

"There are no secular reasons persuasive to most reflective people in the case of abortion."[2]
–Robert Audi

This restriction is so pervasive that even a Christian philosopher such as Robert Audi proclaims that it would be illegitimate for a Christian to inject religious arguments into public discourse, so that believers are obligated to remain silent unless they can provide secular arguments. In his own words: "...one has a prima facie obligation not to advocate or support any law or public policy that restricts human conduct, unless one has, and is willing to offer, adequate secular reason for this advocacy or support."[1]

As Christians we should be outraged by that. Not by his statement; by the state of affairs he is describing. If every religious assertion can be rejected out of hand, if the only arguments to be accepted are secular reasons, and if the only thing a believer is permitted to say is the very same thing that the pagans are saying already, then it is no wonder that so many Christians just stay home [and risk getting television-lobotomies!]

One of Audi's statements is particularly heavy. Even if we were already aware of this in our gut, it really hurts to see it in print: "...there are no secular reasons persuasive to most reflective people... in the case... of abortion."[2]

In our discussion of the dimensions of Naturalism in America, we must take even one step further. As we mentioned earlier, at the moment when a woman first discovers an unplanned pregnancy, instinctive or reflexive or socially conditioned reactions are likely to take over. The power of the naturalistic assertions and assumptions must not be underestimated. In the professional opinion of a Christian, C. Ben Mitchell: "Instead of thinking carefully about bioethics from a Christian perspective, Christians, more often than not, capitulate to the naturalistic view of life and death."[3]

3. Nihilism

According to James Sire, "Nihilism is more a feeling than a philosophy. Strictly speaking, nihilism is not a philosophy at all. It is a denial of philosophy, a denial of the possibility of knowledge, a denial that anything is valuable. If it proceeds to the absolute denial of everything, it even denies the reality of existence itself. In other words, nihilism is the negation of everything – knowledge, ethics, beauty, reality. In nihilism no statement has validity; nothing has meaning."[4]

We concluded that Naturalism espoused all seven of our convictions that were anti-orthodoxy except one, Relativism. Nihilism, by contrast, cozies up to all of them except one also, but it likes Relativism and rejects Positivism. Here's how:

Nihilism is the legitimate child of naturalism. Naturalism claims to have killed everything metaphysical, and Nihilism leaves it dead, but it takes naturalism to the max: It begins with Darwinism's repudiation of Creation and divine Design, but instead of exulting in evolution, Nihilism gets really "bummed out": If humans are the mechanical result of millions of years of accidents and mutations and dog-eat-dog natural selection... If people evolved from slime and grubs and mice and monkeys, and are to be viewed as primitives by the next higher species to evolve, then what does that say about this life and about *my* life? Number one, confidence in science to discover truth is as much *blind faith* as the belief in heaven and hell. Thus, no one's religion, or morality, or truth, or knowledge, or *rationality* can be trusted, so nothing

"Some of our elites – professors, journalists, makers of motion pictures and television entertainment, delight in nihilism and destruction as much as do the random killers in our cities. Their weapons are just different."[8]
–Robert H. Bork

can be known, everything is relative. Belief in Relativity gives me Autonomy in all things, and my autonomy means that I may reject Positivism as readily as I rejected Commandments and Universalism: there can be no legitimate authority over me. Since there is no purpose and no meaning to this short, pathetic life of mine, my own Pleasure is my only goal. Since there are no valid standards of morality and ethics, Pragmatism in getting what I want is just fine: The end justifies the means.

Phew. That is a scary chain of conclusions. Unfortunately, this is not just a philosophical discussion. A widespread and deep-seated Nihilism is as American as applesauce. Robert Bork talks about nihilism several times in *Slouching Towards Gomorah: Modern Liberalism and American Decline.* Here are some of his chilling statements: "One who is absorbed in himself and his sensations, believing in few or no moral or religious principles, in nothing transcendental, is a nihilist. A culture that preaches narcissistic nihilism is asking for trouble... The extrovert, the hedonist, the madman, the criminal, the suicide, or the exhibitionist can rise to heroic stature in [the American 'hard rock' culture of today's youth]."[5]

"Nihilism was the order of the [Sixties decade, which] combined domestic disruption and violence with an explosion of drug use and sexual promiscuity; it was a decade of hedonism and narcissism."[6]

In its "mature stage," "impatient, destructive, nihilistic Sixties radicalism" is transformed into "modern liberalism... the radicals control the institutions they formerly attacked."[7]

Mr. Bork tells us that nihilism is spreading in our culture, and that when the subject is bioethics, it "finds killing for convenience acceptable... Convenience is becoming the theme of our culture. Humans tend to be inconvenient at both ends of their lives."[9]

4. Existentialism

Existentialism and Postmodernism are the two world views to next be addressed. Both are born of the Nihilistic urge to reject Enlightenment Naturalism's confidence in scientific certainty. Thus, they both strongly repudiate not only *divine* Design but *any* presumption that *the truth* can be known through the rational approach to a Mechanistic cosmos. From that starting point, both Existentialism and Postmodernism reason that they can be absolutely certain [the irony is clear] about the rightness of Relativism and individual Autonomy, and the wrongness of Universalism and spiritual Accountability. This fixation on Relativism and Autonomy which seems to begin in Nihilism is characteristic of six of the eight secular world views we are considering, and in every case, that pair of convictions engenders a strong commitment to Pleasure and Pragmatism.

There is, however, much that is unique about Existentialism. Skepticism was one of the engines that drove the enlightenment to reject all things religious and traditionally authoritative. It was inevitable, then, that in the course of time skepticism would turn inward on modernism and begin questioning *its* faith in science. The conclusion: "There is no rational answer for anything that exists. The universe is meaningless and absurd. Life has no real meaning, and death is the greatest absurdity of all."[10]

The Nihilistic stance, above, was penned by Anderson to describe where Existentialism began. Like a world-class sales trainer greeting a room full of discouraged rookies, existentialism has *the cure* for nihilism! If truth is relative and everything lacks meaning, well then, everything is a blank slate, the universe is moist clay in the hands of each Autonomous individual – people are free to make of it, and of themselves, whatever they choose. *Choice* is the icon of existentialism. A person's freedom of choice, his/her right to

*** REMEMBER ***
that every pair of pages contains this nifty OUTLINE, with the current topics underlined:

SCOPE and FOCUS
I. CONVICTIONS
- Polarizing Certainties
- Worldview Confusion
  - Deism
  - Naturalism
  - Nihilism
  - Existentialism
  - Postmodernism
  - Eastern pantheistic monism
  - New age
  - "Humanism"
- Human Condition & Life
- Stewards vs. Masters

II. PRETEXTS
III. MANDATE
IV. LEGACY
V. ABORTIVE LINKS
VI. DILEMMA
VII. DESTINY

1 Robert Audi and Nicholas Wolterstorff, *Religion in the Public Square: The Place of Religious Convictions in Political Debate*, 31.
2 Robert Audi, 31.
3 Mitchell, in Kilner, *Bioethics and the Future of Medicine, A Christian Appraisal*, 131.
4 James Sire, 75.
5 Robert Bork, 125-6.
6 Robert Bork, 50-1.
7 Robert Bork, 34.
8 Robert Bork, 95.
9 Robert Bork, 192.
10 Kerby Anderson, 38.

choose, is the bedrock, the foundation of everything. James Sire says that the heart of Existentialism is "creating meaning by subjective choosing... The *objective* world is a world of essences. Everything comes bearing its nature. Salt is salt; trees are tree; ants are ant. Only human beings (subjective) are not human before they make themselves to be so. Each of us makes himself or herself to be human by what we do with our self-consciousness and our self-determinacy."[1]

For those us who are pro-life, here is the horror in what Sire is saying: It is *consistent* with their world view for existentialists to call a new*born*, much more a *pre*born child, '*potential* human life' – they still believe that about a ten-year-old!

The roots of existentialism are in the Enlightenment, with Kant,[2] and on the theological side with Kierkegaard.[3] Existentialism and nihilism appear to have been undercurrents [within Modernism] which emerged in the United States after World War I. Intellectuals entertained them as philosophies, but the public acceptance of them is attributed to national confidence-shakers, beginning with the Great Depression and World War II.[4]

While the broad course of events was turning American culture toward the Relativism and Autonomy of atheistic Existentialism, another Existentialism – in theology – was having a comparable effect within the Church, particularly in what became the mainline denominations. The positive side of Christian existentialism is its emphasis on the individual's conscious decision-of-will to believe in Christianity, to make a 'radical leap of faith'. The harm was that its "subjective, choice-centered basis" pushed what had been Protestant individualism firmly into the camps of Relativism and personal Autonomy.[5]

5. Postmodernism

It was the view of Socrates "that the 'universal doubt' of all opinions would lead us, not into the heart of the truth, but into a void."[6] Sire says that "Both modernism and postmodernism rest on [the conviction] that the cosmos is all there is – no God of any kind exists... We are therefore on our own."[7] But Postmodernism contains "a skepticism that denies truth exists at all or, if it does exist, that it can be known – or, even if it can be known, that it can be expressed and communicated."[8]

In *The Universe Next Door* we are told that "existentialism is a step in the postmodern direction. Sarte said, 'Existence precedes essence.' We make ourselves by what we choose to do... The postmodern pundit says, 'We are only what we describe ourselves to be.'"[9] The same volume also explains, "The first question postmodernism addresses is not what is there or how we know what is there but how language functions to construct meaning itself [Sire calls this building 'a story']. In other words, there has been a shift in 'first things' from being, to knowing, to constructing meaning."[10]

Developing within *The Sensate Culture*, "The existentialism movement in philosophy found human existence absurd. It was succeeded by postmodernism... All truth became relative... Religious doctrines were no longer exalted as objectively and absolutely true *or* denounced as objectively false; instead they were praised as 'true for you,' or 'true for me.'"[11]

For a postmodernist, according to Sire, "Truth is whatever we can get our colleagues (our community) to agree to... Most of us have our *selves* constructed by the conventional language of our age and society... Ethics, like knowledge, is a linguistic construct. Social Good is whatever society takes it to be."[12] It is clear that postmodernism begins by turning its back dramatically on [the discernability of any] Mechanism, and thus builds its case for both Relativism and Autonomy.

1 James Sire, 97-9.

2 James Hunter, 124-5.

3 James Sire, 96.

4 Sire, 96: "World War I had not made the world safe for democracy. The generation of flappers and bathtub gin, the rampant violation of an absurd antiliquor law, the quixotic stock market that promised so much – these prefaced in the United States the Dust Bowl thirties. With the rise of National Socialism in Germany and its incredible travesty of human dignity, students and intellectuals the world over were ready to conclude that life is absurd and human beings are meaningless. In the soil of such frustration and cultural discontent, existentialism in its atheistic form sank its cultural roots. It was to flower into a significant worldview by the 1950s and is now in full bloom."

"Our age... called postmodern, finds itself afloat in a pluralism of perspectives... but with no dominant notion of where to go or how to get there. A near future of cultural anarchy seems inevitable."[16] –James Sire

SCOPE and FOCUS
I. CONVICTIONS
Polarizing Certainties
Worldview Confusion
Deism
Naturalism
Nihilism
Existentialism
Postmodernism
Eastern pantheistic monism
New age
"Humanism"
Human Condition & Life
Stewards vs. Masters
II. PRETEXTS
III. MANDATE
IV. LEGACY
V. ABORTIVE LINKS
VI. DILEMMA
VII. DESTINY

This brings us back to the Supreme Court, which has proven to be a pawn of Naturalism for the last several decades, but which in 1992 in the *Casey* decision legitimized and institutionalized postmodernism with its *mystery passage*: "At the heart of liberty is the right to define one's own concept of existence, of meaning, of the universe, and of the mystery of human life."[13] Harold Brown says that "we are in the era of postmodernism, where reality is fluid and truth depends entirely on the beholder."[14]

The Universe Next Door sums up the historical swing: "There has been a movement from 1) a 'premodern' concern for a just society based on revelation from a just God to 2) a 'modern' attempt to use universal reason as the guide to justice, to 3) a 'postmodern' despair of any universal standard for justice. Society then moves from medieval hierarchy to Enlightenment democracy to postmodern anarchy."[15]

6. Eastern pantheistic monism

Six of our eight secular world views are passionate in their rejection of everything metaphysical, and of Christian monotheism in particular. But it is widely acknowledged that "Man has a God-shaped void in his soul," and that "Man is the religious animal." Two of our popular world views begin with attempts to satisfy that natural spiritual hunger: Eastern pantheistic monism, and the New Age. An important clarification must be made as we begin: In their hearts both of these world views deify the Self, not God or even gods. Neither one contains commitment or altruism; both are self-absorbed philosophies centered on Autonomy, Relativism and Pleasure. But both encourage devotees to engage in a spiritual quest, to look inward to see beyond themselves to tap into metaphysical truths and to embrace universal realities.

Both Eastern pantheistic monism and the New Age are fascinated with the notion of reincarnation [the idea that each person's spirit has a series of earthly lives, inhabiting first one person – or animal – for a lifetime and then another, in a sort of spiritual recycling program. This conveniently negates a major source of naturalistic nihilism regarding the finality of death]. Both address karma, the idea that reincarnation is a vehicle of universal justice whereby a person's next incarnation will be pleasant or debased as their just deserts for the moral quality of *this* earthly test [It may be noted that those well situated in this life seem to be more eager to discuss karma than those whose life experiences are at the "unfortunate" end of the spectrum].

Both reincarnation and karma erect major obstacles to those who would argue that abortion violates the right to life of the preborn. Reincarnation counters that the abortion doesn't harm the aborted souls at all, except the very minor cosmic inconvenience of having to miss this chance and getting bumped to the end of the line for the next cycle. Karma solves even that nuisance: any injustice that might be ascribed to the abortion itself, and also the missed-opportunity dilemma both are transformed to karma-equity, assuring even more favorable circumstances in the next life [perhaps being born into a pro-life family for starters!].

To a greater degree than with the New Age, Eastern pantheistic monism does tap into some authentic religious traditions, Hinduism and Buddhism in particular. *Eastern* simply means from Asia, *pantheism* is the belief that God is everywhere and in everything, not a Person/divine being like the Christian God, but almost exactly like *The Force* as portrayed in the *Star Wars* movies. *Monism* is, in the strictest sense, the belief that all spirit is one; at death what has ignorantly been considered the individual soul of a particular person merges, like a single falling raindrop, into the vast ocean of Soul. To the eastern mind, reincarnation, karma, and monism can coexist with no apparent conflict. Not so in America; as one might guess, Americans

5 James Sire, 97-100.

6 Leo Strauss, *Natural Right and History*, 124.

7 James Sire, 189.

8 Harold O.J. Brown, *The Sensate Culture*, 54: "Today there is a growing trend to dismiss even the assured facts and scientific evidence of the natural sciences as interpretations that will naturally vary from observer to observer" [Relativism].

9 James Sire, 181-2.

10 James Sire, 175.

11 Harold O.J. Brown, 60-1.
Robert Bork reiterates: "Sometimes called postmodernism or poststructuralism, this denial of truth... the arrogant relativism [is asserted by] critics of science who contend that truth in science depends on one's point of view, not on any absolute content" (268-70).

12 James Sire, 180-2.

13 *Family News From Dr. James Dobson*, October 1997, 2.

14 Harold Brown, 49.

15 James Sire, 175.

16 James Sire, 174.

pick and choose from the smorgasbord of Eastern philosophy, displaying a particular fondness for *individual* reincarnation – with a Hollywood twist: *remembered* past lives which, strikingly, all seem to have been heroic and historically significant.

Pantheistic monism and the New Age have a third ally in their distrust of the faculty of human reason, Nihilism. For all three, this entails a distrust of both Commandments and Positivism. But while Nihihlists rejected rationalism through skepticism, the other two abandoned it in their infatuation with these two children of Autonomy and Relativism: intuition and subjective experience.

To the degree that Americans subscribe to the principles of pantheism and monism, bioethical concerns arise. James Sire explains: "So death is no big deal. Nothing of value perishes; everything of value is eternal. This may help explain the remark Westerners often make about the cheapness of life in the East. Individual embodiments of life – this man, that woman, you, me – are of no value."[1]

So how does Eastern pantheistic monism differ from the New Age? It is the only one of our eight secular world views which offers even a glimmer of moral responsibility. If adherents get past the me-ism of Autonomy and moral Relativism, they may be instructed by the *reincarnation* and *karma* principles of pantheistic monism. In so doing they buy-in to Universal moral principles and acknowledge their personal Accountability within a system that requires moral Justice in thought and deed. Unfortunately this aspect of the world view seems to be much more talked about that lived out, and there would appear to be a greater de facto commitment to Autonomy than to Accountability.

As concerns abortion, it seems highly unlikely, given the facility of rationalizing a karmic benefit to the aborted child, that pantheistic monism asserts any moral restraint on the decision to abort.

7. New Age

The major difference between New Agers and those who subscribe to pantheistic monism is that the New Age, along with Naturalism, places a high value on the individual person. Lest we jump to the hasty conclusion that they value *preborn* persons, it must be said that they do not.

One effect of the popularity of Eastern pantheistic monism and the New Age is that they definitely skew the results of popular opinion polls. In *Megatrends 2000: Ten New Directions for the 1990s*, John Naisbitt explains this about the American public in general: "Spirituality, Yes. Organized Religion, No. A 1987 Gallup poll found 94 percent of Americans believe in God... But are Americans 'religious' or 'spiritual'? ...The evidence from a number of polls suggests the more correct term is 'spiritual.'"[3]

James Hitchcock agrees. "New Age spirituality, in the broadest sense, is simply an attempt to ransack the religions of the world to find whatever is spiritually tasty, whatever will enhance the individual's egotistical hedonism. Traditional religion is rejected and despised precisely to the degree that it makes demands on people rather than simply offering them shallow comfort."[4] Hitchcock also describes the 1970s as "a religious tropical jungle in which no plant was so exotic (or so archaic) that it could not bloom – Eastern religions, American Indian religions, astrology, witchcraft, pantheism, etc. ...American culture is almost drowning in [an] unfocused, unsystematic religiosity... What is sometimes called New Age spirituality."[5] Sire says that whatever spiritual morsel the New Age plucks from whatever source will always be "demythologized by psychology," and that the constant in the New Age is that "Self is the kingpin – the prime reality."[6]

SCOPE and FOCUS
I. CONVICTIONS
Polarizing Certainties
Worldview Confusion
Deism
Naturalism
Nihilism
Existentialism
Postmodernism
Eastern pantheistic monism
New age
"Humanism"
Human Condition & Life
Stewards vs. Masters
II. PRETEXTS
III. MANDATE
IV. LEGACY
V. ABORTIVE LINKS
VI. DILEMMA
VII. DESTINY

"Karma is the Eastern version of you reap what you sow."[2]
–James Sire

1 James Sire, 130.
2 James Sire, 128.
3 John Naisbitt, *2000*, 275.
4 Hitchcock, in Ball, 38
5 Hitchcock, in Ball, 35.
6 James Sire, 144-6.
7 James Sire, 177.
8 James Sire, 139.
9 James Sire, 64-5.
10 Whitehead, *Second*, 124.

"It's almost as if the species (humanity) were taking a quantum leap into a whole new way of being... so that our great-great grandchildren may look back upon us as Neanderthals, so different will they be."[8] -Jean Houston

Among the eight popular world views we are discussing, says James Sire, the New Age is the only one that contains "the slightest bit of optimism" about the human condition:[7] "Basing much of their hope on the evolutionary model – a leftover from Western naturalism – a number of avant garde thinkers are prophesying the coming of a New Man and a New Age," about which Jean Houston of the Foundation for Mind Research could effuse, in 1973, that "...the species [seems to be] taking a quantum leap into a whole new way of being..." [8]

8. "Humanism"

As indebted as we are to James Sire for the treasure of information that is contained in *The Universe Next Door*, we find it curious that he does not grant secular Humanism a place in that *World View Catalog*. It is not an oversight, certainly, because he gives humanism two pages. Here is the essence of his views: "Two forms of naturalism deserve special mention... [Christian humanism and secular humanism]. Humanism itself is the overall attitude that human beings are of special value... Calvin... Erasmus... Spenser... Shakespeare... and Milton [all] wrote from a Christian theistic worldview [and] are sometimes today called *Christian humanists... Secular humanism* is another specific form... well expressed in *Humanist Manifesto II*... [and one which is] completely framed within a naturalistic worldview."[9]

Sire sees secular Humanism as just a subgroup under Naturalism. Our research indicates that it is much more than that, that it can be contrasted with Naturalism, and that its identification as a distinct world view [and more], both socially and politically, makes it an entity of singular significance.

As is customary in popular discourse, the term Humanism in this work will designate what Sire more precisely identifies as *secular* Humanism. The reader is referred to a number of major writers who have made important references to humanism.[11]

"Secular humanists have declared a war on Christianity in this country and are making great strides toward victory."[10] –John Whitehead

11 **Here is what a number of significant writers have said about secular Humanism:**

James T. Draper, et. al., *If the Foundations Be Destroyed*, 1984, 169: "The history of the United States has been the story of the steady rise of humanistic statism to power. Today, the control of civil government, public schools, and many churches has fallen into the hands of humanistic men who are fervent, even fanatical enemies of Christ and His Church."

John Eidsmoe, *God and Caesar*, 1984, 132-4: Direct quotes from the Humanist Manifesto [both I (1933) and II (1973)]: "God is either nonexistent or irrelevant to modern man... Man is the supreme value in the universe... Evolution is the unifying principle of all life... Man is purely a physical or biological creature... No absolute morals or values exist... Man, through the use of his scientific reason, will solve his own problems."

Jean Staker Garton, *Who Broke the Baby?* 1979, 96: "...secular humanism views the Christian faith itself as 'harmful.' Not to be accommodated are those religions which the *Humanist Manifesto* describes as 'dogmatic and authoritarian.' Humanists believe that those with 'faith in the prayer-hearing God, who is assumed to love and care for persons... do a disservice to the human species.'"

Normal L. Geisler, *Is Man the Measure? An Evaluation of Contemporary Humanism*, 1983, 121-2: Summarizes five common beliefs of secular humanism: nontheism, naturalism, evolutionism, ethical relativism and human self-sufficiency.

William R. Hutchison, *American Protestant Thought in the Liberal Era*, 1968, 194-5: Quotes directly from the 1934 book *The Decline of Liberalism* by Walter Marshall Horton, describing the social climate in the early 1930s when the first *Humanist Manifesto* was written: "It was an era of mounting faith in man's ability to control his own destiny through creative intelligence, and to make a heaven on earth with the aid of science and machinery...."

Gary North, *Backward Christian Soldiers*, 1983, 145: "As Christians have begun to recognize the religious impulse of modern humanism, they have seen that there are battle lines drawn between the kingdom of God and the kingdom of Satan – battle lines that affect every area of life."

Randall A. Terry, *Operation Rescue*, 1988, 159: "The reason the church has not stood against abortion is because Christians have bowed the knee to America's god – the god of self. Humanism is the worship of man, or self-worship. It makes life man-centered instead of God-centered... We seek convenience, pleasure, and gratification."

John W. Whitehead, *The Second American Revolution*, 1982, 38: "Humanism can be defined as the fundamental idea that men and women can begin from themselves without reference to the Bible and, by reasoning outward, derive the standards to judge all matters. For such people, there is no absolute or fixed standard of behavior. They are quite literally autonomous..., a law unto themselves... There are no standards that cannot be eroded or replaced by what seems necessary, expedient, or even fashionable at the time. Man is his own authority."

One reason that Humanism deserves special attention is that it does have a national identity. As long ago as 1933, there was a magazine called the *New Humanist*,[1] and in that year it published a remarkable document, "Humanist Manifesto." Just like the *Declaration of Independence*, the manifesto carried the signatures of many prominent Americans who were willing to go public about their humanism.[2] The staying power of humanism is reflected in the fact that an expanded version, "Humanist Manifesto II," was issued in 1973.

More significantly, as contrasted with Naturalism and all of the other world views for that matter, Humanism has received official recognition and standing from the U.S. Government. As a baseline, it should be noted that in 1952 the Supreme Court was declaring, "We are a religious people whose institutions presuppose a Supreme Being... [The state] respects the religious nature of our people and accommodates the public service to their spiritual needs. To hold that it may not... would show a callous indifference to religious groups. That would be preferring those who believe in no religion over those who do believe."[3]

Just nine years later, in 1961, the Court was stating: "Among religions in this country... would generally be considered... Buddhism, Taoism, Ethical Culture, Secular Humanism, and others."[4] John Eidsmoe commented on that finding: "In that decision humanism received official recognition as a religion, and humanists became entitled to free exercise of religion... Therefore, just as the government cannot actively promote Christianity, so also the government *should* not actively promote secular humanism."[5] George Grant says, "By 1963, the courts were protecting and favoring a new religion – humanism (declared a religion by the Supreme Court) – while persecuting and limiting Christianity..."[6]

Several salient features set Humanism apart from the seven world views on James Sire's basic list: 1) It is the only one that has received governmental recognition; 2) More than any of the others it has produced official documents establishing its identity; 3) It deliberately identifies itself as the antithesis of Christianity. It repudiates every foundational conviction of Christian theism: Creation, Design, Commandments, Justice, Virtue, Universalism and Accountability. It strongly embraces and vigorously promotes all of the opposites: Accident, Mechanism, Positivism, Pragmatism, Pleasure, Relativism and Autonomy.[7]

In the bitter contest with orthodox Theism, seven of the eight secular world views function as a team. *Humanism* is the player-coach who does it all. *Naturalism* is the grizzled veteran who specializes in the attack of Accident, Mechanism and Positivism against Creation, Design and Commandments. *Nihilism, Existentialism, Postmodernism, Eastern Pantheistic Monism* and the *New Age* make up the core of the team, to push Relativism, Autonomy, Pleasure and Pragmatism in the faces of Universalism, Accountability, Virtue and Justice. ....*Deism*, long since retired, is mostly ignored.

1 Dale Jorgenson, *Christianity and Humanism*, 53.

2 William Ball, 112, quoting Norman Geisler: "John Dewey and other influential Americans signed the *Humanist Manifesto* that proclaimed... 'Values derive their source from human experience. Ethics is autonomous and situational, needing no theological or ideological sanctions.'"

3 Justice Douglas, in *Zorach v. Clauson*, 1952, quoted in Ball, 88.

4 *Torcaso v. Watkins*, 1961, in Eidsmoe, 138.

5 Eidsmoe, 138.

6 Grant, *Grand Illusions: The Legacy of Planned Parenthood*, 236: "It banned posting the Ten Commandments in school rooms, allowed the Bible to be read only as an historical document, forbade prayer in the public domain, censored seasonal displays... regulated Church schools and outreach missions, demanded IRS regulation of religious institutions, and denied equal access to the media for Christian spokesmen."

7 The secular Humanist is the purist among the eight popular world views that challenge Christian faith. In its eyes, each of the other world views falls short of that mark. Humanism scorns *Deism* for the fatal flaw of owning a Creator. *Naturalism* would score especially high marks for its effectiveness in legitimizing Accident, Mechanism and Positivism; it would be credited with an "assist" to Autonomy and Pleasure, but it would be chastised for its lame performance against Justice and Universalism: by maintaining that human reason, intuition or consensus could produce experience-based standards of morality and codes of ethics, Naturalism fails to be hard-line enough in favor of Pragmatism and Relativism.

From the standpoint of Humanism, five of the world views either waffle or wimp out on the subject of Positivism. *Nihilism* flatly rejects it, although it does earn praise for its promotion of Pleasure, Relativism and Pragmatism. *Existentialism* waffles too much on Positivism, gets high marks for Autonomy and Relativism but is booed for deserting Mechanism in favor of its "create-your-own-reality" program. Just like Existentialism, *Postmodernism* is so-so on Positivism and is best at Autonomy and Relativism, but its Waterloo is Mechanism, because it gets bogged down in the "no-such-thing/can't-be-known/or can't-be-communicated" hang-up. *Eastern pantheistic monism* is too aloof to even notice Positivism, but it makes the team because of Autonomy and Mechanism, commits fouls by supporting Universalism and Justice with its belief in reincarnation and karma, and gets thrown out of the game on the technicality that its Relativism got too big and included metaphysical realities. The *New Age* is a superstar with Autonomy, Relativism, Pleasure and Pragmatism, but it sits out the season with injuries: irrationality and delusional behavior. It even claims to hear the voices of spirits.

"The great divisive issues of American society, such as the abortion issue, involve at root a conflict between radically different notions about what it means to be human and how humans fit into the rest of reality."[8] –Phillip E. Johnson

SCOPE and FOCUS
I. CONVICTIONS
Polarizing Certainties
Worldview Confusion
Deism
Naturalism
Nihilism
Existentialism
Postmodernism
Eastern pantheistic monism
New age
"Humanism"
Human Condition & Life
Fallen & sinful vs. Naturally good
Redeemable vs. Perfectable
Sanctity of the unborn vs. Potentiality
Right-to-Life of preborns vs. Expendability
Stewards vs. Masters
II. PRETEXTS
III. MANDATE
IV. LEGACY
V. ABORTIVE LINKS
VI. DILEMMA
VII. DESTINY

C. Human-Condition Convictions Which Impact Life Decisions

We are coming to terms with the realities that our society is polarized by opposite and mutually exclusive metaphysical convictions, and that our culture is awash with enticing and popular world view alternatives which conspire, intentionally, to destroy the Church and any who would seriously enter Christ's Kingdom. Before addressing the cultural fortifications that have been mounted in defense of publicly approved and legally sanctioned abortion – the subject of Part Two – we must pause to consider those specialized convictions concerning the human condition, and how those certainties impact life-and-death decision making.

In *The Doctor as Judge of Who Shall Live and Who Shall Die*, written in 1970, Helmut Thielicke sharpens our focus: "It is precisely at the point of man's supreme achievements in biology... that a public statement of bankruptcy may be in order... We are so preoccupied with the question of what man 'can do,' that we are in danger of forgetting what he 'is.'"[9] He goes on to say, "When it comes to deciding who or what man is, and whether he is to be understood in terms of his utility or in terms of his 'alien dignity,' science is of no help to us. We must already have made a decision on this question before we can even begin our scientific research..."[10]

We Christians hold that Man was created by God in His own image. The Humanist's perspective of the human condition is summed up in *The Lessons of History*, by Will and Ariel Durant. Shaped by the Naturalistic theory of evolution, their conclusion is that "human beings are normally equipped by 'nature' (here meaning heredity) with six positive and six negative instincts, whose function it is to preserve the individual, the family, the group, or the species... Their totality is the nature of man."[11]

The pairs of instincts they identify are as follows [presented as Positive instinct/Negative instinct]: Action/Sleep; Fight/Flight; Acquisition/Avoidance; Association/Privacy; Mating/Refusal; Parental Care/Filial Dependence. We must keep in mind that survival is the key to the listings. According to Darwin's *survival of the fittest*, to "win" in life is to have lots of descendants, and the extinction of your family line defines failure. By that standard – the best set of ethics Naturalism can come up with – the *winners* will be those who follow the rules of good *breeding*: stay awake, be macho, get rich, mingle, mate and raise lots of children. The losers in the posterity game will be those who stay poor, run away, like privacy, sleep a lot, uphold moral values and have lots of friends. If the evolutionists are right that these principles have been in operation for millions of years, it is amazing that there is any gentleness or friendship left in the world.

8 Johnson, *Reason in the Balance: The Case Against Naturalism in Science, Law and Education*, 182.

9 Helmut Thielicke, *The Doctor as Judge of Who Shall Live and Who Shall Die*, 38.

10 Helmut Thielicke, 39.

11 Durant, 32-33.

12 Russel Shaw, *Abortion on Trial*, 174.

"The issue of abortion law inevitably involves one's most fundamental views on human life and human destiny."[12] –Russel Shaw

1. Fallen & Sinful vs. Naturally Good

John Kilner presents a concise summary of the Christian view of human nature: "Paul's distrust of human-centered ethics stems from his understanding of the human condition. In Adam all 'fell' (became separated from God), and human fallenness entails, among other things, that people cannot always know and do what is right. By nature people are slaves to sin (Rom. 6:17-20). Part of the problem is that the mind has become distorted. It is blinded by the 'god of this age' (2 Cor. 4:4)..."[1]

Michael Bray gives us a second look at it: "The temptations which come from without do not encounter neutral ground. Nor do they make impressions upon a Lockean *tabula rasa* (blank slate). Temptations encounter an original sin nature. So declare the Scriptures (Jas. 1:13-15); so declared the Council of Orange in the sixth century against Pelagius (who denied original sin)."[2]

Regarding the Church's effectiveness in getting the gospel message disseminated within the American populace, the Associated Press issued some very interesting results from Gallup and Harris polls: 90% of Americans believe there is a heaven, and 78% say their prospects for going to heaven are excellent or good. 73% believe there is a hell, and 6% say their own prospects for going to hell are good.[3]

What can we infer from this? 1) The Humanists have only convinced 10% of the people that death is extinction. 2) The Church has failed to teach 17% of the folks that hell is a part of the heaven package. 3) 78% is a big group; that group must certainly include everyone who goes to work, pays most of the bills, feeds the kids and doesn't engage in drive-by shootings. We have failed miserably if we have let all of those people think that they have done what it takes to go to heaven.

Somebody needs to do a poll on the percentage of people who believe that there is no such thing as sin. *That* would undoubtedly be a very big number. Relativism and Autonomy have made their marks on this culture. Ask an evangelist – if you can find one – how you explain repentance and confession to people to whom sin is a foreign language, an *extinct* foreign language. Michael Bray says that faith in the goodness of man is a product of the Renaissance.[4]

Nelson Mandela describes a highly respected and influential man, elected chief of his tribe, educated, and the son of Christian missionaries who, as a victim of Apartheid for his entire life, was nonetheless firmly convinced of "the innate goodness of man."[5]

Keith Miller makes this Christian confession: "We wear masks of success and happiness and integrity so much that we have even convinced ourselves that we are not such a bad people."[6]

Robert Bork says, "Unconstrained human nature will seek degeneracy often enough to create a disorderly, hedonistic, and dangerous society. Modern liberalism and popular culture are creating that society."[7]

"The Noble Savage theory: It's the idea that people living close to nature tend to be noble. It's seeing all those sunsets that does it. You can't watch a sunset and then go off and set fire to your neighbor's teepee."[13]
–Daniel Quinn

1 Kilner, *Life on the Line: Ethics, Aging, Ending Patients' Lives, and Allocating Vital Resources*, 17.

2 Michael Bray, 20.

3 *Press-Enterprise*, 4-12-97, B9.

4 Michael Bray, 71.

5 Nelson Mandela, *Long Walk to Freedom*, 204.

6 Keith Miller, *A Taste of New Wine*, 92.

7 Robert Bork, *Slouching Towards Gomorrah: Modern Liberalism and American Decline*, 153.

8 Eidsmoe, *God and Caesar*, 75-6.

Researcher's note: It would appear that our view of the human condition can be boiled down to very few choices. We may conclude one of three things about the essential character of humanity: 1) With the Bible as our guide, we can affirm that Man was created in the image of God, but willfully chose to rebel, and now exists in a *sinful, fallen* state. 2) If we rely on the Naturalistic theory of evolution for our answer, we will have two options. The rationally logical one is that the law of survival of the fittest imposes the *law of self-interest* as the exclusive moral ethic – we admit that humans are essentially looking-out-for-number-one, and that any apparent kindness or generosity is in reality a devious self-serving sham. It will be noticed that this comes very close to agreement with Christians that mankind is by nature sinful. 3) Perhaps for that very reason, as well as for others best explained by a good psychologist, the majority of Humanists – without troubling themselves to come up with any philosophical or historical justification for it – assert that people are *by nature good*. What seemed to be three choices, turns out to be two. Concerning human nature, Christians say "*bad* to the core," and Humanists say "*Selfish*, but basically *good*."

9 Durant, *The Lessons of History*, 43.

SCOPE and FOCUS
I. CONVICTIONS
Polarizing Certainties
Worldview Confusion
Human Condition & Life
Fallen & sinful vs. Naturally good
Redeemable vs. Perfectable
Sanctity of the unborn vs. Potentiality
Right-to-Life of preborns vs. Expendability
Stewards vs. Masters
II. PRETEXTS
III. MANDATE
IV. LEGACY
V. ABORTIVE LINKS
VI. DILEMMA
VII. DESTINY

2. Redeemable vs. Perfectible

John Eidsmoe has a fascinating theory about political orientation as it relates to convictions about mankind: "...one's view of human nature affects one's theory of government. And here is the most basic difference between liberals and conservatives: liberals generally believe human nature is basically good, while conservatives believe human nature is basically bad. Furthermore, liberals believe human nature can be improved given the right environmental stimuli (which government can supply), while conservatives believe human nature is basically unchanging and unchangeable. Christian conservatives are likely to say that there is little prospect for improving human nature save through the grace of God; secular conservatives are likely to say that there is little prospect for improving human nature, period."[8]

When we inquire as to the prospects for an improvement over basic human nature, there are three distinct possibilities: 1) God offers a radical *heart transplant*, free of charge, to those who apply through Jesus. 2) There is *no hope* for change; human nature – by whatever view – cannot change. This view is predominantly engendered by the evolutionary belief in the congenital me-ism of the survival instinct, but a similar prejudice is also noted in the particular group of Christians who buy-in to a jaded mutation of Calvinism which holds that those God has not "predestined" for heaven are forever doomed. 3) The potential for positive *moral evolution is unlimited*, through intelligent conditioning and social engineering.

When convictions about the human condition are combined, here is what we find. Those who are pessimistic about the human condition – be they pagans or Christians – can be discounted in this discussion because they take no active role in social change. This leaves two distinctly opposite factions: evangelists who hold that Man is sinful and redeemable, and social reformers who are determined to capitalize on basic human goodness.

The Durants say of history that, "Heaven and utopia are buckets in a well: when one goes down the other goes up."[9] After pausing to appreciate the ingenuity of using two buckets, a rope and a pulley to lift water for one's livestock, we can observe that the utopia bucket in America seems now to be full and rising, and the evangelism container looks to be empty and falling.

The *good and perfectible* view of man has a long history. When the United States of America was in its infancy, the German Philosopher G.W.F. Hegel was asserting that the goal of history is a perfect or ideal human society.[10] No doubt Americans took Hegel's writings as a personal compliment. In the early twentieth century, America was making quantum leaps of progress undreamed of fifty years before: automobiles, airplanes for heaven's sake, and all of those electrical gadgets. Leslie Fishbein tells us that the progressive social reformers in the early 1900s were driven by "a relatively new assumption, namely that behavior of both individuals and society can be controlled and regulated, and [by] its corollary, a belief in human and social perfectibility."[11]

Beginning in the mid-1930s, the intelligentsia of America was much influenced by the essays and other writings of Aldous Huxley. Norman Geisler tells us that "Huxley was not a wide-eyed optimist about the nature of man. He believed that 'there is evil in man as well as good.' He recognized man's evil urges and activities such as greed, arrogance, fanaticism, sadism, and self-indulgence. He believed, however, that man is capable of saving himself from these evils."[12]

---

10 James Sire, 67.
Hegel saw in the sweep of history a purposefulness, a traceable line of progress – what we might call social engineering. His *dialectical* theory described a cycle that has come to be called *Thesis, Antithesis*, and *Synthesis*. The idea was that human progress is inevitable, and that the steps in that progress consist of one stage of social development [the dominance of the Christian world view in the West, let us say] being overturned by its opposite [Naturalistic Humanism, for instance], and that ultimately the culture arrives at a third stage of progress, consisting of a synthesis of the two earlier stages. To the degree that there is truth in Hegel's theory, and if it is accurate to say that America is today in the throes of an inevitable, revolutionary replacement of traditional Christianity with secular Humanism, then intelligent Christians should be figuring out what position our faith should hold in the ultimate synthesis, and get busy making that happen... *Unless* God has other plans, of course!

11 Fishbein, in Altherr, 119.

12 Geisler, *Is Man the Measure?*, 16.

13 Quinn, *Ishmael: An Adventure of the Mind and Spirit*, [novel] 146.

The subtitle of Robert Bork's *Slouching Towards Gomorrah* is *Modern Liberalism and American Decline*. He charts the dimensions of our current social and political difficulties, and traces the developments which brought us here, particularly the events of the Sixties. He tells us that "The Sixties were born" in a particular place, Port Huron, Michigan, in June of 1962. At that early convention of the Students for a Democratic Society [the SDS, later notorious for campus disturbances and – many would stress – acts of terrorism] issued the *Port Huron Statement*, "...the SDS agenda for changing human beings, the nation, and the world." Bork describes it as "the most widely circulated document of the Left" in the '60s. The *Statement* declared, "We regard men as infinitely precious and possessed of unfulfilled capacities for reason, freedom, and love." Central to the *Port Huron Statement* was Tom Hayden's conviction that man is "infinitely perfectible."[1]

In the introduction to *Bioethics and the Future of Medicine, A Christian Appraisal*, authors Kilner, Cameron and Scheidermayer observe that, "If we have forgotten who we are, if we have no means of agreeing as a human community as to the kind of beings that human beings are, it is hard to predict how the culture can survive."[2]

1 Robert Bork, *Slouching Towards Gomorrah: Modern Liberalism and American Decline*, 25-27.

2 John Kilner, Cameron and Schiedermayer, *Bioethics and the Future of Medicine: A Christian Appraisal*, x.

3 J.C. Willke, *Handbook on Abortion*, on the cover.

4 Jean Garton, *Who Broke the Baby?*, 69.

5 J.P. Moreland, *Life and Death Debate*, 25.

"If a man loses reverence for any part of life, he will lose his reverence for all life."[3]

–Albert Schweitzer

3. Sanctity of the Preborn vs. Potentiality

In the second major part of this work, we will be examining how each of the secular answers to metaphysical questions [Accident, Mechanism, etc.] impacts a person's concept of what an abortion is. Underlying each of those discussions will be this fundamental dilemma: Is there a sanctity which adheres to a person from the instant of conception, or is the essence of the unborn to be described only in terms of its potentiality?

Jean Garton says that there are four principles that constitute the "Judeo-Christian ethic concerning the sanctity of life": Gift from God; Created for eternal life; Created for fulfillment; and Life and Death as God's realm of sovereignty.[4]

Moreland and Geisler say that there are three views of the essence of the preborn which will determine one's stance on abortion: *sanctity, potentiality* and *sub-humanity*. They say that the belief in sanctity holds that the unborn are fully human, so that abortion is precluded by the primacy of the human right to life over the mother's right of privacy, etc. If the unborn represents human potentiality, then abortion is sometimes justified, based upon a weighing of conflicting rights, those of the mother versus those of an emergent human life. Finally, if the child in utero is classed as sub-human, then abortion is justifiable at any time for any reason.[5]

Throughout this work we will be comparing clashing views regarding just *what* it is that gets aborted. For those of us who labor to build defenses around the womb, the first reality we must accept is that "religious reasons" will be rejected out of hand; we must understand how God views the unborn child, because that must become our view too, but although *sanctity*, the *image of God*, and *eternal soul* are the convictions which compel us to act, they are disqualified as arguments in the public forum. Human rights, equality, equal protection, due process and non-discrimination should be ample protection, but they are inapplicable until we can establish the full humanity, if not personhood, of the preborn. There is extreme discrimination and injustice in the legal status of a wanted child versus that of an unwanted child, by statute and in both civil and criminal judgments. But no wrong will be acknowledged as long as wantedness, gestational age and quality of life issues are presumed to alter status and standing.

SCOPE and FOCUS
I. CONVICTIONS
Polarizing Certainties
Worldview Confusion
Human Condition & Life
Fallen & sinful vs. Naturally good
Redeemable vs. Perfectable
Sanctity of the unborn vs. Potentiality
Right-to-Life of preborns vs. Expendability
Stewards vs. Masters
II. PRETEXTS
III. MANDATE
IV. LEGACY
V. ABORTIVE LINKS
VI. DILEMMA
VII. DESTINY

If *religious arguments* such as the sanctity of life are excluded, and full *humanity* can not yet be established, then *potentiality* may be the only game in town. For starters, an abortion robs the aborted one of her future: there are trophies and diplomas that would have been won, a spouse and children of a family that would have been, there are wages that would have been earned and taxes that now won't be paid, there were potential social contributions that are now lost... perhaps even the cure for AIDS or cancer...

There is an additional line of defense which we will pursue in depth later. The secular word for *sanctity* is *dignity*. While human rights now apply only to human beings who are born and alive, dignity transcends those thresholds. At death a person's physical remains are no longer of importance to him. The vast majority of both Humanists and Christians see the transplanting of available organs as a moral good. But it is the concept of human dignity that causes us to recoil from the picture of the body of a dead American pilot being dragged behind a jeep through a dirt street amid the cheers of our enemies.

When President Clinton proposed a five-year ban on human cloning, it was on the basis of human dignity.[6] He says that abortion should be "safe, legal and rare." Why rare?[7] He's the Abortion President, after all. If all abortions are morally good – even partial birth abortions – then why not *the more the merrier*? Human dignity may be the key. Whatever prompts Bill Clinton to say *rare*, should compel our entire society to rise up and say *Never!* with one voice. Human – or at least humane – dignity for the unborn, by secular norms that are already well established, must be the minimum measure of what we demand.

4. Right-to-Life of the Preborn vs. Expendability

We have just begun to address the question of how the pro-life Christian community can impact the convictions and actions of a pluralistic society and secular government. This heading, *Right-to-life versus Expendability* could simply be a rephrasing of the same question, but it is not. What we must also decide as Christians is, *Are WE willing to embrace religious reasons*, wholeheartedly and completely, in our own approach to abortion? One drop of poison in the Kool-Aid is the end of the party. We will be examining a large assortment of abortion justifications which emerge from each of the seven secular metaphysical convictions we have defined. The frightful fact we must keep in mind is that the *life of the mother* exception is the *only* exception, if we are authentically pro-life. If we forfeit the preborn's right to life and hold her to be expendable in any other situation, we must turn in our "pro-life" badges, pick up our marbles and simply go home. We are out of the game.

6 *Press-Enterprise*, 1-30-98, A3.

7 Bork, 179: "Why rare, if it is merely a choice, a medical procedure without moral problems?"

8 Kilner, Cameron and Schiedermayer, *Bioethics and the Future of Medicine: A Christian Appraisal*, x.

"At the heart of western culture, like any other, lie key assumptions about the nature of human being. The culture is in chaotic disarray, and tending toward a slow disintegration. And this loss of our common understanding of our own nature is evident above all in that cultural context in which human life is most in jeopardy."[8]

–Kilner, Cameron & Schiedermayer

D. Stewards vs. Masters: Our Polarized Culture

We have examined seven pairs of mutually exclusive convictions that divide our society today. We have seen that the combined forces of seven popular world views are doing battle under the secular Humanist banner in a mortal struggle with the Christian Church. We know that it is *open season* on preborn children in America, and we will soon feel the depth of conviction that secular allegiances create in support of abortion. We will ask, later, if the Pro-life movement is on the way to Tianenmen Square.

We would do well to remember the lessons of the spies Moses sent to determine the strength of the fortifications in the Promised Land.[1] Ten of the twelve came back with an accurate report and a faithless recommendation: "... the people who live there are powerful, and the cities are fortified and very large... The land we explored devours those living in it. All the people we saw there are of great size... We seemed like grasshoppers in our own eyes, and we looked the same to them."[2]

But Caleb "silenced the people before Moses and said, 'We should go up and take possession of the land, for we can certainly do it.'"[3] Later, in the book of Joshua, Caleb looks back on that event: "I brought [Moses] back a report according to my convictions, but my brothers who went up with me made the hearts of the people melt with fear. I, however, followed the Lord my God wholeheartedly."[4] Christians who are pro-life can easily relate to the grasshopper thing: fear. May we even more strongly devote ourselves to the Caleb thing: commitment and trust!

Our configuration of the forces defining our national schism is consistent with James Davison Hunter's analysis of the *Culture Wars: The Struggle to Define America*. He assigns the label *Progressive* to the group we have been calling secular Humanists, and calls the defenders of traditional Christian and Jewish faith *Orthodoxy*. We propose alternative names: the Stewards and the Masters. In our view *Masters* is an appropriate title for secular Humanists because they are in total agreement with Protagoras, who said, "Man is the measure of all things."[5]

They clearly aspire to become masters of the universe in their commitments to evolutionary accident and mechanism, positivism and pragmatism, pleasure, relativism and autonomy. By contrast, Stewards are those whose commitment to God transforms their identities and wills to conform to God's creation and design, commandments and justice, virtue, universalism and accountability.

What is the heritage of the Masters? "In 1944, a physician in Germany could participate in genocide with legal sanction; In America he would have been a murderer. In 1977, in America, a physician can perform an abortion with legal sanction; in Germany, he would be a murderer. We have come [180] degrees on the moral compass."[6]

"The official American witness at the Nuremberg doctor's trials, Dr. Leo Alexander commented on the *genesis of the medical atrocities* revealed during the proceedings. 'Whatever proportions these crimes finally assumed, it became evident to all who investigated them that they had started from small beginnings... a subtle shift in emphasis... acceptance of the attitude... that there is such a thing as a life not worthy to be lived.'"[7]

In the United States in 1968, pro-abortion attorneys William Kopit and Harriet F. Pilpel were expounding the "utilitarian" principle that "no person has an absolute right to life."[8] In 1974, Kenneth Vaux, a Professor of Ethics [what an appropriate title!] at Baylor College of Medicine, responded to the *Roe v. Wade* decision: "We now have the possibility, which means the responsibility, of deciding whom we will admit to the human community."[9]

"The most important single issue facing this generation is the devaluation of human life."[16]

–John Whitehead

"As we move through the next millennium, biotechnology will be as important as the computer."[17]

–John Naisbitt

SCOPE and FOCUS
I. CONVICTIONS
Polarizing Certainties
Worldview Confusion
Human Condition & Life
Fallen & sinful vs. Naturally good
Redeemable vs. Perfectable
Sanctity of the unborn vs. Potentiality
Right-to-Life of preborns vs. Expendability
Stewards vs. Masters
II. PRETEXTS
III. MANDATE
IV. LEGACY
V. ABORTIVE LINKS
VI. DILEMMA
VII. DESTINY

Here is another spokesperson for the Master class. Beverly Harrison, Professor of Christian Ethics [I'm *liking* these titles] at Union Theological Seminary: "Infanticide is not a great wrong. I do not want to be construed as condemning women who, under certain circumstances, quietly put their infants to death."[10]

Now a solemn warning to members of that Master race who will someday be old, with children – the ones they didn't abort – wondering what to *do* with their parents: "Kids are not stupid... They know... they were not even deemed to be *human beings* unless their mothers willed it."[11]

So what's up with the Stewards? How stewardly are we in thought and deed? Harold O.J. Brown makes the general observation that "Religious convictions for which thousands willingly suffered martyrdom are [today] dismissed as dangerous illusions."[12]

Paul D. Simmons, writing in 1982, found the constituency of the pro-life movement fascinating: "...not since the Prohibition era have [Fundamentalists] been so involved politically... this is a peculiar brand of Puritanism mixing religious zeal with political leverage to reform society. At stake is what fundamentalists regard as the central moral issues of the time – abortion being a primary concern. This gives them common ground for a coalition with the antiabortion stance of traditional Roman Catholics and creates a powerful voting bloc. Never before have these two groups been allies in American politics."[13] Hunter makes a similar observation: "...this cleavage is so deep that it cuts *across* the old lines of conflict, making the distinctions that long divided Americans – those between Protestants, Catholics, and Jews – virtually irrelevant... To come right to the point, the cleavages at the heart of the contemporary culture war are created by what I would like to call the *impulse toward orthodoxy* and the *impulse toward progressivism*."[14]

Joseph Foreman lays it on the line: "Protecting the lives of babies may be among the fundamental issues of any society and even a watershed test of faith in the living God. Protecting innocent children is not 'activism.'"[15]

We must admit all too readily that, everywhere we look in America today, we see the Masters of secular Humanism living lives that are in nearly perfect harmony with their bedrock convictions [Yes, theirs are easier to live by. Yes, living by their "convictions" comes *naturally*!] But if the same judgment of moral consistency cannot be made of us, we who are to be known as the Stewards and ambassadors of the living God, then shame on us. Our spiritual flabbiness and apostasy have nearly ceased to be a cause for scorn and jokes – now the Church is simply ignored.

"We must do more than make people aware that the unborn are human. We must raise up a generation which will do what it takes personally and corporately to defend the innocent."[18]

–Joseph L. Foreman

1 *Numbers* 13 and 14.
2 *Numbers* 13: 28, 32-33.
3 *Numbers* 13:30.
4 *Joshua* 14: 7-8.
5 Reuben Abel, xxi.
6 M. Baten and W. Enos, in Willke, *Handbook on Abortion*, 134. [They say, "360 degrees" but mean "180."]
7 Eugene F. Diamond, in Dennis Horan, *Infanticide and the Handicapped Newborn*, 55.
8 Russel Shaw, *Abortion on Trial*, 38-40.
9 Vaux, in Clowes, page 50.11.
10 Harrison, by Francis Beckwith, *Politically Correct Death: Answering the Arguments for Abortion Rights*, 174.
11 Brian Clowes, page 45.9.
12 Harold O.J. Brown, *The Sensate Culture*, 8.
13 Simmons, in Batchelor, *Abortion: The Moral Issues*, 176-7.
14 James Hunter, 43.
15 Joseph L. Foreman, *Shattering the Darkness: The Crisis of the Cross in the Church Today*, 13.
16 John Whitehead, *Arresting Abortion: Practical Ways to Save Unborn Children*, ix.
17 John Nisbitt, *Megatrends 2000*, 247.
18 Foreman, 69.

WRITTEN IN 1957:

"It seems unlikely
that the judges will
EVER

feel themselves
ABLE to STRETCH
either the words of the statutes
or
the doctrine of necessity
to permit abortion for

ANY of these considerations:

...raped...
...feeble-minded...
...transmittable disease...
...incest...
...economic ground...
...cannot well support another child...
...mother is unmarried...
...losing her employment...
...interrupt an expensive course of training."

–Glanville Williams
The Sanctity of Life and the Criminal Law
© 1957, pages 171-2

> "When there must be coercion, liberal democracies try to justify it in terms of considerations... that any rational adult citizen would find persuasive."[1]
>
> –Robert Audi

> "There will be no secular solutions to abortion... because abortion is itself the best secular solution to the problem of unwanted pregnancy."[2]
>
> –Joseph Foreman

1 Audi, *Religion in the Public Square*, 16.

2 Foreman, *Shattering the Darkness: The Crisis of the Cross in the Church Today*, 151-2.

II. The Abortion Pretexts: Allegations of Expendability

There is no shortage of secular arguments in support of abortion. The most exhaustive list our research has uncovered was compiled by Francis Beckwith in *Politically Correct Death: Answering Arguments for Abortion Rights*. He found sixty-eight arguments currently being voiced to justify legalized abortion – and persuasively refuted every one of them, we might add. We will give you page-citations along the way. *The Life and Death Debate: Moral Issues of Our Time*, by J.P. Moreland and Norman Geisler, has a great chapter on abortion, and Jean Garton produced a book worthy of its title: *Who Broke the Baby? A Brilliant Disclosure of What the Abortion Slogans Really Mean*. Most pro-lifers do not need to read these books to learn that pro-abortion sloganeering is illogical, but we *should* all read them to sell ourselves on the soundness of our reasons for being *against* abortion.

Firm logic and fine philosophical footwork, unfortunately, are of limited usefulness in winning the abortion war. This is why we began *Orphans in Babylon* with the section on the clash of convictions instead of this one. Our approach to the abortion pretexts will not be to examine the weaknesses in the argumentation, but rather, to learn – as we must – what the pro-abortion arguments can tell us about the fundamental convictions of those who express them.

As will be noted in scanning the outline on this page, we have attempted to categorize the pro-abortion arguments according to the metaphysical convictions which tend to make the slogans seem – to those who voice them – like *what anyone with a brain would understand!*

SCOPE and FOCUS

I. CONVICTIONS

II. **PRETEXTS**

AUTONOMY
- Fundamental Right
- Privacy
- Equality
  - Don't absolutize
  - Zygote vs. adult
  - Compulsory preg.
  - Poor discriminated
  - Men can't vote
  - Equity: soc. / pol.
- Tolerance
  - Pro-lifers are free
  - Pluralism of belief
  - Church & state
  - Imposing morality
  - Capital punishment
- Cost-free right

RELATIVISM
- Personhood Denied
  - Potential life
  - Criteria of persons
- Humanity Challenged
  - Blob of cells
  - Woman's body
  - Speciesism
  - Sperm & ova
  - Cloneability
  - Products of conception
  - Twinning
  - Blueprints
  - Chromosomes, 46+/-
  - Miscarriages legitimize

MECHANISM
- When life begins?
- Implantation
- Heartbeat
- Looking like a child
- Brain functioning
- Pain response
- Quickening
- Viability
- Birth only, nothing less

PLEASURE
- Personal Tragedy
  - Rape / Incest
  - Imperfection
- Burden-Bearing
  - Career interruption
  - Pro-lifers should adopt
  - Abused children result
- Anonymous & Different
  - Mourned less
  - Naming, age, baptism

ACCIDENT
- (Justifies Remedy)
- Birth control failed
- Incapacitated mom

PRAGMATISM
- Self Defense
  - Mother's life
  - Pro-life contradiction
  - Health of mother
  - Alien invasion
- Political Expediency
  - Safe & legal
  - Medical responsibility
  - Population bomb
- Social Benefits
  - Safer than childbirth
  - Fetal research
  - Fetal tissue
  - Organs for transplant

POSITIVISM
- Political Arguments
  - Legal system havoc
  - Consensus lacking
  - Rights are man-made
- Futility of Criminalizing
  - Imposible to stop
  - Birth control homicide?
  - Birth control illegal?
  - Medical restrictions
  - Smoking criminal?
  - Miscarriage, huh?
  - Mom's a murderer!

III. MANDATE

IV. LEGACY

V. ABORTIVE LINKS

VI. DILEMMA

VII. DESTINY

"Abortion may be the characteristic crime of the twentieth century. Our times have lost respect for human life. Dachau, Hiroshima – these are landmarks testifying to how cheaply life is held today."[1]
–Russel Shaw in 1968

Pro-abortion convictions

In 1942, World War II was raging and Pearl Harbor had already been bombed. The New York Medical Academy was having a conference – nothing unusual about a hotel full of doctors talking medicine. What was amazing was that the good doctors were engaged in *philosophical* discussions – about why abortion should be decriminalized. Marvin Olasky tells us that, "Conference speakers overall enumerated themes that received great play over the coming years: anti-abortion laws violated church-state separation, attempted to save that which is not yet human, and did not stop abortion anyway. The underlying argument, however, was that the anti-abortion position lacked compassion for the mother and realism in a world which did not need more poor mouths to feed."[3]

America's medical community had been a significant contributor to the groundswell of public opinion which resulted in nationwide criminalization of abortion in the second half of the nineteenth century. It is therefore ironic that the doctors played such a key role in the reversal of that national consensus and in the sweeping invalidation of all of that hard-won legislation.

The New York conference presenters in 1942 clearly reveal that the positive inclination toward abortion was not a matter simply of emotion and rhetoric, but that rational arguments were being presented whose persuasiveness can be attributed to the depth of moral conviction upon which they were based.

The medical speakers display an Autonomy-and-tolerance conviction in raising the church-and-state issue. The fact that they subscribe to the ethics of Relativism and Mechanism is evidenced by the bold assertion that the unborn are not-yet-human. Their Pain vs. Pleasure orientation is shown in the appeal to compassion for the pregnant unwilling-mother. They are Positivistic in their justification of political expediency to combat the population bomb ("more poor mouths to feed"), and the reference to the futility of trying to enforce anti-abortion laws shows a commitment to Pragmatism. The conference topics of 1942 were sounding major chords of the redirected allegiances of a changing American populace.

Joseph Foreman punctuates the shift: "In the fifties and sixties abortion was an 'issue' – some argued for it and some against it. But by 1973, it stopped being an issue and became a national fact. Those who believed that killing the unborn was right were free to practice their faith... Those who boldly proclaim what they believe, *and then live consistently with it*, will gain credibility. They did. We did not."[4]

That *Roe* was a monumental reversal of public policy is underscored by John Whitehead: "If any is doubtful that the decision in *Roe v. Wade* established abortion-on-demand, I refer them... to Justice Byron White's dissent in *Planned Parenthood v. Danforth* in 1976: 'In *Roe v. Wade*... this Court recognized a right to an abortion free from state prohibition.'"[5]

R.C. Sproul's was one of innumerable voices which have been raised in protest that beliefs which were persuasive in permitting a trickle of abortions have been re-engineered to release a torrent. He says, "The national issue is abortion-on-demand. Even if it were decided in extreme cases that abortion is an ethical option, the extreme cases should not dictate the general law."[6]

1 Russel Shaw, *Abortion on Trial*, 168.

2 F. LaGard Smith, *When Choice Becomes God*, 81.

3 Olasky, *Abortion Rites: A Social History of Abortion in America*, 262.

4 Foreman, 115-6.

5 John Whitehead, *The Second American Revolution*, 124.

6 R.C. Sproul, *Abortion, a Rational Look at an Emotional Issue*, 134.

7 Aldo Leopold comments, "When god-like Odysseus returned from the wars in Troy, he hanged all on one rope a dozen slave-girls of his household whom he suspected of misbehavior during his absence. This hanging involved no question of propriety. The girls were property. The disposal of property was then, as now, a matter of expediency, not of right and wrong" [in Stone, Foreword].

8 Stone, 5.

9 Naisbitt, *Megatrends 2000: Ten New Directions for the 1990s*, 13.

10 Beckwith, *Politically Correct Death: Answering the Arguments for Abortion Rights*, 124-5.

It will be noticed that the assertion, "It's my body!" should be discussed in at least two veins: women's autonomy, and also the implication, "The 'fetus' is part of my body," which will be treated under Relativism, among various challenges to the humanity of the preborn.

Beckwith also addresses the concept of "Noninterference," 20.

11 James Hoffmeier, *Abortion: A Christian Understanding and Response*, 122.

12 Brian Clowes, *Pro-Life Activist's Encyclopedia*, page 14.14.

"What irony that a society confronted with plastic bags filled with the remains of aborted babies should be most concerned about the problem of recycling the plastic."[2]

SCOPE and FOCUS
I. CONVICTIONS
II. PRETEXTS
Autonomy of Mother
Fundamental Right
Privacy
Equality
Don't absolutize
Zygote vs. adult
Compulsory preg.
Poor discriminated
Men can't vote
Equity: soc. / pol.
Tolerance
Pro-lifers are free
Pluralism of belief
Church & state
Imposing morality
Capital punishment
Cost-free right
Relativism of Value
Mechanism & Gradualism
Pleasure vs. Pain
Accident Justifies Remedy
Pragmatic Justifications
Positivism
III. MANDATE
IV. LEGACY
V. ABORTIVE LINKS
VI. DILEMMA
VII. DESTINY

A. Autonomy of the Mother

The strongest assertion of the abortion movement is that it is the Autonomous decision of the pregnant woman: it is no one else's business; end of conversation.[7] But as Hohfeld pointed out in 1923, the "jural opposite" of someone's right is someone else's "no-right."[8] In the case of abortion, declaring a woman's autonomy requires that the unborn child be held right-less. Nonetheless, the assertion that women are supreme in this regard is consistent, perhaps, with the fact that three of John Naisbitt's ten *Magatrends* for the '90s were listed as the Age of Biology, the Triumph of the Individual and of Women in Leadership.[9]

Francis Beckwith's first engagement with the concept of the mother's autonomy is called "Argument from a Woman's Right over Her Own Body."[10] Hoffmeier lists three kinds of rights which might support the concept of the woman's Autonomy: her Right to life; her Right to control her own body ["reproductive freedom" is a popular phrase]; and in general, her Right to manage her own existence.[11] In an example that many would call an extreme attempt to justify the woman's autonomy under the Constitutionally-protected right of free speech, we are told that Laurence Tribe of Harvard has "argued that women 'speak with their bodies' when they kill their preborn babies!"[12]

Dr. Robert D. Orr explains that four basic principles of secular medical ethics are widely accepted – beneficence, non-maleficence, justice, and autonomy – and that, today, autonomy is the dominant one of the four.[13]

A multifaceted defense of women's autonomy is laid out by Sidney Callahan: "Only with reproductive freedom can a woman have the moral autonomy necessary to make mature commitments, in the arena of family, work, or education... The chance biological process of an involuntary pregnancy should not be allowed to override all the other personal commitments and responsibilities a woman has: to others, to family, to work, to education, to her future development, health, or well-being. Without reproductive freedom, women's personal moral agency and human consciousness are subjected to biology and chance."[14]

1. Fundamental Right of the Mother to Abort

Not only has the Supreme Court engrafted women's Autonomy over abortion into the Constitution, it has done the same for a pregnant minor's right to an abortion avenue, "judicial bypass," that permits her to void parental rights. It obliterated husband's rights in the process.[15]

It is interesting that a woman's fundamental right to reproductive autonomy is such an integral part of *American* abortion policy, but that this *product* is not for export: "The hypocrisy gets especially nauseous when we consider Planned Parenthood's government-mandated sterilization programs in developing countries where women's personal rights are conveniently expendable."[16]

---

13 Orr, in Kilner, Cameron and Schiedermayer, *Bioethics and the Future of Medicine, A Christian Appraisal*, 147-8: "... beneficence (the duty to do good for patients)... non-maleficence (do no harm)... justice (fairness, treating people equally)... autonomy, the patient's right to self-determination [which] is a rather new concept in medicine. Declarations about individual rights which began in the 1960s have propelled this principle to its position today as the dominant influence in medical ethics."

14 Callahan, in Jersild, *Moral Issues and Christian Response*, 346.

15 Clowes, page 89.10: The Supreme Court in 1976 let stand the District Court decision in *T H v. Jones*, which elevated a minor's right to abortion on the basis of privacy to the level of a fundamental right.

Paul Ramsey, *Edges*, 18-9: In *Planned Parenthood v. Danforth* [1976], the Supreme Court asserted that "Just as with the requirement of consent from the spouse [previously denied], so here, the State does not have the constitutional authority to give a third party [the parent of a pregnant minor] an absolute, and possibly arbitrary veto [of an abortion]."

Clowes, page 89.11: In his dissent [to *Danforth*], Justice Byron White stated that "It is truly surprising that the majority finds in the United States Constitution, as it must in order to justify the result it reaches, a rule that the State must assign a greater value to a mother's decision to cut off a potential human life by abortion than to a father's decision to let it mature into a live child."

Clowes, page 89.13: The necessity that judicial bypass be permitted under any state effort to require parental consent was asserted by the Supreme Court in 1979 in the two *Baird* cases.

16 F. LaGard Smith, *When Choice Becomes God*, 216.

How could the "Abortion Right" *become* Fundamental?

In 1964 a preborn needed a blood transfusion in order to survive because of an Rh blood problem. The New Jersey Supreme Court ruled that the mother could refuse her own transfusion on religious grounds, but that her fundamental right to practice her religion, and also her right to her own body, are both subordinate to her unborn baby's right to life.[1]

The case law regarding privacy will be discussed next, but the 1992 Supreme Court case, *Planned Parenthood v. Casey*, went beyond privacy to establish abortion as a fundamental right. *Casey* "...put the right to abortion in concrete," says James Dobson. "Therefore, nothing short of a constitutional amendment will protect the unborn child."[2]

The ultimate "pro-CHOICE" victory was the *Casey* decision

R. C. Sproul says that many consider the freedom of choice to be "the most fundamental democratic right of all."[3] The concept of *choice* was hitched to the abortion wagon early and it has been driven hard. A barrage of lobbying yielded a pro-choice pronouncement, in 1930, by the Federal Council of Churches [soon after, renamed the National Council of Churches], and George Grant tells us that "It was not long before an avalanche of compromise occurred. One denomination after another turned a deaf ear on the unborn innocents and capitulated [to *choice*]."[4]

"In the ongoing debate about abortion," says Sproul, "the pro-*choice* position has become pivotal to public opinion. In a poll conducted in 1989 in the United States, seventy-four percent of those questioned agreed with this statement: 'I personally feel that abortion is morally wrong, but I also feel that whether or not to have an abortion is a decision that has to be made by every woman herself.'"[5] Think about it. This is a world-class good-news-bad-news situation: Three-fourths of America thinks abortion is morally wrong [yea!]. Three-fourths of Americans are pro-choice [boo!]. Three-fourths of America thinks that it is possible to be both pro-preborn and neutral-on-abortion at the same time! It is tragic that we, the church, have let the public embrace such a delusion. It is criminal that the Supreme Court, in *Casey*, has presumed to empower each individual with sovereignty to "define one's own concept" of the "mystery of human life."[6]

"Out of the womb, child abuse is everybody's business. But inside the womb, it's *a woman's right to decide*," says F. LaGard Smith.[7] Is that an exaggeration? In our lifetime, the Supreme Court's decisions have enshrined abortion as a fundamental human right of women. Esther Langston says: "What we are saying is that abortion becomes one of the choices, and the person has the right to choose whatever it is that is best that they need as necessary and best for them in the situation for which they find themselves, be it abortion, to keep, to adopt, to sell, to leave in a dumpster, to put on your porch, whatever; it's the person's right to choose."[8]

> **"Christians are properly fearful when decisions about the life and death of other persons are interpreted as matters of personal choice and private decision."[21]**
> **–Christine D. Pohl**

1 *Fitkin v. Anderson*, in Willke, *Handbook on Abortion*, 170.

2 *Focus on the Family* newsletter, July 1997, 2. "...There IS no other way. According to the Supreme Court, the Constitution now explicitly defends a woman's right to kill an unborn baby, and neither the Congress, state legislatures nor lower courts have the power to override that ruling."

3 R.C. Sproul, 15.

4 George Grant, *Third Time Around: A History of the Pro-Life Movement from the First Century to the Present*, 125-6.

5 R.C. Sproul, 117.

6 *Focus on the Family* newsletter, July 1997, 2.

7 F. LaGard Smith, 238.

8 Esther Langston, professor of social work, University of Nevada, Las Vegas, in Beckwith, *Politically Correct Death*, 174.

9 F. LaGard Smith, 257.

10 Gregory Koukl, *Stand to Reason* radio broadcast transcript, "Sanctity of Life Sunday," 1.

11 *Prudential Insurance Company v. Cheek*, in Clowes, page 89.9.

12 John Whitehead, *The Second American Revolution*, 120: "The Supreme Court... [held Connecticut's law against contraceptive devices] unconstitutional on the basis that it violated the Fourteenth Amendment's prohibition against denial of liberty without due process of law. Justice Arthur Goldberg, in a concurring opinion, grafted the principle of the right to privacy onto the Constitution. In essence he proclaimed that the right to contraceptives, which is based upon the right to privacy, was found in the Ninth Amendment [retained rights]."

13 Clowes, pages 89.8 and 89.9: Justice Steward also said: "I can find no such general right of privacy in the Bill of Rights, in any other part of the Constitution, or in any case ever before decided by this Court..."

The *9th Amendment*, 1791, includes the *retained rights* passage: "The enumeration in the Constitution of certain rights shall not be construed to deny or disparage others retained by the people."

The *14th Amendment*, 1866, which is generally about civil rights, includes the *due process* clause: "nor shall any state deprive any person of life, liberty, or property without due process of law, nor deny to any person within its jurisdiction the equal protection of the laws.

SCOPE and FOCUS
I. CONVICTIONS
II. PRETEXTS
Autonomy of Mother
Fundamental Right
Privacy
Equality
Don't absolutize
Zygote vs. adult
Compulsory preg.
Poor discriminated
Men can't vote
Equity: soc. / pol.
Tolerance
Pro-lifers are free
Pluralism of belief
Church & state
Imposing morality
Capital punishment
Cost-free right
Relativism of Value
Mechanism & Gradualism
Pleasure vs. Pain
Accident Justifies Remedy
Pragmatic Justifications
Positivism
III. MANDATE
IV. LEGACY
V. ABORTIVE LINKS
VI. DILEMMA
VII. DESTINY

2. Privacy of the Mother

"A woman may have a "right of privacy," says Smith, "but the killing of an innocent life is never a private matter."[9] Gregory Koukl asks, "Can you go into a closet and murder someone and then claim protection on grounds of your right to privacy? Of course not... Life always preempts the right to privacy. The law routinely invades our privacy for much less weighty reasons."[10]

In 1922 the Supreme Court was adamantly declaring that there is no right to privacy: "As we have stated, neither the 14th Amendment nor any other provision of the *Constitution* of the United States... confers any right to privacy upon either persons or corporations."[11]

Whitehead says that "The cornerstone case for the right to privacy was a 1965 Supreme Court Case, *Griswold v. Connecticut*,"[12] The result was that married people had the liberty – based upon the 14th Amendment's *due-process* guarantee – to buy contraceptives unless prevented by court order. This right was also supported by a newly discovered right, *privacy*, based on the retained-rights tenet of the 9th Amendment – the idea that if the government is not given a power by the Constitution, then the people have retained ownership of that right. In dissenting to *Griswold*, Justice Potter Stewart said, "...it is not the function of this court to decide cases on the basis of community standards."[13] The *Griswold* right to privacy for married people to buy contraceptives was held to extend to the unmarried and the married alike in the *Eisenstadt v. Baird* case in 1972.[14]

The *Eisenstadt v. Baird* case was heard just a year before *Roe v. Wade*, which – based primarily upon the right of privacy – made abortion legal, nationwide. Whitehead comments, "...privacy is *not* a God-given, natural law on the same level as the right to life. But the [Supreme] Court [in *Roe v. Wade*] in effect ignored the natural law argument and considered privacy a constitutional, man-made right."[15]

Privacy was extended to protect infanticide in 1986 in *Bowen v. American College of Obstetricians and Gynecologists*.[16]

We will deal with the 1989 *Webster v. Reproductive Health Services, Inc.* decision in other contexts, but here it is crucial to note that, as explained by Brian Clowes, "Chief Justice William Rehnquist asserted that the 'key elements' of the 'abortion right' – the right to privacy and the 'Constitutional right to abortion' – 'simply do not exist.'"[17]

Casey's liberation of pregnant teens [1992] from their parents, as we have shown, had the effect of upholding Autonomy, Privacy and a Fundamental right to abortion for any pregnant person. Beckwith's *Politically Correct Death* has a section on the "Argument from Privacy"[18]

The *privacy* debate is very much alive. When, in 1997, a California pharmacist cited moral objections in refusing to fill a prescription calling for the use of birth control pills as a *morning-after* method of birth control [to prevent implantation of a fertilized egg], he was supported by his colleagues and his professional association, but Planned Parenthood called his actions "horrifying" and asserted that "no third party has the right to intervene in a *personal decision* made between a woman and her doctor."[19]

It seems clear that virtually everyone on both sides of the abortion issue was "blindsided" by *Roe v. Wade*. That undoubtedly included Russel Shaw and Paul Ramsey. But those two, way back in 1968, were aware of a possibility relating to privacy that has still to occur to many in the pro-life movement today. Shaw wrote, "It may very well be, as Paul Ramsey says, that the controversy over abortion and the law will become irrelevant once the abortion pills now being developed become generally available. Abortion then will be an issue in a *private* sphere which law cannot reach."[20]

14 Clowes, page 89.9: The Court held: "If the right to privacy means anything, it is the right of the individual, married or single, to be free from unwarranted governmental intrustion into matters so fundamentally affecting a person as the decision whether or not to beget a child."

15 John Whitehead, *The Second American Revolution*, 116.

16 Clowes, page 89.15. "The Court found a parent's *right* to refuse treatment [for their handicapped, newly BORN children], based upon the 'right to privacy.' This right to privacy is paramount – even over the [born] child's right to be spared an agonizing death by thirst and starvation."

17 Clowes, page 89.16.

18 Beckwith, 85-6.

19 *Press-Enterprise*, 3-28-97, B1.

20 Russel Shaw, *Abortion on Trial*, 1968, 169.

21 Pohl, in Kilner, *Bioethics*, 212.

3. Equality for Women Requires Freedom of Choice to Abort

One of the major pillars of the pro-abortion edifice, built on the rock of women's Autonomy, is the assertion that the right to abort her unborn child is essential in order for a woman to achieve full equality with men. Just what equality means, not to mention "full equality with men," would certainly be helpful information. We can trace the notion of equality at least back to Plato, who said that equality is just, and inequality unjust. That puts equality in the category of very *good* things. Plato's definition of equality is that it means to treat likes alike and things which are unalike differently, in proportion to the degree of likeness and differentness.[1]

As long as men were making the rules, and since it was obvious that women were *very different* from men, then the subject of equality between them – presumably – never came up. So the Founding Fathers, in saying that all *men* were created *equal* , were not – we can conclude – *thinking* of women, or black people of either sex, for that matter. Despite that, in the opinion of Gordon Wood, equality became "the single most powerful and radical ideological force in all of American history."[2] In the 1830s, Alexis de Tocqueville remarked that Americans loved equality more than freedom.[3]

Peter Westen says that "fifty years ago equality was dismissed as a legal argument of 'last resort,' one to be eschewed until all available 'rights' had been tried and rejected; today equality is becoming the argument of first choice, one that threatens to swallow 'rights' that once ranked far above it."[4] "The great political upsurge of equality occurred," according to Robert Bork, "with Franklin Roosevelt's New Deal and Harry Truman's Fair Deal... [T]he egalitarian passion must always lead to greater centralized power and coercion. Lyndon Johnson's Great Society carried forward what Roosevelt and Truman had begun and accomplished the most thorough-going redistribution of wealth and status in the name of equality that this country had ever experienced."[5]

In *Slouching Towards Gomorrah: Modern Liberalism and American Decline*, we are told that the Sixties "students wanted an end to status... They carried with them the belief that hierarchies are presumptively illegitimate... From there it is a short step to the rejection of the achievement principle."[6] The Sixties ethic and the Sixties generation have seized the reins of leadership in every sector of society, and their emphasis on equality – including disdain for the inequality that motherhood places upon women – is a pervasive element of that takeover. We are told that "Justice Harry Blackmun, who wrote *Roe* and who never offered the slightest constitutional defense of it, simply remarked that the decision was a landmark on *women's march to equality*. Equality in this view, means that if men do not bear children, women should not have to either."[7]

Joseph Foreman points out that the [gender-] feminist movement calls pregnancy the central tool of male domination, and holds that killing her child is an act of liberation for a woman, freeing her to take her rightful place in Western civilization."[8]

Francis Beckwith, in *Politically Correct Death: Answering the Arguments for Abortion Rights*, both raises and refutes a handful of pro-abortion justifications which all center on the theme that equality for women demands the right to abort. **[ ]** will be utilized throughout the "Pretexts" part of *Orphans in Babylon* to identify the **page number** where that topic is addressed in ***Politically Correct Death.***

1 Peter Westen, "The Empty Idea of Equality," 542-3.

2 Wood, in Bork, 66.

3 Bork, 67.

4 Peter Westen, 538.

5 Bork, 67.

6 Bork, 78: "Karl Mannheim... proposed that three principles for the selection of elites – blood, property, and achievement – have marked different historical periods... If we recognize reward according to race, ethnicity, and sex as aspects or analogues of the blood principle, it is obvious how far the achievement principle has been discarded in America in the name of equality."

7 Robert Bork, 183.

8 Joseph Foreman, 118.

9 Moreland and Geisler, *Life and Death Debate, Moral Issues of Our Time*, 26.

10 Described in Focus on the Family *Citizen*, 7-28-97, 4.

[John Swomley, in Jersild, 344, explains that others have taken the argument a step further. They would liken the infant in the womb to a drowning person, for whom an act of rescue by another might entail considerable cost and risk, and doing so would be a virtuous thing to do. But they conclude that the person in the water is not justified in claiming – on the basis of his right to life – that another must jump into the water to save him].

11 Clowes, page 89.9.

12 *Press-Enterprise*, 11-25-96, A10.

[A second result of the elimination of compulsory pregnancy through the availability of abortion is that defendants in paternity suits, and fathers ordered to pay child support, are protesting that they are being discriminated against as victims of *compulsory fatherhood*!]

13 *Press-Enterprise*, 8-1-96, A2.

14 Clowes, page 89.11.

15 Clowes, pages 89.16 and 89.17.

16 Stearns, in Jonathan Black, *Radical Lawyers: Their Role in the Movement and in the Courts*, 1971, 265 and 268: In 1966, Nancy Stearns prepared a legal brief which was widely reprinted and which undoubtedly played a part in swaying public opinion and shaping public policy: "The New York Abortion Laws Effect A Denial Of Equal Protection Of The Law Guaranteed To Women By The Fourteenth Amendment... It is often said that if men could become pregnant or if women sat in the legislatures there would no longer be laws prohibiting abortion. This is not said in jest. It reaches to the heart of

SCOPE and FOCUS
I. CONVICTIONS
II. PRETEXTS
Autonomy of Mother
Fundamental Right
Privacy
Equality
Don't absolutize
Zygote vs. adult
Compulsory preg.
Poor discriminated
Men can't vote
Equity: soc. / pol.
Tolerance
Pro-lifers are free
Pluralism of belief
Church & state
Imposing morality
Capital punishment
Cost-free right
Relativism of Value
Mechanism & Gradualism
Pleasure vs. Pain
Accident Justifies Remedy
Pragmatic Justifications
Positivism
III. MANDATE
IV. LEGACY
V. ABORTIVE LINKS
VI. DILEMMA
VII. DESTINY

the unequal position of women with respect to the burdens of bearing and raising children and the fact that they are robbed of the ability to choose whether they wish to bear those burdens... And it is not sufficient to say that the woman 'chose' to have sexual intercourse, for she did not choose to become pregnant. As long as she is forced to bear such an extraordinarily disproportionate share of the pains and burdens of childrearing... then, to deprive her of the ultimate choice as to whether she will in fact bear those burdens violates the most basic aspects of 'our American ideal of fairness' guaranteed and enshrined in the Fourteenth Amendment."

a. Don't absolutize the unborn's right to life [115]

The implication in the accusation that pro-lifers absolutize the right to life of the preborn is that even if the pregnancy is going to kill the mother pro-lifers assert that no abortion should ever be performed. [See *Orphans in Babylon*, 81, and 256.]

b. Zygote is not the equal of an adult woman [118-20]

As with so many of the comparative arguments made to defend abortion, this assertion confuses the characteristics normal to particular degrees of human development with a difference in nature, of essence, which of course should more properly be the focus of the discussion.

c. Compulsory pregnancy is barbaric [84-5]

This is one of Joseph Fletcher's pet slogans: "No woman should be forced to have a child against her will."[9] Some writers have thrown in the concept that no woman's womb should be used without her "consent."[10]

As we have mentioned, the 1972 Supreme Court case, *Eisenstadt v. Baird*, held that "If the right to privacy means anything, it is the right of the individual... to be free from unwarranted governmental intrusion into matters so fundamentally affecting a person as the decision whether or not to beget a child."[11]

Legalized abortion means that there is no longer such a thing as compulsory pregnancy. This is creating some unexpected dilemmas. It is reported that some insurance companies and HMOs are using test results that indicate a high probability that a preborn is imperfect to pressure a woman to have an abortion, with the threat that, should the abortion offer be rejected, the baby would be excluded from medical coverage under the plan. [12]

d. Poor women are discriminated against if abortion is criminalized [59-60]

e. Men can't get pregnant, so can't vote on abortion [90]

Beyond this assertion than men in general must be kept out of the loop in abortive decisionmaking, the questions of a man's role and rights concerning the impending abortion of his own child are extremely critical. In the swirl of global attention that focused on Britain when it was revealed that 3,000 frozen embryos had been ordered thawed-to-death, the public learned of the British law which requires that embryos cannot be *preserved* unless the father agrees.[13]

In America, in 1976, the Supreme Court's *Planned Parenthood of Central Missouri v. Danforth* decision ruled that a man has absolutely no say, either way, in a woman's autonomous decision to abort or to birth his child, even if the father is the woman's husband. In his dissent, Justice Byron White stated that "It is truly surprising that the majority finds in the United States Constitution... a rule that the State must assign a greater value to a mother's decision to cut off a potential human life by abortion than to a father's decision to let it mature into a live child."[14] Brian Clowes also observes that the effect of *Danforth* is to impose "mandatory fatherhood" on the husband if the wife wants to keep the child he does not want.

In 1992, the *Planned Parenthood v. Casey* case, which was seen as a partial pro-life victory, found all portions of the Pennsylvania Abortion Control Act constitutional [informed consent, 24-hour waiting period, parental consent-with-judicial-bypass, and required reporting of information to the State] *except* that it held the spousal notification provision to be unconstitutional.[15]

f. Free choice is required for social & political equality [76-7]

[This footnote explores the social and political equality theme.] [16]

"Not one of us is going to say, 'I'm personally against lynching and genocide, but I don't want to impose my values on others. When innocent life is at stake, we realize that we can no longer be pro-choice. At that point, pro-choice is license to kill."[1]

–F. LaGard Smith

4. Tolerance & Multiculturalism Support Freedom of Choice

Simon Wiesenthal was zealous in seeing that Nazi leaders were brought to justice. In Los Angeles is a cultural treasure called the Simon Wiesenthal Museum of Tolerance. Prominent in its displays are, of course, the Holocaust, and also the civil rights struggle in America. The name of the museum is perplexing. The overall message of the institution seems to be *people must be taught to tolerate those who are different.* But a parallel reality virtually shouts from the content: How could the people [of Germany, of the South] *tolerate* Hitler [and the KKK]? So are we *for* tolerance, or *against* it? Hitler was intolerant of Jews so he killed them; the German people were tolerant of Hitler so he got away with it.

F. LaGard Smith applies that paradox to the bulk of Americans who have been seduced into thinking that they are "pro-choice." "Just let the Ku Klux Klan resurrect lynching, or have some group of neo-Nazis talk about exterminating Jews again, and we will all throw down our pro-choice banners and become the most intolerant people you ever saw – and rightfully so. They could talk all day long about their 'right to decide,' but we wouldn't tolerate it. Under those circumstances not one of us is going to say, 'I'm personally against lynching and genocide, but I don't want to impose my values on others.' When innocent life is at stake, we realize that we can no longer be pro-choice. At that point pro-choice is license to kill."[1]

The push for tolerance as a virtue emerged in the 1700s as an antidote to the religious bloodshed – Catholics vs. Protestants – which convulsed Europe. "Voltaire dedicated himself to an intellectual crusade against religious fanaticism... He believed [but did not directly say]: "I disapprove of what you say, but I will defend to the death your right to say it."[2]

In the early days of the U.S.A., British law was getting stiffer – making abortion before quickening a criminal offense, in 1803, for instance – but "the common law in the United States... was becoming more flexible and more tolerant... especially in sex-related areas, not more restrictive."[3]

As can be seen in the "Politics" entries in the Timeline [at the end of this volume] the Republican Party platform began in 1976 with a tentative mention of support for a right-to-life amendment, got stronger in 1980, mentioned "sanctity" in 1984 and 1988 and began to waffle in 1992, and by 1996 the press was reporting that pro-lifers "have lost political ground. Sen. Bob Dole, the presumptive Republican presidential nominee, reaffirmed Thursday his opposition to abortion but called for his party's platform to include a 'declaration of tolerance' recognizing differing views."[4]

a. Pro-lifers aren't forced to have abortions [86-7]

Randy Alcorn counters this assertion. "The fact that we are not forced to get abortions does not settle the moral issue... The law did not require that the German people kill Jews. The law only required that they stand passively by while others killed them. Likewise, our law 'only' requires that no one be able to go to the killing place and stand between the baby and the knife."[5]

1 F. LaGard Smith, *When Choice Becomes God*, 244.

2 Michael Hart, *The 100: A Ranking of the Most Influential Persons in History*, 410-3,

3 James Mohr, *Abortion in America: The Origins and Evolution of National Policy, 1800-1900*, 5.

4 *Press-Enterprise*, 6-9-96, A1, A4.

5 Randy Alcorn, *Is Rescuing Right? Breaking the Law to Save the Unborn*, 68.

6 Michael Hart, *The 100: A Ranking of the Most Influential Persons in History*, 153.

7 Michael Hart, 286-8.

8 Amendment 1. "Freedom of religion, speech, and the press; rights of assembly and petition. Congress shall make no law respecting an establishment of religion, or prohibiting the free exercise thereof; or abridging the freedom of speech, or of the press; or the right of the people peaceably to assemble, and to petition the government for a redress of grievances."

"There are a number of things demanding intolerance: rape, bigotry, wife and child abuse, to name a few... The question is, what should we physically prevent others from choosing to do?"[19]

–Joseph Foreman

SCOPE and FOCUS
I. CONVICTIONS
II. PRETEXTS
Autonomy of Mother
Fundamental Right
Privacy
Equality
Don't absolutize
Zygote vs. adult
Compulsory preg.
Poor discriminated
Men can't vote
Equity: soc. / pol.
Tolerance
Pro-lifers are free
Pluralism of belief
Church & state
Imposing morality
Capital punishment
Cost-free right
Relativism of Value
Mechanism & Gradualism
Pleasure vs. Pain
Accident Justifies Remedy
Pragmatic Justifications
Positivism
III. MANDATE
IV. LEGACY
V. ABORTIVE LINKS
VI. DILEMMA
VII. DESTINY

b. Religious pluralism shows there is no "right" answer [80-1]

This argument – although it proves nothing about the value of the unborn – underscores the valid point that "pro-choice" pastors, Christians and denominations have negated pro-life attempts to impact the culture.

c. Separate church & state [80-1]

One of the things Martin Luther protested was the Church's interfering in civil government.[6] On the other hand, the second most influential leader of the Reformation, John Calvin, was the *de facto* head of government in Geneva, Switzerland. "...after 1555 he was a virtual autocrat... Attendance at church during prescribed hours [very *long* hours] was required by law."[7]

The demand for the "separation of church and state" is alleged to be found in the First Amendment to the *Constitution*.[8] James Draper says, "...The First Amendment... was included at the insistence of the clergy. It was intended to keep the federal government out of the life of the churches."[9]

Robert Audi dissects the "liberal version of the separation view" and finds that it contains these three strands of conviction: 1) Tolerance, the libertarian principle, freedom from state interference; 2) Impartiality, the equalitarian principle, no preference shown by the state; 3) Neutrality on the part of the state, among religions and between the religious and the non-religious.[10]

"The First Amendment would read like this if it were stated in contemporary language," says John Whitehead, "'The federal government shall make no law having anything to do with supporting a national denominational church, or prohibiting the free exercise of religion.'"[11] The new assertion that the church had no business in politics was evidenced in 1830, when the booklet *Abolition a Sedition* protested the intrusion of religion [argument regarding "higher law"] into the civil realm.[12]

Here is Robert Bork's analysis of *church and state*: "...Within the last several decades, the Supreme Court, at the urging of organizations such as the ACLU, has read the [First Amendment's establishment] clause as though it commanded the separation of religion and society... The first Congress, which proposed the First Amendment for ratification by the states, also appointed chaplains for the House, Senate, and the armed forces [at public expense]."[13]

"Under the First Amendment's prohibition of the establishment of religion, the Court has steadily made religion a matter for the private individual by driving it out of the public arena," says Bork.[14]

Charles Colson thinks, "A showdown between church and state may be inevitable. This is not something for which Christians should hope. But it is something for which they should prepare."[15]

d. Imposing your morality on others is not legitimate [81-2]

Hart tells us that in 1095 Pope Urban II "delivered what was perhaps the single most effective speech in history; [his] call for a Christian war to recapture the Holy Land from the Moslems inaugurated the Crusades."[16] For roughly a hundred years various waves of Crusaders attempted to "impose Christianity" on the Near East.

Five hundred years later, on the very threshold of the Protestant Reformation, Nicolaus Copernicus – because he correctly feared the Church's earthly and ungodly wrath – delayed the publication of the writings which were to launch modern astronomy and science until he was on his deathbed in 1543.[17] At the time, the Church was intent on "imposing its *science*" on the world.

After the Reformation, for a couple of hundred years, it looked like the Protestants and Catholics were going to kill each other off, each side intent on "imposing its *theology*" on the other.[18]

9 James Draper and Forrest Watson, *If the Foundations be Destroyed*, xi.
10 Robert Audi, *Religion in the Public Square: The Place of Religious Convictions in Political Debate*, 3-4.
11 John Whitehead, *The Second American Revolution*, 98.
12 Donald Dayton, *Discovering an Evangelical Heritage*, 76.
13 Robert Bork, *Slouching Towards Gomorrah: Modern Liberalism and American Decline*, 289.
14 Robert Bork, 102.
15 Cal Thomas, columnist, *Press-Enterprise*, 10-23-96, A10.
16 Michael Hart, 269.
17 Michael Hart, 155-7.
18 Michael Hart, 151.
19 Joseph Foreman, *Shattering the Darkness*, 96-7.

In the United States, the Methodist General Conference in 1836 voted, 120-to-14, to express themselves as "decidedly opposed to modern abolitionism, and wholly disclaim any right, wish or intention to interfere in the Civil and political relationship between master and slave..."[1]

A major impetus for the whole democratizing thrust in Europe was to get the various factions of Christianity to stop trying to impose their *doctrines* on each other, and to just tolerate one another. Indeed the word *denomination* carries the implication of a group separated by distinct differences but accepting each other's legitimate existence.[2]

Today, not just critics of the Church, but Christians also urge sensitivity and moderation. Larry Braidfoot says, "The effort to shape society in a way that reflects Christian values must recognize certain limits..."[3] William Ball suggests that a Christian should "...imagine himself living in the late Ayatollah's Iran. If this is unacceptable, then on what grounds can we choose to impose the Christian's divine law on non-Christians?"[4]

Russel Shaw would counter, at least in the case of abortion, that "the *imposing* is on the side of those who favor abortion, since they are imposing death on an innocent human life."[5] Dr. Willke would agree. He says, "Perhaps the question should be turned around? What right does a mother have to impose her morality upon her unborn child... fatally?"[6]

In the words of Vatican II [1962-1965], "Where public authority oversteps its competence and oppresses the people, these people should nevertheless obey to the extent that the objective good demands. Still it is lawful for them to defend their own rights and those of their fellow citizens against any abuse of this authority..."[7]

"Where Christians believe a course of action to be Scripturally based," says Doug Bandow, "they should be uncompromising in their support for it."[8]

Franky Schaeffer says that our society "ridicules, ignores and rejects the Christian point of view... It is time to confront the godlessness of the day with Christian commitment and action."[9]

e. Capital punishment advocates aren't really pro-life [89-90]

The accusation asserts that it is a contradiction for someone who believes in the death penalty to say she is pro-life. The error consists in the persistent notion among pro-abortionists that pro-lifers absolutize the right to life, as was mentioned a bit earlier. There is a simple biblical explanation: the distinction is between the innocent and the guilty. Exodus 21:12 makes it very clear: "Anyone who strikes [an innocent] man and kills him shall surely be put to death [by man]." It is not inconsistent for a pro-lifer to favor capital punishment for capital criminals and the protection of life for the innocent.

While nearly all of the rest of the Western nations have outlawed capital punishment, both the citizens and the government of the United States still think it is an appropriate measure.[10]

One skill pro-abortionists have raised to an art form is distracting listeners from the lives of the innocent by raising emotionally charged tangential issues. Brian Clowes brings this one back to dead center: "Every *day* in this country, more innocent unborn babies die than all the criminals executed in this country's history! ...[Pro-abortionists are saying that] the problem of the deaths of 20 guilty murderers per year is far more important than the problem of the deaths of 1,555,000 innocent babies per year."[11]

1 Donald Dayton, *Discovering an Evangelical Heritage*, 75.

2 See an interesting view of Locke's writings in Hart, 261-2. Hart says that, concerning tolerance, Locke did not practice what he preached – that his tolerance did not extend to the Catholics because he held that they were sworn to the pope as opposed to their civil government.

3 Larry Braidfoot, 121.

4 William Ball, 114.

5 Russel Shaw, *Abortion on Trial*, 173.

6 J.C. Willke, *Handbook on Abortion*, 147.

7 Michael Bray, 160.

8 Doug Bandow, *Beyond Good Intentions, A Biblical view of Politics*, 31.

9 Franky Schaeffer, *A Time for Anger: The Myth of Neutrality*, flyleaf.

10 *Press-Enterprise*, 3-14-97, A7: "Majorities of men and women, Democrats and Republicans and all ethnic groups continue to back capital punishment... Of those polled... 59 percent believe capital punishment is appropriate for juveniles convicted of capital murder. Current law forbids the death penalty for those under 18."

11 Brian Clowes, page 84.2.

12 Focus on the Family *Citizen*, 7-28-97, 2.

13 Gregory Koukl, *Stand to Reason* radio broadcast transcripts, "Female Feticide," 2.

14 Harold Brown, in Ball, *National Morality*, 70.

15 Michael Braun, *The Christian in an Age of Sexual Eclipse*, 38.

16 Brian Clowes, page 89.12: *Beal v. Doe*, Social Security; *Maher v. Roe*, Medicaid; *Poelker v. Doe*, public hospital.

**"Pro-*Choice*? What does that mean?
Why would the mere act of choosing something
make it an acceptable thing to do?
Is everything a woman chooses permissible –
drunk driving, drug dealing, child abuse?
Isn't abortion an act of violence?
In court, doesn't 'deciding' to do violence
simply mean it was premeditated?"[12]**

–Focus on the Family

SCOPE and FOCUS
I. CONVICTIONS
II. PRETEXTS
Autonomy of Mother
Fundamental Right
Privacy
Equality
Don't absolutize
Zygote vs. adult
Compulsory preg.
Poor discriminated
Men can't vote
Equity: soc. / pol.
Tolerance
Pro-lifers are free
Pluralism of belief
Church & state
Imposing morality
Capital punishment
Cost-free right
Relativism of Value
Mechanism & Gradualism
Pleasure vs. Pain
Accident Justifies Remedy
Pragmatic Justifications
Positivism
III. MANDATE
IV. LEGACY
V. ABORTIVE LINKS
VI. DILEMMA
VII. DESTINY

We are asked to tolerate "freedom of choice"

A major difficulty has arisen for those who have been adamant about the need for tolerance of a woman's autonomous right to choose: "Up to this time [radical feminists] have always claimed that abortion on demand is a woman's right. Now all of a sudden they object. Now, there are apparently limitations to this constitutional, universal, God-given right to abortion on demand, and that limitation is if you want to abort the child if it's a female."[13]

Harold Brown declares, "It is morally and ethically fraudulent to defend the right to abort with the slogan 'freedom of choice.'"[14]

5. Free Abortions are Every Woman's Right

"Radical feminists advocate universal access to 100 percent federally funded abortions as a means of implementing their goal of equalizing women with men. They contend that this would free women from the 'burden' of childbirth."[15]

Believe it or not, the Supreme Court did three things right in 1977. It upheld the concept that Social Security does not require the funding of "non-therapeutic" abortions, and that Medicaid funds may be denied for such procedures, and also held that a city may refuse to provide publicly-financed abortions to indigent women in a public hospital.[16]

It happened again in 1980 when the Court upheld the constitutionality of the Hyde Amendment's refusal to fund abortions for women on welfare.[17] In 1989, one of several good things about the *Webster* case was its validation of a state law requiring that public funds, employees, and hospitals may not be used to provide or counsel for abortions.[18]

Best of all, perhaps, was the 1991 decision *Rust v. Sullivan*, which upheld the constitutionality of the government's decision to cut off Title X family planning funds to those organizations that promote or perform abortions. "Planned Parenthood lost tens of millions of annual tax dollars due to this decision."[19]

An additional note regarding the funding of abortions: Life Dynamics, Inc., founded by Mark Crutcher, has verified that the personal cost of abortion – as well as the proximity of an abortionist to one's home – affects the abortion rate. The fact that the number of abortions committed varies according to the laws of supply and demand proves that women, in practice, treat abortion like an option rather than a necessity.[20] As tragic as the implications are for the moral state of our society, the attitude clearly is: "Oh, the price went up? Then I'll keep the kid."

17 Brian Clowes, page 89.13: *McRabe v. Secretary of Health, Education and Welfare*, and also *Zbarez v. Quern*.

18 Brian Clowes, page 89.16: *Webster v. Reproductive Health Services, Inc.*

19 Brian Clowes, page 89.16.

20 Mark Crutcher, *Access: The Key to Pro-Life Victory*, 19.

B. Relativism and the Worth of the Preborn

The Autonomy conviction raised a variety of reasons to defend a woman's right to choose abortion on the basis that "It's nobody's business but my own!" – the woman's exclusive domain of moral authority. We will now address justifications which arise, from the Relativism and Mechanism convictions, on the basis that what is killed by abortion has no right to be protected. The three main types of defense which will be raised are assertions that the unborn is either not a person, or not a human being [Relativism], or not *yet* a human person [Mechanism].

The application of relativistic reasoning is clear in Britain's Abortion Act of 1967, which permitted abortion if continuing the pregnancy would involve "injury to the physical or mental health of the pregnant woman or any existing children of her family greater than if the pregnancy were terminated."[1] This particular example of Relativism, it is noted, also typifies the Pleasure/pain orientation to life: the "injury" to "existing children" easily translates into "hardship" or "burden," rather than to "life and health."

In *Roe v. Wade*, Relativism was hard at work in convincing the Justices to try to convince America that it might be legitimate for a State to restrict abortion after viability, but that before that, preborns are not worth anything. In 1976, the *Danforth* case employed relativism in deciding that a wife's desire to kill their child is more valid than a husband's wish to keep their baby alive. The relativism within the verdict was compounded by the fact that the child's worth or right to life was considered so negligible that it didn't even fit into the equation.

Christians, too, have gone out on some very shaky relativistic limbs. John Klotz published in 1973 – the year we got *Roe*'d – a book called *A Christian View of Abortion*. Add it to the mountain of "pro-choice Christian" writings that convinced the government that there would be no significant moral opposition to legalized abortion. He said, "Since from a Scriptural point of view any abortion involves the taking of a human life... we must recognize that there are instances when a life must be taken and that such taking of a life does not involve a violation of the Fifth Commandment. The government has the right to take the life of a murderer and also has the right to take lives in a just war."[2] It relativizes the value of the preborn to ignore its innocence – which does place it within the Fifth Commandment – and to class it with murderers and enemy soldiers, as OK to kill if the government so chooses.

Relativism is the error which permitted the Lutheran Church [Missouri Synod] prior to *Roe* – to conclude that "The commandment [Thou shalt not kill] cannot be directly applied to every act of abortion, since *no hatred or malice* may be involved in a given case."[3] It is said that the consciences of young gang members are so diminished that they feel no emotion when they drive-by and "off" a stranger. Those Lutherans, to be consistent, must hold that no murder has occurred in this case, either.

Relativism is employed at the abortion clinic every time an abortion is justified as saving the world from another unwanted child. There is a kind of relativism that holds one *adult* person to be more valuable than another: A news report stated that John Salvi had killed two women at an abortion clinic, "...one of them a *magna cum laude* Boston College graduate."[4] If we permit ourselves to become "respecters of persons,"[5] then the step of relativizing away the personhood or the humanity of the preborn gets easier to take.

It is relativism that prevents Congressman Ron Wyden [D-Ore.], who is an abortion enthusiast and a primary promoter of the French abortion pill, RU-486, from seeing his hypocrisy when he lectures tobacco industry executives: "I just can't understand how each of you is engaged in an enterprise that is sure to kill some of our children."[6]

SCOPE and FOCUS
I. CONVICTIONS
II. PRETEXTS
Autonomy of Mother
Relativism of Value
Personhood Denied
Potential life
Criteria of persons
Humanity Challenged
Blob of cells
Woman's body
Speciesism
Sperm & ova
Cloneability
Products of conception
Twinning
Blueprints
Chromosomes, 46+/-
Miscarriages legitimize
Mechanism & Gradualism
Pleasure vs. Pain
Accident Justifies Remedy
Pragmatic Justifications
Positivism
III. MANDATE
IV. LEGACY
V. ABORTIVE LINKS
VI. DILEMMA
VII. DESTINY

1 David Brown, *Choices: Ethics and the Christian*, 122-3.

Researcher's note: The British legalized abortion just six years before *Roe* ... Is there any chance that the U.S. Justices are *still* looking over their shoulder to see what the *Mother Country* is doing?

2 John Klotz, 49.

3 Klotz, 48.

4 Gregory Koukl, *Stand to Reason*, "Abortion Rhetoric," 1.

5 *Acts* 10:34: "God is no respecter of persons."

6 *Life Advocate*, 6/'94, 4.

7 Moreland and Geisler, *The Life and Death Debate: Moral Issues of Our Time*, 33.

8 John Eidsmoe, *God and Caesar*, 181-2.

"If the fetus is presumed to be a person, neither the mother nor any other individual has the right to kill that person. But if the fetus is presumed not to be a person, it must be presumed to be part of the pregnant woman's body, in which case no one else has the right to make decisions regarding it."[14] –B. and P. Berger

1. Personhood of the Preborn Denied

Several different assertions may be contained in the statement, "The preborn child is not a person." We will reserve, for the moment, consideration of the meaning, "Society does not choose to recognize the unborn child as a member of the human family until birth." First, we will explore the interpretation, "The government has decided to withhold the status and protections afforded to human persons until after the unborn gets born."

Since that is one of the assertions the Supreme Court made in *Roe v. Wade*, it would be instructive to note how divergent the statement was from our historical position. Moreland and Geisler explain, "The 'right to life' is an inalienable God-given right according to the *Declaration of Independence* (1776), our national birth certificate. The fact that abortions were forbidden by law at the time of the Fourteenth Amendment and that an embryo was defined as 'child in the womb' shows that the constitutional right to life included unborn children as well."[7]

"There is an interesting parallel between *Roe v. Wade*," says John Eidsmoe, "and the *Dred Scott* decision of 1857 and the *Antelope* decision of 1828. These latter cases concluded that blacks were not 'persons' as defined by the Fifth Amendment. Even still, this did not mean that blacks could be legally killed, ...[A] person who killed a black could be tried for murder. In other words, personhood is not to be equated with the right to life."[8]

In 1927, the Massachusetts Supreme Court held that the unborn child was a "person" in the eyes of the law.[9] More significantly, just three years before *Roe v. Wade*, the U.S. Supreme Court itself referred to the unborn as a "person."[10] Just three months before *Roe*, the Missouri Supreme Court declared, "...unborn children have all the qualities and attributes of adult human persons differing only in age or maturity. Medically, human life is a continuum from conception to death."[11]

As fundamental convictions, Relativism and Mechanism cause people to conclude that a "fetus" is not alive, or is not human, or is not yet a person. Pro-lifers declare that she is a living human child. Guess what. Within the text of *Roe v. Wade*, along with a tendency to use the medical terms [fetus, embryo], the Justices themselves refer to the preborn as some combination of "living... human... child(ren)," sixty-eight times.

In *Roe*, the Court's primary rationale was the woman's supposed right to kill her child privately [Autonomously]. As a secondary precaution, it invoked the denial of personhood, to forestall any possibility that the child's right to life might be seen to compete with the mother's privacy right.[12]

It will be recalled that in 1862 President Lincoln issued the *Emancipation Proclamation* freeing all slaves. In 1988, President Reagan issued a *Right to Life Proclamation* in which he said, "[I] do hereby proclaim and declare the unalienable personhood of every American from the moment of conception until natural death..."[13]

At the time of the *Emancipation Proclamation*, the Civil War was raging, and as commander-in-chief, Lincoln directed – within the Proclamation itself – that the Army and Navy should enforce the freeing of the slaves. The North won the War, and the slaves were freed. President Reagan's Proclamation has been virtually unnoticed, and totally unheeded by government.

9 *Torrigan v. Watertown News Co*. In Willke, *Handbook on Abortion*,169.

10 *Steinberg v. Ohio*, in Moreland and Geisler, *Life and Death*, 33-4.

11 Missouri Supreme Court: *Rogers v. Danforth*, in Willke, 171.

12 John Whitehead, *The Second American Revolution*, 124.

Here is what the *Fourteenth Amendment*, ratified by the States in 1868, says about personhood: "All persons born or naturalized in the United States and subject to the jurisdiction thereof, are citizens of the United States and of the State wherein they reside." It is not talking about how an entity becomes a person. Let's simplify it by setting aside the non-essential parts: **"All persons born or naturalized in the United States... are citizens..."** Here are three things it specifically says: 1) If you are a person who was born here you are a citizen; 2) If you are a person who went through the "naturalization" process you are a citizen; 3) Even if you are a person, if you weren't born or naturalized here you aren't a citizen. Number one is crucial. It clearly does *not* say that getting born is what makes someone into a person. To the contrary, getting born here is one of two things that can make a person *into* a citizen.

What is important about being a person, according to the *Fourteenth Amendment*, is that no *person* can be deprived by the State of "life, liberty, or property," without "due process of law;" nor can they be denied "equal protection of the laws." What is crucial here is that the unborn, in getting aborted, are being denied both due process of law and equal protection under the law. The Court, in *Roe*, said in effect, "Too bad: you're not a person, so these protections don't apply."

13 Ronald Reagan, in Grant, *Grand Illusions*, 264.

14 B. and P. Berger, *The War Over the Family*, 82.

"The same legal tradition which in our society guarantees the right to control one's own body firmly recognizes the wrongfulness of harming other bodies, however immature, different looking, or powerless."[14] –Sidney Callahan

a. Potential human life - acorns aren't oak trees [117]

It is relativism that prompts someone to assert that preborn babies are only *potential* people. One of the earliest slogans to make this claim was the phrase, "Acorns aren't oak trees." Greg Koukl responds that "both are oaks but they are at different stages of development."[1] Moreland and Geisler agree: "It is a misunderstanding of botany to say an acorn is a potential oak tree. An acorn is a tiny living oak tree inside a shell."[2] Nonetheless, the Supreme Court, in *Roe*, referred to the unborn as merely a "potential life."[3]

A "pro-choice Christian" says, "The most one can say, perhaps, is that the fetus is potentially a person."[4] As an official bow to relativism, "The largest Lutheran communions worldwide," George Grant tells us, stated that "the key issue is the status of the unborn fetus... the organic beginning of human life... A qualitative distinction must be made between its claims and the rights of a responsible person made in God's image who is living in relationships with God and other human beings... On the basis of the evangelical ethic, a woman or couple may decide responsibly to seek an abortion."[5]

b. Criteria of personhood [105-10]

A second relativizing denial of personhood is to make a list of characteristics of a person and check how the unborn child measures up. James Q. Wilson wrote: "The moral debate over abortion centers on the point in the development of the fertilized ovum when it has acquired those characteristics that entitle it to moral respect."[6]

John Swomley wants to convince us that when the Bible says people are created "in the image of God," "...this does not refer to biological similarities but to the abilities to love and to reason, self awareness, transcendence, and freedom to choose, rather than to live by instinct."[7] Swomley uses the list to demonstrate that the unborn do not qualify as persons, but the same could be said about all five-year-olds and the majority of teenagers and adults. Beckwith tells us that Warren has come up with a similar list: consciousness, reasoning, self-motivated activity, communication, self-concept/self-awareness.[8] If the goal was to create a list that would exclude all of the unborn but include more youngsters and born people in general, this test seems to do better than the first.

Dr. Bernard Nathanson invites us to apply the Harvard criteria for the pronouncement of death [applied in reverse, to define human life]. On that basis, the unborn child "does respond to pain, makes respiratory efforts, moves spontaneously, and has electroencephalographic activity – life must be present."[9]

Ankerberg and Weldon warn us to distinguish personality from personhood. They quote Norman Geisler: "Personality is a property, but personhood is the substance of being human... Thus, personality is developed gradually, but personhood comes instantly at conception."[10] Moreland and Geisler, in *The Life and Death Debate*, reason through the implications of the *personality* approach: "Since personality involves consciousness, those who lack consciousness would cease to be human. Is it OK to kill the unconscious?"[11]

1 Gregory Koukl, *Stand to Reason*, "Does a Fetus Have a Soul?" 1.

2 Moreland and Geisler, *The Life and Death Debate*, 33.

3 Moreland and Geisler, *Life and Death*, 26.

4 Waldo Beach, *Christian Ethics in the Protestant Tradition*, 67.

5 George Grant, *Third Time Around*, 127.

6 Wilson, in Bork, 176.

7 Swomley, in Jersild, 341.

8 Francis Beckwith, *PC Death*, 106.

9 Nathanson, in Robert Orr, *Life and Death Decisions*, 55.

10 Geisler, in Ankerberg, *When Does Life Begin? And 39 Other Tough Questions About Abortion*, 29.

Geisler: "Personality is a psychological concept; personhood is an ontological [property and knowledge of being] category."

"People function as humans because they are human; they do not become human by performing human functions."[15]

–John Warwick Montgomery

SCOPE and FOCUS
I. CONVICTIONS
II. PRETEXTS
Autonomy of Mother
Relativism of Value
Personhood Denied
Potential life
Criteria of persons
Humanity Challenged
Blob of cells
Woman's body
Speciesism
Sperm & ova
Cloneability
Products of conception
Twinning
Blueprints
Chromosomes, 46+/-
Miscarriages legitimize
Mechanism & Gradualism
Pleasure vs. Pain
Accident Justifies Remedy
Pragmatic Justifications
Positivism
III. MANDATE
IV. LEGACY
V. ABORTIVE LINKS
VI. DILEMMA
VII. DESTINY

Getting back to the preliminary problem, the Supreme Court has held that preborn children do not qualify for due process and equal protection because they are not persons. That doesn't necessarily follow. In this country, the government long ago decided to give legal protection to entities which are not human beings and never will be. By statute, a *corporation*, has been elevated to the status of a "legal person" for the express purpose of affording it protections under the law.[12] Where, in the Constitution, can we find that the founding Fathers intended *that*?

Whitehead continues, "The argument that fetuses lack constitutional rights is simply irrelevant... Dogs are not 'persons in the whole sense' nor have they constitutional rights, but that does not mean the state cannot prohibit killing them... Come to think of it, draft cards aren't persons either... [but they are protected by law from certain harms]. ...it is against the law to burn a draft card but not to kill an unborn child."[13]

2. Humanity of the Preborn Challenged

Ignoring the obvious, multitudes who call themselves pro-choice charge that the preborn are not human beings. Whitehead tells us that "When Hitler determined to exterminate the Jews, some German humanists objected on the basis of the sanctity of life and of natural justice. Hitler simply defined the Jews as less than fully human, and his critics were anesthetized [by Relativism]."[16]

Most, but not all, pro-abortionists maintain that a "fetus" is not human. One exception is renegade feminist Naomi Wolf, who favors the right to abort, but who "has challenged the feminists whose rhetoric seeks to disguise the truth that a human being is killed by abortion. She asks for 'an abortion-rights movement willing publicly to mourn the evil – necessary though it may be – that is abortion.'"[17]

a. Blob of cells is all it is, garbage

Perhaps the strongest relativizing of the aborted-ones is to call them worthless tumors or parasites. Graeser says that "Jean-Jacques Rousseau 200 years ago... called the fetus a 'witless tadpole' which is actually more descriptive but no more accurate than today's popular term 'blob of tissue.'"[18]

It is possible to pinpoint the span of time during which Planned Parenthood [then] president Alan Guttmacher was bitten by the Relativism bug: He "stated in 1961 when speaking of human reproduction that 'Fertilization, then, has taken place; a baby has been conceived.' ...He said in 1968 that 'My feeling is that the fetus, particularly during its intrauterine life, is merely a group of specialized cells that do not differ materially from other cells.'"[19] Two other medical doctors, Walter Char and John McDermott, were afflicted by Relativism and in 1972 declared: "What is aborted is a protoplasmic mass and not a real live individual."[20]

These profound lapses of scientific rationality among doctors prompted Thomas Hilgers to write, also in 1972, that "The blob theory, the main tenet of the tissue-of-the-mother school of embryology, has been advanced for public scrutiny without so much as a note of public criticism from the scientific community or the medical profession."[21]

Governmental endorsement of the blob theory came in 1983 with the Supreme Court's *Akron* pronouncement that preborn babies who are killed by abortion don't have the right to be buried, because they are nothing but "biological waste."[22]

11 Moreland and Geisler, *The Life and Death Debate: Moral Issues of Our Time*, 32-3.
12 John Whitehead, *The Second American Revolution*, 124.
13 Whitehead, *Second*, 124.
14 Sidney Callahan, in Jersild, 348-9.
15 John Warwick Montgomery, "The Rights of the Unborn Children," *Simon Greenleaf Law Review*, vol. 5, '85-86, 65-67.
16 John Whitehead, *The Second American Revolution*, 118.
17 Naomi Wolf, in Bork, 179.
18 Ronald E. Graeser, in *Life Advocate*, 6/'94, 36.
19 Clowes, page 15.12.
20 Clowes, page 53.15.
21 Thomas Hilgers, *Abortion and Social Justice*, 3.
22 Clowes, page 89.15.

The "blob of garbage" theory, asserted by doctors who should be ashamed of themselves and by Justices who undoubtedly know better, has long been practiced by abortion clinics, whose disdain for human dignity has been occasionally brought to light by discoveries of a few – or of hundreds – of mangled bodies in trash bags, boxes, and outdoor refuse bins.[1] Whitehead is one of several who report that a crass Chicago enterprise for a time was advertising the availability of human embryos and other organs encased in "paperweight" novelty items.[2]

Dr. Martti Kekomaki conducted "medical experiments" which involved slicing open the stomachs and cutting off the heads of *live* late term aborted babies. In 1980, echoing the relativism that was heard at the Nuremberg trials, the experimenter justified those actions with the statement, "An aborted baby is just garbage and that's where it ends up. Why not make use of it for society?"[3] The reader may think of this again when we discuss fetal research under the influence of Pragmatism.

A major factor in many of the abortion-justifying pretexts we will consider – particularly Relativism – is the incredible difference that *wantedness* makes. *Un*wanted 'embryos' and 'fetuses' are alleged to be garbage, but if an embryo is *wanted*, everything changes. Example: Two women who threatened to sue because their "*eggs* were allegedly *stolen* by doctors at a University of California, Irvine, fertility clinic," were paid $1.1 million – of California taxpayer money, we might assume – to drop the charges.[4]

Hold that thought. In Britain there is a law which requires that, if no contact can be made with the "owners" for five years, frozen embryos must be destroyed. Even though there are requests from all over the world from people who would love to "adopt" them, without "permission" from the parents the embryos must be thawed to death.[5] Assuming that the California payoff would have been the same if only *one* egg had been "stolen" from each woman, if we apply the established value of $550,000-each to the 3,000 embryos Britain needed to destroy, the monetary value of the catastrophe is 1.65 Billion dollars. ...The magnitude of the *moral* disaster, of course, is even greater, for those of us who believe in the sanctity of human life.

b. Part of the woman's body [41-6, 92-5]

If we progress past the blob theory, the next relativistic argument we encounter is the overworked "It's part of *my* body" assertion, in the words of Jersild, "...essentially tissue belonging to the woman, having no independent humanity."[6]

Guttmacher claims that "Abortion is precisely equivalent to operating on an appendix or removing a gangrenous bowel."[7] Gloria Steinem, as do many, tags the preborn as an alien aggressor, "...[A woman] has a right to remove any parasitic growth from her body."[8] Since *part of my body* implies ownership, it is helpful to recall that under early common law, it was held that the landowner "...may waste or despoil the land as he pleases."[9]

Beyond that, whether the voiceless preborn is held to be property or a biological growth, there are legal limits which pertain to what individuals are permitted to do. While American Autonomy permits the *choice* of whether or not to remove tonsils – or babies now Relativized to be equal to tonsils – there is the understanding that the state has a duty to intervene to protect one from physical mutilation. If someone goes to a public place, chops off one of his own feet with a hatchet, and declares the intention to off the other, society has a right – and the will, that's important – to intervene. Whether the person's *own* feet or someone else's are being chopped does not make a difference.

1 George Grant, *Grand Illusions: The Legacy of Planned Parenthood*, 19.

2 John Whitehead, *The Stealing of America*, 56.

3 *National Examiner*, 8-19-80, 20-1 [not in bibliography].

4 *Press-Enterprise*, 10-24-96, A4.

5 Associated Press, *Press-Enterprise*, 8-1-96, A2.

6 Jersild, *Moral Issues and Christian Response*, 337.

7 Alan Guttmacher, quoted in *Life Advocate*, 4/'94, 4.

8 Gloria Steinem on CNN television, 9-9-81 [not in bibliography].

9 Christopher Stone, 13.

10 *Dietrich v. Northampton*, in Charles Kindregan, *Abortion, the Law, and Defective Children*, 1969, 28.

11 *Bombrest v. Katz*, in Kindregan, 29. [Since then the new precedent has largely been followed in tort cases.]

12 Chicago Circuit Court, May 1971, Judge Kvistadt, in Willke, 170-1. [Previously in *Orphans in Babylon*, we mentioned the case in which a transfusion was ordered for a baby with an Rh blood problem. In the Chicago case, a woman dying from a loss of blood was told that she had a right to refuse the transfusion on religious grounds even if refusing it killed her, but that she would not be permitted to do so this time because she would be taking her unborn baby with her.]

13 Moreland and Geisler, *The Life and Death Debate*, 28: Their list: sex of the baby [is this penis "part of the woman's body"?]; independent brain waves; finger prints; place of residence; birth changes only address and source of food & oxygen; is a nursing baby part of the breast?; is a test tube baby part of a petri dish?; does an Asian embryo transplanted into a black woman become black?

14 "Life Before Birth" pamphlet, Good News Publishers, Westchester, IL 60153. [Not in bibliography.] "Forms penis by 42 days."

SCOPE and FOCUS
I. CONVICTIONS
II. PRETEXTS
Autonomy of Mother
Relativism of Value
Personhood Denied
Potential life
Criteria of persons
Humanity Challenged
Blob of cells
Woman's body
Speciesism
Sperm & ova
Cloneability
Products of conception
Twinning
Blueprints
Chromosomes, 46+/-
Miscarriages legitimize
Mechanism & Gradualism
Pleasure vs. Pain
Accident Justifies Remedy
Pragmatic Justifications
Positivism
III. MANDATE
IV. LEGACY
V. ABORTIVE LINKS
VI. DILEMMA
VII. DESTINY

Actually, the *part of the mother* claim was for a long time an established judicial precedent in America. The Supreme Court in 1884 rejected a suit for prenatal injuries on the basis that a fetus was simply a part of the mother and not a separate human being.[10] By 1946, however, a federal district court abandoned the 1884 precedent and upheld a similar action on the basis of the individuality of a viable 'fetus.'[11] There have been notable cases in which the right to life of the preborn was upheld over the mother's right to refuse medical treatment – for herself, but not for her child – on religious grounds.[12]

Beyond all that we have mentioned, the allegation that an unborn child is "part of my body" is simply biologically ridiculous. Moreland and Geisler list eight biological facts, any one of which establishes conclusively that this is a separate human being,[13] and they don't even mention the fact that, from the moment of conception, DNA analysis can establish a unique genetic "fingerprint."

Pro-abortionists are adamant that a right to abortion is a necessary part of their "Reproductive Rights." Perhaps sexual realities will most dramatically underscore the biological fact that preborns are not just *part of the mother's body*. One aspect of personhood is establishing one's "human sexuality." This turns out to be one of the early priorities. It is usually the eighth week before a woman has confirmed that she is pregnant and schedules an abortion. By that time, the "part of her body" she intends to eliminate – if it is a boy child – has already grown a penis and a brain with measurable brain waves.[14] What have girl babies been doing? "At 10 weeks, a female fetus has made all the eggs she will carry as a woman."[15]

R.C. Sproul notes: "In *The Silent Scream* [pro-life video], we saw what looked [using ultrasound during an actual abortion] like a formed human being going through obvious pain and distress in trying to escape the destructive instruments of the abortionist... the drama on screen did not resemble removal of a 'tumor' or a 'parasite.'"[16]

c. Speciesism: you're absolutizing human life [114-5]

If someone accuses a pro-lifer of speciesism, it tells us more about him than about us. It says that he is committed to an evolutionary view of the universe which sees even born humans as just the kind of animal we happened to evolve into – it relativizes not just preborns but all of humanity. Oliver Wendell Holmes said, "I see no reason for attributing to man a significance in kind different from that which belongs to a baboon or a grain of sand."[17]

d. Sperm & ova are genetically human too [114]

This argument is an attempt to counter the valid assertion that each fertilized ovum is a unique person because its genetic identity is already complete. It tries to relativize the individuality of the child by comparing it to that which is only a component part.[18]

e. Cloneability makes every cell a "person" [114]

This argument reveals a misunderstanding of the cloning process. In cloning, only the DNA is removed from that cell, and it is inserted into a complete ovum. Not the ovum nor the cell nor its DNA is a person. Once the clone's DNA is complete, a new person exists.

f. "Products of conception" can be nonhuman (placenta, etc.) [96]

The phrase "products of conception" is not normally used by pro-lifers but by pro-abortionists as one of many aliases they employ to relativize the humanity of the preborn child. You will not hear pro-lifers asserting that "The products of conception are human beings."

---

15 *Time*, 1-17-94, 19: "An Edinburgh researcher sparked an international ethical debate with his suggestion that women who cannot provide viable eggs of their own might be able to become pregnant with ovaries transplanted from aborted female fetuses."

[If the gender feminists are going to be consistent, they must certainly raise a ruckus about the violation of reproductive rights which takes place if you steal that unborn girl's *ovaries* containing a lifetime supply of those $550,000 human eggs!]

16 R.C. Sproul, 45.

17 R.C.Sproul, 39.

18 Charles Kindregan, 22.

19 Moreland and Geisler, *The Life and Death Debate*, 39.

g. Twinning and recombining must precede ensoulment [97]

In addition to Beckwith's treatment of this objection, on page 97 of *Politically Correct Death*, as indicated above, Moreland and Geisler also mention this puzzling dilemma. Here is the argument: Sometimes an 'embryo' divides, becoming twins. Occasionally, after the twinning, the "twins" recombine and remain a single baby. This is presented as refutation of the argument that a person is created at the moment of conception, because only one of the twins seems to have been created at conception, and in the case of the recombining – where did the "other" twin "go?"[1]

Though of interest biologically, this presents no pro-life challenge. Prolifers are under no obligation to "count the babies" prior to implantation, and are consistent in our contention that from the moment of conception a complete human being exists – at least one – so that no human action should be permitted to thwart normal development.

h. Blueprints are not houses [117]

There are at least two major problems with this relativistic challenge to the humanity of the preborn. First of all, the baby isn't the blueprint; its DNA is. Second, human beings aren't built like a construction project, one stick of wood added to another until – only at the very end – a house finally exists. Rather, a person is a growing organism. Its essential nature is completely formed in an instant. Its identity is set for its lifetime, which will be a continuous process of development.

i. Zygotes occasionally don't have 46 chromosomes [116-7]

An occasional incomplete or imperfect conception has nothing to do with whether a normal 'embryo' is a human being.

j. Spontaneous abortions legitimize surgical abortion [96-7]

The first problem with this argument is that no one knows what percentage of children conceived fail to successfully implant in the womb under normal conditions. It is very common for writers to estimate "up to fifty percent," but nobody really knows. Pro-abortionists contend that spontaneous abortions legitimize intentional abortions. Their rationale usually – whether expressed or implied – is that if God "lets" those millions of embryos get flushed away naturally, then the destruction of other "embryos" or "fetuses" can't be too big a deal to God, either. Moreland and Geisler offer these words of rebuttal: "We have no unqualified moral duty to interfere with natural death [the miscarriages]... It is not inconsistent to preserve natural life, and allow natural death... There is a crucial distinction between spontaneous death and homicide."[2]

This relativizing argument employs faulty logic. The fact that many children are killed accidentally by automobiles every year does not make it OK to drive up on the sidewalk to run over one.

Windows on the womb make a world of difference.

One very positive development in *The Life and Death Debate* is the fact that "modern fetology has placed 'windows' on the womb. In so doing it has brought to light some amazing things about the growth of this tiny person in his/her mother's womb... vivid testimony to the full humanness of the prenatal child."[3]

We are told that showing a woman her baby on the ultrasound screen is the most persuasive anti-abortion strategy there is. Pro-abortion Pollster Harrison Hickman admits: "Nothing has been as damaging to our cause as the advances in technology which have allowed pictures of the developing fetus, because people now talk about that fetus in much different terms than they did 15 years ago. They talk about it as a human being."[4]

"Religion did not discover when life begins; biologists did. Religion did not establish that at the moment of conception a unique and separate individual exists; geneticists did."[5] –Jean Garton

1 Moreland and Geisler, 39; also David Brown, 121.

2 Moreland and Geisler, *The Life and Death Debate*, 38-9.

3 Moreland and Geisler, 35.

4 Focus on the Family, *Citizen*, 7-28-97, 2.

5 Jean Garton, *Who Broke the Baby?*, 71.

6 Garton, 100.

7 Swomley, in Jersild, 341-2.

8 Glover, quoted in David Brown, *Choices: Ethics and the Christian*, 117-8.

9 David Brown, 121.

10 Gareth Jones, *Brave New People: Ethical Issues at the Commencement of Life*, 175.

"Abortion is not the solution to a problem; it is the elimination of a human being perceived to be the problem."[6] –Jean Garton

"Nature or God is the greatest killer, because there are more spontaneous preventions of implantation than those performed medically. In other words, God does not will that every conception should eventuate either in implantation or birth. This is consistent with our previous assertion that a fetus, as well as a fertilized egg, is a potential rather than an actual human being."[7]
–John M. Swomley.

SCOPE and FOCUS
I. CONVICTIONS
II. PRETEXTS
Autonomy of Mother
Relativism of Value
Personhood Denied
Potential life
Criteria of persons
Humanity Challenged
Blob of cells
Woman's body
Speciesism
Sperm & ova
Cloneability
Products of conception
Twinning
Blueprints
Chromosomes, 46+/-
Miscarriages legitimize
Mechanism & Gradualism
When life begins?
Implantation
Heartbeat
Looking like a child
Brain functioning
Pain response
Quickening
Viability
Birth only, nothing less
Pleasure vs. Pain
Accident Justifies Remedy
Pragmatic Justifications
Positivism
III. MANDATE
IV. LEGACY
V. ABORTIVE LINKS
VI. DILEMMA
VII. DESTINY

C. Mechanism, Gradualism

Right to life is achieved by degrees [Beckwith 110-3]

We have seen that Relativism can give rise to a number of strong views which deny either that the preborn are human or that they are persons. Closely related to those beliefs are several which arise from a commitment to Mechanism. A large percentage of Americans fully accept the evolutionary principles. Their world view accepts it as fact that more complex life forms have emerged from simpler ones over millions of years, and that one species – through mutation and natural selection – slowly evolves into another. From that foundation, it is natural to conceive of "fertilized ovum," "blastocyst," "embryo" and "fetus," as subhuman life forms which gradually change into [born] human infants.

If a Gradualistic pro-abortionist took the time to explain such a concept to a pro-lifer, the pro-lifer would most likely keep interrupting with a series of *Yes, buts*. Our view of God's instantaneous creation of Man in His own image is so radically different from their Mechanistic understanding that we would have the same amount of success in converting each other to our views if we were speaking two totally different languages.

The extreme Mechanistic view is presented in *Causing Death and Saving Lives* by J. Glover. He says, "Being a person is a matter of degree. A one-year-old is much more of a person than a newborn baby or a foetus just before birth, but each of these is more of a person than the embryo."[8] The predictable outcome of such convictions is that Glover, along with Joseph Fletcher, not only sees abortion as a positive good but "is also willing to admit the legitimacy of infanticide."[9]

Relativistic and Mechanistic views of abortion are very seductive; they are therefore very prevalent in our society, even among those who may be faithful Christians who would seem to be pillars of orthodoxy. Gareth Jones says, "As we consider the personhood of a fetus, we rely heavily on its potential and on what it will become. As development proceeds, less weight is placed on future potential and more on actual status, and this continues until adulthood is reached."[10]

As we investigate discrete stages of development which a preborn person achieves one by one, we must acknowledge that not only evolutionists and pro-abortionists in general, but probably everybody, at the *feeling* level, experiences a higher level of "like-me" recognition with an unborn child as each successive threshold is reached. To illustrate this point: We would be surprised to see one of our Operation Rescue friends struggling up the steps of the Supreme Court building with a five-foot-tall photograph of a four-cell frozen embryo thawing in a fertility clinic sink.

1. When life begins is unknown [41-6, 92-5]

Our baseline for this exploration is the pro-life conviction that a complete human person instantaneously comes into being at the moment when a sperm unites with the ovum. If the thawing of a frozen embryo seems like less of a tragedy than the dismembered twelve-week-old preborn, the fault is in our perception and in our depth of conviction, because the sanctity and the atrocity are the same, in God's eyes and in His heart. We know when human life begins.

The reader may recall that when we explored Universalism vs. Relativism [page 18], we discussed the Supreme Court's *Casey* decision and its "mystery passage." In the earlier, 1973, *Roe v. Wade* decision the Supreme Court declared *its* inability to determine when human life begins,[1] but as of 1992, in *Casey*, the Court declared that *anybody* could figure that out. It said that every individual has "the right to define one's own concept of existence... and of the mystery of human life."

William Brennan says, "The cultural environment for a human holocaust is present whenever any society can be misled into defining individuals as less than human and therefore devoid of value and respect."[2]

2. Implantation is the beginning of human life [95-6]

The embryo normally implants in the womb six or seven days after conception. As the pro-life community belatedly comes to terms with the abortifacient nature of all American birth control pills, we should expect to face an onslaught of disinformation,[3] asserting that since implantation is the moment when *pregnancy* begins, destruction of an embryo before that time, or preventing the embryo from implanting in the womb, are totally innocent activities, morally. Those arguments have been in print for decades[4] but are simply waiting for the moment when they are needed to counter the punch the Church has not had the heart to deliver, as yet.

That punch is long overdue. Birth control pills in normal use – some polls seem to indicate that they are as prevalent in the Churches as in the general population – are committing an incalculable number of anonymous [undetected] abortions-by-prevention-of-implantation. Add to that the widespread and exploding use of the normal Pill as a morning-after "remedy," Norplant and Depo-provera, and an assortment of other abortifacient prescription cocktails. Chemical abortion must immediately be recognized by the pro-life community as a problem equal to, if not greater than, surgical abortion.

3. Heartbeat tells that someone is alive

A baby's heart is beating, and its own blood – often a different blood type from the mother's – is flowing through its veins one month after conception.[5]

4. Looking like a child is necessary [97-8]

Robert Bork cautions us, "...the more recognizably a baby the fetus becomes, the more our emotions reject the idea of destroying it. But those are uninstructed emotions, not emotions based on a recognition of what the fetus is from the beginning."[6]

"All creatures reproduce after their own kind," says Greg Koukl, "A human being is a human being regardless of what it looks like at any stage of development, because humanness is a 'be-like' kind of thing and not a 'look-like' kind of thing."[7]

It is self-evident that pro-lifers get more passionate in opposition to the various late-term and "partial-birth" abortion techniques than we do about even first-trimester suction abortions, not to mention the general lack of interest, to date, in discussion of the abortifacient nature of the Pill. The fact that *we* obviously look at abortion through Mechanistic eyes gives credence to all of the arguments of pro-abortionists.

1 Jersild, 338, tells us that in *Roe v. Wade*, "Justice Blackmun's majority opinion declared, 'We need not resolve the difficult question of when life begins...' [but] by its legal discussion and its preference for the phrase 'potentiality of life,' the Court took a clear position on the question of when life begins, the issue it wanted to avoid!"

• Kerby Anderson, 208: "Amazingly, in dealing with the *Roe v. Wade* case, the Court was unwilling to *decide* whether or not an unborn child is fully human, yet they *were* willing to open the abortion floodgates."

• President Ronald Reagan, in Sproul, 115: "If we don't know, then shouldn't we morally opt on the side that is life? If you came upon an immobile body and you yourself could not determine whether it was dead or alive, I think that you would decide to consider it alive until someone could prove it was dead. You wouldn't get a shovel and start covering it up. And I think we should do the same thing with regard to abortion."

2 Brennan, in John Powell, *Abortion: The Silent Holocaust*, page i.

3 *Life Advocate*, 6/'94, 35.

4 Randy Alcorn, in *Life Advocate*, September-October 1997, 21.

5 Joe Scheidler, 248.

6 Robert Bork, 175-6.

7 Gregory Koukl, *Stand to Reason* radio broadcast transcript, "Are Humans Persons?" 3-4.

8 Right to Life Crusade, Inc, Tulsa. [Not in bibliography]

9 David Brown, *Choices: Ethics and the Christian*, 121.

10 David Brown, 121.

11 Joseph Fletcher, in 1971, by Stanley Reiser, *Ethics in Medicine: Historical Perspectives and Contemporary Concerns*, 391.

SCOPE and FOCUS
I. CONVICTIONS
II. PRETEXTS
Autonomy of Mother
Relativism of Value
Personhood Denied
Potential life
Criteria of persons
Humanity Challenged
Mechanism & Gradualism
When life begins?
Implantation
Heartbeat
Looking like a child
Brain functioning
Pain response
Quickening
Viability
Birth only, nothing less
Pleasure vs. Pain
Accident Justifies Remedy
Pragmatic Justifications
Positivism
III. MANDATE
IV. LEGACY
V. ABORTIVE LINKS
VI. DILEMMA
VII. DESTINY

5. Brain functioning defines life [101-3]

The preborn child's brain waves have been recorded as early as six to eight weeks after conception,[8] and by the twelfth week the brain structure is complete.[9] We are told that there are theologians who have put forth the argument "that it is the brain which makes possible characteristically personal activity, and so one should not regard the potential for personhood as being present until the brain's basic structure is present."[10] Pro-lifers strongly disagree.

But Joseph Fletcher says: "In light of medical proposals to redefine death in terms of irreversible coma or a loss of the higher brain function... if such ex-cerebral patient is no longer alive in any human sense or personal sense, would it not follow that a pre-cerebral embryo or fetus is not yet alive in any human and personal sense?"[11]

Even this threshold is much too early for many pro-abortionists to accept as evidence of human activity. R.C. Sproul tells us: "Science has joined with philosophy and reached equally gloomy conclusions. Nuclear physicist Winston C. Duke stated, 'A philosophy of reason will define a human being as life which demonstrates self-awareness, volition and rationality. Thus it should be recognized that not all men are human... It would seem... to be more inhumane to kill an adult chimpanzee than a newborn baby, since the chimpanzee has greater mental awareness.'"[12]

6. Pain response is first sign of human action [103-4]

Fetal pain is an area of great controversy – a clear indication that the pro-death camp recognizes the potential for future pro-life victories. The United Methodist Church earned the title "the abortion church" by its zealous efforts to lend religious credence to the pro-abortion rhetoric. With one sentence – a blatantly false one – in the *United Methodist Social Principles*, all question of fetal pain was rejected by the pronouncement that in the "tragic conflict of life with life that may justify abortion," there is no brain or neocortex, and hence no pain in cases of early abortion.[13] David Brown, in *Choices: Ethics and the Christian*, relates the assertion that "an aborted foetus is aborted painlessly."[14]

The pro-life movement has provided abundant documentation that the aborted ones do, indeed, feel pain. "The unborn child can feel pain and is sensitive to touch, light, heat, and noise as early as 11 weeks after conception. Using closed-circuit television cameras [it has even been] shown that if an unborn child is pricked with a needle, the infant will recoil in pain. But if a beep sounds before the prick, and this is repeated several times, the tiny baby will begin to recoil at the beep in anticipation of the pain he knows will come."[15]

Ankerberg and Weldon say "...there is little doubt that the vast majority of abortions cause pain to the child."[16] We mentioned earlier the graphic testimony provided by the video which shows – on the ultrasound screen – the panic of a child being aborted, including its *Silent Scream*.[17]

The partial-birth abortion procedure is now well understood. There can be no doubt that the stabbing of a scissor-like tool in the back of the head and opening it to create a hole, the exchanging of the scissors for the suction device, and then the experience of having one's entire brain sucked out, all without benefit of anesthesia, involves outrageous pain.[18]

Robert Bork summarizes medical evidence that neither local nor general anesthesia administered to the mother provides any effective painkilling benefit to the unborn baby.[19]

12 R.C. Sproul, *Abortion: A Rational Look at an Emotional Issue*, 28.

13 John Swomley, in Jersild, *Moral Issues and Christian Response*, 341.

14 David Brown, 114.

15 Kerby Anderson, *Living Ethically in the '90s*, 206.

16 John Ankerberg and John Weldon, *When Does Life Begin? And 39 Other Tough Questions about Abortion*, 43.

17 R.C. Sproul, 45.

18 *Press-Enterprise*, 3-20-97, A6.

19 Robert Bork, 182.

"Even infanticide and an agonizing death of a *born* – but handicapped – child by thirst and starvation has been found legally permissible under a parent's right to refuse treatment, based upon the 'right to privacy.'"[1]

The painfulness of virtually every abortion technique – not to mention that they are "cruel and inhuman" outrages against fundamental human dignity – has been underplayed by the pro-life movement, unrecognized by society, and rejected by the courts. The Supreme Court, in the 1976 *Danforth* decision, ruled that for a State to prohibit abortion by salt poisoning – because of its agonizing process of bringing about the baby's death – was unconstitutional.[2]

When a London mother decided that she could afford one more child but not two, she had one of her unborn twins killed. They stabbed it in the heart with a needle.[3] Since it was such big news, one has to wonder at what age the "lucky" twin will learn the truth... and – when disciplined – if this child will some day ask, "I bet you wish *I'd* been the one you had killed, huh, mum?"

7. Quickening is the moment of "ensoulment" [99]

Quickening has a long tradition but a very imprecise definition. It is described as the first moment when the mother feels the baby *move*. The obvious variables include how active this particular preborn is, and how sensitive, preoccupied or interested the mother is. Nonetheless, for centuries, before modern medicine arrived, the cessation of menstruation, the enlargement of the abdomen – along with a few more physiological modifications – and "quickening" were as much predictive information as biology could provide. Quickening tends to be felt midway through a pregnancy.

The history of Christian theology records the rise and fall of the theory that quickening marked the moment of ensoulment. This idea was supported, in part, by the reference to John the Baptist "leaping" in Elizabeth's womb at the greeting of Mary, who was pregnant with Jesus.[4]

The belief that ensoulment did not occur until quickening found its way into the courts, both religious and civil, and persisted – through common law – in the early decades of the United States of America. The earliest statutes outlawing abortion, in eleven states beginning with Connecticut in 1821, while they made abortion illegal, did so only after quickening.[5]

By the late 1800s, the notion of quickening had been abandoned and all abortion was prohibited, in every state. In spite of this fact, the historical references to quickening and its links to ensoulment theories are persistently resurrected as challenges to the pro-life contention that human life – including ensoulment – begins at conception.

8. Viability denotes an independent human being [99-101]

The concept of viability remains a very important distinction for those who are pro-life. Defined as the point in pregnancy when the preborn baby could survive outside the womb, viability is an imprecise and problematic label. Answering the question *Is this baby viable?* requires, first, the answer to several others: What is the current level of medical technology? What resources and expertise are available to *this* child, here and *now*? What are this child's prospects, in terms of her own health and developmental level? What mandates and restrictions are imposed by law and by this medical institution? Who would assume the costs involved? And, finally, Does the mother want this baby to live?

1 *Bowen v. American College of Obstetricians and Gynecologists*, 1986, in Clowes, page 89.15.

2 *Planned Parenthood of Central Missouri v. Danforth*, in Brian Clowes, *Pro-Life Activist's Encyclopedia*, page 89.11.

3 *Press-Enterprise*, 8-18-96, A18.

4 *Luke* 1:44.

5 Douglas Butler and David Walbert, *Abortion, Medicine, and the Law*, 249.

6 United Nations, *Abortion Policies: A Global Review*, 3 vols.

7 Glanville Williams, *The Sanctity of Life and the Criminal Law*, 230.

8 *Press-Enterprise*, 10-28-96, A3.

9 Charles Kindregan, *Abortion, the Law, and Defective Children*, 1969, 30.

10 James Bopp, *Restoring the Right to Life: The Human Life Amendment*, 4.

11 Carol Lefcourt, *Women and the Law*, page 10A-3.

12 *Planned Parenthood of Central Missouri v. Danforth*, in Brian Clowes, page 89.11.

13 *Coalutti v. Franklin*, in Carol Lefcourt, page 10A-5.

About *Coalutti*, Brian Clowes says, "This decision actually stated that, should the abortionist become aware that the unborn baby is viable, he is under no obligation to try to save its life or even to decrease its suffering" (page 89.13).

14 *Thornberg v. American College of Obstetricians and Gynecologists*, in Clowes, page 89.15.

15 Ronald Graeser, in *Life Advocate*, 6/'94, 36.

"There is no doubt that seven month old unborn babies hear, cry, dream, learn, and feel pain and pleasure just as infants do. In fact they can show a preference for their mother's voice and can discriminate between two languages, preferring the 'mother tongue.'"[15]
–Ronald Graeser

SCOPE and FOCUS
I. CONVICTIONS
II. PRETEXTS
Autonomy of Mother
Relativism of Value
Personhood Denied
Potential life
Criteria of persons
Humanity Challenged
Mechanism & Gradualism
When life begins?
Implantation
Heartbeat
Looking like a child
Brain functioning
Pain response
Quickening
Viability
Birth only, nothing less
Pleasure vs. Pain
Accident Justifies Remedy
Pragmatic Justifications
Positivism
III. MANDATE
IV. LEGACY
V. ABORTIVE LINKS
VI. DILEMMA
VII. DESTINY

The *Roe* Court justices equated viability with the beginning of the third trimester of the pregnancy, the 24th week. Internationally, abortion restrictions are increased variously, at 16, 20, 22, 24, and 28 weeks, for instance.[6] The lower limit at which a preborn has left the womb and lived to be taken home as an infant continues to drop as technology improves. In 1957, Glanville Williams identified viability at 28 weeks.[7] Currently survival is not considered miraculous at 22 or even 20 weeks. In 1996, a Michigan baby, just 14 ounces at birth, gained four pounds in four months and went home a healthy infant.[8]

Historically in the United States, viability has been an important distinction in both civil and criminal cases. Something of a new precedent was set by a New York case in 1953, in which the judgment came down in favor of a plaintiff who had been injured during the third month of his mother's pregnancy; the court held that non-viability at the time of the injury did not mean that the plaintiff was not a separate human being.[9]

The *Roe v. Wade* case, in 1973, went to lengths to explain the significance of viability as the [earliest] point at which "state interest" in "preserving potential human life" becomes compelling. While *Roe* specifically declared that a State was free to prohibit abortion after viability,[10] that privilege was immediately revoked by *Roe*'s companion case, *Doe v. Bolton*, in which the Court so liberally granted the range of abortion justifications under the category of "health of the mother," that abortion-on-demand throughout the entire pregnancy became the result.[11]

The next big change came in 1976 with the Court's *Danforth* decision, which upheld Missouri's right to prohibit abortion of viable babies [unless the pregnancy endangered the woman's life],[12] but in 1979 the court struck down a similar Pennsylvania law which it said was too vague about what constitutes viability.[13] The Supreme Court hit Pennsylvania again in 1986, finding unconstitutional another law which had attempted to protect viable babies from abortion.[14]

1989, however, became a good year for viability. Seeming to reverse its previous trend, the Supreme Court in the *Webster* decision upheld a Missouri requirement that abortionists must test for viability in pregnancies over 20 weeks, and which prohibited abortion of viable babies.[16]

Along with fetal pain and cruel and inhumane abortion procedures, viability seems to offer another avenue for future progress in protecting the lives of at least some unborn children who would otherwise be killed.

16 *Webster v. Reproductive Health Services, Inc.*, Associated Press, *Press-Enterprise*, 7-9-89, A5.

Here are some attitional anecdotes regarding viability: 1) the success of *in vitro* fertilization proves that unborn children are viable – can live outside the mother's body – at the earliest moments after *conception* (Horn, 75-6); 2) Viability does not imply independence. Prior to viability, the preborn is dependent upon the oxygen and and nutrition supplied through the umbilical cord. From the point of viability, the child can survive outside the womb, but is still dependent upon a multitude of people and technologies (Hunt, 133). Infants are dependent minute by minute on others to provide warmth, nutrition, protection and care. Many three-year-olds would probably starve if locked inside a grocery store; 3) The statutes in California, as in all states, provide that the State *should assume custodial responsibility* for those defined as incompetent, including anyone "who by reason of old age, disease, **weakness of mind, or other cause, is unable, unassisted, properly to manage and take care of himself**..."(Stone, 18); 4) If a baby who turned out to be viable at 20 or 22 weeks, once outside the womb is acknowledged to be a 100% human person, why is its older cousin, 28 weeks along but still in the womb, not a person? (Moreland, *Life and Death*, 35).

9. Only *birth* confers human-being status

"In the minds of pro-abortionists, an unborn baby is not considered a living human person. Once birth occurs, however, a different set of rules apply."[1]

It was big news when two Delaware students delivered their baby in a motel, put it into a plastic bag and hurled it into a dumpster. The *Time* magazine article, itself, was equally as shocking as the young couple's callous act. The headline screamed, "Children Without Souls." The article explained, "When a poor, black 13-year-old from the Bronx leaves her newborn to die, we go on about our business, but we are gripped when two affluent white teenagers do the same thing... The dark side of kids who have everything is that they cannot tolerate one blemish on their smooth lives..." The article concludes: "There are monsters among us who, with wealthy parents and a battalion of lawyers, tap a culture ready to forget the victim and forgive the accused, especially if they remind us of ourselves. But not this time, not this evil."[2]

We can taste the contempt, the loathing that this writer, this national magazine, this secular culture feels toward the "monsters" who could commit such an "evil" act. As pro-lifers we have to be amazed by this. How can anyone see this act as morally any different from what we assume the writer – and the Clintons – would have deemed a fine, intelligent, appropriate, even honorable solution to the dilemma: a partial-birth abortion? Doing the "right thing" would have cost more; maybe Yankee frugality just led the two to decide on a do-it-yourself kinda-like abortion so they could apply the money saved toward a prom dress or skiing trip. That is sensible thinking, isn't it? Pragmatism is the rule, after all.

In a culture that has no problem with 4,000 abortions a day, what's the big deal over a detail like born/not born? From the baby's perspective, what's the difference? Given only two choices, there is really little advantage to having your brains sucked out and then being dropped into a "medical waste" container, over death by being hurled against the side of a steel dumpster.

The message within this story – loud and clear – is that to the culture that is fundamentally rooted in relativism and mechanism, the fact – the technicality – of *birth* is a very big deal. Within that mindset, the difference between a full term baby, half delivered, and the same child one minute later – if not killed but having taken its first breath – is beyond description. Until we pro-lifers can comprehend that there is a difference to be seen, and can see what it is that they see when they believe it, we will have no hint of the diabolical dragon we awaken when we declare ourselves to be pro-life.

And we must *feel* what the culture feels toward those two confused, miserable kids; and we must personally experience the smashing of our skulls into mush against that dumpster. But we must also feel more. We must own that the same violence, the same sacrilege, occurs in the case of every abortion, of every chemical prevention of implantation, of every thawing of a frozen embryo. Each, every one, and all of them. And then we must resolve to do whatever it takes to convey our sense of outrage in a way that the culture can comprehend, so that one by one, they might see, and turn and be healed and reborn.

What is our message? "Did you 'come from' an infant? No. You once were an infant who grew and developed into the child or adult you are today... Did you 'come from' a fertilized ovum? No, you once were a fertilized ovum who grew and developed into the child or adult you are today. Nothing has been added to the fertilized ovum who you once were except nutrition... *You* were all there at the beginning."[3]

"Today, the evidence that human life begins at conception is a scientific fact so well documented that no intellectually honest and informed scientist or physician can dare deny it."[4]

–Ankerberg & Weldon

1 R.C. Sproul, *Abortion: A Rational Look at an Emotional Issue*, 15-6.

2 *Time*, 12-2-96, 70.

3 J.C. Willke, *Handbook on Abortion*, 10-11.

4 John Ankerberg and John Weldon, *When Does Life Begin? And 39 Other Tough Questions About Abortion*, 5.

5 Carl F.H. Henry in William Ball, *In Search of a National Morality: A Manifesto for Evangelicals and Catholics*, 22.

6 F. LaGard Smith, *When Choice Becomes God*, 189.

7 John Klotz, *A Christian View of Abortion*, 1973, 47-8.

SCOPE and FOCUS
I. CONVICTIONS
II. PRETEXTS
Autonomy of Mother
Relativism of Value
Personhood Denied
Potential life
Criteria of persons
Humanity Challenged
Mechanism & Gradualism
When life begins?
Implantation
Heartbeat
Looking like a child
Brain functioning
Pain response
Quickening
Viability
Birth only, nothing less
Pleasure vs. Pain
Personal Tragedy
Rape / Incest
Imperfection
Burden-Bearing
Career interruption
Pro-lifers should adopt
Abused children result
Anonymous & Different
Mourned less
Naming, age, baptism
Accident Justifies Remedy
Pragmatic Justifications
Positivism
III. MANDATE
IV. LEGACY
V. ABORTIVE LINKS
VI. DILEMMA
VII. DESTINY

D. Pleasure / Pain:

"In 1942 Pitirim A. Sorokin, professor of sociology at Harvard University, wrote the book *The Crisis of Our Age* in which he took a dim view of Western Civilization. It had become, he affirmed, essentially sensate – that is, the masses were now prone to believe only what they feel, taste, smell, hear and see."[5]

What are the convictions that would cause a culture with an historical allegiance to the Christian worldview to become "sensate?" For starters, they might embrace evolution and rejection-of-God in the form of Accident and Mechanism. Next, they might restructure their traditions of individualism and democracy into the unabashed me-ism of Autonomy. Finally, they could adopt Relativism in morality and institute Pleasure and Pain as the working definitions of the moral good and what is morally bad. A sensate culture is one whose fundamental life assumptions are based upon accident, mechanism, autonomy, relativism and pleasure.

Citizens in a sensate culture always look for the easy way out. That is why America loves abortion. "The stage had already been set with other convenient escape routes: bankruptcy, divorce, drugs, and suicide. Abortion is the consummate escape route."[6] A sensate culture, committed to personal pleasure and the avoidance of every unpleasantness above all else, will prize abortion as a handy antidote to personal tragedies, undesired burdens, and unfulfilling relationships.

1. Personal tragedy can be diminished by abortion

The Commission on Research and Social Action of the American Lutheran Church proposed in 1970 that abortion could be justified on the basis of the physical or mental health of the mother, rape, incest, or a child with grave physical or mental defect. It said, "Such permissiveness strikes us as more consistent with Christian love and responsible freedom than does the denial-of-choice forced by law."[7]

Here is some insight provided by Brian Clowes: "Both of the January 22, 1973 abortion decisions were based upon lies. They were both supposedly brought to aid two 'hard-luck' abortion cases (rape in *Roe*, and spousal abuse in *Doe*), but one plaintiff was lying for her own benefit, and pro-abortion lawyers were lying for the other plaintiff (neither woman ever got an abortion). It is extremely significant that the plaintiff's attorneys could not even find a *real* 'hard case' to pursue."[8]

a. Rape / Incest [Beckwith, *PC Death*: pages 68-72]

Less than .06 percent [that's six out of ten thousand] of all pregnancies result from rape.[9] A meticulous study of 3,500 rape cases in the Minneapolis-St. Paul area over a 10-year period revealed that not one pregnancy occurred.[10]

Moreland and Geisler explain why "appealing to sympathy for the rape victim does not avoid the question of justice for the abortion victim": 1) there is no way to become unraped. Abortion does not take away the evil of the rape; it adds another evil to it. 2) The rape problem is not solved by killing the baby. 3) Even if abortion were justified in a few extreme cases such as rape, this would not thereby justify abortion on demand. 4) Immediate medical attention prevents conception. 5) Few rape pregnancies occur. 6) Adoption is very often the best decision.[11]

The rape and incest pleas are a smokescreen to win sympathy that can be parlayed into support for abortion on demand. As Russel Shaw says: "Despite the frequent mention in pro-abortion propaganda of pregnant, mentally defective, 13-year-old girls who have been raped by their fathers, the vast majority of women who undergo abortions are married, pregnant by their husbands, middle-class and mothers of other children."[12]

8 Brian Clowes, *Pro-Life Activist's Encyclopedia*, page 89.7.

9 John Ankerberg, 94.

10 *The Presbyterian Journal*, 10-18-78, reported by Right to Life Crusade, Inc., Tulsa. [Not in bibliography]

11 Moreland and Geisler, *The Life and Death Debate: Moral Issues of Our Time*, 30-1.

12 Russel Shaw, *Abortion on Trial*, 17.

b. Imperfection / quality of life of the child [65-8]

Karl Barth said, "A community which regards its weak members as a hindrance, and proceeds to their extermination, is on the verge of collapse."[1]

The rubella epidemic broke the heart of America

The United States suffered an epidemic of rubella, "German measles," in 1964 – 65. Statistically, 25% to 50% of the women who contract rubella during the early stages of pregnancy give birth to a deformed child. An estimated 30,000 imperfect children were born in America during that epidemic.[3]

Russel Shaw, in *Abortion on Trial* in 1968, predicted: "A campaign of agitation for abortion in cases where foetal damage as a result of rubella is judged likely... *Life* magazine speedily decreed an 'almost fifty-fifty chance' of deformities... [and] gave a pat on the back to physicians who performed abortions on these grounds, calling them 'conscientious doctors of highest integrity who acted in defiance of community convention and state law.'"[4]

America's dedication to the Pleasure principle made the public putty in the hands of a media that played up the devastating experience of giving birth to a "defective" child, and which was already so committed to abortion that *Life* magazine would applaud doctors who were breaking the law.

The Thalidomide tragedy focused on one desperate woman

Thalidomide was a prescription sedative widely used in Europe in the early Sixties. The lack of drug-testing standards resulted in the widespread distribution of the drug before it was discovered that it caused extreme deformities in children born to women who had taken it. Newspapers around the world told of thousands of babies being born with missing or useless arms and hands, feet and legs. In Belgium, in 1962, the mother of one such child confessed to killing her infant daughter in order to save her from a lifetime of suffering; she was acquitted by twelve male jurors.[5]

In the United States the moral dilemmas were widely discussed, and the pro-abortion forces exploited every opportunity to play on sympathy for the mothers, as well as on the quality-of-life issue for the Thalidomide children. As it happened, one American wife became the de facto "poster child" of the Thalidomide nightmare. Sherri Finkbine's husband, returning from a trip to Europe, bought some Thalidomide in London and brought it home to Arizona. When the disaster hit the news, she realized that she had taken *that drug* and that she was pregnant too.[6]

What should Sherri Finkbine do? became the topic of national debate. Much was made of the disgrace that – because abortions were still illegal in America – she had to fly to Stockholm in order to solve her terrible problem. The situation also provided an opportunity for the question, "What if she had been poor – or even middle class – but couldn't afford to fly to Europe? She would be trapped in a compulsory-pregnancy country; she and her pathetic child would be doomed by their government to lives of misery."

In the rubella epidemic and the Thalidomide tragedy, pro-abortion forces won major public opinion victories by harnessing emotion and sympathy for innocent victims to the "Legalize Abortion – for just the Hard Cases" wagon.

If anything, the media oversold the *tragedy of an imperfect child* theme. No sooner had abortion become legal than giving birth to a less-than-perfect child became an embarrassment, to be defended by such statements as "If I had only *known* I could have had an abortion." Wrongful-birth suits began to win awards in the hundreds of thousands of dollars.[7]

The spin-off from the financial liability of doctors has now produced prenatal tests to determine probabilities of a preborn suffering any one of nearly 200 identified abnormalities.[8]

Doctors seem to want to administer every possible test in order to avoid being sued for negligence. Parents of *in utero* children feel the pressure – particularly from insurance companies and HMOs that fear their costs of treating imperfect children – to abort on the basis of the slightest indication that there might be "something wrong."

"Giving some people, whether parents, doctors, or government officials, the power to choose who is normal enough to live is enormously dangerous."[2] –Doug Bandow.

1 Karl Barth, in Mall and Watts, *The Psychological Aspects of Abortion*, 125-6.

2 Doug Bandow, *Beyond Good Intentions, A Biblical View of Politics*, 168.

3 Pilpel and Norwick, *When Should Abortion Be Legal?* 1969, 13.

Harriet F. Pilpel was, in 1969, on the boards of directors of both the American Civil Liberties Union and Planned Parenthood Federation of America.

4 Russel Shaw, 21.

5 Shaw, 18-19.

6 Shaw, 19-20.

7 John Whitehead, *The Stealing of America*, 58.

8 Butler, *Abortion, Medicine, and the Law*, 260.

SCOPE and FOCUS
I. CONVICTIONS
II. PRETEXTS
Autonomy of Mother
Relativism of Value
Personhood Denied
Humanity Challenged
Mechanism & Gradualism
Pleasure vs. Pain
Personal Tragedy
Rape / Incest
Imperfection
Burden-Bearing
Career interruption
Pro-lifers should adopt
Abused children result
Anonymous & Different
Mourned less
Naming, age, baptism
Accident Justifies Remedy
Pragmatic Justifications
Positivism
III. MANDATE
IV. LEGACY
V. ABORTIVE LINKS
VI. DILEMMA
VII. DESTINY

We are a consumerist nation. Everything is backed by a 100% satisfaction guarantee. The Pleasure commitment entails the rejection of the imperfect. Brian Clowes tells us that, "already in this country, we forcibly abort the mentally handicapped, coercively sterilize the unwanted, and systematically euthanize the inconvenient. Such individual actions, because they are so universally repulsive, are committed under a cloak of the strictest secrecy. Only the family, the doctors, and the judges know, and they aren't telling."[9]

2. Burden-bearing should not be required of a woman

The Pleasure and Pain orientation which demands the right to abort in situations of personal tragedy, as we have discussed, also contends that if "continuation of the pregnancy" can be expected to result in any inconvenience or disruption at all, then "termination" of that pregnancy should be an option. The United Methodist Church expressed the view that every termination of potential human life is a normal problem to be justified only because of the "damage that may result from an unacceptable pregnancy."[10]

Sissela Bok even finds a painless way to describe such an act: "Abortion can be looked upon, also, as the withdrawal of bodily life support on the part of the mother."[11]

a. Career interruption is unacceptable [68]

b. Pro-lifers aren't willing to adopt all of the unwanted [88-9]

c. Abused children result from unwanted pregnancies [63-5]

From 1972 to 1990 the rate of child abuse has increased 600%, and four times as many children now die each year from child abuse.[12] "Abortion IS child abuse of the worst kind."[13]

3. Anonymous fetuses seem much different from born babies

If the things which are done in aborting babies were being done, even once in a while, to born children, the national uprising would exceed anything the world has ever seen. The reason that does not happen is because humans are not rational creatures; we are emotional beings. Preborn babies just naturally seem different to us – to the pro-lifers as well as all others. It is evidence that the Pleasure-and-Pain conviction has seized every one of us that our pro-life activism is driven not by what the preborn *is* but rather by how we *feel* about her. How we feel about unborn children is clouded – shrouded – by the fact that their invisibility and facelessness makes them anonymous to us, and thus – to a large degree – unreal.

a. Sentiment and mourning are less for a fetus [98-9]

The contention that an aborted baby is not mourned to the same degree as a born child who has died, where it is true, may be attributed to the invisibility we have noted. Various writers have described what is lacking as "life in relationship," "an immediacy is lacking," and "not yet regarded as a member of the human community."

Some women tell us – from personal experience – that a woman's guilt-and-grief combination after submitting to an abortion can be much more intense than the grief over the born child lost through no fault of her own.

Some pro-abortionists maintain that the value of fetal life is contingent upon the woman's free consent and subjective acceptance, and that "Prior to her own free choice and conscious investment, a woman cannot be described as a 'mother' nor can a 'child' be said to exist."[14]

b. Naming, baptizing and age all wait until birth [104-5]

The idea that because naming, *birth*-day and baptism are reserved for born children, preborns aren't fully human and can be aborted, might seem farfetched, but a major Protestant denomination has actually used the baptism argument in its justification of abortion.[15]

9 Brian Clowes, page 50.12.

10 John Swomley, in Jersild, 341.

11 Sissela Bok, in Reiser, *Ethics in Medicine*, 433.

12 *Statistical Abstract of the United States*, 1990. [Not in bibliography]

13 Moreland and Geisler, *The Life and Death Debate*, 29.

14 Sidney Callahan, in Jersild, 347.

15 George Grant, *Third Time Around*, 127. "The largest Lutheran communions worldwide..."

E. Accident Justifies Abortion as a Remedy

The most audacious challenge to the Christian world view is that there is no God and that the universe and life all came into being by accident. That is really where the rest of the assaults begin. It is no surprise, then, that accident should be the underlying presupposition from which some powerful pro-abortion arguments arise.

1. Birth control was used but it failed

When it is asserted that a particular pregnancy is the "fault of" failed technology – as opposed to the more essential reality that a procreative act has taken place – the speaker isn't really opening a discussion, but rather closing one. Attributing the cause to an accident brings into play the whole constellation of beliefs engendered by evolution, all of which combine to make abortion not only a morally neutral option but a perfectly logical and normal remedy. Accident absolves the parent of all responsibility.

2. Incapacitated woman (drunk / naive / retarded / in a coma)

This category of unplanned pregnancies is particularly problematic, and it is closely related to the rape/incest situations for which the pleasure-and-pain orientation legitimizes abortion. The distinction that accounts for placing the two categories at this distance from one another is that in the case of rape and incest you begin with a traumatic, life-changing sex crime, and it is the emotions surrounding that outrage which drive the abortion decision. In the case of an incapacitated woman, while there is perhaps an equal element of outrage that the act has taken place, the woman who was victimized has little or no recollection of the act which caused her to become pregnant. The volition toward an abortive solution here arises from the "accidental" nature of the pregnancy, from the woman's perspective.

F. Pragmatism and the Fate of the Unborn

Brian Clowes helps us to see that a great number of the justifications presented for abortion emerge from a commitment to pragmatic problem solving. Pro-abortionists assert: "Abortion is really no big deal. All we are doing is getting rid of unwanted children who would just be abused anyway. Safe and legal abortion is a great benefit to our nation, because it cuts down on overpopulation, culls out the unwanted human beings who would just wind up on the welfare rolls anyway (thereby saving us billions of tax dollars per year), and demonstrates that our society is progressive and caring."[1]

Jean Garton counters with a Christian perspective: "If what we are interested in is a stopgap measure, then abortion seems reasonable. If what we desire are results, then abortion seems like an answer. But it is an option which does not exist in a vacuum, for it involves the sacrifice of not only the unborn child, but a way of life, an entire ethic. As the seamless robe of Christ, to unloose but one thread of its fabric is to eventually unloose it all."[2]

1. Self-Defense

Philosopher Thomas Hobbes concluded that the most natural and fundamental principle of ethics is the right of self-defense. Whenever self-defense is invoked, what we must carefully measure is the proportionality between the harm threatened and the act of protection. We have learned, too, the difference between the inch of permission that abortion legislation intends and the mile of license the abortion industry takes.

1 Brian Clowes, *Pro-Life Activist's Encyclopedia*, page 48.1.

2 Jean Garton, *Who Broke the Baby? A Brilliant Disclosure of What the Abortion Slogans Really Mean*, 97.

3 Russel Shaw, *Abortion on Trial*, 39. Researcher's note: Public opinion polls are very deceptive. One which is typical asked people, *yes* or *no*, did they think abortion should be legal in the situation of... [The list of situations seemed to measure the spectrum from the most trivial to the most crucial reasons] The strongest statement listed was "Mother's health seriously endangered." A pro-lifer who approves of only the life-of-the-mother exception might tend to answer *no* to all of the other options and to be thinking *ONLY if* while firmly checking *yes*, next to "Mother's health is *seriously* endangered." But when legislators and judges read the results of the poll they will come to believe – incorrectly – that 71% of Americans want abortion laws to permit "mother's health" as a justification to abort.

4 James Bopp, *Restoring the Right to Life*, 14.

5 Doug Bandow, *Beyond Good Intentions: A Biblical View of Politics*, 168.

6 Francis Beckwith, *PC Death*, 12.

7 Alan Guttmacher, in Brian Clowes, page 51.1.

• Dr. Roy Heffernan of Tufts University Medical School says, "Anyone who performs a therapeutic abortion is either ignorant of modern medical methods or unwilling to take the time and effort to apply them" [in Clowes, page 51.4.].

• "C. Everett Koop says that in his thirty-six years of pediatric care and surgery he had never once seen a mother's life in danger that could not be solved by inducing labor or by Caesarean section. Killing the fetus to save the mother was never an alternative that required consideration." [Al Haffner, *The High Cost of Free Love*, 174].

*** REMEMBER ***
that every pair of pages contains this nifty OUTLINE, with the current topics underlined:

SCOPE and FOCUS
I. CONVICTIONS
II. PRETEXTS
Autonomy of Mother
Relativism of Value
Personhood Denied
Humanity Challenged
Mechanism & Gradualism
Pleasure vs. Pain
Personal Tragedy
Burden-Bearing
Anonymous & Different
Accident Justifies Remedy
Birth control failed
Incapacitated mom
Pragmatic Justifications
Self Defense
Mother's life
Pro-life contradiction
Health of mother
Alien invasion
Political Expediency
Safe & legal
Medical responsibility
Population bomb
Social Benefits
Safer than childbirth
Fetal research
Fetal tissue
Organs for transplant
Positivism
III. MANDATE
IV. LEGACY
V. ABORTIVE LINKS
VI. DILEMMA
VII. DESTINY

a. To save the mother's life, an abortion is OK

The life-of-the-mother exception is the only one permitted if we are to be authentically pro-life. Abortion advocates have been masterful in their manipulation of the language to capitalize on shadings of meaning which distort public opinion and sway governmental policy. The life of the mother exception holds that abortion is only acceptable if the continuation of the pregnancy will result in the death of the mother. Period.[3]

Prior to 1965, abortion was illegal in every State, but the life-of-the-mother exception was allowed in all of them but four.[4]

There is confusion, however, as to what is implied by this exception. Some assume that it recognizes a qualitative difference between a born mother – a wife, maybe a mother of other children – and that anonymous, mournedless, not-yet-a-person entity that secular convictions have described to us. Some may believe that her public identity gives her more moral value than the preborn child. "There is no Scriptural basis for making such a choice," says Doug Bandow.[5]

But the life-of-the-mother dilemma is not a case of deciding *between* the child and the mother. If the pregnancy kills the mother, the nonviable baby dies too. As Francis Beckwith explains: "It is a greater good that one human should live (the mother) rather than two die (the mother and her child)."[6]

Back in 1967 Alan Guttmacher was still thinking and talking like a doctor; his rhetoric had not yet caught up with his trade as an abortionist. In 1967 he was saying:

> **"Today it is possible for almost any patient to be brought through pregnancy alive, unless she suffers from a fatal disease such as cancer or leukemia, and if so, abortion would be unlikely to prolong, much less save the woman's life."[7]**

When an abortion advocate says *self-defense,* the meaning is very broad: "No woman should be required to give up her life or health or family security to save the life of a fetus that is threatening her well-being. At the very least she is entitled to self-defense."[8] Abortionist Willard Cates refers to abortion as a standard "treatment for the sexually transmitted disease of unwanted pregnancy."[9]

For verification of the *give 'em an inch* truism, in sworn court testimony, abortionist Jane Hodgson explained how she applies the legal phrase "to save the life of the mother." "I feel there is a medical indication to abort a pregnancy where it is not wanted. In good faith, I would recommend on a medical basis... 100%. ...I think they are all medically necessary... I am concerned with the quality of life, not physical existence."[10]

b. Life-of-the-mother exception, when endorsed by "pro-lifers," is a contradiction [117-8]

Pro-abortionists have often portrayed the pro-life position as "absolutizing" the baby's right to life even over the mother's right to life. Then, when it suits their purpose, they reverse their rhetoric and say, "Aha! You say it is OK to abort to save the life of the mother – that proves that you are a hypocrite." As we have observed, people did not arrive at a pro-abortion stance through a series of logical arguments and proofs; rather, abortion *feels* like a natural and good solution to problems because they have subscribed to philosophical principles such as Relativism, Mechanism and Pragmatism. Their sloganeering and argumentation are to be understood as what floats to the surface in the cauldron of their lives – they are not the fire that makes it boil.

8 John Swomley, in Jersild, 345.

9 Cates, in Clowes, page 53.15.

10 Jane Hodgson, in Clowes, page 51.1.

c. Health of the mother must be preserved above all.

History will remember that the ambiguity within the phrase *health of the mother* was a major factor in the growing practice of abortion by reputable doctors, its acceptance by the popular culture, and the governmental approval of abortion in the second half of the 20th century.

Kenneth Niswander identified two trends in the twenty years from 1947 to 1967. First, medical technique and technology were making abortion much safer, resulting in a reduction in the number of legitimate abortions justified by the mother's physical health. Secondly, there was a significant rise in the number of legal abortions certified as necessary by psychiatrists as required to preserve the mental health of the mother.[1]

This mental health loophole unleashed a flood. Pro-abortion attorneys were arguing mightily for a "broad interpretation" of the language of abortion statutes "so as to include every variety of economic and mental ill within the rubric of 'endangering the health of the mother.'"[2] Robert Orr tells us that it eventually became true that "any perceived threat to the woman's mental well-being could justify an abortion... since any unwanted pregnancy can induce considerable emotional turmoil."[3]

In 1961, the National Council of Churches approved hospital abortion "when the health or life of the mother is at stake."[4] As of 1967, the American Medical Association was officially approving of abortion in cases where "health" as well as life is threatened, including "threat to the mental or physical health of the patient," and by 1969, 80% of therapeutic abortions in a major city were certified as necessary for psychiatric reasons.[5]

The Supreme Court issued a preview of *Roe v. Wade* in 1971, when it upheld as constitutional the laws of the District of Columbia [by extension, of any State] which permitted abortion on the grounds of "mental health" under the umbrella of "maternal health." This ruling, two years before *Roe*, legitimized *de facto* "abortion on demand" in many States.[6]

The effect of *Roe v. Wade*, therefore, was to extend throughout the nation what had been granted – in 1971 – to a checkerboard pattern of states. *Roe* "stated that abortions could be performed in the second and third trimesters for the 'mother's physical or mental health.' In *Doe v. Bolton*, the companion decision to *Roe*, the Court expanded this definition so that the abortionist has legal discretion to kill children for virtually any reason whatever throughout the entire nine months of pregnancy."[7]

Informed by the new law of the land, government doctors would describe, in 1976, unwanted pregnancy as "the second highest sexually transmitted disease" with gonorrhea being number one.[8] In 1979, Garton told us that "...the most widely read obstetrical text refers to unwanted pregnancy as a 'venereal disease.'"[9]

Less than a week after President Clinton's [first] veto of the partial birth abortion ban, the eight U.S. Catholic Cardinals sent him a letter in which they stated, "...as you know and we know, an exception for 'health' means abortion on demand."[10]

John Eidsmoe speaks for all pro-lifers: "Even if we were to concede that abortion could heal the mental health of the mother, we would then be faced with a conflict of rights: the mother's right to mental health versus the child's right to life. I would argue that the child's right to life is paramount."[11]

1 Niswander, in David Smith, *Abortion and the Law*, 37-8.

2 Russel Shaw, *Abortion on Trial*, 38.

3 Robert Orr, *Life and Death Decisions*, 49-50.

4 Pilpel and Norwick, *Should Abortion be Legal?*, 8.

5 Pilpel and Norwick, 14.

6 *United States v. Vuitch*, in Clowes, page 89.9.

7 Clowes, page 89.10. Quoted from *Doe v. Bolton*: "...the medical judgement may be exercised in the light of all factors – physical, emotional, psychological, familial, and the woman's age – relevant to the well-being of the patient."

8 In Garton, *Who Broke the Baby?*, 87 and 107: "...a paper presented by three physicians from the U.S. Center for Disease Control before an annual convention of Planned Parenthood Physicians, 1976, entitled, "Abortion as a Treatment for Unwanted Pregnancy: The Number Two Sexually Transmitted Disease."

9 Jean Garton, 87 and 107: the text: *Williams Obstetrics*, Fifteenth Edition, p. 842.

10 Focus on the Family, *Citizen*, 6-24-96. The Cardinals also pointed out, "It was instructive that the veto ceremony included no physician able to explain how a woman's physical health is protected by almost fully delivering her living child, and then killing that child in the most inhumane manner imaginable before completing the delivery."

11 John Eidsmoe, *God and Caesar*, 180.

12 Swomley, in Jersild, *Moral Issues and Christian Response*, 345.

13 John Noonan, *The Morality of Abortion*, 1970, 162-3.

14 Rosalind Pollack Petchesky, in Jersild, 346.

15 Dr. Natalie Shalness, 1968, in Clowes, page 53.15.

16 Eileen McDonagh, by Frederica Mathewes-Green, in Focus on the Family *Citizen*, 7-28-97, 1; "mugger" on page 4.

17 Sidney Callahan, in Jersild, 348.

SCOPE and FOCUS
I. CONVICTIONS
II. PRETEXTS
Autonomy of Mother
Relativism of Value
Mechanism & Gradualism
Pleasure vs. Pain
Accident Justifies Remedy
Pragmatic Justifications
Self Defense
Mother's life
Pro-life contradiction
Health of mother
Alien invasion
Political Expediency
Safe & legal
Medical responsibility
Population bomb
Social Benefits
Safer than childbirth
Fetal research
Fetal tissue
Organs for transplant
Positivism
III. MANDATE
IV. LEGACY
V. ABORTIVE LINKS
VI. DILEMMA
VII. DESTINY

d. Alien invasion: "unplugging a violinist" is morally OK [128-35]

John Swomley asserts that "No woman should be required to give up her life or health or family security to save the life of a fetus that is threatening her well-being. At the very least she is entitled to self-defense."[12] We are told that "In traditional Jewish and Catholic thought, the mother-threatening fetus was called an 'innocent pursuer' or 'innocent aggressor.'"[13]

The child in the womb is blissfully unaware that it is being called a "biological parasite,"[14] and that a doctor is accusing that "a parasite can commit murder."[15] The baby can hear, but fortunately not understand, the advice to the mother, "...you have the power to defend yourself, to repel this intruder with deadly force... Get an abortion... expel the agent of coercion... Imagine you are being held prisoner."[16] The same woman who gives that advice says that having an unwanted pregnancy is like jogging through the park at midnight and getting mugged; even if you took a foolish risk, you did not ask to get mugged, and the government has the responsibility to free you from the attacker and pay the cost [provide an abortion].

This avalanche of pragmatic protest is countered by Beckwith [128-35, as indicated in heading, above] and by others. Callahan says that "having a baby is not like rescuing a drowning person, being hooked up to a famous violinist's artificial life-support system, donating organs for transplant – or anything else."[17]

Moreland and Geisler's position can be summed up as follows: 1) We do not have the right to kill human beings in private; 2) Abortion is more like killing an indigent person in our home because he will not leave; 3) In 99 percent of abortions the "guest" entered with the consent of the host... It is more like inviting a guest into our home who is indigent and then killing him simply because we decided we did not want him there.[18]

In the words of Randy Alcorn, "Babies are not cancerous tumors to be desperately avoided and dramatically removed. That they are unplanned by us does not mean they are unplanned by God."[19]

2. Political Expediency

Political expediency has a very long – if not proud – tradition. In an article called "Cities of Blood," Curtis Blair explains. "Killing sometimes finds justification when made a means of serving a greater and higher cause, and in the case of the ancient Americans [Mayan and Aztec human sacrifice], the greater cause was the welfare of society. For them it was a matter of survival. Their gods needed a steady diet of hearts and blood in order to bless the land with rain, sun, and abundant crops."[20]

On the same subject, Hans Jonas tells us that "human sacrifices in early communities... were not acts of blood-lust or gleeful savagery; they were the solemn execution of a supreme sacral necessity. One of the fellowship of men had to die so that all could live, the earth be fertile, the cycle of nature renewed. The victim often was not a captured enemy but a select member of the group: 'the king must die.'"[21]

Pro-lifers tend to see more parallels than pro-abortionists do between a Mayan pyramid and an American abortion clinic. One easy connection is that both are tragic examples of the result of the pragmatic approach to solving a problem of huge moral dimensions, and the conclusion that it is permissible to sacrifice human lives on the altar of some presumed "greater good."[22]

18 Moreland and Geisler, *The Life and Death Debate: Moral Issues of Our Time*, 30.

19 Randy Alcorn, "Does the Birth Control Pill Cause Abortions?" in *Life Advocate*, September–October, 1997, 28.

20 Curtis Blair, in *Life Advocate*, 2/'94, 27.

21 Hans Jonas, *Ethical Aspects of Experimentation with Human Subjects*, 223.

22 Earl J. Reeves, in Robert Clouse, *Protest and Politics*, 191: In 1968, Earl J. Reeves was writing about the conflicting factors which impinged on the moral question of whether teenagers should be given easy access to contraceptives. His comments are extremely instructive about the kinds of concerns and priorities that were weighing heavily on Christian hearts and consciences in the late '60s. "...any increase in temptation must be weighed against the benefits of avoiding the psychological damage of an unwanted pregnancy for those who already find the temptation overwhelming. Furthermore, it is apparent that once a teenager has become pregnant, been expelled from school, and has had either a baby or an abortion, the chances are great that she will soon be pregnant again."

a. End acts of desperation ("safe and legal") [125-8]

The slogan *Safe and Legal* has been the workhorse that has pulled the pro-abortion movement through four decades. The architects of that movement successfully packaged the image of back-alley butchers into a positive slogan that fit nicely on a poster beside a drawing of a coathanger, slightly rusty, slightly bent.

Christian voices have assisted the pro-abortion champions of pragmatism. The United Church of Christ – which had led the pro-life charge [in the nineteenth century] – in *this* century proclaimed: "The right of men and women to have access to adequately funded family planning services, and to safe and legal abortions as one option among others."[1] The "safe" part of *safe and legal* really came not from legalization so much as from the ready access to antibiotics "and improved medical techniques" which began in the 1940s.[2]

When C.W. Scudder, in 1964, wrote a book called *Crises in Morality*, abortion didn't even make the list. But Scudder did give it a passing mention, although not by its actual name. This was one of the many books which, in exhorting Christians to show more love to their neighbors, raised the awareness of and sympathy for the plight of unmarried teens who get pregnant. Pregnancy was always a tragic *condition*, never a *baby*. Scudder said, "...failure to [provide assistance and love to unwed mothers] will continue to leave thousands of young girls, pregnant out of wedlock, at the mercy of those who will use their condition for selfish gain."[3]

Dr. Bernard Nathanson has admitted that he and most others in the pro-abortion camp "lied about the highly inflated claim of 5,000–10,000 [maternal] deaths per year from [illegal] abortion," and the U.S. Bureau of vital Statistics reported that in 1973 there were only 45 maternal deaths from abortion.[4]

Those fabricated figures were so readily and so widely repeated that they became common knowledge [common deception]. In 1967 Kenneth Niswander's words fed the fiction: "Legal abortion in a well-equipped hospital is not hazardous, but criminal abortion currently accounts for thousands of deaths annually in the United States. If a realistic relaxation of state laws on legal abortion will decrease this toll of needless deaths, society owes this protection to desperate women."[5] We can't really tell if Mr. Niswander is a Christian, but we can be certain that he is a pragmatist.

In 1966, the American Medical Women's Association "joined with the American College of Obstetricians and Gynecologists and the American Law Institute in urging limited legalized abortion, [noting] that there are an estimated one million abortions performed in the United States each year and few of them are performed under sanitary medical conditions."[6]

Russel Shaw reports that a very prevalent argument in 1968 was that "If more than a million women are violating the existing laws each year, the laws are clearly unacceptable in the contemporary American social climate and should be changed."[7] "In order to get *Roe v. Wade* passed, the number of back-alley abortion deaths had to be exaggerated by a hundredfold," Surgeon General C. Everett Koop said... "The greatest number of deaths ever in one year was 373. That's a terrible number, but it wasn't 10,000."[8]

"Safe and legal" takes on new meaning in light of these figures provided by Whitehead: "We are told that legalized abortions are much safer than illegal abortions... In 1967 there were 275 deaths in this country as a result of abortion. That was when only a few states had legalized abortion. Interestingly, 164 of those deaths were from legal abortions. That was more than the deaths from illegal abortions at that time."[9] "So-called 'safe and legal' abortions have killed more than 500 women since the United States Supreme Court committed *Roe v. Wade* in 1973."[10]

1 George Grant, *Third Time Around*, 126.
2 Robert Bork, 179.
3 C.W. Scudder, page vi.
4 Moreland and Geisler, *Life and Death Debate*, 29.
5 Niswander, by D. T. Smith, *Abortion & the Law*, 59.
6 Earl Reeves, Clouse, 193.
7 Russel Shaw, *Abortion on Trial*, 34.
8 Carr, *Celebrate Life: Hope for a Culture Preoccupied with Death*, 145-6.
9 John Whitehead, *Arresting Abortion: Practical Ways to Save Unborn Children*, 20.
10 Clowes, page 19.5.
11 Clowes, page 89.15.
12 *Life Advocate*, 6/'94, 14.
13 *Press-Enterprise*, 2-19-97, B3.

When that woman checked in for her *safe and legal* abortion she had no way of knowing these details about the abortionist, who is now on trial for her negligent homicide: In 1992 he had perforated a woman's uterus and left her baby's head inside her; a hospital had to do a hysterectomy. Eight months later he lacerated the uterus and ruptured the colon of a woman who then was hospitalized for an 8-hour surgery and a hysterectomy. In 1993 he ruptured another uterus and lacerated a bowel on that woman. Subsequent problems led the state attorney general, in 1995, to ask the state medical authorities to declare that abortionist "grossly negligent." He was put on probation, which means it was still OK for him to perform the abortion on the 27-year-old during which he ruptured her uterus; he sent her home, where she died. [*Press-Enterprise*, 12-19-96, A1, A10].

The owner of that California clinic is also an abortionist. Nine years ago he lost his Florida medical license for "gross negligence," so he came to California, where the commanding officer of a marine base kicked him out for "unprofessional conduct." While operating the clinic where the 27-year-old was fatally injured, the owner was disciplined for starting an abortion on a woman who turned out to be six and a half months pregnant. He is the *doctor* who is supposed to be offering *safe and legal* abortions, but he was either unable or unwilling to determine the developmental age of the baby. Based on that act of "gross negligence," he was placed on five years'

SCOPE and FOCUS
I. CONVICTIONS
II. PRETEXTS
Autonomy of Mother
Relativism of Value
Personhood Denied
Humanity Challenged
Mechanism & Gradualism
Pleasure vs. Pain
Personal Tragedy
Burden-Bearing
Anonymous & Different
Accident Justifies Remedy
Birth control failed
Incapacitated mom
Pragmatic Justifications
Self Defense
Mother's life
Pro-life contradiction
Health of mother
Alien invasion
Political Expediency
Safe & legal
Medical responsibility
Population bomb
Social Benefits
Safer than childbirth
Fetal research
Fetal tissue
Organs for transplant
Positivism
III. MANDATE
IV. LEGACY
V. ABORTIVE LINKS
VI. DILEMMA
VII. DESTINY

Another feature of *safety* in abortion is the setting. Two Supreme Court decisions in 1983 struck down State attempts to increase the safety of abortions [requiring that they be performed in hospitals beginning with the second trimester]. The *Ashcroft* ruling said that the statute "unreasonably infringes upon a woman's constitutional right to obtain an abortion," and the *Akron* verdict held that the other state had thrust "a significant obstacle in the path of women seeking an abortion."[11]

According to the Supreme Court, Tommy Tucker's late-term abortion clinic is safe enough. Angela Hall paid abortionist Tommy Tucker $1,800 to kill her 22-week unborn baby... She died too.[12] Here is another tragedy:

> In California, in 1996, an autopsy report states that an abortionist's "gross negligence." resulted in the death of a 27-year-old woman[13] The Riverside, California, *Press-Enterprise*, continuing the story the next day, stated that "Overall, the incidence of death associated with pregnancy has decreased during the past 20 years. In the early 1970s, one in every 30,000 legal abortions resulted in [maternal] death. Today, that number is one in every 167,000 abortions."[14]
>
> We must not fail to notice that just the day before, the deputy coroner was quoted as saying that because it was the result of a therapeutic [legal] abortion, even though the abortionist was going to be charged with negligent homicide, the 27-year-old woman's cause of death would be officially listed as "accidental."[15] Knowing that this is how criminal deaths of aborted women are documented, it is no wonder that we have statistical "proof" that *legal* abortion procedures are getting *safer and safer* all the time.

Maybe it was George Grant who first observed that abortion is the only surgical procedure in America that is totally unregulated. The Pennsylvania State Legislature has tried to require that abortion clinics at least submit some basic medical statistics to the state. The Supreme Court in 1986 ordered that they must not do that; it would be unconstitutional.[16]

It is unclear whether the State reworded the statute or the Court had a change of constitution – or both – but in the 1992 *Casey* case, the Court allowed that Pennsylvania could, indeed, require that an abortion clinic send them reports.[17]

It is a sad commentary on our culture that we pro-lifers count it a major victory that states are now *permitted* to require [certain, limited] information reporting from abortionists. One would hope that this is at least one small step toward the day when zero will be the number of deaths at abortion clinics – both of mothers *and* of babies.

Mark Crutcher is the founder and director of Life Dynamics, Inc, in Denton, Texas, which documents injuries and deaths of women due to abortions, and assists in the litigation of such cases. Mr. Crutcher says that in 1998 "We are currently active in almost 100 abortion-injury cases, including 13 which involve the death of the woman who was having the abortion."[18]

Mark Crutcher's book, *Lime 5: Exploited by Choice*, details case histories of women who have suffered over 23 major types of injuries and malpractice.[19]

One set of statistics from California reveals that a clinic was aware of complications developing in 15.5% of their patients [it is impossible to know how many problems the clinic did not find out about]. Specific types of difficulty were indicated. During the period of time covered by the report, if you had a "safe and legal" abortion at that clinic, you would have a 10% chance of one of these four problems: part of baby not removed; infection requiring treatment; anesthetic complication; or perforated uterus.[20]

probation in September which meant he was still authorized to perform abortions and to supervise the other abortionist who caused the woman's death. [*Press-Enterprise*, 12-20-96, A1, A12].

14 *Press-Enterprise*, 12-20-96, A1, A12.

15 *Press-Enterprise*, 12-19-96, A1, A10.

16 *Thornberg v. American College of Obstetricians and Gynecologists*, 1986, in Clowes, page 89.15.

17 *Planned Parenthood v. Casey*, 1992, in Clowes, pages 89.16 and 89.17.

18 Mark Crutcher, *Access: The Key to Pro-Life Victory*, 24.

19 Crutcher, *Lime 5*, 19 to end.

20 Kristin Luker, *Taking Chances: Abortion and the Decision Not to Contracept*, 173.

b. Shift responsibility from government to medical authority

Suppose that instead of a democratic republic, the U.S. were a kingdom. Suppose that our laws were simply the pragmatic fabrications of a nine member tribunal appointed by the monarch for life. Were that the case, what do you suppose that *great council* would have decided about the abortion hubbub back in 1973? ...Very likely they would have handed down a *Roe v. Wade*. *Roe* was the perfect *pragmatic* solution the dilemma the country was facing: social confusion – perhaps anarchy – as the states lurched forward, first one and then another, toward what seemed clearly to be inevitable: a dismantling of the statutes criminalizing abortion, which had been enacted one by one over a fifty-year period in the late nineteenth century.[1]

But there is one simple solution that would spare the nation – and the justice system – all of that grief. Just give the medical community what it's asking for: Hand the problem to the doctors; let them make all of the abortion decisions. What's the worst that could come of it? A handful of Bible-thumpers might huff and puff for a decade or two; it would create who-knows-how-many of those para-church organizations, but that's good for the economy: lots of conventions and printing and postage.

In *Women and the Law*, Carol Lefcourt tells us that "since the early nineteenth century in the United States, when childbirth was seized from the hands of midwives and placed under the aegis of male gynecologists, the medical profession has sought to control the means of reproduction."[2] Jachemsen says that in "*modern* humanity's view and experience of life, former religious ways of dealing with human fragility and disease have, at least in public life, virtually been replaced by an absolutizing of health and medicine."[3]

Roe v. Wade declared: "The abortion decision in all its aspects is inherently and primarily a medical decision and basic responsibility for it must rest with the physician." *Doe v. Bolton* embellished the theme: "...the medical judgement may be exercised in the light of all factors – physical, emotional, psychological, familial, and the woman's age – relevant to the well-being of the patient. All these factors may relate to health. This allows the attending physician the room he needs..." The Autonomy granted the abortionist was defended and enlarged in 1986, in *Thornberg*, when the Court struck down Pennsylvania's attempt to create mandatory testing for viability and to demand that viable babies be spared. The Supreme Court declared that viability [to paraphrase the words of Forrest Gump] *is like a box of chocolates; only the abortionist knows what you get*. The effect of *Thornberg* is that nothing shall hamper the abortionist's appraisal of viability, and none may question the results.[4]

Here is the situation. All questions of morality and ethics relating to abortion are now the province of the medical establishment, which just happens to be the premier institutional embodiment of the Accident, Mechanism, and Pleasure/pain orientations to the universe, and whose ethical standards are the best that Relativism and Pragmatism can provide.

"One's life, one's right to vote, one's property, can all be taken away," says Christopher Stone, "But those who would infringe on them must go through certain procedures to do so; these procedures are a measure of what we value as a society."[5]

Regarding the fate of preborn children, our government's policy is that there is absolutely no procedure by which any defense of their right to life can even be raised. Because the fox has been assigned to guard the henhouse, the official value of human life has just fallen off of the bottom of the scale. J.C. Willke observed that "Never [before] in western civilization have we legally allowed innocent humans to be deprived of life without due process of law."[6]

1 It looked like the recipe for fifty years of courtroom chaos. It could be imagined that every unwanted pregnancy would require its own law firm, courtroom and jail house to determine who had the right to decide who *should* decide who *could* decide what to do next, and all of this to the incessant accelerated ticking of those 9-month biological clocks! [It's not like you can go on vacation and decide about the abortion when you get back.]

2 Lefcourt, page 8.2.

3 H. Jochemsen, in Kilner, *Bioethics and the Future of Medicine: A Christian Appraisal*, 14.

4 *Thornberg v. American College of Obstetricians and Gynecologists*, Clowes, page 89.15.

5 Stone, *Should Trees Have Standing?*, 35.

6 J.C. Willke, *Handbook on Abortion*. [Sorry. Page reference deleted; you needed to read his whole book anyway.]

7 We will later discuss Thomas Malthus [in part IV.C.5], who singlehandedly created the population bomb hysteria which remains a pervasive and powerful force in public policy, both nationally and globally. We will here take a look at some of the ways that theory has impacted the abortion debate.

8 Hilgers, *Abortion and Social Justice*, 161.

9 George Grant, *Grand Illusions*, 34-5.

10 In 1966 there was a World Congress on Evangelism in Berlin. "One of the dominant features in the Hall for this conference was a population clock. This giant thirty foot display flashed pictures of eleven babies every second to dramatize the rapidity of the growth of the world's population... It was estimated that the population of the world increased by two million persons during the ten days the congress was in session." [Earl Reeves, in Robert Clouse, 183].

11 Mary Calderone, in Beckwith, *PC Death*, 53.

SCOPE and FOCUS
I. CONVICTIONS
II. PRETEXTS
Autonomy of Mother
Relativism of Value
Personhood Denied
Humanity Challenged
Mechanism & Gradualism
Pleasure vs. Pain
Personal Tragedy
Burden-Bearing
Anonymous & Different
Accident Justifies Remedy
Birth control failed
Incapacitated mom
Pragmatic Justifications
Self Defense
Mother's life
Pro-life contradiction
Health of mother
Alien invasion
Political Expediency
Safe & legal
Medical responsibility
Population bomb
Social Benefits
Safer than childbirth
Fetal research
Fetal tissue
Organs for transplant
Positivism
III. MANDATE
IV. LEGACY
V. ABORTIVE LINKS
VI. DILEMMA
VII. DESTINY

c. Population bomb gets de-fused [60-3]

Legalized abortion is seen as having provided fine pragmatic solutions to three thorny political problems: saving women from becoming back-alley statistics, transferring abortion decisions from the judges to the doctors, and defusing the population bomb.[7]

"There are three problems that are often cited as posing a real crisis for the future of mankind," says Thomas Hilgers, "environmental deterioration, starvation, and poverty."[8] A rapidly expanding population could negatively impact all three of these crises. One of the favorite themes of Margaret Sanger and her Planned Parenthood Federation has been that abortion is necessary to curtail the exponential grown of the world population.[9]

Their dedicated efforts have kept that theme on the political front-burner for many decades. In the '60s we were told, "There will be 180,000 more persons for breakfast tomorrow."[10]

The president of Planned Parenthood in 1968 was saying "We are still unable to put babies in the class of dangerous epidemics, even though this is the exact truth."[11]

"If we continue to increase at the same rate for 500 to 600 years, there will be one square yard per person over the whole face of the earth," wrote Leroy Augustein in 1969.[12]

"The population explosion is a myth," say Ankerberg and Weldon.[13]

Philip Ney brings it home: "Although overpopulation has been touted as the most critical problem in the world, *under*population in Western countries has become perhaps the most burning issue in recorded history. A rapid decline in population is something that Western countries cannot deal with. There is no mechanism for enabling the major institutions and the economy to adjust."[14]

"Since 1973," Carr and Meyer tell us, "American women have been having babies at less than the 2.1-per-lifetime rate needed to keep population constant. The current fertility rate [in 1990] is 1.8 births per woman."[15]

From 1940 to 1980, the U.S. population growth averaged 18% each ten years; from 1980 to 1990 it was only 11%.[16]

Brian Clowes shows us the real result of trying to make abortion the pragmatic cure for the supposed over-population problem of America: "The direct loss of life caused by abortion exceeds that of all this country's wars put together, not only in baby deaths and injuries to women, but in lost wages, consumed services and goods, and taxes totaling more than forty-seven trillion dollars ($47,460,000,000,000.00), or ten times the entire national debt."[17]

---

12 Augustein, *Come, Let Us Play God*, 54-5.

13 Ankerberg, *When does Life Begin?*, 151: "4.5 billion people, the world's population [in 1989], could be placed in the state of Texas in one gigantic city with the population density less than that of many existing cities, leaving the rest of the globe completely empty. The problem is not too many people as much as it is the distribution of resources."

14 Ney, in Mall, *The Psychological Aspects of Abortion*, 34. [For those of us who are adults today – of whatever age – the pool of youngsters whose demand for housing is supposed to preserve the equity value of our houses, and the pool of taxpayers who are supposed to be paying in so that we can draw out some Social Security... That pool of our posterity has been diminished by one-third by abortion.]

15 Steven Carr, *Celebrate Life*, 146-7.

16 Derived from figures in Ball, *In Search of a National Morality*, 22.

The financial "case" upon which abortion has been sold, pragmatically, to the American people and to our government presupposes that the babies who are being aborted are the ones who would have been on welfare, dragging the rest of us down and the government too. This is fatally flawed logic. All of the demographics indicate that the composition of the population of aborted babies would be virtually identical to the existing society. The average person in our culture is not a taker but a producer and a giver. When you add up all of the welfare recipients, jailbirds, sociopaths, blue-collar workers, white-collar workers, and professional athletes together you find that the average American earns – and pays taxes on – $346,678.00 in his / her lifetime [Derived from Beckwith, *PC Death*, 60-1].

17 Clowes, page 48.2.

3. Social Benefits

Pragmatism does not only view abortion as justified by a mother's right to self-defense from internal alien attack, and as a logical solution to pressing political problems, but pragmatism also contends that abortion is a total plus for society. "Even before *Roe*, on the basis of the liberalized laws in several states, Lawrence Lader could call the rapid increase in abortion figures 'a triumph of the human spirit,' exulting that 'an act of faith can become a revolution.' Illustrations abound in which abortion advocates now speak of abortion not only as a right but also as virtually a morally good deed."[1]

Because of abortion, pragmatists contend, women are protected from the hazards of child-bearing labor, medical knowledge is advanced through fetal research, tissue from aborted babies is useful in treating the medical conditions of those born people we choose to keep alive, and by the transplanting of fetal organs into bigger people the aborted one is part of an heroic act.

a. "Safer than childbirth" [125-8]

James Bopp tells us that "health has been broadly interpreted by doctors who support abortion. Dr. David Zbaraz, for instance, declared that *all* first-trimester and most second-trimester abortions were medically necessary since, during that time, abortion was medically safer than childbirth."[2]

This allegation is refuted by Moreland and Geisler,[3] as well as by Ankerberg and Weldon, who reveal that "the maternal death rate from childbirth is roughly .01 percent or 1 in 10,000; therefore, it is one of the safest of medical procedures. The maternal death rate from abortion is at least twice this and possibly as high as 20 times this figure [citations given]. Thus, for the average healthy woman, abortion is far more risky than childbirth. But regardless, the child mortality rate from abortion is 100 percent – it is the most fatal surgical procedure in existence. Even saving hundreds of women cannot justify killing millions of babies."[4]

b. Fetal research contributes to medical progress

Just two years after *Roe*, doctors Gaylin and Lappe were saluting the boon to medicine that abortion was providing: "In this case of abortion, the fetus is doomed to death anyhow, but perhaps its death can be ennobled when the research has as its objective the saving of the lives of other wanted fetuses."[5] By contrast, also in 1975, in *The Ethics of Fetal Research*, Paul Ramsey warned that "both the foes and the proponents of abortion frequently confuse research using fetal tissue or the dead abortus with research using the [live] human fetus *in situ,* or the previable living abortus."[6]

Here are the implications of what Paul Ramsey is saying. When we authorize "fetal research" we are giving the green light to someone who – with the mother's consent but not the father's or baby's – wants to give the mother a light case of rubella and then wait a few weeks, do the abortion, and check to see how deformed the baby has become. We are saying "go for it" to a researcher who wants to make a series of tests to see how drugs given to the mother affect the baby while it is still in the womb, by putting things into the mother, checking a watch or a calendar, and then extracting parts or fluids from the baby to see how much of the substance has shown up. The attitude here is, "It's going to be killed anyway, so we can do whatever we want." That same pragmatic attitude gets carried further. "Yes" to fetal research permits curious doctors to surgically remove a baby from the womb, leave it connected by the umbilical cord so it stays alive, and do any number of things to it in that context. "Yes" also means that once removed from the mother entirely, even while it is still alive, anything may be done to it to "find out what happens if..." **Actual examples will illustrate the point. See Citations column, this page and next, starting at note seven.**[7]

SCOPE and FOCUS
I. CONVICTIONS
II. PRETEXTS
Autonomy of Mother
Relativism of Value
Personhood Denied
Humanity Challenged
Mechanism & Gradualism
Pleasure vs. Pain
Personal Tragedy
Burden-Bearing
Anonymous & Different
Accident Justifies Remedy
Birth control failed
Incapacitated mom
Pragmatic Justifications
Self Defense
Mother's life
Pro-life contradiction
Health of mother
Alien invasion
Political Expediency
Safe & legal
Medical responsibility
Population bomb
Social Benefits
Safer than childbirth
Fetal research
Fetal tissue
Organs for transplant
Positivism
III. MANDATE
IV. LEGACY
V. ABORTIVE LINKS
VI. DILEMMA
VII. DESTINY

1 Harold O.J. Brown, in Ball, 69-70.

2 James Bopp, *Restoring the Right to Life*, 13.

3 Moreland and Geisler, *The Life and Death Debate*, 29.

4 Ankerberg and Weldon, *When Does Life Begin?*, 137-8.

5 Willard Gaylin and Mark Lappe, 1975, by Clowes, page 53.11.

6 Paul Ramsey, page xii.

7 Ramsey, 23: Doctors wondered if premature babies can be made to 'breathe" through their skin. The pragmatic way to test the method was to take 40 preborns and immediately after removing them from the mother's body, immerse them in an oxygenated saline solution and keep track of how long it took them to die; the "winner" lasted eleven days.

[Examples Continue at the top of the next page]

• John Eidsmoe, *God and Caesar*, 185; also in Willke, 129: We are not told what future benefit is anticipated from this next study, but researchers found ways to decapitate aborted children immediately after an abortion and keep the brain alive for as long as five months.

• Eidsmoe, 185: One such researcher responded to criticism with, "Once society's declared the fetus dead, and abrogated its rights, I don't see any ethical problem... Whose rights are we going to protect, once we've decided the fetus won't live?" Good question. Apparently, the answer is, "No one's."

• John Whitehead, *The Stealing of America*, 49-50; also Willke, 128: A twenty-four week preborn has a good chance of survival. Nonetheless, researchers, because it is legal to ignore viability, removed such a baby from its mother, and while it was still alive – without anesthetic – sliced its chest open to do experiments on its still-beating heart.

• Paul Ramsey, *The Ethics of Fetal Research*, 21-2: A 26-week-old baby was removed from a 14-year-old girl. The baby was so healthy that even after 5 hours, 8 minutes of research had been conducted on it, when they disconnected it from the experimental apparatus, its "gasping respiratory efforts increased to 8 to 10 per minute," and it took 21 minutes for it to die. "The researcher was given a prize."

• Stanley Reiser, *Ethics in Medicine: Historical Perspectives and Contemporary Concerns*, 473-4. [With the possible exception of the brain research noted above – which may have been conducted in Europe – the experiments just described have all been permitted in the United States under the *Regulations of the U.S. Department of Health, Education, and Welfare Governing Fetal Research*, which imposes no moral constraint at all, and merely states that any type of fetal research is permissible, provided that "the purpose of such research is the development of important biomedical knowledge that cannot be obtained by alternative means." That is a prime example of Pragmatism in action.]

The mother is deemed autonomous over the choice to authorize fetal research, just as she is for the abortion.[8] *Technically* the father of the child has veto power over fetal research under the Uniform Anatonomical Gift Act (UAGA), but in practice his wishes may be ignored. The Act does not require his *consent* – the mother's is sufficient – and he need not even be told that this is contemplated. Unless he is aware of the possibility *and* takes the initiative to "object," he is out of the loop.[9]

The Environmental Protection Agency has spent $300,000 of your tax money to have an Ohio medical research company find out how much harm was done to the brains, hearts and other vital organs of 100 preborn babies when pesticides were injected into their bodies.[10]

c. Fetal tissue is valuable in treating born people

"The use of fetuses as organ and tissue donors is a ticking time bomb of bioethics," says ethicist Arthur Caplan of the Hastings Center.[11] On the other hand, a University of Colorado professor says, pragmatically, "A fetal cadaver shouldn't be treated any differently from another cadaver, as long as society agrees that we can use cadaveric tissue."[12]

One man's cadaver is another man's child. The reader will recall that, earlier, we raised the question of human dignity regarding the body of a downed American pilot in enemy hands. Perhaps the professor's cavalier attitude toward the bodies of the aborted ones might be pierced by the knowledge that aborted babies are considered health food delicacies in China, where state doctors "hand out bottles of thumb-sized aborted babies to be made into meat cakes or soup with pork and ginger."[13]

But procedure, not morality, is the only thing to be questioned according to one UCLA doctor who said, "Research on fetal tissue should be allowed as long as it is carefully done."[14] The tantalizing prospects of potential beneficial use of fetal tissue lures many into the pragmatic trap. Both hope and success are reported for treatment of scourges like diabetes, blood diseases, paralysis, and liver, kidney and eye diseases.[15]

Doctors are excited about possible fetal tissue treatments for Alzheimer's and Huntington's diseases, about implants of fetal tissue and fetal brain grafts; they talk of fetal tissue enabling them to genetically engineer super cells, growing them in cultures, of freezing and storing fetal brain tissue, and of neural-tissue banks full of deposits for future surgeries.[16]

Researchers are looking hopefully at fetal tissue for possible breakthroughs regarding epilepsy and strokes, sickle-cell anemia, hemophilia and Tay-Sachs disease; they want to use brain tissue from aborted babies to produce dopamine to relieve Parkinson's disease symptoms, and they theorize that since the cells of preborns are growing and developing so much more rapidly than those of plain-old born people, those cells might be used to "make new nerve connections" in some cases of blindness or spinal-injury paralysis.[17]

If the question is as simple as "Should we maximize the potential human benefits by recycling this resource, or ought we let it go to waste?" then a lot of vital Christians will probably be voting to "make the best of it."

8 Ramsey, *Fetal*, 38.

9 Reiser, 458.

10 Whitehead, *The Stealing of America*, 56.

11 "Help from the Unborn," *Time* magazine, 1-12-87, 62.

12 "Should Medicine Use the Unborn?" *Newsweek* magazine, 9-14-87, 63.

13 Gregory Koukl, *Stand to Reason* radio broadcast transcripts, "Velocitizing Morality," 1.

14 "Should Medicine Use the Unborn?" *Newsweek* magazine, 9-14-87, 63.

15 "Help from the Unborn," *Time* magazine, 1-12-87, 62.

16 "Steps Toward a Brave New World," *Time* magazine, 7-13-87, 56-7.

17 "Should Medicine Use the Unborn?" *Newsweek* magazine, 9-14-87, 62.

d. Organs for transplant make the "fetus" an *involuntary* hero

The same factors which argue for the medical use of fetal tissue are equally compelling toward approval of organ transplants from aborted children. This is already beyond the theoretical stage and in practice. "Soviet physicians and [American Dr. Robert] Gale tried a controversial new technique on six of the most severely irradiated Chernobyl [Soviet nuclear power plant disaster] workers: fetal surgery. In a desperate attempt to reconstitute the blood-forming tissues of those victims, the doctors transplanted liver cells from human fetuses aborted in the first months of pregnancy."[1] Thymus glands have been transplanted from aborted babies to born children.[2] In similar fashion, kidneys have been transplanted.[3]

Critics of the direction in which we are headed include a member of England's Parliament who remarked, "This consumerist approach to the creation of life puts it on a par with an American fast-food outlet," and another Londoner added, "Obviously, the fetus will just become a spare parts box for medical science."[4] There is a sizable – and very pragmatic – segment of the American populace who think that a box of human spare parts is a great idea: *Time* magazine reported in 1993 that **"24% of Americans approve of cloning to produce babies whose vital organs can be used to save the life of others."**[5]

Earlier, under the heading of the humanity of the preborn, and the "part of the woman's body" argument, we shared the information that "At ten weeks, a female fetus has made all of the eggs she will carry as a woman."[6] Even short of transplanting fetal ovaries into born women, researchers have long had the techlology needed to implant, in a previously infertile woman, eggs from aborted babies – fertilized or not, at her option.[7] In at least one instance, reported by Willke, the testicles from an aborted baby were "successfully" transplanted into a 28-year-old man who "had previously been unable to become fully sexually active."[8]

All of the pro-abortion arguments which hinge on doubts of the full humanity or personhood of the unborn child, or on that child's wantedness – plus particularly, those which assert the "reproductive rights" of the mother – must all be reexamined in light of the obvious *wantedness* of the aborted child as the source of valuable *human* components and capacities.

Some are raising flags of caution regarding the moral and ethical pitfalls attendant upon fetal research, the use of fetal tissue, and fetal transplants. First is a question which arises from transplants of the more standard variety: organs harvested from a suddenly deceased born person. Given the perishability of the product it has been asked if there is not a temptation to hasten pronouncement of death in order to maximize the *freshness* of the organ.

Turning to the subject of organs and tissue from aborted children, there arise legitimate questions regarding death, pain and dignity.[9] The very child whose rights were denied on the basis that his mother did not want her may arguably have attained standing by the sheer fact that bioethical value implies human-worth. *Newsweek* raised the danger of profiteering in the sale of fetal products.[10]

Greg Koukl turns over the "cadaver" argument to see what's on the other side. He says of the already aborted baby, "There's no human inside there, the person is gone. But... if legalizing the use of fetal tissue, which [by itself] has no moral ramifications... causes more abortions [to be performed because of the demand for fetal products], then the act that was initially non-moral becomes immoral."[11]

On the topic of human dignity, Hans Jonas brings up the concept of *inviolability*. Here is what he says: "It may well be the case that the individual's interest in his own inviolability is itself a public interest such that its publicly condoned violation, irrespective of numbers, violates the interest of all."[12]

1 "Help from the Unborn," *Time* magazine, 1-12-87, 62. [In spite of the effort, the patients died within one week of the accident.]

2 Ramsey, *Fetal*, 25; and Willke, *Handbook*, 54.

3 "Should Medicine Use the Unborn?" *Newsweek* magazine, 9-14-87, 63.

4 *Life Advocate*, 2/'94, 5.

5 *Time*, 11-8-93, 65-70. Researcher's comments: Other parts of this survey on cloning are most enlightening: 63% think cloning is against God's will; *but only 58% think it is morally wrong* – can this really mean that 5% believe that "God is against it, but *I say* it's morally OK"? Here is the part that reflects a polarization of America, right down the middle: 46% think that human cloning should be made illegal, but an opposing 45% approve of cloning to produce extra embryos to increase the chance of infertile couples being able to produce a child. Remember the "fast-food" analogy? This report says that 16% of Americans think that cloning should be used to stock "embryo banks from which prospective parents could select a child with genetic characteristics they desire." We shall presume that catalogs would show photos of the already-born clones who are identical to the frozen ones offered.

6 *Time* magazine, 1-17-94, 19.

7 *Life Advocate*, 2/'94, 19.

8 Willke, *Handbook on Abortion*, 129.

9 Hans Jonas, *Ethical Aspects of Experimentation with Human Subjects*, 222.

10 "Should Medicine Use the Unborn?" *Newsweek* magazine, 9-14-87, 63.

11 Gregory Koukl, *Stand to Reason* radio broadcast transcripts, "Pulling the Trigger on Abortion," 5.

12 Hans Jonas, *Ethical Aspects of Experimentation with Human Subjects*, 222.

SCOPE and FOCUS
I. CONVICTIONS
II. PRETEXTS
Autonomy of Mother
Relativism of Value
Personhood Denied
Humanity Challenged
Mechanism & Gradualism
Pleasure vs. Pain
Personal Tragedy
Burden-Bearing
Anonymous & Different
Accident Justifies Remedy
Birth control failed
Incapacitated mom
Pragmatic Justifications
Self Defense
Mother's life
Pro-life contradiction
Health of mother
Alien invasion
Political Expediency
Safe & legal
Medical responsibility
Population bomb
Social Benefits
Safer than childbirth
Fetal research
Fetal tissue
Organs for transplant
Positivism
Politics
Futility of Criminalization
III. MANDATE
IV. LEGACY
V. ABORTIVE LINKS
VI. DILEMMA
VII. DESTINY

G. Positivism & the Abortion Problem

A Positivistic orientation predisposes a person in favor of legalized abortion with arguments of two basic types: Why abortion *should* not be re-criminalized, and Why criminalization of abortion, at this point in history, *could* not be enforced. In a sense, this second type leans toward pragmatism, just as many if not most of the pro-abortion justifications we have considered seem to rest on two or more deeply held convictions.

1. The Politics of an Abortion Policy for the Nation

Beckwith acknowledges and counters three pro-abortion assertions as to why, politically, we should not re-criminalize abortion: **a)** The legal system would be wrecked by granting preborns a "right to life" [Beckwith,120]; [Details of the expected problems constitute the next subsection below this one]; **b)** Abortion is extremely controversial and there is no political consensus [82-3]; Mnookin testifies to this reality: "Few issues have been as divisive politically as abortion. Opinion polls suggest part of the reason: There is no consensus on what policy is appropriate. Somewhere between 20 percent and 41 percent of American adults now support abortion on demand. A much smaller, but nonetheless substantial minority of approximately 15 percent believe that abortion should never be permitted;"[13] **c)** Rights are society's to grant or to withhold as it wishes, and at the moment it has been decided that the "right to choose" is right and the fetus's "right to life" is wrong [113].

2. The "Futility" of Criminalizing Abortion

Making much of the lessons learned from Prohibition, pro-abortionists play on the "You can't legislate morality" theme in arguing that abortion must not be re-criminalized because it would be impossible to enforce:

a) Stopping abortions would be impossible [83-4]; Pro-abortionists have ranted that Rescuers who trespassed to passively sit before a clinic door were "anarchists" who advocate the breaking any law they don't like. One would think from their judgmentalism that pro-abortionists hold the law in high esteem. Their own words and deeds have, however, proven the opposite about them; this is consistent with their orientation to Positivism, as opposed to divine Commandments of right and wrong. The pro-abortion leaders have vowed, defiantly and repeatedly, that if abortion were to be re-criminalized, or if even the slightest impediment were raised to "abortion on demand," they would not hesitate to violate such law [see *Orphans*, 273].

In Birmingham in January of 1998, the bomb did not kill two employees of a safe-and-*legal* abortion clinic. Those two were working as paid assistants at what was once a legal abortion clinic, but which, as soon Alabama's new law criminalized "a certain type of late-term abortions," had publicly announced that it was continuing that procedure in defiance of State law.[14] As Paul Harvey would say, "Now you know the rest of the story." **b)** Homicide-by-birth-control might become a crime, if one's "contraceptive" is proven to be abortifacient [115]. **c)** Outlawing birth control might be necessary – those which are abortifacients – if a right-to-life of the preborn were enforced [115-6]. **d)** Treatment of some medical conditions might need to be prohibited: a D & C procedure which is used for an abortion is also used to remove a cyst from the uterus [116]; **e)** Smoking and other "harm to fetuses" might criminalize the mother [120-1]; Doug Bandow, in his ...*Biblical View of Politics*, addresses this concern about smoking: "The threat to the fetus seems too small to justify such government micromanagement of a mother's life."[15] On the other hand, the possibility of such defense of the preborn is not totally theoretical: "...passive smoking by a preborn child has been held to be child abuse, and a mother has been convicted for 'providing cocaine to another' because of its effects on her unborn baby."[16] **f)** Miscarriages would become suspect [121]; **g)** Prosecuting the women as murderers would logically follow [72-4].

13 Robert Mnookin, *In the Interest of Children: Advocacy, Law, Reform, and Public Policy*, 154.

14 *Press-Enterprise*, 1-30-98, A1, A10.

15 Doug Bandow, *Beyond Good Intentions, a Biblical View of Politics*, 169.

16 Robert Orr, *Life and Death Decisions*, 55.

So many excuses – so little love...

We have seen that a person's
foundational metaphysical convictions,
rooted even more deeply than the world view labels that
attempt to describe them,
cause those whose hearts and minds
are shaped by those presuppositions
to view the procedures called
abortion
as either a natural boon to humanity,
or alternatively,
as a diabolical outrage against the holiness of God.

The person who has rejected
creation, design, commandments,
justice, virtue, universalism
and accountability to God,
has embraced their opposites.
If she is **unhappily pregnant**, alone and afraid,
a hundred pretexts for
abortion
will arise spontaneously
from deep within her,
each one seeming sensible and true.
In her mind she will explain to the child within her:

This isn't fair / I feel trapped... (pleasure / pain)

This wasn't in my plan / it's not my fault... (accident)

You can't communicate / you can't even think... (mechanism)

Nobody will know / You won't know the difference... (relativism)

The law says it is OK... (positivism)

The doctors will fix everything / you'll be better off... (pragmatism)

It's my decision to make; mine alone... (autonomy)

Some day,
when the time is right,
she *will* have a child she can keep.
She and *that* daughter will be very close.
...And when the mother grows old they'll still be close.
Then one day, the daughter will draw near to *her* and say,
"This isn't fair / I feel trapped..."

SCOPE and FOCUS
I. CONVICTIONS
II. PRETEXTS
III. MANDATE
Biblical Authority
Pro-Abortion View
Pro-Life View
Roles of a Disciple
Alien & Pilgrim within God's Creation
Theologian, revealing Divine Design
Priest, proclaiming God's Commandments
Prophet, crying out for Godly Justice
Loving Neighbor, displaying Virtue
Zealot, fighting for Universal Truths
Evangelist, witnessing to our Accountability
IV. LEGACY
V. ABORTIVE LINKS
VI. DILEMMA
VII. DESTINY

III. The Mandate: Seeking Biblical Guidance

Before we address the Roles of a Biblical Disciple, we must come to understand, as best we can, God's view of Abortion. That knowledge will inform our perception of what God may be calling his people to do – both individually and as His Church – in this era and nation.

A. Biblical Authority Relating to Abortion

Because there are so many denominations, pastors, congregations and individuals who identify themselves as "pro-choice," we – as pro-life Christians – must find out how they can hold such a view. There are at least three possible answers to that question. Some Christians have simply been brainwashed, and they sincerely think that "pro-choice" is a neutral position, even though those folks assuredly do not take a "pro-choice" stand on drive-by shootings and gang-rape. A second group of Christians are consciously in favor of abortion, at least in a particular set of situations which they will be happy to name for you. This second group, in the main, have no biblical or theological basis for accepting abortion, but have simply embraced enough humanistic convictions that the pro-abortion slogans now make sense to them, and God's will just got shoved out of the picture. A third group is even more scary than the first two. This group has become certain that God is pro-choice, even that God and His Word hold abortion to be an acceptable act. These are beliefs we must take most seriously.

Fortunately – not fortunately for the Church, but fortunately in that it helps us know what we are up against – at least one writer has written a biblical interpretation of a pro-abortion God. John Swomley asserts that the Bible is "Pro-Choice." We will examine Mr. Swomley's attempt to find scriptural support for abortion first, and then see what biblical realities he might have overlooked. Finally, this researcher will present the argument that the God of the Bible is radically "Pro-Life."

1. Evidence from a Pro-Abortionist's Bible

In 1990, *Christian Social Action* was published by the General Board of Church and Society of the United Methodist Church. As part of that document, John M. Swomley wrote "Human Beings: In God's Image," which was reprinted in 1993 in *Moral Issues and Christian Response*, edited by Paul T. Jersild and Dale A. Johnson.[1]

Synopsis of John Swomley's contentions

Mr. Swomley proclaims and defends a number of liberal "pro-choice Christian" assertions which cry out for correction: **1)** That abortion was "widely practiced" in biblical times, that Israel's neighbors were anti-abortion but the God of the Bible was not; that in Exodus 21:22-25 "the woman, undeniably, had greater moral and religious worth than the fetus;" **2)** That "There is also reference in the Mosaic law to 'abortion on request' (*Numbers* 5:11-31);" **3)** He states "Aside from these passages, the Bible does not deal with the subject of abortion... there is no condemnation or prohibition of abortion anywhere in the Bible in spite of the fact that techniques for inducing abortion had been developed and widely used by the time of the New Testament;" **4)** Regarding the beginning of human life, he declares, "The Bible's clear answer is that human life begins at birth with breathing."

An analysis of John Swomley's case

Mr. John Swomley, author of "Human Beings: In God's Image," is not just a "pro-choice Christian;" he claims to speak for the entire Protestant branch of Christianity, as – supposedly – contrasted with the Catholic Church. He also does violence to the Bible by grossly distorting its content and message:

> **A.** "In Assyria the fetus was given more value than the mother... Although the Hebrews were influenced by many of the laws of their Assyrian, Sumerian and Babylonian neighbors, all of which forbade abortion, the Hebrew scriptures had no laws forbidding abortion. This was chiefly because of the higher value placed upon women." [2]

1 John Swomley, in Paul Jersild and Dale Johnson, *Moral Issues and Christian Response*, 340-5.

2 Swomley, in Jersild, 340.

B. "There is also reference in the Mosaic law to 'abortion on request' (Numbers 5:11-31) if a husband suspects his wife is pregnant by another man. The 'husband shall bring his wife to the priest'..."[1]

C. "Aside from these passages, the Bible does not deal with the subject of abortion."[2]

With Assertion **C**, that this is all that the Bible says about abortion, Swomley implies that this is all God's word has to say about willful destruction of one's offspring. This could not be farther from the truth. Infanticide, not abortion, was the "choice" of choice among the pagan peoples of the promised land. A primary result of God's command that the displaced Canaanite cultures should be utterly destroyed was to be protection of the Hebrews from contamination by the cult of child-killing. The efforts were in vain, and infant sacrifice to the blood-thirsty god Molech became a major problem for the Jews, from Jericho to Babylon.

So what John Swomley tries to get us to believe about the Bible with Assertion **A** is the exact opposite of the truth. Israel's neighbors were not pro-life; they practiced infanticide religiously. Assertions **A** and **B** would lead us to believe that the Bible endorses a woman's right [more "highly valued"] to "abortion on request," when even the passage he quotes stipulates the totally "politically *in*correct" situation of the woman held powerless against the husband's "choice" to abort on the grounds of mere suspicion! To understand this passage would require more expertise than this researcher possesses, but it is clear that these verses say the opposite of what Mr. Swomley asserts.

Additionally, contrary to Mr. Swomley's notion that the Bible condones the killing of one's children, an abundance of biblical references makes it clear that for the Jews to become pro-choice like their neighbors was an abhorrent idea. As will soon be demonstrated, it profaned the name of God, desecrated their land, and resulted in rejection by God: in affliction, plundering and exile, and in the destruction of Jerusalem.

Next the author tries to get us to believe that the Bible says the pre-born are not yet human.

D. "The Bible's clear answer is that human life begins at birth with breathing."[3]

E. "The most important determinant of viability is lung development."[4]

F. "99 percent [of abortions occur] by 20 weeks... there is no brain or neo-cortex, and hence no pain in cases of early abortion."[5]

Does Swomley's copy of the Bible lack the many crucial verses which attest not only to the child's humanity but *personhood* before birth? More key verses will follow, but these two will suffice for now:

[Elizabeth:] *"As soon as the sound of your greeting* [Mary] *reached my ears, the baby in my womb* [John the Baptist] *leaped for joy."* *Luke 1:44*

Before I formed you in the womb I knew you, before you were born I set you apart; I appointed you as a prophet to the nations. *Jeremiah 1:5*

As for the lack of awareness of pain [Assertion **F**], the author asserts that sentience is lacking before 20 weeks. We have previously cited documentation that babies experience pain in the great majority of abortions.[6]

Next, the writer grants us profound insights into the psyche of the Almighty:

G. "God does not will that every conception should eventuate either in implantation or in birth. This is consistent with our previous assertion that a fetus, as well as a fertilized egg, is a potential rather than an actual human being."[7]

H. "'In the image of God' ...does not refer to biological similarities but to the abilities to love and to reason, self awareness, transcendence, and freedom to choose, rather than to live by instinct"[8]

It is simply illegitimate to assert that whatever eventuality God allows as a consequence of the outplaying of His master plan is, first of all, an act of His "will" and, second, whatever God allows as an accident of natural processes, a human is morally justified in committing as a volitional act. If Assertion **G** is sufficient justification for abortion, then the fact that "crib death" claims the lives of many infants should legitimize suffocation with a pink or blue blanket as a cure for midnight crying.

With Assertion **H**, the writer attempts to delete the implication of sanctity from the biblical phrase "in the image of God" and to twist those words to support the act of abortion, but it is simply not defensible to say that a pre-born child can be killed because it has failed to match the "abilities" of God.

SCOPE and FOCUS
I. CONVICTIONS
II. PRETEXTS
III. MANDATE
Biblical Authority
Pro-Abortion View
Pro-Life View
Roles of a Disciple
Alien & Pilgrim within God's Creation
Theologian, revealing Divine Design
Priest, proclaiming God's Commandments
Prophet, crying out for Godly Justice
Loving Neighbor, displaying Virtue
Zealot, fighting for Universal Truths
Evangelist, witnessing to our Accountability
IV. LEGACY
V. ABORTIVE LINKS
VI. DILEMMA
VII. DESTINY

In spite of what he says, Mr. Swomley probably would not feel that a person would be justified in killing a former President of the United States simply because he is now in the process of *losing* the abilities of "reason, self awareness, transcendence, and freedom to choose..."

It was earlier observed that Mr. Swomley would claim that his opinions on these subjects are those of "most" Protestants, and that he would attempt to cast Protestantism as pro-choice, in opposition to pro-life Catholicism. In doing so, the writer has jettisoned several million pro-life evangelicals (and others) from the ranks of Protestantism – the pro-life denominations outnumber "pro-choice" denominations, by far.[9] In fact, there are 250 million Americans. Over half of them, 128 million are *members* of pro-life churches![10]

Assertion **J** [below] seems to be intended to equate the Catholic position on a pre-born child's right to life with Swomley's own contention that "In Assyria the fetus was given more value than the woman"[11] This assertion about Catholicism is in error, and is directly refuted by the writer's own Assertion I, from his previous page, which took pains to build a case that even the Catholics occasionally agree that "the fetus does not have equal value with the mother." [12]

> **I.** "A further illustration comes from Roman Catholic doctrine. Although the Roman Catholic hierarchy strongly opposes intentional abortion, in practice it sometimes recognizes the priority of the woman over the fetus... the Roman church argues that although the death of the fetus is foreseen, it is not intended because the intention is to preserve the health and life of the woman... the fetus does not have equal value with the mother" (342, pars. 4, 6).

> **J.** "Thus far I have contrasted Catholic and Protestant doctrine... Given these differences about legalism, the phrase 'sacredness of life' means one thing to Catholic bishops – that the life of the fetus is all-important. But to most Protestants and many others it means that there is a presumptive right to life which is not absolute but conditioned by the claims of others" (343, par. 7 - 344, par. 1).

The greatest tragedy of Mr. Swomley's verbal exercise is that he came to all of those erroneous conclusions after framing the wrong question. The reason he ended up omitting so much of what the Bible has to say on the real subject is that he seems to be answering, "What does the Bible specifically say about *abortion*?" This is a totally inappropriate method of seeking moral direction from the Bible. It is like a factory worker asking his pastor, "Does the Bible say anything about theft of computer chips by employees?" A negative answer does not mean "The Bible says it's a fine thing to do"!

Here are two honest questions for anyone who really seeks biblical answers:

1) Are there biblical examples of people who conceived children they did not raise, because they killed them?

and 2) What does the Bible reveal about God's view of those acts?

1 Swomley, in Jersild, 340, par. 3.
2 Swomley, in Jersild, 340, par. 4.
3 Swomley, in Jersild, 340, par. 5.
4 Swomley, in Jersild, 340, par. 5.
5 Swomley, in Jersild, 341, par. 5.
6 *Orphans in Babylon*, 59. If Mr. Swomley really believes that these criteria [**E** and **F**] – if they were true – are justifications for killing, then we must assume that if he ever had the misfortune to be confined in an iron lung, he would deem it morally acceptable for anyone to give him a lethal injection, as long as it was preceded by a shot of morphine.
7 Swomley, in Jersild, 342, par. 1.
8 Swomley, in Jersild, 341, par. 3.
9 John Naisbitt, *Megatrends 2000*, 274.
...also Clowes, page 42.9.
10 Clowes, page 42.9, and *World Almanac and Book of Facts, 1991*, 34 and 554.
11 Swomley, in Jersild, 340, par. 1.
12 Swomley, in Jersild, 342, par. 6.

2. Evidence from a Pro-Lifer's Bible

Here, again, are our "two biblical questions:"

1) Are there biblical examples of people who conceived children they did not raise, because they killed them?

and 2) What does the Bible reveal about God's view of those acts?

We will now explore the Biblical foundations for the assertion that the above questions produce these seven PRO-LIFE answers:

a. CHILD-KILLING, "infanticide," was the paramount overarching abomination of the idolatry and immorality of Israel's neighboring cultures, which constantly threatened to infect and destroy God's holy people.

b. THE NATIONS surrounding Israel were obsessed with infanticide much as America is fully committed to abortion today; their cultures were saturated with pagan religions and cults of fertility and death.

c. GOD'S PEOPLE fought a constant battle, from Jericho to Babylon, to resist the contagion of pagan rites; on many occasions, the Israelites, from commoners to kings, indulged in child-killing, always with catastrophic results.

d. BLOODGUILT is a theme tightly woven into the fabric of biblical morality. Infanticide was demonstrated as particularly offensive to God, a defilement of the land, and resulted in the most dire of consequences, for the willing-killing parents and their descendants, for the community that failed to punish the guilty ones, for the land and nation, and for God's relationship with His people.

e. God's JUDGMENT & WRATH were certain to fall – *far and wide*, as they say – as a consequence of infanticide. Punishment was delivered by famine, disaster, the sword and pestilence.

f. REPENTANCE & OBEDIENCE of God's people is the only corrective for the bloodguilt of infanticide.

g. RESTORATION of harmony with God and of peace to the land were never guaranteed. As Forrest Gump once said, "Sometimes, there's not enough rocks."[1]

a. CHILD-KILLING

INFANTICIDE was the overarching abomination of the idolatry and immorality of Israel's neighboring cultures, which constantly threatened to infect and destroy God's holy people. In the book of *Ezekiel*, God tells the prophet to compare His chosen people to the most pathetic example possible, a wretched newborn child, rejected by her own parents, not even offered to the bloodthirsty god Molech as a sacrifice to gain a benefit, but simply cast on the town's *golgotha* to succumb to the elements or to be ravaged by predators.

...confront Jerusalem with her detestable practices; ...You were thrown out into the open field, for on the day you were born you were despised. Then I passed by and saw you kicking about in your blood, and as you lay there in your blood I said to you, "Live!" But... you took your sons and daughters... My children, and sacrificed them to the idols.

Ezekiel 16:1-6, 20-21

Not only is the God of the Bible pro-life; He performs the first Rescue Operation. He says that He took pity on the outcast child and adopted her. But God's rescued orphan is now practicing infanticide![2]

In *Beyond Good Intentions: a Biblical View of Politics*, Doug Bandow states, "Scripture relates manhood back to conception, suggesting that that instance, rather than birth, is the point when life begins in God's eyes. For example, the Lord told Rebekah after she had conceived Esau and Jacob:"[3]

Two nations are in your womb, and two peoples from within you will be separated.

Genesis 25:23

Note also:

Before I formed you in the womb I knew you, before you were born I set you apart; I appointed you as a prophet to the nations.

Jeremiah 1:5

SCOPE and FOCUS
I. CONVICTIONS
II. PRETEXTS
III. MANDATE
Biblical Authority
Pro-Abortion View
Pro-Life View
Child-killing
The Nations
God's People
Bloodguilt
Judgment
Repentance
Restoration
Roles of a Disciple
Alien & Pilgrim
Theologian
Priest
Prophet
Loving Neighbor
Zealot
Evangelist
IV. LEGACY
V. ABORTIVE LINKS
VI. DILEMMA
VII. DESTINY

Recall this part of Job's prayer to God:

"Your hands shaped me and made me... Remember that you molded me like clay... Did you not pour me out like milk and curdle me like cheese, clothe me with skin and flesh and knit me together with bones and sinews? You gave me life and showed me kindness, and in your providence watched over my spirit." *Job 10:8-12*

For you created my inmost being; you knit me together in my mother's womb. I praise you because I am fearfully and wonderfully made; your works are wonderful, I know that full well. My frame was not hidden from you when I was made in the secret place. When I was woven together in the depths of the earth, your eyes saw my unformed body. All the days ordained for me were written in your book before one of them came to be. *Psalm 139:13-16*

The previous verses make clear that God has an intimate creative relationship with each individual person from the moment of conception, but the following passage, in addition to reiterating man's sin-nature, in doing so reveals that our full *essential being* exists at conception, *including* that sinful identity:

"Surely I was sinful at birth, sinful from the time my mother conceived me." *Psalm 51:5*

When Elizabeth heard Mary's greeting, the baby [John the Baptist] *leaped in her womb, and Elizabeth was filled with the Holy Spirit...* [Elizabeth:] *"As soon as the sound of your greeting reached my ears, the baby in my womb leaped for joy."* *Luke 1:41, 44*

In the above passage, pro-lifers often note that the in utero *person* John the Baptist was obviously aware of being – and excited about being – in the presence of the in utero *person*, Jesus. But verse 41 is even more revealing: Jesus and John are already at *work*. It could be described in this way: The Holy Spirit zapped from Jesus into John at that instant, clearly irradiated Elizabeth, and surely ricocheted between the two women for quite a while, and has been bouncing all over the planet ever since! In the next scripture, Jesus is obviously talking about the born children He is with, but it belongs here if for no other reason than to remind us that it is not just adults but *all persons* who are valuable and special to God. Jesus is speaking to his disciples about God's children:

"Your Father is not willing that any of these little ones should be lost." *Matthew 18:14*

Abraham is the patriarch, the father of the entire Jewish race. But this first recruit to God's program has a very important lesson to learn:

God tested Abraham... "Take your son, your only son Isaac, whom you love... sacrifice him... on one of the mountains I will tell you about..." [God calls and stops him:] *"Do not lay a hand on the boy... Do not do anything to him."* *Genesis 22:1-2, 12*

Abraham, everybody else will always be "doing it," but get this straight, this killing-your-own-children thing is *not* for you. Not for your family and descendants. Not now. Not ever.

Do not give any of your children to be sacrificed to Molech, for you must not profane the name of your God. *Leviticus 18:21*

This day I call heaven and earth as a witness against you that I have set before you life and death, blessings and curses. Now choose life, so that you and your children may live and that you may love the Lord your God, listen to His voice, and hold fast to Him. *Deuteronomy 30:19-20*

---

1 The title character in the movie *Forrest Gump*, watching a young woman throw stones at the abandoned house in which her father had regularly raped her.

2 Note Jesus' parable of the unmerciful/ungrateful servant, *Matthew* 18:23-35.

3 Doug Bandow, 166.

b. THE NATIONS

The cultures surrounding Israel were saturated with pagan religions and cults of fertility and death.

When a land falls into the hands of the wicked, he blindfolds its judges.
Job 9:24

Woe to those who call evil good and good evil, who put darkness for light and light for darkness, who put bitter for sweet and sweet for bitter... Their roar is like that of the lion... They growl as they seize their prey and carry it off with no one to rescue.
Isaiah 5:20, 29

Satan... deceives those who are perishing. They perish because they refused to love the truth and so be saved. For this reason God sends them a powerful delusion so that they will believe the lie.
2 Thessalonians 2:9-11

This concept of a "powerful delusion" warrants a great deal more study. The idea that the global acceptance of – and acquiescence to – abortion has a metaphysical dimension beyond mere self-deception needs to be explored. To this researcher, the real puzzle concerns the church. The *non*-believers reared in a modernist, evolutionist, hedonistic culture are being 100 percent consistent when they flush away "potential human life." But for Christians, who believe that the preborn are fully human persons created by God in the "image of God," to be complacent about abortion – which they acknowledge to be murder – defies understanding.

Also, for a Christian who claims to be repentantly pro-life to sit at this computer keyboard typing *ideas* about abortion while 4000 abortions are being committed in America *today*, simply makes no sense. The slogan of Operation Rescue in 1988, and the title of a cassette-taped speech by Randall Terry in that year, was "If You Believe Abortion is Murder, Then Act Like It Is Murder." But when Michael Griffin and Paul Hill did exactly that – used deadly force to stop abortionists – the sloganeering disappeared.

SCOPE and FOCUS
- **I. CONVICTIONS**
- **II. PRETEXTS**
- **III. MANDATE**
  - Biblical Authority
    - Pro-Abortion View
    - Pro-Life View
      - Child-killing
      - The Nations
      - God's People
      - Bloodguilt
      - Judgment
      - Repentance
      - Restoration
  - Roles of a Disciple
    - Alien & Pilgrim within God's Creation
    - Theologian, revealing Divine Design
    - Priest, proclaiming God's Commandments
    - Prophet, crying out for Godly Justice
    - Loving Neighbor, displaying Virtue
    - Zealot, fighting for Universal Truths
    - Evangelist, witnessing to our Accountability
- **IV. LEGACY**
- **V. ABORTIVE LINKS**
- **VI. DILEMMA**
- **VII. DESTINY**

They have given the dead bodies of Your servants as food to the birds of the air, the flesh of Your saints to the beasts of the earth. They have poured out blood like water all around Jerusalem, and there is no one to bury the dead.
Psalm 79:2-3

Any Israelite or any alien living in Israel who gives any of his children to Molech must be put to death. The people of the community are to stone him... If the people of the community close their eyes when that man gives one of his children to Molech and they fail to put him to death, I will set My face against that man... and all who follow him...
Leviticus 20:1-2, 4-5

Forgoing a deep biblical analysis, let's just explore what the opening of Leviticus 20 seems to clearly indicate about abortion. If it is valid to equate giving one's child to Molech with submitting to an abortion, then it seems to – in God's eyes – be an offense, a capital crime in fact. It would follow that a just government would impose the ultimate sanction on this crime. Should the government fail in this duty, there may be room to interpret this passage as indicating that the responsibility might revert to the "people of the community" [perhaps the Church?] to put an end to the offense. In any event the passage surely stands as yet another indication that God is *very* pro-life.

Even jackals offer their breasts to nurse their young, but My people have become heartless... Because of the sins of her prophets and the iniquities of her priests... now they grope through the streets like men who are blind. They are so defiled with blood that no one dares to touch their garments.
Lamentations 4:3, 13-14

c. GOD'S PEOPLE

The Chosen Ones fought a constant battle to resist the contagion of pagan rites; the Israelites, from commoner to kings, repeatedly indulged in child-killing, with catastrophic results. The Bible abounds in references to Higher Law, with abundant examples of the mandate to put God's law above man's when they conflict.

They [converts to the faith] *would not listen, but persisted in their former practices. Even while these people were worshiping the Lord, they were serving their idols. To this day their children and grandchildren continue to do as their fathers did.*
2 Kings 17:40-41

Jesus said: *"...your enemies will build an embankment against you and encircle you and hem you in on every side. They will dash you to the ground, you and the children within your walls... because you did not recognize the time of God's coming to you."*
Luke 19:43-44

On a hill east of Jerusalem, Solomon built a high place for Chemosh the detestable god of Moab, and for Molech the detestable god of the Ammonites. He did the same for all his foreign wives, who burned incense and offered sacrifices to their gods.
1 Kings 11:7-8

Ahaz... walked in the ways of the kings of Israel and even sacrificed his son in the fire, following the detestable ways of the nations the Lord had driven out before the Israelites.
2 Kings 16:2-3

The children rebelled against Me: They did not follow My decrees, they were not careful to keep My laws... I also gave them over to statutes that were not good and laws they could not live by; I let them become defiled through their gifts – the sacrifice of every firstborn – that I might fill them with horror so they would know that I am the Lord.
Ezekiel 20:21, 25-26

Not only the nation has become defiled by abortion, but the Church, pastors and trusting flocks of believers as well. What is lacking is the "filling with horror" that legalized abortion should engender in every godly heart.

Manasseh... did evil in the eyes of the Lord, following the detestable practices of the nations the Lord had driven out before the Israelites. He rebuilt the high places his father Hezekiah had destroyed; he also erected altars to Baal and made an Asherah pole, as Ahab king of Israel had done... In both courts of the temple of the Lord, he built altars to all the starry hosts. ***He sacrificed his own son in the fire****, practiced sorcery and divination, and consulted mediums and spiritists. He did much evil in the eyes of the Lord, provoking Him to anger... the people did not listen* [to God's warnings]. *Manasseh led them astray, so that they did more evil than the nations the Lord had destroyed before the Israelites.*
2 Kings 21:1-6, 9

Jehoiakim was twenty-five years old when he became king... And he did evil in the eyes of the Lord, just as his fathers had done... The Lord sent Babylonian, Aramean, Moabite and Ammonite raiders against him. He sent them to destroy Judah, in accordance with the word of the Lord proclaimed by his servants the prophets. Surely these things happened to Judah according to the Lord's command, in order to remove them from his presence ***because of the sins of Manasseh and all he had done, including the shedding of innocent blood****. For he had filled Jerusalem with innocent blood, and the Lord was not willing to forgive.*
2 Kings 23:36-37; 24:2-4

As we transition from examining the abortion complacency of the church into the dynamics of defilement by the shedding of innocent blood, it would be well to contemplate the hopeful note that the Bible contains for the righteous remnant, the faithful few. Sometimes, maybe often, there is protective exemption from God's holy justice – remember Noah – for those to whom He grants His mercy and grace:

[God to His messenger:] *"...put a mark on the foreheads of those who grieve and lament over all the detestable things..."* [to the guards of the city:] *"Follow him through the city and kill* [all others]. *Begin at My sanctuary... The land is full of bloodshed and the city is full of injustice... I will bring down on their own heads what they have done."*
Ezekiel 9:4-6, 9-10

d. BLOODGUILT

The theme of bloodguilt is tightly woven into the fabric of biblical morality. Infanticide was particularly offensive to God, a defilement of the land. It resulted in the most dire of consequences, for the willing parents and their descendants, for the community that failed to punish the guilty ones, for the land and nation, and for God's relationship with His people. "When Noah got off the boat, in Genesis chapter nine, the only negative thing God warned him about was bloodshed"[1]

> "And from each man too, I will demand an accounting for the life of his fellow man. Whoever sheds the blood of man, by man shall his blood be shed; for in the image of God had God made man."
> *Genesis 9:5-6*

> [Losing in battle, the king of Moab], took his firstborn son, who was to succeed him as king, and offered him as a sacrifice on the city wall. The fury against Israel was great; they withdrew and returned to their own land." *2 Kings 3:26-27*

A particularly horrific truth is contained in the above account. In the economics of spiritual warfare, blood sacrifice trumps everything. Here's the story: God's army has victory in their grasp. The king of Moab is desperate. Chemosh, the national god, delights in human sacrifice. The crown prince is slain and presented as a burnt offering to Chemosh. We are left to speculate the nature of the "fury against Israel" that the act engendered. Social psychologists might suggest that the emotional reaction to their king's desperate act prompted his troops to renew the battle with super-human vigor. Beyond that, however, is the possibility that the shedding of innocent blood unleashed in the spiritual realm a hoard of diabolical furies [Frank Peretti could make this come alive for us]. The fact remains: The innocent blood of one man's child changed the course of battle. God's army packed it in and went home.

In the modernist war between faith and secularity, many crucial battles have been fought with mixed results: prohibition, evolutionary science, prayer in schools, church-and-state, and so forth. But the abortion battle has been the Moab for the Church. Prior to 1973 it was all a "My daddy is tougher than your daddy" debate. With *Roe v. Wade* the secularists put it all on the line: *We'll bet you 4000 mangled babies a day that Darwin was right!* History may report that a flustered Church essentially cashed in its chips and skulked back home in the dark.

> Do not pollute the land where you are. Bloodshed pollutes the land, and atonement cannot be made for the land on which blood has been shed, except by the blood of the one who shed it. Do not defile the land where you live and where I dwell, for I, the Lord, dwell among the Israelites.
> *Numbers 35:33-34*

> [Nathan to David, for God, about the arranged death of Uriah]: "You struck down Uriah the Hittite with the sword and took his wife to be your own. You killed him with the sword of the Ammonites. Now, therefore the sword will never depart from your house, because you despised Me and took the wife of Uriah..." *2 Samuel 12:9-12*

King David's tragic tale reveals a couple of truths: The guilt remains even when one gets someone else to do the killing, and the consequences are far-reaching and permanent. Note that the forgiveness that followed David's confession did not eliminate the moral debt:

> Then David said to Nathan, "I have sinned against the Lord." Nathan replied, "The Lord has taken away your sin. You are not going to die. But because by doing this you have made the enemies of the Lord show utter contempt, the son born to you will die." ...on the seventh day the child died. *2 Samuel 12:13-14, 18*

The guilt of mothers and fathers who have aborted their children is a problem for society, for the Church, and for them as individuals and marriage partners. Jody Clemens of Open Arms, a ministry to women post-abortion, in Columbia, Missouri, gets to the root of the dilemma: "I had been told by many in the pro-life movement, and wanted to believe it, that I was the second victim of abortion. What that did to me was not bring me to a point of humility and brokenness before the Lord. It appeased my conscience because I did not have to admit to myself the depravity of my own heart that I could go to the depths of taking the life of my own child"[2]

Biblically, there is no alternative to the fact that people who consent to the killing of their children are guilty in God's eyes. Circumstances may mitigate the degree of culpability – civil laws for involuntary manslaughter and justifiable homicide are based in the Bible, after all – but no one who skips repentance and confession to God should presume to receive His forgiveness. Saint Augustine's words are timeless:

SCOPE and FOCUS
I. CONVICTIONS
II. PRETEXTS
III. MANDATE
Biblical Authority
Pro-Abortion View
Pro-Life View
Child-killing
The Nations
God's People
Bloodguilt
Judgment
Repentance
Restoration
Roles of a Disciple
Alien & Pilgrim within God's Creation
Theologian, revealing Divine Design
Priest, proclaiming God's Commandments
Prophet, crying out for Godly Justice
Loving Neighbor, displaying Virtue
Zealot, fighting for Universal Truths
Evangelist, witnessing to our Accountability
IV. LEGACY
V. ABORTIVE LINKS
VI. DILEMMA
VII. DESTINY

"Why do I tell these things? It is that I myself and whoever else reads them may realize from what great depths we must cry unto you. And what is closer to your ears than a contrite heart and a life of faith?"[3]

...There was a famine for three successive years; so David sought the face of the Lord. The Lord said, "It is on account of Saul and his bloodstained house... because he put the Gibeonites to death..." [after seven of Saul's descendants were killed, then] *God answered prayer in behalf of the land.* *2 Samuel 21:1, 6, 14*

Curtis Blair says, "The Old Testament reveals that God always gave special regard to a nation's practice of shedding innocent blood. Those nations which did such things received warning of a coming bloodshed – one that would be their own!"[4]

They mingled with the nations and adopted their customs. They worshipped their idols, which became a snare to them. They sacrificed their sons and their daughters to demons. They shed innocent blood, the blood of their sons and daughters... and the land was desecrated by their blood. *Psalm 106:35-38*

e. JUDGMENT & WRATH

In the Bible, God's judgment was always certain to fall as a consequence of infanticide. Punishment was delivered by famine, disaster, the sword and pestilence. "We modernist Christians make the mistake of refusing to truly believe in divine judgments in history and the pending judgment of our own American nation"[5]

What right have you to recite My laws or take My covenant on your lips? You hate My instruction and cast My words behind you... These things you have done and I kept silent... consider this, you who forget God, or I will tear you to pieces, with none to rescue. *Psalm 50:16-22*

God says: "I cannot stand your assemblies... Away with the noise of your songs! I will not listen to the music of your harps. But let justice roll on like a river, righteousness like a never-failing stream!" *Amos 5:21-24*

The days are coming when I will send a famine through the land... A famine of hearing the words of the Lord. Men will stagger from sea to sea and wander from north to east, searching for the word of the Lord, but they will not find it. *Amos 8:11-12*

I will give you over to ruin and your people to derision... The day of your watchmen has come, the day God visits you. Now is the time of their confusion. *Micah 6:16; 7:4*

1 Randall Terry, "If You Believe..." cassette.
2 *Life Advocate*, 5/'94, 25.
3 Augustine, *Confessions*, 67.
4 *Life Advocate*, 2/'94, 27.
5 Michael Bray, 84.

They rejected His decrees and the covenant... they sacrificed their sons and daughters in the fire... Therefore the Lord rejected all the people of Israel; He afflicted them and gave them into the hands of plunderers, until He thrust them from His presence. *2 Kings 17:15-20*

...This city has so aroused My anger and wrath that I must remove it from My sight... They built high places for Baal... to sacrifice their sons and daughters to Molech. *Jeremiah 32:31, 35*

...this [by sexual sins and child sacrifice] *is how the nations that I am going to drive out before you became defiled... and if you defile the land, it will vomit you out as it vomited out the nations that were before you.* *Leviticus 18:24-25, 28*

I will give you over to bloodshed and it will pursue you. Since you did not hate bloodshed, bloodshed will pursue you. *Ezekiel 35:6*

Preaching about the wrath of God is very much out of fashion, but this reflects a change in man's view, not necessarily God's. "To an age which has unashamedly sold itself to the gods of greed, pride, sex, and self-will, the Church mumbles on about God's kindness, but says virtually nothing about His judgment"[1]

Israel has sinned... that is why the Israelites cannot stand against their enemies; they turn their backs and run because they have been made liable to destruction. I will not be with you any more unless you destroy whatever among you is devoted to destruction. *Joshua 7:11-12*

Their silver and gold will not be able to save them... I will turn My face away and robbers will enter and desecrate My treasured place... Because the land is full of bloodshed and the city is full of violence... teaching of the law by the priest will be lost... By their own standards I will judge them. *Ezekiel 7:19-27*

[God's enemies boast:] *"We have made a lie our refuge and falsehood our hiding place."* [God says to them:] *"Your covenant with death will be annulled; your agreement with the grave will not stand..." When the overwhelming scourge sweeps by, you will be beaten down by it.* *Isaiah 28:15, 18*

W.E.B. DuBois spoke out about the failure of most Christians to lead – or even follow – in the abolition of slavery, but he could as accurately have been criticizing today's Christian acquiescence to abortion: "There is always a certain glamour about the idea of a nation rising up to crush an evil simply because it is wrong. Unfortunately, this can seldom be realized in real life, for the very existence of the evil usually argues a moral weakness in the very place where extraordinary moral strength is called for"[2] Pro-life activists chide their own with, "The abortuaries remain open by permission of the churches of the neighborhood"[3]

Ephraim's glory will fly away like a bird – no birth, no pregnancy, no conception... Ephraim will bring out their children to the slayer... What will You give them? Wombs that miscarry and breasts that are dry... because of all their wickedness... *Hosea 9:11-15*

O Lord God almighty, how long will Your anger smolder against the prayers of Your people...? Our enemies mock us. *Psalm 80:4, 6*

Another king will arise... He will speak against the Most High and oppress His saints and try to change the set times and the laws. The saints will be handed over to him for a time... *Daniel 7:24-25*

As Operation Rescue neared the zenith of what the media and the authorities would allow, founder Randall Terry observed, "There are two types of judgment: the judgment unto restoration, or judgment unto annihilation. Judah was judged and then restored... but the ten tribes were just annihilated... So the question is not, Will America be judged and will the church in America be judged? The question is, Will we be judged and then restored, or will we just be completely wiped out? ...I don't know the answer... [with reference to German Christian complacency about Hitler:] What the church tolerates today, she may be despised for tomorrow"[4]

Martin Niemoller's wisdom is widely published... and seldom applied: "In Germany they came first for the Communists, and I didn't speak up because I wasn't a Communist. Then they came for the Jews, and I didn't speak up because I wasn't a Jew. Then they came for the trade unionists, and I didn't speak up because I wasn't a trade unionist. Then the came for the Catholics, and I didn't speak up because I was a Protestant. Then they came for me, and by that time no one was left to speak up"[5]

We Evangelical Christians are clearly in denial about what the Bible says about child-killing, blood-guilt and judgment. Who knows what sort of "watchman" it would take, and what kind of alarm would call God's army to muster. But the Bible abounds with history we insist on repeating.

Prepare for war! Rouse the warriors! ...Beat your plowshares into swords and your pruning hooks into spears. Let the weakling say, "I am strong!" ...Multitudes, multitudes in the valley of decision! *Joel 3:9-10, 14*

No doubt a multitude *will* rise up – but only to notify this researcher that the scriptural order is exactly reversed in *Isaiah* [2:4] and *Micah* [4:3]. Because those who presume to be "the Church" choose to major in minor things, preferring [as any *rational* person would] the grandstand to the arena, they will be unfazed by the fact that "Until the time of Constantine, Christians were the focus of ten major periods of persecution. Jerome stated that at the height of one persecution, any day in the year saw five thousand believers martyred for their faith"[6]

SCOPE and FOCUS
I. CONVICTIONS
II. PRETEXTS
III. MANDATE
Biblical Authority
Pro-Abortion View
Pro-Life View
Child-killing
The Nations
God's People
Bloodguilt
Judgment
Repentance
Restoration
Roles of a Disciple
Alien & Pilgrim
Theologian
Priest
Prophet
Loving Neighbor
Zealot
Evangelist
IV. LEGACY
V. ABORTIVE LINKS
VI. DILEMMA
VII. DESTINY

There will be terrible times in the last days. People will be lovers of themselves, lovers of money... unholy, without love... without self-control... lovers of pleasure rather than lovers of God – having the form of godliness but denying its power. Have nothing to do with them... Everyone who wants to live a godly life in Christ Jesus will be persecuted. 2 Timothy 3:1-5, 12

Thoreau's speech about the martyrdom of John Brown echoed the pre-Constantinian apologist's "the blood of the martyrs is seed" and declared, "...when you plant, or bury, a hero in his field, a crop of heroes is sure to spring up. This is a seed of such force and vitality, that it does not ask our leave to germinate"[7]

Amy Carmichael, the rescuer of child temple prostitutes in India, laid it all on the line: "...our Master has never promised us success. He demands obedience. He expects faithfulness. Results are His concern, not ours. And our reputation is a matter of no consequence at all"[8] Miss Carmichael also said, "...the hallmark of the true missionary... is refusal to be weakened or hardened or soured or made hopeless by disappointment"[9] Can it be that someone has stolen from our *Declaration of Independence* – or perhaps just from our vocabularies and our wills – the line that said "We mutually pledge to each other our lives, our fortunes, and our sacred honor"?

f. REPENTANCE & OBEDIENCE

The only corrective for the bloodguilt of infanticide is the repentance and obedience of God's people.

If a man is found slain, lying in a field... and it is not known who killed him... Then all the elders of the town nearest the body... shall declare, "Our hands did not shed this blood, nor did our eyes see it done. Accept this atonement for your people Israel... and do not hold your people guilty of the blood of an innocent man... Deuteronomy 21:1, 6, 7-8

Randall Terry, founder of Operation Rescue, said of the above passage, "We cannot pray that prayer. We share in the guilt of the blood; it's on our hands just as much as it is on the rest of the nation's because we *can* go to these death camps... [we *have* seen, we *do* know]"[10]

When you spread out your hands in prayer, I will hide my eyes from you; even if you offer many prayers, I will not listen. Your hands are full of blood... Stop doing wrong, learn to do right! Seek justice, encourage the oppressed. Defend the cause of the fatherless, plead the case of the widow. Isaiah 1:15-17

Echoes of the words of William Penn should resonate in patriot hearts today: "Always put justice above the law, and when the law is unjust challenge it directly"[11]

Because they have rebelled against their God their little ones will be dashed to the ground, their pregnant women ripped open. Return, O Israel, to the Lord your God. Your sins have been your downfall! Take words with you and return to the Lord. Hosea 13:16 – 14:2

Rescue those being led away to death; hold back those staggering toward slaughter. Proverbs 24:11

Why are you silent while the wicked swallow up those more righteous than themselves? You have made men like fish in the sea... the wicked foe pulls all of them up by hooks... By his net he lives in luxury and enjoys the choicest food. Is he to keep on emptying his net, destroying nations without mercy? Habakkuk 1:13-17

1 J.I. Packer, *Knowing God*, 134, quoted by Bray, 152.
2 W.E.B. duBois, *The Suppression of the African Slave-Trade to the United States of America, 1638-1870*, 195.
3 Michael Bray, 18.
4 Randall Terry, "If You Believe" cassette.
5 Niemoller, in Chuck Colson, 125.
6 Randall Terry, *Operation Rescue*, 100. [Some of us are convinced that Ronald Reagan was our last Constantine, and that persecution awaits those who will take Christian discipleship seriously.]
7 Howard-Johnson, 109; Michael Bray, 89-90.
8 Terry, *Operation Rescue*, 70.
9 Terry, *Operaton Rescue*, 68.
10 Randall Terry, "If You Believe" cassette.
11 *Life Advocate*, 2/'94, 5.

Saint Augustine said, "When God commands something contrary to the customs or laws of a people, it must be done, even if it had never been done before; if it has been neglected, it must be restored; and if it has never been established, it must be established."[1]

[God asks:] *Who will rise up for Me against the wicked? Who will take a stand for Me against evil-doers? ...Can a corrupt throne be allied with you – one that brings on misery by its decrees? They band together against the righteous and condemn the innocent to death.*
Psalm 94:16, 20-21

Is not this the kind of fasting I have chosen: to loose the chains of injustice and untie the cords of the yoke, to set the oppressed free and break every yoke? *Isaiah 58:6*

...whatever you did for one of the least of these brothers of mine, you did for me.
Matthew 25:40

Jesus went out as usual to the Mount of Olives... [To His disciples He said:] *"Pray that you will not fall into temptation."* [The Mount of Olives was, or was near, the high place Solomon built for Molech – 1 Kings 11:7-8] *Luke 22:39-40*

[Solomon's prayer:] *"When they sin... if they have a change of heart... repent... plead with You... If they turn back to You with all their heart and soul... then... hear their prayer and their pleas, and uphold their cause. And forgive Your people who have sinned against You."*
2 Chronicles 6:36-39

...If My people who are called by My name will humble themselves and pray and seek My face and turn from their wicked ways, then I will hear from heaven and will forgive their sin and will heal their land. *2 Chronicles 7:14*

[You, God] *have shaken the land and torn it open... You have shown Your people desperate times... But for those who fear You, You have raised a banner to be unfurled against the bow... God has spoken from His sanctuary: "Who will bring Me to the fortified city?"* *Psalm 60: 2-6, 9*

"Dietrich Bonhoeffer, a young German pastor who lived during the rise and fall of the third Reich... warned... rebuked... dissented... ran an illegal pastoral training school... smuggled Jews to safety and freedom, and finally was martyred for his work against Hitler about one week before the war ended."[2]

Bonhoeffer's obedience to God included being part of a nearly-successful plot to assassinate Hitler. William Purcell tells us, "As it happened, Bonhoeffer was in America when war came. He could have remained there. But he chose to return, and because of this decision he was to die. He became involved in the plot, in which many of the finest Germans were concerned, to kill Hitler."[3] As John Whitehead said in another context, "Only individual conscience, sincerity, and, most importantly, obedience to the Higher Law can prescribe where those boundaries are..."[4]

This is what you are to do to them [godless nations]: *break down their altars, smash their sacred stones, cut down their Asherah poles and burn their idols in the fire.* *Deuteronomy 7:5*

This researcher has a particular fondness for Gideon. There are many practical truths in his adventure stories, but most exciting of all is this: At some point in his life Gideon had perhaps heard *Deuteronomy 7* read from an old scroll. He listened, and he remembered what it said. But not only that. He did it! The verse tucked away in his brain was retrieved by God in the fullness of time, and,

In the morning when the men of the town got up, there was Baal's altar, demolished, with the Asherah pole beside it cut down and the second bull sacrificed on the newly built altar! They asked each other, "Who did this?" When they carefully investigated, they were told, "Gideon..." *Judges 6:28-29*

Hezekiah did what was right... He removed the high places, smashed the sacred stones and cut down the Asherah poles. He broke into pieces the bronze snake... Hezekiah trusted in the Lord... held fast to the Lord... He kept the commands the Lord had given Moses. *2 Kings 18:1-6*

"The Lord is with you when you are with Him..." When [the king of Judah] *Asa heard these words... he removed the detestable idols... repaired the altar... assembled the people...* [All who would not seek the Lord were to be put to death!] *They took an oath... rejoiced... because they had sworn it wholeheartedly. They sought God eagerly, and He was found by them.*
2 Chronicles 15:2, 8-15

[A great revival]: *Josiah desecrated Topeth... so no one could use it to sacrifice his son or daughter in the fire to Molech... He also desecrated the high places that were east of Jerusalem... and slaughtered all the priests of those high places on the altars.* *2 Kings 23:10, 13, 20*

SCOPE and FOCUS
I. CONVICTIONS
II. PRETEXTS
III. MANDATE
Biblical Authority
Pro-Abortion View
Pro-Life View
Child-killing
The Nations
God's People
Bloodguilt
Judgment
Repentance
Restoration
Roles of a Disciple
Alien & Pilgrim within God's Creation
Theologian, revealing Divine Design
Priest, proclaiming God's Commandments
Prophet, crying out for Godly Justice
Loving Neighbor, displaying Virtue
Zealot, fighting for Universal Truths
Evangelist, witnessing to our Accountability
IV. LEGACY
V. ABORTIVE LINKS
VI. DILEMMA
VII. DESTINY

1 Augustine, *Confessions*, 87.
2 Randall Terry, *Operation Rescue*, 33.
3 William Purcell, *Martyrs of Our Time*, 83.
4 John Whitehead, *Right to Picket*, 3.
5 William Purcell, 83.
6 Terry, "If You Believe" cassette.
7 Bandow, 23-24.

"When Bonhoeffer was in Geneva at the outset of the war he was asked what it was which he prayed for in those times. He replied: 'If you want to know the truth, I pray for the defeat of my nation, for I believe that that is the only way to pay for all the suffering which my country has caused in the world.'"[5]

"There reaches a point when the blood cries from the ground, and God says, 'Enough!' And even though Josiah was the greatest king Judah had ever had [he instituted great reforms], God sent a prophet and said, 'It's too late, Josiah.' And part of it was because it was a top-down repentance, Josiah was trying to institute reform and the people weren't really repenting... WE are in grave danger as a nation..."[6]

[Mordecai to Esther:] *"Who knows but that you have come to royal position for such a time as this?"* [Esther's reply:] *"I will go to the king, even though it is against the law. And if I perish, I perish."* *Esther 4:14-16*

g. RESTORATION

The return of harmony with God and of peace to the land was never guaranteed. Doug Bandow is convinced that ""Believers have a biblical responsibility to apply their beliefs in their civic as well as private lives. An important aspect of that duty is simply responding to attacks from an increasingly hostile secular state"[7]

Defend the cause of the weak and fatherless; maintain the rights of the poor and oppressed. Rescue the weak and needy; deliver them from the hand of the wicked. *Psalm 82:3-4*

Let this be written for a future generation, that a people not yet created may praise the Lord: "The Lord looked down from His sanctuary on high... to hear the groans of the prisoners and release those condemned to death." *Psalm 102:18-20*

He will deliver the needy who cry out, the afflicted who have no one to help. He will take pity on the weak... and save the needy from death. He will rescue them from oppression and violence, for precious is their blood in His sight. *Psalm 72:12-14*

Why should the nations say, "Where is their God?" Before our eyes, make known among the nations that You avenge the outpoured blood of Your servants. May the groans of the prisoners come before You; by the strength of Your arm preserve those condemned to die. *Psalm 79:10-11*

Hate evil, love good; maintain justice in the courts... Why do you long for the day of the Lord? That day will be darkness, not light. It will be as though a man fled from a lion, only to meet a bear, as though he entered his house and rested his hand on the wall only to have a snake bite him. *Amos 5:15, 18-19*

Our struggle is not against flesh and blood, but against the rulers, against the authorities, against the powers of this dark world and against the spiritual forces of evil in the heavenly realms. ***Ephesians 6:12***

"When the church isn't being persecuted, it is being corrupted"[1]

–Chuck Colson

SCOPE and FOCUS
I. CONVICTIONS
II. PRETEXTS
III. MANDATE
Biblical Authority
Pro-Abortion View
Pro-Life View
Child-killing
The Nations
God's People
Bloodguilt
Judgment
Repentance
Restoration
Roles of a Disciple
Alien & Pilgrim within God's Creation
Theologian, revealing Divine Design
Priest, proclaiming God's Commandments
Prophet, crying out for Godly Justice
Loving Neighbor, displaying Virtue
Zealot, fighting for Universal Truths
Evangelist, witnessing to our Accountability
IV. LEGACY
V. ABORTIVE LINKS
VI. DILEMMA
VII. DESTINY

Restoration, for the Church in America, will never be achieved without persecution, repentance, discipline, hardship, sacrifice and loss.

[The Lord, to Rehoboam, through Shemaiah:] *"Since they have humbled themselves, ...My wrath will not be poured out on Jerusalem through Shishak* [king of Egypt]. *They will, however, become subject to him, so that they may learn the difference between serving Me and serving the kings of other lands."* *2 Chronicles 12:7-8*

As a shepherd saves from the lion's mouth only two leg bones or a piece of an ear, so will the Israelites be saved. *Amos 3:12*

He [Jesus] *was with wild animals, and angels attended Him.* *Mark 1:13*

"Don't be afraid," Elisha answered. "Those who are with us are more than those who are with them..." The Lord opened the servant's eyes, and he looked and saw the hills full of horses and chariots of fire all around Elisha. *2 Kings 6:16-17*

Dr. Martin Luther King Jr. provided inspiration for all: "Man is not a helpless drifter in the river of existence, but an active agent in the unfolding events by which he is surrounded."[2]

The advice of 17th century bishop St. Francis de Sales was "Pray as though everything depends on God. Work as though everything depends on you."[3] He was certainly a brother to C.S. Lewis, who said, "The greatest thing is to be found at one's post as a child of God, living each day as though it were our last, but planning as though our world might last a hundred years."[4]

"When Adoniram Judson saw his missionary work in Burma destroyed, his presses smashed, his converts killed or scattered, and he himself in a filthy dungeon, his captors taunted him, asking, 'What are your prospects now?' Judson answered, 'As bright as the promises of God!'"[5]

Pope John Paul II, addressing a large group of Americans in Denver, Colorado, warned us all,

"Woe to you if you do not succeed in defending life."[6]

1 Charles Colson, 113.
2 King, in Purcell, page v.
3 De Sales, in Ball, 5.
4 Lewis, in Colson, 253.
5 James Draper, *If the Foundations be Destroyed*, 174.
6 *Life Advocate*, 2/'94, 5.
7 Stringfellow, by Hoffmeier, 133.
8 In Thomas Hilgers, *Abortion and Social Justice*, page x.
9 James Atkinson, *Church and State Under God*, 36.
10 Bandow, 1.

It was He who gave some to be apostles... prophets... evangelists... pastors... teachers... to prepare God's people for works of service. Ephesians 4:11-12

B. The Roles of a Biblical Disciple

We have explored the humanistic world view assumptions which foment the clashes of conviction which have made "abortion rights" the focal point of our curent culture war. Having examined the biblical mandate for a Christianity that is radically pro-life, we should now investigate the ways in which Christians, both individually and communally as members of the Body of Christ, should be impacting our culture. We shall see that Stewards are: Pilgrims and Aliens on earth, demonstrating the primacy of the Creation conviction over evolutionary Accident theories; Theologians who defend Divine Design against allegations that Accident can explain life; Pious Priests who proclaim God's holy Commandments to be a higher source of law than man's Positivism; Prophets crying out for Justice for the multitudes who are abused by Pragmatic structures and systems; Loving Neighbors exemplifying Virtue in contrast to the Pleasure and Pain measure of the good life; Zealots fighting to uphold Universal Truths against the flood of Relativism; Evangelists witnessing to human Accountability before God in the face of claims of individual Autonomy.

1. Pilgrim & Alien
Stewardship of the Creation conviction

William Stringfellow wrote that the "most obstinate misconception associated with the gospel of Jesus Christ is that the gospel is welcome in this world."[7] In the second century, the *Epistle to Diognetus* revealed that Christians "live in their own countries, but only as sojourners. They have a share in everything as citizens, and endure everything as aliens. Every foreign land is their fatherland, and yet for them every fatherland is a foreign land."[8]

Atkinson is one of many who hold that when the Roman persecution of Christians ended in the fourth century, Christianity became the state religion "at tremendous cost to the spiritual integrity of the church and therefore to its message and function. It could be argued (and has been) that it has never been right since, except for some rare moment of prophetic insight and witness on the small scale."[9]

"Each man's life is but a breath. Man is a mere phantom as he goes to and fro... I dwell with you as an alien, a stranger, as all my fathers were."

Psalm 39:5, 12, also 1 Peter 2:11

Surely we are to be like Paul who confronted others with the truth, and who, when they opposed him and became abusive, left and went to the house next door [Acts 18:6-7]. He reminds us that "our citizenship is in heaven" [Philippians 3:18-20], and warns us,

Do not be yoked together with unbelievers... We are the temple of the living God. As God has said, "I will live with them and walk among them... Therefore come out of them and be separate."

2 Corinthians 6:14, 16-17

Doug Bandow warns of the danger of failing to maintain our spiritual distance from the world: "Unfortunately, Christianity, no less than any other religion, has often allied itself with the governments of its day... The closer the relationship of church and state, the more spiritualy irrelevant and institutionally fractured the Body of Christ..."[10] Tragically, parishioners lulled by the gentle words of Jesus often are startled when reminded that he also said:

I have come to bring fire on the earth, and how I wish it were already kindled! ...Do you think I came to bring peace on earth? No, I tell you, but division. Luke 12:49,51

The Master warns us: *If you belonged to the world, it would love you as its own. As it is, you do not belong to the world, but I have chosen you out of the world. That is why the world hates you.* John 15:19

We are the ones who are called to bear the torch that was carried in the days of Nehemiah: *All who separated themselves from the neighboring peoples for the sake of the law of God... all these now join their brothers the nobles, and bind themselves with a curse and an oath to follow the law of God.*

Nehemiah 10:28-29

Let us follow in the footsteps of Paul, who said: *I press on to take hold of that for which Christ Jesus took hold of me... Forgetting what is behind and straining toward what is ahead, I press on toward the goal... God has called me heavenward.* Philippians 3:12-14

"It is a general law of human society for men to obey their rulers – how much more must God, ruler of all creation, be obeyed without hesitation in whatever he imposes upon it! Just as among the authorities in human society the greater authority is set above the lesser in the order of obedience, so God stands above all others."[1] –Saint Augustine

2. Theologian
Stewardship of the Design conviction

"What the problem has been for the past forty or fifty years in American Christendom is that Christianity has been reduced to a religion of doctrine instead of duty and behavior. Look at Matthew 25: Judgment of sheep and goats... you fed... you clothed... you visited... It's based upon our actions."[2]

"We have imbibed some bad theology. We have glanced at Jesus through the glasses of the New Testament and seen the brief example of the Lamb who came to be slain. And we have mistaken His passive, sacrificial role for the norm of Christian life... We have defined His nature on the basis of a narrow mission of Christ on earth..."[3]

We need to heed this warning from C. Ben Mitchell: "Unless denominational leadership... recaptures the vision for theological instruction in the local church, the battle for the Christian world view will be lost, perhaps for generations to come. Furthermore, Christians will be unable to bring scriptural truth to bear on bioethical dilemmas... We will be aiding and abetting the assault on human life!"[4]

The urgent need for sound biblical theology is underscored by Joseph Foreman: "It is not enough to determine whether or not the *world* permits something. We have to ask whether God allows *us* to permit it... The day may come when we are in danger of being too intolerant of child-killers. Until then, what must be explained is why we are so cooperative with them."[5]

Bray pinpoints the fallacy of liberal secularized theology: "Modernist, liberation theologians have argued for [foreign, political] revolution to secure 'human rights' with no vision for the establishment of true justice [under] the law of God."[6]

The prophecies of Amos apply well to our modern plight: *The days are coming when I will send a famine through the land... A famine of hearing the words of the Lord. Men will stagger from sea to sea and wander from north to east, searching for the word of the Lord, but they will not find it.*

Amos 8:11-12

Paul's words convict the complacent: *Continue to work out your salvation with fear and trembling, for it is God who works in you to will and to act according to His good purpose.*

Philippians 2:12-13

The true theologians among us today must be recognized as those who wear the mantle of Elijah, challenging: *How long will you waver between two opinions? If the Lord is God, follow him; but if Baal is god, follow him.* *I Kings 18:21*

Let us leave the elementary teachings about Christ and go on to maturity... Enlightened... we have tasted the heavenly gift, have shared in the Holy Spirit, and have tasted the goodness of the word of God, and the powers of the coming age.

Hebrews 6:1-5

There is great counsel in the book of Joshua: *Do not let this book of the law depart from your mouth; meditate on it day and night, so that you may be careful to do everything written in it.*

Joshua 1:8

Likewise: *These commandments that I give you today are to be upon your hearts... Talk about them when you sit... walk... lie down... get up. Tie... bind them on your foreheads. Write them on the doorframes...* *Dueteronomy 6:6-9*

Paul must have the last word on the importance of sound theology: *All scripture is God-breathed and is useful for teaching, rebuking, correcting and training in righteousness, so that the man of God may be thoroughly equipped for every good work.*

2 Timothy 3:16-17

SCOPE and FOCUS
I. CONVICTIONS
II. PRETEXTS
III. MANDATE
Biblical Authority
Pro-Abortion View
Pro-Life View
Child-killing
The Nations
God's People
Bloodguilt
Judgment
Repentance
Restoration
Roles of a Disciple
Alien & Pilgrim within God's Creation
Theologian, revealing Divine Design
Priest, proclaiming God's Commandments
Prophet, crying out for Godly Justice
Loving Neighbor, displaying Virtue
Zealot, fighting for Universal Truths
Evangelist, witnessing to our Accountability
IV. LEGACY
V. ABORTIVE LINKS
VI. DILEMMA
VII. DESTINY

Written in 1956:

"If the church is to help in restoring the world to moral sanity, there must first be revolt and recovery of moral sanity within the church."[7]

–Bernard Iddings Bell

3. Pious Priest

Stewardship of the Commandments conviction

The name taken by the Salvation Army seems outdated to many people today, probably because we have been conditioned to view Jesus as our best friend or "co-pilot," rather than our Commander-in-Chief. Pastor-priests must not be perceived as leaders of pep rallies for God but recruiters, enlisting soldiers for spiritual combat.

When John Brown was hanged, ending his plan to free slaves by force, the clearest voice raised was not a pastor's but that of Henry David Thoreau: "Newspaper editors argue that it is a proof of [John Brown's] insanity that he thought he was appointed to do this work which he did... They talk as if it were impossible that a man could be 'divinely appointed' in these days to do any work whatever; as if vows and religion were out of date... They talk as if a man's death were a failure, and his continued life, be it of whatever character, were a success... What shall we think of a government to which all the truly brave and just men in the land are enemies, standing between it and those who it oppresses? A government that pretends to be Christian and crucifies a million Christs every day!"[8]

We are told that "The modernist recoils in horror when someone presumes to have been inspired or actually 'called' by God to a given task... there is a low tolerance for people who claim to be led by God to do anything extraordinary. Joan of Arc's biographer says: 'In our own day, Joan of Arc would probably be regarded as deranged.'"[9]

One lasting result of abortion clinic Rescues, Foreman tells us, is that they, "showed people that saving a baby's life is as normal and expected a part of a Christian life as church attendance, prayer, and Bible reading,"[10] and that, "More pastors were arrested with [Operation Rescue] than with any other organization in the history of this country."[11]

Rescue was controversial, and increasingly costly. It was no surprise that Rescuers were intimidated and chilled by ever-longer jail sentences and bigger fines, and by fear of reprisal from secular and governmental employers. When it comes to pastors generally, however, those [who are paid full time to act on the commandments of God-alone] were often even less likely than their parishioners to venture into Rescue, or were frequently the first to abandon that godly enterprise.

Pastors who Rescued – or who even acknowledged biblical support for the act of Rescuing – often paid a penalty: in attendance, in contributions, some even being censured or fired. Most readers will be shocked to learn that the government that supposedly guarantees freedoms of religion and of speech took action in 1990 to muzzle pastors in their own pulpits: a U.S. District Judge in New York issued an injunction against "Project Rescue and member ministers of the Western New York Pro-Life Clergy Council, who preach in support of rescue missions at abortion clinics. The injunction specifically prohibited these ministers from quoting Proverbs 24:11 ['Rescue those being dragged to the slaughter...'], even when the verse would not be used in conjunction with a sermon on rescues. Any mention whatever of this scripture passage would mean an immediate $10,000 fine."[12]

1 Augustine, *Confessions*, 88.
2 Randall Terry, cassette.
3 Michael Bray, 155.
4 Mitchell, in Kilner, *Bioethics...*, 132.
5 Foreman, 59.
6 Michael Bray, 162.
7 Bell, *Crowd Culture*, 1956, 67, quoted by Roche.
8 Thoreau, by Bray, 93.
9 Bray, 84.
10 Joseph Foreman, 18-9.
11 Foreman, 54.
12 Brian Clowes, pages 14.11 to 14.12.

The heart of a pastor's dilemma is that his vocation is also his job. Some even call him an "entrepreneurial franchisee." Setting aside the cynicism, it is true that the clergyman with the purest motives for biblical ministry must still keep an eye on the parish's bottom line, for the most godly programs seem only to be viable so long as a satisfied congregation attends and contributes.

As long ago as 1941, Elton Trueblood was warning that it is "the good opinion of his fellow Christians which a Christian leader naturally most covets."[1]

In the Sixties, Robert Raines shared the observation that "Most congregations look to their ministers to provide the spiritual life of the church, depending upon them, in a sense, to pre-digest the teachings of Christ and spoonfeed the more palatable portions to the passive pew-sitter."[2]

By 1988, George Grant was sounding the alarm: "Part of the reason the church is in such bondage today is that it has failed to preach the truth. Instead of nurturing God's People with the rich truths of practical Biblical instruction, we have indulged in theological junk food..."[3]

Also in 1988, Randall Terry gave a warning to rescuers which is timeless in the context of any Christian ministry, whether it be of the paid or tentmaking variety: "There is *no life*, no life-giving power, in the abortion battle. If you make abortion your life focus, you will die... We cannot warn against this snare enough. Your heart must be filled with a love for Jesus more than a hatred for child killing. Your mind must focus on thoughts of Christ... If we put the work first in our hearts instead of Christ, it becomes idolatry. God will not tolerate idolatry even when the idol is ministry."[4]

Another leader of Rescues, Pastor Matt Trewhella, says,

"When God calls us to defend the innocent, He is simply calling us to do what He has always called us to, namely, to be willing to give up our agendas and our goals to follow Him."[5]

As we consider the divine calling of pastor-priests to declare and uphold God's Commandments, and come to terms with the incessant pressure to avoid controversy and painful experiences, the subject of post-abortive Christian women is paramount. Michael Bray identifies this as an arena in which sensitivity and compassion have obscured God's commandments and scriptural theology. He calls it a case of "bad doctrine," centered in "the victim status bestowed upon aborting or 'post-abortion' women... Under pressure to respond to accusations that prolifers cared only for the baby, the prolife movement [along with most prolife pastors] walked into a public relations trap... Abortion on the part of the woman became more mistake than murder."[6]

He goes on to say that "women who aborted their children were not duly charged with murder. They were denied, we might say, the biblical grieving process which involves a true confession. A true confession results in true forgiveness and reconciliation... There have always been acknowledged 'degrees of murder' – but the guilt of murder in some degree ought to be proclaimed without apology by those who would declare the truth."[7]

Dawn Stover of Advocates for Life Ministries agrees. In reporting on "healing services," conducted by eight pro-abortion women pastors, which offered "words of comfort" and "statements of acceptance" along with candle-light prayers and singing, but devoid of biblical confession, repentance or forgiveness, Dawn says "These 'pastors' are just salving the conscience of women who have aborted their children. They're paving their road to hell with false comfort."[8]

The testimony of Jody Clemens, quoted earlier [page 86] is worth reading again: "I had been told by many in the pro-life movement, and wanted to believe it, that I was the second victim of abortion. What that did to me was not bring me to a point of humility and brokenness before the Lord. It appeased my conscience because I did not have to admit to myself the depravity of my own heart that I could go to the depths of taking the life of my own child."[9]

Repentance is not only mandatory for women who have aborted their children. It is a normal experience of life for every Christian, especially those of us who share in the indictment that the Church has failed, miserably, to respond biblically to legalized abortion.

SCOPE and FOCUS
I. CONVICTIONS
II. PRETEXTS
III. MANDATE
Biblical Authority
Pro-Abortion View
Pro-Life View
Child-killing
The Nations
God's People
Bloodguilt
Judgment
Repentance
Restoration
Roles of a Disciple
Alien & Pilgrim within God's Creation
Theologian, revealing Divine Design
Priest, proclaiming God's Commandments
Prophet, crying out for Godly Justice
Loving Neighbor, displaying Virtue
Zealot, fighting for Universal Truths
Evangelist, witnessing to our Accountability
IV. LEGACY
V. ABORTIVE LINKS
VI. DILEMMA
VII. DESTINY

In writing *What's Wrong with the World* in 1910, G.K. Chesterton remarked: **"The Christian ideal has not been tried and found wanting. It has been found difficult and left untried."**[10]

Randall Terry, in his historic "Letter from Atlanta," was pleading for pious priests to proclaim accountability to God's holy law: "Remember folks, when Pearl Harbor was bombed, *everybody* stopped *everything*, and the *nation went to war*. If even a fraction of the Evangelical and Catholic community would get serious, *really serious*, about ending child-killing, even if it meant we suffered for a while, we could bring an end to this holocaust. God help us rise to the occasion."[11]

On the front lines of skirmishes, Rescuers often suggest that the arresting officers should join them. At least one patrolman was prompted by God to do just that. When Las Vegas motorcycle officer Chet Gallagher was sent to arrest Rescuers, he simply removed his badge [effectively resigning from the force] and sat down among them at "the doors."[12] In 1988, Jackson, Mississippi police detective Joe Daniels, "after completing his paperwork, which read: 'Subject was arrested trespassing at an abortion clinic in an attempt to prevent the massacre of unborn children,' typed out his letter of resignation. Daniels explained later that, as pro-lifers prayed for him, he realized he was compromising his Christian beliefs."[13]

"Sheriff Hickey of Corpus Christi, Texas, announced in January 1990 that if abortuary blockaders were to come to town he would not send his men to arrest them... Congressmen, looking for a way to justify passing the FACE [Freedom of Access to Clinic Entrances] bill with its intended federal intervention, summoned the sheriff to D.C. to hear him testify. He said: 'I will not be party to the slaughter of an innocent human being. If requested to remove rescuers from abortuary doors, I have said I will not.' The sheriff cited other examples of the type of civil disobedience he was championing: '*The Declaration of Independence*, the Boston Tea Party, the American Revolution, nonenforcement of the Fugitive Slave Act, and civil rights protests of the Sixties.'"[14]

"Michael Gerrety, chief of police for twelve years in Redwood Falls, was jailed in Fargo in June 1991. He had joined with others in a blockade of North Dakota's only abortuary. Married for thirty years and father of five children, he risked losing a comfortable retirement which would have been his in six years. In a telephone interview from jail, he said, 'I've spent 22 years in law enforcement. During that time I've dedicated my life to protecting innocent people. This is a continuation of that, only these are small people.'"[15]

In the early days of Operation Rescue, Randall Terry's pastor "participated in a Rescue, was arrested, tried, found guilty, and fined. He refused to pay the fine. The judge was quite perplexed and very uncomfortable about sentencing Pastor Little to ten days in jail... Soon after handing down this sentence, the judge confided to a friend that sentencing good people to jail was more than he could bear. He wrote his letter of resignation and stepped down from the bench."[16]

---

1 D. Elton Trueblood, *Vocational Christian Pacifism*, in Hutchison, 208.

2 Raines, *Reshaping the Christian Life*, 28.

3 Grant, *Grand Illusions*, 237.

4 Terry, *Operation Rescue*, 217-8.

5 Trewhella, in Foreman, 175.

6 Bray, 19.

7 Bray, 22.

8 *Life Advocate*, 4/'94, 24.

9 *Life Advocate*, 5/'94, 25.

10 Chesterton, 48.

11 Terry, in Foreman, 168-70.

12 Bray, 132.

13 Terry, *Operation Rescue*, 245-6.

14 and 15 Bray, 132-3 [two quotes].

16 Terry, *OR*, 238.

"Always put justice above the law, and when the law is unjust challenge it directly."[1]

–William Penn

4. Prophet

Stewardship of the Justice conviction

So fearful are we of intruders whose prophetic claims might stem from delusion or diabolical design, that we in the church have banished, along with those, any authentically prophetic voice from our midst.

When Atlanta, in 1989, sentenced Randall Terry to two years in jail for misdemeanor trespass, he penned *An Open Letter to the Pastoral Community of Atlanta*. In it he declared, "I fear we will be remembered with scorn and contempt – a disgrace to Church history – because in an hour when we could have turned the tide in America, we chose not to... I'm talking about God judging America, the way that He has judged every civilization in history that turned its back on Him."[2]

When a trumpet sounds in a city, do not the people tremble? ...Surely the sovereign Lord does nothing without revealing His plan to His servants the prophets. The lion has roared – who will not fear? The sovereign Lord has spoken – who can but prophecy? Amos 3:6-8

Prophecy never had its origin in the will of man, but men spoke from God as they were carried along by the Holy Spirit. 2 Peter 1:21

I was neither a prophet nor a prophet's son... but the Lord took me from tending the flock and said to me, "Go, prophecy to my people." Amos 7:14-15

Joseph Foreman tells us that, "God's true prophets never had God's blessing to walk out on His people. They set us the example of staying within the confines of the Church of their day without toning down their message. Anyone who considers himself prophetic must do the same."[3]

God said to Ezekiel: "When I speak to you, I will open your mouth and you shall say to them, 'This is what the sovereign Lord says,' Whoever will listen let him listen, and whoever will refuse, let him, for they are a rebellious house." Ezekiel 3:27

In the year of *Roe v. Wade*, 1973, J.I. Packer wrote *Knowing God*. In it, Packer said, "To an age which has unashamedly sold itself to the gods of greed, pride, sex, and self-will, the Church mumbles on about God's kindness, but says virtually nothing about His judgment."[4]

Then the Lord reached out his hand and touched my mouth and said to me, "Now, I have put My words in your mouth. See, today I appoint you over nations and kingdoms to uproot, and tear down, to destroy and overthrow, to build and to plant." Jeremiah 1:9-10

If the watchman sees the sword coming and does not blow the trumpet to warn the people... I will hold the watchman accountable... I have made you a watchman... so hear the word I speak and give them warning from me. Ezekiel 33:6-7

Raise your voice like a trumpet. Declare to my people their rebellion... For day after day they seek Me out; they seem eager to know My ways, as if they were a nation that does what is right and has not forsaken the commands of its God. Isaiah 58:1-2

SCOPE and FOCUS

I. CONVICTIONS

II. PRETEXTS

III. MANDATE

Biblical Authority

Pro-Abortion View

Pro-Life View

Child-killing

The Nations

God's People

Bloodguilt

Judgment

Repentance

Restoration

Roles of a Disciple

Alien & Pilgrim within God's Creation

Theologian, revealing Divine Design

Priest, proclaiming God's Commandments

Prophet, crying out for Godly Justice

Loving Neighbor, displaying Virtue

Zealot, fighting for Universal Truths

Evangelist, witnessing to our Accountability

IV. LEGACY

V. ABORTIVE LINKS

VI. DILEMMA

VII. DESTINY

1 *Life Advocate*, 2/'94, 5.

2 Terry, in Foreman, 173.

3 Foreman, 58.

4 Packer, 134. [Also quoted earlier, *Orphans*, 89.]

5 Terry, in Foreman, 168-9.

6 Mandela, *Long Walk to Freedom*, 277.

7 Voltaire, in Clowes, page 81.4.

8 Atkinson, 26.

9 Grant, *Third Time*, 147.

10 Luther, in Alcorn, *Is Rescuing Right?*, 234.

11 Justin Martyr, *Apology*, in Roberts, *The Ante-Nicene Fathers*, Vol. I, 163.

Randall Terry said, "Winning the war for America's soul will not come easily, cheaply, nor quickly. Child-killing is entrenched in our culture and the death forces will not be dethroned overnight, or without a serious fight. It's going to cost us to reform this country. We're going to have to suffer. If we won't pay the price, we will most assuredly lose all our 'safety, comfort, and possessions' anyway, and with them the future for our children. America will lie in the ash heap of history, testifying against our cowardice and selfishness, with our children and grandchildren bearing the full brunt of the brutality and chaos that is coming. The cost of *not* fighting is too great."[5]

I will search Jerusalem with lamps and punish those who are complacent... They will build houses but not live in them... Listen... a day of trumpet and battle cry... I will bring distress on the people... because they have sinned against the Lord.
Zephaniah 1:12-17

As [a heavenly voice] *spoke, the Spirit came into me... He said... "Whether they listen or fail to listen... They will know that a prophet has been among them... Do not be afraid, though briers and thorns are all around you and you live among scorpions." Ezekiel 2:2, 5-6*

Nelson Mandela, who served 27 years in South Africa's prisons before being released and elected president in that country's first free election, says, "History shows that penalties do not deter men when their conscience is aroused."[6]

I am ridiculed all day long; everyone mocks me... The word of the Lord has brought me insult and reproach all day long. But if I say, "I will not mention Him, or speak any more in His name," His word is in my heart like a fire, a fire shut up in my bones. I am weary of holding it in; indeed, I cannot. Jeremiah 20:7-9

In the 1700s, the French philosopher Voltaire concluded, "To announce truths, to propose something useful to mankind, is an infallible recipe for being persecuted."[7]

The officials said to the king, "This man should be put to death. He is discouraging the soldiers..." So they took Jeremiah and put him into the cistern... in the courtyard of the guard... It had no water in it, only mud, and Jeremiah sank down into the mud. Jeremiah 38:4,6

God said to Ezekiel: "I will make your forehead like the hardest stone... Go now to your countrymen in exile and speak to them..." So I sat among them for seven days – overwhelmed... God said, "I have made you a watchman... I will hold you accountable [if you do not warn them], *but if you do warn the wicked man and he does not turn... you will have saved yourself." Ezekiel 3:9, 11, 15-19*

When you are brought before synagogues [churches], *rulers and authorities, do not worry about how you will defend yourselves or what you will say, for the Holy Spirit will teach you at that time what you should say. Luke 12:11-12*

In *The Church and State Under God*, James Atkinson declares, "The State has every right to ask the Church to give an account of its stewardship, to ask what it is doing with its vast resources of men, money and buildings... with its many committees and commissions; or, all the empty and redundant churches [buildings] in our towns and countryside; or, its feeble and ineffective witness to a permissive and secularized society."[8]

What I tell you in the dark, speak in the daylight; what is whispered in your ear, proclaim from the rooftops. Matthew 10:27

George Grant says, "The theology of deliverance runs all throughout the Bible. Again and again, Scripture exhorts the faithful to rescue the weak, in one way or another, out of the strong jaws of death. God Himself is the great rescuer."[9]

Speak up for those who cannot speak for themselves, for the rights of all who are destitute. Speak up and judge fairly; defend the rights of the poor and needy. Proverbs 31:8-9

Martin Luther spoke a prophetic word that applies directly to our situation in America today: "If I profess with the loudest voice and clearest exposition every portion of the truth of God *except* precisely that little point which the world and the devil are at that moment attacking, I am not confessing Christ, no matter how clearly I may be professing Christ. Where the battle rages, there the loyalty of the soldier is proved, and to be steady on all the battle fronts besides is mere flight and disgrace if he flinches at that point."[10]

One of the Church Fathers, Justin Martyr, warns us, "If, when ye have learned the truth, you do not what is just, you will be before God without excuse."[11]

"The real problem which the early Christians faced was this: how a small community professing the true religion could exist within another and larger community professing a false one."[1]
–James Atkinson

SCOPE and FOCUS
I. CONVICTIONS
II. PRETEXTS
III. MANDATE
Biblical Authority
Pro-Abortion View
Pro-Life View
Child-killing
The Nations
God's People
Bloodguilt
Judgment
Repentance
Restoration
Roles of a Disciple
Alien & Pilgrim within God's Creation
Theologian, revealing Divine Design
Priest, proclaiming God's Commandments
Prophet, crying out for Godly Justice
Loving Neighbor, displaying Virtue
Zealot, fighting for Universal Truths
Evangelist, witnessing to our Accountability
IV. LEGACY
V. ABORTIVE LINKS
VI. DILEMMA
VII. DESTINY

5. Loving Neighbor
Stewardship of the Virtue conviction

C. Ben Mitchell says that, "Part of the task of the church is to create a moral community and, beacon-like, display to the world what such a community looks like."[2] "George W. Forell has identified three basic patterns of social teaching which have emerged in the course of history and which have been elaborated in various ways in the Christian church. These patterns he calls the *separation* [detached and uninvolved], the *domination* [enforce Christian morality on all], and the *integration* ['dialogical' relationship, to be *in the world*, although not of the world]."[3]

Martin Luther said: "It is out of the question that there should be a Christian government even over one land... since the wicked always outnumber the good. Hence a man who would venture to govern with the gospel would be like a shepherd who should place in one fold wolves, lions, eagles and sheep together and let them freely mingle."[4]

Colonel V. Doner, author of *The Samaritan Strategy: A New Agenda for Christian Activism*, says "We must discover once and for all whether God expects us to serve others or whether God's sole purpose for us is to get saved, get 'spiritual' and go to heaven."[5]

This researcher disputes Mr. Doner's assertion, or at least the way he expresses it. Clearly we are called to be servants in the world, not just escapees from the world. But this researcher can not agree that we are called to "serve others" or to "serve the world." Too many Christian testimonies and ministries have ended in bankruptcy [moral and spiritual as well as financial] because of the mistaken notion that their calling was to serve the world. It is a major distinction, not minor, to say that we are called to serve GOD *in* the world.

Two of the books by Elton Trueblood provide clues to this significant truth. In *The Incendiary Fellowship*, Trueblood says, "The Christian who understands his calling is humble for two reasons: first, the demand exceeds his powers, and, second, the essential calling is that of a servant."[6] The servant role is not in dispute. But beyond that, Elton Trueblood is correctly echoing the Apostle Paul, who said "Therefore I will boast all the more gladly about my weaknesses, so that Christ's power may rest on me... When I am weak, then I am strong"[7]

We will always fail if we try to minister to "one of the least of these" directly, with the attitude that God will notice how we perform, or that we are serving because Christ sent us. The crucial distinction is that we must be lending our bodies to the work that we see God performing; if we get *that* right, God ministers *through* us, and *we* might even become, in effect, observers of His miraculous ministry. Our obedience in making ourselves available to God is the key; we must understand the process of serving God IN the world.

1 James Atkinson, *Church and State Under God*, 4.
2 Mitchell, in Kilner, *Bioethics*, 132.
3 Perry Cotham, *Christian Social Ethics*, 9-10.
4 Luther, in Colson, 117-8.
5 Doner, 98.
6 Trueblood, *Incendiary Fellowship*, 92.
7 *2 Corinthians* 12:9-10.
8 Trueblood, *New Man*, 41.
9 Tucci, in Terry, *Operation Rescue*, 244. [Pastor Keith Tucci succeeded founder Randall Terry as National Director of Operation Rescue in 1990.]

The Lord confides in those who fear Him.
Psalm 25:14

Jesus Himself testified, *The Son can do nothing by Himself; He can do only what He sees the Father doing... By Myself I can do nothing; I judge only as I hear.* John 5:19, 30

The Counselor, the Holy Spirit, ...will teach you all things and will remind you of everything I have said to you. John 14:26

Blessed are those who have learned to acclaim You, who walk in the light of Your presence, O Lord. Psalm 89:15

The Holy Spirit is not just the warm fuzzy feeling we get when we light candles and sing along with the guitar. We must decide, above all else, that God really does speak to us, lead us, and minister through us. We must believe *that*, experience it, and testify to it... not only in our congregations, but on main street and at city hall.

The only thing that counts is faith expressing itself through love... Since we live by the Spirit let us keep in step with the Spirit.
Galatians 5:6, 25

They will be a people blessed by the Lord, they and their descendants with them. Before they call I will answer; while they are still speaking I will hear. Isaiah 65:23-24

I was the craftsman at His side, I was filled with delight day after day, rejoicing always in His presence, rejoicing in His whole world and delighting in mankind. Proverbs 8:30-31

In *The New Man for Our Times*, Trueblood says, "It is not enough to give a cup of cold water; it is necessary also to tell why."[8]

If we apprehend these lessons aright, we will join the Savior who has rolled up His sleeves and is at work in the world. We will experience His leadership; we will feel His power ministering through us, and we will at all times confess His presence and His love. With these understandings, these are our marching orders:

Do not withhold good from those who deserve it, when it is in your power to act. Do not say to your neighbor, "Come back later; I'll give it tomorrow" – when you have it with you.
Proverbs 3:27-28

Is not this the kind of fasting I have chosen: to loose the chains of injustice and untie the cords of the yoke, to set the oppressed free and break every yoke? Is it not to share your food with the hungry, and to provide the poor wanderer with shelter, when you see the naked, to clothe him... Isaiah 58:6-7

I was hungry... thirsty... a stranger... in need of clothes... sick... in prison... Whatever you did for one of the least of these brothers of Mine, you did for Me. Matthew 25:35-36, 40

May the groans of the prisoners come before you; by the strength of your arm preserve those condemned to die. Psalm 79:11

True religion and undefiled... is to visit the orphan and widow in their distress, and to keep one's self unstained by the world. James 1:27

Shadrach, Meshach and Abednego told the king: If we are thrown into the blazing furnace, the God we serve is able to save us from it... But even if He does not, we want you to know, O king, that we will not serve your gods or worship the image of gold you have set up. Daniel 3:16-18

In round numbers, roughly a hundred thousand Christians have been present at an abortion clinic when a Rescue was taking place, half of them taking part and getting arrested. The rest of the Church in America is laden with the false notions and images which were carefully contrived and portrayed through the media in order to discredit Rescues and Rescuers. If the reader has concluded that a Rescuer is a crass, boisterous self-absorbed anarchist, then the media campaign has been a great success. Few who have not attended a Rescue understand the truth: that 99% of Rescuers are contrite, prayerful, humble and quiet.

On the subject of loving neighbors, who exemplify Christian virtue, we offer this testimony of Pastor Keith Tucci regarding the character of the Rescuers he has known: "Many rescuers didn't just have zeal over the abortion issue – they had a zeal for God. They loved people. I saw pro-lifers at Operation Rescue reach out to pregnant girls, drug addicts, and the people in the porno districts. They invited street people to come to their hotel rooms to take showers. They bought them lunch and ministered to them. Then it really hit me. Unborn babies are people. If you care about people, you've got to care about the unborn. If you care about them then it's natural to care about all the needy of this world."[9]

6. Zealot
Stewardship of the Universalism conviction

After the "cleansing of the temple" by Jesus, John 2:17 records that "His disciples remembered that it is written: 'Zeal for your house will consume me.'" Zeal implies public action born of a passionate conviction. Zeal is what has been lacking in most pro-life activity. Many pro-lifers have shown the world dogged persistence, but few have exemplified biblical zeal.

In the Fifties and Sixties, Elton Trueblood was already reflecting on the Church's loss of zeal, particularly in his writings *The New Man for Our Time,* and *The Incendiary Fellowship*. Mr. Trueblood characterized two types of Christian as the activist and the pietist, "both of which are valuable, [and which] have been harmed by mutual isolation. The problem, therefore, is that of a new isolationism [within the church]."[1]

In 1988, Colonel V. Doner revealed how completely the activist had been eclipsed by the pietist: "For the average Christian, who since the day of his conversion has never been taught anything different, service is clearly optional. We may choose to serve, or we may not, depending upon our schedule, level of talent or energy, or our general disposition."[2]

In 1996, Robert Bork declared, "Religion, while pervasive, seems increasingly unable to affect actual behavior."[3] Many modern observers of the Church lament its failure to be "salt and light." Trueblood, forty years ago, was sounding the same alarm: "To be baptized by water is the merely symbolic experience of being cleansed or forgiven; to be baptized by fire is to be ignited... What we need is 'quiet fanatics.'"[4]

This researcher concludes that the Zealot is uniquely commissioned by God to be the steward of the Universalism conviction, while all Christians are to live lives reflecting the hierarchy in which God's higher law supersedes man's law. Bray tells us that when Scripture speaks "about submission to authority: parents, church elders, and governments... the principle is qualified from the beginning. The people of God are never enjoined to unconditional submission. When tyrants ruled, God sent deliverers to the people. The Scriptures are full of examples of righteous disobedience and revolution."[5]

Charles Colson agrees: "Once government promotes disorder or so abuses human rights that it undercuts the dignity of humanity, or when government becomes an instrument for the taking of innocent human lives, then the Christian has a higher duty, which is to obey God's law and not man's."[6] Foreman is even more precise: "The task of the Church is to call forth, train, lay hands on, send out, and support people who will obey God, whether it is legal or illegal to do so."[7]

He also pinpoints why so few Christians have displayed holy zeal, and why the Church has recoiled from identification with those who have: "The world's idea is that protecting children before they are born is, even for Christians, a mere political issue. They do not believe that we will act as if children in the womb are equal to us just because God tells us they are... The suffering with which society threatens us becomes their intimidating yardstick of our faith: 'How much suffering is that little life worth?'"[8]

Over four hundred years ago, one of the early voices of the Protestant Reformation wrote: "The resistance of Moses against Pharaoh, of Ehud against Eglon, and of Jehu against Jehoram were not, as they perhaps appear, the deeds of private individuals. Since all of them were specially called by God, they possessed an authority surpassing even that of magistrates."[9]

SCOPE and FOCUS
I. CONVICTIONS
II. PRETEXTS
III. MANDATE
Biblical Authority
Pro-Abortion View
Pro-Life View
Child-killing
The Nations
God's People
Bloodguilt
Judgment
Repentance
Restoration
Roles of a Disciple
Alien & Pilgrim within God's Creation
Theologian, revealing Divine Design
Priest, proclaiming God's Commandments
Prophet, crying out for Godly Justice
Loving Neighbor, displaying Virtue
Zealot, fighting for Universal Truths
Evangelist, witnessing to our Accountability
IV. LEGACY
V. ABORTIVE LINKS
VI. DILEMMA
VII. DESTINY

1 Trueblood, *New Man*, 18.

2 Doner, *The Samaritan Strategy: A New Agenda for Christian Activism*, 97.

3 Bork, *Slouching Towards Gomorrah: Modern Liberalism and American Decline*, 64.

4 Trueblood, *Incendiary Fellowship*, 105 and 118.

Other biblical examples of holy zeal include these:

The king of Egypt said to the Hebrew midwives, "...If it is a boy, kill him." The midwives, however, feared god and did not do what the king of Egypt had told them to do; they let the boys live.

Exodus 1:15-17

Pharaoh gave this order: "Every boy that is born you must throw into the nile." ...She became pregnant and gave birth to a son [Moses]. ...When she saw that he was a fine child, she hid him for three months... *Exodus 1:22; 2:1-2*

All the royal officials knelt down and paid honor to Haman, for the king had commanded this... But Mordecai would not kneel down or pay him honor... Day after day they spoke to him but he refused to comply. *Esther 3:2-4*

[Mordecai said to Esther:] *"Who knows but that you have come to royal position for such a time as this?"* [Ester replied:] *"I will go to the king, even though it is against the law. And if I perish, I perish."* *Esther 4:14-16*

...There was a famine for three successive years; so David sought the face of the Lord. The Lord said, "It is on account of Saul and his blood-stained house... because he put the Gibeonites to death..." [After seven of Saul's descendants were killed, then:] *God answered prayer in behalf of the land.* *2 Samuel 21:1, 6, 14*

Ahab summoned Obadiah, who was in charge of his palace. Obadiah was a devout believer in the Lord. While Jezebel was killing off the Lord's prophets, Obadiah had taken 100 prophets and hidden them in two caves... and had supplied them with food and water. *1 Kings 18:3-4*

When Athaliah saw that her son was dead, she proceeded to destroy the whole royal family. But Jehosheba... took Joash and stole him away from among the royal princes who were about to be murdered. She put him and his nurse in a bedroom to hide him... [and then] *at the temple of the Lord for six years while Athaliah ruled...*

2 Kings 11:1-3

5 Michael Bray, 158.

6 Colson, in Alcorn, *Is Rescuing Right?*, 71.

7 Foreman, *Shattering the Darkness: The Crisis of the Cross in the Church Today*, 35.

8 Foreman, 10.

9 Philip du Plessis-Morney, in Bray, 166.

10 King, in Clowes, *Pro-Life Activist's Encyclopedia*, page 81.1.

11 Clowes, page 81.1.

12 Robert Lee and Martin Marty, *Religion and Social Conflict*, 178-9.

Holy zeal, stewardship of the Universalism conviction, and allowing ourselves to hear and heed God's call to dynamic public action, are subjects that require sustained prayerful examination on the part of every serious Christian. In this quest, we will be greatly hampered by the historically recent trend of pietism at the expense of activism, and also to the degree that we ourselves have been infected by the doctrines of Autonomy, Pleasure, Relativism, Pragmatism and Positivism.

An additional impediment to our right understanding of God's will for our responsiveness to abortion is engendered by the media's intentional skewing of the truth about Rescue, particularly, and about pro-life convictions in general. There has been a wholesale identification of the pro-life movement as "just like" the civil rights movement. The errors within this comparison are not self evident.

Dr. Martin Luther King Jr., who was arrested 22 times for civil disobedience, said, "An individual who breaks a law that conscience tells him is unjust, and who willingly accepts the penalty of imprisonment in order to arouse the conscience of the community over its injustice, is in reality expressing the highest respect for the law."[10]

Brian Clowes responds to lingering civil rights assumptions: "No pro-life action has been so misunderstood by the public, the pro-aborts, and even Christians as [have] rescue missions. A rescue is *not* organized to make a statement; it is *not* a mere 'sit-in'; it is an actual and earnest attempt to save lives! ...A rescue mission is mounted to save unborn lives and mother's health by placing oneself between the victims and the killer – the abortionist. The philosophy of rescue is as simple as that."[11]

When a civil rights activist staged a sit-in at a lunch counter it was *not* primarily an attempt to get lunch; it was a strategy designed to sway public opinion against the injustice of segregation. But when a rescuer blocks access to an abortion clinic the *primary* objective is to save the life of the child who is about to be aborted. Any hope that the collective American conscience might be influenced is secondary to the direct aim of achieving an immediate rescue of the child from death. A rescuer is peacefully making real the Psalm's imperative:

Defend the cause of the weak and fatherless; maintain the rights of the poor and oppressed. Rescue the weak and needy; deliver them from the hand of the wicked.

Psalm 82:3-4

In 1964, Lee and Marty were testifying, "Conflict of some sort or other is inevitable when the faithfully religious person is confronted with the need to 'obey God rather than men' in a concrete area of human choice."[12] Dr. D. James Kennedy, in the forword to Randall Terry's 1988 book on the biblical and philosophical basis of *Operation Rescue*, said: "I feel that this approach [rescue] is biblically correct. These peaceful protesters are obeying God's law in a peaceful, nonviolent manner. As a result no babies are killed at the abortion clinic while the protesters are there. In addition, the pro-life movement gains momentum, adding to the social pressure necessary to bring about political change."[1]

Even though Dr. Kennedy fell into the media-conditioned pattern of calling rescuers *protesters*, he correctly expressed the primacy of the *intervention* to rescue, and that the *strategy* of influencing public opinion, increasing social pressure and bringing about political change is secondary to that.

We must discard our rose-colored glasses when reading the Bible. Paul's obedience to God did not increase his popularity with government and society:

> *While they were trying to kill [Paul], news reached the commander... When the rioters saw the commander and his soldiers they stopped beating Paul. The commander came up and arrested him.*
>
> *Acts 21:31-3*

Likewise, when commissioned to do God's holy work, the apostle did not go out of his way to surrender. To put this next passage into modern perspective we might say that Paul was listed as number one on the FBI's "most wanted" list, his hotel was surrounded by police, and the SWAT team was in place... What was a zealous Christian to do?

> *In Damascus the governor... had the city guarded in order to arrest me. But I was lowered in a basket from a window in the wall and slipped through his hands.* *2 Corinthians 11:32-3*

The warrants for his arrest and the question of his public image, at least in this instance, were secondary to the urgency of carrying on the work God had set before him. Randall Terry wrote: "God always calls His people to action in times of moral crisis."[2] Franky Schaeffer says, "In a misguided generation, God raises up shepherds to do the work of those leaders who have abdicated their responsibility to lead His people."[3]

The words of Nelson Mandela are worth noting: "In South Africa, a man who tried to fulfill his duty to his people was inevitably ripped from his family and his home and was forced to live a life apart, a twilight existence of secrecy and rebellion... In attempting to serve my people, I found that I was prevented from fulfilling my obligations as a son, a brother, a father, and a husband."[4]

Joseph Foreman declares, "In all arenas of life, we have strayed so far from our heritage of sacrificial obedience to God, that peacefully stopping a baby-murderer seems extreme. Because we do not Rescue in any area of life, Rescue at an abortion clinic seems pushy. Face it: Rescuers – that is to say, Christians – *are* pushy where life and death or heaven and hell are at stake. The Cross does not wait until a more polite, humane era when people can be crucified with their clothes on, and take anesthesia for the pain. We take up our cross, period."[5]

Nelson Mandela says that as a young black lawyer in South Africa he "discovered for the first time people of my own age firmly aligned with the liberation struggle, who were prepared, despite their relative privilege, to sacrifice themselves for the cause of the oppressed."[6]

Joseph Foreman is clear: "We want to strive to be in a position where jail, beatings, or lawsuits are not the significant factor in the decisions we make about how and where we will obey God. It is only recently, and in America, that prison was not considered a live possibility for the faithful believer... The experience of Rescuers is a return to what is far more normal in the experience of God's people through the centuries."[7] Dr. Martin Luther King, Jr. was jailed for protesting denial of equality to black Americans. Someone asked him: "Why are you in jail?" His only response was: "Why are you not in jail?"[8]

In the introduction to *Shattering the Darkness*, Foreman says,

"My goal is not that you get arrested, but that you never again fear what men do to you. I want you to set your affairs in order so that when it comes to obeying God you do not make lawsuits, tax exemptions, going to jail, losing your job, popularity, or success, your main considerations."[9]

SCOPE and FOCUS
I. CONVICTIONS
II. PRETEXTS
III. MANDATE
Biblical Authority
Pro-Abortion View
Pro-Life View
Child-killing
The Nations
God's People
Bloodguilt
Judgment
Repentance
Restoration
Roles of a Disciple
Alien & Pilgrim within God's Creation
Theologian, revealing Divine Design
Priest, proclaiming God's Commandments
Prophet, crying out for Godly Justice
Loving Neighbor, displaying Virtue
Zealot, fighting for Universal Truths
Evangelist, witnessing to our Accountability
IV. LEGACY
V. ABORTIVE LINKS
VI. DILEMMA
VII. DESTINY

The Apostle Paul characterized the Christian life:

As servants of God... in great endurance... in troubles... hardships... distresses... beatings... imprisonments... riots... hard work... sleepless nights... hunger... With weapons of righteousness in the right hand and the left. *2 Corinthians 6:4-5,7*

Though we live in the world we do not wage war as the world does. The weapons we fight with are not he weapons of the world. On the contrary, they have divine power to demolish strongholds. *2 Corinthians 10:3-4*

"Don't be afraid," Elisha answered. "Those who are with us are more than those who are with them..." The Lord opened the servant's eyes, and he looked and saw the hills full of horses and chariots of fire all around Elisha. *2 Kings 6:16-17*

[God said to Jeremiah] *"Do not say, 'I am only a child.' You must go to everyone I send you to and say whatever I command you. Do not be afraid of them for I am with you... Get yourself ready! Stand up and say to them whatever I command you... Today I have made you a fortified city, an iron pillar and a bronze wall to stand against the whole land."* *Jeremiah 1:7, 17-18*

In 1972, most Christians in America still presumed that their government was supportive – or at least tolerant – of Christianity. In the Soviet Union at that time, there was no such illusion, and some Christians were breaking the civil law in order to obey God's law with a "'Christian publishing house,' an organization which on its clandestine press has been producing Bibles, hymn books and magazines. This has been one of the most daring and effective ways of protest by the break-away Baptists... And the K.G.B. have so far failed to shut down the illegal printing works."[10]

We are warned by Joseph Foreman: "If our goal is not to transform society, but just tinker with it, then we will fail. God is playing for keeps. If we want to take back the power bases of our society, we must first learn to lay down our lives in service."[11]

Cut down the trees and build siege ramps against Jerusalem. This city must be punished; it is filled with oppression. As a well pours out its water, so she pours out her wickedness; violence and destruction resound in her; her sickness and wounds are ever before Me. *Jeremiah 6:6-7*

In the words of John Whitehead: "It is now time for another revolution, a revolution in the reformative sense... A revolution in the minds and the souls of human beings – a revolution promulgated to be a total assault on the humanistic culture. A Second American Revolution founded upon the Bible in its totality. In this, and only this, is there hope for the future."[12] George Grant declares that it is "crucial" for "prophets and priests guiding and guarding the land, to do more than point out the dangerous idolatries of Planned Parenthood. We must destroy every idol and we must tear down the high places. Whatever the cost."[13]

Israel has sinned... That is why the Israelites cannot stand against their enemies; they turn their backs and run because they have been made liable to destruction. I will not be with you any more unless you destroy whatever among you is devoted to destruction. *Joshua 7:11-12*

This is what you are to do to them [the godless nations]: *break down their altars, smash their sacred stones, cut down their Asherah poles and burn their idols in the fire.* *Deuteronomy 7:5*

Josiah desecrated Topeth... so no one could use it to sacrifice his son or daughter in the fire to Molech... He also desecrated the high places that were east of Jerusalem... and slaughtered all the priests of those high places on the altars.
2 Kings 23:10, 13, 20

1 Kennedy, in Terry, Forword.
2 Terry, *Operation Rescue*, 36.
3 Scheaffer, in Scheidler, 14.
4 Mandela, *Long Walk to Freedom*, 543.
5 Foreman, 1.
6 Mandela, 80.
7 Foreman, 177-8.
8 King, in John Powell, *Abortion: the Silent Holocaust*, 5-6.
9 Foreman, Introduction, xx.
10 Howard-Johnson, *Aida of Leningrad*, 110.
11 Foreman, Introduction, xxii.
12 Whitehead, *The Second American Revolution*, 180.
13 Grant, *Grand Illusions*, 262.

They are swift to shed innocent blood... the Lord looked and was displeased that there was no justice. He saw that there was no-one, He was **appalled** that there was no-one to intervene.

Isaiah 59:7, 15-16

The Lord was with Jehoshaphat because in his early years he walked in the ways of his father David... His heart was devoted to the ways of the Lord; furthermore, he removed the high places and the Asherah poles from Judah. 2 Chronicles 17:3-6

In *Martyrs of Our Time*, William Purcell quotes Dietrich Bonhoeffer: "If we claim to be Christians there is no room for expediency. Hitler is anti-Christ; we must go on with our work and eliminate him..."[1] Michael Bray explains: "Samson fought a one-man guerilla war against the Philistine government. The people of Israel acknowledged this *de facto* government and opposed Samson's conduct (Judges 15:11)... The downfall of the Philistine rule came about through incessant pursuit of justice on the part of one man. Samson's countrymen arrested him, bound him, and delivered him over to the lawful Philistine authorities."[2]

Joseph Foreman is optimistic: "I believe the days of ten-thousand-person Rescues are still ahead. I believe we will see huge crowds of Christians descend on free-standing [abortion] clinics and each take a brick home with them. I know for a fact that most abortionists expect this of us... This transformation in the Church will come as a result of enough Christians trading their lives for others, thereby purchasing the right to speak to our society."[3]

The great hymn, in the words of Martin Luther, warns: "Were we in our own strength to confide, Our striving would be losing."[4] In 1988, Randall Terry wrote: "The church has *no chance* of restoring our quickly disappearing liberties, no chance of bringing America back to moral sanity unless we repent of our idolatry and compromise. But if we repent, God can and will do wonders – even through a *remnant* of his people."[5]

Each of the [wall] *builders wore his sword at his side as he worked...* [Nehemiah said:] *"We are widely separated from each other along the wall. Whenever you hear the sound of the trumpet, join us there. Our God will fight for us."*

Nehemiah 4:17-20

The Israelites camped opposite them like two small flocks of goats while the Arameans covered the countryside... The Israelites inflicted 100,000 casualties in one day. The rest of them escaped to the city of Aphek, where the wall collapsed on 27,000 of them.

1 Kings 20:27-30

Whenever you are arrested and brought to trial, do not worry beforehand about what to say. Just say whatever is given you at the time, for it is not you speaking but the Holy Spirit.

Mark 13:11

In the words of C.S. Lewis: **"It is not your purpose to succeed, but to do right; when you have done so, the rest lies with God."[6]**

There will be no lasting solution at law, in alternatives, nor through education, "until enough people treat the preborn as their human equals."[7] –Joseph Foreman

SCOPE and FOCUS
I. CONVICTIONS
II. PRETEXTS
III. MANDATE
Biblical Authority
Pro-Abortion View
Pro-Life View
Child-killing
The Nations
God's People
Bloodguilt
Judgment
Repentance
Restoration
Roles of a Disciple
Alien & Pilgrim within God's Creation
Theologian, revealing Divine Design
Priest, proclaiming God's Commandments
Prophet, crying out for Godly Justice
Loving Neighbor, displaying Virtue
Zealot, fighting for Universal Truths
Evangelist, witnessing to our Accountability
IV. LEGACY
V. ABORTIVE LINKS
VI. DILEMMA
VII. DESTINY

1 Purcell, 83.
2 Bray, 159.
3 Foreman, Introduction, xxi.
4 Luther, in Haffner, *The High Cost of Free Love*, 186.
5 Terry, *Operation Rescue*, 174.
6 Lewis, in Alcorn, *Is Rescuing Right?*, 150.
7 Foreman, 165
8 Aeschliman, 98.
9 Niebuhr, in Raines, *The Secular Congregation*, 61.
10 *Christian Times*, 11/'97, 1.
11 *1 Timothy* 1:15.
12 *1 John* 1:8.
13 *James* 2:10.

"We gave you strict orders not to teach in this name, yet you have filled Jerusalem with your teaching..." Peter and the other apostles replied: "We must obey God rather than men!" *Acts 5:28-29*

7. Evangelist

Stewardship of the Accountability conviction

In *Global Trends: Ten Changes Affecting Christians Everywhere*, Gordon Aeschliman writes: "The temptation is there, when facing the evils of our day, to blame 'secular humanists,' 'liberals' or 'the press.' The truth is, if the United States is 99 per cent evangelized, as mission statistician David Barrett suggests, then the church is to blame for the mess we are in. Is this where our evangelism leads? Is this what a society looks like after the gospel has been unleashed without restraint for 300 years? The plight of society is nothing more than an indictment on the church."[8] In the 1960s, Robert Raines, in *The Secular Congregation*, quoted Richard Niebuhr: "We Christians are not those who are being saved out of a perishing world, but those who know the world is being saved."[9]

This researcher must confess that he is so focused on the culture wars – and on abortion particularly – that for a season he pulled back from the Promise Keepers phenomenon, judging it as having failed to take a biblical pro-life stand. Now it is clear that Promise Keepers was divinely appointed to fulfill a particular, and different, mandate: to proclaim Christianity to be a commitment-thing, and a public-testimony thing. Promise Keepers made great, obedient strides in fulfilling that mission. An acknowledgment of commitment and public witness as central features of Christianity is prerequisite to a Christianity that can call Stewards to muster in fighting the culture war.

This foundational role of Promise Keepers was well stated by its president, Randy Phillips: "Why are we here? ...Is it to demonstrate political might? No... Is it to take back the nation by imposing our religious values on others? No... We have come to display our spiritual poverty that Almighty God might influence us."[10]

Promisekeepers helped to bring, among many other things, confession and repentance back into the Church. This is crucial, for perhaps the greatest lie that has pervaded both the culture and local congregations is that Christians view themselves as people who once were sinners *but now are not*. To the contrary, even the apostle Paul admitted, to Timothy and to us, "Christ Jesus came into the world to save sinners of whom I *am* the worst."[11]

John said, "If we claim to be without sin, we deceive ourselves and the truth is not in us,"[12] and James agrees: "Whoever keeps the whole law and yet stumbles at just one point is guilty of breaking all of it."[13]

The sin problem in America is of three types: Christians who think that they have ceased sinning; pagans who deny that they are sinful; and church members who have been permitted to think that they became Christians without having experienced either confession or repentance. We have spoken previously about the travesty of post-abortive women being granted victim status and false comfort, devoid of biblical accountability and divine healing.[14]

The widespread denial of guilt before God, particularly where it is promoted by denominations and clergy, prompts us to speculate that perhaps modern society has been inoculated against guilt and is therefore now practically immune to biblical evangelism. As long ago as the Sixties, writers like Keith Miller were concluding, "If one goes about trying to capitalize on men's conscious guilt to get them to a personal relation with God, he may miss many of the sharpest people altogether and drive them away from Christ, since they simply don't experience their basic problem as guilt."[15]

Miller went on to say, "Our attitude betrays our lack of real faith. We act as if we were selling tickets to something, or memberships, instead of introducing people to Almighty God in an eternal and conscious relationship."[16]

Trueblood declared that, **"Committed Christianity... is a faith marked by a burning conviction and the consequent desire to see it spread."**[17]

14 *Life Advocate*, 4/'94, 31, and 6/'94, 43.

15 Miller, *A Taste of New Wine*, 92.

16 Miller, *A Taste of New Wine*, 92.

17 Elton Trueblood, *Incendiary Fellowship*, 24.

"All that is taking place around you was fore-announced... the swallowing up of cities by the earth; the theft of islands by the sea; wars, bringing external and internal convulsions; the collision of kingdoms with kingdoms; famines and pestilences, and local massacres, and widespread desolating mortalities... the decay of righteousness, the growth of sin, the slackening interest in all good ways..."[1]

–Tertullian [c. 200 A.D.]

SCOPE and FOCUS
I. CONVICTIONS
II. PRETEXTS
III. MANDATE
Biblical Authority
Pro-Abortion View
Pro-Life View
Child-killing
The Nations
God's People
Bloodguilt
Judgment
Repentance
Restoration
Roles of a Disciple
Alien & Pilgrim within God's Creation
Theologian, revealing Divine Design
Priest, proclaiming God's Commandments
Prophet, crying out for Godly Justice
Loving Neighbor, displaying Virtue
Zealot, fighting for Universal Truths
Evangelist, witnessing to our Accountability
IV. LEGACY
V. ABORTIVE LINKS
VI. DILEMMA
VII. DESTINY

In *Megatrends 2000* we are told: "At the dawn of the third millennium there are unmistakable signs of a worldwide multidenominational religious revival. American baby boomers who rejected organized religion in the 1970s are returning to church with their children in tow or joining the New Age movement... the worldwide charismatic movement has tripled in the last decade to nearly 300 million, including millions of Roman Catholics."[2]

The trends raise more questions than they answer, among them, Is the "religious revival" a mark of increasing Christian *commitment*, or rather consumerist shopping in a spiritual marketplace where Christianity and the New Age are merely viewed as brand names for essentially similar products? And, Is the burgeoning charismatic movement a signal that the Holy Spirit is on the move in conscription warriors for God's battlefields, or is much of the apparent growth merely the noise of "resounding gongs and clanging cymbals"?[3]

At the heart of our evangelism must be this question: "How can the 4,500 unreached people who are scheduled for murder [abortion] today be reached by the gospel? ...There is no way to reach these needy children without crossing to the other side of the iron curtain of American law which has descended protectively around the abortion industry."[4]

Joseph Foreman continues, saying that from our traditional view of evangelism "...we know that we must send people where it is illegal for them to go, with a message it is illegal to preach... such as Eastern European Missions... The Christian missions to Korea and Japan were begun when the missionary was forbidden by law even to enter the country – on penalty of death. But they came anyway, and Christians were martyred, by the thousands."[4] Traditional evangelism has never been a subject of personal satisfaction but always one of radical commitment to a risen Lord. Obedience, not individual "spiritual fulfillment," has always been the goal:

> *Go and make* ***disciples*** *of all nations, baptizing them in the name of the Father and of the Son and of the Holy Spirit, and teaching them to* ***obey*** *everything I have commanded you.*
> *Matthew 28:19-20*

Our Mandate as Christ's Church

The policies engendered by the convictions of secular humanism have resulted in a clash of cultures – with abortion at its heart – which places the Church in a defensive posture, struggling for the right to exist. The Bible mandates a pro-life position. In America's present culture war, the Body of Christ is only complete if it is composed of pilgrims, theologians, priests, prophets, loving neighbors, zealots and evangelists, who each recognize the crucial roles played by the others, and who all exhibit inspired commitment and the working of the Holy Spirit. The Church must be filled with Stewards of unshakable convictions regarding Creation, Design, Commandments, Justice, Virtue, Universalism and Accountability.

1 Tertullian, *Apology*, in Roberts, *Ante-Nicene Fathers*, Vol. III, 33.
2 John Naisbitt, *Megatrends 2000*, 270.
3 *1 Corinthians* 13:1.
4 Foreman, 152-3.
5 Foreman, 153.

SCOPE and FOCUS
I. CONVICTIONS
II. PRETEXTS
III. MANDATE
IV. LEGACY
Christian Tradition
Early Church
Reformation Era
World Precedents
Holocaust
Nuremberg
Geneva
United Nations and Int'l. Human Rights
Unborn Child's Rights
Global Abortion Norms
Apartheid
United States History
Independence
Liberty & Rights
Abolition of Slavery
Pretexts for slavery
Links in slave chains
Discipleship & slavery
Slavery and Abortion
Women's Passage Rites
Protection & Rights
Anti-Family Changes
Feminism
Seeds of Destruction
Nietzsche
Malthus
Darwin
Marx
Freud
Between World Wars
Techno-prosperity
Modernism
Fundamentalism
Scopes
Capone & Ness
Pivotal Developments
Public education
Great Depression
Post-war materialism
Synthetic heroes
Post-war paranoia
Kinsey-Elvis-Madonna
Clinton generation
Civil Rights
Parental Responsibility
Humaneness
Animal rights
Endangered species
Environmentalism
Illegal aliens
Criminal rights
Children's rights
V. ABORTIVE LINKS
VI. DILEMMA
VII. DESTINY

IV. The Legacy: Stewards vs. Masters, Endless Struggle

As if in response to George Santayana's "Those who do not remember the past are condemned to relive it,"[1] Will and Ariel Durant declare that "The present is the past rolled up for action, and the past is the present unrolled for understanding."[2]

The current culture war in America, which we have characterized as a battle between the Masters and the Stewards, is in one sense just the latest expression of an ageless struggle. George Grant, in *Third Time Around: A History of the Pro-Life Movement from the First Century to the Present*, makes it clear that this is the third revolution of an historical cycle of Christian activism undertaken to counter an upsurge of pagan childkilling. On the other hand, the biblical record clearly describes history as linear, having a "beginning," a middle, and an apocalyptic "ending." There is as much reason to *doubt* that the American church will triumph over abortion as there is to believe that it will.

Thus far we have examined the depths of conviction that drive both the Masters and the Stewards, particularly with reference to the conflict over abortion. Before examining the dynamics of the present abortion dilemma, in Part V, it would be prudent to "unroll the past" for understanding.

A. Christian Tradition

Jean Garton asserts that "The fundamental and most serious question of this century is: What does it mean to be human? ...while some obvious differences exist between the first and the twentieth century, never before has Christianity been in a world as similar to the one in which it was born."[3]

David Braine's summary is this: "For the whole of Christian history until appreciably after 1900, so far as we can trace it, there was virtually complete unanimity amongst Christians – evangelical, catholic, orthodox – that, unless at the direct command of God, it was in all cases wrong directly to take innocent human life. Abortion and infanticide were grouped together as early as the writing called the [Christian] *Didache* which comes from the first century after the crucifixion."[4]

1. Early Church

"The Christian's refusal to recognize Caesar worship was regarded as a political offence," says James Atkinson. "To deny the religious priority of the state was an act of treason... It is significant that the early Christians were described by Roman officials as 'atheists,' in that they did not believe in the Roman gods."[5]

Christianity was born in an era when childkilling was widespread and common, whether by abortion, by abandonment, or by ritual sacrifice. George Grant details the practices in Greece, Rome, Persia, and by the Chinese, Hindus and Arabs. He also confirms that "Primitive Canaanites threw their children onto great flaming pyres as a sacrifice to their god Molech."[6]

By contrast, Grant tells us that, "The wholehearted consensus [of the Christians] of the Apostolic Era was that all life was a sacred gift from God and that any breach of that gift was nothing less than murder."[7]

1 Santayana, in Whitehead, *Stealing of America*, xiii.
2 Durant, *Lessons of History*, 12.
3 Garton, *Who Broke the Baby?*, 92.
4 Braine, *Medical Ethics and Human Life*, 11.
5 Atkinson, *Church & State Under God*, 5.
6 Grant, *Third Time*, 12.
7 Grant, *Third Time*, 23-4.

"Knowing that the struggle for life would not be won in a day, the early Christians worked hard, educating their children, involved themselves in their culture, lobbied their magistrates, and built for the future. They knew that theirs was a multi-generational task. And so, they laid the groundwork for a multi-generational victory. The pro-life ethic was not an isolated single-interest issue for them. It was integrated into a comprehensive covenantal worldview that touched every area of life."[1] –George Grant

Grant quotes a wide assortment of writings of the Church Fathers denouncing abortion and infanticide as murder.[2] Michael Gorman says, "Writers of the first three Christian centuries laid the theological and literary foundation for all subsequent early Christian writing on abortion. We will see that three important themes emerged during these centuries: the fetus is the creation of God; abortion is murder; and the judgment of God falls on those guilty of abortion."[3]

In *Third Time Around*, Grant tells us that, "They rescued the perishing, confronted injustice, and tore down the high places" [pages 31-2]. The writer lists the names of many who were martyred for rescuing abandoned infants [27-8]. Grant also details the boldly illegal pro-life activism of Callistus of Rome [27] and of Basil [21], and many other Christians, which contributed to the eventual full criminalization of child-killing by decree of the Emperor Valentinian in 374 A.D. [21].

As related by Howard-Johnson, "Tertullian, looking back on three centuries of tribulation under the Romans, shortly before Constantine accepted the new faith... said: 'The more you persecute us, the more we grow. The blood of the martyrs is the seed of the church.'"[4]

George Grant, in his first pro-life masterpiece, *Grand Illusions: The Legacy of Planned Parenthood*, observed: "It was not until the rapid spread of Christianity throughout the Mediterranean world in the second and third centuries that a consistent and convincing pro-life message began to sound. When it did, the whole civilized world stopped to listen. It was not long until laws were passed and a cultural consensus was reached to protect both women and children. The church's pro-life message was arresting."[5]

What is clear is this pattern: Christians whose convictions compel them to confront the ungodliness of their culture will be persecuted; faithfulness in the face of sanctions and death results in Church growth; when the number of uncompromising believers reaches a particular level, the scales of justice shift and the hard-won cultural victory is achieved.

Doug Bandow is one of many Christian writers who consider the Roman turnabout and embrace of Christianity to have been a kiss of death for faith: "...There may have been no greater disaster for the cause of the gospel, in contrast to the material interests of the clerical class, than the marriage of church and state which first occurred under Constantine... [Earlier,] in the face of organized repression and a paganistic culture, Christianity spread throughout the entire Roman Empire. But once the church became the official state religion, it degenerated spiritually..."[6]

CONCLUSIONS. From Pentecost to Constantine, Christians: • Courageously proclaimed the Bible's one-God of creation, and Jesus His Son [creation vs. accident]; • Declared the sanctity of every human life, born or unborn [design vs. mechanism]; • Acted faithfully but "illegally" in obedience to a Higher Law than man's [commandments v. positivism]; • Rescued the abandoned infants, and cared for the handicapped and destitute [justice vs. pragmatism]; • Self-sacrificially showed love to their neighbors [virtue vs. pleasure]; • Declared the right to life from conception [universalism vs. relativism]; • And – uncounted thousands – willingly endured persecution and martyrdom for refusing to compromise their commitment to God [accountability vs. autonomy].

SCOPE and FOCUS
I. CONVICTIONS
II. PRETEXTS
III. MANDATE
IV. LEGACY
Christian Tradition
Early Church
Reformation Era
World Precedents
Holocaust
Nuremberg
Geneva
United Nations and Int'l. Human Rights
Unborn Child's Rights
Global Abortion Norms
Apartheid
United States History
Independence
Liberty & Rights
Abolition of Slavery
Women's Passage Rites
Seeds of Destruction
Between World Wars
Pivotal Developments
Civil Rights
Parental Responsibility
Humaneness
V. ABORTIVE LINKS
VI. DILEMMA
VII. DESTINY

1 Grant, *Third Time*, 32.

2 Grant, *Third Time*, 23-5; see also Shaw, *Abortion on Trial*, 141, and Williams, *Sanctity of Life*, 148.

3 Gorman, *Abortion & the Early Church*, 47.

4 Howard-Johnson, 109.

5 Grant, *Grand Illusions*, 190.

6 Bandow, *Beyond Good Intentions: A Biblical View of Politics*, 223.

7 Hunter, 131-2.

8 Brown, in Garton, 68.

9 Jean Garton, *Who Broke the Baby?*, 68.

10 John Jefferson Davis, *Abortion and the Christian*, 5.

2. Reformation Era

A startling assertion is made by James Hunter as he puts today's *Culture Wars* in historical perspective: "The rise of Christianity as a world religion between the first and third centuries, and the success of the Protestant Reformation in the sixteenth century created the most fundamental cultural divisions in the history of Western civilization."[7]

Harold O.J. Brown declares "Every major Protestant theologian from John Calvin, in the days of the Reformation, through Dietrich Bonhoeffer, whom the Nazis killed, through Francis Schaeffer, today, is strongly anti-abortion."[8] Jean Garton adds to this list of pro-life theologians, "Ramsey, Williams, Outler, Barth, Thielecke and many others."[9]

It is interesting to note that Brown's list begins with Calvin. J.J. Davis clarifies: "While Martin Luther apparently did not directly address the question of abortion, his teachings on original sin and the origins of the human soul had the effect of personalizing the unborn child... For Calvin, the unborn child is 'already a human being,' a judgment in harmony with the early church fathers such as Tertullian."[10]

At about the time of the Reformation, Ignatius Loyola – founder of the Society of Jesus – wrote, "Life is God's most precious gift. To scorn it by any sort of murderous act – such as the abortion of a child – is not merely an awful tyranny, it is a smear against the integrity of God as well. Suffer as we must, even die if need be, such rebellion against heaven must not be free to run its terrible courses."[11]

"In 1652 Vincent [De Paul] was horrified to discover that a guild of midwives had begun performing illicit abortions in the slums of Paris. He quickly went to work, organizing relief... He lobbied the magistrates... He prodded the church... He also launched a complete investigation of the grisly trade, drawing public attention to the issue and provoking public ire against the whole sordid affair. At one point, he actually went undercover to infiltrate the covert meetings of the guild."[12]

As to theology, Davis explains that "by the middle of the eighteenth century, Catholic teaching had moved away from the earlier position of Aristotle and Aquinas and had identified conception as the time of ensoulment. The change was, in part, due to new embryological information unavailable to Aquinas."[13]

The Renaissance marked a cultural shift in literature and the arts from heavenly to earthly themes. The "sensate" shift from virtue to pleasure and from brotherly love to self-serving "love" was mentioned earlier.[14] "Toward the end of the Middle Ages... the official church was too embroiled in its own political conflict to see the idle, pagan-inspired ['love stories'] as a significant problem... The love stories became the wellspring of what [is now] known as romantic literature... The newly defined *love* undermined the Christian view of the purposes of marriage. The word *heart* became an idiom for emotion rather than mind. These new definitions of *love* and *heart* challenged the spiritual and natural hierarchy of authority within man and placed emotions in control of acts."[15]

Linda Bird Francke seems to continue deParrie's survey of history: "...abortion was receiving high acceptance as the only effective form of reproduction regulation and was being practiced with increasing frequency throughout Europe and America. The movement was capped off by a highly popular book by the Marquis de Sade published in 1795, which not only attacked the restrictions the church put on abortion, but actually extolled the values of abortion."[16]

11 Grant, *Third Time Around*, 59.

12 Grant, *Third Time Around*, 52.

13 Davis, *Abortion and the Christian*, 5.

14 *Orphans in Babylon*, 14, note 4.

15 Paul deParrie, *Romanced to Death*, 63-4.

16 Franke, *The Ambivalence of Abortion*, 14.

The seeds of the modern culture wars were contained in the most fundamental premises of the Protestant Reformation: individualism and the questioning of authority. Whitehead explains: "First, Luther argued that the Bible was the final authority. Nothing was considered superior or even equal to it in authority. This meant that man and all his institutions, including the state as well as the church, were under the authority of God and the Bible... Second, ...was Luther's argument for the priesthood of all believers. Up to this point in time, men passed through hierarchies and mediators as the pathway to God. Luther's doctrine attacked this idea. He asserted that all men, without need of a king (claiming divine rights) or any other human agency, had immediate access to God. This doctrine gave us individualism (but with responsibility)."[1]

Allen Verhey links Luther to the modern fixation on autonomy: "In 1520... Luther wrote *The Freedom of a Christian*... Indeed, the case could be made that the Protestant contribution to medical ethics is precisely its emphasis on freedom, on the patient's autonomy."[2]

Southern Baptist ethicist Paul Simmons makes this distinction: "Those Protestants who stress the biblical notion of the priesthood of all believers will be inclined to stress the right and responsibility of the woman in making the abortion decision. Those who rely more on rules and church or religious leader authority models will advocate legal controls."[3]

The modern demand for the separation of church and state may well have begun as a reaction to the Protestant *wedding* of church and state in Geneva, Switzerland, where, "In practice, Calvin dominated the city, and after 1555 he was a virtual autocrat... Attendance at church during prescribed hours was required by law."[4]

The Durants outline developments within Catholicism which also greatly impacted the church-state debate: "Though the Church served the state, it claimed to stand above all states, as morality should stand above power... The Church offered itself as an international court to which all rulers were to be morally responsible... The majestic dream broke under the attacks of nationalism, skepticism, and human frailty... More and more the hierarchy spent its energies in promoting orthodoxy rather than morality, and the Inquisition almost fatally disgraced the Church."[5]

Michael Bray says that "Medieval political theory [and also the Lutherans' *Magdeburg Confession* in 1550] recognized a contractual bond between rulers and subjects. Violation of the contract on the part of the king justified revolt... Theodore Beza (1519-1605) [wrote]: 'But if the tyrant forbids you to do what God has commanded, then you will not have done your duty merely by refusing to obey the tyrant, but you must render obedience to God. Thus, Obadiah not only refused to kill the prophets, but gave them refuge and nourishment [hid 100 of them in caves] against the will of Ahab and Jezebel'"[6]

Just how far Calvin felt Christians should go in defense of bedrock convictions was clearly stated: "Those who draw the conclusion that the teaching of the Gospel and the pure worship of God should not be defended by arms are wrong and ignorant."[7]

Hart says that, "A second important consequence of the Reformation was the widespread religious warfare in Europe which followed it. Some of these religious wars (for example, the Thirty Years' War in Germany, which lasted from 1618 to 1648) were incredibly bloody. Even aside from the wars, political conflicts between Catholics and Protestants were to play a major role in European politics for the next few centuries."[8]

Hunter addresses those earlier Culture Wars: "The Enlightenment thinkers... were particularly anxious to see the end of hostilities between Protestants and Catholics and between Christians and Jews in their own societies..."[9]

Wolterstorff summarizes: "For seventeenth-century England, ...peace did depend on getting citizens to stop invoking God, canonical scriptures, and religious authorities when discussing politics in public – to confine such invocations to discussions within their own confessional circles."[10]

Will and Ariel Durant chronicle the theological decline and the rise of naturalism, beginning in the Middle Ages, in *The Lessons of History*: "The 'death of God' ...required many causes besides the spread of science... First, the Protestant Reformation, which originally defended private judgment. Then the multitude of Protestant sects and conflicting theologies, each appealing to both Scriptures and reason. Then the higher criticism of the Bible... as the imperfect work of fallible men. Then the deistic movement in England, reducing religion to a vague belief in a God hardly distinguishable from nature."[11]

SCOPE and FOCUS
I. CONVICTIONS
II. PRETEXTS
III. MANDATE
IV. LEGACY
Christian Tradition
Early Church
Reformation Era
World Precedents
Holocaust
Nuremberg
Geneva
United Nations and Int'l. Human Rights
Unborn Child's Rights
Global Abortion Norms
Apartheid
United States History
Independence
Liberty & Rights
Abolition of Slavery
Women's Passage Rites
Seeds of Destruction
Between World Wars
Pivotal Developments
Civil Rights
Parental Responsibility
Humaneness
V. ABORTIVE LINKS
VI. DILEMMA
VII. DESTINY

Cal Thomas also traces *The Death of Ethics in America* back to beginnings in the Middle Ages, citing a problem that arose "from the medieval nature-grace dualism of Thomas Aquinas that divided human life into two spheres – the *supernatural*, revealed to man by God's Word in the Bible, and the *natural* that is known to man by his own reason."[12]

Paul deParrie agrees: "The new naturalism defined all beings and events as *natural*. The supernatural was either denied outright or reduced to being unknown natural phenomena... The seventeenth-century philosopher, Baruch Spinoza exemplified this belief saying, 'Nature always observes laws and rules... although they may not all be known to us... What is meant in Scripture by a miracle can only be a work of Nature.'"[13]

Elsewhere, deParrie says of naturalism, "This 'science' propounded a world in which the natural order was an ultimate truth... Right and wrong, it taught, could be discerned by what was natural... The conclusions of naturalism laid the foundations for the later acceptance of premarital sex and hedonism."[14]

CONCLUSIONS: • Christians in the Middle Ages considered their theological beliefs to be worth fighting and dying for, even as an expanding secular culture sought to reject God completely [creation vs. accident, and design vs. mechanism]; • In the face of an aggressive naturalism, the orthodox reasserted the primacy of God's law over man's law, but rampant religious strife argued for the wisdom of the privatization of religious faith [commandments v. positivism]; • An expanding abortion culture was aggressively challenged by some of the faithful [justice vs. pragmatism]; • Self-sacrificial ministries served "widows and orphans," while much of society shifted its focus from heavenly to earthly delights [virtue vs. pleasure]; • Persecution and martyrdom tested convictions about right and wrong, as earlier unanimity was lost to extreme doctrinal diversity [universalism vs. relativism]; • Protestantism stressed direct, personal Accountability to God alone, but that individuality opened the door to Autonomy and to the questioning of all authority – the Bible, and particularly its miracles, came under unrelenting attack;

• Every branch of Christianity was pro-life to the core, defending humanity from the moment of conception.

1 Whitehead, *Stealing of America*, 10.
2 Verhey, in Kilner, *Bioethics and the Future of Medicine*, 81.
3 Simmons, by Swomley, in Jersild, *Moral Issues & Christian Response*, 344.
4 Hart, 286-8.
5 Durant, 44-5.
6 Bray, 164-6.
7 Calvin, from vol. 5 of *Calvin's New Testament Commentaries*, in Bray, 60.
8 Hart, 151.
9 Hunter, 41.
10 Wolterstorff, in Audi and Wolterstorff, 79.
11 Durant, 47.
12 Thomas, *Death of Ethics*, 31.
13 DeParrie, *Romanced to Death*, 70.
14 DeParrie, *Romanced to Death*, 65.

B. World Precedents

The secular world labors tirelessly to remove credit from Christianity for any historical movements that have benefited humanity, even as it loudly trumpets the dark chapters in church history. Wolterstorff observes: "Many of the social movements in the modern world that have moved societies in the direction of liberal democracy have been deeply and explicitly religious in their orientation: the abolitionist movement in nineteenth century America [and in Europe], the civil rights movement in twentieth century America, the resistance movements in fascist Germany, in communist Eastern Europe, in apartheid South Africa."[1]

He continues: "...movements are often analyzed by Western academics and intellectuals as if religion were nowhere in the picture... The people in Leipzig [resistance movement in East Germany in the late 1980s] assembled in a meeting space that just happened to be a church to listen to inspiring speeches that just happened to resemble sermons; they were led out into the streets in protest marches by leaders who just happened to be pastors."[2]

We will consider civil disobedience later [part V.C.], but as a preview, Chuck Colson asks and answers this question: "When is civil disobedience justified? ...Inadequate though it was, the resistance of the German church to Hitler was a clear modern example of this necessity. In the Sixties we saw it in the Civil-rights Movement, as we do today in the Right-to-Life Movement and nonviolent resistance to Apartheid in South Africa."[3]

As we begin to look for historical precedents for socio-political movements in some way related to America's present culture war, our preliminary observation must be that property rights have an extremely long and strong history – as contrasted with Human Rights, which are a much more recent phenomenon. Aldo Leopold captures an essential feature of Homer's myths: "When god-like Odysseus returned from the wars in Troy, he hanged all on one rope a dozen slave-girls of his household whom he suspected of misbehavior during his absence. This hanging involved no question of *propriety*. The girls were *property*. The disposal of property was then, as now, a matter of expediency, not of right and wrong."[4] We reflect that some of the most persuasive pro-abortion arguments begin by reducing the status of the preborn to that of a piece of property.

A general historical rule has been that individuals have enjoyed autonomy in the disposition of their property, and states have exercised sovereignty in their treatment of the people within their borders. As international protocol evolved, it was asserted that a state could be constrained from abusing the citizens [read *property*] of another state who happened to be inside its territory. Subsequent to that development, we are told by Thomas Buergenthal, "...the doctrine of humanitarian intervention was the first to give expression to the proposition that there were some limits to the freedom states enjoyed under international law in dealing with *their own* nationals." He continues, "The doctrine of humanitarian intervention, as expounded by Hugo Grotius in the 17th century... recognized as lawful the use of force by one or more states to stop the maltreatment by a state of its own nationals when that conduct was so brutal and large-scale as to shock the conscience of the community of nations."[5]

Here we have the beginnings of global recognition that *individuals* have rights that governments must respect. When we raise the question of abortion, however, it must be acknowledged from the start that the "community of nations" seems now to be firmly resolved that abortion is a pragmatic *solution* to a host of problems, as opposed to viewing abortion as a moral *problem*.

Related to the question of when a state is justified in intervening in the internal affairs of another state is the issue of when one individual is permitted to raise a hand against another. The right of self-defense has been among the most fundamental in virtually all societies. Beyond self-defense, Bray tells us, "The Christian just war theory (*Justum Bellum*) was built not upon a principle of self-defense, but upon that of defense of another. Accordingly, force may be lawfully wielded by the... citizen authorized by the state [as a soldier or peace officer, for instance], or by the private citizen authorized as it were by God (and in fact most states of the United States) for the purpose of protecting a neighbor from harm."[6]

"Although the internationalization process continues to this day every time a human rights treaty enters into force, it began in the 19th century with the conclusion of treaties to ban the slave trade and international agreements to protect Christian minorities in the Ottoman (Turkish) Empire." [See *Treaty of Paris* of 30 March 1856, and *Treaty of Berlin* of 13 July 1878][7]

SCOPE and FOCUS
I. CONVICTIONS
II. PRETEXTS
III. MANDATE
IV. LEGACY
Christian Tradition
Early Church
Reformation Era
World Precedents
Holocaust
Nuremberg
Geneva
United Nations and Int'l. Human Rights
Unborn Child's Rights
Global Abortion Norms
Apartheid
United States History
Independence
Liberty & Rights
Abolition of Slavery
Women's Passage Rites
Seeds of Destruction
Between World Wars
Pivotal Developments
Civil Rights
Parental Responsibility
Humaneness
V. ABORTIVE LINKS
VI. DILEMMA
VII. DESTINY

We begin with these observations:

In the earliest ages, governments protected the property rights of individuals and recognized the principle of personal self-defense. The states themselves regarded people as their property. Christians in whatever society acted on the biblical imperative to minister to those less fortunate, and to rescue the innocent victim [including infants legally abandoned by their parents]. It was Christians, by and large, who founded orphanages, hospitals, schools and prison ministries.

In an intermediate stage, governments came to acknowledge that there were limits on their right to abuse nationals of other states and, more recently, their own people. States also began to institute human welfare programs, often patterned after Christian models. The Christian duty – and right – to intervene to prevent harm to an innocent victim took shape globally in the just war theory and in the concept of humanitarian intervention. At the personal level, the Defense of Necessity was acknowledged to condone individual acts of force to prevent injury to another.

As if acting on the principle that an ounce of prevention is worth a pound of cure, the community of nations began to enact treaties [cited above] to constrain some of the more flagrant abuses of humanity, such as slavery and religious persecution. After World War I, however, the League of Nations proved to be only a paper tiger, and when Hitler won control of Germany there was no international deterrent capable of preventing World War II.

1. Holocaust

Justice vs. Pragmatism

"When [Friedrich 'Martin'] Niemoller, the great independent Christian, ...told Hitler that he was troubled about the future of Germany, Hitler replied bleakly: 'Let that be my concern.'"[8]

F. R. Bienenfeld, in *Rediscovery of Justice* , says: "Hitler, like a despotic father, permitted his mature children the delight of indulging in all those cruelties to which children by nature are inclined and which it is the natural task of education to combat. He induced the German nation to return to the happy condition of irresponsible childhood and commit unbelievable atrocities without remorse because the leader had assumed all responsibility."[9]

According to John Powell, "...the seeds of human destruction in Germany were planted in the growing acceptance of the Hegelian pragmatic morality: If it provides a solution for a practical problem, it is morally justifiable. The (desirable) end justifies the (evil) means."[10]

John Whitehead says that under Hitler's philosophy, "all life became relative. If, as it did, it became convenient to exterminate people at Auschwitz, it was done. This was still easier to do with evolution as a foundation. After all, man is yet an evolving animal. The Jews, labeled subhumans, became nonbeings. It was both legal and right to exterminate them in the collectivist and evolutionist viewpoint. They were not considered part of the whole and thus were not persons in the sight of the German government."[11]

Whitehead goes on to say:

> The German people were clearly not ignorant of Hitler's goals when they voted for him. The voters were very aware of the Nazi ideology. Nazi literature, including statements of the Nazi plans for the future, had papered the country for a decade before Hitler came to power. In fact, Hitler's book, *Mein Kampf* [1925], which is his blueprint for totalitarianism, sold more than 200,000 copies between 1925 and 1932... When German President Hindenburg died in August 1934, Hitler assumed the office of president as well as that of chancellor... This new move was approved in a general election in which Hitler obtained 88 percent of the votes cast... The essence of the political system which Hitler intended to establish in Germany was clear. Thus, the German people, in essence, asked for Auschwitz.[12]

1 Audi and Wolterstorff, 80.
2 Audi and Wolterstorff, 80.
3 Colson, 247-9.
4 Garrett Hardin, echoing Leopold, in Stone, foreword, x.
5 Buergenthal, *International Human Rights, in a Nutshell*, 3-4.
6 Michael Bray, 67.
7 Thomas Buergenthal, *Nutshell*, 6.
8 William Barclay, *Ethics in a Permissive Society*, 182.
9 Bienenfeld, 121.
10 Powell, *Abortion: the Silent Holocaust*, 28.
11 Whitehead, *The Stealing of America*, 15.
12 Whitehead, *Stealing*, 15-6.

In *When Light Pierced the Darkness,* Nechama Tec tells us:

> As a general rule, in each country mass murders were preceded by a carefully orchestrated sequence of violations of rights. In the first phase, laws were introduced defining who was and who was not a Jew and requiring the identification of all those who were now defined as Jewish. Next came the expropriation of Jewish property and the denial to Jews of gainful employment. The beginning of the end was signaled by the removal of Jews from their homes to specially designated areas, usually sealed-off ghettoes, out of sight of Christian populations. Isolation of the Jews in the ghettoes before moving them to the death camps was a rigidly enforced part of the master plan in virtually all countries under the Nazi direct control. This was followed by the final mass annihilation.[1]

Joseph Foreman, as usual, makes an astute observation: **"Hitler never required the common people to kill Jews. He merely required them to permit him to kill them."[2]**

Christian Complicity with Hitler

Randy Alcorn tells us that within six months after the Nazis came to power in Germany, "In September 1933 the German Evangelical Church elected Hitler's puppet to [church] leadership. They submitted to the decree that all Jews by race, as well as those married to Jews, would be disqualified from church office. Considering it to be a biblical responsibility to government, they also passed a ruling that pastors take an oath of loyalty to Hitler and the government of Germany. An outraged Bonhoeffer urged that all pastors resign from a church that was selling out to the state."[3] George Grant tells us that the Lutherans also gave in to Hitler's demands.[4]

As to leadership in Nazi government, William Barclay says, "When Hitler came to power, at first he did not threaten the church as such, but he took good care that no real Christian ever held any power. He deliberately got rid of them, for he openly admitted that he wanted no one in his government who knew any other loyalty than loyalty to the state."[5]

"Without the cooperation and support of the scientific and medical professions, much of what the Nazi powers were able to do could not have been accomplished... Germany's most brilliant scientists, educators, and physicians, as well as the Christian church, were deceived into supporting a system which later brought destruction to that land and many of its people."[6]

According to Nechama Tec, "It seems likely that had the Pope, Pius XII, come out in support of the Jews, or had he condemned Nazi atrocities, Catholic ambiguities might have been resolved in favor of the persecuted Jews. This, however, did not happen. In fact the Pope's official silence, if anything, suggested tacit approval of these policies."[7]

It wasn't until 1995, that: "In an unusually blunt confession of guilt, Germany's Roman Catholic bishops have asserted that Catholics share responsibility for the Nazi Holocaust. The bishops deplored the failure of German Catholics to act against Nazism... [saying,] 'During the period of the Third Reich, Christians did not carry out the required resistance to racist anti-Semitism.'"[8]

Tec observes: "Faced with Nazi extermination of Jews, devout Catholics had many choices. They could... defy the urgings of a priest and save Jews. Or they could try to ignore what was happening to the Jews, rationalizing their decision by saying that it was a political rather than a church matter and that the church taught obedience to temporal authority in political matters... They could urge others to denounce Jews [turn them in to the authorities] and, if the opportunity presented itself, to denounce Jews themselves."[9]

John Whitehead notes: "The lack of resistance of the Christian churches to the Nazi state's Jewish policies has been the concern of extensive and still unconcluded literature. The Nazis noticed early that the churches took their stand, not on the issue of human rights of all Jews, but on an expedient and self-serving concern for 'Christian Jews.' The church by its expediency [pragmatism] and lack of political involvement was eventually neutralized by the state."[10]

"On April 1, 1933, Adolf Hitler called a national boycott of all Jewish businesses. The boycott was honored by most German citizens. After three days the boycott ended. Hitler had learned what he wanted to know: no one would stand up for the Jews. On the very day the boycott began, a group called 'The German Christians,' which included a number of well-known church leaders and theologians, held their first national rally in support of Hitler and the 'new Germany.'"[11]

1 Tec, *When Light Pierced the Darkness: Christian Rescue of Jews in Nazi-Occupied Poland*, 6.

2 Foreman, 98.

3 Alcorn, *Is Rescuing Right?*, 111-2.

SCOPE and FOCUS
I. CONVICTIONS
II. PRETEXTS
III. MANDATE
IV. LEGACY
Christian Tradition
Early Church
Reformation Era
World Precedents
Holocaust
Nuremberg
Geneva
United Nations and Int'l. Human Rights
Unborn Child's Rights
Global Abortion Norms
Apartheid
United States History
Independence
Liberty & Rights
Abolition of Slavery
Women's Passage Rites
Seeds of Destruction
Between World Wars
Pivotal Developments
Civil Rights
Parental Responsibility
Humaneness
V. ABORTIVE LINKS
VI. DILEMMA
VII. DESTINY

Anecdotal Acts of Heroism

Unarmed Against Hitler: Civilian Resistance in Europe, 1939-1943, records: "On April 5, 1942, Easter Sunday, Norway's bishops and pastors officially broke all administrative ties with the state and thereby lost their salaries. They insisted nonetheless on continuing their spiritual responsibilities. Quisling[12] considered this to be 'active insurrection' and threatened those who would not change their minds with worse censures. Of 850 pastors, [only] 50 gave in to this blackmail. Several dozen resisting bishops and pastors were arrested, and the primate was placed under house arrest. Hundreds of intellectuals and teachers signed a petition in favor of liberating Berggrav and others from prison... Several pastors were arrested and deported, but this changed nothing. Norway had no national church until the end of the war."[13]

"Forcing the Jews to wear a distinctive sign [often a large Star of David] was one of the tactics of harassment that enabled the Germans to recognize Jews as such on sight, and was designed to create a gulf between the Jews and the rest of the population."[14] Instant identification was essential to the Nazi objectives: if there were any uncertainty as to whether a particular stranger on the street was a Jew, the unrelenting process of debasement, abuse and persecution could not have been carried out as intended.

There are examples of widespread civil disobedience against Hitler's puppet governments. As early as 1941, "with Germany at its peak of conquest, the Bulgarian government began to introduce the package of anti-Jewish laws that had to do with the definition, expropriation, and concentration of Jews. The public disapproved of these steps. Thus, for example, the law requiring Jews to wear the yellow Star of David was attacked with special vigor. Under pressure, the government had to back down."[15]

There was also heroism in high places, among those who had nothing to gain and a great deal to lose for their bold stand, "King Boris III of Bulgaria, ruler from 1918 to 1943, was continually pressured by Hitler to join the Nazi effort. He steadfastly refused to cooperate. Even though Bulgaria was officially allied with Germany, not one soldier did he send to Hitler's army, nor did he allow one Bulgarian Jew to be deported to Poland. King Boris is one of the lesser-known heroes of that time."[16]

Here is testimony from a concentration camp survivor: "On a cold morning in the late fall of 1944 when I was a prisoner in Buchenwald... I saw a large group of shivering men in green uniforms penned into the enclosure next to mine. It was the police force of Copenhagen, rounded up because they refused to cooperate with the Nazis.. Throughout their internment, they were engaged in a systematic effort to sabotage any Nazi attempts to exploit their labor... Denmark and its police force surely deserve our highest admiration."[17]

"When [the Nazis] invited the Dutch doctors to rehabilitate people for the sole purpose of putting them to forced labor, the Dutch doctors adamantly refused... When these Dutch physicians were threatened with revocation of their licenses, they simply mailed in their licenses and took down their shingles. Even when the Reich Commander had one hundred Dutch doctors arrested and sent to concentration camps, the whole Dutch medical profession continued to stand firm."[18]

During World War II a priest bombed a Nazi freight train.[19]

4 Grant, *Third Time Around*, 127.

5 Barclay, *Ethics in a Permissive Society*, 182.

6 Glenn M. Hultgren, citation lost, So sorry!

7 Tec, *When Light Pierced the Darkness*, 138.

8 *Press*, 1-22-95, A2.

9 Tec, 137.

10 Whitehead, *The Stealing of America*, 59.

11 Randy Alcorn, *Is Rescuing Right?*, 111.

12 Vidkun Quisling was the Norwegian politician who betrayed his country to the Nazis and became a puppet ruler. Hence, his name has entered the world vocabulary: *quisling* is now a synonym for *traitor*.

13 Jacques Semelin, *Unarmed Against Hitler*, 67.

14 Israel Gutman, *Encyclopedia of the Holocaust*, vol. 1, 8.

15 Tec, 10.

16 Letter from "Roxana, Ill," to Ann Landers, *Press*, 4-19-97, B10.

17 Letter from "Annandale, Va.," to Ann Landers, *Press*, 4-19-97, B10.

18 John Powell, *Abortion: The Silent Holocaust*, 33.

19 Kerby Anderson, *Living Ethically in the '90s*, 12.

What Kinds of People Defied Hitler?

We have evidence that a broad spectrum of people took risks in opposition to the Nazis, including both the king and the citizens of Bulgaria, the police force of a major city, a solid majority of one nation's doctors, and the preponderance of the clergy of another country's state-church.

"Historians and military experts have wondered over the years if a civilian population itself could ever organize a nonmilitary civilian defense... Since they saw this kind of struggle as reserved for 'saints,' they thought it unlikely to be carried out by an entire population unless it contained millions of saints."[1] In this regard two unique examples come to mind: Gandhi's use of non-violent civil disobedience to rid India of foreign colonial rule by England, and black South African victory over apartheid [perhaps as much due to the lack of guns as to pacifistic convictions]. The fact that both of these examples required a bloody and protracted struggle is proof that power will never be relinquished without conflict. Despite the considerable amount of violence involved, it is clear that both of these were moral victories, not military.

A major difference separates the contests in India and South Africa from heroism under Hitler. Gandhi and Mandela led monumental majorities in a quest for political liberty, a struggle of self-interest for the victims of tyranny. In Germany [as in America's pro-life movement] the heroism asked is exclusively altruistic – individuals abandoning a safe and comfortable situation for the statistically improbable possibility of rescuing a stranger from imminent death. Under the Nazis, the chance of success was fractional, and the probability of a failure – fatal to both rescuee and rescuer – was astronomical. Every time such risk was taken is testimony that *holiness*, the very image of God, *is* a component of the human spirit.

Nechama Tec, author of *When Light Pierced the Darkness: Christian Rescue of Jews in Nazi-Occupied Poland*, provides several insights into the character of those heroic souls: "Pious rescuers had to rely on personal rather than on official religious values. It is certain that religion played a positive and significant role in the protection of Jews by pious rescuers, but these helpers seemed to be religious in a special way. They were independent in their interpretation of religious values, and this independence prevented them from blindly following the teachings of the Church... It was these moral convictions rather than religion *per se* that made them rescue Jews even when faced with opposition from the clergy."[2]

"Normative altruism refers to helping behavior demanded, supported, and rewarded by society. In contrast, autonomous altruism refers to selfless help, which is neither reinforced nor otherwise rewarded by society. Indeed, autonomous altruism may be opposed by society and may at times involve grave risks not only of physical injury but of social ostracism... Indeed, saving Jews in Nazi-occupied Poland put the actor in conflict with his society's expected values."[3]

Here we take the liberty of summarizing Tec's general profile of the kind of person who rescued Jews in Nazi-occupied Poland: (1) Individuality, separateness, positive-marginality; (2) Independence, self-reliance, unmoved by criticism; (3) Long-standing strong commitment to help the needy; (4) Humility, doing the right thing, not feeling 'heroic'; (5) Spontaneous rescue, not pre-planned; (6) Broad commitment to all the helpless and needy.[4]

All of the insights from *When Light Pierced the Darkness* are fascinating, but these are astonishing: "Only a minority of those [Jews] saved reported having been saved by friends. Many reported approaching friends first, being turned down, and then being aided by strangers. More than half simply said they were protected by strangers."[5]

SCOPE and FOCUS
I. CONVICTIONS
II. PRETEXTS
III. MANDATE
IV. LEGACY
Christian Tradition
Early Church
Reformation Era
World Precedents
Holocaust
Nuremberg
Geneva
United Nations and Int'l. Human Rights
Unborn Child's Rights
Global Abortion Norms
Apartheid
United States History
Independence
Liberty & Rights
Abolition of Slavery
Women's Passage Rites
Seeds of Destruction
Between World Wars
Pivotal Developments
Civil Rights
Parental Responsibility
Humaneness
V. ABORTIVE LINKS
VI. DILEMMA
VII. DESTINY

Governments Vanquish Enemies

Nechama Tec says, "The most formidable barrier to Jewish rescue was the degree to which Nazi occupying forces gained control of the government machinery. Where the Nazis were in virtual control, they were prepared to do whatever was necessary to annihilate the Jewish populations and would brook no interference from any individual or group in regard to the carrying out of their policies."[6]

"In 1941 as the initial anti-Jewish measures were being introduced, the citizens of Amsterdam protested by calling for a general strike that lasted three days. The Germans reacted swiftly with severe reprisals against both Christians and Jews. From both groups many arrests and deportations to concentration camps followed. In the climate of resignation... even the great powers of the continent seem to have conceded the irresistibility of Nazism."[7]

Michael Bray tells us, "To anyone turning in a Jew, the Gestapo usually paid one quart of brandy, four pounds of sugar, and a carton of cigarettes, or a small amount of money... The host was usually executed on the spot, or hanged in a public place as an object lesson to 'Aryans' who entertained the notion of hiding a Jew."[8]

Heroism Defies the Odds

"Traditionally, the Danes had perceived the Jews as Danes, and now they refused to hand them over to the Nazis, even when ordered to do so. At this point the Danish underground gained in stature and, with the cooperation of other Danes, moved the country's Jewish population to Sweden. Danish opposition to the Nazi measures saved even the 472 Jews [of the 8,000 originally in Denmark] who were seized by the Germans before they could be evacuated..."[9]

It is reported that with the support of King Christian X, Danish churches, and Danish Resistance, 7200 Jews were evacuated in three weeks, and that Danes set up a system of visitation and supply for the roughly 500 Jews who were deported to Theresienstad, which enabled all but 51 of them to survive the war.[10]

An otherwise unremarkable American high school Latin teacher named Varian Fry thrust himself into the Holocaust in 1940, "with the reluctant permission of the U.S. government. He was supposed to rescue 200 Jewish artists and intellectuals [in Marseille, France] from the Nazis and get out in three weeks. But Fry... stayed 14 months. Aided by a few expatriate Americans and French volunteers, he saved nearly 4,000 people, sneaking them out with forged passports or smuggling them across the mountains into Spain... The U.S. State Department repeatedly warned Fry to desist and the U.S. Consulate in Marseille confiscated his passport."[11]

Tec tells us that the Netherlanders who helped Anne Frank and her family were sent to concentration camps,[12] and George Grant reveals that Corrie Ten Boom's father and sister both died in German camps for their central role in the Dutch underground and for hiding Jews in their Holland home.[13] Remarkably, Dutch Christians attempted to hide 25,000 Jews from the Nazis. Tragically, three-fourths of those were "denounced" [turned in by their neighbors]. Miraculously, 7,000 Dutch Jews were *successfully* protected by the Dutch.[14] In 1942, a Ukrainian doorkeeper agreed to hide and secretly provide for 21 fugitive Jews. When the doorkeeper's brother-in-law found out and was going to turn him in to the Gestapo, the doorkeeper "grabbed an ax and killed him." He fled with the Jews to escape revenge by his wife and her family.[15]

"Yad Vashem was established in 1953 in Jerusalem as a memorial to European Jews who perished during World War II... This memorial also pays tribute to Christians who, during this period, saved Jews. The formal Hebrew title of these saviors is... The Righteous Ones of the Nations of the World... As a rule, it is next to impossible to receive this title without a request from Jewish beneficiaries; survivors usually petition the committee to honor their protectors."[16]

This honor is not afforded, then, if the Jews ultimately perished in spite of heroic efforts to save them, or if the benefactor's name is either not known or not remembered. Tec continues: "Earlier I described righteous Poles who lost their lives because they were protecting Jews. As a rule they died with their charges, and Yad Vashem distinctions thus will not be offered to them... Recalling that at times the Germans would surround and burn entire villages accused of harboring Jews, annihilating every inhabitant, it is obvious that neither the names nor the numbers of the resulting fatalities can ever be known" [Roughly 6,000 have been honored, and it is estimated that the actual number directly deserving that honor is ten times that, or 60,000].[17]

1 Jacques Semelin, *Unarmed Against Hitler: Civilian Resistance in Europe, 1939-1943*, 64.
2 Tec, 148-9.
3 Tec, 152.
4 Tec, 154.
5 Tec, 129.
6 Tec, 6.
7 Tec, 10.
8 Bray, 96.
9 Tec, 8.
10 "The Rescue of Danish Jewry 1943-1993" display at Simon Wiesenthal Center, Los Angeles, November, 1996.
11 *Press*, 2-16-96, A2.
12 Tec, 3.
13 Grant, *Third Time Around*, 132.
14 Tec, 9.
15 Bray, 96-7.
16 Tec, 3-4.
17 Tec, 84.

Intolerance of Dissent

A factor of ten was a typical measure used by Hitler in exacting his style of revenge. *Associated Press* reports that "the last Nazi" was tried in Italy in March of 1998. Following a 1944 ambush which had killed 32 German soldiers in Italy, Hitler had demanded tenfold retaliation. The SS captain had marched 335 civilians of all ages, including 71 Jews and several Catholic priests into a cave, which was then blown up. The aging captain told the newspaper reporter, "I was just following orders."[1]

How do you Measure a Holocaust?

In 1941, Elton Trueblood wrote *Vocational Christian Pacifism*. In it he declared, "We are now [at the beginning of World War II] in the midst of a revolution produced by a combination of forces, ideological, psychological and technological, which have given us a new problem. Since the combination of forces never existed before, the present situation has no true counterpart in history."[2] Trueblood's statement is equally true of the United States today.

In the foreword to his 1988 manifesto *Operation Rescue*, Randall Terry said "Let us not repeat the lesson of the German church in the 1930s and '40s that stood apathetically by and watched as the unwanted of their generation were marched off to unspeakable death. We need Corrie Ten Booms of the 1980s who will stand up to man's repudiation of God's law and follow Jesus' command to love our neighbors as ourselves."[3]

In 1996, the medical director of a London fertility clinic was given an order that can be compared to those Hitler gave his underlings. A 1990 British law requires the destruction of frozen four-cell human embryos after five years unless donor couples seek an extension. He had been ordered to defrost 3,000 embryos. His view of his dilemma mirrors the plight expressed by Hitler's officers and troops: "I have been told that, if I make a stand and refuse to destroy them, then I will be sent to prison and someone else will come in and do it anyway."[4]

"The situation under Hitler drove Bonhoeffer to abandon pacifist tactics and participate in a plot to assassinate the [elected] president of his own country. [He said:] 'It is not only my task to look after the victims of madmen who drive a motorcar in a crowded street, but to do all in my power to stop their driving at all.'"[5]

America's Holocaust, and Rescue

R.C. Sproul is willing to reveal his own confusion when he compares the two Holocausts: "Rescue, which involves intentional civil disobedience, is hotly disputed even within the ranks of pro-life advocates... The Bible has a high view of the sanctity of life and of civil disobedience. This is the issue that divides Christians. It's the same issue that Dietrich Bonhoeffer had to struggle with when he was invited to join a plot to assassinate Adolf Hitler. We must draw the line between what is a legitimate form of protest and what is not... I must confess that I have not resolved it in my own mind. However, the urgency of the abortion issue requires us to protest to the very limit that our consciences allow."[6]

We must add Sproul to the list of godly Christian authors who have "missed it" when it comes to the distinction between rescue and protest. When I ignore my neighbor's "no trespassing" sign and dive into his swimming pool to save the kid who is drowning, I am not *protesting* that the gate was left unlocked, I am *rescuing* a human being from death.

Time magazine works very hard to deny pro-life views a sympathetic hearing. Yet just two weeks after Paul Hill killed abortionist Britton, *Time* published an amazing article by Michael Kinsley which is either serious or sarcastic, and it is impossible to tell which. The piece clearly acknowledges the Holocaust link to abortion in America, but it is probable that *Time*'s editors expected readers to conclude, "Aren't pro-lifers a bunch of hypocrites?" as opposed to, "Yeh, Kinsley's right, Paul Hill really did the country a great service." Here is a key quote: "On July 29 [1994, Paul] Hill shot and killed Dr. John Britton and a clinic volunteer at an abortion clinic in Pensacola, Florida. Almost all elements of the right-to-life movement condemned the killings. But why? After all, the practical effect of such actions is not merely to put one baby killer out of business but to chill the entire practice of abortion in America. Surely during the real Holocaust it would have been 'justifiable homicide' to kill a German camp guard, if that would have slowed the feeding of the gas chambers."[7]

1 *Associated Press, Press*, 3-11-98, A2.
2 Trueblood, in Hutchison, in 1968, 210.
3 Terry, *Operation Rescue*, foreword.
4 *Associated Press, Press*, 8-1-96, A2.
5 Bray, *A Time to Kill*, 96.
6 Sproul, *Abortion: A Rational Look at an Emotional Issue*, 155-6.
7 Michael Kinsley, in *Time*, 8-15-94, 64.
8 *Press*, 8-27-94, H3.

"Justifiable Homicide?"

Although we do not know where Michael Kinsley really stands, Rev. David Trosch does not mince his words; shortly after signing the "defensive action" statement affirming a biblical justification for Paul Hill's act, and after publishing his view that it was "justifiable homicide" in a local newspaper, Father Trosch was defrocked. Newspapers reported that he draws "an historical analogy to the French Resistance during world War II. 'When they killed the enemy soldiers, did anybody admonish them?' he asked. 'In fact, they were considered heroes.' In recent weeks, Trosch has elaborated his views in letters to religious and secular authorities. Writing last month to members of Congress, he warned of a possible civil war marked by 'massive killing' of abortion doctors and their staffs."[8]

CONCLUSIONS CONCERNING TWO HOLOCAUSTS

There are so many parallels between the Nazi Holocaust and abortion in American that this researcher has concluded that the degree to which an individual will claim that there is a difference between the two is basically the measure of how great a difference that person sees between a preborn child in an abortion clinic and a Jew in a concentration camp. If one sees both as innocent human persons targeted for an unjust death, then both holocausts are virtually identical.

Both German Nazism and American abortionism are philosophically rooted in Pragmatism, nourished by Positivism and evolution [Accident and Mechanism]. Both Relativize the value of human life and deem selected categories of humanity as subhuman and malignant. In both cases a radical doctrine seduced the intelligentsia, captured the bases of power, and then harnessed existing social winds and currents to forge an impregnable political machine.

The abortion culture, like Nazism, has successfully neutralized church leadership, winning the support of the blind and gullible and systematically marginalizing most of the rest. As in Europe, a smattering of American clerics have sounded the trumpet, but few have ventured into more than a tentative skirmish, and the trumpeting has grown less frequent and more muted. The great majority of overt Christian opposition to abortion, as to Hitlerism, has come from "laymen," many of whom report that their shepherd is either unsupportive or even critical of their actions.

SCOPE and FOCUS
I. CONVICTIONS
II. PRETEXTS
III. MANDATE
IV. LEGACY
Christian Tradition
Early Church
Reformation Era
World Precedents
Holocaust
Nuremberg
Geneva
United Nations and Int'l. Human Rights
Unborn Child's Rights
Global Abortion Norms
Apartheid
United States History
Independence
Liberty & Rights
Abolition of Slavery
Women's Passage Rites
Seeds of Destruction
Between World Wars
Pivotal Developments
Civil Rights
Parental Responsibility
Humaneness
V. ABORTIVE LINKS
VI. DILEMMA
VII. DESTINY

Both governments pushed for the privatization of religion, and acted with unfettered determination to eliminate any opposition to their most cherished programs, taking particular care to deter potential foes by aggressively demonizing and punishing all offenders to the maximum degree possible.

The primary differences between the two holocausts can be seen in the variety of options available to those who oppose the regime, and the numbers of citizens who pursue those options. Numerically, six million Jews were exterminated by Hitler, and more than five times that many preborn American children have met a similar government-assured fate. In both cases the argument could be made that the program is the work of a democratically elected government in pursuit of publicly supported goals.

A difference is that most Americans are still convinced that a pro-life political solution can be achieved through normal democratic processes, while practically nobody ever thought that there was a political remedy for Nazism. Hitler, then, allowed for no safe avenue of opposition, while the United States citizenry sustains untold scores of pro-life parachurch ministries, some boasting hundreds of thousands of financial supporters, and conducting an unprecedented volume of lobbying and educational activity. So upwards of a half-million Americans can "fight abortion" in total safety, sacrificing only the dollar amount they choose to contribute, while there was absolutely no comparable niche throughout the totality of Nazi-occupied Europe. To voice even a word of concern about what was happening to the Jews often marked the "protester" for an identical fate.

When is a Rescue NOT a Rescue?

The next level of opposition beyond protest is ministry to victims. Unfortunately, when a victim is under a sentence of death, simply offering "a cup of water in His Name"[1] [while it may be greatly appreciated] affords no rescue. But American sidewalk counselors and crisis pregnancy centers [particularly when working as a team] sometimes are able to effect a true rescue of a baby from death, while still affording relative safety and security for the rescuers. However, even such peaceful, loving and socially beneficial ministries are increasingly demonized and persecuted, although not [yet?] to the degree that Hitler would have crushed a comparable intrusion on his plans.

In Europe direct rescue always carried grave risks. It typically took either the form of an "underground railroad" to spirit Jews away to safe havens, or lacking that opportunity, hiding Jews in one's home or place of business; the decision to participate in either one of these forms of rescue instantly transformed one's own life into a nightmare, and made it more likely than not that the rescuer, and perhaps his family and other innocents, would meet an early and violent death.

Abortion clinic "rescuers" in the United States do nothing of that kind. Of the estimated sixty thousand Europeans who attempted to rescue Jews, perhaps forty to fifty thousand of them were apprehended, nearly all dying at their captors' hand. Of roughly fifty thousand "Rescue" arrestees in the United States, the vast majority spent no more than a few days in jail, and it is conceivable that less than one thousand were jailed for weeks, that only a few hundred did a number of months, and that only a handful have logged incarceration that totals more than a year. World War II Europe afforded no such opportunity to wear a "good guy" hat at so paltry a cost.

In America, no more than three authentic pro-lifers have [to date, according to the public record] taken risks comparable to those of most of the rescuers of Jews. Paul Hill, Michael Griffin and Shelley Shannon [by their own testimony] each attempted to protect specific preborn human babies by shooting the serial killer who was determined to kill them. Each of those three can be likened to a person in Germany who protected a Jew being chased by an SS trooper by killing that Nazi. We may assume from their acts that Paul, Michael and Shelley *truly see no difference* between a preborn child and a European Jew. There can be only one explanation for why the rest of us who claim to be pro-life have not acted as they did: our vision is clouded and we see unborn babies less clearly than they do [Turnstyle Ministries invites dialogue on this assertion].

There is one more point of comparison between these two holocausts. During Hitler's reign of terror, there were active resistance movements throughout Europe, conducting sabotage and guerilla warfare. Their counterpart in the American pro-life struggle is composed of the individuals who attempt to save babies by eliminating the chief "tool" of the abortionist's trade: the abortion clinic itself. By and large these folks take care to prevent injury to persons and to avoid causing damage to adjacent businesses in their attempt to burn abortion clinics to the ground. While it is not their practice to turn themselves in, their amateur status has proved it likely that they will be either tracked down by the highly-motivated law enforcement community or turned in by some civic-minded acquaintance. There are many pro-lifers who have been convicted of pro-life arson. Our very incomplete research has discovered twelve who have been sentenced to ten years or more in prison; two of those received twenty-year sentences, and one was sentenced to 42 years in prison [see the Timeline at the end of *Orphans*, beginning at about 1980].

SCOPE and FOCUS
I. CONVICTIONS
II. PRETEXTS
III. MANDATE
IV. LEGACY
Christian Tradition
Early Church
Reformation Era
World Precedents
Holocaust
Nuremberg
Geneva
United Nations and Int'l. Human Rights
Unborn Child's Rights
Global Abortion Norms
Apartheid
United States History
Independence
Liberty & Rights
Abolition of Slavery
Women's Passage Rites
Seeds of Destruction
Between World Wars
Pivotal Developments
Civil Rights
Parental Responsibility
Humaneness
V. ABORTIVE LINKS
VI. DILEMMA
VII. DESTINY

1 *Matthew* 10:42; *Mark* 9:41.
2 Abe Fortas, *Concerning Dissent and Civil Disobedience*, 1968, 56.
3 Fortas, 57.
4 Fortas, 56. See additionally: Robert H. Jackson, *The Case Against the Nazi War Criminals*, 12.
5 *Orange County*, Calif., *Register*, 11-23-95, A1.
6 Scheidler, 353.
7 *Orange County,* Calif., *Register*, 11-23-95, A1.
8 F.L. Smith, *When Choice Becomes God*, 163.
9 Whitehead, *The Second American Revolution*, 88.
10 *Press*, 12-25-96, A16.
11 DeMar, in Foreman, xv.
12 Randall Terry, *Operation Rescue*, 31-2.

2. Nuremberg

Justice & Accountability

The basic defense of every member of the Nazi machine that did Hitler's bidding was Positivism: "Everything we did was perfectly legal," and "I was just following orders." Abe Fortas, a U.S. Supreme Court Justice at mid-century, pointed out that the London Agreement and the Nuremberg Trials defined new international laws which were applied *retroactively* to the Nazi leaders.[2] He went on to explain that the difficulty was in stating new international law which would condemn Hitler's atrocities without automatically indicting "the allied command responsible for bombing German cities and destroying their urban [civilian] population, or for the use of flame throwers in the [Pacific] command."[3]

Here is the list Abe Fortas compiled of the crimes that were ascribed to the Nazi leaders: "(1) **crimes against peace**, defined as planning, preparing, initiating, or waging a war of aggression; (2) **crimes of war**, defined as violations of the laws or customs of war; (3) **crimes against humanity**, defined to include murder, extermination, enslavement, deportation, and other inhuman acts committed against any civilian population."[4] Defense lawyers at Nuremberg objected that one of the main charges against their clients – waging an aggressive war – "had never been established as an offense in international law."[5] **The judgments at Nuremberg can be nothing more nor anything less than a sober acknowledgment that the world is Accountable to Higher Law!**

"It seemed appropriate, when the Allies conquered Germany, to make Nuremberg the scene of the trials to judge the crimes against humanity committed during the Third Reich," Scheidler tells us. "Nuremberg, Germany, was the seat of the Nazi party. The Nazis held a huge rally there every year."[6] If "Crimes against Posterity" trials are ever held for the architects of American abortion and their henchmen, the selection of an apt location will perhaps be narrowed down to New York City and San Francisco.

At the first Nuremberg International Military Tribunal, 21 were tried, 19 convicted, and twelve executed "for their roles in the murder of 6 million Jews, torture of prisoners of war, enslavement of the citizens of occupied nations and sadistic medical experiments," and beyond that first trial, "nearly 200 more Nazis were tried in 12 successive international military trials at Nuremberg. Thousands more were tried by national courts..."[7]

Several have identified significant parallels between the German experience under Hitler and America's present abortion culture. F. LaGard Smith quotes Dr. Leo Alexander's testimony as a consultant at the Nuremberg Trials: "The beginnings at first were merely a subtle shift in emphasis in the basic attitude of physicians. It started with the acceptance of the attitude, basic in the euthanasia movement, that there is such a thing as a life not worthy to be lived."[8]

John Whitehead discusses the result when a marriage of moral Relativism and legal Positivism is consummated: "...man cannot know, according to a higher law, what is just or right in a given situation, he cannot protest and criticize legitimately any particular course of action as unjust... During the Nazi era in Germany positivism disarmed the German jurists against law of an arbitrary and criminal nature. The very same thing has now happened in America."[9]

Does Whitehead overstate the situation? We think not. The *Associated Press* reported:

> A new federal rule allows doctors to experiment on certain dying patients without their consent. "1996 is the 50th anniversary of Nuremberg, where trials of Nazi doctors concluded [in the *Nuremberg Code*, that] humans should never again undergo such horrific, involuntary experimentation," noted the Georgetown University bioethicist Robert Veatch. "In the United States, we are commemorating that event by adopting regulations that flat-out are in violation of the Nuremberg Code."[10]

Are Nuremberg-style trials justified by the American [and the world's] embrace of a modern "bioethics" founded upon Relativism, Pragmatism and Positivism? Gary DeMar certainly thinks that they are:

> The principle that an individual is bound by a higher moral authority, beyond what civil sanctioned laws provided, was established in West Germany decades ago, during the trials of Nazi war criminals... Why doesn't America applaud those who seek to rescue the preborn from the border guards of the abortion industry? ...Operation Rescue is not only an indictment of Congress, the courts, and the abortionists, it is first and foremost an indictment of the Christian church.[11]

"Everything we do is being recorded... by the courts of heaven..." said Randall Terry. "In addition, the next generation will weigh our lives against our words, our deeds against our doctrines, our strength and courage against this hour of crisis... How do we view the German Christians who stood by and did nothing to rescue Jews from mass slaughter? ...What the church tolerates today, she may be despised for tomorrow."[12]

3. Geneva

Universalism & Justice

Under John Calvin's leadership, Hart tells us, Geneva, Switzerland, "became the leading Protestant center of Europe."[1]

Geneva's Christian convictions thrust it into leadership in, among other things, the struggle to restrain the abuses of power. Buergenthal tells us "Humanitarian law [rules of restraint, applied to warfare] is much older than international human rights law. Its modern development is usually traced to a series of initiatives undertaken in the 19th century by the Swiss... These initiatives produced the Geneva Convention of 1864, which was designed to protect medical personnel and hospital installations... [It also promoted the rule: 'Don't shoot the wounded']."[2]

In a modern world where it sometimes seems that practically any violence can be justified by "He *deserved* it!" we would do well to remember this hallowed international principle: even the enemy soldier who just moments ago killed your best buddy must be *protected* from further injury from the moment that he becomes incapacitated by injury, sickness, capture or surrender. This principle must be factored-in when we begin to discuss the human rights equation for the helpless and vulnerable ones we call preborn human beings.

The *Geneva Convention* of 1864 and the subsequent *Hague Convention*, Number III, of 1899, were combined and expanded after World War II to form the four *Geneva Conventions of 1949* and the two *Protocols Additional* to these Conventions. *Respect for Life in Medicine, Philosophy and the Law* tells us that Geneva also birthed another historical document a year earlier: "In 1948, when the horrors of the Nazi concentration camps were fresh in everybody's mind, the World Medical Association adopted what is known as the *Declaration of Geneva*. On admission to his profession the young doctor was [henceforth to pledge, among other things,] 'I will maintain the utmost respect for human life, from the time of conception; even under threat, I will not use my medical knowledge contrary to the laws of humanity.'"[3]

4. United Nations & Human Rights

Justice & Positivism

With all of its shortcomings, the United Nations is the best international advocate of peace and human rights that has ever existed. Just as a weak and ineffective *Articles of Confederation* preceded the more effective *Constitution* of the United States, the League of Nations, created after World War I, proved itself impotent against Hitler and was replaced by the United Nations in 1948.

Whereas the United States is founded upon Universal and godly principles [more about that soon], the *United Nations Charter* is clearly a *contract* between the governments of member nations, a monument to Positivism in a pluralistic world. Couched within the preamble to the *U.N. Charter*, however, is this tip of the hat to Universalism: "We... reaffirm faith in *fundamental* human rights, in the *dignity* and *worth* of the human person..." Belief in fundamental human rights, those which are affirmed to be *beyond all agreements*, imply that there are Universal moral truths, and if dignity and worth are inherent in being human, not bestowed or granted by governments and societies [not options but standard factory equipment], then humans have a dignity [we Christians say, *sanctity*] beyond the ability of others to bestow it and which no one has the right to deny or to violate.

There are two philosophical camps concerning human rights, one committed to Universalism and the other predicated upon Positivism. The latter group would maintain that no human rights exist until they are *created* through the signing of a formal written document [the social contract theory is alive and well, internationally]. The former group believes that the task of humans is to discover and to formally *recognize* those rights which are inherently owned by each and every person. These contrasting philosophical approaches greatly influence their respective groups whenever human rights documents are being written, adopted, or implemented.

There are some key terms which are essential to understanding international human rights documents. A *declaration* is a non-binding statement of principles agreed upon by certain countries ["states," with a small "s"]. International human rights *law*, on the other hand, is contained in *treaties*, which may also be called *covenants* or *conventions*. Compared with civil law, which generally applies to everybody within a given geographical area, human rights law seems more complex because some states are obligated to obey it and others are not, depending on a variety of factors.

SCOPE and FOCUS
I. CONVICTIONS
II. PRETEXTS
III. MANDATE
IV. LEGACY
Christian Tradition
Early Church
Reformation Era
World Precedents
Holocaust
Nuremberg
Geneva
United Nations and Int'l. Human Rights
Unborn Child's Rights
Global Abortion Norms
Apartheid
United States History
Independence
Liberty & Rights
Abolition of Slavery
Women's Passage Rites
Seeds of Destruction
Between World Wars
Pivotal Developments
Civil Rights
Parental Responsibility
Humaneness
V. ABORTIVE LINKS
VI. DILEMMA
VII. DESTINY

1 Hart, *The 100: A Ranking of the Most Influential Persons in History*, 286-8.

2 Buergenthal, *International Human Rights, in a Nutshell*, 17.

3 Owsei Temkin, *Respect for Life*, 1; and J.C. Willke, *Handbook on Abortion*,13.

5. The Unborn Child's Human Rights

Pragmatism & Positivism

What Rights do the Unborn have under the International Human Rights documents? The liberal forces have successfully kept the door open for abortion in virtually all of the International Human Rights treaties. The Inter-American System does recognize full humanity and personhood from conception. Article 4 (1) of the *American Convent on Human Rights* states, "Every person has the right to have his life respected. This right shall be protected by law, and, in general, from the moment of conception. No one shall be arbitrarily deprived of his life."

Back to the International arena, the *Declaration of the Rights of the Child* [two versions, 1924 and 1959] prefigured the *Convention on the Rights of the Child*. In the framing of this *Convention*, valiant attempts were made to secure protection for the preborn, but these efforts were effectively thwarted. The specific articles of this *Convention* do not provide any protection to the preborn, and only in the Preamble [thus nonbinding] is there a mention of protecting children "before as well as after birth." The complete preambular clause is as follows: "Whereas the child, by reason of his physical and mental immaturity, need special safeguards and care, including appropriate legal protection, before as well as after birth..."

In 1990, Philip Alston published in the *Human Rights Quarterly*, "The Unborn Child and Abortion Under the *Draft Convention on the Rights of the Child*." One of his generalizations is that "**The *Convention* conforms with existing international human rights law. While recognizing that the fetus is deserving of appropriate protection, its right to life *per se* is not recognized**." Alston's article details the wide variety of viewpoints that were given a hearing and consideration for inclusion in the *Convention*. These included the proposal from the U.N. Commission on the Status of Women that the "right to abortion" be included in the *Convention on the Rights of the Child*! The International Humanist and Ethical Union wanted the *Convention* to guarantee that "every child has a right to be born a wanted child." On the other hand, The Holy See submitted, "...the rights of the child begin before birth; life exists from the moment of conception; human life shall absolutely be respected and protected from that moment." The United States Delegation asserted that the *Convention* "must be worded in such a manner that neither proponents nor opponents of abortion can find legal support for their respective positions in the *Draft Convention*." The American plea for tolerance was sustained in the final vote. It must be noted that this ambivalence is not neutrality, for the lack of protection is an open door to abortion.

The *Convention on the Rights of the Child* [including its protections of the right to life] does pertain to "human beings below the age of eighteen," which avoids the additional problem which would have been raised had the word been "persons" rather than human beings, but to date, no action has been initiated to test whether a ***preborn*** human being is covered by the designation "human being under eighteen."

Similarly, Article 3(1) of the *Convention* clearly states that "In all actions concerning children, whether undertaken by public or private social welfare institutions, courts of law, administrative authorities or legislative bodies, **the best interests of the child shall be a primary consideration**." This article clearly *should* provide significant protection to *unborn* children from abortion and live fetal research, etc., but the preponderance of evidence shows that the international community accepts the legitimacy of abortion, even while much of that community is bound to the *Convention of the Rights of the Child*, including this particular article.

6. Global Norms Regarding Abortion

Pragmatism & Positivism

"But *everybody's* doing it!" is frequently the plaintive defense by teenagers of behavior criticized by their parents. In the United States, where the media seems to have appointed itself apologist and propagandist for abortion,[1] it would be easy to form the assumption that the whole world shares this government's view that only a fundamentalist lunatic anarchist would object to abortion on demand.

A three-volume resource recently published by the United Nations now makes it possible to appraise our country's stance within the community of nations. *Abortion Policies: A Global Review*, uses a standard format to reflect the statutes, policies and practices of 190 nations – one by one – concerning fertility, contraception and abortion. In the preparation of *Orphans in Babylon*, the country-by-country statistics contained in these three volumes has been entered into a database in order to generate the comparisons summarized herein.

US Abortion Policy: Globally Normal?

"A woman's right to choose," and "abortion on demand" are the popular phrases that best distinguish America's abortion policies from those of the rest of the world. Only 42 nations out of the 190, just 22%, permit any form of abortion on request, and all but six of those specify the number of weeks' gestation after which request can no longer justify an abortion. Abortion on request is only permitted during the first ten weeks in seven countries, and it is limited to the first twelve weeks in another twenty-four of them. What this means is that only five nations in the world permit abortion on request after the first trimester, only 2.6% of them. Sweden permits it up to the 18th week; Singapore and China stop at 24 weeks. It must be noted that China, which is much criticized by the United States for its unconscionable population-limiting practices,[2] still does not permit a woman to abort a child she has carried into the third trimester just because she decides she wants to have an abortion then. But all of this leaves only Canada and the United States, a scant 1% minority in the community of nations, permitting abortion upon request throughout the entire pregnancy . . . in the case of America, and at the insistence of its President, even when a baby is half delivered in what is called a "partial birth abortion." Clearly the United States, by its abortion policy, stands as far from the mainstream as is possible, the fuzz at the edge of the fringe.

Beyond mere choice, there are various other justifications for abortion, all of which the United States finds acceptable. Predictably, the majority of nations agree that if continuation of the pregnancy would endanger the life of the mother, an abortion is the equivalent of self-defense and is therefore permitted. Even so, there are four nations that do not say yes to that, and four more that specifically say no to all abortions, even in that situation. Additionally, there are nine countries of the world that hold all abortions to be illegal, but which by policy overlook abortions performed for the purpose of saving the woman's life. So the United States stands with 96% of the globe in permitting abortion to save the life of the mother.

The next levels of acceptance come in the categories of the mother's health and, beyond that, the mother's mental health. Because these terms are so vague, it is probable that a large percentage of abortions performed with these justifications are in situations far less compelling than was intended by those who authorized these reasons for abortion. Yet half of the states in the world join the United States in permitting abortions for both of these reasons. The flipside of that coin, of course, is that almost half of the world disagrees with the United States, holding that the life of the unborn is more important than the concept of "risk to the mother's mental health." [Twenty-three countries – 12% – say *yes* about mother's health but draw the line at "mental health." Another sixty-eight countries – 36% – are on record as stating that neither the concept of mother's mental health nor that of mother's health is sufficient justification for destroying the child in the womb.]

One of the most controversial arguments for abortion is the situation of rape or incest. Another is in the case of known imperfection of the preborn child. As in other categories, some states declare an official policy of tolerance toward circumstances which are technically unlawful. For simplicity those "No, but" responses will be considered as *yeses* in this section. The United States accepts rape and incest, and imperfect-child justifications for abortion. In the rest of the world, seventy-nine states, 42%, also accept both justifications. Seven countries allow abortions in the case of rape or incest but not for imperfect babies, and seven nations permit the second but not the first of those two justifications. Once again, more than half of the world disagrees with the United States when it argues for permitting abortions on those grounds.

SCOPE and FOCUS
I. CONVICTIONS
II. PRETEXTS
III. MANDATE
IV. LEGACY
Christian Tradition
Early Church
Reformation Era
World Precedents
Holocaust
Nuremberg
Geneva
United Nations and Int'l. Human Rights
Unborn Child's Rights
Global Abortion Norms
Apartheid
United States History
Independence
Liberty & Rights
Abolition of Slavery
Women's Passage Rites
Seeds of Destruction
Between World Wars
Pivotal Developments
Civil Rights
Parental Responsibility
Humaneness
V. ABORTIVE LINKS
VI. DILEMMA
VII. DESTINY

The United States also holds that abortion is an acceptable remedy for economic or social hardships. Only 29% of the world agrees with that, just fifty-five countries.

The myth that abortions in the United states are "safe and legal" is perpetuated by the media[3] with the complicity of health agencies[4] Thus the public remains ignorant of essential truths and realities. Citizens have been convinced that the abortion delivery system in place in the U.S. is the one the Supreme Court sanctioned in the case of *Roe v. Wade*. This is far from true. Within the text of their decision in *Roe*, the justices quoted the American Medical Association's 1970 resolution, "RESOLVED, That abortion is a medical procedure and should be performed only by a duly licensed physician and surgeon in an accredited hospital acting only after consultation with two other physicians..."[5] Because the Justices implied, rather than required, that abortions be performed in a hospital, the Planned Parenthood model of an abortion clinic has become the norm in the U.S. and elsewhere, a type of operation the Supreme Court Justices in their *Roe v. Wade* decision referred to as "abortion mills."[6]

Despite Planned Parenthood's huge success at spreading its clinic concept around the globe,[7] eighty-seven countries, 46%, permit abortions only inside hospitals. An additional nine nations permit early abortions outside hospitals but require a hospital setting after a certain stage in the pregnancy. Bangladesh requires this after the sixth week. Bosnia and Herzegovina, Croatia and Cuba do so after ten weeks, and twelve weeks is the cutoff in Barbados, Bulgaria, Cape Verde and Georgia. In China, abortions may be performed elsewhere during the first two trimesters, but after the twenty-fourth week of pregnancy the setting must be a hospital. American-style abortion clinics, especially late-term and full-term, are clearly not the norm internationally.

Here is the most shocking statement in the U.N. documents: The United States section of the United Nations abortion-statistics volumes states that **Federal law no longer requires that an abortion be performed by a physician, leaving that question up to the States to decide.**[8]

Only 22 nations, just 11.5%, are with the U.S. in allowing non-physicians or the woman herself to perform abortions. At the other end of the spectrum, of course, are the four countries that permit no exceptions to their no-abortion policy. Next, twenty-five nations, 13%, require a consultation among three or more physicians prior to any abortion being performed. Another thirty-three, 17%, require that the abortion be performed by a physician who consults with at least one other physician regarding the medical and legal grounds for that abortion. This leaves more than a hundred countries, 53%, that permit some abortions by lone physicians; second opinions are required after the early stages of pregnancy in nineteen of those, another 10% of the globe. Thus, America stands opposed by 30% of its peers who require a second opinion in every case, and another 10% who require one after the earliest phases of development.

1 Grant, *Grand Illusions*, 167-185.

2 Grant, *Grand Illusions*, 25.

3 Grant , *Grand Illusions*, 33-4, and 167-85.

4 Crutcher, *Lime 5: Exploited by Choice*, 135-170.

5 Supreme Court, *Roe v. Wade*, 722.

6 Supreme Court, *Roe v. Wade*, 725.

7 Grant, *Grand Illusions*, 1-2.

8. United Nations, *Abortion Policies: A Global Review*, Vol. III, 163.

Earlier it was shown that eight countries have anti-abortion laws that stand even when the pregnancy endangers the mother's life. Among the rest of the countries , those that permit abortions to save the mother's life, there are thirty-five that have determined the maximum stage of development beyond which no abortions may be performed, even when the mother's life is at risk. Sixteen of them permit no abortions after the twenty-eighth week. Algeria's law prohibits abortions after viability. Japan and the United Kingdom do so after the twenty-fourth week, Spain after twenty-two, and India and Bulgaria after the twentieth week. In Antigua and Barbuda, Portugal, and Seychelles the latest that abortion is permitted is the sixteenth week. Nine nations permit abortions only in the first trimester – the first twelve weeks – and Morocco outlaws abortion after the sixth week of pregnancy.

What does this last section mean to you if you're a preborn child? It means that in 4% of the world's countries, eight of them, you are protected from abortion at the moment of conception. There are ten more countries, for a total of 9% of the world, in which you are protected if you make it through the first trimester. Weeks sixteen, twenty, twenty-two and twenty-four are critical, but if you get through all of them there will be another 9 nations, for a total of 14% of the world, that will protect you. Making it past the twenty-eighth week will bring sixteen additional states to your aid, for a total of 22% of the globe in which you are protected by law. Even so, in the third trimester, when most lives could be sustained outside the womb, 78% of the world's nations permit abortions. In some of those, including the United States, it is legal to kill a child during natural childbirth, if the mother simply wants it done.

7. Apartheid... "Truth & Reconciliation" Accountability and Mercy

The struggle for equality waged by the black population of South Africa against Apartheid provides invaluable lessons for the pro-life movement in America today. The similarities are striking. In South Africa, a minuscule white minority seized political dominance and ruthlessly asserted that power against a seemingly helpless majority. Apartheid was a social and political policy that institutionalized the doctrine that a class of humans could be denied rights, and life itself, because of its ascribed inferiority. As with the whites in South Africa, American liberals used their ascendancy in the realm of education to gain control of other institutional power bases and, ultimately, to achieve total ownership of governmental power.

In South Africa the black majority was denied the vote outright. In the United States secular humanism's tyranny over a *voting* Christian majority is made possible by the masterful marginalization of all orthodox Christian leadership, and by propaganda campaigns so effective that significant factions of Christianity are either conscripted into the liberal ranks outright or cowed and brainwashed into political impotence.

The resultant differences are significant. Every nonwhite member of South African populace chafed under daily injustices, which created the fierce resolve to break their chains regardless of the cost. The escalating repression, which affected every nonwhite inhabitant, only fanned the flames of revolution. Only a handful of South African whites exhibited altruism by supporting the people's struggle, certainly far less than a decisive contribution to the entire liberation movement.

The situation in America, not by accident, is very different. The successful privatization of faith has created a complacent throng of Christians who enjoy the blessings of national prosperity and who appreciate the freedom to practice their religion in any way they please [just so long it is confined to the "church property"]. A conspiracy of silence ["don't ask, don't tell"] hides the church's participation in the culture of abortion, both surgical and chemical. Thus if abortion is mentioned as a problem at all, it is usually expressed as a contagion of "the world," out *there*, as opposed to *everywhere*. Since pre-born humans as a class are invisible, voiceless and powerless, there is absolutely no self-interested political block that can demand its rights in the way that blacks could do in South Africa. The entire pro-life movement consists of not even one victim; it is made up entirely of altruistic defenders of the rights of those helpless and faceless others. This fact alone translates into an inferior brand of motivation. Among your pro-life friends, does anyone's determination resemble that of a bloody man with a broken broomstick, shouting at the approaching tanks, "Come and get me, because I'm not taking it any more!"?

SCOPE and FOCUS
I. CONVICTIONS
II. PRETEXTS
III. MANDATE
IV. LEGACY
Christian Tradition
Early Church
Reformation Era
World Precedents
Holocaust
Nuremberg
Geneva
United Nations and Int'l. Human Rights
Unborn Child's Rights
Global Abortion Norms
Apartheid
United States History
Independence
Liberty & Rights
Abolition of Slavery
Pretexts for slavery
Links in slave chains
Discipleship & slavery
Slavery and Abortion
Women's Passage Rites
Seeds of Destruction
Between World Wars
Pivotal Developments
Civil Rights
Parental Responsibility
Humaneness
V. ABORTIVE LINKS
VI. DILEMMA
VII. DESTINY

1 Mandela, *Long Walk to Freedom: The Autobiography of Nelson Mandela*, 1994. Because they will be numerous, citations from this work will be identified by page numbers, in [brackets].

2 *TIME for Kids*, 3-6-98, 4-5. Not in bibliography.

Part of the South African white government's successful strategy was to label and divide the groups it dominated. Racially, they differentiated between the Blacks, the Asians [mostly from India], and the Coloureds [those of mixed races]. Politically they pitted the historic tribal leaders against the various political organizations as they emerged, including the African National Congress, the Pan Africanist Congress, and the socialists and communists.

Our primary source of data regarding Apartheid has been the autobiography of Nelson Mandela, *Long Walk to Freedom.*[1]

What is profoundly evident in this study is that a vastly outnumbered minority of whites, when they controlled all basic institutions of society – government, criminal "justice," education and communications – were able to abuse and subdue even an impassioned and well-organized majority's opposition for nearly a hundred years. The lessons of Apartheid should be a stark antidote to the glib optimism of the naive within the pro-life movement.

European colonization of South Africa began in the 1600s. South Africa was often an arena of the ongoing European struggle between the Dutch and British, complicated by local rivalries and by discoveries of natural treasures of diamonds and gold. When British colonial rule seemed to end in 1910, what really happened was that control passed from the governments of Europe to the whites residing in South Africa.[2]

Excluded from any voice in the government, blacks within two years founded the African National Congress, in 1912, to combat racialism [Mandela, 74-5]. They were in for 77 years of bloody failure before their amazing series of victories, beginning in 1990. In 1921, police killed 183 unarmed peasants [256-7]. In 1943, Nelson Mandela marched with 10,000 others in a nine-day bus boycott that successfully reversed a fare increase from fourpence to five [75].

Thirty-seven years of peacefully "working within the system" demonstrated two things: that civil *obedience* won no correction of a government's unjust policies, and that "cool heads" in the organizations that shape public protest simply gave the green light to the government to become more oppressive.

In 1949, while the Nuremberg trials were punishing Nazi "crimes against humanity," the South African government was establishing new, racially discriminatory laws. They prohibited mixed marriages. They demanded registration of all citizens by race, which created social and geographic divisions between the races. The *Group Areas Act* required that whites, Blacks, Asians and Coloureds all live in separate areas. And *Pass Laws* required that all nonwhites receive prior, written, government permission to travel beyond their race's area [for instance, to go to work as a domestic servant in a white home, or to travel through the area of another race in order to visit a relative's home]. Mandela relates: "This [brought] a radical change: the ANC's policy had always been to keep its activities within the law... [the ANC Annual Conference adopted its Youth League's – Mandela and his friends' – Program of Action] which called for boycotts, strikes, stay-at-homes, passive resistance, protest demonstrations and other forms of mass action... The ANC's leaders [finally realized that they] had to be willing to violate the law and if necessary go to prison for their beliefs, as Gandhi had" [98-9].

For the African National Congress's "Freedom Day" in 1950, a one-day general strike calling for the abolition of the pass laws and all discriminatory legislation, "two thirds of African workers stayed home" [101]. During a peaceful march that night [a specific new law prohibited "all meetings and gatherings" for May 1], "mounted police galloped into the crowd, [beating and shooting]. Eighteen Africans died and many others were wounded in this indiscriminate and unprovoked attack" [102].

The South African government's response to Freedom Day was the *Suppression of Communism Act* which, "made it a crime, punishable by a maximum of ten years' imprisonment, to be a member of the [Communist] party or to *further the aims* of communism... a crime to *advocate any doctrine that promoted 'political, industrial, social or economic* ***change*** within [South Africa] by the ***promotion*** *of* disturbance or disorder'" [102].

All major militant groups were united in outrage over the Freedom Day murders and the *Suppression of Communism Act*, joining for a National Day of Protest less than two months after the original Freedom Day. Mandela says, "Mass action was perilous in South Africa, where it was a criminal offense for an African to strike, and where the rights of free speech and movement were unmercifully curtailed... a political strike is always riskier than an economic one... [but it] *sent a warning... that we would not remain passive in the face of apartheid.* June 26 [1950] has since become [the new] Freedom Day" [102-3].

One of the most odious features of the 1950 *Suppression of Communism Act* was "Banning." This, Mandela says, "was a legal order by the government, and generally entailed forced resignation from indicated organizations, and restriction from attending gatherings of any kind. It was a kind of walking imprisonment. To ban a person, the government required no proof, offered no charges; the minister of justice simply declared it so. [This was] a strategy designed to remove the individual from the struggle... To violate or ignore a banning order was to invite imprisonment" [118].[1]

Just before the ANC's conference was to begin in 1952, fifty-two leaders from around the country were banned for six months from meeting with more than one person at a time [Therefore Mandela could not attend his son's birthday party] [125-6].

Mr. Mandela summarizes apartheid: "It was a crime to walk through a Whites Only door, a crime to ride a Whites Only bus, a crime to use a Whites Only drinking fountain, a crime to walk on a Whites Only beach, a crime to be on the streets past eleven, a crime not to have a pass book and a crime to have the wrong signature in that book, a crime to be unemployed and a crime to be employed in the wrong place, a crime to live in certain places and a crime to have no place to live" [130].

The 1953 *Western Areas Removal* scheme was designed to disperse all minorities into the countryside, undermining their political cohesiveness, and to effectively reserve cities *for whites only*. In the same year, the *Public Safety Act* "empowered the government to declare martial law and to detain people without trial, and the *Criminal Laws Amendment Act* authorized corporal punishment for defiers" [those engaged in peaceful civil disobedience] [116].

The Defiance Campaign was announced by the ANC, and the government's plan to evacuate the black residents of Sophiatown became "the first major test of strength" [134-5]. "We ran the [Sophiatown] antiremoval campaign on the slogan, 'Over Our Dead Bodies,' a motto often shouted from the platforms and echoed by the audience... Ten thousand people gathered [for a rally]... [On the night before the scheduled removal] more than five hundred youthful activists expected the ANC to give them an order to battle the police and the army... They assumed our slogan meant what it said... [but] an insurrection required careful planning or it would become an act of suicide. We were not yet ready to engage the enemy on its own terms..." [142-3].

The government sent four thousand police and army troops who removed resident families just before their homes were bulldozed into rubble. "Sophiatown died" [143].

In 1953, in Sophiatown, Nelson Mandela ended a speech by declaring that nonviolence had become "a useless strategy and could never overturn a white minority regime bent on retaining its power at any cost... Violence is the only weapon that will destroy apartheid, and we must be prepared, in the near future, to use that weapon" [136]. In his autobiography, he notes: "Henceforth, all of my actions and plans... would become secret and illegal... My bans drove me from the center of the struggle to the sidelines" [140].

Mandela reports that by 1954, "Newspapers would not publish our statements; printing presses refused to print our leaflets, all for fear of prosecution..." [141]. The degree of governmental oppression brought rival factions together. Two hundred organizations – white, Black, Indian, and Coloured – were invited to a "Congress of the People." Mandela reports that "three thousand delegates braved police intimidation" and took part [148-50].

In 1955-56 the government raided the homes and businesses of 500 people, seizing anything they thought might incriminate anyone of anything illegal [163-4]. In 1956, Mandela received his third banning and "resolved not to become my own jailer" [166-7]. His subsequent activities, and a pile of "evidence" confiscated from wherever, resulted in his arrest – along with 143 others – and trial for high treason ["a hostile intention to disturb, impair, or endanger the independence or safety of the state." The punishment was death]. They also were charged with an alleged conspiracy to overthrow the state [166-7]. They were in jail for two years and eight months before their trials began [201].

Women receive high praise from Nelson Mandela: "Few issues touched a nerve so much as that of [requiring] passes for women... They could be fined ten pounds or imprisoned for a month for failing to produce their 'reference book.' In 1957 [they] reacted with fury... their protest against passes set a standard for anti-government protest that was never equaled. As [a respected leader] said, 'When the women begin to take an active part in the struggle, no power on earth can stop us from achieving freedom in our lifetime.' In Johannesburg... a large group of women gathered at the central pass office, and chased away women who had come to collect passes and clerks who worked in the office, bringing the office to a standstill. Police arrested [more than a thousand] of the women" [191].

SCOPE and FOCUS
I. CONVICTIONS
II. PRETEXTS
III. MANDATE
IV. LEGACY
Christian Tradition
Early Church
Reformation Era
World Precedents
Holocaust
Nuremberg
Geneva
United Nations and Int'l. Human Rights
Unborn Child's Rights
Global Abortion Norms
Apartheid
United States History
Independence
Liberty & Rights
Abolition of Slavery
Pretexts for slavery
Links in slave chains
Discipleship & slavery
Slavery and Abortion
Women's Passage Rites
Seeds of Destruction
Between World Wars
Pivotal Developments
Civil Rights
Parental Responsibility
Humaneness
V. ABORTIVE LINKS
VI. DILEMMA
VII. DESTINY

In 1959, perhaps taking a page from America's success at exiling Native Americans to *reservations*, South Africa created eight separate *bantustans*, "whereby 70 percent of the people would be apportioned only 13 percent of the land" [200].

Also in 1959, the Pan Africanist Congress emerged as a militant rival to the African National Congress [197]. When a 1960 PAC protest involving 30,000 people turned into a riot, the government concluded that anarchy would erupt unless all protest was eliminated. Shortly thereafter, when the 75 members of the Sharpeville police force found themselves surrounded by several thousand peaceful demonstrators, they panicked: "Suddenly, the police opened fire on the crowd and continued to shoot as the demonstrators turned and ran in fear. When the area had cleared, sixty-nine Africans lay dead, most of them shot in the back as they were fleeing. All told, more than seven hundred shots had been fired into the crowd, wounding more than four hundred people, including dozens of women and children. It was a massacre, and the next day press photos displayed the savagery on front pages around the world" [206-7].

Mandela reflects: "A freedom fighter learns the hard way that it is the oppressor who defines the nature of the struggle" [144]. The *Associated Press* refers to Sharpeville as, "...where police gunned down 69 black protesters in a 1960 massacre that galvanized the anti-apartheid movement."[2]

A call went out for a nationwide stay-at-home and a "National Day of Mourning and Protest for the atrocities at Sharpeville." Mandela's view is: "The country responded magnificently as several hundred thousand Africans observed the call" [207]. A stay-at-home in the United States would cost participants only a day's pay – and raise the *possibility* of adverse consequences from employers for some. By contrast, we must remember that in South Africa there was a wide assortment of crimes the government could attribute to those who took part, and a trip to jail, a beating, or the loss of a job could be among the minor consequences. Keeping that in mind, we would agree that "the country responded magnificently" if 2% to 5% of the population took part in spite of the risks.

Unfortunately, rioting broke out in many areas, giving the government an excuse to declare a State of Emergency, to suspend habeas corpus, and to place the country under martial law [207-8]. Both the ANC and the PAC were declared illegal organizations, making mere membership a felony punishable by a term in jail and a fine. "The penalty for furthering the aims of the ANC was imprisonment for up to ten years. Now even nonviolent law-abiding protests under the auspices of the ANC were illegal. The struggle had entered a new phase. We were now, all of us, outlaws" [211].

John F. Kennedy is widely quoted as having said, "**Those who make peaceful change impossible, make violent change inevitable.**"[3] His sentiments were echoed by Nelson Mandela: "**When a man is denied the right to live the life he believes in, he has no choice but to become an outlaw**" [223]. This was the conclusion drawn by Mandela: "Nonviolent passive resistance is effective as long as your opposition adheres to the same rules as you do. But if peaceful protest is met with violence, its efficacy is at an end. For me, nonviolence was not a moral principle but a strategy; there is no moral goodness in using an ineffective weapon" [137]. "The South African government saw the [Defiance] campaign as a threat to its security and its policy of apartheid. They regarded civil disobedience not as a form of protest but as a crime" [116]. Mandela also reflected: "**I went from having an idealistic view of the law as a sword of justice to a perception of the law as a tool used by the ruling class to shape society in a way favorable to itself. I never expected justice in court, however much I fought for it**" [226], and "**We saw the trial as a continuation of the struggle by other means**" [314].

1 Mandela, *Long Walk to Freedom: The Autobiography of Nelson Mandela*, 1994. Because they will be numerous, citations from this work will be identified by page numbers, in [brackets].

2 *Associated Press, Press*, 12-11-96, A9.

3 JFK, in Schlesinger, 254-5.

In 1961 Nelson Mandela founded the unofficial, illegal, militant arm of the African National Congress, called the *Spear of the Nation*, "MK" for short. His rationale for this move and for its strategy is crucial: "*Spear of the Nation* considered four types of violent activities: sabotage, guerilla warfare, terrorism, and open rebellion. For a small and fledging army, open revolution was inconceivable. Terrorism [indiscriminate violence against persons] inevitably reflected poorly on those who used it, undermining public support... Guerilla warfare [clandestine attacks on the personnel and machinery of the enemy] was a possibility, but since the ANC had been reluctant to embrace violence at all, it made sense to start with the form of violence that inflicted the least harm against individuals: sabotage. Because it did not involve loss of life it offered the best hope for reconciliation among the races afterward" [239 and 246].

Mandela explains the need to divorce the two branches of the same movement: "A military movement should be a separate and independent organ... fundamentally autonomous. There would be two separate streams of the struggle... nonviolence had failed us, for it had done nothing to stem the violence of the state nor change the heart of our oppressors... The [ANC] congresses authorized me to go ahead and form a new military organization, separate from the ANC. The policy of the ANC would still be that of nonviolence" [238-9].

He continues, amplifying his approach to sabotage: "Our strategy was to make selective forays against military installations, power plants, telephone lines, and transportation links; targets that would not only hamper the military effectiveness of the state, but frighten National Party supporters, scare away foreign capital, and weaken the economy. This we hoped would bring the government to the bargaining table" [246].

"Strict instructions were given to members of the MK that we would countenance no loss of life... All MK members were forbidden to go armed into an operation and were not to endanger life in any way... But if sabotage did not produce the results we wanted, we were prepared to move on to the next stage: guerilla warfare and terrorism" [246]. Mandela quotes the view that guerilla warfare is "not designed to win a military victory so much as to unleash political and economic forces that would bring down the enemy" [260].

In 1961, Nelson Mandela, "released a letter to South African newspapers from underground: 'I am informed that a warrant for my arrest has been issued, and that the police are looking for me... I will not give myself up to a government I do not recognize... Under present day conditions in the country, to seek for cheap martyrdom by handing myself to the police is naive and criminal... I will not leave South Africa, nor will I surrender. Only through hardship, sacrifice and militant action can freedom be won" [240-1]. He was ultimately arrested, convicted, and sent to prison.

The government increased repression in response to a perceived threat. Under a new Sabotage Act in 1962, "Sabotage itself now carried a minimum penalty of five years without parole, and a maximum of death. Because the wording of the act was so broad, even activities such as trespassing or illegal possession of weapons could constitute sabotage. Another act of Parliament prohibited the reproduction of any statement made by a banned person. Nothing I said or had ever said could be reported in the newspapers... Possession of a banned publication became a criminal offense, punishable by up to two years in prison" [296].

In 1963 the *Ninety-Day Detention Law* "waived the right of habeas corpus and empowered any police officer to detain [without a warrant] any person on the grounds of suspicion of a political crime... The ninety-day detention could be extended, until 'this side of eternity.' The law helped transform the country into a police state; no dictator could covet more power than the *Ninety-Day Detention Law* gave to the authorities" [295].

By 1964, Nelson Mandela says, "I was forty-six years old, a political prisoner with a life sentence... I was entitled to have only one visitor, and to write and receive only one letter every six months" [The letters were so heavily censored that not much more than the salutation was left] [336 and 349].

"International public opinion," says Mandela, "is sometimes worth more than a fleet of jet fighters" [259-60].

In 1968, the International Conference on Human Rights produced the *Proclamation of Teheran*. It declared that, "Gross denials of human rights under the repugnant policy of apartheid is a matter of the gravest concern to the international community. This policy of *apartheid*, condemned as a crime against humanity, continues seriously to disturb international peace and security. It is therefore imperative for the international community to use every possible means to eradicate this evil. **The struggle against *apartheid* is recognized as legitimate**."[1]

SCOPE and FOCUS
I. CONVICTIONS
II. PRETEXTS
III. MANDATE
IV. LEGACY
Christian Tradition
Early Church
Reformation Era
World Precedents
Holocaust
Nuremberg
Geneva
United Nations and Int'l. Human Rights
Unborn Child's Rights
Global Abortion Norms
Apartheid
United States History
Independence
Liberty & Rights
Abolition of Slavery
Pretexts for slavery
Links in slave chains
Discipleship & slavery
Slavery and Abortion
Women's Passage Rites
Seeds of Destruction
Between World Wars
Pivotal Developments
Civil Rights
Parental Responsibility
Humaneness
V. ABORTIVE LINKS
VI. DILEMMA
VII. DESTINY

In 1973 the United Nations General Assembly adopted the *International Convention on the Suppression and Punishment of the Crime of Apartheid*. By 1976 it entered into force internationally, having received the necessary ratification by twenty nations. This treaty restated that apartheid is a crime against humanity, and went on to "declare criminal those organizations, institutions and individuals committing the crime of *apartheid*," and also those who "directly abet, encourage or cooperate" in its commission, regardless of where such individuals may be at the time of the crime. It went even further: "Persons charged with the acts enumerated... [in] the present Convention may be tried by a competent tribunal of any State Party to the Convention which may acquire jurisdiction over the person of the accused or by an international penal tribunal" [think *Nuremberg*][2]

This meant, among other things, that if a member of South Africa's government took a vacation to [or mysteriously appeared some morning in] a country that had ratified this Convention, he could be arrested, tried, convicted, and imprisoned for the international crime of *apartheid*.

Mandela was encouraged when [after eleven years in prison] he "learned of the successful liberation struggles in Mozambique and Angola in 1975... the tide was turning our way... *I was confident* the world was moving toward our position, not away from it" [435 and 437].

Nine years later he was still optimistic: "The anti-apartheid struggle as a whole had captured the attention of the world; in 1984, Bishop Desmond Tutu was awarded the Nobel Peace Prize... the South African government was under growing international pressure, as nations all across the globe began to impose economic sanctions" [452].

In 1985 Mandela was offered what he called "a tempting trap," his freedom, *if* he "unconditionally rejected violence as a political instrument." His response was to "reaffirm to the world that... if I emerged from prison into the same circumstances in which I was arrested, I would be forced to resume the same activities for which I was arrested" [455].

In 1986, "the ANC had called for the people of South Africa to render the country ungovernable, and the people were obliging. The state of unrest and political violence was reaching new heights. The anger of the masses was unrestrained... International pressure was growing stronger every day. On June 12, 1986, the government imposed a State of Emergency in an attempt to keep a lid on protest... " [457]. Mandela says, "Even with all their bombers and tanks, they must have sensed they were on the wrong side of history. We had right on our side, but not yet might" [457].

In 1990 apartheid ended, and Nelson Mandela was released from prison. He says, "My people had been waiting for me for twenty-seven years and I did not want to keep them waiting any longer... I entered prison at the age of forty-four, but I was no longer a young man, I was seventy-one, and I could not afford to waste any time" [481, 490, 497].

The *Associated Press* reports, "Political fighting between the [black] Zulu nationalist Inkatha Freedom Party and Mandela's [black] ANC... killed more than 10,000 [of each other's] people [between 1984 and 1994]."[3]

In 1992, "The mass action campaign culminated in a general strike on August 3 and 4 in support of the ANC's negotiation demands and in protest against state-supported violence. More than four million workers [one tenth of the 40 million population] stayed home in what was the largest political strike in South African history" [527].

In 1993, Mandela says, "I was notified that I had won the 1993 Nobel Peace Prize jointly with Mr. de Klerk" [the last white President of South Africa, who presided over the end of apartheid and the transition to democracy] [532]. By 1994, Nelson Mandela had been elected President of South Africa, and the Truth and Reconciliation Commission had been created.[4]

1 *Proclamation of Teheran*, United Nations, *Human Rights*, First Part, 51-4.

2 United Nations, *Human Rights*, First Part, 80-6.

3 Associated Press, *Press*, 3-13-97, A14.

4 *Christianity Today*, 2-9-98, 20. Not in bibliography.

In February, 1998, *Christianity Today* gave broad treatment to South Africa's Truth and Reconciliation Commission. The Commission was given four primary tasks: 1) to grant amnesty to "persons who make full disclosure of all the relevant facts relating to acts associated with a political objective," 2) to give victims "an opportunity to relate the violations they suffered," 3) to report to the nation on its findings, 4) to make recommendations "aimed at the prevention of similar violations in the future."[1]

The article reflects, "Many people worry that this Commission, both through its offer of amnesty and its focus on reconciliation, undermines the importance of justice."[2] The central element of the Commission's process is confession. In the first two years after the first Truth and Reconciliation hearing in April 1996, "more than 7,000 people have volunteered to tell the truth about past crimes... Some hearings are even broadcast on television."[3]

A COMPELLING QUESTION: How far would we have to look to find American parallels to South African excesses in repressing dissent?

To defend apartheid, South Africa enacted laws specifically intended to chill protest, even though they clearly violated basic human rights such as the freedom of speech. In the United States, F.A.C.E., the *Freedom of Access to* [abortion] *Clinic Entrances* statute, is precisely such a law.

In its quest for law and order, South Africa's government was willing to contort basic legal terms in order to compound the consequences of a lesser offense: trespass could become an act of "sabotage." In America, the simple Operation Rescue practice of peaceful noncooperation when arrested, going limp as a sign of solidarity with the helpless abortee, has sometimes been improperly charged as "resisting arrest." In California, for instance, "resisting arrest" actually means to attempt to *prevent* an arrest "by the use of force or violence," and carries a one-year penalty. Also, at trial, people who gave speeches at a rally the night before a Rescue have been tried for a contrived felony, "*conspiracy* to commit trespass," even though trespass is only a misdemeanor.

Nelson Mandela says, "No dictator could covet more power than the *Ninety-Day Detention Law* gave to the [South African] authorities" [295]. An Atlanta judge presumed to have that same unfettered power in 1990, when 13 Rescuers, because we were accused of *repeating* the misdemeanor of trespass, were denied bail and kept in jail for ninety days before the beginning of our trials [see Timeline at the end of *Orphans*, "1990"].

In 1994, pro-life leaders with squeaky-clean records of peaceful protests, and impeccably documented commitments to non violence were convicted in a federal kangaroo court of "threats, violence, extortion and violation of federal ***Racketeering*** law" and ordered to pay $258,000 to the very abortion providers whose profession is considered to be professional-killer-of-babies under the leaders' deeply held religious faith.[4] In 1995, the Supreme Court let stand a ruling that peaceful anti-abortion protesters must pay nearly $100,000 to the Sacramento, California, abortion clinic they had picketed.[4] Also in 1995, Jeff White, the director of Operation Rescue California, was ordered to pay $880,000 in damages for "harassing and trespassing" on the property of four San Diego abortionists.[4] Was Nelson Mandela ever forced to buy rifles and bullets for the Sharpeville police force?

President Clinton has twice-vetoed the Partial Birth Abortion Ban, and in 1998 the Supreme Court let stand the ruling that Ohio's Partial Birth Abortion Ban unduly interfered with a woman's right to choose abortion.[5] Did South Africa's president or highest court ever formally protect a private citizen's "right" to defend a Whites Only drinking fountain by shooting a black child just as she was taking a drink?

CONCLUSIONS: During America's Vietnam War, perhaps not far in time or geography from the "My Lai Massacre," a U.S. officer reported, "In order to liberate the village, it was necessary to destroy the village." In South Africa, sixty or seventy years of constant internal strife had only served to make the government more entrenched and more repressive. Had Nelson Mandela been wrong about the direction of the tides of history, and had the world press and the International Human Rights community turned a deaf ear to the struggle, **it seems probable that the oppressed majority would have been required to destroy the nation before they could free their nation from white rule.**

With that preface, it would be hard not to observe two things: **1) The pro-life "movement" in the United States lacks even the tiniest fraction of the passion** demonstrated by the South Africans who, propelled by righteous self-interest, sustained an unrelenting, intensifying crusade against tyranny for three-quarters of a century; **2) The global tide of history is flowing in the direction of abortion-acceptance** rather than toward recognition of the right to life of the preborn. Rather than leaning toward censure of the United States for its passionate embrace of abortion, the world community seems increasingly eager to emulate and to adopt America's abortion standards.

1 *Christianity Today*, 2-9-98, 20. Not in bibliography.
2 *Christianity Today*, 2-9-98, 21. Not in bibliography.
3 *TIME for Kids*, 3-6-98, 4-5.
4 *Press*, 4-21-98, A1. Three citations.
5 *Press*, 3-24-98, A3.

SCOPE and FOCUS
I. CONVICTIONS
II. PRETEXTS
III. MANDATE
IV. LEGACY
Christian Tradition
Early Church
Reformation Era
World Precedents
Holocaust
Nuremberg
Geneva
United Nations and Int'l Human Rights
Unborn Child's Rights
Global Abortion Norms
Apartheid
United States History
Independence
Liberty & Rights
Abolition of Slavery
Pretexts for slavery
Links in slave chains
Discipleship & slavery
Slavery and Abortion
Women's Passage Rites
Protection & Rights
Anti-Family Changes
Feminism
Seeds of Destruction
Nietzsche
Malthus
Darwin
Marx
Freud
Between World Wars
Techno-prosperity
Modernism
Fundamentalism
Scopes
Capone & Ness
Pivotal Developments
Public education
Great Depression
Post-war materialism
Synthetic heroes
Post-war Paranoia
Kinsey-Elvis-Madonna
Clinton generation
Civil Rights
Parental Responsibility
Humaneness
Animal rights
Endangered species
Environmentalism
Welcome aliens!
Criminal rights
Children's rights
V. ABORTIVE LINKS
VI. DILEMMA
VII. DESTINY

C. United States of America

Nelson Mandela alerted us to the necessity of assessing the ebb and flow of the global tides of history.. The chart of a nation sometimes runs with those forces, while at other times it can demonstrate the presence of strong countercurrents along man's course. If we are to learn our place in history and rightly play our part in the divine plan, then it is essential that we know the design of the vessel in which we travel, assess any modifications and damages it has sustained during travel, and divine the character and commitments of the captain and crew, so that we might rightly judge our best prospects for arriving safely at our intended port.

"From the seventeenth through the early nineteenth centuries," Olasky tells us, "at no time was abortion considered legitimate and legal, but the practice did occur when some women fell through the cracks, taking their unborn children with them."[6]

James Hitchcock helps us understand some currents and countercurrents: "In ways which are perhaps not sufficiently appreciated, the Calvinist origins of the American Northeast seem to have stamped a permanent religiosity on the American soul, a reality already noticed as early as the 1830s by Alexis de Tocqueville and others. Classical Puritanism disappeared in time, and New England eventually became (apart from its Catholic immigrants) one of the more secular parts of the country."[7]

1. Independence

Universalism & Justice

"Religion got mixed up with American democracy when George Washington started praying at Valley Forge."[8]

"If words could make us free, then men would not have died because of the Gospel, or for the *Declaration of Independence*... If education could make us free, then Jesus would not have bothered to die; He would simply have set up a new and better rabbinical school," observes Foreman.[9] "Rebellion to tyrants is obedience to God," said Thomas Jefferson.[10]

In his historic *Letter from Atlanta* in 1989, Randall Terry asked us all, "What are you willing to pay to see this holocaust [abortion] ended and our nation reformed? At the close of the *Declaration of Independence* our founding fathers said, '...with a firm reliance on the Protection of Divine Providence, we mutually pledge to each other our Lives our Fortunes and our Sacred Honor.' It took that kind of commitment and sacrifice to give birth to this nation; it will take the same level of dedication and courage to reform her."[11] In the words of Jefferson, "The care of human life and happiness, and not their destruction, is the first and only legitimate object of good government."[12]

6 Marvin Olasky, *Abortion Rites: A Social History of Abortion in America*, 41.

Summary of examples of "typical cases" from American court records, by Olasky, 20-26: suspicion of infanticide in 1629; execution for infanticide in 1648; conviction for intention to abort in 1652; a wormwood abortion in 1656; an abortion following rape in 1663; killing a bastard child in 1665; abortifacients used in the 1680s; murder of a newborn in 1719; and fifty-one infanticide convictions from 1670 to 1807.

7 Hitchcock, in William Bentley Ball, *In Search of a National Morality: A Manifesto for Evangelicals and Catholics*, 32.

8 Citation lost; only the truth remains, as it should.

9 Joseph Foreman, *Shattering the Darkness: The Crisis of the Cross in the Church Today*, 70.

10 Jefferson, in *Life Advocate*, 2/'94, 4.

11 Terry, in Foreman, 168-71.

12 Jefferson, in F. LaGard Smith, *When Choice Becomes God*, 95.

There Would Be No U.S.A. Had Men Not Owned Principles Worth Fighting and Dying For

Thomas Jefferson's letter from Paris, of November 13, 1787, is to the point: "What country before ever existed a century and a half without a rebellion? And what country can preserve its liberties if the rulers are not warned from time to time that their people preserve the spirit of resistance? Let them take arms... The tree of liberty must be refreshed from time to time with the blood of patriots and tyrants. It is its natural manure."[1]

Here is a portion of a Samuel Davies sermon, based on *Jeremiah* 48:10: "The art of war becomes part of our religion. Blessed is the defender of his country and the destroyer of its enemies... This denunciation, like the artillery from heaven, is leveled against the mean, sneaking coward, who, when God, in the course of His providence, calls him to arms, refuses to obey and consults his own ease and safety more than his duty to God and his country."[2]

Bray translates the message well, for our own day: "The right of resistance is in the community. It is the right of revolution, which God sanctions, and which good men in past ages have exercised to the salvation of civil and religious liberty. When a government fails to answer the purpose for which God ordained it, the people have a right to change it."[3]

In controversy, Public Opinion is Fickle

Mid-century Supreme Court Justice Abe Fortas wrote: "From our earliest history, we have insisted that each of us is and must be free to criticize the government, however brashly; even to advocate overthrow of the government itself..."[4]

Joseph Scheidler, who has blazed a pro-life path through the swamps and brambles, says: "During the American Revolution, the colonists were expert in the use of the leaflet; people like Tom Paine and Paul Revere regularly printed articles and handed them out to the people. Since the press at that time was under the sway of England, it was generally hostile to the colonists' ideas. If the colonists wanted to express their views on independence or some other facet of English oppression, they had to resort to the leaflet. We have a similar problem in this country today, with media hostile to the pro-life movement."[5]

Abe Fortas reminds us that all major policy issues are marked by controversy and conflict: "Most of our wars have met bitter and violent condemnation as 'immoral' and 'barbarous.' In the Revolutionary War, only about half of the people supported the Revolution. Churchmen led the vocal opposition. Wealthy families bitterly assailed the politicians like George Washington whom they charged with base and selfish motivation."[6]

While Fortas says that pastors "led the vocal opposition," Randall Terry claims that "the clergy of this country were the greatest stimulants and sustainers of the American Revolution."[7]

There is no contradiction; both are probably right. At the time of the Revolution there was no electronic media. Newspapers, books, and leaflets [print on a lifeless page], and public speeches, were the primary means by which thoughts were replicated in society. Sermons were the most prevalent form of speechmaking. Combined with the pastors' near monopoly on the cutting edge of communications, their tendency to both hold and to enthusiastically share their strong convictions made it likely that they would be listed prominently as leaders on both sides of *any* issue.

Colonel Doner believes that, "The Evangelical bodies... quickly rose to cultural dominance mainly because they were all organizing the same basic impulse, sharing common convictions about purpose and destiny, and participating in the common task of creating a Christian republic."[8]

"If you read the *Declaration of Independence*," says Greg Koukl, "some form of the word God is used four different times and it is the very foundation of their entire case against England, the foundation for the *Constitution*, and our Republican way of government."[9]

Randy Terry says about the *Declaration of Independence*: "That sacred document to which Rev. Witherspoon affixed his name was an act of outright treason against King George. When Witherspoon and scores of other clergy participated in or encouraged this rebellion, they were breaking the law. But these men incurred no guilt for their actions, for they were based squarely on the concept of Higher Law."[10]

John Adams, the second president of the United States, in a letter to his wife, Abigail, wrote: "The fourth day of July... ought to be commemorated as the day of deliverance, by solemn acts of devotion to Almighty God."[11]

SCOPE and FOCUS
I. CONVICTIONS
II. PRETEXTS
III. MANDATE
IV. LEGACY
Christian Tradition
Early Church
Reformation Era
World Precedents
Holocaust
Nuremberg
Geneva
United Nations and Int'l Human Rights
Unborn Child's Rights
Global Abortion Norms
Apartheid
United States History
Independence
Liberty & Rights
Abolition of Slavery
Pretexts for slavery
Links in slave chains
Discipleship & slavery
Slavery and Abortion
Women's Passage Rites
Seeds of Destruction
Between World Wars
Pivotal Developments
Civil Rights
Parental Responsibility
Humaneness
V. ABORTIVE LINKS
VI. DILEMMA
VII. DESTINY

2. Liberty & Rights

Universalism & Autonomy

R.C. Sproul reminds us that compromises of conviction were already being made by the founding fathers in deference to what we now call the plurality of faiths represented in our nation: "The framers of the *Declaration of Independence* and the *Constitution* clearly appealed to norms [Universalism] beyond human legislation or judicial opinions [Positivism] in defining our most basic rights. Natural law was a chief consideration and served as a convenient middle ground to satisfy religious as well as nonreligious people."[12]

"The essential liberal principle has been at work wherever reformers have sought to change doctrines or institutions in such a way as to increase individual freedom," says William Hutchison. "The words 'Protestant liberalism' have come to refer especially to a set of religious ideas that flourished in Europe and America from the opening of the nineteenth century through the first quarter of the twentieth."[13]

"Freedom and equality are sworn and everlasting enemies, and when one prevails the other dies," say the Durants. "Leave men free, and their natural inequalities will multiply almost geometrically... Utopias of equality are biologically doomed."[14] John Adams wrote this prophetic word: "Our *Constitution* was made only for a moral and religious people. It is wholly inadequate for the government of any other."[15]

According to Greg Koukl: "The argument in the *Constitution* is this: Men have rights as men... These are transcendent rights. They are not rights that are given or taken away by government, but are rights that come from God. Therefore, government must acknowledge them."[16]

When Randall Terry and other prophetic voices speak of God's certain judgment on the nation that sponsors abortion, they are echoing Thomas Jefferson, who in 1781 expressed the same concern over our national tolerance of slavery: "Can the liberties of a nation be thought secure when we have removed their only firm basis, a conviction in the minds of the people that their liberties are the gift of God – that they are not to be violated but with His wrath? Indeed, I tremble for my country when I reflect that God is just; that his justice cannot sleep forever..."[17]

Many have recognized the hand of God's judgment in the Civil War that was fought on the battlefield over a moral issue too deep to be resolved by the ballot box. Michael Bray asks: "Is pursuit of 'Liberty' a cause higher than protection of innocent children from slaughter in abortion chambers? Were American revolutionaries in such selfish pursuit of their own liberty that they ignored that of a million enslaved Africans? ...What are patriots to do? ...We think there is moral ground greater many times over for a revolution in these times than there was in 1776."[18]

---

1 Jefferson, in Michael Bray, *A Time to Kill*, 65.

2 Davies, in Bray, 66.

3 Bray, 158.

4 Fortas, in John Whitehead, *The Right to Picket*, 3.

5 Joseph Scheidler, *Closed: 99 Ways to Stop Abortion*, 36.

6 Abe Fortas, *Concerning Dissent and Civil Disobedience*, 52.

7 Terry, "If You Believe..." cassette.

8 Colonel V. Doner, *The Samaritan Strategy: A New Agenda for Christian Activism*, 75.

9 Gregory Koukl, *Stand to Reason* radio broadcast transcripts, "Slavery, Abortion & Inalienable Rights," 1.

10 Randall Terry, *Operation Rescue*, 110.

11 *Citizen* magazine, 7-28-97, 8.

12 Sproul, *Abortion: A Rational Look at an Emotional Issue*, 21.

13 Hutchison, *American Protestant Thought in the Liberal Era*, 1.

14 Will and Ariel Durant, *The Lessons of History*, 20.

15 Adams, in Doug Bandow, *Beyond Good Intentions, A Biblical View of Politics*, 30.

16 Gregory Koukl, *Stand to Reason* radio broadcast transcripts, "Slavery, Abortion & Inalienable Rights," 1.

17 Jefferson, in William Ball, *In Search of a National Morality*, 82.

18 Michael Bray, *A Time to Kill*, 169-70.

3. Abolition of Slavery

Universalism & Justice

If a slave has taken refuge with you, do not hand him over to his master. Let him live among you wherever he likes and in whatever town he chooses. Do not oppress him.

Deuteronomy 23:15

American slavery and the modern abortion dilemma have much in common. Both involved the widespread acceptance and legal sanction of grave injustices to human beings, made possible only by the extreme re-definition of what it means to be human. Both were seen as Pragmatic solutions to monumental social and economic problems, and in both, positivism enhanced the liberty, autonomy and "happiness" of one class of people, immorally, at the expense and loss of another.

In both instances, the ascendancy to power for the oppressors came by incremental concessions and compromises won from a moral opposition which proved to be too weak and too internally conflicted to resist. In each case, the abomination came to be so entrenched and so protected politically that its place of predominance on the national landscape seemed permanent, and its quixotic foes seemed like mere flies to be swatted.

In the example of slavery, but not [yet?] with abortion, a groundswell of public controversy began to find weaknesses in the institutional defenses, and wrenches began to be thrown into machinations of power, both socially and politically. Intensifying clashes over slavery made it clear that the moral strife exceeded the capacity of political containment. As was more recently demonstrated in South Africa, the American pro-slavery power bases demonstrated a preference of death [and killing] to surrender. Lacking international forces comparable to those which made South Africa's government cry "Uncle!" America faced only two options: dissolution of the Union, or Civil War.

R.C. Sproul tells us, "Those struggling for the unborn's fundamental right to live should be encouraged by William Wilberforce's struggle to abolish slavery in the British empire. Year after frustrating year, his efforts were defeated by Parliament. He was harassed, maligned, ridiculed, and slandered. Wilberforce was sharply criticized for raising religious objections against the slave trade."[1]

Lord Melbourne is quoted as saying, "Things have come to a pretty pass when religion is allowed to invade public life."[2]

Randy Alcorn gives us an intimate look at Wilberforce's style of abolitionism: "Wilberforce, a devout Christian, was the British parliamentarian whose single-minded efforts finally brought an end to the slave trade in England. For many years his colleagues would not pay attention to his words about the realities of slavery. Wilberforce would periodically reach under his chair and pull out chains, draping them over himself to symbolize the inhumanity of slavery. His fellow parliamentarians would roll their eyes, snicker, mock him, and call him a fool. But it is Wilberforce, not they, who is remembered – by God and men – as the one who stood for justice and mercy."[3]

He goes on: "Wilberforce suffered sleepless nights, plagued by dreams of the suffering Black man. Finally, in 1807, against incredible odds, Wilberforce saw the slave trade outlawed. But even then, he was to fight eighteen more years for the emancipation of existing slaves [in England]. Wilberforce died in 1833 – three days after the *Bill for the Abolition of Slavery* passed its second reading in the House of Commons, bringing slavery in England to its final end."[4]

John Wesley, the founder of Methodism, sent Wilberforce an encouraging letter in which he wrote: "Unless God has raised you up for this very thing, you will be worn out by the opposition of men and devils, but if God is for you who can be against you? Are all of them together stronger than God? Oh, be not weary of well-doing. Go in the name of God, and in the power of His might, till even American slavery, the vilest that ever saw the sun, shall vanish away before it..."[5]

In 1970, when practically nobody could anticipate that *Roe v. Wade* was on the horizon, W.E.B. DuBois wrote in his survey of American slavery, "No American can study the connection of slavery with United States history, and not devoutly pray that his country may never have a similar social problem to solve..."[6]

Thomas Jefferson, as a legislator in 1783, introduced a proposal that slavery be prohibited in all new states. By only one vote, it failed to pass.[7]

Before the Civil War (1861-5), there were approximately four million Negroes in the United States. Robert Linder tells us: "Of these, only about a quarter of a million were free and theoretically enjoyed the individual rights guaranteed by the Constitution. The remainder of the Negroes in the U.S. were slaves and not considered legally to be 'people.'"[8]

For the black slave, as for the preborn child today, personhood was within the power of another to either grant or to deny, autonomously; the slave's owner could grant or withhold freedom, and preborn's mother can sustain or terminate life.

SCOPE and FOCUS
I. CONVICTIONS
II. PRETEXTS
III. MANDATE
IV. LEGACY
Christian Tradition
Early Church
Reformation Era
World Precedents
Holocaust
Nuremberg
Geneva
United Nations and
Int'l Human Rights
Unborn Child's Rights
Global Abortion Norms
Apartheid
United States History
Independence
Liberty & Rights
Abolition of Slavery
Pretexts for slavery
Slaves as property
Political expedience
Links in slave-chains
Irrepressible trade
Governmental action
Social dynamics
Church controversy
Methodism shifts
Discipleship & slavery
Prophetic voices
Zeal against slavery
Campus turmoil
Oberlin-Wellington
Pre-War violence
Evangelists shine
Pious priestly voices
Slavery and Abortion
Women's Passage Rites
Seeds of Destruction
Between World Wars
Pivotal Developments
Civil Rights
Parental Responsibility
Humaneness
V. ABORTIVE LINKS
VI. DILEMMA
VII. DESTINY

a. Pretexts for retaining slavery

Even though one-sixteenth of the blacks were no longer slaves in 1860, they were still not free Americans. Jonathan Black tells us, "It took the Dred Scott case 10 years to reach the Supreme Court... In March 1857, the Court ruled that 'people of African descent are not and cannot be citizens of the United States and cannot sue in any court of the United States,' and the black people had 'no rights which whites are bound to respect.'"[9]

The Supreme Court asserted that it could justify the denial of citizenship to blacks, "as a subordinate and inferior class of beings, who had been subjugated by the dominant race..."[10]

(1) Property of the slave-owner: Positivism & Autonomy

In the Introduction to the *Dred Scott* decision, Dr. J.H. Van Evrie acknowledged both the magnitude of the cleft in society, and the precipice near which the nation was tottering:

> ...henceforth and forever the status of the Negro, his relation to the white citizens, and the rights of the latter in respect to "slave" property, are now clearly defined within the Federal jurisdiction. And this decision must be accepted and sustained by the northern masses, or there must be disunion and dismemberment of the Union... Therefore if the northern people, led astray by the agents and dupes of the enemies of Democracy refuse to abide by it... it remains, then for the honest and patriotic citizens of the North... to regard as enemies to the peace of the country, and indeed to the safety of society, all those who, under the pretense of Negro liberty, would render liberty for the white man impossible.[11]

R.C. Sproul says, "Once a decision has been reached in a nation's highest court, the subsequent influence on shaping public opinion is enormous. We learned this painful fact in the history that followed the Supreme Court's infamous Dred-Scott decision, which perpetuated slavery in the United States."[12]

> There is a footnote in history that says Abraham Lincoln met Harriet Beecher Stowe, the author of *Uncle Tom's Cabin*. He addressed her, "So you're the little lady who started the big war." Her story about slavery had to be told, in graphic, emotional terms because she needed to arouse a sleeping nation. The story of abortion must also be told that way.[13]

(2) Political expediency: Pragmatism & Positivism

It would be much too simplistic, as well as a distortion of history, to assert that the North's motivation in fighting the Civil War was primarily to free the slaves. As Terry put it, "Lincoln stated in a conversation with abolitionists during the first part of the war, 'It appears to me that the great masses of this country care comparatively little about the Negro, and are anxious only for military successes.' ...The Civil War was not started primarily because of slavery, but slavery was crushed because of the Civil War."[14]

Abe Fortas says that during the Civil War, "President Lincoln was badgered by both hawks and doves... In the spring of 1863, New York was convulsed by draft riots. Homes and buildings were burned; pitched battles were fought between police and rioters; over a thousand people were killed or wounded... A powerful movement began to force Lincoln not to stand for reelection. In August, 1864, Lincoln himself wrote that 'this administration will not be re-elected.'"[15]

1 Sproul, 149.
2 Lord Melbourne, in F.L. Smith, *When Choice Becomes God*, 49.
3 Alcorn, *Is Rescuing Right?*, 213-4.
4 Alcorn, *Is Rescuing Right?*, 234.
5 Sproul, 149-50.
6 DuBois, *The Suppression of the African Slave-Trade to the United States of America, 1638-1870*, 197.
7 Hart, 368-9.
8 Linder, in Clouse, 125.
9 Jonathan Black, 127.
10 *Dred Scott v. Sanford*, 60 US (19 How.) 396, 404-05 (1856), in Stone, 6.
11 Van Evrie, in Black Heritage Library Collection, *The Dred Scott Case*, ix.
12 Sproul, 70.
13 Joseph Scheidler, 368.
14 Terry, *Operation Rescue*, 104.
15 Fortas, 54.

b. Links in the chains of slavery

Autonomy, Positivism & Pragmatism

According to W.E.B. DuBois, America's solution to its slavery problem can be credited to "...three classes of efforts made during this time – moral, political, and economic: that is to say, efforts which sought directly to raise the moral standard of the nation; efforts which sought to stop the trade by legal enactment; efforts which sought to neutralize the economic advantages of the slave-trade."[1]

(1) Irrepressible slave trade

America was willing to prohibit the importation of additional slaves to the country before it was ready to "intrude" on the conduct of Americans who bought, sold and exploited the slaves who were already here. The prospect of prohibiting the importation of slaves, according to DuBois, raised these questions: "How shall illegally imported Africans be disposed of? How shall violations be punished? How shall the Interstate Coastwise Slave-Trade be protected?"[2]

One of the consequences of our *Constitution*'s division of powers is that one branch of government is charged with the responsibility of implementing laws which were enacted by another. Apprehension of illegal slave importers was largely prevented by the difficulty of proving that interdicted boats carried newly-arriving blacks as opposed to existing slaves being transported to new workplaces or to new owners. Beyond that, if the sympathies of the enforcers are with the institution of slavery rather than the plight of the slave, then enforcement of the law [a lesson we later re-learned during Prohibition] can be expected to be less than enthusiastic. In the opinion of DuBois, "...When the law needed executive interpretation, the decision was usually in favor of the looser construction of the law... [The slave trade] from New Orleans to Mobile was, for instance, declared not to be coastwise trade, and consequently, to the joy of the Cuban smugglers, was left utterly free and unrestricted... In the courts it was still next to impossible to secure the punishment of the most notorious slave-trader."[3]

In summary, DuBois says, "In reviewing efforts toward the suppression of the slave-trade from 1820 to 1850, it must be remembered that nearly every [president's] cabinet had a strong, if not a predominating, Southern element... Naturally, under such circumstances, the government displayed little activity and no enthusiasm in the work... Indeed, all that an American slaver need do was to run up a Spanish or a Portuguese flag, to be absolutely secure from all attack or inquiry on the part of United States vessels."[4]

He says that as a result there was "such a remarkable increase of illicit traffic and actual importations [of slaves] in the decade 1850-1860, that the movement may almost be termed a reopening of the slave trade."[5] Nevertheless, says DuBois: "The one great measure which finally stopped the slave-trade forever was, naturally, the abolition of slavery... The abolition of slavery itself, while due in part to direct moral appeal and political [wisdom], was largely the result of the economic collapse of the large-farming slave system."[6]

(2) Governmental action and slavery

"The abolitionist movement," Whitehead tells us, "came under particular fire after 1830. During this era, every Southern state except Kentucky passed laws restricting the press, speech, and discussion regarding slavery."[7] What's more: "The penalty for printing or circulating anything 'tending to incite slave insurrections' varied from the lash to imprisonment. The death penalty was the prescribed punishment for the second or third such offense (depending upon the state). Under many such statutes mere possession of abolitionist *literature*, regardless of the source, was punishable by fines and imprisonment. As a consequence: by about 1828 freedom of speech against slavery was dead in the South."[8]

A specific example of this suppression is provided by Donald Dayton: "In 1847 Adam Crooks answered a call to North Carolina.. to pronounce that Gospel which proclaims liberty to the captives, and the opening of the prisons to them that are bound... Crooks eventually had to leave the state to escape imprisonment on the charge of '...bringing into the state with the intention to circulate, a printed pamphlet named and styled the Ten Commandments.'"[9] "Abolitionists often met with whippings, brandings, beatings, tar and featherings, and occasionally hangings merely for advocating abolitionism or for merely possessing abolitionist literature."[10] According to Whitehead, Georgia's legislature passed and Governor Lumpkin signed an act which offered a $5,000 reward to any person who could bring publisher Lloyd Garrison to Georgia to be tried. This, says Whitehead, "in effect, was [intended to be a payment from the Georgia state treasury] for the commission of the crime of kidnapping."[11]

"In the North," says DuBois, "with all the hesitation in many matters, there existed unanimity in regard to the slave-**trade**; and the new Lincoln government [in 1862] ushered in the new policy of uncompromising suppression by hanging the first American slave-trader who ever suffered the extreme penalty of the law."[12]

SCOPE and FOCUS
I. CONVICTIONS
II. PRETEXTS
III. MANDATE
IV. LEGACY
Christian Tradition
World Precedents
United States History
Independence
Liberty & Rights
Abolition of Slavery
Pretexts for slavery
Slaves as property
Political expedience
Links in slave-chains
Irrepressible trade
Governmental action
Social dynamics
Church controversy
Methodism shifts
Discipleship & slavery
Prophetic voices
Zeal against slavery
Campus turmoil
Oberlin-Wellington
Pre-War violence
Evangelists shine
Pious priestly voices
Slavery and Abortion
Women's Passage Rites
Seeds of Destruction
Between World Wars
Pivotal Developments
Civil Rights
Parental Responsibility
Humaneness
V. ABORTIVE LINKS
VI. DILEMMA
VII. DESTINY

(3) Social Dynamics and slavery

When the New York Anti-slavery Society was founded [by "the Tappans, Garrison, and a number of other revival and reform leaders"] in 1833, the landlord cancelled their lease just before the first meeting, fearing anti-abolitionist violence. The fears were well founded; the meeting was held in Charles Finney's church and was interrupted by an angry mob.[13]

"A mob had earlier ransacked Lewis Tappan's home, burning his furniture in the streets... Tappan left his home unrepaired all summer as a 'silent Anti-Slavery preacher to the crowds who will flock to see it,' ...The Tappans lived in [constant fear] of assassination or destruction of their property. They had to seek insurance out of the city in Boston at an 'abolitionist premium.' ...The South began to boycott the Tappans' business enterprises and threatened economic sanctions to those with whom they did business."[14]

"Tappan money and organizational skill were also behind the abolitionist propaganda campaigns. Lewis Tappan created the plan of publishing four monthly journals (one to be issued each week) to be mailed free to influential persons throughout the country. This more than any other abolitionist activity united the South in opposition. Mobs broke into post offices to destroy shipments of the journals."[15]

According to DuBois: "Each generation sought to shift its load upon the next, and the burden rolled on, until **a generation came which was both too weak and too strong to bear it longer.** One cannot, to be sure, demand of whole nations exceptional moral foresight and heroism; but... The most obvious question which this study suggests is: How far in a State can a recognized moral wrong safely be compromised [indulged]?"[16]

He summarizes: "A lethargy [had] seized the country, and it did not awake until slavery was about to destroy it. Even then, **after a long and earnest crusade, the national sense of right did not rise to the entire end of slavery**. It was only a peculiar and almost fortuitous commingling of **moral, political, and economic motives** that eventually crushed African slavery and its handmaid, the slave-trade in America."[17]

(4) Church controversy and risks

According to Whitehead, "As a result of the public hostility toward his [abolitionist] writings, [Elijah] Lovejoy's [printing] press was destroyed on four separate occasions in Alton, [Illinois]... 'If the civil authorities refuse to protect me, I must look to God, and if I die, I have determined to make my grave in Alton.' On November 6, 1837, Lovejoy was shot five times and died shortly after a mob attempting to destroy his fourth press was dispersed."[18]

Dayton says that prior to the death of Elijah Lovejoy, pastor Luther Lee "had assumed that since abolitionists were 'attacked by the religious press... they must be a set of desperate fanatics,'" but that Lovejoy's murder convinced Lee that it was wrong to remain silent any longer.[19] Former President John Quincy Adams wrote: "That an American citizen in a state whose Constitution repudiates all slavery, should die a martyr in defense of the freedom of the press, is a phenomenon in the history of this Union. **Martyrdom [has been called] the only test of sincerity in religious belief.** It is also the ordeal through which all great improvements in the condition of men are doomed to pass."[20] Dayton tells us that "abolitionist missionaries" to the South, "were mobbed, dragged into court, and imprisoned. At least one Wesleyan minister in the South was lynched. But these preachers set about founding churches with such names as Freedom Hill and Lovejoy Memorial Chapel."[21]

1 DuBois, 195.
2 DuBois, xiii.
3 DuBois, 161.
4 DuBois, 158.
5 DuBois, 178.
6 DuBois, 197.
7 Whitehead, *The Right to Picket*, 35.
8 Whitehead, *The Right to Picket*, 35.
9 Dayton, *Discovering an Evangelical Heritage*, 79.
10 Whitehead, *The Right to Picket*, 35.
11 Whitehead, *The Right to Picket*, 36.
12 DuBois, 191.
13 Dayton, *Discovering an Evangelical Heritage*, 67-8.
14 Dayton, 69.
15 Dayton, 69.
16 DuBois, 198-9.
17 DuBois, 196.
18 John Whitehead, *The Right to Picket*, 36-7.
19 Dayton, 81.
20 Adams, in Whitehead, *The Right to Picket*, 37.
21 Dayton, 79.

Robert Linder says, "Many people do not realize that major denominations like the Methodists, Baptists, and Presbyterians attacked slavery as an institution long before the Civil War, even in the South."[1] He goes on: "As tensions between North and South mounted and the Civil War approached, Baptists, Methodists, and Presbyterians split along regional lines over the question of whether or not slavery was a sin... the morality of slavery was only one of several issues leading to the Civil War, but for the churches it was the fundamental question. The scars of the great conflict of the last century are yet visible in American Protestantism and the basic question of whether it is sinful and immoral to deny other human beings their basic rights lingers on to the present."[2]

Doug Bandow agrees: "Christians in both North and South firmly believed that God was on their side... The Baptist, Methodist, and Presbyterian denominations split apart... Clerics and parishioners again ended up on different sides of another regional split a century later: civil rights."[3]

Methodism's particular metamorphosis

England's founder of Methodism, John Wesley, in his 1774 *Thoughts Upon Slavery*, condemned "every gentleman that has an estate in our American plantations; yea, **all slaveholders** of whatever rank and degree; seeing men-buyers are exactly on a level with man-stealers. You therefore are guilty, yea **principally** guilty, of all these frauds, robberies, and murders. **You are the spring that puts all the rest into motion.**"[4]

"In 1780, the General Conference of the Methodist Church declared that slavery was contrary to the laws of God and required all of its itinerant preachers to free their slaves."[5] "The 1784 founding conference of the [American] Methodist Episcopal Church had called for the expulsion of any member engaged in the slave trade, but with the growth of Methodism into the largest American denomination, this stance was gradually abandoned. When faced with the alternative of growth into a national church or maintaining discipline on the slavery issue, Methodism chose growth and prosperity. By the 1820s and 1830s the Methodists had largely accommodated to the institution of slavery."[6]

One Methodist pastor combined the roles of prophet and zealot. Orange Scott "studied the *Liberator* of William Lloyd Garrison and other abolitionist writing for a year before declaring himself an abolitionist. He then spent one hundred dollars of his own money (no small amount in that time for a Methodist preacher!) to subscribe to the *Liberator* for three months in the name of one hundred ministers of the New England [Methodist] Conference... As a result the New England delegation to the [Methodist] General Conference was abolitionist and included Orange Scott."[7]

In spite of Orange Scott's valiant efforts in lengthy debates over slavery, the conference delegates resolved, by a vote of 120 to 14, to express themselves as "decidedly opposed to modern abolitionism, and wholly disclaim any right, wish or intention to interfere in the civil and political relationship between master and slave..."[8]

That 1836 Methodist *decision, to avoid imposing Christian morality on the South*, had a chilling effect on antislavery discussion. Orange Scott was demoted from his position as presiding elder [like a district superintendent] because he refused to cease lecturing and writing on the subject of slavery.[9] Dayton says that after 1836, Methodism "assigned abolitionist ministers either to 'hard scrabble' circuits or to churches where the antiabolitionist feeling was so strong that they would be crushed, [and it] brought ministers to [church] trial for attending abolitionist meetings or even reading abolitionist literature."[10]

Because Methodism had become so repressive of abolitionism, Orange Scott – and a few others – broke away, founding the Wesleyan Methodist Church. George Pegler, who left Methodism to become a Wesleyan, wrote these five reasons why "the churches of the North are responsible for the continuance of slavery:" 1) including slaveholders in fellowship; 2 and 3) voting for pro-slavery candidates and parties; 4) segregated seating in church; 5) silencing/persecuting abolitionists.[11] Dayton observes: "The Wesleyan Methodists have been vindicated in recent years. What appeared as revolution and insurrection to their contemporaries now appears to us to have been responsible social witness."[12]

At the time of Orange Scott's untimely death in 1847, Luther Lee said of him: "If it be insisted that he was ultra and rash, it was because he lived in advance of his age. He advocated no sentiments, and resorted to no measures, which are not destined, very soon, to become the moderate sober views of the world."[13]

SCOPE and FOCUS
I. CONVICTIONS
II. PRETEXTS
III. MANDATE
IV. LEGACY
Christian Tradition
Early Church
Reformation Era
World Precedents
Holocaust
Nuremberg
Geneva
United Nations and Int'l Human Rights
Unborn Child's Rights
Global Abortion Norms
Apartheid
United States History
Independence
Liberty & Rights
Abolition of Slavery
Pretexts for slavery
Slaves as property
Political expedience
Links in slave-chains
Irrepressible trade
Governmental action
Social dynamics
Church controversy
Methodism shifts
Discipleship & slavery
Prophetic voices
Zeal against slavery
Campus turmoil
Oberlin-Wellington
Pre-War violence
Evangelists shine
Pious priestly voices
Slavery and Abortion
Women's Passage Rites
Seeds of Destruction
Between World Wars
Pivotal Developments
Civil Rights
Parental Responsibility
Humaneness
V. ABORTIVE LINKS
VI. DILEMMA
VII. DESTINY

c. Discipleship and slavery

"Every discussion of attempts to end slavery, discrimination, and segregation," says Charles McCoy, "must take account of [both] the assistance and opposition of churches."[14] James Draper gets specific: "The abolitionists... mainly Unitarian, rose up in righteous wrath against slavery and demanded its immediate abolition. In emotional terms which sent alarm through the South, they spread their gospel of abolition by means of stirring up hatred against Southern slaveholders. Interestingly enough, in the South, Unitarians were advising the slave owners to react violently. Ultimately, it was Southern Unitarians who persuaded the South to secede from the Union..."[15]

Donald Dayton highlights the "alienation of the abolitionists during the 1840s as traditional churches refused to embrace reform [abolitionism]."[16] He cites the example of two sisters, Angelina and Sarah Grimke, of whom he says, "though usually identified as Quakers, they were originally converted from Southern aristocratic Episcopalianism under the influence of Presbyterian revivalism. They apparently turned to Quakerism because that sect most fully expressed their newfound antislavery sentiments."[17]

Dayton identifies a pattern that is undoubtedly as applicable to abortion-fighting as it was to abolitionism: "The failure of the church to embrace the great moral concerns of an age can drive out sensitive youth who will find moral leadership in other circles."[18] Colonel Doner minces no words: "The Church's pre-Civil War withdrawal from actively influencing political decisions is credited by some historians with playing a major role in provoking the Civil War in the first place. They hold that the Church, through its involvement, could have persuaded the government to outlaw slavery without the necessity of a terrible and tragic war that claimed over a half million American casualties."[19]

(1) Prophetic anti-slavery voices: Universalism & Justice

Readers will recall that when Moses challenged Pharaoh to free the Hebrew slaves, the immediate effect was that a harsh penalty was laid on those slaves [Exodus 5:6-9], and that what we would call *public opinion* came down heavily upon Moses [Exodus 5:19-21]. In recent years, not only abortion clinic burnings, and shootings of abortionists, but even peaceful Rescues have been blamed by many pro-life leaders for alienating supporters of the pro-life movement. Prior to the Civil War, "Three particular occurrences," says John Whitehead, "raised the national sensitivities *against antislavery* free speech activities and writings." These were William Lloyd Garrison's newspaper *The Liberator*; a booklet, "Appeal to the Colored Citizens of the World," written in 1829 by David Walker, a free black in Boston; and Nat Turner's slave uprising in 1831. Whitehead notes that writings seen to incite slave insurrections carried penalties of the lash and imprisonment for the first offense, and death for repeat offenders.[20]

Although Garrison's *Liberator* had been willing to print a rationale-of-defense for Nat Turner's efforts,[21] when John Brown's raid at Harper's Ferry failed in 1859, what might be termed a "more mature" *Liberator* called it "a misguided, wild, and apparently insane effort."[22]

Henry David Thoreau's outspoken advice had been that those who opposed slavery "should at once effectually withdraw their support, both in person and property [taxes], from the government."[23] His opinion was that if the government "requires you to be the agent of injustice to another, then I say, break the law... What I have to do is to see, at any rate, that I do not lend myself to the wrong which I condemn... By paying taxes to an unjust government, the citizen condones wrongs committed by the state."[24]

In 1846, Thoreau was arrested in Massachusetts for refusing to pay his poll tax on the grounds that the tax essentially sponsored slavery and the Mexican War, both of which he believed were immoral.[25] It was not Thoreau's one-man tax protest that impacted society, but rather, his famous essay, "On the Duty of Civil Disobedience," which is not only credited with inspiring many who opposed slavery, but which is said to have also helped to shape the philosophies of Gandhi, M. L. King, and Nelson Mandela.[26]

Robert Downs includes Harriet Beecher Stowe's *Uncle Tom's Cabin* as one of sixteen titles in *Books that Changed the World*.[27]

Among the pastors who took a courageous, prophetic stand against slavery was Luther Lee who, Dayton tells us, "opposed all decisions based on expedience, insisting that right must be responded to, regardless of worldly considerations."[28]

1 Linder, in Clouse, 125.
2 Linder, in Clouse, 125-6.
3 Bandow, *Beyond Good Intentions, A Biblical View of Politics*, 18.
4 Wesley, in Dayton, 73-4.
5 Linder, in Clouse, 125.
6 Dayton, 74.
7 Dayton, 75.
8 Dayton, 75.
9 Dayton, 75.
10 Dayton, 75-6.
11 Dayton, 78.
12 Dayton, 84.
13 Luther Lee, in Dayton, 84.
14 Mccoy, in Lee, *Religion and Social Conflict*, 37.
15 Draper, *If the Foundations Be Destroyed*, 103.
16 Dayton, 34.
17 Dayton 89.
18 Dayton, 34.
19 Doner, 47.
20 Whitehead, *The Right to Picket*, 35.
21 Whitehead, *The Right to Picket*, 35.
22 Bray, *A Time to Kill*, 89-92.
23 Robert Downs, *Books that Changed the World*, 69.
24 Downs, 69.
25 Randy Alcorn, *Is Rescuing Right?*, 119.
26 Randy Alcorn, *Is Rescuing Right?*, 119.
27 Downs, 76.
28 Dayton, *Discovering an Evangelical Heritage*, 81.

(2) Zealots against slavery: Justice & Pragmatism

It is clear that – as we are rediscovering with abortion – the polarization and confusion engendered by strong clerical and denominational stands, both for and against slavery, neutralized the Christian impact on society and weakened confidence in the church as the source of moral authority. It remained for lone Christian activists, and isolated communities of faith to stand in the gap for the rights of the slave.

Calvin Fairbanks spent nearly 20 years in jail in Kentucky, between 1844 and 1961 for having helped four slaves to escape to freedom. He had served five years for helping a family of three escape. He next helped a female slave escape and served nearly 15 years for that.[1]

Turmoil on Campus

Most American colleges in the decades preceding the Civil War pragmatically cleansed their faculties of abolitionists in an effort to avoid antagonizing their supporters. This tactic was largely successful in assuring that future pastors and church leaders would be fed a *tolerant, pro-choice gospel* regarding slavery.

An unusual "rebellion" occurred, however, at Lane Theological Seminary in Cincinnati. A student, Theodore Weld, initiated 18 days of debates between abolitionists and a "colonization society." Members of the campus anti-slavery society infuriated their elders by insisting on "treating blacks as social equals." The only staff member who sided with these students was fired, and the campus forbade future discussions of controversial issues such as slavery for fear that harm would be done to the "prosperity of the Institution..."[2]

It is notably unusual that, rather than knuckling-under, 40 of the abolitionist students withdrew from the college and set up a "free seminary" across town.[3] The "Lane Rebellion" became the nucleus of a unique Christian experiment which centered at Oberlin, Ohio [near Cleveland]. Oberlin College was founded in 1833 and pledged to admit students of any color [and by 1841 had become the first U.S. school to award college degrees to women]. Dayton says, "Oberlin wished to make the whole Christian church an 'antislavery society.' The means was 'moral suasion' or the use of Finney's 'new measure revival techniques.' ...the wider Congregational association of which Oberlin was a part... vowed to have 'no Christian communion with those who practice slavery, or with any who justify the system.'"[4]

Crucial to the success of the Oberlin experiment [the "colony" and the school] was the fact that Arthur Tappan chose to support it financially: "He pledged his entire income (about one hundred thousand dollars a year – quite a sum in those days!) to the project, holding back only enough to provide modestly for his family..."[5]

The Oberlin-Wellington Rescue

Federal fugitive slave laws had been enacted beginning in 1793. When Congress and various states systematically strengthened those laws in the 1830s and 1840s, "Oberlin's response was based on a doctrine of civil disobedience that appealed to 'higher' or divine law."[6]

The Oberlin community had become a major hub of the underground railroad, some members invading the South to free slaves. But in 1858, four armed men – operating to enforce the fugitive slave laws – seized an escaped slave who had taken refuge at Oberlin, and were holding him in a hotel room in nearby Wellington, awaiting the next train. Dayton affirms that "several hundred Oberlinites stormed the hotel" and rescued the slave. John Price, the fugitive slave, was hidden in the home of Oberlin professor and *president* J.H. Fairchild. Subsequently 21 identifiable Oberlinites were tried for their crimes. In their defense they appealed to "higher law," and stated, "We must obey God always, and human law, social and civil, when we can."[7]

The Wellington community, not to mention the prosecutor and judge in Cleveland, were extremely hostile to Oberlin and all it stood for. Despite predictable convictions, "One historian of Oberlin has ranked the episode with the publication of *Uncle Tom's Cabin* and John Brown's raid on Harper's Ferry as events that stirred the public imagination before the Civil War."[8]

Pre-War Violence & Commentary

"Nat Turner was a Christian slave, suffering under the often times brutal conditions of a racist brand of slavery," says Michael Bray. "In 1831, he and several fellow slaves slew thirteen men, eighteen women, and twenty-four children. Horrific as this deed was, (today) the horror of turner's deed gives way to praise of his heroic efforts to stop slavery. And his execution is lamented more than the deaths of the innocent children."[9]

Donald Dayton establishes links between Oberlin and John Brown. He says that John Brown "had been preparing for his raid on Harper's Ferry during the Oberlin-Wellington Rescue Trial. Two Oberlin blacks [died along with John Brown]... The Oberlin chapel bell tolled for an hour on the day of Brown's execution... A member of the Oberlin board of trustees declared in a funeral sermon, 'We can see no signs of hallucination nor of infatuation in John Brown. We esteem him as one of the Wise Men of our times.'"[10] Bray reveals, "Immediately after the raid regular citizens and even abolitionists denounced Brown."[11]

SCOPE and FOCUS
I. CONVICTIONS
II. PRETEXTS
III. MANDATE
IV. LEGACY
Christian Tradition
Early Church
Reformation Era
World Precedents
Holocaust
Nuremberg
Geneva
United Nations and Int'l Human Rights
Unborn Child's Rights
Global Abortion Norms
Apartheid
United States History
Independence
Liberty & Rights
Abolition of Slavery
Pretexts for slavery
Slaves as property
Political expedience
Links in slave-chains
Irrepressible trade
Governmental action
Social dynamics
Church controversy
Methodism shifts
Discipleship & slavery
Prophetic voices
Zeal against slavery
Campus turmoil
Oberlin-Wellington
Pre-War violence
Evangelists shine
Pious priestly voices
Slavery and Abortion
Women's Passage Rites
Seeds of Destruction
Between World Wars
Pivotal Developments
Civil Rights
Parental Responsibility
Humaneness
V. ABORTIVE LINKS
VI. DILEMMA
VII. DESTINY

(3) Evangelists and slavery: Justice & Virtue

The pietist-activist polarization was very much at work in pre-Civil War America. Colonel Doner says: "The real problem was the perception on the part of the Evangelicals that an anti-slavery Church would necessarily remain a very small Church... The churches persuaded themselves that their main mission was to 'Christianize the nation' by multiplying converts, and their phenomenal success on this score seemed to justify the priority that placed 'winning souls' above freeing slaves. But [most of] the soul-winning campaigns maintained their emotional momentum only by studious avoidance of all controversial issues."[12]

Just as Oberlin became the notable exception to the anti-abolitionist climate on campuses, there were salutary exceptions among evangelicals and evangelists. Dayton says that the New York Anti-Slavery Society was founded "by the Tappans, Garrison, and a number of other revival and reform leaders."[13]

Evangelist Theodore Weld [earlier a central figure in the Lane Rebellion] was like an abolitionist Johnny Appleseed; converts in the towns where he preached revivals established "nearly 100 new American Anti-Slavery Society chapters in Ohio in one year," and the AAS national committee was so impressed with Weld's effectiveness that they had him share his techniques with a hand-picked cadre, and they "sent out seventy such agents as Jesus had sent out seventy disciples to preach."[14]

Another like-minded group was the American Missionary Association. "Lewis Tappan said of the AMA that 'Its single object is to send out a pure gospel free from any compromise.' The AMA supported as many as two hundred missionaries (including a number sent to the South) and expended a million dollars in its first decade."[15]

(4) Pious priests and slavery: Commandments & Virtue

Despite the pragmatic pressures that kept most local pastors from taking a biblical stand against slavery, a significant number of them took courageous and costly action. Charles McCoy salutes "those Rhode Island ministers of the eighteenth century who denounced the slave trade while some of their wealthiest members derived their incomes from that source..."[16]

Among the martyred pastors was Rev. Charles Turner Torrey, who died in a Baltimore prison "while serving a sentence for invading the South to help slaves escape."[17] Dayton says that, "Wesleyans often spoke of the conjunction of 'piety and radicalism,'" striving to excel in both areas.[18] In 1864, pastor Luther Lee said, "The gospel is so radically reformatory, that to preach it fully and clearly is to attack and condemn all wrong, and to assert and defend all righteousness."[19]

1 Randall Terry, *Operation Rescue*, 105.
2 Dayton, *Discovering an Evangelical Heritage*, 29 and 36.
3 Dayton, 37.
4 Dayton, 41.
5 Dayton, 37.
6 Dayton, 46.
7 Dayton, 48-50.
8 Dayton, 61.
9 Bray, 87.
10 Dayton, 61-2.
11 Bray, 89-90.
12 Doner, *The Samaritan Strategy: A New Agenda for Christian Activism*, 47.
13 Dayton, 66-7.
14 Dayton, 30.
15 Dayton, 70-1.
16 McCoy, in Lee and Marty, *Religion and Social Conflict*, 39.
17 Dayton, 82.
18 Dayton, 77.
19 Dayton, 81.

d. Parallels between slavery and abortion

When The Civil War came, the slavery/abolition split was not simply South/North; it severed states, towns and families, and revealed that within any particular *individual* the huge assortment of pro/con arguments waged an *internal* war of their own. Any future conflagration over abortion would surely entail comparable conflicted tragedies at every level, with the exception that on the national scene the North/South geographical split of slavery would have no counterpart [unless slight rural/urban leanings toward pro-life/pro-abortion, respectively, are considered]; there could be no seceding but only a to-the-death, winner-take-all, mortal combat for total national dominance. While we must all recoil in horror at such a prospect, it is imperative that we examine our nation's current embrace of **abortion** with the plumbline of history, as we candidly assess all of the dimensions of America's abortion policy: past, present and future.

In 1993, a *Time* magazine article quoted an unnamed pro-lifer's comment: "You can draw a lot of comparisons between the fight over abortion and slavery. The abolitionists' movement lasted some 60 years, and it could be the same with abortion."[1]

CONCLUSIONS: This researcher would have to confess that sixty years seems to be a very optimistic projection for the end of abortion, given the obviously greater difficulty of the abortion struggle. To explain: **1**) The slave was a constant, visible testimony of his own humanness, and could actively participate in his escape to freedom; the preborn is faceless, invisible and helplessly enwombed by a mother who may be resolved to making him dead. **2**) A single successful effort could liberate a slave from a lifetime of misery; preventing the intended abortion of one preborn would require kidnapping and restraining her mother for nine months. **3**) Enslaving one victim required a capture in Africa, trans-Atlantic shipment, marketing and transportation, feeding, housing and overseeing; aborting one's child can be accomplished during a lunch break from work. **4**) An emancipated slave or slave family could soon achieve financial independence; each thwarted abortion demands an 18-year commitment to every facet of parenthood of that child. **5**) The only direct advantage of slavery was the economic gain to the slave holder; abortion is claimed to be an economic boon to the mother, the government, and society at large, while it is alleged that criminalizing abortion would result in an incalculable financial burden and overpopulation catastrophe for all concerned.

John Eidsmoe also uses the 60-year figure: "It often seems that nothing is being done, that no [pro-life] progress is being made. However, I believe more people are coming to realize that the unborn child is in fact a human being, and that his right to life deserves protection. Let us remember that the battle to abolish slavery took over sixty years, and the battle for full racial equality is still being waged a century later. But few would deny that progress has been made and victories have been won."[2]

Actually, the "sixty years" understates the span of 76 years between the *Constitution* [1787] which validated slavery by establishing that a slave equals three-fifths of a person, and the *Emancipation Proclamation* in 1863.

In 1998 we are 25 years into the abortion era. Twenty-five years after the ratification of the *Constitution*, as of the year **1812**, the English Parliament had already abolished the British slave trade, but abolitionism in America was little more than a minor intellectual debate, and it would be eight years before the U.S. would *begin* to constrain the importation of new slaves. The first fugitive slave act had already been imposed with little opposition. It would be another 20 years before William Lloyd Garrison would begin agitating for the "immediate" abolition of slavery, and the various anti-slavery societies would emerge. Compared to Abolitionism, the pro-life movement is decidedly ahead of the game in organization and activity, but it would be difficult to count even a single step of progress in the long march toward recriminalization and the elimination of abortion.

SCOPE and FOCUS
I. CONVICTIONS
II. PRETEXTS
III. MANDATE
IV. LEGACY
Christian Tradition
Early Church
Reformation Era
World Precedents
Holocaust
Nuremberg
Geneva
United Nations and Int'l Human Rights
Unborn Child's Rights
Global Abortion Norms
Apartheid
United States History
Independence
Liberty & Rights
Abolition of Slavery
Pretexts for slavery
Slaves as property
Political expedience
Links in slave-chains
Irrepressible trade
Governmental action
Social dynamics
Church controversy
Methodism shifts
Discipleship & slavery
Prophetic voices
Zeal against slavery
Campus turmoil
Oberlin-Wellington
Pre-War violence
Evangelists shine
Pious priestly voices
Slavery and Abortion
Women's Passage Rites
Seeds of Destruction
Between World Wars
Pivotal Developments
Civil Rights
Parental Responsibility
Humaneness
V. ABORTIVE LINKS
VI. DILEMMA
VII. DESTINY

1 *Time*, 4-19-93, 40.
2 Eidsmoe, *God & Caesar*, 182-3.
3 Scheidler, 368.
4 Foreman, 42-3
5 F. LaGard Smith, 112.

Progressive Stages of the Abolition Movement

We render, here, a generalized timetable of the anti-slavery movement: 1) The *Constitution* sets slavery in stone, and 30 years of political debate begins; 2) After **30** years, in the 1820s, public moral debate intensifies, as do efforts to chill protest and activism, by governmental act. 3) After **40** years, in the 1830s, zealous activists, publications and organizations emerge; the critical change is that actions have begun to match the moral rhetoric; the resulting damage to the enshrined evil evokes retaliation in the form of mob violence and official repression under the cloak of "preserving law-and-order;" 4) After **50** years, in the 1840s, public debate invades the churches [shouldn't it be reversed, the Church declaring a righteous moral truth to the society?]; denominations are rocked by the resultant schisms, and the self-contradicting "Christian voice" is a public joke. 5) After **60** years, in the 1850s, lacking a Church-based legitimacy, true Christian character must express itself through para-church and even secular avenues. Even so, a viable political challenge eventually becomes a possibility. 6) After **70** years, in the 1860s, as the political scales shift to win the upset of the Old Order through legitimate democratic methods, the deposed powers resolve to destroy the nation rather than relinquish control, and a bloody Civil War becomes necessary.

Joseph Scheidler says: "The solution to slavery was a terrible war. Abortion, the most bloody war in our country's history, is going on now in abortion clinics and hospitals and doctors' offices across the nation. We are witnessing a civil war. There must be an all-out effort to end the tragedy of this century, the murder of our helpless unborn, one every twenty seconds in the [surgical] abortion industry."[3]

"The underground railroad was not a strategy to abolish the 'slavery issue,'" says Joseph Foreman, "It is what the serious Christian did to abolish slavery for this slave, then that slave, and then the next slave. They did not look at slavery as an 'issue.' They looked at the slave personally... the Underground railroad was not primarily a strategy, it was a way of life – it was Rescue."[4]

F. L. Smith is confident that "in its heart," America knew that slavery and racial discrimination were wrong, and "In its heart, America knows that human life begins before birth."[5]

4. U.S. Women's Rites of Passage

"Historians have wondered what happened to the abolitionist impulse after the Civil War. To some extent it died out with the emancipation of the slaves, though many Christians, sensitive to the broader problems of prejudice and injustice, devoted their lives to work among the freedmen. But the major force of the antislavery struggle was in the postwar era rechanneled into the 'purity crusade' and the temperance movement [which] were more amenable to a 'personal morality' orientation. While the slaveholder was the sinner in the case of slavery, the prostitute and the drunkard were more directly engaged in sin and needed to be 'rescued' from their plight."[6]

George Grant divides Western history into five "significant eras."[7] His fourth era is the Missions Movement, 1800 to 1914 when World War I began. The turn of the century marked the zenith of Protestant Christianity's influence over American culture. President Theodore Roosevelt spoke these prophetic words in 1904: "The measure of our civilization will not be *that* we have done much, but *what* we have done with that much. I believe that the next half century will determine if we will advance the cause of Christian civilization or revert to the horrors of brutal paganism. The thought of modern industry in the hands of Christian charity is a dream worth dreaming. The thought of industry in the hands of paganism is a nightmare beyond imagining. The choice between the two is upon us."[8]

Roosevelt's 1905 State of the Union message was equally prophetic: "The transformation of the family is one of the greatest sociological phenomena of our time; it is a social question of the first importance, of far greater importance than any mere political or economic question can be... There are those who believe that a new modernity demands a new morality. What they fail to consider is the harsh reality that there is no such thing as a new morality. There is only one morality. All else is immorality. There is only true Christian ethics over against which stands the whole of paganism. If we are to fulfill our great destiny as a people, then we must return to the old morality, the sole morality."[9]

6 Dayton, *Discovering an Evangelical Heritage*, 100.

7 Grant, *Third Time Around: A History of the Pro-Life Movement from the First Century to the Present*, 3-4. His five eras: **Patristic**: Founding of the Church to fall of Rome (476); **Medieval**: 476 to fall of Constantinople (1453, also the end of the 100 Years' War between the French and English); **Renaissance and Enlightenment**: 1500 to French Revolution (1789); **Missions Movement**: 1800 to World War I (1914); **Modern Era**: 1900 to date.

8 Roosevelt, in Grant, *Third Time Around*, 118. Grant's summary of 19th century industrial progress: "That century had produced steamships, railroads, streetcars, bicycles, rollerskates, the air brake, the torpedo, telephones, telegraphs, transatlantic cables, harvesting machines, threshers, cotton gins, cooking ranges, sewing machines, phonographs, typewriters, electric lights, illuminating gas, photographs, x-rays, motion pictures, and cottonseed oil" (116-7).

9 Roosevelt, in Grant, *Third Time Around*, 118-9.

Where has all the virtue gone?

Regina Morantz analyzes the basic reasons for the erosion of Christian morality: "Nineteenth-century moralism gradually succumbed in the first decades of the twentieth century to the combined attack [against the] purity advocates: idealistic physicians inspired by bacteriological discoveries facilitation the control of venereal disease, and the diverse but insistent proponents of the Freudian revolution. Social and economic factors also underlay the emergence of new sexual attitudes."[1]

She continues: "As early as 1907 Simon Patten predicted the gradual economic shift away from austerity and production [Virtues] to a concern with consumption. An interest in leisure and luxury fostered **pleasure** and personal fulfillment as positive goods, and undermined Victorian prescriptions of thrift, self-denial, and personal control [virtues]. Urbanization eroded community and religious controls on behavior. In addition, the increasingly visible women joining the labor force were freed from some of the constraints of home and family."[2]

In 1975, Shana Alexander summarized: "As woman's place began to change three-fourths of a century ago, ...the great temples of the new religion became the powerful ladies' magazines... What all women's magazines were giving women to read was largely illusion, fantasy, and too often cruel deception... Exploitation of women's needs and dreams... abounded in the closed, essentially fake world of ladies' magazines."[3]

a. Protection & rights movements
Justice & Positivism

There is no doubt that Victorian rigidity was widely renounced after the turn of the century. We will next be exploring a series of twentieth century movements which can be grouped together as social drives designed to improve the lot of women. This optimistic social engineering clearly began in the nineteenth century, particularly with the successes of evangelistic revivalism, the abolition of slavery through the Northern victory in the Civil War, and the campaigns that criminalized abortion throughout the nation.

(1) Abortion...
Women and unborn children as victims

The reader is invited to scan the Timeline at the end of *Orphans* to note the evolution of public sentiment against abortion between 1800 and 1880. In 1800, not one state had statutes prohibiting abortion, but by 1900 every state prohibited abortion, and most had made it a criminal offense. "Most of the legal changes came during a short twenty-year period from 1860 to 1880."[4] Assorted sources attribute this phenomenon to a variety of trends and movements. Here follows this researcher's best rendering of the details.

The nineteenth century saw a marked weakening of moral standards as pioneers turned their backs on their roots and exulted in American opportunity, autonomy and independence. A relaxing of moral standards was accompanied by increased frequency of abortive remedies, and there was a subsequent national awakening to the nature and magnitude of the abortion problem. This social concern led to a grassroots, broadly-based, successful movement to outlaw abortion.

In the first decade of the 1800s, two European developments introduced conflicting themes into America's view of abortion. Responding to the horrors of poisons being imprecisely administered in an attempt to induce miscarriage, England's Parliament outlawed all poison-induced abortions. This statute abandoned the common law distinction of quickening, and prohibited chemical abortions at any stage of pregnancy.[5] It may be assumed that Parliament's motivation was primarily to protect the pregnant woman from harm, and only secondarily to protect the life of the child.

It should be noted, however, that British common law still delayed the execution of a woman who was convicted of some capital crime, if she happened to be pregnant, until after delivery of her child, clearly an early recognition of the right-to-life of the preborn.[6]

In the same year when Parliament outlawed chemical abortion, 1803, Thomas Malthus published the second edition of his 1798 *Essay on Population*, which launched the "population-bomb" hysteria which persists, world wide, today.[7]

So at a time when the American libertarian spirit was already being evidenced in increased "problem pregnancies," two conflicting news items from Europe stirred the emotional mix on this side of the Atlantic: 'Babies can be bad news,' and 'Abortions are dangerous.'

SCOPE and FOCUS
I. CONVICTIONS
II. PRETEXTS
III. MANDATE
IV. LEGACY
Christian Tradition
Early Church
Reformation Era
World Precedents
Holocaust
Nuremberg
Geneva
United Nations and Int'l Human Rights
Unborn Child's Rights
Global Abortion Norms
Apartheid
United States History
Independence
Liberty & Rights
Abolition of Slavery
Pretexts for slavery
Links in slave chains
Discipleship & slavery
Slavery and Abortion
Women's Passage Rites
Protection & Rights
Abortion's victims
Anti-prostitution
Employment rights
Suffrage
Anti-alcohol
Anti-saloon
Prohibition
Legislating Morals
Anti-Family Changes
Anti-motherhood
Anti-child
Sexual equality
Feminism
Equal opportunity
Equal results
Seeds of Destruction
Between World Wars
Pivotal Developments
Civil Rights
Parental Responsibility
Humaneness
V. ABORTIVE LINKS
VI. DILEMMA
VII. DESTINY

Early efforts to protect women from the evils of abortion

Elizabeth Ann Seton founded the first Catholic religious order in America, now the Sisters of Charity, and her "efforts to expose the horrors of illicit abortions... enabled her to effect a number of changes in both legislation and enforcement" before her death in 1821.[8]

Legislative action to curb abortion began in Connecticut in 1821. The unique pattern followed by a number of other states in the next 20 years deviated from the British model in that America tended to include exceptions in order to save the life of the mother.[9] This first round of anti-abortion laws usually applied only after quickening, and prohibited only the administering of poisons to the pregnant woman, but not mechanical or surgical abortion methods.[10] Thus, the supporters of legalized abortion are partially right *if they stipulate* that these *early laws* were enacted to protect the pregnant woman but not to preserve the life of the child.

In the 1840s, "The *National Police Gazette* was undoubtedly the most sensational newspaper in America [perhaps the forerunner of modern tabloids]... edited by George Wilkes... Though the paper regularly filled three of its eight pages with advertising... Wilkes refused to provide any space for abortionists. He regularly wrote editorials calling for the criminalization of the industry – calling the practitioners 'professional murderers,' and 'child destroyers.' The prominent pastor Gardiner Spring and the famed editor Louis Jennings would both later credit Wilkes with having provoked them to action."[11] "In 1845, Massachusetts became the first state to make abortion, or attempted abortion, at any point in pregnancy a criminal offense."[12]

Scientific research began to open windows on the womb. The human egg was first discovered in 1827. Prior to this the woman was regarded as an incubator for the "man's seed," and in the 1840s the union of sperm and egg at conception was demonstrated.[13] The research of prominent embryologist Hugh Hodge "had convinced him beyond any shadow of a doubt that life began at conception and that the destruction of that life before or after birth was unmitigated murder."[14] Grant says that Hodge trained a generation of young doctors at the University of Pennsylvania medical school to revere human life, and that, "In 1854, he began to lobby the American Medical Association... to call a halt to the slaughter of children."[15]

Dr. H.R. Storer, a third generation Boston Ob/Gyn, began in 1855 to write two widely-read pro-life medical books, and was soon chosen to be the head of the first national right-to-life organization, a "select committee" of the American Medical Association![16]

In 1856, Samuel Taylor "was a prototypical mild-mannered small town pharmacist... a lifelong Methodist... But when the daughter of one of his customers nearly died from a dose of mail-order abortifacient pills [enormously popular and widely advertised], he sprang into action... He began a one-man educational campaign – first with his fellow pharmacists, later expanding to physicians, and finally with state legislators... He drafted model legislation that was approved by [sixteen states]."[17] In Congress, the 1866 Assimilative Crimes Statute included strong anti-abortion laws.[18]

1 Regina Markell Morantz, in Altherr, *Procreation or Pleasure?: Sexual Attitudes in American History*, 147.

2 Morantz, in Altherr, 147.

3 Shana Alexander, 11-12.

4 George Grant, *Third Time Around: A History of the Pro-Life Movement from the First Century to the Present, 109.*

5 James C. Mohr, *Abortion in America: The Origins and Evolution of National Policy, 1800-1900*, 5.

6 Charles Kindregan, *Abortion, the Law, and Defective Children*, 32.

7 Robert Downs, *Books that Changed the World*, 54.

8 Grant, *Third Time Around*, 104.

9 Russel Shaw, *Abortion on Trial*, 43.

10 James Mohr, 20-1.

11 Grant, *Third Time Around*, 107.

12 J. Douglas Butler, *Abortion, Medicine, and the Law*, 249.

13 Debra Evans, *Without Moral Limits: Women, Reproduction, and the New Medical Technology*, 69.

14, 15 and 16 Grant, *Third Time Around*, 105.

17 Grant, *Third Time Around*, 107-8.

18 Garton, 63-4.

Almost immediately after the Civil War ended, in the late 1860s, denominations like the Congregationalists and Presbyterians issued strong anti-abortion pronouncements, and Methodist and Baptist churches were widely circulating pro-life sermon booklets which "showed that the Bible teaches that life begins at conception – in more than forty different passages from Genesis to Revelation – and that abortion is thus 'no less than murder.'"[1]

Catholic bishops in America had begun reaffirming pro-life policies in the 1850s, and when Pope Pius IX "renewed the medieval censures against abortion in 1869, each local parish was encouraged in an encyclical to become involved in pro-life activity."[2]

As to activism, the 1840s had seen not only a heating up of anti-*slavery* conflict, but of anti-abortion zeal as well. For example, "Leslie Printice... also organized regular protests in front of Anna Lohman's five [New York] area abortion franchises... Tenacious and unrelenting, Leslie led a rally outside Lohman's lavish home in 1846 that was by turns emotional, physical, and fierce. When Lohman went to trial for the first time the next year, Leslie was there – despite innumerable threats on her life from a number of the gangsters on Lohman's payroll – to testify with several children 'saved from the butcher's knife.'"[3]

James Mohr offers an analysis of why the events of the 1840s were so crucial: "In the early 1840s three key changes began to take place in the patterns of abortion in the United States. These changes profoundly affected the evolution of abortion policy for the next forty years. First, abortion came out into the public view [thanks to the *Police Gazette*, perhaps]... Second, the overall incidence of abortion began to rise sharply in the 1840s and remained at high levels through the 1870s [social and political instability and war time excesses?]... Third, the types of women having recourse to abortion seemed to change [Mohr says: white, married, Protestant, middle- and upper-class women exercising personal reproductive choice, as opposed to immigrants and prostitutes, who were the stereotypical abortion clients]."[4]

Mohr gives a large measure of credit for the anti-abortion movement to the medical community, calling it "The Physicians' Crusade Against Abortion, 1857-1880," and stating that "The founding of the American Medical Association in 1847... dramatically affected the evolution of a number of social policies... Opposition to abortion was definitely one of them."[5]

Marvin Olasky, however, disagrees: "Mohr's story of how abortion was fought in the late nineteenth century is also wrong. The American Medical Association did not have the power to do what Mohr said it could do. Laws by themselves, while important as educational tools, were not grandly effective. Laws clearly dissuaded some women from having abortions, but... thousands of other abandoned, unmarried women were not dissuaded. Sixty thousand prostitutes were not dissuaded [some say that they averaged 1.8 abortions per year, each. And an abortionist] was able to build a millionaire's mansion on Fifth Avenue."[6]

George Grant is convinced that Christian ethics and the commitment of religious leaders as well as zealous "laymen" were the elements essential to success in criminalizing abortion. He draws these conclusions with caution: "Actually, the nineteenth century American church seemed uniquely impotent to lead such an important struggle. The Catholic community was still largely comprised of immigrants and was thus excluded from the mainstream of American discourse. And the divisive moral and political dilemma of chattel slavery dominated the thinking of most Protestants – to the exclusion of almost everything else – in both the North and South. [But] a number of courageous pioneers shook the church out of its doldrums... As impressive as all these efforts were – in the press, in the medical community, and in the political arena – it was the church that led the pro-life movement toward a consummate victory... In less than two decades, the church was able to marshal hostile journalists, ambivalent physicians, reticent politicians, and even radical feminists to the cause of exploited mothers and their helpless unborn. They succeeded overwhelmingly."[7]

SCOPE and FOCUS
I. CONVICTIONS
II. PRETEXTS
III. MANDATE
IV. LEGACY
Christian Tradition
Early Church
Reformation Era
World Precedents
Holocaust
Nuremberg
Geneva
United Nations and Int'l Human Rights
Unborn Child's Rights
Global Abortion Norms
Apartheid
United States History
Independence
Liberty & Rights
Abolition of Slavery
Pretexts for slavery
Links in slave chains
Discipleship & slavery
Slavery and Abortion
Women's Passage Rites
Protection & Rights
Abortion's victims
Anti-prostitution
Employment rights
Suffrage
Anti-alcohol
Anti-saloon
Prohibition
Legislating Morals
Anti-Family Changes
Anti-motherhood
Anti-child
Sexual equality
Feminism
Equal opportunity
Equal results
Seeds of Destruction
Between World Wars
Pivotal Developments
Civil Rights
Parental Responsibility
Humaneness
V. ABORTIVE LINKS
VI. DILEMMA
VII. DESTINY

1 Grant, *Third Time Around*, 97-9.
2 Grant, *Third Time Around*, 97.
3 Grant, *Third Time Around*, 106. Hey, Reader: Have you ordered this book yet?
4 James Mohr, *Abortion in America: The Origins and Evolution of National Policy, 1800-1900*, 46-7.
5 Mohr, 147 and 152.
6 Marvin Olasky, *Abortion Rites: A Social History of Abortion in America*, 292.
7 Grant, *Third Time Around*, 97 and 100.
8 Grant, *Third Time Around*, 106.
9 *Esther* 4:14.
10 Grant, *Third Time Around*, 95.
11 Grant, *Third Time Around*, 95-6.
12 Grant, *Third Time Around*, 100. Anthony: "I deplore the horrible crime of child murder." Gage decried the "crime of child murder, abortion, or infanticide."
13 James Mohr, *Abortion in America*, 224.
14 Grant, *Third Time Around*, 108.
15 Grant, *Third Time Around*, 110.
16 Olasky, *Abortion Rites: A Social History of Abortion in America*, 283.
17 Olasky, 293.

This researcher's tentative conclusion is that 1870 was a pivotal year. It appears that the earliest concern over abortion arose at the "grass roots" and, without benefit of much organization or expertise, began to shape preliminary legislative reforms. Non-mainstream journalism started to raise the public consciousness level. When societal changes began to alter the abortionists' volume of business and the "caliber" of their clientele, physicians and pharmacists became alarmed by the personal tragedies abortion left in its wake. Concurrently, embryologists were making pro-life discoveries. And the fledgling American Medical Association was eager to clean up the image of health professionals, define its turf, and test its political muscle; attacking abortionists was the perfect vehicle to accomplish all three objectives.

The Church, shamed by its pathetic collective performance in the *abolition* struggle – and discovering that a massive moral victory [the Civil War] had been won without them – perhaps resolved to perform more honorably in this next crusade. By 1870, however, although the moral, medical and legal arguments were all in place, the MEDIA establishment [apart from fringe publications like the *Police Gazette*] had not yet decided that its *moment* had arrived. **The publishing voice was essential to delivering the message that would raise the clamor that would deliver the vote to outlaw abortion.**

Providentially, Louis Jennings was a pioneer in American journalism, a committed Christian, pro-life, and editor of the New York *Times*. "In 1870, Jennings began a crusade against abortion on the editorial pages of his paper that finally lead to the criminalization of the procedure in every state in the Union. He understood the power of the printed page and utilized it expertly. He knew only too well that it would be necessary to provoke a public outrage over the issue, not simply a stiffening of legislation that might go unenforced."[8] Jennings was joined by a *Times* reporter, Augustus St. Clair, another pro-life Christian. Because of these two obedient zealots, who were placed in a crucial position for "such a time as this,"[9] "America awoke in a jolt to the horror of abortion... It became a moral crusade. It became a movement, an outcry."[10] Despite the decisive leadership of the *Times*, there is room to speculate that the rest of the journalistic community had the power to defeat the cause, simply by excluding abortion news from their own reporting, or by giving the same stories an opposite "spin."

"At first, the press was disinclined to expose the homicidal details of the abortion industry due to the possibility of their own loss of income – abortionists accounted for as much as a quarter of all classified advertising dollars for a number of local newspapers... [However,] all around the country, the same newspapers, magazines, and digests that had previously accepted advertising from abortionists began to throw the searchlight of truth on their detestable deeds of darkness."[11] "So monolithic was the consensus... that even the most ardent feminists [Susan B. Anthony and Matilda Gage, by name] had to rally under the pro-life banner."[12]

Unlike the preliminary anti-abortion restrictions prior to 1850, the ultimate sanctions were explicitly framed to protect the unborn child's right to life, from conception: "After 1860, legislators dropped traditional quickening rules, revoked common law immunities for women... In short, established the official abortion policies that most Americans would live with through the first two-thirds of the twentieth century... Reflecting the legislative trend of the 1870s, Georgia enacted the first explicitly anti-abortion law in its history in 1876. The measure made the abortion of 'any woman pregnant with a child... an assault with intent to murder.'"[13] Not only were laws enacted, they were sometimes enthusiastically enforced: Anthony Comstock was a federal special prosecutor. "Between 1872 and 1880 he oversaw the arrest and conviction of fifty-five abortionists operating up and down the east coast."[14]

Those who hold up the nineteenth century anti-abortion crusade as a goal for what today's pro-life movement should expect to accomplish are strongly urged make these comparisons: **1**) Is today's society as open to the possibility that an anti-abortion campaign can be both pro-child *and* pro-woman as were 19th century Americans? **2**) Can the medical, political and legal communities be convinced that the pro-life position is once again in their best interests, and right? **3**) Are pastors and denominations ready to take pro-life risks, and have congregations been trained in the virtue of taking a bold moral stand in the public arena? **4**) Do pro-life leaders have access to media technology adequate to unite the faithful and lead them into battle, AND is there a righteous remnant tuned-in and anticipating that leadership? **5**) Does anyone have a plan for what the faithful must do – and what those in positions of secular power must be persuaded to do – in order for God's will to be accomplished in this time and place? **6**) Who has a picture of what victory will look like, so we will know it if and when we achieve it?

As to what results to expect, George Grant asserts, "It was the church that catalyzed and spearheaded the wildly successful pro-life efforts of the nineteenth century."[15] Marvin Olasky would clearly take issue with Grant: "I have found that pro-life forces have been wrong to assume that abortion was rare in the nineteenth century, that tough laws virtually ended the practice, that doctors and ministers led the way, and that the anti-abortion consensus remained philosophically intact until the 1960s."[16]

As if in response to Grant's estimate that the 19th century pro-life movement was "wildly successful," Olasky takes pains to compare the most valid data on the prevalence of abortion in both 1860 and in 1910, and to factor-in population growth, etc., in order to determine how effective the full criminalization of abortion was at reducing the prevalence of abortion. **The most reliable conclusion is that the imposition of anti-abortion laws nationwide reduced the incidence of abortion by no more than fifty percent.**[17]

(2) Anti-prostitution developments

The Evil That Men Do, an 1889 novel, helped to bend the social conscience in the direction of sympathy for the plight of women and empathy for prostitutes, as it "described in graphic detail oppression at places of work and the degrading conditions of tenement life which impelled working women to prostitution."[1]

Two books in the early twentieth century, *Sister Carrie* and *Susan Lenox: Her Fall and Rise*, centered on "heroines who escaped the harsh realities of a working girl's life through selling their sex and who achieved success and glamor beyond that available to the average woman who preserved her virtue intact."[2]

The public was being conditioned to be more tolerant of prostitution, and women were being taught that virtue was boring and prostitution was glamorous. But prostitution itself was ugly, exploitative and dangerous. The legacy of the 19th century Christian reformers combined with an increasing 20th century "faith in the ability of republican institutions and economic opportunity to cure social problems in the United States" creating a movement to unite police and the medical community in order to "safeguard both the prostitute and the public... By the early twentieth century, the agitation against prostitution had become a national preoccupation."[3]

"The early film industry quickly discovered the profits to be derived from cinematic treatment of commercial vice [prostitution]... *Inside of the White Slave Traffic* (1913) did not do much more than depict a nationwide vice organization so efficient that its female victims never escaped its deadly grasp, and deplore a police system that arrested fallen women and let their clients go free."[4]

A sign of growing Positivism, progressives believed that prostitution could be controlled by governmental action. Two examples were the Mann Act of 1910, which made interstate transportation of women for use as prostitutes a federal crime, and the U.S. Army's control of prostitutes during World War I.[5]

"The double standard tacitly accepted prostitution not merely as a necessary evil but also as an ally of the nuclear family since it allowed men to go to prostitutes, who presumably had knowledge of effective contraception, instead of causing unwanted pregnancies in their wives, who did not."[6]

(3) Employment for women

The mass exodus of men to fight in world War I opened the door to heroic – if exhausting – employment for women, who soon made up 20% of the work force.[7] A comparable situation occurred during World War II. We are told, "Although 70% of American women employed outside the home during the war wanted to remain on the job after the war ended, they would not get their wish. As in World War I and its aftermath, they would be pressured back into the parlor and kitchen. The birthrate soared – a postwar baby boom."[8]

A popular song asked, "How 'ya gonna keep 'em [the soldiers] down on the farm, after they've seen Par-EE?" The flip side of that platter should have asked, "How will you keep 'em in the kitchen and nursery, after they've had some *paychecks*?" The phenomenal influx of women into the workplace in the twentieth century undoubtedly both reflects and increased social orientations toward materialism and Pleasure, individualism and Autonomy.

(4) Suffrage for women

"Turn-of-the-century suffragists actually attributed prostitution to the exclusion of women from public affairs; once women obtained the vote, feminists believed, they would vote consistently for the elimination of vice. Feminists held, moreover, that enfranchised women would find more opportunities for work and would not be coerced into selling sexual favors to men, either within marriage or outside it."[9] When the 19th Amendment, proposing that women be allowed to vote, was put to the states for ratification in 1919, it took less than a year for the deed to be done.[10]

(5) Alcohol's impact on women & society

The campaigns waged against the evils of alcohol were arguably as much a *feminist* thing and a *political progressivist* thing as they were a *Christian crusade*, but when Prohibition failed, the blame was effectively attributed to bigoted Fundamentalists "trying to impose their morality on others."

SCOPE and FOCUS
I. CONVICTIONS
II. PRETEXTS
III. MANDATE
IV. LEGACY
Christian Tradition
Early Church
Reformation Era
World Precedents
Holocaust
Nuremberg
Geneva
United Nations and Int'l Human Rights
Unborn Child's Rights
Global Abortion Norms
Apartheid
United States History
Independence
Liberty & Rights
Abolition of Slavery
Pretexts for slavery
Links in slave chains
Discipleship & slavery
Slavery and Abortion
Women's Passage Rites
Protection & Rights
Abortion's victims
Anti-prostitution
Employment rights
Suffrage
Anti-alcohol
Anti-saloon
Prohibition
Legislating Morals
Anti-Family Changes
Anti-motherhood
Anti-child
Sexual equality
Feminism
Equal opportunity
Equal results
Seeds of Destruction
Between World Wars
Pivotal Developments
Civil Rights
Parental Responsibility
Humaneness
V. ABORTIVE LINKS
VI. DILEMMA
VII. DESTINY

1 Leslie Fishbein, in Thomas Altherr, *Procreation or Pleasure?: Sexual Attitudes in American History*, 119.

2 Fishbein, in Altherr, 120.

3 Fishbein, in Altherr, 115 and 118.

4 Fishbein, in Altherr, 118-9.

5 Fishbein, in Altherr, 119.

6 Fishbein, in Altherr, 120.

7 Geoffrey Perrett, 157.

8 Harvey Green, *The Uncertainty of Everyday Life, 1915-1945*, 152.

9 Fishbein, in Altherr, 118.

(a) Anti-saloon movement

Harvey Green says that the battle against demon rum lasted nearly a hundred years.[11] Certainly it was an aggressive multi-pronged attack for more than fifty years: the Prohibition Party was founded in 1869, and its allies included Wayne Wheeler's Anti-Saloon League, the Evangelical Protestant Churches, and "the Women's Christian Temperance Union, which numbered hundreds of thousands of members."[12] Geoffrey Perrett tells us that in addition to the Prohibition Party, "Prohibition had been taken up by both the Populists and the Progressives, the principal reform movements in American politics at the turn of the century."[13]

The era from 1915 to 1945, Harvey Green tells us, "embraced the nation's greatest attempt at regulating behavior and transforming the social fabric since the abolition of slavery in 1863. Prohibition... was part of a larger reform effort to counter the changes that seemed to endanger the established order. Jazz, the movies (as yet uncensored), radio, 'new' women, 'flaming youth,' and the 'crime wave' in corrupt mobster-ridden cities and the nation's small towns were – to those who wished to see it – the proof of a culture that was out of control."[14]

Green also provides insight into the clash of cultures and convictions which was focused in Prohibition: "The anti-saloon movement was an attempt to impose a middle-class small-town and suburban vision of community life from the American historical context upon workers who were situated in urban areas more closely resembling European cities in at least one important sense: By 1915, the American industrial working class was living in conditions so crowded... that, for many, housing presented the barest minimum of space for sleeping and shelter."[15] Thus, the saloons had become the living rooms for poor workers who literally had no such space to call their own.

Geoffrey Perrett paints a picture of how the culture war over alcohol was played out in Washington state: "By 1903 there were thousands of miles of railroad track, thousands of saloons – and a flourishing arm of the Anti-Saloon League. The arrival of the ASL 'Flying Squad' in a town to back up the Prohibition crusade of the local churches was an event, with torchlight parades, brass bands, speakers, singers, and fireworks."[16]

Alcohol was attacked not only for moral and sociological [pragmatic] reasons, but at the turn of the century scientific studies had begun to reveal harmful physical effects of the consumption of alcohol. "The scientific case against the saloon won over millions who had never been persuaded by clergymen or women's groups."[17]

(b) Prohibition, the Amendment

"Contrary to the usual impression, Prohibition did not arrive like a thief in the night, taking an unprepared country by surprise. There were five completely dry states by 1908, and twenty-three by 1914."[18] A parallel situation preceded *Roe v. Wade*. There was abundant evidence that, state-by-state, abortion statutes were being both eroded and abandoned in the years before *Roe*. The difference is that, unlike the drinkers who got prepared for Prohibition, evangelical Christians did not mobilize in response to the incremental losses, or in preparation for a nationwide legitimizing of abortion.

The war on alcohol had the effect of dividing the various religious bodies in America: "Jews and Catholics wanted temperance, not Prohibition. But Baptists, Methodists, and other evangelicals considered any attack on the Anti-Saloon League as an attack on themselves."[19]

"In the elections of 1916, Prohibition was the principal issue in nearly every state poll, and the prohibitionists won."[20] The 18th Amendment was submitted to the states in 1917, ratified in 1919, and entered into force in 1920. "It was no crime to buy a drink, or an entire case if you wished. The crime was to sell it."[21]

"Prosecution was fitful, judges indifferent. Juries proved reluctant to convict in Prohibition cases... 'What the law enforcement bodies of the large cities wanted was not enforcement but a safe sort of regulation of the liquor-selling traffic,' said one New York editor. They did not believe for a moment that drinking was wrong... The police in any town or city could have shut down every speakeasy and kept it shut had they wanted to do so."[22] Prohibition was repealed by the 21st Amendment in 1933.

"Speakeasies were, oddly, one more forward step for women's rights," says Geoffrey Perrett. "Saloons had barred women customers; speakeasies welcomed them. There was, in fact, an easy, democratic air to these places: all of the customers, men and women alike, were breaking the law together. That they were owned by gangsters seemed to trouble no one."[23]

10 Perrett, 157.
11 Green, 214.
12 Perrett, 167.
13 Perrett, 167-8.
14 Green, 9.
15 Green, 214.
16 Perrett, 167.
17 Perrett, 167.
18 Perrett, 168.
19 Perrett, 167.
20 Perrett, 168.
21 Perrett, 169.
22 Perrett, 172.
23 Perrett, 177.

(c) "You can't legislate morality" gets etched in nation's psyche

Nelson Mandela speaks with authority: **"It is no use to take action to which the masses are opposed, for it will then be impossible to enforce."**[1] In *Altered Landscapes: Christianity in America, 1935-1985*, we are told that some of the "opposition to abortion shows remarkable similarities in stance and tactics to the anti-drink crusades that resulted in Prohibition. Just as the one group attacked saloons, so the other bombs abortion clinics. Just as did the one, so the other would amend the Constitution if appeals to legislative action prove fruitless."[2]

James Atkinson, author of *Church & State Under God*, takes a dim view of all Christian social-crusading: "Had the Apostles and early Christians set about the reformation of those desperate social evils of their day, as so many of our activist contemporaries seek to do, Christianity would have run out in the sand and be now remembered in similar terms to those we use to refer to the slave revolt of Spartacus."[3]

Troy Duster has compiled an insightful list of assertions about the legislating of morality: **1**) Laws which **supplement** the existing moral order may be effective in preventing the spread of behavior that is immoral [i.e. prostitution]; **2**) Laws which create conditions for the development of a **new** morality [where no norms exist] may be successful in creating a new set of moral attitudes about behavior [i.e. drug use in 1914]; but, **3**) Laws which attempt to **change** the existing moral order are doomed to failure [i.e. Prohibition].[4]

To the degree that Duster's assertions are correct, a future legislative, judicial, or Constitutional re-criminalization of abortion could be expected to be only marginally effective. Duster has another way of stating his dire premise: "Passing a law can not change the strong feelings that people have about right and wrong."[5]

b. Anti-family developments; Sanger

Pleasure & Autonomy

As the 20th century began, Victorian assumptions about female sexuality predominated in the social consciousness. "The idea of a female sex drive equal to that of men would have been inconceivable," even among feminists, who were "repelled by incessant male appetite, which was obviously unreciprocated."[6]

Margaret Sanger, the founder of Planned Parenthood, singlehandedly, it sometimes seems, engineered the radical reshaping of attitudes regarding sex, marriage, the family, and contraception in the 20th century. In the process, our nation's orientation was decisively reversed, from virtue and accountability to pleasure and autonomy. "The great unifying theme at the conclusion of the 20th century is the triumph of the individual," says John Naisbitt in *Megatrends 2000,* "the individual as the foundation of society and the basic unit of change. [All of America's 'mass movements'] were built one consciousness at a time by an individual persuaded of the possibility of a new reality."[7]

George Grant says that "In America, Margaret Sanger made Malthusian [population bomb] thinking the cornerstone of her endeavors – her attempts to smuggle contraband contraceptives into the country [and] her advocacy of promiscuous sex and abortion."[8]

In 1921 when Sanger stood up to give her first speech as president of the American Birth Control League, she was interrupted and arrested by a police raid instigated by the Roman Catholic archbishop of New York. "When this became known there were cries of outrage the length and breadth of the country. It was the best send-off the ABCL could have asked for... By 1926 the ABCL had nearly 40,000 members."[9] Catholicism had inadvertently boosted the organization it had tried to quash.

One of the reasons Margaret Sanger was such a bitter foe of Christianity was because of her conviction that Malthus was right about the dangers of overpopulation. She was convinced that "Christian 'charity' to ethnic minorities and the poor" actually inflicted terrible harms to humanity, and was a "symptom of a malignant social disease" because it thwarted nature's plan to eliminate "defectives, delinquents, and dependents" through such remedies as plagues and famines.[10]

Grant gives Sanger a compliment of sorts, linking her accomplishments to five of the most famous persons in history: "For the first time since the time of Plato and Aristotle, a consistent pagan philosophy had been formulated [by Malthus in 1798] to ethically defend genocide – and, for the first time it was systematically implemented [in the 1900s by Hitler, Stalin and Sanger]. Abortion, infanticide, abandonment, and euthanasia were advocated as social *virtues* and traditional Christian values were derided as *vices*."[11]

1 Mandela, *Long Walk to Freedom*, 116.
2 David Lotz, 308.
3 Atkinson, 11.
4 Duster, *The Legislation of Morality: Law, Drugs, & Moral Judgment*, 24.
5 Duster, 4.
6 Fishbein, in Altherr, 118.
7 Naisbitt, *Megatrends 2000: Ten New Directions for the 1990s*, 298.
8 Grant, *Third Time Around*, 123.
9 Geoffrey Perrett, *America in the Twenties: A History*, 163.
10 Grant, *Third Time Around*, 123-4.
11 Grant, *Third Time Around*, 124.
12 Hunter, *Culture Wars*, 186.
13 Perrett, *America in the Twenties*, 161.
14 Perrett, 162-3.
15 Harvey Green, *The Uncertainty of Everyday Life, 1915-1945*, 131-2. Green says in the '20s, *Lysol*'s advertising promoted the product as a disinfecting and deodorizing douche, and "euphemistically suggested" its effectiveness as a spermicide by affirming that its "germ-killing action could help alleviate 'calendar fear.'"
16 Perrett, 160.
17 Grant, *Third Time Around*, 125.
18 Grant, *Third Time Around*, 136-7.
19 Brian Clowes, *Pro-Life Activist's Encyclopedia*, page 42.2.
20 Jonathan Black, *Radical Lawyers*, 265-8.
21 Francis Beckwith, *Politically Correct Death*, 53.

SCOPE and FOCUS
I. CONVICTIONS
II. PRETEXTS
III. MANDATE
IV. LEGACY
Christian Tradition
Early Church
Reformation Era
World Precedents
Holocaust
Nuremberg
Geneva
United Nations and Int'l Human Rights
Unborn Child's Rights
Global Abortion Norms
Apartheid
United States History
Independence
Liberty & Rights
Abolition of Slavery
Pretexts for slavery
Links in slave chains
Discipleship & slavery
Slavery and Abortion
Women's Passage Rites
Protection & Rights
Abortion's victims
Anti-prostitution
Employment rights
Suffrage
Anti-alcohol
Anti-saloon
Prohibition
Legislating Morals
Anti-Family Changes
Anti-motherhood
Anti-child
Sexual equality
Feminism
Equal opportunity
Equal results
Seeds of Destruction
Between World Wars
Pivotal Developments
Civil Rights
Parental Responsibility
Humaneness
V. ABORTIVE LINKS
VI. DILEMMA
VII. DESTINY

(1) Woman as victim: motherhood as a burden
Autonomy through contraception

"The struggle over abortion is ultimately a struggle over the concept of motherhood," says James Hunter.[12]

Just as was the case in Margaret Sanger's career, America's acceptance of contraception inevitably led it to abortion. As defined by the federal *Penal Code* in 1873, birth control information was considered pornography, but "It was only in the struggle to check venereal disease, which by World War I had reached epidemic proportions [considered incurable and fatal, like HIV/AIDS is today – penicillin was not developed until 1927], that condoms became legally available."[13]

Our government had provided condoms free to WWI soldiers, and when the boys came home, contraception was deemed essential. Margaret Sanger's business career had begun in 1915 when she opened her first birth control clinic in Brooklyn, "was arrested, spent 30 days in jail, and then helped publish the *Birth Control Review*."[14]

"Contraceptive devices transformed sexual behavior by the 1920s. They were available in most gas station rest rooms and even in the Sears, Roebuck mail-order catalog, and contraceptive information was available, if sometimes difficult to find. Throughout the era the middle class used condoms, diaphragms, coitus interruptus, abstinence, and spermicides."[15]

In the 1920s, says Perrett, "Novels, plays, and works of social criticism steadily derided marriage as an outmoded institution, something the modern world could well do without. There were confident predictions that marriage would die out before the end of the century."[16]

"In 1930," Grant tells us, "after an all-out lobbying effort by Margaret Sanger's staff, the Committee on Marriage and the Home [of the] precursor to the National Council of Churches became the first major organization in the history of Christendom to affirm the language and philosophy of 'choice' [regarding birth control 'for just the hard cases'], Soon after, the Quakers, the Northern Presbyterians, the Congregational church, the Methodist-Episcopal church, and several Baptist denominations followed suit."[17]

Here is Grant's assessment of the changes: "Disunity racked the church during much of the twentieth century, not just an institutional and a denominational disunity, but a fundamental disunity of focus and purpose. Working at cross purposes with itself, the church tragically nullified its import and impact at the very time it was most needed, ...yielding to a new cultural and scientific high priesthood. A rapid slide into neo-paganism resulted, evidenced by the ascendancy and acceptance [as national leaders] of Hitler, Stalin and Sanger."[18]

"Any real hope for reconciliation between the Catholic church and the Protestant denominations [who had earlier been divided over Prohibition] was probably dashed by the split on artificial contraception."[19]

(2) Children as the enemy ...abortion & eugenics
Autonomy & Relativism

The widespread conception of motherhood as a burden to be avoided by all means was articulated in a 1966 legal brief: "A woman who has a child is subject to a whole range of *de jure* and *de facto* punishments, disabilities, and limitations to her freedom from the earliest stages of pregnancy."[20] Margaret Sanger's contribution to the propagation of that theme, in 1920, was this: "The most merciful thing a large family can do for one of its infant members is to kill it."[21]

The "new freedom" unleashed by the proliferation of contraception in the 1920s produced a tragic and deceptive chain of results: 1) False confidence reduced inhibitions and increased sexual activity;[22] 2) High rates of contraceptive failure were concealed from the public, and the pregnancy rates kept climbing;[23] 3) Expectations of non-pregnancy prompted a scapegoating of the contraceptive, and the justification for an abortion; 4) The number of [illegal] abortions skyrocketed, perhaps reaching a million a year;[24] 5) Consequently, the birth rate *declined*, giving a false "confirmation" that contraception was working.[25]

---

22 Perrett, 153, 164; Altherr, 127-8.

23 *Newsweek*, 3-13-95, 61; *Press*, 8-8-96, A6.

24 G. Williams, 209; Perrett, 160: "Thriving abortion clinics operated all over... [Also] there was abortion by knitting needle, coat hanger, and buttonhook. Desperate women swallowed poisonous concoctions in an attempt to induce a miscarriage."

25 Green, 132.

(3) Woman as victim ...all sex as exploitation by men

Autonomy & Pleasure

"A handful of nineteenth-century social feminists challenged the prevailing view of prostitution," says Leslie Fishbein. They argued that "all women were prostitutes, whether married or not, as long as they were coerced economically into bestowing their sexual favors upon men."[1]

"Toward the end of the nineteenth century American sexual attitudes were beginning to undergo a fundamental alteration, for the dominant sexual ideology of sex as restraint [virtue] was being challenged increasingly by the hitherto radical doctrine of sex as pleasure. The implications of this change in ideology [extended] to the very formation of character and the organization of society."[2]

Whitman, Ellis, and Margaret Sanger all "argued the naturalness of sex as though its very naturalness meant there should be no restriction... Sanger insisted feverishly that liberated sex would usher in a golden age of peace and prosperity. In fact, she saw inhibitions about sex as the single greatest problem facing mankind."[3]

Altherr says that "by the 1920s in the United States the older middle-class beliefs that sex was only for procreation [were] being replaced by a belief in which pleasure, independent of conception, was as equally legitimate an end of sexual activity in marriage as was procreation."[4] Geoffrey Perrett says that "the sexual liberty of the Twenties is nothing less than amazing when compared with the sexual repression only a decade or so earlier."[5] Not only that, one of Margaret Sanger's favorite themes was that "sex could no longer be forced on women as a duty. They had to be persuaded, their consent had to be won [Autonomy]."[6]

In the 1930s, Hollywood continued to condition the public in the revised attitudes toward social values. W.C. Fields was one who did so, through an "unrelenting attack on small-town life, [portraying the] conviction that the outlanders were narrow-minded, sexually repressed, ill-educated, and hostile to anything that smacked of pleasure," and Mae West "exuded sex and thumbed her nose at nearly every social, gender, and sexual convention. She was in command, and she demanded to be satisfied."[7]

c. Feminist movements

Justice

We have devoted the previous ten pages of *Orphans in Babylon* to an exploration of various "rites of passage" for American women during the past 150 years. Little mention seems to have been made by historians of one possible factor which may account for much of the social upheaval and cultural flux our nation has experienced: When the women of America began picking up the pieces of their lives after the Civil War, it most surely occurred to them, individually or in groups of confidants, that the result of the great national bloodbath had been to secure rights and privileges for black men that were still denied to white women, particularly a political voice, the right to vote. The spirit we have come to call *feminism* was surely born of thoughts such as these.

We earlier shared Donald Dayton's opinion that after the Civil War the "abolitionist impulse" was rechanneled into the "purity crusade and the temperance movements" [*Orphans*, page 147, note 6]. This researcher could more easily be convinced that those and the other "rights of passage" for women were simply the necessary battlefields of a larger war, a campaign for women to achieve full equality with men: civil [rights and protections], political, social and sexual, and economic. In short, a 150-year-old feminist revolution on a male-dominated planet. The list of almost exclusively male heroes in the nineteenth century crusade which succeeded in the full criminalization of abortion only underscores the fact that women have long been excluded from positions of power and influence.

As to prostitution, the "oldest profession" has never been seriously attacked but only harassed and regulated, and the greatest factor in reducing the numbers who ply that trade has been the sexual revolution's creation of singles bars where the transactions are more complicated but the results are essentially the same.

1 Fishbein, in Altherr, 120.

2 Altherr, 127.

3 Paul deParrie, *Romanced to Death*, 74.

4 Altherr, 127-8.

5 Perrett, 156.

6 Perrett, 165.

7 Green, 208-9.

8 Beckwith, *Politically Correct Death*, 60-1.

9 John Naisbitt, *Megatrends 2000: Ten New Directions for the 1990s*, 216-7 and 224-5.

10 19th Amendment, 1920; 15th Amendment, 1870.

11 Perrett, 157-8. The ERA was resurrected and "passed" by Congress in 1972, but it died two more deaths, in 1979 and 1982, narrowly failing to accumulate the required number of state-legislative ratifications on both tries.

12 Roger Betsworth, *Social Ethics...*, 174.

13 Peter Westen, 538.

SCOPE and FOCUS
I. CONVICTIONS
II. PRETEXTS
III. MANDATE
IV. LEGACY
Christian Tradition
Early Church
Reformation Era
World Precedents
Holocaust
Nuremberg
Geneva
United Nations and Int'l Human Rights
Unborn Child's Rights
Global Abortion Norms
Apartheid
United States History
Independence
Liberty & Rights
Abolition of Slavery
Pretexts for slavery
Links in slave chains
Discipleship & slavery
Slavery and Abortion
Women's Passage Rites
Protection & Rights
Abortion's victims
Anti-prostitution
Employment rights
Suffrage
Anti-alcohol
Anti-saloon
Prohibition
Legislating Morals
Anti-Family Changes
Anti-motherhood
Anti-child
Sexual equality
Feminism
Equal opportunity
Equal results
Seeds of Destruction
Between World Wars
Pivotal Developments
Civil Rights
Parental Responsibility
Humaneness
V. ABORTIVE LINKS
VI. DILEMMA
VII. DESTINY

Women have made phenomenal gains in the workplace, although the average lifetime income of women remains only half that of the average man.[8] But John Naisbitt's *Megatrends* should give every woman cause to cheer: since World War II the number of employed women has increased 200 percent; women now hold nearly 40 percent of the executive, administrative and management jobs; consistently since the '70s, women have been assuming two-thirds of the new jobs created in the Information Sector [the wave of the future], and women are now starting their own businesses at twice the rate of men![9]

It is a national disgrace that women were not granted the right to vote until fifty years after the same right had been granted to black men.[10]

Although Prohibition failed, the major goals of the Anti-Saloon movement have been achieved, thanks to the combined effects of Alcoholics Anonymous, equal-access rights of women at bars, and televised sports to guarantee that Joe Sixpack will spend most of his free time at home.

"Thanks" in large part to Margaret Sanger and her Planned Parenthood Federation, both abortion-on-demand and abortifacient birth control are perfectly legal and federally protected, men and women and boys and girls are encouraged to freely enjoy what comes naturally, and American men have been placed on notice that anything they say or do "can and will be used against them in a court of law."

(1) Women and equal opportunity: "Equity Feminism"

The nineteenth-century feminist movement is said to have peaked and faded with the apparent demise of the Equal Rights Amendment in 1923.[11]

Sexual discrimination was outlawed by the 1964 Civil Rights Act even though no women "had established a civil rights-type organization or lobbied for its passage. The new feminist civil rights organization, the National Organization for Women (NOW), was formed in 1966 in response to the complaint of women that the law that made sexual discrimination illegal was not being enforced."[12]

"Equality" is the watchword of modern feminism.[13] *Time* magazine, in 1969, reported that the first black woman ever elected to Congress, Shirley Chisholm, "feels she has been more discriminated against as a woman than as a Negro."[14]

Equality for women struck a very responsive chord in the liberal Christian denominations, particularly in the '60s and since then. "The barriers against the ordination of women were crumbling, and women had won unprecedented positions of church authority and power... The pro-choice position ['as American as baseball'] rode the coat tails of the pro-women position in the [liberal] churches."[15]

(2) Women and equal results: "Gender Feminism"

There are really two varieties of modern feminism. The first type, "equity feminism," asks only for a fair chance, equal *opportunity*, what it calls "a level playing field." On the other hand, "Gender feminism" requires equal *results* and fervently demands reparations and affirmative action.[16]

In his book on *Modern Liberalism*, Robert Bork tells us that "the radical [gender] feminist branch of modern liberalism sees all male-female interactions, including marriage, as power relationships – a view that scorns such values as marriage and the family."[17]

Joseph Foreman says that a gender feminist "calls pregnancy the central tool of male domination, and holds that killing her child is an act of liberation for a woman, freeing her to take her rightful place in Western civilization."[18]

14 *Time*, 11-21-69, 53.

15 R.C. Sproul, *Abortion: A Rational Look at an Emotional Issue*, 117-8.

16 Robert Bork, *Slouching Towards Gomorrah: Modern Liberalism and American Decline*, 193-4.

17 Bork, 29.

18 Joseph Foreman, *Shattering the Darkness: The Crisis of the Cross in the Church Today*, 118.

5. Seeds of Social Destruction

The answer to the question, Is history cyclical or linear? is complex. In some ways, history is cyclical [Plato is often credited with the political theory that monarchies tend to evolve into oligarchies, which are capable of maturing into democracies, which if they are not vigilant might be toppled by dictatorships, which often perpetuate themselves in the form of monarchies...], yet in other ways it is linear ["In the beginning...,"[1] "God so loved the world..."[2] "...and books were opened..."[3]. Some *parts* of history are cyclical ["Do not be surprised at the painful trial you are suffering, as though something strange were happening to you..."[4], but some doors once passed through can never be reopened ["Cursed is the ground because of you... By the sweat of your brow you will eat your food..." "Never again will I curse the ground because of man..."[5] "God's gifts and His call are irrevocable."[6] "So you are no longer a slave, but a son... also an heir."[7].

One of the most crucial projects facing the pro-life community is the task of determining which historical developments of the last 150 years are cyclical – and can thus be reversed – and which ones constitute linear developments which are effectively "irrevocable." *Orphans in Babylon* is a preliminary attempt to compile the data which will help us [all of us, *together*] to make those determinations.

This volume is intended to raise more questions than it answers.

Phillip Johnson says that "Any list of the thinkers who most profoundly influenced the twentieth century mind would contain four names: Darwin [1809-1882], Marx [1818-1883], Freud [1856-1939] and Nietzsche [1844-1900]."[8] To this list, your researcher would add the name of Thomas Malthus, whose immense global influence demands that he be included.

Colonel Doner links three of these figures when he describes the developments which followed Christianity's major shift – early in this century – from a gospel that *balanced* pietism and activism, to a fixation on pietism and an abandonment of "the world." He says, "Within a few decades after unilaterally disarming itself, the Church was left defenseless for the attack of the century: the onslaught of Freudian psychology (liberation from moral restraint), Darwinian evolution (invalidating the biblical act of creation and the very nature and purpose of man), and Marxian sociology (anti-God as well as anti-capitalist).

Robert Bork underscores how profoundly these three have damaged the theological foundations of American culture: "The major obstacle to a religious renewal is the intellectual classes, who are highly influential and tend to view religion as primitive superstition. They believe that science has left atheism as the only respectable intellectual stance. Freud, Marx, and Darwin, according to the conventional account, routed the believers."[9]

Phillip Johnson agrees: "Together with Marx's materialistic theory of history and society, and Freud's attribution of human behavior to influences over which we have little control, Darwin's theory of evolution was a crucial plank in the platform of mechanism and materialism [naturalism]... that has since been the stage of most Western thought."[10]

In a 1996 issue of *Time* magazine, Marty Kaplan rounded out this historical intellectual revolution: "The educated person knows that love is really about libido, that power is really about class, that judgment is really about politics, that religion is really about fantasy, that necessity is really about chance. These views come from an Enlightenment that began with Galileo and Newton and a modernity begun by Darwin, Marx and Freud. We are Nietzsche's children, shivering in the pointless void."[11]

a. Nietzsche

Mechanism & Positivism

"The purported death of God, proclaimed explicitly by Nietzsche," says Johnson, "was the foundational event of modernism."[12] The Durants credit Copernicus [1473-1543], John Donne [1573-1631], and Francis Bacon [1561-1626], with helping to form the foundation, "the growing awareness of man's minuscule place in the cosmos," upon which Nietzsche [1844-1900] built his assertion that God was dead.[13]

Chuck Colson interjects an important distinction: "Nietzsche's point was not that God does not exist, but that God has become irrelevant. Men and women may assert that God exists or that He does not, but it makes little difference either way. God is dead not because He doesn't exist, but because we live, play, procreate, govern, and die as though He doesn't."[14]

In *Megatrends 2000*, John Naisbitt says, "Since the 18th century Enlightenment, Westerners have worshiped science almost as a religion. Bolstered by the thinking of... Nietzsche, this trend culminated in the secular 'God is dead' philosophy articulated by radical theologian Thomas J.J. Altizer in the 1960s and 1970s,"[15]

SCOPE and FOCUS
I. CONVICTIONS
II. PRETEXTS
III. MANDATE
IV. LEGACY
Christian Tradition
Early Church
Reformation Era
World Precedents
Holocaust
Nuremberg
Geneva
United Nations and Int'l Human Rights
Unborn Child's Rights
Global Abortion Norms
Apartheid
United States History
Independence
Liberty & Rights
Abolition of Slavery
Women's Passage Rites
Seeds of Destruction
Nietzsche
Malthus
Darwin
Marx
Freud
Between World Wars
Pivotal Developments
Civil Rights
Parental Responsibility
Humaneness
V. ABORTIVE LINKS
VI. DILEMMA
VII. DESTINY

1 *Genesis* 1:1.
2 *John* 3:16.
3 *Revelation* 20:12.
4 *I Peter* 4:12.
5 *Genesis* 3:17-19 and 8:21.
6 *Romans* 11:29.
7 *Galatians* 4:7.
8 Phillip Johnson, *Reason in the Balance: The Case Against Naturalism in Science, Law & Education*, 194-5.
9 Robert Bork, *Slouching Towards Gomorrah: Modern Liberalism and American Decline*, 294.
10 Johnson, 195.
11 Kaplan, in *Time*, 6-24-96, 62.
12 Johnson, 195.

b. Malthus

Mechanism & Pragmatism

The influence of the "population bomb" theory of Thomas Malthus is impossible to exaggerate. Gordon Aeschliman wrote *Global Trends: Ten Changes Affecting Christians Everywhere* in 1990. Three of his ten chapters, "The Shrinking Globe," "Reaching the World's Poor," and, especially, "The Earth Groans," reflect how universally these themes are espoused.[16]

Here is one of the central assertions of Thomas Malthus: "All children born, beyond what would be required to keep up the population to a desired level, must necessarily perish, unless room is made for them by the deaths of grown persons... if we dread the too frequent visitation of [famine, plague, and] ravaging diseases."[17]

Aeschliman's use of abundant statistics assures that we will comprehend the magnitude of the problems which demand *recruits and support for Christian missions*: "According to one expert, by the year 2000 more than two billion people will live in underdeveloped cities, and of that number, 846 million will live as squatters – virtual refugees locked into despair and disease..."[18]

Here is the problem. The vast majority of the factions within the Christian Church which beat the Malthusian drum of alarm over world population growth are participating in three immense tragedies: 1) Either intentionally or naively, they "load the guns" of Planned Parenthood and others who aggressively promote ungodly, pragmatic "solutions" to those problems; 2) They do not mount an opposition to those immoral programs; and 3) They fail to propose, develop and implement godly answers to the dilemmas. [Note: In part V.B of *Orphans*, we will address the kinds of reproductive technology an obedient Church ought to demand, and devise.]

The *Essay on Population* was written by Malthus in 1798. The second edition, published in 1803, added the author's suggestions as to how the natural cycles of war, famine and pestilence could be averted. His recommendation was that abortion and birth control should *not* be used, but that only those who desire to parent a child should engage in sexual intercourse![19]

The intellectual world has madly expounded his dire predictions but has universally ignored the wise, if perhaps impractical, counsel of Thomas Malthus. They believed that coldly pragmatic solutions were demanded: "The physically unfit, the materially poor, the spiritually diseased [those 'duped' by Christianity, for instance], the racially inferior, and the mentally incompetent had to be eliminated. The question was how? ...The vast majority of Malthusians felt that the solution was genetic – restrict or remove 'bad racial stocks,' discourage charity and benevolence, and 'aid the evolutionary ascent of man.'"[20]

Both Adolf Hitler and Josef Stalin based their ruthless programs of human destruction on the population theories of Malthus.[21] More recently, "respectable," "professional" and "compassionate" self-proclaimed apostles of Malthus have used his theory to justify worldwide programs of mass abortion, abortifacient birth control, infanticide, and coerced or involuntary sterilization. Not only that, but in the industrialized countries where *declines* in total population guarantee future economic chaos, Malthusian theory continues to be expounded so as to increase the use of birth control and abortion, when their reduction is clearly what is needed.

Will and Ariel Durant, whom we have frequently held up as examples of Darwinian, pragmatic and relativistic attitudes, must be congratulated for providing a wise view of Thomas Malthus: "The advances of agricultural and contraceptive technology in the nineteenth century apparently refuted Malthus... The multiplication of consumers was also a multiplication of producers: new 'hands' developed new lands (and ways) to raise more food... If existing agricultural knowledge were everywhere applied, the planet could feed twice its present population."[22]

Here is where we stand as a country, relative to the "population explosion." If you subtract daily deaths from daily births it will be seen that America's resident population is growing by 4,400 per day.[23] Coincidentally, an equal number [4,400] of American babies are surgically killed ["aborted"] every day, with the effect of cutting the *growth* of the resident population in half. If we were willing to leave our calculating at that point, someone might be tempted to invoke Malthusian theory and conclude that the American government can justify abortion to keep the population at an "optimum" level. But such an assertion is rendered ludicrous when it is learned that federal policy permits roughly three foreigners to immigrate into the U.S. for every two American babies we abort. That's right: our welcome-mat-is-out to 6,300 *legal* aliens every day.[24]

In 1968, when they wrote *The Lessons of History*, the Durants noted with irony that a Darwinian *principle* seemed to be stacking the biological deck against future belief in Darwin's *theory*: "In the United States the lower birth rate of the anglo-Saxons has lessened their economic and political power; and the higher birth rate of Roman Catholic families suggests that by the year 2000 the Roman Catholic Church will be the dominant force in national as well as in municipal or state governments."[25]

13 Durant, *The Lessons of History*, 46-7.
14 Charles Colson, *Kingdoms in Conflict*, 181.
15 John Naisbitt, *Megatrends 2000: Ten New Directions for the 1990s*, 272.
16 Aeschliman, Global Trends.
17 Malthus, in Grant, *Third Time Around*, 121-2.
18 Aeschliman, 72-3.
19 Durant, 21-22.
20 Grant, *Third Time Around*, 122-3.
21 Grant, *Third Time Around*, 123.
22 Durant, *The Lessons of History*, 22.
23 *World Almanac*, 549; [10,600 births minus 6,200 deaths].
24 *World Almanac*, 549.
25 Durant, 23.

c. Darwin

Accident & Mechanism

Michael Hart says that in 1838 a man "read and was greatly influenced by Thomas Malthus's *An Essay on the Principle of Population."*[1] That man was Charles Darwin. In Robert Bork's opinion, "The three most influential thinkers of the modern era, men who advanced their theories as science, either were bitterly hostile to religion or espoused theories that could be read to undercut faith. Sigmund Freud [attacked religion directly]. Karl Marx viewed religion as superstition that opposed the progress of the working class. Charles Darwin offered the theory of evolution that was taken by many to disprove the theory of a Creator."[2]

"The theory of evolution, long toyed with by naturalists," says James Sire, "was given a 'mechanism' by Darwin and has won the day. There is hardly a public school text that does not proclaim the theory as fact."[3] The crucial effect of evolution, according to Paul deParrie, is that "With Darwin's hypothesis, humanists were at last free from that final restraint – God. God had become a vestigial appendage – and He was the final reason for any moral standards."[4]

Another effect, less obvious, is that "Darwinism also fostered racism," asserts James Draper. "It is not commonly known, but his book *Origin of the Species* has a most revealing subtitle which has been suppressed: *The Origin of the Species by Means of Natural Selection, or, The Preservation of Favored Races*."[5]

Michael Hart reflects: "Even on a secular level, Darwin's theory has caused a great change in the way that human beings think about their world. The human race as a whole no longer seems to occupy the central position in the natural scheme of things that it once did. We now have to regard ourselves as one species among many, and we recognize the possibility that we may one day be superseded."[6]

Darwin's *Origin of Species* is listed among the *Books that Changed the World* by Robert Downs.[7]

d. Marx

Positivism & Pragmatism

In 1848, Karl Marx and Friedrich Engels invented communism when they wrote *The Communist Manifesto*. Most folks would probably be hard pressed to find any link between communism and America's abortion battle or our culture war in general. But it must be remembered that the Soviet Union and China were our *allies* when we were fighting the Germans and the Japanese in World War II, and that among our university intellectuals a significant number were quite enamored with socialism and communism. This was particularly true when communist theories about the weaknesses of capitalism seemed to be validated by the stock market crash and the Great Depression.

Because those academics played such a dominant role in launching our culture wars, it is interesting to explore the threads of Marxist thought which run through the Sixties counterculture which has grown into the public culture of America today. The hub of communist theory is the allegation that capitalists exploit the masses and that revolution against the rich and powerful is justified.[8] Today we note society's victim mentality, defiance of authority, materialism, distrust of the government and of others, and generalized dishonesty – from cheating on taxes to cheating on spouses.

e. Freud

Pleasure & Autonomy

"In the early years, Freud was strongly attracted by Darwin's theories," says Downs.[9] According to Harvey Green, "the new sexual norms for which the young of the 1920s are remembered were a result of the popularization of elements of Freudian psychology, in particular the idea that sex could be pleasurable for women, and that the act of coition could be physically separated from the responsibility of reproduction by the use of newly mass-produced contraceptive devices..."[10] Hart's view is that Freud is probably best known for expounding the notion that "repressed sexual feelings often play a causative role in mental illness or neurosis."[11]

Robert Bork says that the significant thing about Freud is that he "assailed religion in all its forms as an illusion and therefore recast it as a form of neurosis," and that "Many people were particularly attracted to what they took to be the message of the new science of psychology: sex is the driving force of life and inhibitions are not only passe but dangerous."[12]

"Sigmund Freud began dismantling the fallen nature of man by presenting man as a mechanistic, materialistic bundle of experiences and responses. Guilt and sin were useless, even harmful concepts. Civilization had abandoned reason guided by Scripture, and the basis for even simple morality was undercut... Freud added that even man's evil doings were not evil, but natural..."[13]

"It was in the Twenties that Freud became famous," says Perrett. "The young celebrated him because he stood as a complete break with the past. Freudianism rejected two of the most important elements in traditional Protestantism: its absolute moral judgments and its asceticism... America's entire history was portrayed as three centuries of puritanical repression, thwarting all that was healthy, spontaneous, life-affirming, and gracious."[14]

Geoffrey Perrett summarizes: "Throughout the Twenties there was a steady decline in the vitality of religious belief... Religious faith appeared less and less relevant when set alongside the claims made by science, behaviorism, and psychoanalysis."[15]

SCOPE and FOCUS
I. CONVICTIONS
II. PRETEXTS
III. MANDATE
IV. LEGACY
Christian Tradition
Early Church
Reformation Era
World Precedents
Holocaust
Nuremberg
Geneva
United Nations and Int'l Human Rights
Unborn Child's Rights
Global Abortion Norms
Apartheid
United States History
Independence
Liberty & Rights
Abolition of Slavery
Women's Passage Rites
Seeds of Destruction
Nietzsche
Malthus
Darwin
Marx
Freud
Between World Wars
Techno-prosperity
Modernism
Fundamentalism
Scopes monkey trial
Capone & Ness
Pivotal Developments
Civil Rights
Parental Responsibility
Humaneness
V. ABORTIVE LINKS
VI. DILEMMA
VII. DESTINY

6. Between two World Wars

Having taken a peek at some of the major players whose thoughts and works greatly reshaped the intellectual and moral landscape in this century, let us now learn what has been noted about how those new orientations played out in American culture itself.

The changes within the Church were profound. Perry Cotham highlights the contrast. He says that in the late nineteenth century, "evangelicals helped to found: the Salvation Army, the Florence Crittenton homes, schools for immigrants, industrial training institutes, antislavery and temperance societies... The early twentieth century saw evangelicals completely shift their attitude away from social and political activism, a shift that has been called 'the great reversal.'"[16]

Mr. Cotham goes on to say that "the causes for this almost 180-degree turn were several: renewed concern for biblical doctrine, the continuing ideological conflict between the fundamentalists and modernists, the association of social activism with the social gospel (which was deemed to be little more than humanistic optimism), and the movement of evangelical activists into the liberal camp."[17]

Just how monumental the changes were in the roles and status of women is emphasized by Geoffrey Perrett: "Before the first World War women were arrested for smoking cigarettes in public, for using profanity, for appearing on public beaches without stockings, for driving automobiles without a man beside them... and for not wearing their corsets... [They were] summoned before the courts, not only of small towns, but of big cities such as Chicago."[18] The author points to the beginning of the changes: "During [World War I] young women had been encouraged to be assertive in public for the first time. They handed out flags and badges, collected money for war charities, sold bonds..."[19]

According to Robert Bork, "By the 1940s antiauthoritarianism had become dominant. Mid-twentieth century seems to be when envy and egalitarianism became rampant together... The wisecrack... is a leveler, a means of bringing down the person at whom it is directed... Why egalitarianism should have become an obsession between the two world wars is difficult to say, but that it did cannot be doubted."[20]

"A brief collage of those watershed events and phenomena leading to the enthronement of *Choice* as God," is offered by F. LaGard Smith: "Since the two World Wars, America has been shaken out of its isolation to become aware of cultures that are radically different from our own... Even the Depression of the '30s made its contribution to choice by encouraging the freedom of travel... A pro-choice generation is a generation of upwardly mobile nomads."[21]

Smith continues: "Even when Johnny came marching home again, it seemed natural to many women to keep on marching to work... With the wars had come industrialization and people pouring into the cities from off the farms... City dwellers didn't need as many children as folks back on the farm, so family size dwindled. With smaller families and double paychecks, the 'good life' ushered in an age of consumerism..."[22]

1 Michael Hart, *The 100: A Ranking of the Most Influential Persons in History*, 118.

2 Bork, 281.

3 James Sire, *The Universe Next Door: A Basic Worldview Catalog*, 59.

4 Paul deParrie, *Romanced to Death: The Sexual Seduction of American Culture*, 70.

5 Draper and Watson, *If the Foundations Be Destroyed*, 115.

6 Hart, *The 100*, 120-1.

7 Robert Downs, 162.

8 Hart, 92.

9 Robert Downs, 179.

10 Harvey Green, *The Uncertainty of Everyday Life, 1915-1945*, 131.

11 Michael Hart, 190-1. Hart says that even though Freud's first book was published in 1895, "He was already famous when he came to America to lecture in 1908."

12 Robert Bork, 281.

13 Paul deParrie, *Romanced to Death*, 71.

14 Geoffrey Perrett, *America in the Twenties: A History*, 148.

15 Perrett, 205.

16 Cotham, *Christian Social Ethics*, 11.

17 Cotham, 11.

18 Perrett, *America in the Twenties: A History*, 157.

19 Perrett, 151.

20 Robert Bork, *Slouching Towards Gomorrah: Modern Liberalism and American Decline*, 76-7.

21 F.L. Smith, *When Choice Becomes God*, 24-5.

22 Smith, *Choice*, 24-5.

Modernism and materialism

"What could have led to more freedom of choice than the increasing availability of the automobile [and innumerable 'options']? ...With the advent of the telephone, radio, and television, whole new avenues of communication were opened up... With the computer-generated Information Age, choice became self-perpetuating..."[1]

The materialism index increased, too: "Ours is no longer a nation of savers, but spenders – even if we do not have the money... [We became] the credit-card generation, [and next came] on-demand money at the 24-hour automatic teller machine and on-demand purchases in the shopping malls where we regularly go to worship the god of choice. 'On-demand' has been the creed of a pro-choice generation..."[2]

The ultimate application of consumerism, says Smith, came "when women got the Pill, [and] reproductive freedom begat sexual freedom... [We are] now a nation of body fanatics... Either we control it, or it controls us... [People are] demanding a 'right to control' our bodies..."[3]

The conclusion of this downward moral spiral shows us what happens *When Choice Becomes God*: "Minority rights soon swept beyond racial injustice to sexual equality in the workplace (women's rights), to personal sexual freedom for homosexuals (gay rights), to personal reproductive freedom for women (abortion rights). ...In a pro-choice generation, only two minorities have no rights: the unborn, and those who would defend them."[4]

a. Technology & Prosperity

Pleasure & Autonomy

The prosperity and "labor-saving conveniences" produced by the new scientific technologies created the materialism that has made us the "me" society. Harvey Green says: "The American World's Fairs of the ['30s] decade – the Chicago 'Century of Progress' (1933) and the New York 'World of Tomorrow' (1939) – worshiped the gods of science and technology, and presented Americans with a variation of the promise that religion had offered in previous centuries – a future with no problems... Equally powerful for the middle class and the wealthy was a yearning for the past that they thought simpler, and therefore more comforting. Images of idyllic rural small towns of harmony and unity coexisted with the new world of the future."[5] We were rapidly becoming a schizophrenic culture, clinging to the old even as we chased after the new.

The theme of women's inequality was a driving force in the new materialism: "Multiple consumption – two or more radios and even automobiles – became a tactic to fuel the consumption boom of the twenties. The two-car family would, the advertisers said, free the woman of the house from isolation."[6]

In *American Protestant Thought in the Liberal Era*, William Hutchison says, "It was an era of mounting faith in man's ability to control his own destiny through creative intelligence, and to make a heaven on earth with the aid of science and machinery."[7] He goes on to pinpoint just how these developments contributed to the undoing of liberal Christianity: "When the humanists appeared upon the scene, with their Gospel of salvation by scientific research and cooperative effort, the dilemma of liberalism became acute... Was there in fact any shore to which they could return, now that they had cut loose from churchly tradition and infallible revelation?"[8]

It would appear that the liberal Christians endorsed the modern criticisms of traditional Christian faith in a doomed effort to remain "with it" and to woo the intellectual movers and shakers. It is obvious that the secular humanist Masters indulged the mainline denominations as long as it was useful to them, and then scorned and utterly rejected them. The National Academy of Sciences, by 1984, clearly stated: "Religion and science are mutually exclusive realms of human thought whose presentation in the same context leads to misunderstanding of both scientific theory and religious belief."[9]

Reproductive technology will be given a major treatment [in Part V.B of *Orphans*], but here it should be noted that medical research developed penicillin in 1927, and therefore, according to Robert Bork, "It was the availability of antibiotics beginning in the 1940s and improved medical techniques that made abortion safe well before *Roe*."[10]

1 Smith, *Choice*, 25-6.
2 Smith, *Choice*, 26.
3 Smith, *Choice*, 27.
4 Smith, *Choice*, 28.
5 Green, *The Uncertainty of Everyday Life, 1915-1945*, 11.
6 Green, *Uncertainty*, 9.
7 Hutchison, 194.
8 Hutchison, 192.
9 National Academy of Sciences, in Kilner, *Bioethics and the Future of Medicine*, 50.
10 Bork, 179.
11 Johnson, *Reason in the Balance: The Case Against Naturalism in Science, Law & Education*, 201.
12 Hunter, *Culture Wars: The Struggle to Define America*, 131-2.
13 MacIntyre, quoted by Carl F.H. Henry, in Ball, 22.
14 Perrett, 147.
15 Sire, *The Universe Next Door: A Basic World-view Catalog*, 42.

SCOPE and FOCUS
I. CONVICTIONS
II. PRETEXTS
III. MANDATE
IV. LEGACY
Christian Tradition
Early Church
Reformation Era
World Precedents
Holocaust
Nuremberg
Geneva
United Nations and Int'l Human Rights
Unborn Child's Rights
Global Abortion Norms
Apartheid
United States History
Independence
Liberty & Rights
Abolition of Slavery
Women's Passage Rites
Seeds of Destruction
Nietzsche
Malthus
Darwin
Marx
Freud
Between World Wars
Techno-prosperity
Modernism
Fundamentalism
Scopes monkey trial
Capone & Ness
Pivotal Developments
Civil Rights
Parental Responsibility
Humaneness
V. ABORTIVE LINKS
VI. DILEMMA
VII. DESTINY

b. Modernism: The Enlightenment Project

Accident & Mechanism

"Modern science is just as imperialistic as it is naturalistic," says Phillip Johnson. "When science gained the authority to tell the culture 'how things really are,' it told the culture that reality excludes God."[11]

The significance of Modernism is underscored by James Hunter: "The secular Enlightenment of the eighteenth century and its philosophical aftermath... is what inspires the divisions of public culture in the United States today. [The key is] the profound philosophical reorientation of the Enlightenment with its rejection of otherworldly 'superstitions' and its emphasis on societal progress through human mastery over nature..."[12]

"The enlightenment experiment," according to Alasdair MacIntyre, is the cause of "the moral bankruptcy of our culture."[13]

"The crisis of belief that colored the entire life of the Twenties had been in the making for decades," says Geoffrey Perrett. "A 2,000-year-old moral order had really been steadily undermined by nineteenth-century scientists and intellectuals."[14]

A spiritually deadly aspect of the Enlightenment project is described by James Sire: "Another factor in the development of deism is a change in the location of the authority for knowledge about the divine; it shifted from the special revelation found in Scripture to the presence of Reason, 'the candle of God,' in the human mind or to Intuition, 'the inner light.'"[15] Sire finds another way to express the same fact about the effect of Modernism: "The notion of the autonomy of human reason liberated the human mind from the authority of the ancients."[16]

Just how early in American history the liberal denominations can be seen to have embraced the Enlightenment project is described by William Hutchison: "The hallmark of modernism is the insistence that theology must adopt a sympathetic attitude toward secular culture and must consciously strive to come to terms with it. By the 1890s, most of the Protestant liberals were ready to join wholeheartedly in the renewed self-congratulation and enthusiasm for modernity with which Americans generally were ringing in the new century."[17]

Paul deParrie agrees, but also holds that the evangelicals have not been immune to the effects of the liberalization of American society: "For the most part, the modern church has accepted the love-as-emotion doctrine for centuries. The mainline denominations began their rapid descent in the earlier decades of this century. Fundamental and evangelical groups were more tenacious, but the grip began to slip in the fifties and sixties. There was still, however, a commitment to morality that forbade unbridled emotionalism."[18]

James Hitchcock finds the key in academia: "From the early nineteenth century, liberal Protestantism, as it came to be known, disregarded its traditions and the authority of Scripture and primarily found its bearings in the writings of secular intellectuals, usually university professors."[19]

"During the 1920s and 1930s theological liberals took charge of several mainline American denominations," says Marvin Olasky. "Although an outright shift in policy regarding abortion took another generation, the practical 'pro-choice' application was a natural outgrowth of a liberal faith that opposed God's sovereignty and placed 'reason' above revelation."[20]

James Hunter is blunt: "The progressive forces in Protestantism (no longer referred to as modernism but simply called mainline Protestantism) held a position of undisputed domination for the first fifty years of the twentieth century."[21]

According to Perrett: "The Twenties saw the breakup of the self-confidence of Protestantism; the self-confidence, that is, of the traditional American faith."[22]

James Hitchcock holds that Modernism vanquished faith hundreds of years ago: "Religious believers in the West since about 1700 have suffered from a permanent inferiority complex."[23]

---

16 Sire, 177.

17 Hutchison, *American Protestant Thought in the Liberal Era*, 4-6.

18 Paul deParrie, *Romanced to Death: The Sexual Seduction of American Culture*, 171.

19 Hitchcock, in Ball, *In Search of a National Morality*, 34.

20 Olasky, *Abortion Rites: A Social History of Abortion in America*, 261.

21 Hunter, *Culture Wars: The Struggle to Define America*, 85.

22 Perrett, 206.

23 Hitchcock, in Ball, *In Search of a National Morality*, 33-4.

c. Fundamentalism

Commandments & Accountability

Early in twentieth-century America, it became clear that traditional Christian faith was under attack: "The major denominations had compromised with Darwinians; there were movements into the social gospel, and a statist, coercive, top-down salvation by politics. Prominent pastors and scholars came together to publicize a series of essays called *The Fundamentals*. As a consequence, the fundamentalist movement was born," says James Draper. He tells us that fundamentalism was so effective that, "by the 1970s, well over 50 million adult Americans identified themselves as born-again Christians."[1]

According to Perrett, "Fundamentalism found most of its recruits among Baptists, with a sprinkling of Methodists and Presbyterians... Orgiastic religion swept the South... This hysterical religiosity came hard on the heels of industrialization, which was pushing hundreds of thousands of simple, impoverished country people into noisome factories and towns. Damned on Saturday night, they were desperate for salvation on Sunday."[2]

Perrett continues: "Fundamentalism was a back-to-basics movement. The five fundamentals of belief were the infallibility of the Bible; the virgin birth of Christ; the Resurrection; that Christ died to atone for the sins of the world; and the Second Coming. By the mid-Twenties it was claimed that roughly one-fourth of the population accepted the Fundamentalist creed."[3]

In keeping with the sentiments of Fundamentalists, "Frederick Lewis Allen correctly noted that the stock market crash was not an event detached from all other events but was the final judgment on a 'me-first' generation."[4]

"Women preachers were not unknown before the Twenties, but they were very rare. It was a prejudice [that Aimee Semple McPherson] challenged head on. [She] arrived in Los Angeles with ten dollars and a tambourine," and went on to build Angelus Temple, "a 3,000-seat arena with a stage that would do credit to a great opera house."[5] Cal Thomas calls Aimee McPherson "the pastor of the five-thousand-member Angelus Temple in Los Angeles where she would hold forth every night of the week to a packed house and a radio audience with over one million listeners."[6] Such success inevitably attracted a host of critics. Hunter says that, "by the time Sinclair Lewis had published his tale of the odious preacher *Elmer Gantry* in 1927, the images of the hypocrite, the swindler, the charlatan, and the bigot had already become an established part of the fundamentalist stereotype."[7]

Colonel Doner says, "Liberal theology, denying Biblical inerrancy and the 'fundamentals of the faith,' invaded American denominations from German theological schools of 'higher criticism' and by the mid 1930s captured our major seminaries and denominations. Confronted by such attacks, the fundamentalists took a last look around, ducked into their bunkers, and pulled the hatches shut behind them. They felt defeated..."[8]

Just a few years before *Roe v. Wade, Time* magazine would declare: "Fundamentalism is a reflection of the people's insecurity and fulfills an emotional need, ...offering the promise of instant salvation, and the opportunity to indulge in emotional spasms."[9]

It would appear that wake-up calls were delivered to Fundamentalists by an assortment of governmental actions, as early as the '50s, particularly by the Supreme Court, and most stridently, of course, through *Roe v. Wade*. Here is Doug Bandow's overview of the ebb and flow: "Though evangelicals involved themselves in politics early in America's history, defeats over Prohibition and the Scopes trial caused many churches to withdraw almost entirely from politics. For a variety of reasons, including the rise of the electronic church and the perception of increasing secular attacks, aided and abetted by government, on religious values, evangelicals became more active in the political process in the latter half of this century. By the 1970s evangelicals were more likely than any other religious group to vote."[10]

In 1988, Colonel Doner was saying, "As the Evangelical Church slowly emerges from its eighty years of self-imposed exile from involvement with government, culture, and social needs, it will invariably get off to a number of false starts."[11]

Don't overlook the section on the Rise and Fall of the Religious Right in *Orphans*, Part V.F.2.a, page 253.

1 Draper, *If the Foundations be Destroyed*, 126. Draper says, "In 1909... two Christian laymen set aside money to issue some volumes setting forth the fundamentals of biblical faith. These publications were sent to three hundred thousand ministers, missionaries, and Christian workers all over the world. Their greatest impact was in the United States" [169-70]. [*See next column.*]

James Hunter, in *Culture Wars*, adds: "This twelve-volume work included the major doctrines of the Christian faith. [As a result,] thirty-seven anti-evolution bills were submitted to twenty state legislatures between 1921 and 1929" [83].

2 Perrett, *America in the Twenties*, 198.

3 Perrett, 197.

SCOPE and FOCUS
I. CONVICTIONS
II. PRETEXTS
III. MANDATE
IV. LEGACY
Christian Tradition
Early Church
Reformation Era
World Precedents
Holocaust
Nuremberg
Geneva
United Nations and Int'l Human Rights
Unborn Child's Rights
Global Abortion Norms
Apartheid
United States History
Independence
Liberty & Rights
Abolition of Slavery
Women's Passage Rites
Seeds of Destruction
Nietzsche
Malthus
Darwin
Marx
Freud
Between World Wars
Techno-prosperity
Modernism
Fundamentalism
Scopes monkey trial
Capone & Ness
Pivotal Developments
Civil Rights
Parental Responsibility
Humaneness
V. ABORTIVE LINKS
VI. DILEMMA
VII. DESTINY

d. Scopes "Monkey" Trial

Accident & Mechanism

It was something of a fundamentalist victory that five states had outlawed the teaching of evolution in the early 1920s.[12]

Defense attorney Clarence Darrow "tried five times to get the [John Scopes] case moved to a federal court, without success. What mattered was not whether Scopes had taught evolution, but whether the state had the right to forbid him to teach it... The defense was forced to depend on arguments that evolution was true... The judge... sat beneath a banner that enjoined, 'Read Your Bible Daily,' [and] refused to allow the scientists the defense had imported as expert witnesses to take the stand. Their testimony, he ruled, could only be hearsay: they were not present when lower life forms evolved into human beings... [It was] the first trial ever carried on the radio... The Dayton [Tennessee] jury took all of eight minutes to find Scopes guilty. He was fined $100... Fundamentalism pitted itself against fifty years of biblical scholarship. What it really amounted to, however, was a sad, distorted protest against the modern world."[13]

During the Scopes trial, William Jennings Bryan, the prosecutor, said, "You believe in the age of rocks; I believe in the Rock of Ages," and "I have as much right as an atheist to begin with an assumption, and I would rather begin with God and reason down than begin with dirt and reason up."[14]

Before the court of public opinion, Clarence Darrow called the prosecutor, Bryan, as an expert witness on the Bible. "It was a brilliant stroke... Darrow repeatedly pressured him to defend the literal truth of the Bible. Each time he did so, Bryan tried to hedge. Having antagonized everyone who did not take the Bible literally, Bryan then managed to antagonize those who did. To Darrow's question, 'Do you think the Earth was made in six days?' Bryan answered, 'Not in six days of 24 hours.'"[15]

In the Scopes trial, says Harvey Green, "Fundamentalism, prohibition, and local control of education were at war with the forces of the city and its godless corruption and licentiousness."[16]

Darrow and his client, John Scopes, lost, while Bryan and Fundamentalism technically won, but it was both the first and the last such trial in our history, and it served to polarize public opinion and to seal the liberal resolve that the courts and other seats of power must be wrested from the hands of fundamentalists by all means. Cal Thomas says, "The John Scopes evolution trial in 1925 was a watershed because it dramatized the view of secularists that one cannot be both a thinker and a biblical fundamentalist."[17]

e. Capone vs. Ness

Pleasure, Positivism, Pragmatism

Both Al Capone and Elliott Ness have become folk heroes of the Twenties, Capone even though he was a ruthless gangster, and Ness as the lawman immune to corruption. Cal Thomas, Green, and Perrett summarize a Prohibition era in which government employees at every level [from president, congress and attorney general to local police] used their power to circumvent the law, and when a very large percentage of society developed an unprecedented contempt for the law,[18] reveling in civil disobedience for no loftier causes than autonomy and personal pleasure.

4 Cal Thomas, *The Death of Ethics in America*, 83.

5 Perrett, 202-3.

6 Thomas, *The Death of Ethics in America*, 79-80.

7 Hunter, *Culture Wars*, 140.

8 Doner, *The Samaritan Strategy*, 51.

9 *Time* magazine, 3-22-68, 62.

10 Bandow, *Beyond Good Intentions, a Biblical View of Politics*, 136.

11 Doner, 3.

12 Geoffrey Perrett, 201. Tennessee's law made it unlawful for any teacher "to teach any theory that denies the story of the Divine Creation of man as taught in the Bible, and to teach instead that man has descended from a lower order of animals" [199].

13 Perrett, *America in the Twenties: A History*, 200-2.

14 Perrett, 201.

15 Perrett, 201.

16 Green, *The Uncertainty of Everyday Life, 1915-1945*, 208.

17 Thomas, *The Death of Ethics in America*, 76.

18 Thomas, 73-4; Green, 10-11, 215; Perrett, 170-3, 176.

7. Pivotal Developments

"John Kennedy's Inaugural 'Ask not...' was a perfect expression of the duty ethic," said *Time* magazine in 1994. By contrast, it said: "The new culture of rights reversed the flow from individual to society: It said, 'Ask what your country can do for you; you are a victim, and everyone owes you."[1] The article was expressing the idea that the end of the cold war had left Americans "in a state of moral disorientation, as if they had lost a defining purpose."[2]

The magazine listed an agenda of controversies now confronting the American people: "They have much to do with the world's problems now (the economy, trade, environment, nuclear proliferation, foreign policy to address immense slaughter and tumult elsewhere), as well as sizable issues at home, moral and otherwise (crime, poverty, drugs, education, abortion, affirmative action)."[3]

a. Public education and *1984*

Mechanism & Pragmatism

There have been a number of pivotal developments that directly affect the state of our current culture wars between the Stewards of Christian orthodoxy, and the Masters of secular humanism. Changes in education in the United States are crucial to this discussion.

Robert Bork can help us put the question of schools in a proper historical perspective: "Prior to the Enlightenment intellectuals were few in number and dependent upon the support of the Church or some great patron... What freed them was the invention of the printing press and the rise of the bourgeoisie, which enabled intellectuals to find support from a new patron, the mass audience."[4]

Bork also says, "In the 1920s, expressive individualism became the ideology of the American intellectual... I suggest that the attitude described went back well before the Roaring Twenties, probably into the 1890s, and that its explosion in the [Nineteen] Sixties was delayed only by two world wars, the Great Depression, and the smaller size of the academic community prior to the Second World War."[5] What has gone wrong in education, Bork says, "appears to flow from a poisonous combination of radical egalitarianism and radical individualism."[6]

According to Thomas Sowell, "anti-religious propaganda in the schools [now] goes beyond an active promotion of moral relativism to textbooks that openly disparage religion."[7]

Sex Education, an old tool, reinvented by Planned Parenthood

Planned Parenthood pioneer Alan Guttmacher once made this remarkable statement: "The only avenue the International Planned Parenthood Federation and its allies could travel to win the battle for abortion on demand is through sex education."[8]

Former United States Secretary of Education William Bennett said, "In the arsenal of weapons to combat teenage pregnancy, school-based programs are but a bent arrow. However, bent arrows do offer the illusion of action."[9]

Evangelical Christians now actively oppose the sexual-promiscuity indoctrination that has been masquerading as "sex education" in the public schools since the Sixties and Seventies. What is fascinating is to learn that the motivation for first instituting sex education in the early decades of this century was Christian in character. Bryan Strong says, "The sex education movement that began around the turn of the century... was not to encourage sexual adjustment but to sustain an old morality that demanded the repression of all sexual activities except those designed for procreation."[10]

Thomas Altherr adds, "Toward the end of the nineteenth century American sexual attitudes were beginning to undergo a fundamental alteration, for the dominant sexual ideology of sex as restraint [Virtue] was being challenged increasingly by the hitherto radical doctrine of sex as pleasure. The implications of this change in ideology extended to the very formation of character and the organization of society."[11]

SCOPE and FOCUS
I. CONVICTIONS
II. PRETEXTS
III. MANDATE
IV. LEGACY
Christian Tradition
Early Church
Reformation Era
World Precedents
Holocaust
Nuremberg
Geneva
United Nations and Int'l Human Rights
Unborn Child's Rights
Global Abortion Norms
Apartheid
United States History
Independence
Liberty & Rights
Abolition of Slavery
Women's Passage Rites
Seeds of Destruction
Between World Wars
Pivotal Developments
Public education
Great Depression
Post-war materialism
Synthetic heroes
Post-war paranoia
Kinsey-Elvis-Madonna
Clinton generation
Civil Rights
Parental Responsibility
Humaneness
V. ABORTIVE LINKS
VI. DILEMMA
VII. DESTINY

Once again, Strong identifies an astonishing reality: "The prospects of moral degradation of the young led the reformers [around 1920] to insist on the necessity of [sex] instruction. Their general belief in the natural purity of the child, however [evidence that the Christian concept of sinful human nature has largely been supplanted by the 'good-human-nature' notion], led them to assume that children and adolescents had no active sexual feelings or desires but simply curiosity about reproductive processes... One government pamphlet declared that the objective of sex education was 'to satisfy normal questionings [so] that the subject of sex may be put into the background of consciousness.'"[12]

Strong continues: "External restraints, which had once acted as effective deterrents against deviation from the communal sexual norms, appeared to be rapidly disintegrating. The city, for example, with its pervasive anonymity, enabled men and women to engage in affairs without fear that their actions would be discovered. Religious faith appeared to be in decline... Finally, the reformers believed that venereal disease, which hitherto had been an argument of last resort in favor of chastity and monogamy, would cease to act as a deterrent if a cure, which seemed imminent, were found."[13]

In summary: "By 1919, within the sex education movement, the advocates of sex education in the school had triumphed over those who desired to restrict it to the home. Their victory was symbolized in a pamphlet issued by the Federal government that declared, 'As in many other instances, the school must take up the burden neglected by others.'"[14]

So we see in the earliest institution of sex education in public schools the seeds of the paternalistic attitude which today in full bloom asserts that governmental surrogates must protect children from the religious irrationality of their parents!

Public education and its long evolutionary path

Thomas Jefferson, in the earliest days of our nation, put forth far-reaching proposals for public education: free elementary education available to all, a state university for the more gifted, and a system of scholarships.[15]

James Draper says that "by 1860, Americans yielded to secular arguments and churches lost their leadership in education. Education became a governmentally dominated sector. This closed the Bible as the primary textbook in the land, [and] thus, we shifted from a God-centered republic to a man-centered democracy. Seeds were planted to weaken the basic character of America."[16]

Today, the National Education Association is saying that "when the founding Fathers drafted the constitution with its Bill of Rights, they explicitly designed it to guarantee a secular, humanistic state."[17]

Here is a surprise: In 1869, the National Teacher's Association, which soon became the N.E.A., was saying at its annual convention, "The Bible should not only be studied, venerated, and honored as a classic for all ages, people and languages... but devotionally read, and its precepts inculcated in all the common schools of the land."[18]

Perrett tells us, "In the 36 years from 1890 to 1926 the population of the continental United States increased 86%; the college and university enrollment increased almost 550%; and the secondary school enrollment increased almost 1100%. This was the transformation of American education – when education became genuinely democratic."[19]

John Dewey has been called the Father of American Education. "His philosophy has affected virtually every American on a practical level. In this regard his humanistic influence can scarcely be overestimated... Dewey was dead set against any form of supernaturalism in religion. In fact, since most religions pay some homage to the supernatural, he was also opposed to religion in general."[20]

"It was in the Twenties when schools became miniature communities," says Perrett. "No longer [a place] where children spent a few hours a day for half the year until they were thirteen or fourteen. It had become the focal point of their life from the ages of six to sixteen. Home and church had for centuries borne the responsibility of turning children into members of society. The school was now expected to relieve them of most of that burden."[21]

He adds: "Every state in the Union by 1930 had compulsory attendance laws. They expressed one of the profound social changes that marks off the modern world from that of the nineteenth century – the belief that education is a right, something that no parent can withhold from a child."[22]

1 *Time*, 12-5-94, 77.
2 *Time*, 12-5-94, 76.
3 *Time*, 12-5-94, 77.
4 Robert Bork, *Slouching Towards Gomorrah*, 92.
5 Bork, 88.
6 Bork, 256.
7 Sowell, in the *Press-Enterprise*, 3-20-96, A6.
8 Guttmacher, in Brian Clowes, *Pro-Life Activist's Encyclopedia*, page 82.1.
9 Bennett, in Clowes, page 82.1.
10 Strong, in Thomas Altherr, *Procreation or Pleasure?: Sexual Attitudes in American History*, 129.
11 Altherr, 127.
12 Strong, in Altherr, 131.
13 Strong, in Altherr, 133.
14 Strong, in Altherr, 130.
15 Michael Hart, 368-9.
16 Draper, *If the Foundations be Destroyed*, 1.
17 N.E.A., in Hunter, *Culture Wars*, 113.
18 N.T.A., in Hunter, 200.
19 Geoffrey Perrett, *America in the Twenties: A History*, 435.
20 Norman Geisler, *Is Man the Measure?*, 48-9.
21 Perrett, *America in the Twenties: A History*, 437.
22 Perrett, 436.

The impact of universal secular education

Will and Ariel Durant say, "As education spreads, theologies lose credence, and receive an external conformity without influence upon conduct or hope. Life and ideas become increasingly secular, ignoring supernatural explanations and fears. The moral code loses aura and force as its human origin is revealed, and as divine surveillance and sanctions are removed."[1]

Former Congressman John Conlan of Arizona has remarked: "There is a significant trend in education today to teach children that there are no values, that there is no right, that there is no wrong, that there is no God, that man is his own God."[2]

Franky Schaeffer writes, "George Orwell has accurately described a godless world in his book *1984*. We hear its echoes in Aldous Huxley's book *Brave New World*, and we learn exactly how such a society is organized from reading *Animal Farm*."[3]

In a 1976 issue of *The Humanist*, Paul Blanshard wrote, "I think that the most important factor moving us toward a secular society has been the educational factor. Our schools may not teach Johnny to read properly, but the fact that Johnny is in school until he is 16 tends to lead toward the elimination of religious superstition."[4]

"Through the avenue of cultural and moral relativism," laments F. LaGard Smith, "*Choice* has become the only god permitted in the classroom."[5]

When is a "Christian college" not a Christian college?

Carl F.H. Henry tells us, "The forfeiture of Christ-centered education, to which Harvard, Duke, Vanderbilt, and a dozen other universities were originally dedicated, has led on to the loss of any abiding center whatever in polytechnic and liberal arts learning."[6]

James Hunter points to what may be seen as a law of attrition: "Most Evangelical colleges and universities (Wheaton, Taylor, Houghton, George Fox, Gordon) were established in the mid-nineteenth century as a response to the secularization of still an earlier generation of Protestant universities (Harvard, Yale, etc.)... So too a new cycle of orthodox and traditionalist colleges and universities have now been founded because of the perceived vacuum of colleges to carry the true traditions on to the next generation."[7]

More recently, William Hutchison tells us, "Liberals were not lacking in organizational interest. They strove with wide success for control of churches, periodicals, denominations, and inter-church bodies; and by the 1920s they had made liberalism the acknowledged point of view in approximately half the Protestant theological seminaries."[8]

Just how significant control of academia has become is illustrated by data supplied by Robert Bork. The figures compared are for twenty-year increments from 1930 to 1950, and to 1970. From 1930 to 1950 the number of college students increased by nearly 70% [1,000,000 to 1,675,000], while faculty size doubled [from 80,000 to 165,000]. But from 1930 to 1970, the faculties grew 600%, and the number of students grew by 700% [to 500,000 faculty, and 7,000,000 students].[9]

Keeping that growth in mind, we are told by Phillip Johnson, "The most influential intellectuals in America and around the world are mostly naturalists, who assume that God exists only as an idea in the minds of religious believers. In our greatest universities, naturalism – the doctrine that nature is 'all there is' – is the virtually unquestioned assumption that underlies not only natural science but intellectual work of all kinds."[10]

Hunter is more than a little concerned: "The struggle over the ivory tower is significant for the contemporary culture war for the simple reason that its outcome will ultimately shape the ideals and values as well as the categories of analysis and understanding that will guide the next generation of American leaders."[11]

He shares another stunning observation: "When the children of the sixties received their professorships and deanships... they did not abandon the dream of radical cultural transformations; they set out to implement it. Now instead of disrupting classes, they are teaching them."[12]

James Hitchcock agrees: "The New Left and the counterculture were fanatically set against all forms of authority, and religion is by its very nature the most authoritarian of all. Many of the ideas of the radicals of the 1970s have simply become a part of the mainstream of American culture, accepted as conventional wisdom by educators, journalists, and professionals of all kinds."[13]

Politically correct academics

"The secular knowledge sector is a crucial influence," James Hunter points out, "because much of it has the patronage and protection of the state itself. Science and education are, in the main, appendages of the state, as are the myriad regulatory agencies dealing with health [and] communications. So too, of course is the judiciary. The knowledge industry and the modern state, then, are linked in complex and fundamental ways."[14]

SCOPE and FOCUS
I. CONVICTIONS
II. PRETEXTS
III. MANDATE
IV. LEGACY
Christian Tradition
Early Church
Reformation Era
World Precedents
Holocaust
Nuremberg
Geneva
United Nations and Int'l Human Rights
Unborn Child's Rights
Global Abortion Norms
Apartheid
United States History
Independence
Liberty & Rights
Abolition of Slavery
Women's Passage Rites
Seeds of Destruction
Between World Wars
Pivotal Developments
Public education
Great Depression
Post-war materialism
Synthetic heroes
Post-war paranoia
Kinsey-Elvis-Madonna
Clinton generation
Civil Rights
Parental Responsibility
Humaneness
V. ABORTIVE LINKS
VI. DILEMMA
VII. DESTINY

b. Market Crash: the nation becomes Greatly Depressed

Halford Luccock paints the larger picture of our nation's Great Depression: "The jazz party of the '20s, paralleled by the optimistic trust in automatic progress, broke up... The elevator loaded with humanity, due to shoot upwards to some sixty-fifth story of a skyscraper of man's own construction, jammed at about the tenth floor and then dropped. In that drop it was not only General Motors and A.T. & T. and other similar hopes of salvation that were deflated, but faiths as well."[15]

c. Television, Mastercard & Trump: Post-war Materialism

In 1910 G.K. Chesterton wrote *What's Wrong with the World*. In it he noted, "Of all the modern notions generated by mere wealth the worst is this: the notion that domesticity is dull and tame. Inside the home (they say) is dead decorum and routine; outside is adventure and variety."[16]

Ken Bryson has written, "In 1946 we had the beginning of the baby boom. Boomers were born during a period of unprecedented prosperity in which America was unchallenged politically and economically. So what we are seeing is [that] they made quite different choices than had their parents, who were born during the depression and experienced World War II."[17]

Helmut Schoeck helps us with the psychology of materialism: "Since the end of the Second World War, however, a new 'ethic' has, astonishingly, come into being, according to which the envious man is altogether acceptable... This public self-justification of envy is something entirely new. In this sense it is possible to speak of the age of envy."[18]

Thomas Altherr tells us that "The twentieth century brought further secularization to American sexual attitudes... In some ways sex became a commodity, the stuff of advertising, or a drug, the stuff of movies and television and rock music. Redefinitions of sex roles, advancements in birth control and abortion technologies, and women's liberation added new tensions into the sexual mix, [to] this American preoccupation with sexuality."[19]

Doug Bandow writes: "Materialism dominates the West today, a sort of consumerist ethic where life largely revolves around consumption and the political process is viewed by many as merely another way to get more money or goods than one's neighbors do... Government has become a battleground of interest groups, seeking to satisfy their members' unending greed and envy."[20]

"In the church," writes Randall Terry, "The God of righteousness and holiness has been replaced by the god of tranquility, the god of prosperity, and the god of self-love. As a result, God's people have become apathetic and selfish. What happens then, in a time of crisis?"[21] Lovelace agrees: "We have, at best, tried to talk about Jesus to others while investing our main energy in pursuing the same things as the world: survival, security and wealth."[22]

Colonel Doner amplifies the thought: "Our church's noninvolvement and apathy are perfectly consistent with our wrong goals. If our churches are motivated primarily by growth in members, finances, buildings, and community prestige, then settling on a course of 'issue evasion' and non-confrontation makes sense."[23]

1 Durant, *The Lessons of History*, 92-3.
2 Conlan, in Powell, *Abortion: The Silent Holocaust*, 79.
3 Schaeffer, in Scheidler, *Closed: 99 Ways to Stop Abortion*, 12.
4 Blanshard, in *The Humanist*, Mar-Apr. '76, 17; quoted in John Eidsmoe, *God & Caesar*, 135.
5 Smith, *When Choice Becomes God*, 29.
6 Henry, in Ball, *In Search of a National Morality*, 21.
7 James Hunter, *Culture Wars*, 221-2.
8 Hutchison, *American Protestant Thought in the Liberal Era*, 4.
9 Bork, 22.
10 Johnson, *Reason in the Balance*, 7-8.
11 Hunter, *Culture Wars*, 211.
12 Hunter, 219.
13 Hitchcock, in Ball, *In Search of a National Morality*, 37.
14 Hunter, 301.
15 Luccock, in Hutchison, *American Protestant Thought in the Liberal Era*, 200.
16 Chesterton, 71.
17 Bryson, in *Press*, 11-27-96, A1, A10.
18 Schoeck, in Bork, 73.
19 Altherr, *Procreation or Pleasure?: Sexual Attitudes in American History*, 1-2.
20 Bandow, *Beyond Good Intentions, a Biblical View of Politics*, 220.
21 Terry, *Operation Rescue*, 170.
22 Lovelace, in Doner, 552.
23 Doner, 49.

Mass entertainment has eroded faith and expanded materialism

Harvey Green believes that the great popularity of movies has given Hollywood enormous leverage over the morality and assumptions of Americans. He says that "Movies such as *Angels with Dirty Faces* (1938) and *Dead End* (1937) portrayed children as basically good, but corrupted by their environment. The burden of blame rested upon the parents."[1]

Green later gives an example of how the portrayal of characters in films can blur the concepts of right and wrong: "In John Ford's Stagecoach (1939), the passengers are a variety of apparent social misfits – a prostitute, a drunk, a gambler, and a crook – who ultimately show themselves to be virtuous Americans who will sacrifice and cooperate for the common good when crises arise."[2]

In the Sixties, H.S. Vigeveno wrote: "Through diversion, through entertainment we still our restlessness, we fill our solitude, we escape from ourselves. Why do we have to have a transistor along when we go for a walk? Why do we have to have background music? Why are we constantly banishing boredom through entertainment?"[3]

As Todd Gitlin observes, the obsession with activity persists: "This is a generation that watches and rewinds. There is a name for what happens when people pursue a pleasure so relentlessly that the more they ingest in the pursuit of happiness, the more they need, and the less happy, in general, they end up... The word is addiction. Entertainment is the national dope."[4]

From Robert Bork, in his own words: "Ours is a culture already lobotomized by television."[5]

He illustrates: "Fifty million people per week want to watch such things as a 13-year-old boy bragging about having sex with twenty-six women and then being confronted on camera by his mother... The entertainment industry is not forcing depravity on an unwilling American public. The demand for decadence is there."[6]

Paul deParrie notes this hypocrisy: "The bleats of the media proclaim both their near hysteria over rising teen pregnancy rates and their tawdry fixation with sexual deviancy. The same issues of magazines and newspapers will bellow denunciations of rape and exploitation of women and children, while displaying obscene amounts of women's flesh."[7]

At a major Conference for Evangelism in 1969, both the nation's materialism and its anticipation of future technologies were obvious: "By [the year] 2000, It should be possible to telephone from anywhere to anywhere – the middle of Richmond Park to the middle of the Sahara – without wired connections, on pocket telephones... By 2000, the world's libraries and museums should have been catalogued electronically and their collections accessible to anyone with a television screen... The average American spends 106% of his income per year!"[8]

At that conference, Leighton Ford made this dire observation: "Put a T.V. set in a ghetto; let a slum mother see ads for low calorie dog foods, and fur coats for cats, and electric toothbrushes, when her baby has had his ears chewed off by rats, and you have set the stage for a revolution."[9]

d. The NFL & MTV:
Athletics + Antics = Synthetic Heroes

It has been observed that the average American in 1850 had only 2.18 hours a day of discretionary time, but that by 1960 we had 7.48 hours of free time each day. When we are told that the average American now spends seven hours a day in a room where the television is turned on, we discover what has become of our leisure time. Clearly, entertainment – translated into "self-absorbed gratification of the senses" – has become our god.

"One who is absorbed in himself and his sensation," says Bork, "believing in few or no moral or religious principles, in nothing transcendental, is a nihilist. A culture that preaches narcissistic nihilism is asking for trouble... The fixation-on-self first became obvious with rock 'n' roll, which evolved into 'hard' rock [where the] extrovert, the hedonist, the madman, the criminal, the suicide, or the exhibitionist can rise to heroic stature."[10]

The index of value in our society is totally artificial, measured by popularity, by box office "draw." Randy Alcorn observes that Christians have bought the plastic heroes of our culture and do not even recognize true heroism when they see it: "It has always fascinated me that Christians can go to Portland's Memorial Colosseum and jump up and down and cheer at a slam dunk or a three-point shot and be respectable 'fans.' But if they go out to the abortion clinic and try calmly to save the lives of babies about to be killed they are derisively called 'fanatics.'"[11]

1 Green, *The Uncertainty of Everyday Life, 1915-1945*, 124.

2 Green, 210-11.

3 Vigeveno, *Jesus the Revolutionary*, 21.

4 Gitlin, in Bork, 259.

5 Bork, 250.

6 Bork, 128 and 132.

7 Paul deParrie, *Romanced to Death: The Sexual Seduction of American Culture*, 18.

8 Congress for Evangelism, 1969. Not in bibliography.

SCOPE and FOCUS
I. CONVICTIONS
II. PRETEXTS
III. MANDATE
IV. LEGACY
Christian Tradition
Early Church
Reformation Era
World Precedents
Holocaust
Nuremberg
Geneva
United Nations and Int'l Human Rights
Unborn Child's Rights
Global Abortion Norms
Apartheid
United States History
Independence
Liberty & Rights
Abolition of Slavery
Women's Passage Rites
Seeds of Destruction
Between World Wars
Pivotal Developments
Public education
Great Depression
Post-war materialism
Synthetic heroes
Post-war paranoia
Kinsey-Elvis-Madonna
Clinton generation
Civil Rights
Parental Responsibility
Humaneness
V. ABORTIVE LINKS
VI. DILEMMA
VII. DESTINY

e. McCarthy & Patty Hearst: Post-war Paranoia

Pragmatism

Once a Supreme Court Justice, Abe Fortas helps us to see one aspect of the national paranoia which has destroyed society's mutual trust and replaced it with alienation, fear and suspicion: "During World War I, two sedition laws were enacted and more than fifteen hundred persons were arrested under their terms. Heavy sentences were imposed on some of the dissenters. The producer of a movie on the American Revolution was sentenced to ten years' imprisonment because his picture [movie] was found capable of arousing anti-British feelings."[12] He goes on, "In World War II, we needlessly and ruthlessly interned 117,000 Americans of Japanese ancestry – an act which will forever be a blot upon this nation's record."[13]

Moreover, Mr. Fortas concludes, "It was during the Korean War – in the bitterness left by the Communist takeover in China – that McCarthyism was born, and the systematic blighting of thousands of lives and the destruction of valuable careers took place. Only a few of those whom McCarthyism injured had opposed this nation's wartime program or subscribed to communism."[14]

It would seem that the entire communications industry, both in entertainment and in the mass media, has resolved – much like the Jews after Hitler – that "Never again" will they permit government to either judge or to control their lives or their work.

f. Kinsey, Elvis & Madonna

Pleasure & Autonomy

"We are not emancipated; we are just unbuttoned," remarked T.S. Eliot.[15]

"I don't think I would find much argument," remarked Paul deParrie, "if I were to say that America has become sexually hyperactive... Our path to this condition could easily be described as a seduction."[16]

Another of the *Lessons of History* from Will and Ariel Durant tells us that, "In our time, as in the times of Socrates (d. 399 B.C.) and Augustus (d. A.D. 14), war has added to the forces making for moral laxity: soldiers who had tasted adventure and had learned to kill. [Add to that these factors:] women dizzy with freedom, multiplying divorces, abortions, and adulteries."[17]

A key date in our national "unbuttoning" seems to have been 1921, when the National Research Council was organized by scientists and social reformers who decried the "enshrouding of sex relations in a fog of mystery, reticence and shame."[18]

In 1939, Alfred Kinsey began receiving financial support from the National Research Council for his project of researching American sexual attitudes and practices.[19]

"Kinsey's first task was to unshackle a generation from its repressive past. Relieving guilt and reassuring readers that everyone had similar sexual impulses, Kinsey's books contributed to a changing sexual climate."[20]

Thomas Altherr tells us that sex researchers like Kinsey "rushed their findings into print and found an audience, shocked at first, but increasingly eager to learn who was doing what with or to whom sexually."[21]

9 Leighton Ford, Congress for Evangelism, 1969. Not in bibliography.
10 Bork, 125-6.
11 Alcorn, *Is Rescuing Right? Breaking the Law to Save the Unborn*, 213.
12 Fortas, *Concerning Dissent and Civil Disobedience*, 21.
13 Fortas, 21.
14 Fortas, 21.
15 Eliot, in Robert Raines, *The Secular Congregation*, 17.
16 Paul deParrie, *Romanced to Death*, 18.
17 Durant, 39-40.
18 Regina Markell Morantz, in Thomas Altherr, *Procreation or Pleasure?: Sexual Attitudes in American History*, 147.
19 Morantz, in Altherr, 147.
20 Morantz, in Altherr, 160. "Writers dubbed Kinsey's 1948 book *Sexual Behavior in the Human Male* 'The most talked about book of the twentieth century.' Others ranked it with *Das Kapital, The Origin of Species*, and *Wealth of Nations* [by Adam Smith]" [146].
21 Altherr, 145.

Kinsey's effect on the Nation

To a society that had been conditioned to equate what is natural with what is morally right, Kinsey's popular writings greatly affected a society eager to become more "normal." Kinsey's statistic that 86 percent of American males experience premarital intercourse implied that only religiously-repressed men were being left out. The reports that 50 percent of men engaged in extramarital intercourse, and the "almost universal occurrence of premarital petting" had predictable results.[1]

When Kinsey released the companion book regarding American women, an even greater response occurred. We were told that 90 percent of American women took part in premarital petting and that 50 percent engaged in premarital intercourse. As with the men, the reports had the effect of normalizing immoral behavior and, for the women particularly, underscored the unequal and disadvantaged position they were in, compared with men.[2]

"Recent sex surveys report... that in an economy characterized by abundance and oriented toward the production of luxury items and consumer goods, sexual pleasure has become a means of recreation for all classes."[3] *Time* magazine concluded, "No single event did more for open discussion of sex than the Kinsey Report, which got such matters as homosexuality, masturbation, coitus and orgasm into most [news]papers and family magazines."[4]

There can be no doubt that a decade of saturation with the attitudes of Alfred Kinsey prepared young Americans for all of the debauchery we associate with the Sixties. Marvin Olasky says, "In the 1960s the advent of birth control pills contributed to the belief that unwanted pregnancy could be eradicated... No longer would women have to worry about a double standard that allowed men to be sexually active outside of marriage, while women were either bound to virginity or left at risk of unwanted pregnancy."[5]

1 Morantz, in Altherr, 151.
2 Morantz, in Altherr, 154.
3 Morantz, in Altherr, 164. "Character structure and child rearing practices have shifted accordingly, away from an emphasis on autonomous self-control and toward the rational acceptance of pleasure, personal fulfillment, and happiness" [164].
4 *Time*, by Morantz, in Altherr, 161.
5 Olasky, *Abortion Rites: A Social History of Abortion in America*, 295.
6 *Time*, 12-5-94, 77.
7 Robert Bork, *Slouching Towards Gomorrah: Modern Liberalism and American Decline*, 32. Bork notes: "A corollary to the politicization of the culture is the tactic of assaulting one's opponents as not merely wrong but morally evil... [*Continued next column*]

g. Bob Dylan & the Clinton generation

Autonomy & Pragmatism

Time magazine has said, "During the 1960s Americans began a decisive journey across the moral border from the old territory of duty to the new land of rights... [In] part because of the disastrous exercise of American 'duty' in Vietnam, duty gave way to the very different universe of rights and, after that, of entitlements (which represent the decadence of the American guarantee)."[6]

The radical SDS [Students for a Democratic Society] "grew from 600 members in 1963 to more than 100,000 in 1968, but then collapsed in 1969 into hostile factions... The New Left student movement appeared ready to attack all existing structures, including the university, and to use tactics which alienated the majority, in order to make manifest their contempt, their total rejection of the intolerable world created by their elders... The revolt was against the entire American culture [which was seen to be] racist, sexist, authoritarian, and imperialistic."[7]

Modern liberalism is simply Sixties radicalism in its "mature stage," says Robert Bork. "They no longer have need for violence or confrontation, since the radicals control the institutions they formerly attacked."[8] Bork says that the Sixties brand of nihilism "came in two varieties: hedonism and political rage... The Sixties combined domestic disruption and violence with an explosion of drug use and sexual promiscuity."[9]

Abe Fortas saw in the youth of the Sixties an unequaled historical development: "We have precedents for the trials and disorders that attend the economic and political breakthrough of a segment of the population. But the breakup of patterns of authority – of the straight line of march – is new. Our prior experience of youth's rebellion has been limited to explosions within the pattern. Presently [1968], the design itself is challenged."[10]

Just how significant the Clinton Presidency is in history can be illustrated by the comment of Kate Michelman [president of NARAL – the National Abortion Rights Action League] that, if Bill Clinton hadn't been elected in 1992, "There'd be no *Roe v. Wade* today."[11]

In *The Lessons of History*, the Durants declare, "Nothing is clearer in history than the adoption by successful rebels of the methods they were accustomed to condemn in the forces they deposed."[12]

It is possible that something different has happened with our generation of Americans. The Sixties revolution caught the "establishment" off guard, and the government proved to be incapable of an effective response to mass rebellion, and made the mistake of coddling the student-criminals it did identify. As a result, the cultural takeover by the Counterculture has become complete, and it is apparent that the new leadership has resolved to utterly vanquish any rebellion it may face. Here is the perspective offered by Joseph Foreman: "Pro-lifers have never rioted, looted, or burned down sections of town as in the Sixties... Compare also the harshness with which pro-lifers are treated: the average [pro-life] bomber gets ten to twenty years of prison; the rioters of the sixties got suspended sentences. First-time [passive] Rescuers can get six months"[13] [two years, if they are in Atlanta!].

SCOPE and FOCUS
I. CONVICTIONS
II. PRETEXTS
III. MANDATE
IV. LEGACY
Christian Tradition
Early Church
Reformation Era
World Precedents
Holocaust
Nuremberg
Geneva
United Nations and Int'l Human Rights
Unborn Child's Rights
Global Abortion Norms
Apartheid
United States History
Independence
Liberty & Rights
Abolition of Slavery
Women's Passage Rites
Seeds of Destruction
Between World Wars
Pivotal Developments
Public education
Great Depression
Post-war materialism
Synthetic heroes
Post-war paranoia
Kinsey-Elvis-Madonna
Clinton generation
Civil Rights
Parental Responsibility
Humaneness
V. ABORTIVE LINKS
VI. DILEMMA
VII. DESTINY

Vietnam, the moral dimensions

"Vietnam will remain a blight on the U.S. image abroad – both as a military defeat and as a moral failure... What is important is the American reputation for interfering in the affairs of other sovereign nations."[14]

The Associated Press has revealed that "Almost a year before he began the large-scale buildup in Vietnam, President Johnson... believed public opinion was already against the war, [but he was] worried that Congress might run him out of office if he tried to withdraw." As a consequence of that act of moral bankruptcy, 500,000 American men per year were soon fighting there, and 58,000 of them died.[15]

The names of those who died are now engraved on the overwhelming 500-foot-long granite Vietnam War Memorial in Washington. "In 1973, toward the end of the Vietnam War, another tragic war began," says Steven Carr. "There are more victims of this war [abortion] in two weeks than there were in the twelve years of the Vietnam War. If we were to build a memorial wall similar to the Vietnam Memorial, the wall [in 1990] would be over forty-four miles long."[16]

In 1968, Robert Clouse wrote: "This country professes that she desires economic betterment of the Vietnamese yet has become identified with a hated, graft-ridden, parasitic landlord class. The United States, a land that loves liberty, has become entangled with a regime characterized by nepotism and tyranny."[17]

"In 1983, both Richard Nixon and Henry Kissinger said that the United States should have won the war in Vietnam [which is ludicrous when you consider that] the whole of Vietnam, in the opinion of the American specialist in Indochina, Joseph Buttinger, had become Communist by 1945."[18]

The CIA-backed coup in Guatemala in 1954 "showed other countries in Central America that the United States was more interested in unquestioning allies than democratic ones. As a result, movements toward peaceful reform in the region were set back, dictators were strengthened and encouraged, and activists of today look to guerilla warfare rather than elections as the only way to produce change."[19]

In *God & Caesar*, John Eidsmoe summarizes our record, internationally: "For the most part we have kept our commitments to our enemies right down to the last detail. But we have shamefully betrayed our friends. Consider Cuba. Consider Vietnam. Consider Laos. Consider Cambodia. Consider Taiwan. Consider Nicaragua. Is it any wonder El Salvador is worried [in 1984]? Is it any wonder our other allies are nervous about our support? Other nations will not trust a country that does not keep its promises."[20]

It is clear that our federal policy is built on pragmatism, not on justice. In February of 1997, the Associated Press reported that at a meeting of the House International Relations Committee, "Committee members were most critical of the Clinton administration for maintaining normal trade relations with China and inviting its defense minister, Gen. Chi Haotian, who led the 1989 Tiananmen Square massacre, to visit the United States and the White House last December."[21]

If that weren't enough, in June 1998, Bill Clinton "looked across the vast plaza called Tiananmen this morning [and] received his official welcome to China with a 21-gun salute... No words were spoken as Clinton and China's President Jiang Zemin stood at attention before a goose-stepping column of troops from the People's Liberation Army."[22]

Surely Clinton's *pragmatism* dictated the wisdom of not making a fuss over the massacre that occurred there nine years earlier when students peacefully demonstrated their preference for political liberty.

Critics of Hillary Clinton's health care plan were not said to be mistaken but were denounced as greedy pharmaceutical companies, doctors, and insurance companies out to protect their illicit profits" [54].

8 Bork, 34.
9 Bork, 50-1.
10 Abe Fortas, *Concerning Dissent and Civil Disobedience*, 60.
11 *Press*, 1-23-97, A1, A10.
12 Will and Ariel Durant, 34.
13 Foreman, *Shattering the Darkness*, 94.
14 Gordon Aeschliman, *Global Trends: Ten Changes Affecting Christians Everywhere*, 92-3.
15 Associated Press, *Press*, 2-15-97, A15.
16 Carr and Meyer, *Celebrate Life: Hope for a Culture Preoccupied with Death*, 259-60.
17 Clouse, *Protest and Politics*, 265.

Stephen Schlesinger, in *Bitter Fruit*, says: "When something happens to shock Washington... we reach for our gun, [for example, to send] Pershing into Mexico chasing Villa and when the Navy bombarded Veracruz. Harding and Coolidge sent the Marines into Latin America like riot squads. They stayed in Nicaragua so long they grew beards. Our forces have routinely moved in and out of Haiti and the Dominican Republic. The use of American force in Central America and the Caribbean has become a way of life... The record of unilateral use of force by the United States would fill a book... Guatemala bears a special distinction. It is one of two countries where the CIA boasts it carried out a successful clandestine military operation. The other, of course, is Iran" [in the Introduction].

18 Harrison Salisbury, *Vietnam Reconsidered: Lessons from a War*, 214-5.
19 Schlesinger, *Bitter Fruit*, 254.
20 Eidsmoe, 212-3.
21 Associated Press, *Press*, 2-1-97, A11.
22 *Press*, 6-27-98, A1.

8. Civil Rights Movement

Justice & Pragmatism

"Martin Luther King, Jr., made a crucial shift in the movement which had been going nowhere for about 60 years," says Joseph Foreman. "He decided that instead of acting like a second class citizen and begging to be given first class rights, he would act like a first class citizen, assume those rights, and let others prove that he was not human enough to deserve them."[1]

Dr. King is highly quotable: "One may well ask: How can you advocate breaking some laws and not others? The answer lies in the fact that there are two types of laws: just and unjust. I would be the first to advocate obeying just laws. Conversely, one has a moral responsibility to disobey unjust laws."[2] Clearly a universalist and not a positivist, Dr. King said, "An unjust law is a code that is out of harmony with the moral law. One has a moral responsibility to disobey unjust laws."[3] For practicing what he preached, Martin Luther King Jr. was arrested more than thirty times.[4]

When pro-lifers draw comparisons between the civil rights and the pro-life movements, a contrast quickly comes to mind concerning just and unjust laws: While it is straightforward to defy an unjust law that says *people of your race may not sit on these seats on the bus*, a pro-life rescuer is breaking a *just* no-trespassing law when she tries to block access to an abortion clinic. Courts today at every level hold to a strict law-and-order line, saying *This case is not about abortion, it is a simple question of trespassing on private property; guilty as charged.* But concerning civil rights cases, Lady Justice was clearly leaning the other way. When 179 black protesters defied the police order to disband and leave the grounds of a state capitol, they were arrested for a "breach of the peace." But the Supreme Court overturned their conviction on the basis that First Amendment Freedom of Assembly trumped a direct police order![5]

The Roots of the Civil Rights Movement

The black civil rights movement was clearly under way before 1920. Marcus Garvey founded the United Negro Improvement Association in 1914, and within five years had more than two million members. "It was the largest and most successful mass movement of urban blacks in the history of the United States."[6]

We must keep in mind that fifty years had passed since the Civil War, and that by 1920, the churches had widened their social vision so that the Social Creed of the Federal Council of Churches [forerunner of the National Council of Churches] included "supporting equal and adequate opportunities for Negroes" and favored "voting rights for all without regard to race."[7]

Segregation, in the law

The Supreme Court in the 1896 *Plessy v. Ferguson* case held that segregation did not constitute discrimination. In 1954 the Court reversed Plessy, and ruled that segregated educational facilities were unconstitutional.[8]

Clearly the tides of history were already turning in the civil rights direction when, on December 1, 1955, Rosa Parks was arrested for refusing to vacate a white seat on a bus in Montgomery, Alabama. That was a Thursday. On Friday there was an emergency meeting of Montgomery pastors [including MLK]. Leaflets were distributed on Saturday. Ministers announced the pending bus boycott from their pulpits on Sunday, and on Monday morning the Montgomery buses ran their routes almost completely empty, **and** the story was front-page news nationwide.[9]

The leaders of the Montgomery Bus Boycott were not unaware that twelve years earlier, in Alexandra, South Africa, ten thousand blacks in nine days had brought that city's bus system to its knees. Nelson Mandela had been just a participant at that historic moment.[10]

"Nothing stamped with the Divine image and likeness was sent into the world to be trodden on, and degraded, and imbruted by its fellows."[18]
–Abraham Lincoln

1 Foreman, *Shattering the Darkness: The Crisis of the Cross in the Church Today*, 43.

2 Martin Luther King, Jr., in Alcorn, *Is Rescuing Right?*, 118.

3 King, in Francis Beckwith, *Politically Correct Death*, 155.

4 Randy Alcorn, *Is Rescuing Right?*, 120-1.

5 John Whitehead, *Arresting Abortion*, 37.

6 Rober Betsworth, *Social Ethics*, 148.

7 Charles McCoy, in Robert Lee, *Religion and Social Conflict*, 39.

8 Jonathan Black, *Radical Lawyers*, 128-9.

9 Robert Lee, *Religion and Social Conflict*, 44.

10 Nelson Mandela, *Long Walk to Freedom*, 75.

11 Charles McCoy, in Robert Lee, *Religion and Social Conflict*, 46.

12 Tigar, in Jonathan Black, *Radical Lawyers: Their Role in the Movement and in the Courts*, 47.

13 Charles McCoy, in Robert Lee, *Religion and Social Conflict*, 37.

14 McCoy, in Lee, 49.

15 King, In Howard Clinebell, *Mental Health Through Christian Community*, 99.

16 McCoy, in Lee, 47.

17 McCoy, in Lee, 50.

18 Lincoln, in Elton Trueblood, *New Man for Our Time*, 81.

SCOPE and FOCUS
I. CONVICTIONS
II. PRETEXTS
III. MANDATE
IV. LEGACY
Christian Tradition
Early Church
Reformation Era
World Precedents
Holocaust
Nuremberg
Geneva
United Nations and Int'l Human Rights
Unborn Child's Rights
Global Abortion Norms
Apartheid
United States History
Independence
Liberty & Rights
Abolition of Slavery
Women's Passage Rites
Seeds of Destruction
Between World Wars
Pivotal Developments
Civil Rights
Parental Responsibility
Humaneness
Animal rights
Endangered species
Environmentalism
Welcome aliens!
Criminal rights
Children's rights
V. ABORTIVE LINKS
VI. DILEMMA
VII. DESTINY

Sit-ins for civil rights and equality

On the First of February in 1960, four Negro college students sat, unserved, at a segregated lunch counter in Greensboro North Carolina, from 4:30 until its 5:30 closing. "Word spread rapidly... In the brief span of two months [sit-ins] had spread to sixty-five cities and during the subsequent two years embraced parks, swimming pools, theaters, restaurants, churches, interstate transportation, voter registration, libraries, museums, art galleries, laundromats, employment, housing, real estate offices, beaches, and courtrooms."[11]

"The first lunch counter demonstration at Greensboro," says Michael Tigar, "no longer looks to us as it did at the time. Today we view it through the smoke and flame of Harlem, Watts, Newark, Detroit, Washington, D.C., and scores more cities."[12]

Freedom Rides on interstate bus transportation

"In mid-May 1961, headlines across the nation told a story of raw and ugly violence in Alabama. A Greyhound bus carrying an interracial group had been burned... Public order was seriously threatened, yet the police seemed indifferent... Federal marshals at last were sent in... What caught the eye of the public through the mass media was not an isolated phenomenon, but formed part of a movement for racial justice which had a long past."[13]

"The Freedom Ride, which was planned by the Congress of Racial Equality, began when an integrated group set out across the South to discover how well federal rulings requiring desegregation of interstate travel facilities were being obeyed. [After the violence and police complicity in Alabama, C.O.R.E. participants], giving up the plan to travel by bus on to New Orleans, ended this Freedom Ride by taking air transportation. [Students, however, stepped up and continued the Freedom Rides.] Eventually 305 persons from every section of the nation were jailed as Freedom Riders."[14]

The sit-ins and freedom rides for civil rights provide this **crucial lesson for the pro-life movement:** minuscule numbers of demonstrators [i.e. "305"] for a valid moral cause, if given broad and sympathetic media coverage, can gain the support of the entire nation. The converse is equally true: fifty-thousand Christian Rescuers of babies from abortion, even when unjustly treated by the police and in the courts, can be demonized and marginalized into extinction by **the media** – at its whim. In a republic such as ours, the media – as long as even the Christians continue to esteem its portrayals of reality as Gospel – will remain the **ultimate seat of power**, with an unchallenged hold on even the reins of government.

The Church and movements for social justice

Martin Luther King Jr. observed: "So often the contemporary church is a weak, ineffectual voice with an uncertain sound. So often it is the archdefender of the status quo. Far from being disturbed by the presence of the church, the power structure of the average community is consoled by the church's silent – and often vocal – sanction of things as they are."[15]

Charles McCoy lends credence to the notion that church "leaders" don't seem to initiate the great moral crusades, but appear more typically to wait until a groundswell becomes evident before stepping forward as organizers and spokesmen for the crusade that is already in progress. McCoy's statement, published in 1964, was this: "Again we see the religion of the churches providing meaning, motivation, and guidance brought to bear on a movement not begun by the churches and about which organized religion, viewed generally, was and remains decidedly ambivalent."[16]

Prior to 1970, the researcher of *Orphans in Babylon* had been a full-time "supply" pastor in the Missouri-West Conference of the United Methodist Church. These three events occurred within one year: 1) The Special General Conference of the United Methodist Church in St. Louis "called for abortion to be removed from the criminal code and placed under medical regulation." 2) The Official Board of the church I pastored, backed by the District Superintendent, put me on notice that I must never again mention the civil rights movement in my sermons; and 3) I left the pastorate, permanently.

Charles McCoy said it well: "Quite clearly, the protest movements for racial justice illustrate the ambiguous position toward which religious organizations tend when confronted with social conflict."[17]

The Civil Rights Movement in a nutshell

In March of 1998 *Parade* magazine featured an article about the black student leaders who were at the center of the sit-ins and freedom rides. The article invites us to "Consider what they did. When they had started out, they were virtually alone. Only the Supreme Court, of all government organs, seemed sympathetic. Even to the young liberal President, John Kennedy, they were in the beginning, in his own words, a pain in the a**. Yet only five years later, both parties of Congress... and the Justice Department [were working for them] and the FBI, however reluctantly, had come aboard; and the President of the United States, Lyndon Johnson was their principal convert. **They did this with the help of television, which made the struggle a national morality play**" [emphasis added].[1]

Parade continued with a summary of the key to civil rights success: "Ordinary young people, hardly favored by circumstances at their birth, changing first the conscience of the nation and then its laws, because their cause was right and because they were willing to risk their lives. That was their simple strategy. By offering up their lives in one dangerous venue after another, they believed, first the media and then the feds would be forced to come with them and witness what happened to them."[2]

Dr. King once predicted, "The Negro will only be truly free when he reaches down to the inner depths of his own being and signs with the pen and ink of assertive selfhood *his own* emancipation proclamation."[3]

Unfortunately, the preborn are incapable of defending their own rights but remain dependent upon others to assert their rights for them. If the pro-life movement is successful in mustering enough self-sacrificial activism to win a victory for those helpless, invisible ones, it will have been a kind of crusade unparalleled in human history.

Dr. Willke wrote that abortion "is a civil rights issue. It is a question of whether an entire class of living humans shall be deprived of their basic right to life on the basis of age and place of residence."[4]

In the words of Daniel Callahan: "The great strength of the movement against abortion is that it seeks to protect one defenseless category of human... Furthermore, it strives to resist the introduction into society of forms of value judgments that would discriminate among the worth of individual lives [relativism]. In almost any other civil rights context, the cogency of this line of reasoning would be quickly respected."[5]

Here is a personal revelation from Randy Alcorn: "I was released from Portland's Justice Center after spending a two-day jail sentence for rescuing innocent babies. When I walked out on the street and looked back at the building in which I had been imprisoned, there in large letters on the cornerstone was this quote: 'Injustice anywhere is a threat to justice everywhere,' Underneath was the date 1963, preceded by the name of the man who said it – Martin Luther King [Jr.]. What irony that twenty years earlier King himself was considered a doer of injustice because he broke civil laws. Indeed, at the date those very words were said, King was being locked up in places just like this one that was now proud to put his quote on its cornerstone!"[6]

SCOPE and FOCUS
I. CONVICTIONS
II. PRETEXTS
III. MANDATE
IV. LEGACY
Christian Tradition
Early Church
Reformation Era
World Precedents
Holocaust
Nuremberg
Geneva
United Nations and Int'l Human Rights
Unborn Child's Rights
Global Abortion Norms
Apartheid
United States History
Independence
Liberty & Rights
Abolition of Slavery
Women's Passage Rites
Seeds of Destruction
Between World Wars
Pivotal Developments
Civil Rights
Parental Responsibility
Humaneness
Animal rights
Endangered species
Environmentalism
Welcome aliens!
Criminal rights
Children's rights
V. ABORTIVE LINKS
VI. DILEMMA
VII. DESTINY

1 *Parade* magazine, 3-22-98, 5. Not in bibliography.

2 *Parade* magazine, 3-22-98, 6. Not in bibliography.

3 King, in *In Faith and Love*, 44. Sorry, remainder of citation has been lost.

4 J.C. Willke, *Handbook on Abortion*, 147.

5 Callahan, in J. Douglas Butler, *Abortion, Medicine, and the Law*, 349.

6 Alcorn, *Is Rescuing Right?: Breaking the Law to Save the Unborn*, 121.

7 Shana Alexander, 39-42.

8 Christopher Stone, *Should Trees Have Standing?* 18. The incomplete citation says: *"In re* Byrn, *L.A. Times*, 12-5-71."

9 Jean Garton, *Who Broke the Baby? A Brilliant Disclosure of What the Abortion Slogans Really Mean*, 86.

9. Parental-Responsibility Statutes

Virtue & Accountability

For a woman to consent to having her preborn child killed, huge emotional hurdles must be surmounted. Even the most avid supporters of evolution and naturalism concede that the maternal instinct for the protection of her offspring is among the strongest found in nature ["Never get between a mother bear and her cub"]. Beyond that, even a positivist will acknowledge that virtually every state has statutory requirements that parents must provide protection and care – warmth and nourishment – to their children. See the notes at this citation for sections of California's Civil Code and Penal Code.[10]

In 1975, a leading feminist was writing *The State-by-State Guide to Women's Legal Rights*. Because Shana Alexander was so clearly pro-abortion, it may be assumed that she had no idea that her words contain truths that should make any abortion unthinkable: "Once a man and a woman have given life to a child, they take on both rights and responsibilities toward that child... It is a crime in almost every state to desert young children who are dependent... Every state has legal provisions to remove minor children from the custody of unfit or unsuitable parents."[7]

In 1971, prior to *Roe v. Wade*, New York was already an abortion mecca due to its liberalized abortion laws, but this anecdote, regarding a preborn's right to protection from a mother who is contemplating abortion, warrants further investigation: "Professor Byrn of Fordham petitioned the New York Supreme Court to appoint him legal guardian for an unrelated foetus scheduled for abortion so as to enable him to bring a class action on behalf of all foetuses similarly situated in New York's 18 municipal hospitals. Judge Holtzman granted the petition of guardianship. There is a traditionally recognized guardian for the object – the mother – and her decision has been in favor of aborting the foetus."[8]

"In a subsequent 1976 case [*Planned Parenthood v. Danforth*] the Supreme Court ruled that a father need not give his consent or even be informed of the mother's decision to abort a child which together they had produced... At a time when society is calling for greater responsibility on the part of fathers and greater involvement in the rearing of children, it seems ironic."[9]

10 **California's Civil Code includes fascinating** – and sometimes terrifying – **provisions**:

§ 29. "A child **conceived**, but not yet born, is to be **deemed an existing person**, so far as may be necessary for its interests in the event of its subsequent birth..." [This means that if a child can get born in California, it is certified by the state to have been **a person from the moment of conception**, and any damage caused prior to birth is subject to the laws that protect born persons! But, in application, here is the result: A California drug addict who is nine months pregnant has these two options: If she delivers a drug-dependent baby, California will throw the mom in jail because she "provided drugs to a minor child," but if she gets an abortion there is no problem because a baby that doesn't get born was never a person!];

§ 34.5 [**Pregnant minors** need no one's permission to get an abortion];

§ 196. "The father and mother of a child have an equal responsibility to support... their child in the manner suitable to the child's circumstances;"

§ 203 (enacted 1872) "The **abuse of parental authority** is the subject of judicial cognizance in a civil action brought by the child, or by its relative..., or by the Supervisors of the county where the child resides; and when the abuse is established, the child may be freed from the dominion of the parent, and the duty of support... [may thus be] enforced;"

§ 204. "The **authority** of a parent ceases: Upon the appointment, by the Court, of a guardian of the person of a child;"

§ 206. "It is the duty of the father, the mother, and the children **of any person in need who is unable to maintain himself** by work, **to maintain such person to the extent of their ability**;"

§ 207. "If a parent neglects to **provide** articles necessary for his child who is under his charge, according to his circumstances, a third person may in good faith supply such necessaries...;"

§ 208.5. The father or mother of a minor child shall not be liable for the **support** of a child of such minor child."

California's Penal [criminal] Code includes these provisions:

§ 187 (a). "Murder is the unlawful killing of a human being, or a fetus, with malice aforethought. (b) This section shall **not** apply to any person who commits an act which results in the death of a fetus if any of the following apply: ...(3) The act was solicited, aided, abetted, or consented to by the mother of the fetus."

§ 188. "Malice... may be express or implied. It is express when there is manifested a deliberate intention unlawfully to take away the life of a fellow creature. It is implied, when no considerable provocation appears, or when the circumstances attending the killing show an abandoned and malignant heart;"

§ 205. "A person is guilty of **aggravated mayhem** when he or she unlawfully, under circumstances manifesting extreme indifference to the physical or psychological well-being of another person, intentionally causes permanent disability or disfigurement of another human being or deprives a human being of a limb, organ, or member of his or her body... Aggravated mayhem is a felony punishable by imprisonment in the state prison for life with the possibility of parole;"

§ 240. "An **assault** is an unlawful attempt, coupled with a present ability, to commit a violent injury on the person of another;"

§ 242. "A **battery** is any willful and unlawful use of force or violence upon the person of another;"

§ 270. "If a parent of a minor child willfully omits, without lawful excuse, to furnish necessary... shelter or medical attendance, or other remedial care for his or her child, he or she is guilty of '**Failure to Provide**;'"

§ 270.5. [Parents have a] "**Duty to accept** minor into parent's home or provide alternative shelter;"

§ 271. "Desertion. Every parent of any child under the age of 14 years... who deserts such child in any place whatever with intent to abandon it, is punishable by imprisonment..."

§ 271a "Abandonment. Every person who knowingly and willfully abandons, or who, having ability so to do, fails or **refuses to maintain** his or her minor child under the age of 14 years... is punishable by imprisonment..."

§ 273a. "Willful cruelty or... endangering life or health. Any person who, under circumstances or conditions likely to produce great bodily harm or death, willfully causes or permits any child to suffer, or inflicts thereon unjustifiable physical pain or... willfully causes or permits the person or health of such child to be injured... is punishable by imprisonment..."

10. Humaneness in Our Culture

Virtue & Accountability

"Societies, like human beings, progress through different stages of sensitiveness," says Christopher Stone.[1]

The key word here is *progress*. Even Charles Darwin, of all people, described a kind of human evolution which denotes an increase of justice and humaneness, not pragmatism: "In *Descent of Man*, Darwin observed that the history of man's moral development has been a continual extension in the objects of his 'social instincts and sympathies.' Originally each man had regard only for himself and those of a very narrow circle about him: later, he came to regard more and more 'not only the welfare, but the happiness of all his fellowmen;' then 'his sympathies became more tender and widely diffused, extending to men of all races, to the imbecile, maimed, and other useless members of society, and finally to the lower animals.'"[2]

Of course, Darwin considered this increasing emotional tenderness and moral generosity to be character flaws, not virtues, because benevolent acts toward "useless members of society" – as he thought Christianity foolishly encouraged – weaken "the race" and defeat the natural process of the "survival of the fittest."

Diverging from the views of Darwin and Malthus, Sidney Callahan says, "In all patriarchal unjust systems, lesser orders of human life are granted rights only when wanted, chosen, or invested with value by the powerful. Fortunately, in the course of civilization there has been a gradual realization that justice demands [that] the powerless and dependent be protected against the uses of power wielded unilaterally."[3]

In *The War Over the Family*, the Bergers ask and answer some key questions. "In the eighteenth century, what led to a new moral consensus to the effect that judicial torture was an intolerable practice? Or, in the nineteenth century, that children should not be subject to the full rigors of the criminal law? In both of these examples the process can be traced; and it involved various institutions, but it was possible only because large segments of society acquired a new vision of the nature of being human and therefore of the limits of humanly tolerable acts. If a new consensus on abortion is imaginable at all, something like this would have to happen here. We would suggest two elements... a revival of awe and a recognition of ignorance."[4]

The Bergers stop just short of quoting Scripture, but this verse comes easily to mind: **"If my people, who are called by my name, will humble themselves and pray and seek my face and turn from their wicked ways, then will I hear from heaven and will forgive their sin and will heal their land."[5]**

SCOPE and FOCUS
I. CONVICTIONS
II. PRETEXTS
III. MANDATE
IV. LEGACY
Christian Tradition
Early Church
Reformation Era
World Precedents
Holocaust
Nuremberg
Geneva
United Nations and Int'l Human Rights
Unborn Child's Rights
Global Abortion Norms
Apartheid
United States History
Independence
Liberty & Rights
Abolition of Slavery
Women's Passage Rites
Seeds of Destruction
Between World Wars
Pivotal Developments
Civil Rights
Parental Responsibility
Humaneness
Animal rights
Endangered species
Environmentalism
Welcome aliens!
Criminal rights
Children's rights
V. ABORTIVE LINKS
VI. DILEMMA
VII. DESTINY

There would seem to be a natural tendency for relativism to come into play when we discuss the subject of humaneness. In *Megatrends 2000*, John Naisbitt wrote: "Although some of us are as dead set against biotechnology as Jeremy Rifkin, others have worked through to a middle ground: They think that manipulating the genes of plant cells seems okay, but that playing around with human genes is definitely not. Animals are somewhere in between; it depends on whether what is being done is humane or not."[6]

As to those benevolent leanings that impel crusaders to defend the rights of the downtrodden, Troy Duster said in 1970, "Some thirty years ago, Svend Ranulf brilliantly developed the thesis that the middle-classes have a near monopoly on moral indignation. Max Weber and Max Scheler had earlier offered similar propositions."[7]

Could it be that the poor are made selfish by hunger and that the rich become miserly through fear of loss, leaving only the middlers to hear and to heed the cries of the needy? Perhaps that is why the biblical prayer asks: **"Give me neither poverty nor riches, but give me only my daily bread. Otherwise, I may have too much and disown You and say, 'Who is the Lord?' or I may become poor and steal, and so dishonor the name of my God."[8]**

By all accounts, the undeniable humaneness of American society should produce outrage in defense of the helpless preborn. "The same legal tradition which in our society guarantees the right to control one's own body firmly recognizes the wrongfulness of harming other bodies, however immature, dependent, different looking, or powerless," says Sidney Callahan.[9]

Beyond the rights of preborn persons, Christopher Stone argues that American humaneness should be reflected in a system of legal protections for even the rocks and trees: "We should have a system in which, when a friend of a natural object perceives it to be endangered, he can apply to a court for the creation of a guardianship... It is no answer to say that streams and forests cannot have standing because streams and forests cannot speak. Corporations cannot speak either; nor can states, estates, infants, incompetents, municipalities or universities. Lawyers speak for them, as they customarily do for the ordinary citizen with legal problems."[10]

Stone later asserts that under the system he proposes, a "guardian would urge before the court injuries not presently [recognized:] the death of eagles and inedible crabs, the suffering of sea lions, the loss from the face of the earth of species of commercially valueless birds, the disappearance of a wilderness area... Indeed, the widespread growth of environmental groups shows that human beings do feel these losses."[11]

Should Trees Have Standing? was written in 1972. Since that time, as it suggested, the *Endangered Species Act* has required that humans go to ridiculous lengths [and expense] to protect any species of life that is found to be failing the "survival of the fittest" test, but of course, the *right to slaughter* endangered preborn humans was guaranteed by *Roe v. Wade*! Does no one in power acknowledge the lunacy in all of this?

a. Animal Rights

Justice & Accountability

The foundational humaneness of the American people is most noticeable in our love of animals, and our particular fondness for dogs, cats, horses, and Mickey Mouse.

In Florida the man who buried puppies alive in a paper bag was "charged with three felony counts of cruelty to animals and six misdemeanor counts of animal abandonment."[12] A jury convicted a California man of animal cruelty because he suffocated two kittens in a plastic bag. The SPCA [Society for the Prevention of Cruelty to Animals] said that the conviction sends a message that "cruelty to animals is a crime and should not be tolerated."[13] In neither case was the right to kill the pets in question, yet no one can deny that the methods used by both men was much more humane than the standard procedures for every legal abortion of a human baby.

The U.S. Wild Horse and Burro Program boondoggle is a case of humanitarianism gone crazy. Wild horses were eating grass that the government would rather have reserved for cattle. Public pressure demanded a humane solution. The program has spent $250 million to see that 165,000 animals have been "adopted" by private citizens. The sweet thought has become a very sweet deal. Ninety percent of the "adoptive owners" wait the mandatory year and then sell the horses for $700 each to be eaten as horsemeat in Asia and Europe. Here is the math for the average humanitarian rescue of a wild horse: The government cost [taxpayer money] is $1,515 to capture the horse and arrange the adoption; the adoptive owner pays zero up to a maximum of $125 to get the animal; the owner feeds the horse for a year and sells it for $700.[14]

The $250 million federal program created a horsemeat industry that has earned unethical citizens over a hundred-million dollars. It would be more humane if the government would just pay people $700 to go out and shoot a horse, leaving it as food for some endangered buzzard!

1 Stone, *Should Trees Have Standing? Toward Legal Rights for Natural Objects*, xii.
2 Stone, 3.
3 Callahan, in Paul Jersild, *Moral Issues & Christian Response*, 349.
4 Brigitte and Peter Berger, *The War Over the Family: Capturing the Middle Ground*, 78.
5 *2 Chronicles* 7:14.
6 Naisbitt, Megatrends 2000: *Ten New Directions for the 1990s*, 247.
7 Troy Duster, *The Legislation of Morality: Law, Drugs, and Moral Judgment*, viii.
8 *Proverbs* 30:8-9.
9 Callahan, in Jersild, 348-9.
10 Christopher Stone, *Should Trees Have Standing*, 17.
11 Stone, 28-9.
12 *Press*, 1-27-95, A3.
13 *Press*, 4-2-97, A4.
14 Associated Press, in *Press*, 1-12-97, A3.

Are we really "saving the seals"?

The International Fund for Animal Welfare has successfully lobbied for Canadian laws that prohibit the killing of the cute little harp seal pups until they shed their white coats at one month of age, and hooded seals until they lose their blue fur at about one year.[1] The regulations are not about the right to life and do nothing to protect the species from decimation, because in neither case does the protection permit enough maturity to allow for reproduction. It clearly caters only to the emotional feeling that *baby* seals should not be killed.

In California a mountain lion killed a young woman, leaving her two young children without a mother. Authorities tracked down the mountain lion, shot it, and arranged for care for its orphaned cub. The public was asked for donations; "more than twice as much money has been pledged" to help care for the cub than for the two children.[2]

Why animals are protected

David Paterson and Richard Ryder assert that the claim for animal rights "rests upon the thesis that if the use of such a concept as 'rights' is appropriate and possible for humans then it is also appropriate and possible for the rest of sentient creation."[3]

The term sentient means having the capacities of perception and feeling. We must observe that by this standard, any preborn human who is the target of standard abortion techniques would qualify fully for such protections as are provided by law for "sentient" animals.

As long ago as 1780, Jeremy Bentham was arguing for animal rights in this fashion: "The day may come when the rest of the animal creation may acquire those *rights* which never could have been withheld from them but by the hand of tyranny... The question is not can they *reason*? Nor, can they *talk*? But, can they *suffer*?"[4]

Paul Ramsey, in analyzing *The Ethics of Fetal Research*, observed that in our society: "One does not protect tissue. Nor do we – if human benefits are seriously at stake – protect animals from more than pain and wanton wastage."[5] It would appear that America's avoidance of "wanton wastage" is not sufficient to protect the *lives* of the preborn from being sacrificed, but that it is sufficient to allow the recycling of the babies' bodies.

Paterson and Ryder go so far as to assert: "A full statement of animals' rights must include a consideration of their: 1) right to life; 2) right to be protected from suffering; 3) right to live free from interference (save possibly for the benefit of the individual); 4) right to live in accordance with their 'natural requirements.'"[6]

The *Declaration Against Speciesism* which garnered 150 signatures at Trinity College, Cambridge, in 1977, asserted that for "species capable of feeling" [this should include preborn humans], "the infliction of suffering" and "curtailment of their enjoyment" should be condemned "unless it be necessary for their own individual benefit."[7]

John Eidsmoe reflects on the Supreme Court's rationale for legalizing abortion: "Animals are not persons under the Fourteenth Amendment; yet we have laws preventing cruelty to animals. Strangely enough, livestock have more protection under the law today than do unborn children!"[8] He continues: "Even animals are entitled to humane treatment, and society has a right to protect itself against practices which brutalize and dehumanize. Laws requiring the administration of painkiller to the unborn prior to an abortion should be upheld with little difficulty... Many mothers might think twice about an abortion, knowing that the unborn child is capable of feeling pain."[9]

In *Living Ethically in the '90s*, Kerby Anderson writes: "It is remarkable that the law protects animals from cruel deaths. A person can kill his dog or cat, but he cannot kill it with cruelty. He would be subject to arrest if he cut off his pet's limbs, dissolved its skin in acid, or starved it to death. Yet the law allows these kinds of atrocities to be carried out against the most defenseless members of the human family."[10]

Tolerance of animal activism vs. intolerance of pro-life activism

Paterson and Ryder wrote in 1979: "The fact that the animal welfare movement is failing is apparent in the actions of the young and impatient animal rights campaigners who, frustrated by lack of action and progress in the animal welfare battle, are burning boats used for hunting seals, rescuing animals from vivisection laboratories and factory farms, and damaging vehicles and buildings used for animal exploitation."[11]

In 1987 the Animal Liberation Front set a $4.6 million fire that destroyed the Veterinary Diagnostic Lab at the University of California at Davis. Ten years later, 31 animal rights activists were arrested for trespassing at the rebuilt lab. They carried "large posters that denounced animal experimentation as 'science gone mad.'"[12]

That one fire at Davis probably exceeded the dollar value of all of the abortion clinic demolitions combined, yet there is a glaring discrepancy between the way animal rights activism and pro-life activism are treated by both the media and the government. Pro-lifers are publicly demonized and get "the book" thrown at them in court, while Greenpeace is painted with a Robin Hood brush, and no governmental task force was ever created by the Attorney General to implicate animal-activists as collaborators and co-conspirators in animal-rights violence.

SCOPE and FOCUS
I. CONVICTIONS
II. PRETEXTS
III. MANDATE
IV. LEGACY
Christian Tradition
Early Church
Reformation Era
World Precedents
Holocaust
Nuremberg
Geneva
United Nations and Int'l Human Rights
Unborn Child's Rights
Global Abortion Norms
Apartheid
United States History
Independence
Liberty & Rights
Abolition of Slavery
Women's Passage Rites
Seeds of Destruction
Between World Wars
Pivotal Developments
Civil Rights
Parental Responsibility
Humaneness
Animal rights
Endangered species
Environmentalism
Welcome aliens!
Criminal rights
Children's rights
V. ABORTIVE LINKS
VI. DILEMMA
VII. DESTINY

b. Endangered Species

Mechanism & Accountability

Congress passed the *Endangered Species Act* in 1973, the same year when the Supreme Court declared open season on preborn humans. Killing an eagle carries up to a one-year prison term and a $100,000 fine.[13]

Many have noted the irony that Darwinism and endangered species advocacy seem to go together. The combined wisdom of Darwin and Malthus, when applied to humans, results in policies such as those of Hitler and Planned Parenthood in which the elimination of unwanted members of the human species is upheld as supporting the "survival of the fittest." But when an endangered species is identified and elaborately protected, the supposed beneficial processes of "natural selection" and "survival of the fittest" are thwarted by human acts. It is unconscionably contradictory for the "scientific community" to embrace the view that it is wrong for Christians to feed the human victims of famine, while at the same time demanding that absolutely no species of life be permitted to die out.

Construction of a $74.5 million complex in Temecula, California, was delayed for six months "so two pairs of endangered songbirds [California Gnatcatchers] can mate."[14] The Santa Ana Sucker, a fat-lipped fish that vacuums scum from stream beds, is threatened with extinction, and one official declared, "It's part of our natural heritage and biodiversity... We're not sure how it fits in, but we don't want to throw away parts. Once it's gone, it's gone for good."[15]

"In its three short years on the endangered species list, the Delhi Sands Flower-Loving Fly has cost San Bernardino [Calif.] County $3.5 million."[16] Additionally, in constructing a new hospital, the county has been ordered to set aside nine acres as a protected habitat for this fly.

Those flies should protest that they aren't being treated as well as the kangaroo rats in the next county! In 1988 the Stephens kangaroo rat was identified as endangered in Riverside County.[17]

They have an abundance of kangaroo rats, mind you, but the ones with a specific hair color and length of tail [only a university expert can tell them apart] are identified as a separate species, and *they* are very rare. Since 1988, the owners of 78,000 acres of prime Southern California land have been denied the right to build homes or other structures, or even to plow their farm land lest they disturb the burrows of the "Stephens" kangaroo rat.[18]

The hard-fought agreement on how to protect the rats requires that owners pay nearly $2,000 per acre to the government, which will then buy and maintain seven Stephens kangaroo rat sanctuaries totaling nearly 43,000 acres.[19] If you take the time to do the math, you will discover that the government has settled the dispute between human land-owners and kangaroo rats over 78,000 acres of land by giving the rats 55% of the land, and charging the humans for the costs. The program guarantees exclusive, undisturbed and government-enhanced living for the rats on 1% of the total land area of Riverside county [43,000 of 4,593,280 acres], some of the best parts, we might add, and the cost of maintaining these preserves will be shared, forever, by the taxpayers of California.

There are 200 protection plans under way for endangered species like the kangaroo rat, nationwide. The number two official of the U.S. Interior Department says that he fears a "national revolt against the Environmental Protection Act."[20] Should anyone be surprised?

When Christopher Stone wrote *Should Trees Have Standing?* in 1974, he argued that not only animal species but rivers and forests have rights [to existence, to life] that should be protected by law. He asserted: "Contemporary public concern for protecting nature's ecological equilibrium should lead to the conferral of standing [the right to be represented in court] upon environmental objects to sue for their own preservation."[21]

We would assert that preborn human children, from the moment of conception, are entitled to a constitutional guarantee of their right to life. When Margaret Rosenberger compiled *Issues in Focus: Gaining a Clear Biblical Perspective on the Complex Issues of Our Time*, she observed: "The penalty for killing an unborn eagle in this country is a fine of up to $5,000 and up to five years in prison. But killing an unborn baby is not considered a crime at all, as long as the mother approves."[22]

1 *The Toronto Globe and Mail*, in *Press*, 11-7-96, A17.
2 *Press*, 5-23-94, A1.
3 Patterson and Ryder, *Animal Rights – a Symposium*, ix.
4 Patterson and Ryder, 3.
5 Ramsey, *Fetal Research*, 28.
6 Patterson and Ryder, x.
7 Patterson and Ryder, viii.
8 Eidsmoe, *God & Caesar*, 181.
9 Eidsmoe, 186-7.
10 Kerby Anderson, 206.
11 Patterson and Ryder, 163.
12 *Press*, 4-21-97, A4.
13 *Press*, 3-6-95, A3.
14 *Press*, 3-9-97, B1.
15 Associated Press, in *Press*, 4-3-97, A3.
16 *Press*, 10-10-96, B1, B12.
17 *Press*, 1-23-96, A1, A12.
18 *Press*, 11-27-95, A10.
19 *Press*, 3-7-96, B1, B8. [$1,950 per acre; 42,959 acres]
20 *Press*, 1-23-96, A1, A12.
21 Stone, xv.
22 Rosenberger, 94.

c. Environmentalism

Mechanism & Accountability

Another very pronounced reflection of the generalized humaneness of America is how environment-conscious our society has become. The controversy centered on loggers and owls in the Pacific Northwest has become a national soap opera.

Internationally, environmentalism is a top priority. There are global conventions, protocols and *programmes of action* concerning the ozone layer, biological diversity, endangered species, the marine environment, climate change, and desertification and drought.[1]

A *Declaration of the Human Rights of the Preborn Child* is being promoted by Louise Ackad of Alliance for Life International,[2] but its goal of instituting global safeguards for the intrauterine environment is destined for a long uphill battle.

An early opportunity for the U.S. Supreme Court to define the parameters of environmentalism came in the Mineral King case [*Sierra Club v. Morton*] The U.S. Forest Service had granted a permit to Walt Disney Enterprises Inc. to 'develop' [translate: Disneyland-ize] the pristine Mineral King Valley in California.[3] The Sierra Club's attempt to protect the environment from such radical commercialization resulted in the opinion of the Ninth Circuit Court that the Club had no "standing" to represent the Valley, since it did not own the property in question nor could it demonstrate that the development would "aggrieve" or "adversely affect" the Club *per se*.[4]

Should Trees Have Standing? was written to promote Christopher Stone's argument that environmental objects [inanimate or wet, as well as living] should have standing in court, and should be entitled to political and legal representation. One of Stone's assertions is that "One can say that we never know what is going to prove useful at some future time. In order to protect ourselves, therefore, we ought to be conservative now in our treatment of nature."[5] It is no less compelling to employ the same line of reasoning to assert that since the child scheduled for abortion might be destined to be tomorrow's Einstein, Gandhi or Michelangelo, we ought not take the risk of killing him today.

The Supreme Court, when it reviewed the Mineral King case in 1972, upheld the lower court's ruling that The Sierra Club lacked standing. Justice Douglas, however, in his dissent to the 4-3 decision, suggested that it would be helpful if the government "fashioned a federal rule that allowed environmental issues to be litigated before federal agencies or federal courts in the name of the inanimate object about to be despoiled, defaced, or invaded by roads and bulldozers and where injury is the subject of public outrage."[6]

Obviously not enough of the justices were concerned one year later in 1973 about the innocent preborn human children "about to be despoiled, defaced" and "invaded" by the abortionists' instruments of death when they committed *Roe v. Wade*. In *Roe* and *Doe*, the Court pointedly declared that the unborn have no standing, and that no amount of "public outrage" would be sufficient to raise a defense of their right to life.

The Supreme Court acted illegally in legitimizing abortion nationwide in at least one way that has not been previously explored. This view is predicated on two simple assumptions: that the Supreme Court is an agency of the federal government, and that the womb is the natural "human environment" of a preborn child. Three years prior to *Roe*, the 1970 National Environmental Policy Act stipulated that **every federal agency must "include in** every recommendation or report on proposals for legislation and other **Federal actions significantly affecting the quality of the human environment, a detailed statement** by the responsible official **on the environmental impact [and] any adverse environmental effects, [and stating] alternatives [and] any irreversible and irretrievable commitments** of resources which would be involved in the proposed action should it be implemented."[7]

Forget the overrated dangers of living on a street where drive-by shootings regularly occur. The Supreme Court's action in *Roe* and *Doe* rendered the *American womb* the most hazardous human environment on earth: one out of every three humans who enters that space will be murdered while there.

SCOPE and FOCUS
I. CONVICTIONS
II. PRETEXTS
III. MANDATE
IV. LEGACY
Christian Tradition
World Precedents
United States History
Independence
Liberty & Rights
Abolition of Slavery
Women's Passage Rites
Seeds of Destruction
Between World Wars
Pivotal Developments
Civil Rights
Parental Responsibility
Humaneness
Animal rights
Endangered species
Environmentalism
Welcome aliens!
Criminal rights
Children's rights
V. ABORTIVE LINKS
VI. DILEMMA
VII. DESTINY

1 United Nations. *For Life on Earth*, interactive CD-ROM. Not in bibliography.

2 Louise Ackad, *Declaring the Human Rights of the Preborn Child*, a master's thesis, 236-42.

3 Stone, 59. In the words of the Supreme Court's opinion in this case: "...an area of great natural beauty nestled in the Sierra Nevada Mountains in Tulare County, California, adjacent to Sequoia National Park... and is designated as a National Game Refuge by special Act of Congress."

4 Christopher Stone, *Should Trees Have Standing?*, Foreword.

5 Stone, 43.

6 Stone, xv.

7 Stone, 36.

8 *U.S. Code*, Title 8, § 1522, in Thomas Jacobs, *Legal Directory of Children's Rights*. Vol. 1 [Federal Statutes], 62.

9 Eidsmoe, 171.

10 Bray, *A Time to Kill*, 26.

11 Bandow, *Beyond Good Intentions, a Biblical View of Politics*, 167.

12 *Press*, 3-14-97, A7.

13 *Press*, 12-5-96, A7.

14 *Press*, 12-5-96, A7.

15 Amnesty International, "The Death Penalty: Cruel & Inhuman Punishment" pamphlet. Not in bibliography.

d. American hospitality toward aliens

Virtue & Justice

When an unborn child of American parents is just moments away from a full term natural delivery, and even if the natural father desperately wants to love and raise that child, if the mother simply decides on a whim that she'd like to abort, that child is held by the American government to be not a person, not a child, not a human being at all, but utterly devoid of value, rights, or a second chance... she will die.

By stark contrast, consider our government's official policy toward an *alien* child born just minutes ago, in a boat, to a *refugee* family that now arrives in U.S. territory. The federal government will "provide assistance, reimbursement to States, and grants to and contracts with public and private nonprofit agencies, for the provision of child welfare services, including foster care maintenance payments and services and health care, furnished to any refugee child... In the case of a refugee child who is unaccompanied by a parent or other close relative... the services described... may be furnished until the month after the child attains eighteen years of age."[8]

Disclaimer: Here follows a theoretical discussion, not a suggestion! Suppose a pro-life man kidnapped his wife who was about to have their full-term child aborted. If the husband held his wife against her will long enough for the baby to be born, left the child on the doorstep of a hospital and fled the country, two significant things would have happened. The man would have become a refugee, fleeing prosecution in America for having acted out his strongly held religious convictions, and his born baby would be the child of a refugee. Would the U.S. government not be obligated to provide for the child's every need until after her eighteenth birthday?

There is another example of the dramatic difference in "standing" before our government that occasions the technicality of birth. In this case we are not considering the plight of refugees but of a pregnant foreign woman, knowledgeable about American law, but who has no legitimate reason to enter this country. This example is not hypothetical; it is acted out regularly along our borders. If the illegal alien can somehow get into the U.S. and can deliver her child while here, the baby is automatically and instantly an American citizen. The child has the constitutionally protected right to remain here for life, and is entitled to welfare, food stamps, education and medical care. The result is that an American father whose government rendered him incapable of preventing the abortion of his own child will also be required by that government, through his taxes, to support for eighteen years the child of the illegal alien. Where is the justice for all of that?

e. Criminal rights and capital punishment

Justice & Mechanism

The reader may recall that on page 48 we briefly responded to the accusation that people who favor capital punishment cannot be authentically pro-life. In *God & Caesar*, John Eidsmoe says, "God values human life so much that he has ordained capital punishment for those who wrongfully destroy human life."[9]

Michael Bray agrees: "It is not inconsistent to be prolife and favor capital punishment... The advocacy of capital punishment for capital crimes is necessary for both communication of the truth (of the sanctity of human life) and deterrence of criminal acts... Those same scriptures which uphold the sanctity of human life call for the execution of capital criminals."[10]

This truth is reconfirmed by Doug Bandow: "Of course, the fact that God considers life to be precious does not mean that it can never be taken. Life is sacred, not inviolate: Mosaic law prescribed death for a variety of offenses, including murder and adultery. In these cases other fundamental interests were considered to be more important than the right to life. The unborn child, however, is innocent of any crime. Thus, only the most compelling of reasons could justify taking his life."[11]

Consistent with the clear biblical endorsement of capital punishment for capital crimes is the American public's belief that it is an appropriate consequence and useful as a deterrent to major crime.[12] "Fifty-six men were executed nationally [in 1995]. It was the largest number in 38 years. More than 3,000 were waiting on death row."[13] By contrast with the 3,000 convicted prisoners on death row, and the 56 capital criminals who were actually executed in one year, more than 4,000 *innocent* American babies have an appointment with death by abortion *tomorrow*, the same number as were killed today, and yesterday, and every day since 1973.

The Supreme Court ruled capital punishment unconstitutional in 1972 but reinstated it in 1976. This, of course, is further confirmation of the instability of the Court, and of its pragmatic, positivistic "legisprudence" during the years during which it committed but failed to rescind *Roe v. Wade*.

Three-hundred-thirteen capital criminals have been executed in the U.S. in the twenty years from 1976 to 1996. In that recent year, the laws of 12 states did not include the death penalty. Among those that did, 32 states authorized lethal injection, 11 electrocution, seven lethal gas, four hanging, and three the firing squad.[14] [If you add these up, you will conclude that some states authorize more than one method.]

Remembering that we are seeking connections between America's humanitarian leanings and abortion, we note that in 1977 the Supreme Court ruled that the death penalty is excessively harsh punishment for the crime of rape.[15] Pro-lifers think that abortion is an excessively harsh punishment for the crime of being unborn and unwanted by your mother.

Reasons asserted for never executing criminals

According to amnesty International, there are many reasons why even the most malevolent capital criminal should never be executed: "The death penalty teaches that killing is sometimes acceptable, while denying the fundamental humanity of all people – including those who commit atrocious acts. With each execution, the United States further numbs itself to the tragedy of state-sanctioned killing... The U.S. was founded on a respect for those fundamental rights each individual deserves for no other reason than because he or she is a human being... The death penalty is irreversible... The death penalty is a lottery... The system of death sentencing is like a lottery determined by countless random factors."[1] The reader is invited to note how slightly the above wording needs to be altered in order to make a far more convincing argument against abortion.

When Supreme Court Justice Harry Blackmun, who was the author of the *Roe v. Wade* opinion, was speaking about the death penalty he said "From this day forward, I no longer shall tinker with the machinery of death."[2] Is it possible that the Justice is not gripped by what strikes instantly at the heart of a pro-lifer when such a statement is made, that Blackmun's *Roe v. Wade* decision was exactly that, "tinkering with the machinery of death"?

f. Children's Rights

Justice & Accountability

The ultimate demonstration of innate humaneness is seen in the fact that most folks naturally agree that babies – and puppies and kittens for that matter – are cute. It's a good thing, too, probably nature's way of assuring that people will go to the trouble it takes to assure a constant supply of future adults!

In the Age of Agrarians, children were valued as extra "hands" to help with the endless list of chores needing to be done on the farm. With the shift to industrial work in urban areas, children became liabilities instead of assets, so it was not long until youngsters were given special niches in the labor force, their meager wages contributing to the family's welfare. The first movements toward child protection were aimed at reducing the deaths and serious injuries to children working long hours in factories, mills and mines. A major boost was given to social awareness of the problem by the publication of *Oliver Twist* by Charles Dickens in 1837.

Geoffrey Perrett, in his *America in the Twenties: A History*, says, "The first [federal] child-labor law [1916] had invoked the power of Congress to regulate interstate commerce, a power that had been used to curb white slavery, adulterated food, and lotteries. In 1918 the [Supreme] Court ruled that using this power to curb child labor was unconstitutional. Congress passed a second child-labor law, putting a 10 percent tax on goods made by child labor. The Court had sanctioned prohibitory taxes on narcotics, phosphorous matches, and yellow margarine, but the line evidently had to be drawn somewhere because the Court in 1922 drew it at child labor. The only course open now was a child-labor amendment."[3]

Perrett continues, saying that child labor "was an issue that generated much passion for most of the Twenties, yet by 1932 only six states had ratified the Child Labor Amendment... As for [President Herbert] Hoover, there was no issue that moved him more deeply than the rights of children... But by setting the upper limit at eighteen instead of sixteen, the amendment's congressional sponsors had made defeat almost certain."[4]

The Fair Labor Standards Act of 1938 began the first effective national reform of child labor abuses. Since then every State has enacted such laws, and the rapid advances in public education and in compulsory attendance statutes removed children from the work force by putting them in school.

Besides schooling and child labor laws, our national commitment to the protection and nurturing of children is reflected in the parental responsibility statutes previously addressed,[5] as well as in the *U.S. Code* Title 42, "Public Health and Welfare" statutes, and in the endless array of activities in the arts, scouting and athletics.

Virtually every indicator of the deeply humane character of American society would seem to predispose us to love, protect and nurture every child from the moment of conception. That our national sympathies have been illogically distorted so as to sympathize totally with the "plight" of the woman "trapped in a crisis pregnancy" to the exclusion of regard for the abortion-doomed child is a tribute to the effectiveness of a superb [diabolical] propaganda campaign waged relentlessly by the Masters of secular humanism for a century or longer.

Doug Bandow says that there is "an obvious Biblical concern over the plight of the helpless – which [a preborn baby] certainly is. The Old Testament prophets frequently attacked Israel's leaders for ignoring the plight of widows and orphans... In fact, with at least one parent committed to ending his life, an unborn child is rather like an orphan."[6]

1 Amnesty International, "The Death Penalty: Cruel & Inhuman Punishment" pamphlet. Not in bibliography.

2. *Life Advocate*, 4/'94, 4.

3 Perrett, 464.

4 Perrett, 464.

SCOPE and FOCUS
I. CONVICTIONS
II. PRETEXTS
III. MANDATE
IV. LEGACY
Christian Tradition
Early Church
Reformation Era
World Precedents
Holocaust
Nuremberg
Geneva
United Nations and Int'l Human Rights
Unborn Child's Rights
Global Abortion Norms
Apartheid
United States History
Independence
Liberty & Rights
Abolition of Slavery
Women's Passage Rites
Seeds of Destruction
Between World Wars
Pivotal Developments
Civil Rights
Parental Responsibility
Humaneness
Animal rights
Endangered species
Environmentalism
Welcome aliens!
Criminal rights
Children's rights
V. ABORTIVE LINKS
VI. DILEMMA
VII. DESTINY

CONCLUSIONS

The lessons of history for the Stewards of Christian faith

Will and Ariel Durant sought to fathom *The Lessons of History* from an evolutionary and naturalistic perspective, beginning at a point of skepticism regarding religious faith in general and toward divine inspiration of the Christian Bible in particular. *Orphans in Babylon* prays that God will reveal the Lessons of History for Christians who are pro-life Stewards as we embark on this new century.

Our **LEGACY** includes a **Christian Tradition** which teaches us that God's ways are so different from the ways of the world that His people will always be labeled as deluded and dysfunctional, and must steadfastly regard themselves as pilgrims and sojourners on this planet. The **Early Church** inspires us with a courage-unto-death in boldly refusing to bow the knee to Caesar, in denouncing the wickedness and idolatry of its culture, and in displaying sacrificial love "unto the least of these" through obedience to a Law higher than man's. In the **Reformation Era** we re-learned the lessons that each of us stands individually accountable before the judgment seat of God, and that Christian salvation is a prize worth dying for.

Numerous **World Precedents** inform our struggles as pro-life Christians today. The Nazi **Holocaust** taught all of us to declare, "Never again!" to any who would presume to assert that any class of human beings is subhuman and unworthy of life. **Nuremberg** stands as a glorious example that mankind must hold all men accountable to God's moral order, at all times, regardless of what the earthly statutes may sanction. **Geneva** has taught us that even in the extremes of war and social upheaval, there is never any excuse for causing injury or death to the innocent and helpless. The **United Nations** and **International Human Rights,** although they at most times further the goals of peace and justice, at best still represent only the mutually-beneficial contracts agreed upon by the powers of *this* world.

The **Unborn Child is utterly Rights-less.** In the United States a pregnant female of any age has been granted a constitutional right to an abortion at any time during the pregnancy and for any reason. The preborn, by definition, is not a person, not a child, not a human being, but truly a cancer and a parasite, if so viewed by her mother.

Global Abortion Norms are apalling. The political, economic, social and moral state of this planet is such that more than a third of the children conceived by humanity are greeted not with rejoicing and thanks to God for a blessing, but rather with curses or cries of lament. Worldwide, there are few places – if any – where women assume that abortion is out of the question because neither their society nor their government will permit it.

Apartheid proved the maxim that "power corrupts, and absolute power corrupts absolutely." We must recognize that the American government's commitment to abortion is as fundamental as South Africa's was to apartheid. Since the preborn are utterly incapable of rising up to demand their own right to life, and their fate rests in the hands of a Church that is fragmented and over the hill [spiritually and morally], their chances of success must be recognized to be but a fraction of that which existed for the black majority who battled desperately and relentlessly for nearly a century before achieving *their own* political rights in South Africa.

5 Carol Lefcourt, *Women and the Law*, page 6.6 discusses the "best interests of the child" standard in custody cases.

6 Bandow, *Beyond Good Intentions, A Biblical View of Politics*, 166.

United States History is linear. When Americans invade a frontier, we subdue it so completely as to render it unrecognizable, and beyond any possibility of restoration to its former state.

Our **War for Independence** and our **Civil War** were essentially the same but for the result. The Colonies felt [as did the South] a rising sense of moral indignation over economic and political injustices perpetuated by the British [Northern] government. They enumerated their grievances and moral justifications, and then Declared their Independence [seceded from the Union]. Since sound moral arguments left Britain [the North] unconvinced of the wisdom of political division, a war was necessary to resolve the impasse.

When we address the underlying cause of the Civil War, we recognize that slavery was a greater moral evil than the mere denial of political and economic liberty in the Colonies; likewise, abortion [*killing* the innocent] is even higher on the moral scale than was slavery. That the notion of fighting a future civil war over abortion in America is now incomprehensible is not a measure of the holocaust but of our failure to feel in our hearts what we know in our heads: Abortion is the very worst form of genocide: familicide.

Christian **Discipleship** with regard to **slavery** is most instructive for our current dilemma. The Church in general was a guardian of the status quo, mostly silent with regard to slavery. Christian abolitionism emerged among various laymen, students and evangelists, with pastoral leadership lagging way behind. When the debate invaded the parish, congregations and denominations polarized and often parted over the complex moral issues.

As would be later evidenced during the Holocaust, bold public testimony against slavery, and self-sacrificial civil disobedience to rescue individual victims via the underground railroad were exhibited predominantly by those who held deeply internalized Christian ethics, rather than by those who had seemed to be outwardly religious. It was only through the valor of the firebrands and the righteous lawbreakers that the social climate heated up and the silent majority [including righteous but timid pastors] became mobilized for action.

Even when the public uproar rose to include rioting and bloodshed, the president's own polls judged the political clout of the World as superior to that of the morally motivated minority. It has been widely recognized that the Civil War was not fought over the moral issue of slavery but was precipitated only because the geographical arrangement of North versus South transformed the institution of slavery into the rallying point of overarching political and economic conflicts.

Slavery and abortion are uniquely similar in that they both represent extreme moral injustices against a class of people defined as subhuman, in which abominations became both entrenched in the society and vigorously protected by government at all levels. For any to assume or to imply that abortion can be abolished with less commitment or at a lower cost than occasioned the elimination of slavery would be both illogical and irresponsible.

Women's Rites of Passage in the United States must be acknowledged to have been linear developments, doors through which our society has passed and which have now closed behind us. The movements in this century that have secured various **Protections & Rights for women** have succeeded in establishing "equality with men" as a minimum standard, and have enshrined autonomy and pleasure as moral virtues, and relativism, pragmatism and positivism as cultural gods.

Anti-Family Changes have branded the stay-at-home wife-and-mom a cultural misfit. Children have ceased to be regarded as gifts from God. Family planning now features a consumerist approach, which warns that a baby in the shopping cart of your life will toss out a lot of your favorite selections and will mess up or eat up most of the rest.

The **Seeds of Destruction** planted by **Nietzsche, Malthus, Darwin, Marx,** and **Freud** have blossomed into godlessness, paranoia, rootlessness, rebellion, and sex-obsession. **Between** the **World Wars** we cast off restraint, lost respect for the law, and came to despise moral crusaders. We exchanged religious faith for a blind confidence in **techno-prosperity.**

The **Great Depression** set the stage for **postwar materialism. Synthetic heroes** transformed those people whose virtue would once have made them into crusaders for universal justice, into couch potatoes who now take great pride in rooting for the winning team. **Kinsey, Elvis and Madonna** reshaped us into a people obsessed with self, who are primarily valued by others on the basis of physical appearance and "sex-appeal." We are now a society in which strong religious convictions, virtue and noble character are considered laughable, if not outright pathological abnormalities.

The **Civil Rights Movement** and the **Clinton generation** have transformed government into the conscience of the nation [positivism], and taught the media that it has the power of God – to create reality out of thin air.

SCOPE and FOCUS
I. CONVICTIONS
II. PRETEXTS
III. MANDATE
IV. LEGACY
V. ABORTIVE LINKS
Recreational Sex
Reproductive Technology
Abortion Industry
Problems with abortion
Excuses for inaction
Goals of intervention
Types of intervention
Justifications offered
Necessity. Justifiable
Higher accountability
Governmental Action
Involuntary Complicity
Supreme Court
Politics
Legislation
Hyde amendment
F.A.C.E.
Blood money
Human life amendment
Partial birth (D & X)
Value of a child
Law Enforcement
Bureaucracy
Police power
Due Process in Court
Injunctions
Crimes charged
"Necessity" defense
"Jury nullification"
Pro-lifer Consequences
Social Climate
Education
Media
World view
Power
Bias
re: Christianity
re: Abortion
re: C.P.C.s
re: Rescue
Elite few
Religious Confusion
Polarization of Believers
Pluralism
Priorities
Theology
Liberalized
Social gospel
Leader crisis
Public Acts of Faith
Religious Right
Self-destructing
Marginalized
Revival time?
Abortion Controversy
"Catholic" view
Image of God
Personhood
Preborn human rights
The exceptions
Choice views
Has Church failed?
Personal Decision to Abort
Dissuade the mother
Last-ditch miracles
Real pro-life choices
VI. DILEMMA
VII. DESTINY

V. The Death Wish:
Links in the Abortive Chain

Thus far in *Orphans in Babylon* we have explored the clash of convictions between the Stewards and the Masters in our society. We have dissected the theoretical pretexts by which abortion is justified in the minds of some. We have examined the roles of a biblical disciple of a pro-life God. And we have looked for guidance in the lessons of history. We must now study the anatomy of this abortion monster in order to rightly discern the magnitude and the nature of the battles which lie before those who are destined to hear and to heed the trumpet call of His angels in this age.

In *Abortion Rites: A Social History of Abortion in America*, Marvin Olasky says: "Pro-abortion groups have been *wrong*... in their typical assertion that abortion was widely accepted before this century, that abortion was diffused throughout the population, that abortion became illegal because regular doctors sought to drive out competitors, and the abortion rates generally are unaffected by illegality or the development of alternatives."[1]

Joseph Scheidler wrote, "This book [*Closed: 99 Ways to Stop Abortion*] is based on the equation that abortion equals murder. It will make sense only to those who believe without question that abortion is the unjust, premeditated taking of an innocent human life... [It] is a collection of methods that can be used, and that have been used successfully, to stop abortions."[2]

"We call abortion *murder*, and yet we don't act like it's murder," said Randall Terry in 1988. "So we have no credibility. A holocaust of this magnitude deserves, in the political, social sense, aside from the religious, deserves massive upheaval to confront it. And that is exactly what we have not done. We have failed to produce the necessary social tension that affects political change."[3]

Olasky stresses this: "A pro-life activist who believes a change of law will eliminate abortion ignores the late nineteenth-century lesson that law by itself avails little unless programs emphasizing prevention and offering true compassion are in place and effective. A pro-life talk show guest who blames abortion on the sexual revolution of the 1960s and the Supreme Court edicts of the 1970s ignores the trends culminating in 1962 that made legalization likely."[4]

"Neither allowing abortion nor prohibiting it," says Thomas Hilgers, "has done anything to correct the underlying social and economic conditions which cause women to seek abortions. In the long run, only by confronting and solving these problems are we likely to find an exit from what has been termed 'the abortion dilemma.'"[5]

"Strategic targets" of anti-abortion activism were identified by R.C. Sproul in 1990 as: "the pro-choice adherents," "liberal churches and liberals," "the medical community," "politicians and public officials," "parents and the family," and "rescuing at abortion clinics."[6]

The strategy and techniques of the pro-life movement, according to Joseph Foreman, "must reflect [these] differences between child-killing in the womb and other forms of brutal physical assault: 1) The mother is willing, and finances it; 2) The Church permits it; 3) Some insurance covers abortion but not childbirth; 4) Intellectuals approve; 5) Feminists say abortion liberates a woman from male domination; 6) We (all) have permitted it to continue for years on end."[7]

1 Olasky, *Abortion Rites*, 283.
2 Scheidler, 17.
3 Randall Terry, "If You Believe" cassette. On the tape, Terry cites examples of movements which he said did "produce the necessary social tension:" the feminist movement, Vietnam war protest, civil rights, the birth of our nation, the end of slavery, women's voting rights movement.
4 Olasky, *Abortion Rites*, 283-4.
5 Thomas Hilgers, *Abortion and Social Justice*, 1972, 100.
6 Sproul, Abortion: *A Rational Look at an Emotional Issue*, 151-6.
7 Joseph Foreman, *Shattering the Darkness: The Crisis of the Cross in the Church Today*, 118.

The anatomy of the abortion monster

The *Roe v. Wade* decision did not unleash the abortion holocaust any more than a right-to-life amendment could end it. As we have seen, innumerable theories, events, movements and convictions have contributed to the cultural meltdown of which abortion is but one major symptom.

Behind the tragedy of a single abortion lies a series of contributing factors. God's loving will for the lives of those who are being aborted is bound by a chain of seven links; an x-ray of the anatomy of the abortion monster reveals seven vital organs.

Abortion is caused by: 1) Recreational [vs. procreational] sex; 2) Reproductive technology; 3) The abortion industry; 4) Governmental action; 5) The social climate; 6) Religious confusion; and 7) The personal decision of the mother to abort.

These are the seven theaters of the war against abortion. Crucial battles must be fought, and decisive victories can be won in each of these arenas, but in every instance we engage a powerful and entrenched enemy, on his own turf. God help us.

A. Recreational (vs. Procreational) Sex[1]

Appearing on "Good Morning America," Jane Fonda "pronounced herself 'stunned' that a 1996 federal law established state grants totaling $250 million for programs stressing abstinence until marriage."[2] Yet it is a simple fact that if people shared sexual intercourse only when they were ready and willing to parent the child they might conceive, there would be no more abortions.

Margaret Sanger, we are told by Joseph Scheidler, "believed strongly in the program of eugenics. Her idea was that society should be made up of a breed of thoroughbreds and the inferior members should not reproduce. She believed sex was an end in itself. Sex could be used for reproduction by those who *should* reproduce, but for those who should not, the poor and minorities, it should serve strictly as a form of entertainment."[3]

"On television," Robert Bork reveals, "recreational sex is pervasive and is presented as acceptable about six times as often as it is rejected... The moral relativism of the Sixties is now television's public morality."[4]

An article in *Newsweek* in 1995 confirmed that use of the Pill results in pregnancy much more frequently than the public has been led to believe. Its statistics showed that false confidence in the Pill's protection increased sexual activity by so much, and the pill allowed "breakthrough pregnancy" so often that more women than ever experienced unwanted pregnancies! Newsweek asserted: "The pill was designed to let women control when and if they got pregnant. Of course, it also freed them and their partners to view sex as recreation. But that was before sexual freedom gave way to increasing numbers of out-of-wedlock births."[5]

The research of Akerlof and Yellen agrees, saying that "reproductive-technology-shock swept away old social mores. It made it harder for women to say 'no' to sex with men who weren't willing to say 'yes' to marriage," [And when a child is conceived,] "Some men now believe that a woman's choice not to have an abortion gives them the choice not to support the child"[6] This is no different from the attitude of health care plans that pressure plan members to abort babies *suspected* of being less than perfect with a threat to deny plan services to the child if it is allowed to live.

The sexual revolution has resulted in the United States having the highest teenage pregnancy rate in the world.[7] Since the U.S. is also the leader in at-school "sex education" and ready access to birth control, one could easily conclude that these factors are contributors rather than remedies of the problem.

During the years between 1971 and 1979, the period when legalized abortion further reduced the fear of unwanted pregnancy, and consequently boosted sexual activity, "the percentage of teen girls who had ever had intercourse increased from 28 to 46 percent. By 1985, about 40 percent of the unmarried teenagers between ages fifteen and nineteen were sexually active."[8]

Here is more shocking news, from 1996: "Two-thirds of the babies born to teenage mothers in a new California study were fathered by adults some four to six years older than the girls, not by fellow classmates, as long suspected... Girls in high school had babies with men on average 4.2 years older, while junior-high girls bore children to men on average 6.7 years older. Among 10 to 14-year-old girls, some 27 percent of the fathers were age 20 to 24."[9]

America's government spent $14.56 Billion on teenage "birth control" programs from 1971 to 1992. They have been as effective as pouring gasoline on a fire: the percentage of teens who are sexually active doubled, from 29.7% to 59.1%; the teen pregnancy rate increased by 55%, from 95 per thousand to 147 per thousand; and teen abortions increased 213%, from 190,000 to 595,000.[10]

American teenagers now conceive over a million babies a year; they abort about half of them.[11]

"In the old days there were three fears which went far to keep a grip on sexual intercourse before and outside of marriage – the fear of detection, the fear of infection, and the fear of conception."[12]

...Young people today aren't afraid of anything.

Recreational sex is more American than baseball – a lot more kids are playing it.

The Church must, without apology, proclaim a godly moral standard, particularly to its young people. It must also intensify current efforts to produce and to promote programs which will raise the moral index of the nation.

Please Note the "Reproductive History Timeline" at the bottom of the next several pages.

SCOPE and FOCUS
I. CONVICTIONS
II. PRETEXTS
III. MANDATE
IV. LEGACY
V. ABORTIVE LINKS
Recreational Sex
Reproductive Technology
Contraception
Birth control
IUD
the Pill
Low-dose Pill
Pill failure rate
Abortifacient, the Pill?
Tough truth re: Pill
the Mini-pill
Vaccines
Depo-Provera
Norplant
RU-486/Mifepristone
Morning-after
the-Pill, the morn.after
Do-it-yourself
The cutting edge
Preferences shift
Victories vs. repro-tech
what Magnitude?
Respect & fear
unlikely Crusaders
Fertility pitfalls
Abortion Industry
Direct Action
Intervention to Defend
Governmental Action
Social Climate
Religious Confusion
Personal Decision to Abort
VI. DILEMMA
VII. DESTINY

B. Reproductive Technology

"The historically sharp dividing line between birth control and abortion has well and truly been obliterated by the New Abortionists: The pharmaceutical companies," says Brian Clowes.[13]

Pragmatic double speak is at its best [worst] in the pro-abortion camp generally, and in the reproductive industry in particular. The people who so totally brainwashed society into substituting the word *choice* for the act of *abortion*, has been successful in blurring the meanings of *birth control* and *contraception* and are now well on their way to a radical and false redefinition of the word *pregnancy*.

Back in 1963, before it perfected the art of speaking with a forked tongue, Planned Parenthood sometimes told the truth: "Is birth control an abortion? Definitely not. An abortion kills the life of a baby after it has begun. It is dangerous to your life and health. It may make you sterile so that when you want a child you cannot have it. Birth control merely postpones the beginning of life."[14]

Well, part of what they said was true. Since abortion was still illegal and their business was birth control, they told the truth about some of the dangers of abortion and particularly that it "kills the life of a baby after [conception]." They were, however, already misleading the public about their own business. *Postpone* does not apply at all, unless they were to say that birth control postpones getting pregnant. So that WE are all on the same page: contraception is the prevention of a conception that would otherwise have occurred when a sperm cell fertilizes an ovum [egg], creating at that instant a unique new human person. Once conception has taken place, contraception can no longer occur, and it will require some form of birth control to kill that child before it gets born.

There is a five- to seven-day window of opportunity for some killing of the tiny person to take place before the little guy implants in the wall of the uterus. Abortifacients, either mechanical, chemical or a combination of the two, are often used to accomplish that act of killing. The master thought-manipulators have been busy for years shifting the emphasis away from conception and toward pregnancy: "Emergency Contraception Pills [ECPs] work during the first 3 days after unprotected intercourse but before pregnancy begins... [They] do not cause an abortion. An abortion is the termination of pregnancy; Emergency Contraceptive Pills work **before** a woman becomes pregnant."[15]

Such propagandists are capitalizing on the fact that in general usage it seems equivalent to say that you don't want to conceive a child and that you don't want to become pregnant. So "birth control" is the industry that seeks to thwart both conception and implantation, in an effort to stop pregnancies. Most accurately, they are in the business of pregnancy prevention. They are not ignorant, they are sly; they know that a pro-life Christian might be interested in reducing the likelihood of conceiving a child right now, but under no circumstances does she want to do anything which would interfere with the normal development of a child she does conceive.

The truth is that an IUD [intrauterine device] is mechanical. It is a plastic or metal "T" which is placed inside the womb to irritate it so much that the lining goes into defense mode and prevents the implantation of any baby who might come knocking. But these same concept-twisters intentionally try to deceive someone who is morally opposed to killing her child into thinking that an IUD is not abortifacient: "Why might an IUD be used? ...If you want to do everything possible to avoid pregnancy because you are unalterably opposed to having an induced abortion should a pregnancy occur."[16]

1 The identification of recreational sex as one of the seven contributing factors behind the abortion holocaust does not mean that the researcher wants to take the bliss out of the marriage relationship. These facts are made available for the edification of a wide variety of readers!
2 *Christian Times* newspaper, 11/'97, 5.
3 Scheidler, 83.
4 Bork, *Slouching Towards Gomorrah*, 127.
5 *Newsweek*, 3-13-95, 61. Not in bibliography.
6 *Press*, 11-25-96, A10.
7 Geoff Tunnicliffe, *One Hundred Ways to Change Your World*, 100.
8 Susan and Marvin Olasky, *More than Kindness: A Compassionate Approach to Crisis Childbearing*, 22-3.
9 *Press*, 4-18-96, A12.
10 Brian Clowes, *Pro-Life Activist's Encyclopedia*, page 82.11.
11 *Press*, 4-18-96, A12.
12 William Barclay, *Ethics in a Permissive Society*, 206.
13 Clowes, *Pro-Life Activist's Encyclopedia*, page 31.2.
14 Planned Parent pamphlet, August, 1963, in J.C. Willke, *Handbook on Abortion*, 187.
15 Robert Hatcher, *Emergency Contraception: The Nation's Best-Kept Secret*, 29, 31.
16 Hatcher, 63.

A narrative overview of how today's birth control came to be

A **Timeline** is provided at the bottom of the next few pages for those who wish to scan the historical development of reproductive knowledge and technology, and our **culture's emerging attitudes**. It is known that from earliest recorded history violence was sometimes inflicted on a woman in such ways as to induce her body to miscarry a child. With the occasional exception of direct physical blows to the abdomen, most of the crude methods consisted of poisons ingested orally or vaginal intrusions – direct chemical, herbal or mechanical attacks on the vulnerable preborn.

By the early decades of our **national history** not much had changed; the surgical instruments began to reflect Yankee ingenuity, and abortion "pills" were creatively advertised in the penny press. Most of the abortionists' trade was from the prostitutes who averaged 1.8 abortions per year, and who also were the primary market for the abortifacient pharmaceuticals. Both forms of birth control were imprecise, to say the least, and Joseph Lister's revolutionary discovery that antiseptic surgical methods could drastically reduce mortality from infections was not made until after the Civil War. As we detailed earlier, a complex marriage of goals and sympathies resulted in the criminalization of abortion in the second half of the 1800s.

Significant developments in reproductive technology included the cervical cap in 1860, sanitary surgery in 1865, the contraceptive diaphragm in 1882, X-rays in 1895, and the IUD in 1909. Condom use was popularized during and after World War I, and through the efforts of Margaret Sanger, who opened her first contraceptive clinic in 1916. The year 1929 saw the development of penicillin and also the discovery of the functions of progesterone. A little-known fact is that a very effective [although equally dangerous] morning-after pill was available from 1940 until 1970. The year 1950 saw the invention of synthetic progesterone and the successful transplanting of an embryo from one cow to another. Amniocentesis was developed in 1952, the first sex-change operation was performed in 1953, and the oral contraceptive Pill was invented in 1954 [approved and hugely popular by 1960], while ultrasound began in 1958.

Much credit for the **sexual revolution of the Sixties** can be given to ten years of sexual-attitude-adjustments from Kinsey, leading up to the availability of the Pill from 1960 on. Thalidomide and rubella brought reproductive tragedy into the national spotlight between 1962 and 1965. The invention of the suction aspiration/suction curettage method of abortion in 1970 was just in time to facilitate the proliferation of abortion clinic start-ups spawned by *Roe v. Wade* in 1973, the same year that the convulsive hormonal drug Prostin F2-Alpha was developed to cause or assist in creating a miscarriage.

TIMELINE

REPRODUCTIVE HISTORY

1600s Microbes are identified & described. Condom is invented.
1677 Sperm are identified & described.
1827 Human egg is first discovered. Prior to this discovery, woman was seen as receptacle for the "man's seed."
1830s Abortion pills through mail-order are widely advertised. **1830 – 1880** Surgical abortion business flourishes – even where "illegal" – with no unified Christian opposition.
1840s Union of sperm and ovum is demonstrated.
1854 Dr. Hugh Hodge, esteemed embryologist, concludes that life begins at conception and that abortion is murder. He impresses his convictions on his pre-med students and on the AMA. **1855** Prominent Boston Ob/Gyn H.R. Storer begins writing anti-abortion books. The AMA will soon tap him to launch the first national right-to-life organization. **1856** When a local girl nearly dies from mail-order abortion pills, pharmacist Samuel Taylor begins a crusade to influence pharmacists, doctors and legislators. He drafts anti-chemical-abortifacient legislation adopted in 16 states.
1857-1880 Physician's Crusade Against Abortion.
1859 Charles Darwin's *Origin of Species is* published.
1860 The contraceptive cervical cap is developed • In spite of high maternal mortality rates due to unsanitary surgical methods and the absence of antibiotics, and the fact that 2/3 of the clients are prostitutes [having 1.8 abortions/year], the surgical abortion rate in 1860 is probably at least 1/3 to 1/2 of what it will be in 1990 [per Olasky's figures].
1865 Joseph Lister develops Antiseptic surgery; [ten years earlier would have *greatly* reduced the fatality rate in the Civil War]. **1869** Widely-circulated booklets of pro-life sermons provide biblical evidence that life begins at conception and that abortion is murder. **1870s** Many states outlaw contraceptives.
1875 Doctors prove that human sperm and egg unite at conception.
1882 Contraceptive diaphragm is popularized.
1895 X-Rays are discovered.
1900 One standard abortion pill used by prostitutes is taken for three days along with hot baths.
1909 IUD The intrauterine device is invented. **1914** Margaret Sanger's *The Woman Rebel* magazine promotes the idea that contraception is an alternative to abortion.
1915-1935 Intrauterine device sales begin. By the mid-1930s multiple companies are exploiting the lucrative IUD market.
1916 Margaret Sanger's first [contraceptive] clinic. **1918** *Medical World* calls for a repeal of birth control bans, but reaffirms that abortion "should not be performed except, if ever, as a last resort to save the life of the mother." **1920-1929** Birth control advocates shrewdly promote the economic plight of large families.
1929 Penicillin is developed. It will dramatically reduce the danger of infection and death in all surgeries, including abortions.
• Progesterone is discovered to do two things: sustain pregnancy and stop ovulation. **1930s-1960s** Conservatives taking a hard line against birth control alienate those moderates who see no biblical prohibition of contraceptives for married couples. Prohibition and contraception controversies yield two generations of ambivalent Christians who believe that "I shouldn't impose my views on others." **1931** The liberalized Council of Churches caves in to Margaret Sanger's staff's lobbying blitz and agrees that contraception should be a matter of personal choice for married people. Many denominations echo the view: Quakers, Northern Presbyterians, the Congregational church, the Methodist-Episcopal church, and several Baptist groups. This shift sabotages any possible united moral stand by Protestants and Catholics on any issue, including abortion. **1933** Hitler comes to power in Germany, and he legalizes abortion.

SCOPE and FOCUS
I. CONVICTIONS
II. PRETEXTS
III. MANDATE
IV. LEGACY
V. ABORTIVE LINKS
Recreational Sex
Reproductive Technology
Contraception
Birth control
IUD
the Pill
Low-dose Pill
Pill failure rate
Abortifacient, the Pill?
Tough truth re: Pill
the Mini-pill
Vaccines
Depo-Provera
Norplant
RU-486/Mifepristone
Morning-after
the-Pill, the morn.after
Do-it-yourself
The cutting edge
Preferences shift
Victories vs. repro-tech
what Magnitude?
Respect & fear
unlikely Crusaders
Fertility pitfalls
Abortion Industry
Direct Action
Intervention to Defend
Governmental Action
Social Climate
Religious Confusion
Personal Decision to Abort
VI. DILEMMA
VII. DESTINY

1978 brought the birth of the first test-tube baby; the first human embryo-transfer was achieved in 1983, and the first fetal surgery was performed one year later. The abortion pill, RU-486 was invented in 1988, in which year forced-twinning of multiple, identical bull calves was also achieved. The FDA approved Norplant in 1990 and gave the green light to RU-486 production and testing in 1994. In 1997 we witnessed the first successful cloning of an adult mammal, a sheep.

Contraception

John Ankerberg reaffirms what we stated earlier: "The word 'contraceptive' is being misused by some people today. They use this word in referring to drugs that really end a pregnancy by destroying the already developing human. But a *true* contraceptive should do no more than *prevent* the sperm and egg from uniting to form a zygote, i.e., a human life."[1]

The word is getting out: "Increasing numbers of women are beginning to realize that certain forms of 'contraceptives' – including the IUD," says F.L. Smith, "and the so-called 'morning after' pill – are in fact abortifacients."[2]

Birth control

"With social and political organizations promoting a pro-choice/pro-abortion agenda, any device that offers simplicity of use, longevity of effect, and little evidence of side effects becomes an attractive product to promote in the United States... under the guise of contraceptive choice and population control," says Lawrence Roberge.[3]

George Grant provides a stark appraisal of the current state of reproductive technology: "Planned Parenthood's program of birth control is nothing but foreplay for abortion. Besides the fact that it is fraught with awful side effects, complications, and medical risks, it is incapable of preventing unwanted pregnancies as well. Planned Parenthood's entire myth is an empty charade. We simply cannot contend or pretend otherwise."[4]

1 Ankerberg, *When Does Life Begin? And 39 Other Tough Questions about Abortion*, 157.

2 F. LaGard Smith, *When Choice Becomes God*, 113.

3 Roberge, in Kilner, *Bioethics and the Future of Medicine, A Christian Appraisal*, 180.

4 Grant, *Grand Illusions: The Legacy of Planned Parenthood*, 30-1.

1935-1938 *Facts and Frauds in Women's Hygiene* reports that 50% of birth control clinic clients who rely on condoms are becoming pregnant. The trade magazine *Manufacturing Chemist* reveals that 9% of condoms fail to contracept. Such information is successfully denied public exposure.
• Sweden becomes the first democratic, Christian nation to legalize abortion in the 1900s.

1940s A very effective morning-after pill is introduced: high-dose estrogen, called DES. Not until the 1970s is its use stopped when research uncovers serious long term dangers to mothers and their children.

1942 In *Skinner v. Oklahoma,* the Supreme Court first recognizes reproductive autonomy as a basic civil right, "the right to have offspring," on equal protection grounds, regarding involuntary sterilization of certain convicted felons.

1946 In *Bombrest v. Katz* a federal district court sets a new precedent, abandoning *Dietrich*'s 1884 "mother's body" ruling in favor of the individuality of a viable preborn who was injured. The federal court defines "child" as "an unborn or recently born human being." **1949** In *Williams v. Marion Rapid Transit,* the Supreme Court of Ohio declares that an unborn child is a person within the meaning of the Ohio Constitution.

1950 Synthetic progesterone is created.
• First successful transplanting of a cow-to-cow embryo.
•Despite protracted schisms over contraception, every major Christian and non-Christian church denomination in the U.S. remains "vigorously and unashamedly" anti-abortion [Clowes, 42].

1952 Amniocentesis is developed.
• First sex-change operation. **1953** *Kelly v. Gregory* is a New York tort case which holds that viability is no longer necessary, and a preborn injured during the third month of his mother's pregnancy was a separate human being entitled to damages. • In *May v. Anderson*, the Supreme Court rules that the right to bear and raise children is "far more precious than property rights."

1954 Oral contraceptive Pill is invented and tested.
•Planned Parenthood holds an international conference calling for "reform" of abortion-restricting laws, worldwide.

1955 In *Mallison v. Pomeroy,* the Supreme Court of Oregon affirms that the state has recognized "the separate entity of an unborn child by protecting him in his property rights and against criminal conduct..." and concludes that an unborn child is a person within the meaning of the state constitution.
• Planned Parenthood Federation of America sponsors a three-day conference in order to win support for legalization of abortion among leaders in medicine, psychiatry, law, sociology and other fields. • PPF's conference proceedings emerge as a book, which *Time* publicizes, and which *Coronet* magazine touts as "the most comprehensive and authoritative book of information ever compiled on the vital subject of abortion."

1958 Ultrasound examination of the preborn begins.

1960 Birth control PILL first marketed. The oral birth control Pill is so masterfully promoted as a "contraceptive" that few voices are raised to suggest its abortifacient effect, and those questions are smothered by nonstop propaganda heralding a new age of sexual freedom and equality for women. Nearly forty years – and countless anonymous lives – will pass before the blissfully ignorant begin to hear the stark truths about the abortifacient nature of the Pill.

1962-1965 Anguish and empathy, nationally and internationally, are focused on the mothers' "nightmare" of birthing deformed babies following the recent American rubella epidemic (20,000), and the thalidomide tragedy in Europe (5,000-7,000). Abortion proponents are cranking up the "hard cases" rhetoric. • The Gallup poll, for the first time, mentions abortion: Asked whether Sherri Finkbine [an American who had taken the European tranquilizer, Thalidomide] did right or wrong "in having this abortion operation" [in Sweden], 52% say "right," 32% say "wrong," and 16% have no opinion.

SCOPE and FOCUS
I. CONVICTIONS
II. PRETEXTS
III. MANDATE
IV. LEGACY
V. ABORTIVE LINKS
Recreational Sex
Reproductive Technology
Contraception
Birth control
IUD
the Pill
Low-dose Pill
Pill failure rate
Abortifacient, the Pill?
Tough truth re: Pill
the Mini-pill
Vaccines
Depo-Provera
Norplant
RU-486/Mifepristone
Morning-after
the-Pill, the morn.after
Do-it-yourself
The cutting edge
Preferences shift
Victories vs. repro-tech
what Magnitude?
Respect & fear
unlikely Crusaders
Fertility pitfalls
Abortion Industry
Governmental Action
Social Climate
Religious Confusion
Personal Decision to Abort
VI. DILEMMA
VII. DESTINY

Abortifacient birth control

In February 1992, writing in opposition to a Louisiana law banning abortion, Tulane Law School Professor Ruth Colker wrote, "Because nearly all birth control devices, except the diaphragm and condom, operate between the time of conception... and implantation... the statute would appear to ban most contraceptives."[1] Colker referred to all those methods including the Pill, which sometimes prevent implantation. Her point was that abortion should not be banned because "nearly all" birth control is abortivacient and would be outlawed by anti-abortion laws! While she used the argument to pragmatically assert that anti-abortion laws would be unenforceable, her logic serves as well to condemn abortifacient birth control.

Truth is better than fiction

In the next few pages we will be contrasting the **claims** made in Hatcher's *Emergency Contraception: The Nation's Best Kept Secret* with more reliable data provided by sources such as: The Christian Center for Bio-Ethics of Portland, Oregon; *The Pro-Life Activist's Encyclopedia*, by Brian Clowes; Dr. J.C. Willke's *Handbook on Abortion*; and Randy Alcorn's *Does the Birth Control Pill Cause Abortions?* which was effectively reprinted in the September/October 1997 issue of *Life Advocate* magazine.

1 Colker, from the *Dallas Morning News*, 2-6-92, 23A, in *Life Advocate*, Sept-Oct/'97, 16.

2 Christian Center for Bio-Ethics, "Keeping The Promise to Protect Your Family: Would You Gamble With the Life of Your Child?" pamphlet.

3 Hatcher, *Emergency Contraception: The Nation's Best-Kept Secret*, 116.

4 Hatcher, 63: "Several studies have examined the insertion of copper IUDs for emergency contraceptive treatment. In studies of over 1,300 women who have used the post-coital IUD, only 1 became pregnant."

5 Hatcher, 2.

6 Hatcher, 68

TIMELINE, continued from previous page.

1964 *Life* magazine gives public praise to physicians who perform illegal abortions on women who have contracted rubella while pregnant, calling them "conscientious doctors of highest integrity who acted in defiance of community convention and state law."

1965 In *Griswold v. Connecticut,* the Supreme Court mandates that state law may not restrict access of married persons to contraceptives. In dissenting, Justice Potter Stewart says, "I can find no such general right of privacy in the Bill of Rights, in any other part of the Constitution, or in any case ever before decided by this Court... it is not the function of this Court to decide cases on the basis of community standards." Clowes [page 89.90] says that *Griswold's* "privacy" makes it a more important case than *Roe*. **1966** National Organization for Women [N.O.W.] is established with the liberalization of abortion laws as a major goal. **1967** In *Gleitman v Cosgrove,* a wrongful-birth suit, the Supreme Court of New Jersey states: "The right to life is inalienable in our society. A court cannot say what defect should prevent an embryo from being allowed life... The sanctity of the single human life is the decisive factor in this suit in tort... We firmly believe the right of their child to live is greater than and precludes their right not to endure emotional and financial injury." • California is the first of 14 states [by 1972] to adopt the [1962] American Law Institute-recommended guidelines for exceptions permitting abortion. California doctors quickly demonstrate that pregnancy itself can be defined as a "grave impairment to health," to justify *any* abortion. •Hawaii's first CPC [Crisis Pregnancy Center]. • The American Medical Association [AMA], abandons 100-years of being pro-life and calls for decriminalization of abortion.

1968 Pope Paul VI, in his *Humanae Vitae* encyclical, reaffirms the sanctity of life. In the public arena, for lack of Protestant voices, opposition to abortion is successfully dubbed the "Catholic" position. • 53% of Catholic couples now use some form of birth control other than the approved rhythm method, according to a Ryder-Westoff survey [Clouse, 189].

1968 The American Baptist Convention endorses abortion on demand in the 1st trimester. • Nationally and internationally there is a strong movement... toward legalized abortion focusing the debate on the exceptions, the hard cases: life of the mother and rape.
• Alan Guttmacher, president of Planned Parenthood, declares, "The fetus... is merely a group of specialized cells that do not differ materally from other cells" [Mnookin, 164]. • Planned Parenthood, like Zero Population Growth, now promotes abortion on demand.
• A Christian missionary doctor has already defined the abortifacient function of both the popular IUD, and the experimental "morning-after pill," calling both "microscopic murder" [Clouse, 191; *also* Shaw, 169]. • These concerns are quashed by many who should be on God's side; Earl J. Reeves says, "Even the question of the possibility of destroying life by destroying a fertilized egg through an IUD or a pill seems likely to be dismissed by most evangelicals as a highly theoretical and legalistic controversy" [Clouse, 193].

1969 First in vitro fertilization [human sperm joins egg].
• The new morning after pill is still experimental. • In parts of America where only "therapeutic" abortions are legal, doctors are willing to certify that 8,000 to 10,000 abortions were necessary to save the life of the mother. • Forty of the 50 United States still hold abortion a crime, except to save the mother's life. • National Council of Churches approves abortion to preserve mother's life *or health*. • The fictitious "statistics" are now routinely repeated: one million illegal abortions causing 8 thousand maternal deaths per year.

1970 The "vacuum" method, later to be called suction curettage, is instantly very popular. At least one entrepreneur makes day time use of one wing of a motel, rolling a suction machine from room to room. • In *Keeler v. Superior Court,* the California Supreme Court rules that the unborn are not human beings as pertains to murder. **1971** Nearly a half-million *legal* abortions this year.

1972 In *Eisenstadt v. Baird,* the Supreme Court extends reproductive privacy to the unwed: access to contraceptives equal to that previously guaranteed only to married couples.
• Thirty of the 50 United States still hold abortion a crime, except to save the mother's life.

IUD, the intrauterine device

The Christian Center for Bio-Ethics says:

"The Intrauterine Device, or IUD is not a contraceptive. That is, it does not prevent fertilization, the joining of an egg and sperm, from occurring (conception). It does nothing to disrupt ovulation, the menstrual cycle, or to thicken the cervical mucous. The IUD is a device which is inserted into the womb and which creates a hostile environment by irritating and thinning the endometrium, the lining of the uterus. Such a state of irritation leaves the uterine wall unprepared for the process of implantation when a newly conceived baby attempts to cleave to the wall of the uterus... Understanding that human life begins at conception, this intentional disruption of the uterine environment produces an early abortion. The unborn child, unable to implant, starves for lack of nutrition, dies, and is sloughed off during the next menstrual cycle."[2]

We showed earlier [page 89] that the Hatcher book recommends IUDs for those who are "unalterably opposed" to having an abortion! Here is its specific summary ["How It Works"] of what a t-shaped mechanical device placed in the womb does in order to keep a woman from getting pregnant: "IUD: A plastic device inserted into the uterus through the cervix to prevent pregnancy, primarily by preventing fertilization. The Copper T 380A IUD (ParaGard) releases small amounts of copper and the Progesterone "T" IUD (Progestasert System) releases progesterone."[3] This was the total summary of how an IUD works.

Since Hatcher correctly states, elsewhere, that conception can only take place within three days of intercourse [because the sperm then die], and makes no mention that an IUD "works" by thwarting implantation, he has no basis upon which to state that: "One type of IUD called the Copper T 380A (and marketed as ParaGard), which is regularly used as a long-term method of birth control, is an extremely effective [99.9%][4] form of emergency contraception when inserted into the uterus within 5 to 7 days after unprotected intercourse,"[5] or that, "If an IUD is inserted as an emergency contraceptive, it may be inserted within the 5 to 7 days following unprotected intercourse (before implantation)."[6]

[*This analysis is continued on the next page.*]

1973 In *Roe v. Wade*, the Supreme Court rules that the "right to privacy" makes abortion on demand a constitutional right, voids the pro-life statutes of 30 states and prohibits legislative protection of preborn life.
- In *Doe v. Bolton*, the Supreme Court gives a green light to abortion *clinics* and expands "maternal health" to include "general maternal well-being," justifying abortion throughout 9 months.
- Immediately after the *Roe* decision, the National Conference of Catholic Bishops proclaims "...no Court opinion can change the law of God prohibiting the taking of innocent human life" (Clowes, 43). • Nobel laureate James Watson asserts that the the only "rational, compassionate" policy would be to give parents a 3-day grace period after a child's birth, during which they may exercise a lethal choice, euthanasia.
- Prostin F2-Alpha, a synthetic hormonal drug developed by Upjohn, is designed to induce violent early labor, causing miscarriage. **1975** The District Court of Utah, in *T H v. Jones*, holds that "privacy" includes a minor's fundamental right to abortion. The Supreme Court lets it stand.

1976 In *Planned Parenthood v. Danforth*, the Supreme Court invalidates spousal or parental consent requirements for abortion [hence men have no reproductive rights], and holds that states may not require abortionists to attempt to sustain viable abortees, and may not prohibit salt-solution abortions in order to decrease a preborn's suffering. • Polls show that barely 1% of the public consider abortion a national election issue. • Dr. Joycelyn Elders [later to become Clinton's Surgeon General] says, "Abortion has had an important and positive public health effect... the number of Down's syndrome infants in Washington state in 1976 was 64% lower than it would have been without legal abortion" [*Life Advocate*, 2/'94, 33.]

1977 In *Carey v. Population Services International*, the Supreme Court finds a constitutional right of minors to have contraceptives. • "Pope Paul VI not only calls abortion a threat to world peace but brands women who have abortions killers who 'freely and consciously murder the fruit of their womb'" [Francke, 249].
- The National Right to Life Committee is boycotting the March of Dimes, which endorses amniocentesis, and thereby possible abortion of handicapped or damaged preborns.

1978 First test-tube baby. • Depo-Provera is available.

1983 First human embryo transfer.

1984 First fetal surgery.

1985 Clowes estimates 55 million surgical abortions [world] annually and "at least twice as many more ...by abortifacient 'contraceptives'" [2-21].
- *The Silent Scream* film, hosted by ex-abortionist Bernard Nathanson, jolts all who see it.

1988 RU-486, "the abortion pill," is invented.
- Seven genetically identical bull calves are produced from laboratory-altered embryos. Forced-twinning in animals by breaking a single embryo into pieces can produce as many as 20 identical [calves] from a single "good-blood-line" mating.

1989 *Webster v. Reproductive Health Services, Inc*. The Supreme Court has been invalidating state efforts to protect viable preborns, but this year it turns, upholding a Missouri requirement that doctors must test for fetal viability if at least 20 weeks old, and prohibiting abortion if the baby is found to be viable. "Additionally, state funds, employees, and hospitals may not be used to provide or counsel for abortions" [Clowes, page 89.16]. Chief Justice William Rehnquist asserts that the "key elements" of the 'abortion right' – the right to privacy and the "Constitutional right to abortion" – simply do not exist.

1990 Norplant is approved by the FDA as a "contraceptive."

1992 **FDA approves Depo-Provera.** • In *Planned Parenthood v. Casey*, the Supreme Court says that a state may not require that a husband be notified of his wife's abortion. It does, however, uphold Pennsylvania's requirements of informed consent, 24-hour waiting period, required reporting of abortion data, and parental consent with judicial bypass. • *Casey* includes Justice O'Connor's "undue burden" criterion which holds that a state may not create "absolute obstacles or severe limitations on the abortion decision." • In *Casey*, Justices O'Connor, Kennedy and Souter reaffirm *Roe*'s mandate that a woman has a right to abortion prior to viability.

1993 Female condom is invented.

1994 RU-486 is to be produced in the USA under a agreement signed between a New York abortion-rights group and the patent holders.
- San Francisco doctors begin testing RU-486 as a "morning-after" pill – it was designed for use after a woman knows she is pregnant. •The Supreme Court refuses to hear the appeal of Alexander Loce, who was convicted of blocking access to an abortion clinic to save the life of his own preborn child.

1997 First cloning of an adult mammal, a sheep.

[*Continued from previous page*]

As a matter of fact, if Hatcher were willing to admit that the IUD's effect is to prevent implantation he would stress that it should be inserted within the first *four* days, because the definition of *implantation* in his own book tells us that implantation is "The process of a fertilized egg becoming attached to the lining of the uterus. Implantation occurs 5 to 7 days after fertilization. Once implantation is complete, a woman is considered pregnant."[1] He has painted himself into a corner. When he wants to assert that Pills used as emergency contraception do not "abort a pregnancy," he says, "Abortion is the termination of a pregnancy. Emergency contraceptive Pills work **before** a woman becomes pregnant."[2] He is caught saying that implantation [the start of pregnancy] occurs between 5 and 7 days after conception, and that the IUD can be used as emergency contraception 5-7 days after fertilization. His contorted mis-definition of abortion is that it is the termination [not of the life of a conceived human, but] of a womb-implanted one. In these statements, Hatcher has tried to imply that the IUD "only" prevents implantation, but he has inadvertently confirmed that for children who implant on the 5th, 6th or early on the 7th day, the pregnancy has already begun when an **abortion** is caused by the insertion of an IUD on the 7th day.

It is not that Mr. Hatcher *should know better*; he knows. His writing is simply a prime example of the incessant, deceptive propaganda campaign waged by the advocates of the killing of unborn babies.

The United States Food and Drug Administration [FDA] states in its *Text of Required Patient Information for IUDs*, that "IUDs seem to interfere in some manner with the implantation of the fertilized egg in the lining of the uterine cavity. The IUD does not prevent ovulation."[3]

Dr. Willke says that the effect of an IUD "is to prevent implantation. This is clearly abortive."[4]

1 Hatcher, 12.
2 Hatcher, 31.
3 FDA, in Clowes, *Pro-Life Activist's Encyclopedia*, page 32.1.
4 J.C. Willke, *Handbook on Abortion*, 183.
5 *Newsweek Extra*, 76.
6 Unnamed writer, in William Barclay, *Ethics in a Permissive Society*, 205.
7 Reeves, in Robert Clouse, *Protest and Politics*, 183.
8 Alexander, *Women's Legal Rights*, 18.
9 Randy Alcorn, *Life Advocate*, Sept.-Oct. 1997, 13.
10 Alcorn, *Life Advocate*, Sept.-Oct. 1997, inside front cover.
11 Brian Clowes, *Pro-Life Activist's Encyclopedia*, page 31.6.
12 J.C. Willke, *Handbook on Abortion*, 184.
13 Hatcher, 114.
14 *Physician's Desk Reference*, in *Life Advocate*, Sept.-Oct. 1997, 14.
15 Brian Clowes, page 31.5.
16 Alcorn, *Pro-Life Answers to Pro-Choice Arguments*, 1992, 118.
17 Shaw, *Abortion on Trial*, 169.
18 *Life Advocate*, Sept.-Oct. 1997, 23.
19 Clouse, 191-2.
20 Cottrell, 33-4.

The Pill

A *Newsweek Extra*, Winter 1997-98, had as its theme "The Power of Invention." It stated, "The Pill remains in common usage, and it's hard to think of a pharmaceutical that's had a greater effect on American life and mores."[5]

With an interesting choice of words, in 1971 a Christian writer in Britain asserted: "Contraception found its peak in the pill, which is easy to take, normally safe in action and almost infallible in effect. The methods of contraception have been so refined and rendered so effective that it is now not necessary for anyone to have a baby unless they want to."[6]

Three years earlier, in 1969, American Earl J. Reeves was only slightly less enthusiastic and more than a bit prophetic: "Most of the practical problems associated with birth control – uncertainty, messiness, interruption of the normal pattern of intercourse – have, therefore been either eliminated or drastically reduced by the advent of the Pill. Even the remaining problems of counting days and remembering to take the daily dosage may soon be eliminated by new techniques."[7]

Feminist Shana Alexander in 1975 heaped massive praise on the Pill for its effect in the emancipation of women: "I wonder anew whether and how the human female will ever transcend the lower, more dependent, less rights-ful station to which her reproductive nature has until the last-minute invention of The Pill confined her."[8]

Problems with the Pill result in the Low-dose Pill

"After the Pill had been on the market fifteen years," says Alcorn, "many serious negative side effects of estrogen had been clearly proven [examples & documentation are cited]... Beginning in the mid-seventies, manufacturers of the Pill steadily decreased the content of estrogen and progestin in their products. The average dosage of estrogen in the Pill declined from 150 micrograms in 1960 to 35 micrograms in 1988... [and] virtually all oral contraceptives used in America [in 1997] are 'low dose' pills, [containing] 20-35 micrograms."[9]

Randy Alcorn documents that about 14 million American women are currently "on the Pill," as are about 80 million worldwide.[10]

"Dr. John Hildebrand, an expert in the field, estimates that more than 500 [American] women die every year because of pill-induced effects [although the resultant malady is listed as the direct cause of death, not the Pill which caused it *in*directly]. It is ironic indeed that the same Pill that the Neofeminists pushed so hard as part of their solution to 'excessive illegal abortion deaths' now kills five times as many women per year as illegal abortions themselves [truly] did before *Roe v. Wade*."[11]

SCOPE and FOCUS
I. CONVICTIONS
II. PRETEXTS
III. MANDATE
IV. LEGACY
V. ABORTIVE LINKS
Recreational Sex
Reproductive Technology
Contraception
Birth control
IUD
the Pill
Low-dose Pill
Pill failure rate
Abortifacient, the Pill?
Tough truth re: Pill
the Mini-pill
Vaccines
Depo-Provera
Norplant
RU-486/Mifepristone
Morning-after
the-Pill, the morn.after
Do-it-yourself
The cutting edge
Preferences shift
Victories vs. repro-tech
what Magnitude?
Respect & fear
unlikely Crusaders
Fertility pitfalls
Abortion Industry
Governmental Action
Social Climate
Religious Confusion
Personal Decision to Abort
VI. DILEMMA
VII. DESTINY

The Pill's failure rate, "breakthrough pregnancy"

Dr. Willke said that in 1979 there were "over 30 'contraceptive' pills on the market, each differing a little from the others. They 'prevent' pregnancy through three separate functions. 1) They thicken the mucous plug at the cervix... 2) They prevent release of the ovum... 3) They render the lining of the womb hostile to implantation. This [third] effect is abortifacient."[12]

Robert Hatcher states the accurate figure when he admits that, despite the triple-punch delivered by the Pill, "3%" of Pill users become pregnant every year.[13] The best confirmation of this statistic [there are many others] comes from *The Physician's Desk Reference*.[14]

Clowes reveals that an "attitude of 'invincibility' naturally leads to carelessness in the use of the Pill... When user error is factored in... the overall effectiveness rate for the low-dose Pill is 89 percent per year... In summary, if a girl of 15 who is fornicating begins to use the Pill and uses it without ceasing, there is a better than 50 percent chance that she will become pregnant by the time she is 22! Most people would intuitively expect that the massive distribution and use of the birth control pill would drastically cut down on the number of 'unwanted pregnancies' in this country. However, research by leading population experts has proven just the opposite."[15]

Is it true that the Pill is an abortifacient?

Randy Alcorn has done a prodigious amount of pure, rigorous research into the data that will answer the question, Is the birth control Pill abortifacient? In a 1992 book, he stated, "Some forms of contraception, specifically the intrauterine device (IUD), Norplant, and certain [he will later stop using the qualifier 'certain'] low-dose oral contraceptives, often do not prevent conception but prevent implantation of an already fertilized ovum. The result is an early abortion, the killing of an already conceived individual. Tragically, many women are not told this by their physicians [and pastors]... On the matter of controlling family size by killing a family member, we all ought to agree. Solutions based on killing people are not viable."[16]

Alarm regarding the possible abortifacient nature of the Pill was sounded as early as 1968, five years before *Roe v. Wade*. In *Abortion on Trial* by Russel Shaw, the prophetic point was made that at some future time abortion might become "an issue in a private sphere which law cannot reach... Indeed, this state of affairs may already be at hand if the intra-uterine devices and birth control drugs now on the market actually produce their effect by preventing the implantation of the fertilized ovum in the uterus, in which case they are acting as abortifacients."[17]

A year before that, in 1967, "at a medical conference, the representatives of a major hormone producer admitted that with OCs [oral contraceptives], ovulation with a possibility of fertilization took place in up to seven percent of cases, and that subsequent implantation of the fertilized egg would usually be prevented [by other effects of the same OC]."[18]

In 1968, Robert Clouse's *Protest and Politics* included a segment by Earl J. Reeves. He revealed that some missionary doctors who wanted to be able to use the Pill to the "benefit" of the peoples they served were trying to hush the Christians who were objecting to the abortifacient nature of the IUD, for fear that the result might be restrictions on the availability of the Pill, in which, besides its anti-ovulant effect, "the progesterone estrogen combinations also make the cervical mucus impenetrable to the sperm *and* render the womb unsuitable for implantation of a fertilized egg. This reaction is similar to the interference charged against the IUD and has been cited by some Catholics as a reason for rejecting the Pill."[19]

The controversy was still alive in 1985 when *Tough Questions – Biblical Answers* was written by Jack Cottrell. As a Protestant, he said, "The Roman Catholic Church has consistently condemned every form of interference with the natural procreational purpose of sex. What is our answer? Yes and no. Contraception *in itself* is not wrong; but certain *forms* of birth control may be wrong... Some contraceptives actually prevent conception, which is proper; but some work by preventing a fertilized ovum from being implanted in the wall of the womb, which is equivalent to abortion."[20]

The *real* Best-Kept-Secret

Not only the public and most Christians remained ignorant of the abortifacient nature of the Pill, but the majority of pastors and most pro-lifers did too. In 1990, when pro-lifer F. LaGard Smith wrote *When Choice Becomes God*, most of that book was right-on, but he made this grave mistake: "Whatever other adverse consequences it may have brought into play, the Pill *prevents* conception of new life rather than *killing* new life once it is conceived. By contrast, RU-486 is specifically designed to kill innocent human life."[1]

Even Randy Alcorn, considered by the researcher of *Orphans in Babylon* to be the most authoritative current voice on this subject, admits that "In 1991, while researching my book *Pro-Life Answers to ProChoice Arguments*, I heard someone suggest that birth control pills can cause abortions. This was brand new to me – in all my years as a pastor and a pro-lifer, I had never heard it before... In fourteen years as a pastor, doing considerable premarital counseling, I always warned couples against the IUD because it causes abortions. I typically recommended young couples use the Pill because of its relative ease and effectiveness."[2]

Pastor Alcorn's subsequent study revealed a vast and overwhelming body of evidence, all of it verifying the abortifacient nature of the Pill. One example: "In its 1984 publication 'Facts About Oral Contraceptives,' the U.S. Department of Health and Human Services stated, '...combined pills (synthetic estrogen and progestogen) ...make it difficult for a fertilized egg to implant, by causing changes in Fallopian tube contractions and in the uterine lining."[3]

Randy Alcorn, after exhaustive research concludes: "There is a clear answer to our question 'does the Birth Control Pill Cause Abortions?' The answer is definitely 'Yes.' ...Every time it causes an abortion the Pill will be thought to have succeeded as a contraceptive."[4]

The Christian Center for Bio-Ethics states, "In the end, [the Pill] does exactly the same work as the much publicized abortion pill, RU-486."[5]

Judie Brown, the President of the American Life League, was quoted in the *Good News* newsletter as to the "abortive nature of the birth control pill."[6]

An interviewer asked "Are there any birth control pills out there that do not have this potential to abort a developing child?" Dr. Thomas Hilgers answered, "There are none!"[7]

Brian Clowes states the tragic truth: "Most women in general either do not know or no longer care that all birth control pills on the market today are abortifacients."[8]

1 Smith, *When Choice Becomes God*, 255.
2 Alcorn, *Life Advocate*, Sept.-Oct./'97, 13.
3 Alcorn, *Life Advocate*, Sept.-Oct./'97, 20. If the reader will do herself the favor of buying Alcorn's book, *Does the Birth Control Pill Cause Abortions?* [see Bibliography], the abundance of corroborative sources will include: Leon Speroff and Philip Darney's "authoritative text" *A Clinical Guide for Contraception*: "The combination pill produces an endometrium which is not receptive to ovum implantation, a decidualized bed with exhausted and atrophied glands;" *My Body, My Health*, Clinician's Edition by Stewart, et. al.; *The Handbook of Obstetrics & Gynecology*; The President of the Food and Drug Administration in 1976; *Ovulation in the Human* by Crosignani and Mishell: "[Birth control pills] affect the endometrium, reducing glycogen production by the endometrial glands which is necessary to support the blastocyst;" *Williams Obstetrics*; Dr. G. Virginia Upton, Regional Director of Clinical Research for Wyeth International [one of the major birth control pill manufacturers], in a study of oral contraceptives published in a major medical journal, confirmed that "the graded increments in LNg in the triphasic OC [oral contraceptive] serve to maximize contraceptive protection by increasing the viscosity of the cervical mucus (cervical barrier), by suppressing ovarian progesterone output, and by causing endometrial changes that will not support implantation;" and many others, including "significant research results" presented in the March 1996 issue of *Fertility and Sterility*.
4 Alcorn, *Life Advocate*, Sept.-Oct./'97, 29, 16.
5 Christian Center for Bio-Ethics, "Keeping The Promise to Protect Your Family: Would You Gamble with the Life of Your Child?" pamphlet.
6 *Good News* newsletter, 2/'97.
7 Hilgers, in Bray, 201-2.
8 Brian Clowes, *Pro-Life Activist's Encyclopedia*, page 31.2.

SCOPE and FOCUS
I. CONVICTIONS
II. PRETEXTS
III. MANDATE
IV. LEGACY
V. ABORTIVE LINKS
Recreational Sex
Reproductive Technology
Contraception
Birth control
IUD
the Pill
Low-dose Pill
Pill failure rate
Abortifacient, the Pill?
Tough truth re: Pill
the Mini-pill
Vaccines
Depo-Provera
Norplant
RU-486/Mifepristone
Morning-after
the-Pill, the morn.after
Do-it-yourself
The cutting edge
Preferences shift
Victories vs. repro-tech
what Magnitude?
Respect & fear
unlikely Crusaders
Fertility pitfalls
Abortion Industry
Governmental Action
Social Climate
Religious Confusion
Personal Decision to Abort
VI. DILEMMA
VII. DESTINY

9 Alcorn, in *Life Advocate*, Sept.-Oct./'97, 25.
10 John Swomley, in Jersild, *Moral Issues and Christian Response*, 341-2: "Up to 50 percent of fertilized eggs do not implant."
11 Alcorn, in *Life Advocate*, Sept.-Oct./'97, 23.
12 Alcorn, in *Life Advocate*, Sept.-Oct./'97, 23.
13 Alcorn, in *Life Advocate*, Sept.-Oct./'97, 14, 21, 24: "...the 3% rate, which is firmly established statistically."
14 Alcorn, in *Life Advocate*, Sept.-Oct./'97, 16: "Dr. Thomas Hilgers, renowned fertility expert, personally heard Dr. Ronald Chez, a scientist with the National Institute of Health (NIH), publicly state that the pills of today, with their lower estrogen doses, allow ovulation up to 50% of the time."

How frequently does the Pill cause an abortion?

Randy Alcorn's monumental 1997 book *Does the Birth Control Pill Cause Abortions?* presented conclusive proof: **"The Pill does result in abortions. Only the numbers are uncertain."**[9]

While it is impossible to positively determine those numbers, there is enough knowable data that we can make some educated guesses. **We will attempt to estimate the <u>number of abortions per year</u> that are caused by the abortifacient feature of birth control pills, and <u>how likely it is</u> that a woman will unknowingly conceive a child but have it fail to implant because she is on the pill.** The simplest error to make in this enterprise would be to blame the Pill for 100% of the failed implantations of women who are on the Pill. However, it is widely estimated that 50% of fertilized eggs *normally* fail to implant.[10]

We will begin with these widely-accepted statistics, which are consistent with those in Randy Alcorn's book:

1) 13,900,000 female Americans are "on the Pill."[11]
2) 25% of sexually active, fertile women, using no birth control, get pregnant in any given year.[12]
3) 3% of women who rely on the Pill nevertheless become pregnant in any given year.[13]

USING NO BIRTH CONTROL, our HYPOTHESIS

For purposes of this hypothesis, we will assume that a sexually active, normally fertile woman ovulates 100% [one egg "drops" each month]. Therefore, of 100 such women, all 100 can be assumed to carry both live sperm and an available egg at least once this year.

IF 50% of the sperm cells that reach the cervix are blocked by the normal mucus accumulation, then of the 100 women who have both live sperm and an available egg, only 50 will conceive a child.

IF, when the womb is normal, only 50% of the fertilized eggs implant [50% x 50 = 25],[10] then of the 50 tiny babies, 25 would implant, producing 25 "pregnancies." ["Twenty-five" is known to be accurate.][12]

USING THE PILL, our HYPOTHESIS

IF a sexually active, normally fertile woman, **on the Pill**, ovulates 50% less than normal,[14] then, of 100 such women, only 50 would carry both live sperm and an available egg at least once this year.

IF 50% of the sperm that reach the cervix are already blocked by the normal mucus accumulation, AND if 50% of those that would otherwise get past are blocked by the pill-produced extra mucus, then of the 50 women who have both live sperm and an available egg only 12 will conceive a child [50% of 50% of 50 women = 25% x 50 = 12½].[15]

IF, when the womb is normal, only 50% of the fertilized eggs implant [50% x 12 = 6], and **IF, because of the Pill**, 50% of those that would normally implant, now **fail to implant** [50% x 6 = **3**], then of the 12 tiny babies, only 3 would implant, producing **3 "pregnancies"** [Three is known to be the accurate number].[13]

The above hypothesis demonstrates a series of reasonable percentages-of-reduction which, if they happen to be accurate, **would explain the Pill's method of creating the fact we do know**, that the **pill reduces** the annual **pregnancy rate** from 25% without birth control[12] **to 3%** for women on the Pill.[13]

IF this line of reasoning happens to be factual, it means that just as 3% of the women on the Pill get pregnant in a given year, another **3% would unknowingly have both conceived and lost babies** because of the Pill's abortifacient effect.

IF all of this happens to be the way the Pill works, **then 417,000American babies** [3% x 13.9 million women on the Pill] **are aborted by the Pill every year.**[16]

IF our hypothesis is accurate, then 3 of every 100 women on the Pill suffer an undetectable, "Pill-induced failure-to-implant" abortion in a given year [3% x 100].

The same percentage, stated differently, would mean that *if 33 women* were on the pill in a *single year*, one of them could expect to conceive a child that fails to implant in the womb because of the abortifacient nature of the Pill.

Using the same ratio, *if two women* are each on the Pill for *sixteen-and-one-half years*, then one of them could reasonably expect to have conceived a child that failed to implant because of the abortifacient nature of the Pill. Since it is reasonable to think that one woman who chooses the Pill as her birth control method **will be on the Pill for 16½ years**, and if our ESTIMATE of the incidence of the Pill-induced failure-to-implant coming into play is correct [3% = 3/100 = 1/33], then that decision might carry a **fifty-fifty chance** that in choosing the Pill she will have **unconsciously chosen to chemically abort her own child**, by the Pill's effect, at some time during that span of years.[17]

The problem is at least this great, because we have taken pains to make our hypothetical calculations as conservative as possible: **A fifty-fifty chance that what I am about to choose will kill my child is plenty of reason to reject that choice!**

Randy Alcorn says that "a Christian woman taking the Pill might over time have no Pill-induced abortions, or she might have one, three or a dozen of them."[18]

15 Our hypothetical figures would suggest that 12 to 12½ percent of women on the Pill experience the fertilization of an egg each year. Alcorn allows that it might be less than that, but on the other hand, perhaps it is as high as 50% [Alcorn, in *Life Advocate*, Sept.-Oct./'97, 24].

16 This estimate, 417,000, is only half [*exactly* half] of the number estimated, "834,000," by Bogomir M. Kuhar, Doctor of Pharmacy and president of Pharmacists for Life, which is quoted by Alcorn in *Life Advocate*, Sept.-Oct./'97, 23. Alcorn himself speculates, "If the same number of children do not survive the hostile endometrium as do survive, it would be 420,000" [24].

[*Notes are continued on page 198.*]

Notes continued from page 197:

17 This estimate, one pill-induced failure-to-implant every 33 years of Pill usage, is very conservative compared to the estimate given by J.C. Espinoza, M.D., "...**one abortion every other year for all women on the Pill**," quoted by Alcorn in *Life Advocate*, Sept.-Oct./'97, 23 .

18 Alcorn in *Life Advocate*, Sept.-Oct./'97, 23 .

The Mini-pill

Always the master of distortion, Robert Hatcher describes the mini-pill as "Birth control pills containing only progestin that prevents pregnancy by thickening cervical mucus."[1] Randy Alcorn, on the other hand, quotes a handful of eminently authoritative sources which all agree that instead of three mechanisms like the Pill, the mini-pill almost never suppresses ovulation, but has two effects: a contraceptive process of thickening cervical mucus, and an abortifacient mechanism which makes the uterine lining "hostile to implantation." Alcorn concludes: "clearly the progestin-only pill (Mini-Pill) by its effects on the endometrium, causes abortions and must be added to the list of abortive birth control methods."[2]

Temporary contraceptive "vaccines"

The World Health Organization arm of the United Nations has been conducting research since the 1970s in an effort to produce abortifacient vaccines, which are sometimes termed antifertility vaccines or contragestational vaccines,[3] and has two types which are stirring global interest and pro-life fears. The first type is called Human Chorionic Gonadotropin Vaccine (HCG). Its specific purpose is to cause a long-term chemical imbalance in the womb making that environment hostile to implantation.[4] The second product is called Trophoectoderm Antigen Vaccine. This type, called a contregestational vaccine, "will actually 'teach' the woman's immune system that the early embryo is foreign and must be destroyed"[5]

With either one of these substances, the woman would never know that she had conceived a child. Both are clearly not contraceptive, but rather, abortifacient, thwarting implantation of, or directly attacking, an already created human being. The old pro-abortion rhetoric will be resurrected to stress that what is eliminated is just a "blob of cells," and the newer fancy linguistic footwork will surely be employed to emphasize that because it acts before implantation it does not abort because the woman wasn't yet "pregnant." *Life Advocate* says that both of these vaccines will "be touted as 'birth control' that is long lasting, low maintenance, and easily available. Both may also lead the recipient into immuniological sterility (permanent immune destruction of developing embryos)."[6]

Lawrence Roberge notes two of the most frightening things about the emerging vaccines: "Abortion vaccines could replace 90% (or more) of the clinical legal abortions," and "will be distributed in the offices of tens of thousands of OB/GYN physicians."[7]

Depo-Provera

While the abortion vaccines are not yet available, Depo-Provera has been in regular use since the 1970s. It is described as a progesterone that "is generally administered by injection intramuscularly (IM) every three months. It [sometimes] acts to suppress ovulation. It also irritates and thins the lining of the uterus, making implantation of the newly conceived person unlikely."[8]

True to form, Robert Hatcher claims that Depo-Provera "prevents pregnancy chiefly by thickening cervical mucus and by suppressing ovulation," and he rates its use as one-tenth as likely to result in pregnancy as using the Pill [.3% versus 3%].[9]

SCOPE and FOCUS
I. CONVICTIONS
II. PRETEXTS
III. MANDATE
IV. LEGACY
V. ABORTIVE LINKS
Recreational Sex
Reproductive Technology
Contraception
Birth control
IUD
the Pill
Low-dose Pill
Pill failure rate
Abortifacient, the Pill?
Tough truth re: Pill
the Mini-pill
Vaccines
Depo-Provera
Norplant
RU-486/Mifepristone
Morning-after
the-Pill, the morn.after
Do-it-yourself
The cutting edge
Preferences shift
Victories vs. repro-tech
what Magnitude?
Respect & fear
unlikely Crusaders
Fertility pitfalls
Abortion Industry
Direct Action
Intervention to Defend
Governmental Action
Social Climate
Religious Confusion
Personal Decision to Abort
VI. DILEMMA
VII. DESTINY

1 Hatcher, *Emergency Contraception: The Nation's Best-Kept Secret*, 114.

2 Alcorn, in *Life Advocate*, Sept.-Oct/'97, 12.

3 Lawrence Roberge, in Kilner, *Bioethics and the Future of Medicine, A Christian Appraisal*, 178.

4 Roberge, in Kilner, 179-80.

5 Roberge, in Kilner, 180.

6 *Life Advocate*, 6/'94, 34.

7 Roberge, in Kilner, 183-4.

8 Christian Center for Bio-Ethics, "Keeping The Promise to Protect Your Family," pamphlet. Randy Alcorn agrees: "It sometimes suppresses ovulation, but also thins the lining of the uterus, preventing implantation" (in *Life Advocate*, Sept.-Oct./'97, 12).

9 Hatcher, *Emergency Contraception*, 114.

10 Hatcher, 116.

11 Hilgers, in Bray, 195.

12 Christian Center for Bioethics pamphlet.

13 Alcorn, in *Life Advocate*, Sept.-Oct./'97, 12.

14 Scheidler, *Closed: 99 Ways to Stop Abortion*, 215.

15 Hatcher, 81.

16 Hatcher, 79.

17 Hatcher, 79.

18 *Time*, 12-5-94, 45-6.

19 *Time*, 12-5-94, 45-6.

20 Associated Press, *Press*, 9-12-96, A3.

Norplant

Here is Robert Hatcher's spin on Norplant: "Six match stick-sized progestin-filled rods inserted under the skin of a woman's upper arm. Prevents pregnancy for 5 years by thickening cervical mucus. During the first year of use, ovulation is completely suppressed in about half of women" [He must consider this mucus barrier against sperm to be made of super-glue because his figures indicate that Norplant prevents pregnancy in 99.91% of the women who use it].[10]

Here is the puzzle. Progestin is what Hatcher himself says is the cause of the Pill's third mechanism of defense against pregnancy – the alteration of the uterine lining – yet when he describes a product with one active ingredient, progestin, he ignores the known effect the substance has on the womb. By contrast, the Christian Center for Bio-Ethics, and Randy Alcorn [12], and Brian Clowes [page 33.2], agree with Thomas Hilgers, who says that Norplant "has as one of its primary mechanisms the disturbance of the lining of the uterus... for the specific purpose of destroying the new life that is created if conception occurs, and with Norplant ovulation and conception probably occurs an alarming percentage of the time."[11]

The media has systematically helped to suppress "bad press" for both the surgical-abortion and birth-control industries. The Christian Center for Bio-Ethics tells us what we hear from no secular source, that as of August 1996 "over 68 federal lawsuits against Norplant's maker, Wyeth-Ayerst Laboratories, have been consolidated in Texas alone. Norplant is linked with loss of vision, migraines, brain tumors, and are often difficult to remove because of a tendency for the capsules to migrate in the body."[12]

One of the most daunting things about Norplant, Depo-Provera, and the Pill is that Operation Rescue and the other pro-life activists have never found an effective way to Rescue women from a quick procedure that can be performed in any doctor's office, or from filling a prescription at their local pharmacy. How could you even protest at so many thousands of locations where the majority of the trade has nothing to do with the death industry? To the degree that reproductive technology is making the abortion clinic obsolete, by that same measure is the pro-life movement losing its best-ever platform and focal point for public debate.

RU-486 / Mifepristone / "The French Abortion Pill"

Mifepristone is popularly know as the "French Abortion Pill" or RU-486. Randy Alcorn calls it a "human pesticide, causing a mother's womb to become hostile to her own child, resulting in an induced miscarriage."[13]

Joseph Scheidler says, "RU-486 is used in early pregnancy, prior to the seventh week. It causes [the body to think it's not pregnant, and] the uterus to shed its lining, and thus the baby is expelled. By itself RU-486 is 65% to 80% effective, so it is used in combination with a prostaglandin to [cause the body to convulsively expel the baby, and to] achieve up to a 96% 'effectiveness' rate in killing unborn babies."[14]

Robert Hatcher informs us that in France an RU-486 abortion requires four trips to the doctor: for an examination, to get the Mifepristone pill, coming back two days later for the prostaglandin, and returning 8 to 10 days later to determine if the "entire pregnancy has been expelled."[15]

Hatcher acknowledges that RU-486, is an abortifacient if used during the pregnancy, but not if used as emergency contraception before implantation has "started" the pregnancy.[16]

Some experts, Hatcher says, "predict that mifepristone will eventually replace Emergency Contraceptive Pills because it is more effective as an emergency contraceptive, causes less nausea and vomiting, and requires only one dose."[17]

Time magazine has said that eventually a Mifepristone abortion is expected to cost about the same as a surgical procedure.[18] That will certainly be the case if Planned Parenthood is successful at cornering the market on post-implantation chemical abortions, as seems clearly to be their goal. This would assure their financial survival under the theory of, "If you can't beat 'em, join 'em."

In some circles the experimental use of RU-486 in the U.S. was called the "M&M trials," because the two drugs involved were Mifepristone and Misoprostol.[19] After all of the political debate over RU-486, a different sort of M&M experiment was begun with little public notice. The FDA approved the plan for Planned Parenthood to combine two drugs currently approved for other applications to be combined to perform chemical abortions. For "$250 to $350, a woman who is no more than seven weeks' pregnant is injected with methotrexate, which stops development of the placenta and embryo. Four to seven days later, misoprostol tablets are inserted into her vagina, causing the uterus to contract and expel the fetus... There is nothing illegal in using the drugs in this way."[20]

The Morning-after-Pill concept

Clowes tells us, "As far back as 1966, Garrett Hardin and other population theorists were dreaming and hoping that the major 'contraceptive' of the future would be an abortifacient pill... The best part (from the anti-lifer's view) is that she would never actually know whether or not she had aborted, and so her conscience could remain clear."[1]

In 1968, Earl Reeves was reporting that William F. Campbell, a missionary doctor in Morocco, was calling the IUD a "mechanism for microscopic murder," and on the same grounds he "would reject the experimental 'morning after' pill as well."[2]

The Pill is being used as a morning-after pill?

Here, in his own words, is why Robert Hatcher calls *Emergency Contraception: The Nation's Best-Kept Secret*: "In the early 1970s, Dr. Albert Yuzpe, a Canadian obstetrician and gynecologist, described the simple method of prescribing a strong dose of birth control pills to women who had unprotected intercourse within the past 72 hours and did not wish to become pregnant. He prescribed 2 pills of Ovral (then a common birth control pill) to be taken immediately after unprotected intercourse and 2 more to be taken 12 hours later. Now called Emergency Contraceptive Pills, Yuzpe's emergency treatment has been used by thousands of women throughout the world to avoid unintended pregnancy."[3]

Time magazine puts the secret into perspective, and its report, without saying so, credits the pro-life movement with a level of influence that is almost never acknowledged in the media: "Drugmakers have been reluctant to market or label their products as emergency contraception pills in the U.S., fearing that it would subject them to lawsuits, protests or even boycotts. Now the U.S. Food and Drug Administration has decided to take matters into its own hands. The agency plans to publish a notice in the *Federal Register* declaring that oral contraceptives can be used safely and effectively to avoid pregnancy as late as three days after intercourse."[4]

"We've been using this procedure for many years in our clinics but were not able to publicize it," says a Planned Parenthood spokesperson. Planned Parenthood "was enboldened by the FDA decision." It will begin urging smaller pharmaceutical firms to package their pills specifically as emergency contraception. "The FDA has gone as far as they can go," says Planned Parenthood, "They're clearly inviting the manufacturers to repackage the Pill."[5]

"Doc's Spread Word: Pill Works on Morning After," was the headline of the *USA Today* cover story on April 29, 1997. It said, "U.S. gynecologists are launching a major nationwide campaign to make sure women know about the best-kept morning-after contraceptive secret: common birth control pills [which] will prevent 75% of pregnancies."[6]

Of course, that was obviously the goal of Robert Hatcher, and his five co-authors, when they wrote *Emergency Contraception: The Nation's Best-Kept Secret.* Here are the three most important things they want American women to know: "1) There are safe, legal and available contraceptives a woman can take to prevent pregnancy after unprotected intercourse if she acts quickly. Emergency Contraceptive Pills are one of our nation's best-kept secrets. 2) Emergency Contraceptive Pills are not mifepristone (RU-486) and they do not cause an abortion. Rather, Emergency Contraceptive Pills are simply a higher than usual dose of regular birth control pills. 3) At the end of this book is a directory of clinicians and clinics offering information about and providing emergency contraception."[7]

This is just one of scores of times that this book asserts that killing a recently conceived person before she implants in the womb is not an abortion. Its second-favorite selling point is that since half of our annual "3.5 million unintended pregnancies" involved intercourse with no effort at contraception, the use of emergency contraception could reduce that number by half, and thereby eliminate the need for half of our "1.6 million" surgical abortions, reducing the number to 800,000.[8]

Hatcher repeatedly uses a question-and-answer format. To the question, "Will women use Emergency Contraceptive Pills repeatedly, instead of adopting ongoing contraception?" he answers, "The nausea [50% of the time] and vomiting [20%] associated with emergency treatment are unpleasant enough to discourage most women from repeatedly using Emergency Contraceptive Pills."[9]

And that's not all. The book owns up to the fact that "Emergency Contraceptive Pills are not nearly as effective as any of the other ongoing methods of birth control," and, "During emergency contraceptive treatment, women may also suffer from headaches, breast tenderness, dizziness, or fluid retention."[10]

There are also warning signs to watch for "over the next couple of weeks": severe abdominal pain/chest pain, shortness of breath, cough/severe headache, dizziness, weakness, numbness/eye problems (vision loss or blurring), speech problems/severe leg pain (calf or thigh).[11]

Oh. If you are among the one in five women who vomit up the pills, you are instructed to take more of the same pills![12]

One of the suggestions of the *Emergency Contraception* book is that a woman should go to a "clinician" and get and fill a prescription to have on hand as part of an "Emergency Contraceptive Kit."[13] Would it be out of line for us to speculate that having the emergency kit on hand might give some women a false sense of security, might increase the incidence of unprotected sex, and might ultimately result in an increase in the number of conceived babies who get chemically aborted?

SCOPE and FOCUS
I. CONVICTIONS
II. PRETEXTS
III. MANDATE
IV. LEGACY
V. ABORTIVE LINKS
Recreational Sex
Reproductive Technology
Contraception
Birth control
IUD
the Pill
Low-dose Pill
Pill failure rate
Abortifacient, the Pill?
Tough truth re: Pill
the Mini-pill
Vaccines
Depo-Provera
Norplant
RU-486/Mifepristone
Morning-after
the-Pill, the morn.after
Do-it-yourself
The cutting edge
Preferences shift
Victories vs. repro-tech
what Magnitude?
Respect & fear
unlikely Crusaders
Fertility pitfalls
Abortion Industry
Direct Action
Intervention to Defend
Governmental Action
Social Climate
Religious Confusion
Personal Decision to Abort
VI. DILEMMA
VII. DESTINY

1 Brian Clowes, page 31.1.
2 Reeves, in Robert Clouse, *Protest and Politics*, 1968, 191.
3 Hatcher, v.
4 *Time*, 7-15-96, 59.
5 *Time*, 7-15-96, 59.
6 *USA Today*, 4-29,97, 1A. Not in bibliography.
7 Hatcher, 55.
8 Hatcher, 3, 13, 32.
9 Hatcher, 55.
10 Hatcher, 30.
11 Hatcher, 41.
12 Hatcher, 41.

Do-it-yourself abortions

Robert Orr's two biggest concerns about the abortion pills now in use in America are that they are prescriptions that can be taken at home, and that abortifacient chemical birth control might replace some of the true contraceptives now in use.[14] "Drugs designed to destroy the unborn very early in pregnancy," say Ankerberg and Weldon, "make abortion much less messy, perhaps safer and much more private."[15]

"This may sound cynical, but this is what would now happen in practice if abortion were illegal," says Bernard Nathanson. "Compounds know as prostaglandins can now be used to bring on contractions and expel [the unborn], and would readily be available for do-it-yourself abortions in vaginal suppository form."[16]

Unwilling to wait, "The Feminist Women's Health Centers and others have distributed 'how-to' abortion guides for women including 'When Birth Control Fails: How to Abort Ourselves Safely.'"[17]

Ankerberg and Weldon describe an experimental drug that "not only kills the [baby], but also acts to expel it quickly with no need for prostaglandins and/or suction... More chilling is the finding that if the drug is given very early in the pregnancy (3-4 weeks), the entire pregnancy will be resorbed, i.e. it will simply disappear, leaving no trace; there is no bleeding, no expulsion of tissue, nothing to identify this as an abortion."[18]

We share again, here, the prophetic words in Russel Shaw's 1968 book, *Abortion on Trial*: "It may very well be, as Paul Ramsey says, that the controversy over abortion and the law will become irrelevant once the abortion pills now being developed become generally available. Abortion will be an issue in a private sphere which law cannot reach."[19]

Innovations and the cutting edge of reproductive technology

In 1990, according to John Naisbitt's *Megatrends 2000*, there were 403 biotech firms in the U.S.[20]

But in 1995, *Newsweek* took a close look at reproductive technology and found that the industry had virtually abandoned birth control research in favor of being on the cutting edge of the lucrative fertility market. They reported, "It's not just RU-486. Companies have fled the entire contraceptive market because the risk of lawsuits outweighed any possible jackpot," and went on to describe the only true contraceptive innovation of the decade, the [1993] female condom, which was "applauded for giving women control over STD [sexually transmitted disease] prevention and criticized for esthetics: it looks like an oversized male condom, feels like Crisco and squeaks. It takes getting used to."[21]

According to *Newsweek*, "The solution, of course, is a method that does it all – microbicides, 'detergent' suppositories or foams that kill off everything from sperm to disease... The promise of a male contraceptive [any time soon] is unlikely... Instead... men could freeze their sperm and then get vasectomies. But that won't protect against AIDS and STDs, and it won't affect men who refuse to get involved."[22]

The magazine asked this pertinent question: "With all the condoms, pills and foams, why are so many women getting sterilized? ...thirty years after the pill promised a contraception revolution, the effort to find a cheap, easy-to-use, safe and effective method has proven a bitter failure... At a time when more than half of all pregnancies are unplanned... the options are shrinking. The manufacturers of the Today Sponge pulled it off the market in January [1995]; the IUD has all but disappeared, and the diaphragm is literally as unpopular as abstinence... For the first time, more women are opting for sterilization than any other form of birth control."[23]

13 Hatcher, 55.
14 Robert Orr, *Life and Death Decisions*, 59.
15 John Ankerberg, *When Does Life Begin? And 39 Other Tough Questions*, 160.
16 Nathanson, in Francis Beckwith, *Politically Correct Death*, 59.
17 Brian Clowes, page 18.4.
18 Ankerberg, 160.
19 Shaw, 169.
20 Naisbitt, *Megatrends 2000*, 267.
21 *Newsweek*, 3-13-95, 61.
22 *Newsweek*, 3-13-95, 62.
23 *Newsweek*, 3-13-95, 60.

Death to your child, in the privacy of your own home

In 1993 *Time* had asked its readers to:

"Imagine if abortion could be a truly private matter. Say, something as easy as visiting a doctor, getting a few pills, returning home to swallow them, then checking back a few days later to make sure that all went as planned."[1]

Just five years later we no longer have to imagine; that future is NOW.

In 1990 we were informed about what happens *When Choice Becomes God*: "That we could even seriously consider the eventual possibility of over-the-counter death of unborn children is a mark of how far we have gone in a pro-choice generation."[2]

Birth control preferences do shift

In the second half of the nineteenth century, the invention of the cervical cap and the diaphragm, and the innovation of condoms made of rubber marked the cutting edge of reproductive technology. The IUD was invented in 1909. Less commonly remembered now, an effective morning-after pill was introduced in the 1940s, and it was thirty years before research revealed its serious long term dangers to both women and their children. The Pill was invented in 1954 and was released to revolutionize American sexual mores in 1960. As of 1982 the Pill remained the most popular type of birth control, but by 1990, as the baby boomers began to abandon baby-making, surgical sterilization became more common than even the Pill.[3]

In the years since the AIDS epidemic began, the condom has enjoyed a resurgence of popularity, joined in 1993 by the female condom, which has not been enthusiastically received.

Some interesting trends were revealed by the results, released in the mid-'90s, of a poll of nearly 10,000 abortion patients. Fifty-eight percent of those polled reported that failed birth control had resulted in the pregnancy they were terminating, while 11 percent admitted that abortion was their first line of defense against childbearing.[4]

Subtracting the 58% and the 11% from 100% leaves 31% whose situation must be that they employ some form of birth control but that human error rather than birth control failure resulted in this pregnancy. It was also interesting that, compared with responses 7 or 8 years earlier in 1987, more than twice as many of the recent group were reporting pregnancy because of condom failure [from 16% to 32%]. It was reported that "'While this reflected an increase in the number of patients who said they used condoms, it did not represent a shift away from the pill. Most of the additional condom-users [were women who had previously been] using other barrier methods or no methods at all."[5]

The *Newsweek* article, in 1995, noted: "Even a few years ago doctors rarely debated that the first choice for a teenager was the Pill. Now they're not so sure... The chances of getting kids to [double-up, with] the pill-and-condom combo are small. So health experts find themselves in the troubling position of having to decide between putting teens at risk for pregnancy or AIDS."[6]

SCOPE and FOCUS
I. CONVICTIONS
II. PRETEXTS
III. MANDATE
IV. LEGACY
V. ABORTIVE LINKS
Recreational Sex
Reproductive Technology
Contraception
Birth control
IUD
the Pill
Low-dose Pill
Pill failure rate
Abortifacient, the Pill?
Tough truth re: Pill
the Mini-pill
Vaccines
Depo-Provera
Norplant
RU-486/Mifepristone
Morning-after
the-Pill, the morn.after
Do-it-yourself
The cutting edge
Preferences shift
Victories vs. repro-tech
what Magnitude?
Respect & fear
unlikely Crusaders
Fertility pitfalls
Abortion Industry
Direct Action
Intervention to Defend
Governmental Action
Social Climate
Religious Confusion
Personal Decision to Abort
VI. DILEMMA
VII. DESTINY

1 *Time*, 6-14-93, 48-54.

2 F. LaGard Smith, *When Choice Becomes God*, 254.

3 *Newsweek*, 3-13-95, 60-1.

4 *Press*, 8-8-96, A6.

5 *Press*, 8-8-96, A6.

6 *Newsweek*, 3-13-95, 62.

7 *Christian Times* newspaper, 11/'97, 5: "A 1996 federal law established state grants totaling $250 million for programs stressing abstinence until marriage."

8 Randy Alcorn, in *Life Advocate*, Sept.-Oct./'97, 27-8. See Couple to Couple League in bibliography.

9 Alcorn, in *Life Advocate*, Sept.-Oct./'97, 23: Figures offered by Dr. Kuhar of Pharmacists for Life: IUD, 3.825 million; Norplant, 2.925 million; Depo-Provera, 1.2 million; The Pill, .834 to 4.17 million.

10 Brian Clowes, *Pro-Life Activist's Encyclopedia*, page 31.4.

11 F. LaGard Smith, 113.

Pro-life victories vs. reproductive technology

Every day for a pro-lifer brings good news and bad news, and if we are not prayerfully vigilant, the overwhelming bad news will eclipse the crucial incidental victories. Above all, we must know the truth, skilfully extracting it from the foolishness and fabrications of this world.

The first unpleasant truth about birth control is that the enemy continues to win the public relations contest through semantic propaganda. Just as in the public mind abortion *is* choice, a baby now has innumerable pseudonyms, including fetus, blastocyst, blob and "the pregnancy." Most critical is the probability that the enemy will succeed in its campaign to redefine implantation and pregnancy as the beginning of moral consideration, in the minds of Christians and even pro-lifers as well as for Joan Q. Public. If the view can be sustained that prevention of implantation is not an abortion, then we are lost before we enter that battlefield.

One pressing order of business is to inform ourselves and each other of the true nature of each of the weapons in the birth control arsenal. When we have divided the components into those which are contraceptive [only] from the ones which have abortifacient mechanisms, the results must become common knowledge throughout the pro-life movement, the churches, and ultimately the society at large. Of first magnitude is for us to overcome our shock and embarrassment [read guilt] over the fact that the Pill kills babies, and then set that aspect of our affairs in order.

The Pill now stands conspicuously *with* the other abortifacient mainstays of the birth control industry: Depo-Provera, Norplant and the mini-pill. The super-abortifacient IUD, which took a public relations nose-dive a few years ago, now threatens to make a significant comeback, particularly because it is being aggressively promoted as a "contraceptive" and because it compares favorably to other Emergency "Contraception" through higher effectiveness and lower side effects. On the immediate horizon is a seemingly inevitable mass popularization of abortifacient emergency "contraception," particularly that which uses standard birth control pills, and also those pills re-packaged and openly promoted as "morning-after pills."

Just out of sight but just around the corner are the imminent onslaughts of RU-486, M&M, and other abortion pills and potions, and the long-awaited [long-feared] "contraceptive" vaccines and microbicide detergents.

Among the best good news is the simple fact that there are non-abortifacient, truly-contraceptive options in the reproductive marketplace. Although of minimal and, some say waning, use, the cervical cap, the diaphragm, the female condom and spermicides are in this category.

There are also non-abortifacient options which can boast wide spread acceptance: the male condom, female sterilization and male sterilization. There are additional victories to report concerning abstinence programs, in availability, acceptance, official endorsement, and even federal funding.[7] "There is also Natural Family Planning, which is not simply the old 'rhythm' method but a very thoughtful and scientific approach. The Couple to Couple League is a good source."[8]

The Magnitude. Is abortifacient birth control a holocaust?

The surgical abortion holocaust involves the conscious complicity of mothers in the deaths of 1.5 million American babies a year. Some of the figures quoted by Randy Alcorn indicate that abortifacient birth control [just IUDs + Norplant + Depo-Provera + the Pill as normally used] may kill 8 million to 12 million tiny babies every year, a holocaust 5 to 8 times as great at surgical abortion.[9]

These figures are consistent with those offered by Brian Clowes: "Some researchers (using very conservative figures) have calculated that the birth control pill directly causes between 1.53 and 4.15 million chemical abortions per year – [meaning] between 1 and 2½ times the total number of surgical abortions committed in this country every year!"[10]

Why have churches and, indeed, the pro-life movement, concentrated their focus on surgical abortion while chemical abortion has been a massacre of greater magnitude? Simply put, because of relativism, emotion. Our actions verify that flushing away a blob of cells matters less to even the pro-life movement than does the bloody dismemberment of a preborn who looks like a baby.

Ignorance, too, perhaps. In 1990, when Smith wrote *When Choice Becomes God*, "Increasing numbers of women [were] beginning to realize that certain forms of 'contraceptives' – including the IUD, or coil ([then] largely in disuse because of adverse side-effects), and the so-called 'morning-after' pill – are in fact abortifacients."[11] No mention was made of the abortifacient nature of the Pill in general use.

More about the magnitude of the abortifacient problem

It was reported that during the ten-year period from the mid-'80s to the mid-'90s, even though the pro-lifers were celebrating a decline in the *numbers* of surgical abortions being performed, more significantly, the abortion *rate*, "the number of abortions per 1,000 women of reproductive age, remained unchanged at 23... There are several reasons for the decline in [actual number of] abortions: aging of female baby boomers... reduced access to abortion, improved use of birth control and changes in attitudes about abortion."[1]

Only one of these stated reasons can be factual: There were fewer abortions, numerically, because there were fewer women of reproductive age. The other three "reasons" cannot be true because the abortion rate would not have "remained unchanged" if access to abortion were really reduced, if birth control use had really been improved, or if attitudes about abortion had really changed. So the report is an indictment of the pro-life movement: even during the years when the Religious Right was flexing its political muscle and when Operation Rescue had moved the abortion debate to the front burner, no real change was made in public attitudes, abortion access, or birth control usage, sufficient to lower the abortion rate in the U.S.A.

"Many people have wondered why the church has seemed to have so little effect when it comes to stopping legal abortion in America. Is it possible that, knowingly or unknowingly, 'contraceptive' practices used by Christians have robbed the church of her moral authority to speak against abortion? When we, as Christians declare the biblical truth that human life begins at conception, and that we oppose abortion, we must be consistent. We must not compromise by refusing to address methods of birth control which result in abortion."[2]

Randy Alcorn asks, "Can God, who creates each human life at the point of conception, fully bless the prolife efforts of CPC volunteers and Right to Life workers and sidewalk counselors and pastors and doctors – and any of us – when we turn right around and use, prescribe or recommend a product that sometimes takes the life of an unborn child? ...**Are we moral relativists and gradualists, different only in degree but not in kind [from] those we call abortionists? ...Perhaps what we thought was a conviction will be proven to be no more than a preference**."[3]

It is no excuse to complain to God that the watchmen did not blow the trumpet,[4] because as long ago as 1976 we were reading the books like *Issues of Life & Death,* in which Norman Anderson quoted R.F.R. Gardner's words: "History is littered with instances where Christians have fought needless battles over non-essentials. There have been others, however, where matters of grave importance have gone almost by default. If there is to be a battle on this matter [Gardner was specifically addressing abortifacient birth control], let it be on ground of our choosing."[5]

We have chosen, at least so far, to avoid fighting this battle at all.

SCOPE and FOCUS
I. CONVICTIONS
II. PRETEXTS
III. MANDATE
IV. LEGACY
V. ABORTIVE LINKS
Recreational Sex
Reproductive Technology
Contraception
Birth control
IUD
the Pill
Low-dose Pill
Pill failure rate
Abortifacient, the Pill?
Tough truth re: Pill
the Mini-pill
Vaccines
Depo-Provera
Norplant
RU-486/Mifepristone
Morning-after
the-Pill, the morn.after
Do-it-yourself
The cutting edge
Preferences shift
Victories vs. repro-tech
what Magnitude?
Respect & fear
unlikely Crusaders
Fertility pitfalls
Abortion Industry
Direct Action
Intervention to Defend
Governmental Action
Social Climate
Religious Confusion
Personal Decision to Abort
VI. DILEMMA
VII. DESTINY

1 *Press*, 3-22-96, A22.

2 Christian Center for Bio-Ethics. "Keeping The Promise to Protect Your Family: Would You Gamble with the Life of Your Child?" pamphlet.

3 Alcorn, in *Life Advocate*, Sept.-Oct./'97, 29-30.

4 *Ezekiel* 33: 6-7, and *I Corinthians* 14:8.

5 Gardner, in Norman Anderson, 67-8.

6 Joseph Scheidler, *Closed: 99 Ways to Stop Abortion*, 218.

7 *Chicago Tribune*, in *Press*, 11-5-96, A5.

8 *Newsweek Extra*, Winter 1997-98, 76.

9 *Newsweek*, 3-13-95, 61.

10 Scheidler, *Closed: 99 Ways to Stop Abortion*, 215.

11 *Time*, 4-28-97, 66.

12 *Press*, 3-28-97, B1.

13 *Time*, 4-28-97, 66.

14 *Time*, 4-28-97, 66.

15 *Press*, 1-8-98, A3.

16 Press, 3-7-96, A13.

17 Williams and Wilkins, *Clinical Gynecologic Endocrinology and Infertility*, 937-9, quoted by Alcorn, in *Life Advocate*, Sept.-Oct./'97, 25-6.

Winning the fear of an adversary

There is at least one area in this whole arena of reproductive technology in which the pro-life movement has had a positive impact: The pharmaceutical corporations have repeatedly revealed their awareness that the Movement could hurt them financially. Their vulnerability to a boycott is real: "In an effort to persuade the UpJohn company to discontinue its manufacture and research on the abortifacient drug, Prostaglandin, for second trimester abortions, [Right to Life of Cincinnati issued a] wallet card suggesting alternative products that could be purchased instead of UpJohn products."[6]

The *Chicago Tribune* reported in 1996 that "because of the controversy surrounding the [RU-486] drug's use in abortion, the [Population Council, which holds U.S. patent rights to that drug] has been unable to convince any major American pharmaceutical company to market the pill."[7]

"The Pill, from launch [1954] to FDA approval [1960] took less than a decade – a remarkable feat... [But] In recent years, expensive litigation and other controversies have slowed investment in alternative methods."[8]

Newsweek reported that "Politics, coupled with the high cost of developing new contraceptives, has taken a mighty toll. 'The pharmaceutical industry has washed its hands of birth control,' says the father of the pill, Stanford University chemist Carl Djerassi. In the space-race '60s... nine major American companies were doing contraceptive research; now only one is still committed. Djerassi blames U.S. regulators for being hypercautious. It took Depo-Provera, a progestin that's injected every three months, 25 years to win Food and Drug Administration approval, in 1992."[9]

The same article expressed the need for "a pill that women could take if they've had unprotected sex," and then added, almost as an aside, "Actually, morning-after methods already exist – a doctor can prescribe large doses of birth-control pills to a woman... but no company is willing to market a morning-after label."

Joseph Scheidler writes of this global pro-life victory: "In June, 1993, a French pro-life activist group asked for international demonstrations against RU-486 in conjunction with the annual stockholders meeting of Roussel-Uclaf in Paris. Pro-lifers held demonstrations at French Consulates in eleven cities in the U.S., eight cities in Canada and in several European and Australian locations, as well as at the pharmaceutical plants of companies owned by Hoechst. Following the shareholders' meeting the chief executive officer of Roussel-Uclaf announced that it would be at least five years until RU-486 would be marketed in the United States, *due to pro-life resistance*."[10]

Pharmacists – the unlikely crusaders

"The 6,000-member California Pharmacists Association [in 1996] adopted a policy allowing pharmacists to refuse to fill prescriptions based on "ethical, moral or religious grounds."[11]

John Boling, a pharmacist at a Temecula, Calif., Longs drug store "cited moral objections and refused birth control pills for a woman wanting to practice a 'morning-after' method to prevent pregnancy [notice the newspaper's politically-correct terminology, not to 'self-abort' or to 'prevent implantation']. A vice president for Planned Parenthood called the actions... 'horrifying' and said no third party has the right to intervene in a personal decision made between a woman and her doctor."[12]

Time magazine reported, "Longs has reprimanded the pharmacist, [and said]: 'Our policy is that a pharmacist, if he has moral objections, should refer the prescription to another on-duty pharmacist, or to another Longs, or to a competing pharmacy, if necessary.'"[13]

The magazine went on to report, "A recent survey of 625 pharmacists showed that 82% of them believe they have the right to refuse to fill a prescription for a drug such as RU-486 that would facilitate abortions. A new era of conscientious objection may be dawning."[14]

At what cost fertility?

Since reproductive research has so clearly abandoned birth control in favor of the greener pastures of fertility engineering, our pro-life witness needs to be asserted there also. "A scientist's claim that he will start cloning humans within two years set off a nationwide clamor... DNA would be removed from a woman's egg and replaced with the DNA from the person to be cloned [male or female]. The fertilized egg would grow into an embryo that would be placed into the woman, who would give birth to the cloned child."[15]

Could it be that gender feminists are more than a little bit thrilled by the prospect of totally removing men from the process of reproduction?

Forced twinning, already perfected in the production of multiple copies of prized farm animals,[16] is a much simpler enterprise, easily duplicated in humans, and yet it has the same result as cloning. What is a Christian to say as the technician gets ready to cut a "blastocyst" into a dozen pieces to find out how many of them have the miraculous ability to grow into complete copies of the tiny person who God says was a unique individual at the moment of conception?

What about this: "When, even under optimal conditions, physicians attempt to implant an embryo conceived in-vitro, it is true that there is a low success rate. According to Dr. Leon Speroff... 29 out of 30 embryos die in the attempt to implant a child."[17]

C. Abortion Industry

Among the seven "links in the abortive chain" we will be exploring, *recreational sex* and *reproductive technology* have thus far been addressed. Because women who do not want to bear a child are having sexual intercourse, and because they either do not use contraception or birth control, or the technologies fail to perform as expected, a few million unwanted pregnancies occur in America each year. Because surgical abortion is a prevalent enterprise, aggressively supported and defended by all levels of government, and encouraged by the professions and the popular culture, one and one half million women have consented to having their preborn children killed by this industry every year for the past quarter-century.

It is time for a comprehensive evaluation of the performance of the Christian community on the topics of its witness against, confrontation of, and impact on the abortion industry that draws clients from every parish in which the Church ministers.

We will begin with a listing of the evils of surgical abortion which demands that Christians respond. We will explore various excuses that may tend to contribute to a state of moral paralysis. An examination of the variety of possible goals of intervention should precede the discussion of types of ministries that tend to be conducted within the abortion arena. Ultimately we must come to terms with the assortment of justifications that may support pro-life activism in order to determine, prayerfully, humbly and sacrificially, what God requires us, individually and corporately, to do.

1. Problems with abortion

Globally, the surgical abortion industry is estimated to collect blood money totaling "ten billion dollars a year."[1]

Planned Parenthood is "a multi-billion dollar international conglomerate with programs and activities in one hundred twenty nations on every continent. In the United States alone, it employs more than twenty-thousand staff personnel and volunteers in over eight hundred clinics, nearly two hundred affiliates, and more than fifty chapters in every major metropolitan area, coast to coast."[2]

God's law. Sanctity. Killing the innocent. Bloodguilt

We began our discussion of the sanctity of preborn life, created in the Image of God, on pages 34-5 of *Orphans in Babylon*, and continued in Part III [pages 70-92]. Joseph Foreman writes that Operation Rescue "showed people that saving a baby's life is as normal and expected a part of a Christian life as church attendance, prayer, and Bible reading. People understood that to refuse to save a child whom we could have saved is to incur the guilt of innocent blood."[3]

Right to life from the moment of conception

We introduced the right to life of the preborn on page 35, and have offered biblical and historical evidence that this right should under no circumstances be infringed. We cited California law [*Orphans*, 177, note 10 §29], which declares the personhood of the preborn from the moment of conception, but which then inanely stipulates that this biological reality is automatically negated if perchance the child dies before birth. As only one of many specific examples, Derrick Riley "was arrested by the Kern County Sheriff's Department on double homicide charges for the murder of his wife, Diana Riley, and their unborn child."[4]

Joseph Foreman asserts the people must treat the preborn as human equals, and that "Christians must act like Christ even though it is illegal."[5]

SCOPE and FOCUS
I. CONVICTIONS
II. PRETEXTS
III. MANDATE
IV. LEGACY
V. ABORTIVE LINKS
Recreational Sex
Reproductive Technology
Abortion Industry
Problems with abortion
God's law. Bloodguilt
Right to life
Cruelty to the preborn
Inhumane acts
Excuses for inaction
Autonomy of woman
Relativism. Subhuman
Mechanism. Potential
Pragmatism. Tactics
Pleasure. Controversy
Positivism. Legality
Goals of intervention
Stop this abortion
Dissuade women
Fewer locations
Society more pro-life
Government pro-life
Church authentic
Types of intervention
Protest. Witness
Interposition. Rescue
Destruction. Burn
Violence. Killing
Guerilla Warfare
Revolution
Justifications offered
Freedoms: speech...
Civil disobedience
Life vs. property
Deter others
"Execute" the guilty
Necessity. Justifiable
Higher accountability
Governmental Action
Social Climate
Religious Confusion
Personal Decision to Abort
VI. DILEMMA
VII. DESTINY

1 George Grant, *Grand Illusions: The Legacy of Planned Parenthood*, 23.

2 Grant, *Grand Illusions*, 23.

Cruelty to the preborn. Pain

We have previously shared evidence that the preborn can experience pain during virtually every abortion procedure [59-60].

Inhumane acts

We have discussed the concept of human dignity and inhumane acts in several contexts: the Nazi medical experimentation on human subjects and lampshades made of human skin; medical experimentation on the tiny, still-living victims of abortion; a dead American pilot dragged behind a jeep; the serious crime of suffocating kittens in a plastic bag. With outrages of these types for points of reference, let us consider various abortive procedures with an eye toward a determination of whether abortion might rightly be classed as cruel and inhumane treatment which should "shock the conscience of humanity."

Eighty to 85 percent of abortions are performed in the first trimester, by suction-aspiration. "The procedure involves paralyzing the cervical muscle ring and then inserting a vacuum tube into the uterus and against the body of the child. The suction is almost thirty times more powerful than a home vacuum cleaner, and literally tears the child's body limb from limb. The scraps are then sucked through the tube and into a bottle,"[6]

"Dilation and curettage (commonly called D&C) is a procedure that involves dilating the cervix with a series of instruments to allow the insertion of a curette – a loop-shaped knife – into the womb. The instrument is used to scrape the placenta from the uterus and then cut the baby apart. The pieces are then drawn through the cervix. The tiny body must be reassembled by an attending nurse to make sure no parts remain in the womb to cause infection [as is also necessary in the case of suction abortions]."[7]

Saline amniocentesis, a "once-common method of abortion is now [1988, even more rare in the '90s] used only when gestation passes the sixteen week mark... A long needle is inserted through the mother's abdomen and directly into the child's amniotic sac. A solution of concentrated salt is then injected into the fluid there. The child breathes in, swallowing the poisonous salt [which is also literally burning-off the baby's skin] After about an hour of convulsing and struggling, the child is overcome and the mother goes into labor. About a day later she will deliver a corpse."[8]

Dilation and Evacuation (D&E) is described by Grant as a "particularly brutal method of abortion, commonly used when pregnancies have reached well into the second and third trimesters. Strips of laminaria – a spongy seaweed – are placed in the cervix to [very slowly] stretch it open. A pliers-like pair of forceps is then used to crush the child's skull and snap its spine. The now pliable corpse is wrenched piece by piece out of the womb. Next the abortionist must reassemble the body parts on the surgical table in order to make certain that nothing was left behind in the uterus."[9]

In a digoxin abortion, that substance is injected by a needle directly into the baby's heart. This kills the child, and the body is subsequently expelled by prostaglandin-induced labor.[10]

During the last three months of pregnancy [which means that often the viable baby could be kept alive, to be adopted, for instance], abortions are performed by hysterotomy, which involves opening the womb surgically and removing the baby as in a caesarean section. However, the purpose of this procedure is to end the infant's life. Instead of being cared for, the baby is wrapped in a blanket, set aside, and allowed to die."[11]

D&X, the "partial-birth abortion," is one in which the person performing the abortion "partially vaginally delivers" a living baby, interrupts the delivery to jab a pointed tool into the back of the child's neck, next uses a suction device to suck the baby's brains out, and then completes the delivery of the suddenly dead infant. Although both houses of Congress twice voted to outlaw this procedure, President Clinton vetoed it both times. More than eighteen states have successfully enacted laws similar to the blocked federal measure. When Ohio passed a law that simply outlawed any abortion that sucked the baby's brains out, the Supreme Court let stand a lower court ruling that this law was unconstitutional, saying that the law would unduly interfere with a woman's right to abortion.[12]

3 Foreman, *Shattering the Darkness*, 18-9.

4 *Life Advocate*, 4/'94, 25.

5 Foreman, 163-6.

6 Grant, *Grand Illusions*, 68.

7 Kerby Anderson, *Living Ethically in the '90s*, 205-6.

8 Grant, *Grand Illusions*, 70-1.

9 Grant, *Grand Illusions*, 69-70.

10 *Life Advocate*, 4/'94, 9.

11 Kerby Anderson, 206.

12 *Press*, 3-24-98, A3.

2. Excuses for inaction by Christians / pro-lifers

Even though it is only one of the seven "links in the abortive chain," the abortion industry [as also the government] has been the target of more than its equal share of pro-life attention and effort. Yet the vast majority of pro-lifers, not to mention Christians in general, have done very little to either confront or impact this conspicuous public abomination.

It must be true that the majority of pastors, congregations and Christians are simply so preoccupied with other, important matters that challenging the abortion industry has not yet seemed to be part of their ministry, their calling. Many others, however, who have included surgical abortion in their list of major *concerns*, have accepted a variety of reasons for not getting involved in this arena. Those reasons/excuses must be addressed.

Autonomy of woman. "It's none of our business"

In pages 41 through 49 of *Orphans* we investigated the pro-abortion arguments for the woman's autonomy in the abortive "choice:" that it is her fundamental right [now constitutionally guaranteed], that privacy protects it, that equality with men demands it, that tolerance should grant it, and that tax payers should fund it.

Every Christian should bristle at the allegation that abortion is none of our business; no person has any right to "choose" to rape or rob or assault or murder another person. Stopping the killing of helpless innocent children is everybody's business.

Relativism. "It's a Subhuman thing. A blob"

Those who buy in to relativism all accept that a preborn child is somehow different from a born baby. In pages 51 to 56 we explored the particulars of some of those alleged differences. To deny the humanity or personhood of the unborn immediately puts them in the "expendable" and "rightsless" categories. Yet the impulse to make a relativistic distinction is very strong. Indeed, the zeal and emotional intensity exhibited by various pro-lifers may be seen as a measure of how much or how little relativism exists in their conception of the *in utero* child. To frame an example for the sake of comparison, there is a difference between lust and adultery: the question of adultery implies a simple yes/no, either/or situation, while lust is subject to a continuum of possibilities with never-an-improper-thought at one end and sex-crazed-dirty-old-man at the other!

It is simplistic and false to assert that pro-abortionists relativize the worth of a preborn as sub-human, while pro-lifers do not relativize but rather hold her to be identical in all respects to a born infant. It is not an either/or thing but a continuum thing. **Every pro-lifer relativizes the unborn to some degree**. If you dispute this, consider this hypothetical situation: you are being held hostage by terrorists, along with a pregnant woman and her three-year-old child. The woman is ordered to swallow RU-486 or they will shoot her born child. One dead hostage on the floor proves that they are serious. What is your advice to this desperate woman? If any part of you feels that chemically aborting the unconscious and invisible one is the lesser of two evils, then you are guilty [as am I] of relativizing the "fetus" as less valuable than the born child. The fact that every pro-life Christian relativizes the worth of the preborn to some degree opens us to the challenge that our anti-abortion rhetoric is hypocritical.

The charge is true. Our embarrassment over that chink in our armor has had two tragic results: 1) we have each constructed an elaborate mental document which details our private brand of pro-lifeism. We are convinced that we ourselves hold a consistent and true pro-life standard. 2) by that standard we have judged other pro-lifers as wise [like us], or somewhat in error, or greatly mistaken, or sinfully deluded. And we have gone public with those judgments of our brothers and sisters.

SCOPE and FOCUS
I. CONVICTIONS
II. PRETEXTS
III. MANDATE
IV. LEGACY
V. ABORTIVE LINKS
Recreational Sex
Reproductive Technology
Abortion Industry
Problems with abortion
God's law. Bloodguilt
Right to life
Cruelty to the preborn
Inhumane acts
Excuses for inaction
Autonomy of woman
Relativism. Subhuman
Mechanism. Potential
Pragmatism. Tactics
Pleasure. Controversy
Positivism. Legality
Goals of intervention
Stop this abortion
Dissuade women
Fewer locations
Society more pro-life
Government pro-life
Church authentic
Types of intervention
Protest. Witness
Interposition. Rescue
Destruction. Burn
Violence. Killing
Guerilla Warfare
Revolution
Justifications offered
Freedoms: speech...
Civil disobedience
Life vs. property
Deter others
"Execute" the guilty
Necessity. Justifiable
Higher accountability
Governmental Action
Social Climate
Religious Confusion
Personal Decision to Abort
VI. DILEMMA
VII. DESTINY

1 Cathy Ramey, *In Defense of Others: A Biblical Analysis and Apologetic on the Use of Force to Save Lives*, 6-8.

2 *Life Advocate*, 4/'94, 16.

3 Jesus, *John* 15:13.

4 Cathy Ramey, 8.

5 Foreman, *Shattering the Darkness: The Crisis of the Cross in the Church Today*, 138.

6 Foreman, 103-4.

Real life-and-death examples of pro-life relativizing

On March 10, 1993, Michael Griffin shot abortionist David Gunn to death. "The pro-life movement was suddenly pulled apart in a debate over the morality of doing harm to an abortionist in order to save the life of an innocent child... By saying that Michael Griffin had 'sinned,' [some] Christians were implying that the abortionist (even as a murderer of unborn children) had a higher degree of value to his life than did a developing in utero child."[1]

This researcher agrees that such judgment of Michael Griffin does imply that the speaker holds the preborn children the abortionist was scheduled to kill today to be of less worth than the abortionist himself. This is relativism. We will soon deal with the possible justifications [vigilante justice, necessity, etc.], but at this point it is important that it be acknowledged that if I believe that a preborn is a 100% human person from the moment of conception but do nothing to protect her, and if Mr. Griffin intervenes to kill the killer, then he is being more consistent than am I. Michael Griffin tapped a policeman on the shoulder to inform him that he had just shot a man around the corner, and later stated, "I killed him [David Gunn] because of my beliefs and convictions, and if I spend the rest of my life in jail it will be worth it to save one baby."[2]

This researcher must confess, along with the candid reader, that I do not value the preborn child that highly. "Greater love has no one than this, that he lay down his life for his friends."[3]

I believe that God sees no difference between a preborn child and a born child. I would not hesitate to shoot a man who was about to stab the third of three helpless five-year-olds. But I would not shoot an abortionist. I may be able to offer you several excuses for this, but the *reason* is simply that in my heart of hearts I do not [yet] see the unborn child as identical to one who is born.

By contrast with the majority of pro-lifers who publicly denounced Michael Griffin, several prominent leaders signed a "Defensive Action Statement," which affirmed among other things, "We the undersigned, declare the justice of taking all Godly action necessary to defend innocent human life, including the use of force. We proclaim that whatever force is legitimate to defend the life of a born child is legitimate to defend the life of an unborn child..."[4]

A crucial distinction is clearly made between the affirmation that a particular type of action is *justified* [morally, under God's eternal law], and *advocating* that others should do such a thing. The Defensive Action Statement was an affirmation that actions such as Michael Griffin's killing of David Gunn can be morally *justified.*

Rescue, by contrast with killing, is an attempt to intervene to protect the preborn from being aborted, while at the same time maintaining a commitment to peaceful non-violence. Yet there are many Christian leaders, and some who are actively pro-life, who have said that saving the life of the unborn does not justify violating a no-trespassing law. This is yet another example of how the relativizing of the value of a "fetus" comes into play. Rescuer Joseph Foreman says that when rescuers are thrown in jail, "our government, by holding us, and our churches by permitting it, say that each unborn child has no value."[5]

Mechanism. "It's just a Potential human person. Less than equal"

There is a distinction to be drawn between forfeiting the rights of the unborn on the basis of relativism and the act of abandoning *some* preborns on the basis of mechanism [see *Orphans*, pages 57-62]. Joseph Foreman makes a radical statement when he says, "We need men and women who are 100% intolerant of child murder whether it is legal or illegal."[6]

While Joseph is one of the most zealous and committed pro-life rescuers ["missionaries to the preborn"] we have known, he is not "100% intolerant of child murder." His is *restrained* outrage. I believe that if one of Joseph's terrific [born] children was being held by kidnappers inside a particular building, Joseph would *not* remain limp and peaceful while the police dragged him away from *that* door. He would more likely kick down the door and kill the kidnappers with his bare hands if he had to in order to rescue *that* child; at least I know that I would abandon my "Rescuer" commitments in such a circumstance.

By the same token, besides relativizing the value of a preborn child versus a born baby, we mechanistically differentiate between the unborn themselves. With much effort Congress twice amassed enough votes to [attempt to] outlaw "partial birth abortions" because they felt the outrageousness of interrupting the birth of a full-term child in order to kill it halfway out of the birth canal. But the same "pro-life majority" gets thinner when the subject is funding the abortion of welfare women, and the "pro-life consensus" evaporates when someone suggests a right-to-life constitutional amendment to outlaw all abortions. Mechanistically, we are opposed to some abortions but not all.

Within the pro-life movement, thousands have braved jail time in order to make a stab at preventing surgical abortions, but because of the effect of mechanistic thinking, no such campaign has been directed at the abortifacient birth control industry or the fertility clinic massacres of microscopic blobs of tissue, even though we claim to believe that those conceived-ones are as fully human as the mangled poster-children we display in front of the abortion clinics. Mechanism causes pro-lifers to selectively neglect some of the defenseless, much as pro-abortionists are disdainful of all those children they define as "potential human life."

Pragmatism. Bad Tactics. It's beyond our control

Pragmatic thinking takes its toll on the pro-life community [see pages 66-76]. Nelson Mandela, in his summary of the black struggle against apartheid in South Africa, notes the pragmatic effect that "riots poisoned the views of some whites who might otherwise have been sympathetic."[1]

Many have noted that the momentum of the peaceful civil rights movement in the United States abruptly died when the TV news images shifted from fire hoses and police dogs abusing black protesters, and began portraying [and thereby stimulating an increase of] rioting, burning and looting in the inner cities.

When Randy Alcorn was writing *Is Rescuing Right?*, published in 1990, he found an abundance of Christians whose opinions were that "Rescuing will turn society against the church," and "What is to prevent pro-abortion people from blocking access to churches, or even entering them to disrupt services? [this has now happened on a number of occasions]. If we allow *lawless protest* to one side, we justify it for all."[2]

Our obvious point in selecting these quotes is that they are examples of pragmatic arguments interjected into what should be a moral debate. A divergent and partly humorous comment needs also to be made: It would be wonderful if Rescue would prompt a wave of "atheist sit-ins in churches;" we have two thousand years of practice at doing things that are keeping *atheists* away from those hallowed places where the gospel is being preached!

When Cal Thomas considered the effects of violent episodes at abortion clinics, part of his response was pragmatic: "Tactically, as well as politically, the bombing of abortion clinics is probably not a good idea. It allows the pro-choicers to shift the debate from what is taking place inside the building to what is taking place outside."[3]

Joseph Scheidler focuses here on the pragmatic results of violence, not the moral implications: "The shooting death of Dr. Gunn, while allegedly committed by a man new to the movement, only served to bring on a rash of restrictive bills, speed up legislation aimed at curtailing totally non-violent pro-life activity [Scheidler wrote this a year before passage of the F.A.C.E. bill], and give the pro-abortionists a 'martyr.' It made it momentarily more difficult to convince the man-on-the-street that pro-lifers had an undisputed claim to the high moral ground."[4]

Not to discount Joseph Scheidler's considerable skills, but we do not know of anyone who is successful at convincing the man-on-the-street of anything, before or after a shooting takes place!

Greg Koukl, on his Christian radio talk show *Stand to Reason*, got to the heart of our point in all of this: "If you answer that [Michael Griffin's shooting] sets the cause back and it's a bad testimony and it's going to make the pro-abortionists angrier – in short, if you answer it's a bad tactic – then you're arguing pragmatically and have skirted the core ethical question: In isolation, was this killing morally justified?"[5]

Pleasure. "We shouldn't make people sad / guilty / mad"

The pain-and-pleasure orientation to life brings on a whole different set of excuses to neglect the plight of the victims of abortion [review pages 63-5]. Suffice it to say that if we are constrained from doing the deeds of Christian servanthood because of what others my think of us, whether we might make them sad or mad, cause them to feel confused or [perish the thought] guilty, then we must go back to the Bible and reconsider what manner of "gospel" we have been fed. Not only is confrontation an essential arrow in the quiver of a soldier of Christ, but Justice William O. Douglas declared that, in addition, "A function of free speech [is] to invite dispute. It may indeed best serve its high purpose when it induces unrest [or] even stirs people to anger."[6]

SCOPE and FOCUS
I. CONVICTIONS
II. PRETEXTS
III. MANDATE
IV. LEGACY
V. ABORTIVE LINKS
Recreational Sex
Reproductive Technology
Abortion Industry
Problems with abortion
God's law. Bloodguilt
Right to life
Cruelty to the preborn
Inhumane acts
Excuses for inaction
Autonomy of woman
Relativism. Subhuman
Mechanism. Potential
Pragmatism. Tactics
Pleasure. Controversy
Positivism. Legality
Goals of intervention
Stop this abortion
Dissuade women
Fewer locations
Society more pro-life
Government pro-life
Church authentic
Types of intervention
Protest. Witness
Interposition. Rescue
Destruction. Burn
Violence. Killing
Guerilla Warfare
Revolution
Justifications offered
Freedoms: speech...
Civil disobedience
Life vs. property
Deter others
"Execute" the guilty
Necessity. Justifiable
Higher accountability
Governmental Action
Social Climate
Religious Confusion
Personal Decision to Abort
VI. DILEMMA
VII. DESTINY

1 Nelson Mandela, *Long Walk to Freedom*, 121.

2 Alcorn, *Rescuing*, 210.

3 Thomas, in Scheidler, 14.

4 Scheidler, 301.

5 Koukl, *Stand to Reason*, "Pulling the Trigger on Abortion," 2.

6 Douglas, in John Whitehead, *The Right to Picket*, 1.

7 Koukl, *Stand to Reason*, "Pulling the Trigger on Abortion," 4.

Positivism. "Christians must obey all laws"

To declare that a Christians must always obey all laws is to confess one's embarrassing ignorance of Christian history, and of the Bible as well [see page 77]. For a Christian to endorse positivism wholeheartedly is a grave error. Since we just recently held up Greg Koukl as being "right on," it may not seem too disrespectful to suggest that he was off-target, at least once, as concerns positivism. When Mr. Koukl discusses the morality of killing an abortionist he dismisses the "necessity" argument [which we will discuss in a little while], but instead reverts to positivism. His point is that since abortion is currently legal in America, then it is technically inaccurate to call an abortionist a murderer. On that basis, he reasons, since the abortionist is innocent of "murder" he is not biblically deserving of death.[7]

Here is the error we feel has been made. Once we embark on the investigation of biblical morality, interjecting a fragment of man-made legal code is an inappropriate reversion to positivism. One should not say that the biblical injunction that one must not take innocent life protects the abortionist because that man is innocent of murder according to man's law. The proper view, we feel, is that under biblical law the fact that the abortionist repeatedly and without remorse takes innocent human life makes him subject to the Bible's condemnation and dictum: "If anyone takes the life of a human being, he must be put to death."[8]

We are not saying that an individual can presume to be "judge, jury and executioner." [The wrongness of such an act will be discussed under "Justifications: Execute the guilty"]. All we assert at this point is that the abortionist has no positivistic claim to innocence under the technicality that abortion is "legal." Remember Nuremberg.

Much condemnation of Operation Rescue began with *Romans* 13:1, "Everyone must submit himself to the governing authorities, for there is no authority except that which God has established." Such shallow prooftexting is a disgrace. Randall Terry wrote well: "Numerous scriptural examples [cited] support two basic reasons to defy civil authority: 1) Saving someone's life... 2) Remaining faithful to God... For those who still aren't sure, I would point out that the man who penned Romans 13 also wrote four prison epistles! Both Paul and Peter were executed by the Roman authorities as lawbreakers."[9]

The secular writer, Michael Hart, reminds us that Martin Luther "was finally pronounced a heretic and an outlaw by the Diet of Worms (1521), and his writings were proscribed... Although Luther had to go into hiding for a period of about a year, his support in Germany was strong enough to enable him to avoid any serious criminal penalties."[10]

Henry David Thoreau wisely clarified, "It is not desirable to cultivate a respect for the law, so much as for the right."[11]

Nelson Mandela gives us a view from the perspective of the anti-apartheid struggle in South Africa. He says that by 1949, the African National Congress "had become too docile in the face of oppression," and that the ANC's leaders learned that they had to become "willing to violate the law and if necessary go to prison for their beliefs, as Gandhi had... This was a radical change: the ANC's policy had always been to keep its activities within the law."[12]

About himself, Mandela says, "I was made, by the law, a criminal, not because of what I had done, but because of what I stood for, because of what I thought, because of my conscience," and "Can it be wondered that such a man, having been outlawed by the government, should be prepared to lead the life of an outlaw?"[13]

The South African government reflexively increased repression as organized opposition grew, and by 1954, "It seemed inevitable that the government would ban the ANC, and many argued that the organization must be prepared to operate underground and illegally."[14]

The reader will recall [130], that banning was a legal designation imposed by the government of South Africa which forced the banned person to resign membership as well as leadership in groups the authorities considered dangerous. When an organization was banned, it became a crime for anyone to belong to or to cooperate with that group. Since the U.S. government does not choose to take exactly those [unconstitutional] steps, it simply accomplishes an equivalent result through judicial procedure. For example: When a court ruled that Jeff White and Operation Rescue California should pay more than $800,000 to the abortionists they had opposed [peacefully, with neither destruction of property nor violence toward persons], the government was able to seize the organization's property [office equipment], assets and post office box, confiscating any income of both the organization and Jeff personally. Exactly as with Mandela, both the man and the organization were forced to live as fugitives in an underground world where to survive, by definition, involved criminal activity [e.g. to receive money to buy food for his family].

8 *Leviticus* 24:17.

9 Terry, *Operation Rescue*, 91-3.

10 Hart, *The 100: A Ranking of the Most Influential Persons in History*, 149.

11 Thoreau, in Robert Downs, *Books that Changed the World*, 68.

12 Mandela, 98-9.

13 Mandela, 288.

14 Mandela, 148-50.

What justifies the breaking of laws, even in a democracy?

Justice Abe Fortas, in *Concerning Dissent and Civil Disobedience*, quoted Robert Bolt: "To break the law of the land is always serious, but is not always wrong," and in his own words said, "The need sometimes may arise to disobey profoundly immoral or unconstitutional laws."[1] John Whitehead has written: "We are commanded to be good citizens until such time as we are ordered by the law and government to do those things contrary to the law of God."[2] Some have taken that truth to a rigid extreme, re-stating the pro-choice fable: "The law does not force Christians to have abortions."

John Eidsmoe wisely counters: "We should resist and disobey government only when that government commands us to do something the Word of God forbids, or forbids us to do something the Word of God commands – either directly or by clear implication."[3] The thought is completed by Joseph Foreman who says that in the United States, "though it is legal to profess your identification with Christ, it has become illegal to act as if you belong to Christ... Today in America it is illegal to protect unborn people. When it is illegal to save a child from murder, it is illegal to be a Christian."[4] Elsewhere he declares, "To confine ourselves to activities which man finds 'legitimate' or 'legal' inevitably confines us to building our anti-murder programs on a commitment to permit murder."[5]

In the opinion of Gen. William Booth, "No great cause ever achieved a triumph before it furnished a certain quota to the prison population."[6]

In *The Gulag Archipelago* Alexandr Solzhenitsyn declared: "To stand up for truth is nothing! For truth you have to sit in jail."[7]

Brother Andrew, global underground evangelist, has written: "The first principle for any Christian work is this: The Lord Jesus Christ, who crushed Satan and conquered death, commands us to invade this enemy-occupied world and reclaim it for God. We march under his exclusive authority and are forbidden to make any deals with the foe. No compromises. No concessions. And no excuses!"[8]

3. Goals of intervention

Paul and Silas were arrested in Philippi for interfering with a lawful (but ungodly) business. They prevented the soothsaying girl – against her will – from pursuing her lawful occupation. Indeed, they destroyed her employer's business.[9] Joseph Scheidler, in the introduction to his book, *Closed: 99 Ways to Stop Abortion*, states, "The activities and methods proposed in this book are intended to interfere with and even stop the business of abortion."[10]

In 1993 *Time* magazine reported a statement by then-executive director of Operation Rescue, Keith Tucci "that his organization wants to abolish totally the practice of abortion through legal and nonviolent means."[11] Joseph Foreman writes, "All pro-lifers have the same goal: End choice in the realm of child murder."[12]

Orphans in Babylon has identified six distinct objectives of pro-life opposition to the surgical abortion industry: to stop abortions from happening at a particular time and place; to dissuade abortion-minded women; to reduce the number of locations where surgical abortions are performed; to cause our society to become more pro-life; to influence the government to move in a pro-life direction; and to assist the Church to more authentically fulfill its mission.

Stop this abortion, today

"Pro-life activists cannot wait for the legislative and judicial process that will make abortion illegal," wrote Joseph Scheidler, "The activist has to save lives now."[13]

Randall Terry expressed the founding goals of Operation Rescue in this manner: "First of all, I felt we needed repentance in the church... Secondly, I saw that if we believed abortion was murder, then we needed to act like it was murder... [We needed to] physically intervene and save them... Our actions would have the secondary benefit of creating positive social tension [seen as the key to getting the government to change the laws]."[14]

1 Fortas, 29, 63.

2 Whitehead, *Arresting Abortion: Practical Ways to Save Unborn Children*, 42.

3 Eidsmoe, *God & Caesar*, 32.

4 Foreman, 153-4.

5 Foreman, 116.

6 Booth in Randy Alcorn, *Is Rescuing Right? Breaking the Law to Save the Unborn*, 133.

7 Solzhenitsyn, in Brian Clowes, page 81.2.

8 Brother Andrew, in John Whitehead, *The Stealing of America*, 110-1.

9 *Acts* 16:16-40.

10 Scheidler, 18.

11 *Time*, 4-19-93, 40.

12 Foreman, 117.

13 Scheidler, *Closed: 99 Ways to Stop Abortion*, 17.

14 Terry, *Operation Rescue*, 22.

15 Grant, *Third Time Around: A History of the Pro-Life Movement from the First Century to the Present*, 151-2.

16 Foreman, 8.

17 Beckwith, *Politically Correct Death: Answering the Arguments for Abortion Rights*, 160.

SCOPE and FOCUS
I. CONVICTIONS
II. PRETEXTS
III. MANDATE
IV. LEGACY
V. ABORTIVE LINKS
Recreational Sex
Reproductive Technology
Abortion Industry
Problems with abortion
God's law. Bloodguilt
Right to life
Cruelty to the preborn
Inhumane acts
Excuses for inaction
Autonomy of woman
Relativism. Subhuman
Mechanism. Potential
Pragmatism. Tactics
Pleasure. Controversy
Positivism. Legality
Goals of intervention
Stop this abortion
Dissuade women
Fewer locations
Society more pro-life
Government pro-life
Church authentic
Types of intervention
Protest. Witness
Interposition. Rescue
Destruction. Burn
Violence. Killing
Guerilla Warfare
Revolution
Justifications offered
Freedoms: speech...
Civil disobedience
Life vs. property
Deter others
"Execute" the guilty
Necessity. Justifiable
Higher accountability
Governmental Action
Social Climate
Religious Confusion
Personal Decision to Abort
VI. DILEMMA
VII. DESTINY

Human speed-bumps to delay the abortionist's parade

George Grant reports, "Over the next two years [1988-1990] Operation Rescue mobilized thousands upon thousands of Christians to place their bodies between the abortionists and the children. Over fifty thousand arrests resulted."[15]

Every Rescue volunteer signed a pledge to remain peaceful and prayerful, and to neither resist nor assist the police who came to clear the abortion clinic doors so that abortions could resume. Because the primary objective was to prevent abortions from taking place for as long as possible non-violently, ingenious tactics were improvised to further that end. Going limp slowed the removal of human obstacles and would lengthen the time before the doors were reopened. As the police became more efficient, and sometimes cruel, and as the amounts of both jail time and fines kept increasing, the movement had to devise strategies whereby fewer Rescuers could buy more time for the babies. Super-glue sometimes found its way into the locks on clinic doors, and Rescuers were using their own handcuffs and giant bicycle locks to secure themselves to the doors and to one another. On occasion derelict cars were disabled in front of the doors.

For some it was clearly true that the lives of the babies were of much greater value than the incidental expenses required [on the part of either the abortionist or the authorities] to reopen the killing center. Well-meaning, if pragmatic, Christians sometimes criticized the fact that police and other emergency crews were spending time arresting Rescuers that might better be invested in serving the public in other ways. The defense was that it was the police department's decision that the most important job they could perform at that time was to get a baby-killing concession back in business.

Joseph Foreman reports that during the Democratic National Convention, Operation Rescue's "siege of the Atlanta death camps in 1988 proved that weekly Rescues cut into the killing business, dramatically eliminating almost 70% of it even on days when no Rescue was scheduled. In the year following that time, abortion clinic personnel [in Atlanta] report that their abortion business was only 50% of what it was before [Operation Rescue's arrival]."[16]

Even Francis Beckwith, a valiant pro-life Christian writer and philosopher but not a great fan of Rescue, concedes that "Rescues produce tangible results of actual lives saved."[17]

Michael Bray, a pastor and pro-life firebrand but not primarily known as a Rescuer, agrees: "To be sure, blockades have saved thousands of lives directly and many more by the witness made which continues to spread."[18]

Operation Rescue, the mass movement, was at its peak from 1988 to 1990. The Alan Guttmacher Institute is an appendage of Planned Parenthood which presents itself as an impartial compiler of statistics regarding abortion and other deathly subjects [naming the firm after a prominent abortionist and once-president of Planned Parenthood should be a clue to its bias]. The Institute reported, "Between 1988 and 1992, abortion rates declined 5 percent nationally and 8 percent in California."[19]

What would seem at first to be a major tribute to the impact of Operation Rescue on the abortion rate was largely fabricated. The abortion rate reduction was undoubtedly much smaller; more reliable studies report little or no change in the rate during those years.[20]

At the time when it reported the significant decline, Guttmacher's goal was to provide "proof" to show the government how financially injured the abortion industry was by the "illegal activities of Rescuers." This allegation was rewarded by the subsequent rash of court judgments that ordered Rescue leaders and various other pro-life activists to pay millions of dollars in "compensation and punitive damages" to abortionists over the next few years.

18 Bray, *A Time to Kill*, 145.

19 *Press*, 8-4-96, A1, A12.

20 *Press*, 3-22-96, A22: "The Centers for Disease Control and Prevention said... the 1993 abortion rate, or the number of abortions per 1,000 women of reproductive age, remained unchanged at 23 and has held steady since the mid-1980s."

Dissuade women from aborting

The reader will note that we list the individual woman's decision to abort her child as the last of the seven links in the abortive chain. Here we will not duplicate that section but will note the invaluable work of valiant Sidewalk Counselors who have been called to the exhausting and heartwrenching ministry of trying to dissuade abortion-bound women as they walk the last few steps to the door of the abortion clinic. Brian Clowes writes, "The only way to eradicate abortion is to convert the hearts and minds of Americans one by painful one. Only *then* will our babies be safe,"[1] and he quotes Notre Dame Law Professor Charles Rice: "Sidewalk counseling is a tactic that can bring down the whole structure of legalized abortion."[2]

The key to the success of sidewalk counselors is that they directly or indirectly are the voice of the saints at the Crisis Pregnancy Centers who make good on the promise that the church sincerely loves the mothers and babies and stands ready to assist them in countless tangible and crucial ways. Brian Clowes says, "In 1983, about 855,000 women were counseled in the nation's 2,900 crisis pregnancy centers. Of these women, about 40 percent had first visited pro-abortion 'counseling' centers or abortion mills. Of these women, about 650,000 decided to keep their babies – a CPC 'success' rate of 76 percent."[3]

As a credit to the impact the sidewalk counselors and CPCs are having, we are told, "The pro-aborts are attempting to create an environment so hostile to CPCs that nobody will even dare try to organize one. The reason for these attacks can be simply stated: The more than half a million babies saved by the crisis pregnancy centers each year means tens of millions of dollars of lost profit for the abortionists."[4]

In view of the crucial role sidewalk counselors have played, unflaggingly, for more than 25 years, there is this sad note presented by Joseph Scheidler in the 1993 revision of his 1988 book: "Since this chapter [How to Control Their Escort Teams] was written, our prediction that this tactic of using deathscorts would be used 'more and more' has come true with a vengeance. The squads of gays and lesbians and other pro-aborts have virtually turned into hordes at many clinics. With the onset of Operation Rescue in 1988, the network of militant clinic defense groups became better organized and often presents a formidable obstacle to doing sidewalk counseling."[5]

The goal of dissuading abortion-bound women by being present and prayerfully obedient at abortion clinics is achieved only by God's grace, and from our earthly perspective, not very often. Each such miraculous event is cause for heavenly and earthly rejoicing. Pro-abortionists taunt pro-lifers with the assertion that an "incompetent" Shelley Shannon may spend the rest of her life in prison for wounding an abortionist so superficially that he was back at his grisly trade the next day. Here is the rest of the story: On August 19, 1993, a woman who was waiting in the abortion business parking lot had an appointment for a pregnancy test and wanted an abortion. After Shelley Shannon shot George Tiller, the woman decided not to get an abortion and delivered a son, Michael, on March 11, 1994.[6]

Fewer locations doing abortion

Another significant goal of pro-life activism directed toward the surgical abortion industry is the desire that fewer and fewer locations will be available to offer the abortion "service" to American women.

This article appeared in a local newspaper in 1993: "A doctor who has been the focus of an Operation Rescue campaign to make him stop performing abortions has done just that... Anderson [had been] the only local doctor willing to perform abortions."[7]

How's this for a victory? "Philadelphia, PA. The former Lawndale Community Hospital... at one time a high volume abortion facility killing approximately 900 unborn children each year, it is now a part of the St. William's Parish School... In 1978, a handful of prolifers... began holding prayer vigils every Sunday morning outside the hospital... In early 1980 [a] relatively large increase, about seventy-five people, was enough to make the hospital cave in. The administrator announced that, in response to 'community sentiment,' the hospital would no longer perform abortions."[8]

"Dallas, TX – Abortionist Norman Tomkins is moving to Gainesville to escape the heat – the heat of continuous and concentrated protests. '[The protesters] just destroyed my practice,' Tomkins said... Protesters have picketed Tomkins' home, office, and church as well as the office where his wife works since October 1992. They have received postcards with photos of dead babies and claim to have received phone calls."[9]

1 Clowes, *Pro-Life Activist's Encyclopedia*, page 19.3.
2 Rice, in Clowes, page 26.2.
3 Clowes, page 47.1.
4 Clowes, pages 47.1 to 47.2.
5 Scheidler, 341.
6 *Life Advocate*, 5/'94, 14; also Bray, 179-80.
7 *The Virginian-Pilot and the Ledger-Star*, July 9, 1993, in Mark Crutcher, *Access: The Key to Pro-Life Victory*, 8.
8 *Life Advocate*, 6/'94, 27.
9 *Life Advocate*, 6/'94, 5.
10 Crutcher, *Access*, 22.
11 Crutcher, *Access*, 26.
12 *Time*, 4-19-93, 40.
13 Focus on the Family, *Citizen*, 7-17-95, 2-3.
14 Associated Press, in *Press*, 1-9-95, A1, A8.
15 *Newsweek*, 3-13-95, 61.
16 Associated Press, in *Press*, 1-22-96, A3.

SCOPE and FOCUS
I. CONVICTIONS
II. PRETEXTS
III. MANDATE
IV. LEGACY
V. ABORTIVE LINKS
Recreational Sex
Reproductive Technology
Abortion Industry
Problems with abortion
God's law. Bloodguilt
Right to life
Cruelty to the preborn
Inhumane acts
Excuses for inaction
Autonomy of woman
Relativism. Subhuman
Mechanism. Potential
Pragmatism. Tactics
Pleasure. Controversy
Positivism. Legality
Goals of intervention
Stop this abortion
Dissuade women
Fewer locations
Society more pro-life
Government pro-life
Church authentic
Types of intervention
Protest. Witness
Interposition. Rescue
Destruction. Burn
Violence. Killing
Guerilla Warfare
Revolution
Justifications offered
Freedoms: speech...
Civil disobedience
Life vs. property
Deter others
"Execute" the guilty
Necessity. Justifiable
Higher accountability
Governmental Action
Social Climate
Religious Confusion
Personal Decision to Abort
VI. DILEMMA
VII. DESTINY

"Limiting access" with gusto

Mark Crutcher is the founder of Life Dynamics in Denton, Texas. One of the group's key projects is to compile evidence and to assist in civil suits and criminal prosecutions in cases of abortion malpractice, injury and death [to mothers, in addition to babies]. His view is that putting abortionists out of business limits "access" to abortions. He says that "access doesn't just *influence* abortion politics; it is now the determining factor in which side wins and which side loses."[10]

This belief is supported by the statement of abortionist Warren Hern in 1994: "I think that we cannot underestimate the determination of Life Dynamics to destroy us – and they have found an exceedingly dangerous tool."[11]

In 1993 *Time* magazine spoke of "the approximately 1,500 increasingly beleaguered abortion clinics in the U.S."[12]

Focus on the Family's *Citizen* magazine reported in 1995: "The number of facilities that offer abortions plummeted almost 20 percent between 1982 and 1992. Some states experienced a nearly 40 percent drop. About 65 facilities discontinue abortion service each year. Only 7 percent of abortions are now performed in hospitals – an 18 percent decline since 1988... Even in metropolitan counties, more than half have no abortion service."[13]

The Associated Press reported in 1995: "The Abortion Wars: Who's Winning? Despite a flurry of laws and court decisions that rein in anti-abortion protesters, the ranks of abortion providers are shrinking. The losses suggested abortion supporters are winning battles but may be losing the war. Some 200 sites that provided abortion, mostly in smaller rural and public hospitals, have halted the procedure in the last four years under threats of violence, financial woes and political opposition."[14]

In March of 1995, *Newsweek* reported, "With anti-abortion protests becoming more violent, the number of counties with doctors willing to perform abortions has shrunk to 16 percent."[15]

Kate Michelman, president of the National Abortion and Reproductive Rights Action League said in 1996, "Today the freedom of choice is in more jeopardy probably than at any other time since [1973]."[16]

"As hospitals end [abortion] services, the number of medical residency programs training doctors in abortion has dropped by half. Fewer doctors are able, or willing to replace veteran abortion doctors as they retire."[17]

Make Society more pro-life

All pro-lifers would agree that winning the hearts and souls of Americans is central to any future victory over abortion. Joseph Foreman asserts that our plans and strategies as pro-lifers must reflect six critical "differences between child-killing in the womb and other forms of brutal physical assault:" 1) the mother is willing, and finances it; 2) the church permits it; 3) some insurance covers abortion but not childbirth; 4) intellectuals approve; 5) feminists say abortion liberates a woman from male domination; 6) We [all] have permitted it to continue for years on end.[18]

In 1988 Randall Terry was saying, "Most major political change in this country is preceded by social upheaval, and the pro-life movement has been too nice... We've wanted to be respectable, ...to write letters, ...maybe carry a sign once in a while. By doing so, we have reduced the murder of a million-and-a-half children a year to the same level as whether or not we want a stop sign up some place, so we write a letter to the editor... We call abortion *murder*, and yet we don't act like it's murder."[19]

In his *Operation Rescue* book, Randall Terry wrote, "The entire abortion industry along with the National Organization for Women began to sit up and take notice... the opponents of Operation Rescue take our stand seriously. Why? Because they know if we can call enough people to repent and participate in a mass uprising to shut down abortion mills, their government funding will be cut off and their selfish 'pro-choice' murders will once again be made illegal."[20]

Unfortunately, after a few months of granting favorable press to Operation Rescue a sternly chastised media resolved to alternately demonize the entire pro-life movement and then ignore it totally. By definition, for the past eight years, Christian witness and activism of all kinds has been either a non-event or a topic of derision.

17 Associated Press, in *Press*, 1-9-95, A1, A8.

18 Foreman, 118.

19 Randall Terry, "If You Believe Abortion is Murder, Act Like It's Murder," cassette, 1988.

20 Terry, *Operation Rescue*, 26.

Stepping back to get a broader view of social change

In South Africa, Nelson Mandela once spoke to a crowd of ten thousand to inaugurate a Defiance Campaign: "I told the people that they would make history and focus the attention of the world on the racist policies of South Africa."[1] The good news is that he was precisely correct; the bad news is that the wheels of social progress turn so slowly that Mandela would spend 27 years in prison before his prophetic vision was realized.

Barbara Ehrenreich offers us the long view of recent pro-life events: "Quite apart from blowing up clinics and terrorizing patients, the anti-abortion movement can take credit for a more subtle and lasting kind of damage: It has succeeded in getting even pro-choice people to think of abortion as a 'moral dilemma,' and 'agonizing decision.'"[2]

Making Government more pro-life

As has been stated already, a primary but indirect goal of pro-life activism towards the abortion industry is to hasten the day when abortion will once again be outlawed in the United States. How we are doing will be discussed at length just a few pages further along. Here is a peek.

George Grant says, "Amazingly, this dangerous and brutal procedure [abortion] is the only surgery which is legally protected from any sort of government regulation. There are laws that dictate how tonsils may or may not be removed... but there are no laws that dictate how abortions may or may not be performed."[3]

He continues, "Planned Parenthood claims to be a privately funded, non-profit family planning organization. But that is an illusion... It is instead one of the largest – if not *the* largest – publicly funded multi-national collectives the world has ever seen."[4]

In 1995, Planned Parenthood affiliates performed 139,899 [nearly 10%] of the nation's abortions. $171,900,000 [that's 171 *million*] of its revenues [that's 34%] come from taxpayers through government grants and contracts. Thus their total annual revenue is more than $505 million, and it turns out that taxpayers effectively paid for nearly fifty thousand Planned Parenthood abortions [34% x 139,899].[5]

An important component of the early Operation Rescue vision was that an overwhelming multitude of Christians would blockade every abortion mill in such numbers that arresting them would "clog the system," filling the jails and courtrooms to the extent that an overwhelmed government would conclude that "The American people will simply not tolerate legalized abortion."

Here it is in Randall Terry's own words: "Only two abortion mills mar our [Binghamton, N.Y.] community. That's 80,000 Roman Catholics and evangelicals against two death camps. If three percent of the group, just 2,400 people, agreed to do multiple sit-ins at the local death camp, what do you think would happen? Probably nothing would happen to us, and we would likely keep the abortion mills from doing their bloody work... We would totally clog the system... that uprising would only consist of three percent of the religious community."[6]

It would appear that Randall Terry both overestimated the zeal of modern American Christians and underrated the resolve of the government to crush rebellion. In the words of Michael Kinsley in *Time* magazine: "The antiabortion movement, like the civil rights movement, may ultimately persuade society that it has been profoundly wrong. But meanwhile, a democratic society cannot fail to protect the exercise of what it has determined to be a fundamental right."[7]

Rescue leader Joseph Foreman reflected in 1992 on the lessons of the previous four years: "We built two defining focal points into Operation Rescue: 'Save a baby at any cost,' and 'Create political clout to change the law.' [Those] created an unresolvable internal conflict... The way we set forth the case of the children – the way we declared our willingness to defend them – left us with a win-or-die stand... We – particularly the leaders – were publicly caught between what we promised and what we could deliver."[8]

The failure of Operation Rescue's vision to materialize in 1990 was not due to internal defects. The blame can be placed equally at the feet of the government's pragmatic injustice, the media's self-serving agenda, and the Church's inertia. It might be candidly observed that the entire pro-life movement's degree of success in moving our abortion-loving government over the past 25 years is as the croaking of so many frogs in the moat outside a mighty castle.

1 Mandela, *Long Walk to Freedom*, 112.

2 Ehrenreich, in Brian Clowes, page 45.3.

3 Grant, *Grand Illusions: The Legacy of Planned Parenthood*, 85.

4 Grant, *Grand Illusions*, 28, 30.

5 Figures derived from California ProLife Council, *California ProLife Update*, Spring 1997, 4.

6 Terry, *Operation Rescue*, 198-9.

7 Kinsley, in *Time*, 8-15-94, 64.

8 Foreman, 5-7.

9 Carol Lefcourt, *Women and the Law*, page 8.2.

10 Associated Press, in *Press*, 1-9-95, A1, A8.

11 Michael Bray, 133-4.

SCOPE and FOCUS
I. CONVICTIONS
II. PRETEXTS
III. MANDATE
IV. LEGACY
V. ABORTIVE LINKS
Recreational Sex
Reproductive Technology
Abortion Industry
Problems with abortion
God's law. Bloodguilt
Right to life
Cruelty to the preborn
Inhumane acts
Excuses for inaction
Autonomy of woman
Relativism. Subhuman
Mechanism. Potential
Pragmatism. Tactics
Pleasure. Controversy
Positivism. Legality
Goals of intervention
Stop this abortion
Dissuade women
Fewer locations
Society more pro-life
Government pro-life
Church authentic
Types of intervention
Protest. Witness
Interposition. Rescue
Destruction. Burn
Violence. Killing
Guerilla Warfare
Revolution
Justifications offered
Freedoms: speech...
Civil disobedience
Life vs. property
Deter others
"Execute" the guilty
Necessity. Justifiable
Higher accountability
Governmental Action
Social Climate
Religious Confusion
Personal Decision to Abort
VI. DILEMMA
VII. DESTINY

What bright spots can be detected on the dark abortive scene?

While abortion has now been declared even more fundamentally a Constitutional right than it was in 1973, there are scattered [we dare not say "points of light"] "candles on the glacier" which give us inklings of what someday may be experienced with far greater frequency:

"Women's health clinics have frequently been closed by state authorities when abortion procedures were undertaken by anyone other than licensed physicians."[9]

"It is an uncontested fact that the number of places women can go for abortions has decreased: Hospitals accounted for most of the decrease. Restrictions on public funding for abortion drove the procedures out of public hospitals; private hospitals acknowledge that pressure from anti-abortion groups helped push them into ending the service."[10]

"The most famous judge who regularly dismissed charges against [abortuary] blockaders is retired Judge Harold Johnson of Bridgeton, Missouri. John Ryan, a man who encouraged blockades in St. Louis and inspired many by his writings and his actions, was dismissed by Judge Johnson *one-hundred times* after repeatedly being arrested for blocking abortuary doors."[11]

The city of Milwaukee "decided not to waste its resources imprisoning the unimprisonable. So... Christians rescued every day the death camps they targeted were open. In September of 1991, Bread and Roses, the highest-volume killing center in Wisconsin, closed; and Jakobowski, the killer, left town for good. Eleven Milwaukee child-killers have now quit killing as well, leaving only six who grimly hang on in the teeth of a groggy but awakening Church [in 1992]."[12]

Make the Church more authentic

Among the most profound reasons for the call for Christians to stand against the abortion industry would have to be the objective of restoring authenticity to the practice of Christianity.

When James Hunter published *Culture Wars: The Struggle to Define America* in 1991, it was not yet widely understood, apparently even by him, that the Religious Right and Operation Rescue had both been decisively pierced and effectively deflated by the concerted efforts of the powers held by secular humanism. For this reason, Hunter still reflected an earlier optimism: "Some observers have argued that the moral vision of the orthodox alliance, particularly as championed by the Evangelical Protestant community, is in a strong position to actually dominate American public discourse in the near future... There is an indigenous passion and intensity of moral commitment that exists in some parts of the orthodox alliance that is just not found in balancing measure by their counterparts on the progressivist side. On some issues this translates into a new militancy. The anti-abortion project, Operation Rescue, and the tactics of civil disobedience it employs, signals this change."[13]

While it is agreed that the Church possesses multiple times the power needed to accomplish fantastic exploits for the kingdom of God among men, what is now apparent is that due to serious deficiencies of vision and will, little flexing of that spiritual muscle should be expected in the near future.

Joseph Foreman reflects: "Our goal was to see churches, not organizations, rise up to defend the children. In the beginning this happened with great success: more pastors were arrested with us than with any other organization in the history of this country. Operation Rescue envisioned God's people led by their pastors going out in simple obedience... We did not intend to replace the Church, but to spur the Church to take on its historic task. When the Church would not, we had no Plan B to fall back on, and still lack such a plan..."[14]

Foreman continues: "The reason we need people willing to spend months in jail for a single Rescue, is not to clog the courts or jail, but to raise the moral stakes for all of us. In jail he becomes a visible representative of the child in the womb who is still invisible to the Church... Moral authority, not clogged courts and jails, will turn the tide."[15]

12 Joseph Foreman, 184.

13 Hunter, 299.

14 Foreman, *Shattering the Darkness: The Crisis of the Cross in the Church Today,* 54,142.

15 Foreman, 54.

Rhoda! Whoever is at the door, tell him we're busy praying![1]

Unfortunately, the beginning of the end of the Operation Rescue phenomenon was contained in the fact that instead of rallying to the support of fellow Christians who were jailed for taking a bold Christian moral stand, most pastors and congregations appeared to be embarrassed by them and to ignore them.

During Christmas week of 1989, Joseph Foreman gathered together the Rescuers from all over the country who had responded to his challenge to "Buy a one-way ticket to Atlanta to Rescue in solidarity with Randall Terry in the city that has tossed him in jail and thrown the key away [a two-year sentence for simple trespass]." When we arrived the headlines blared, "They're Coming Back!" for what Joseph Foreman had billed "The Second Siege of Atlanta." No convention hall was necessary; when all 18 of us crowded into one motel room for our marching orders, Joseph read John 12:24: "Unless a kernel of wheat falls to the ground and dies, it remains only a single seed. But if it dies, it produces many seeds."

It soon became clear that not only did the political machine in Atlanta want us dead and buried, but we had already been written off by the Church, both local and national, as well. Sixteen of us Rescued, were jailed without bail for three months awaiting trial, were convicted and were not released until June. Randall Terry had walked free shortly after our arrest, and while our ministry in the cell blocks was fruitful and rewarding, we knew that to the church we had become as invisible and anonymous as the doomed children of abortion. Once aspiring to become the seed of revival, we came to understand that seed is sometimes cast on the rock, choked by thorns and eaten by the birds.[2]

Foreman has said, "Transformation in the Church will come as a result of enough Christian trading their lives for others, thereby purchasing the right to speak to our society."[3]

Miraculous events in Milwaukee

"In the summer of 1992... from June through August... on the average... each week, 3,000 to 5,000 Milwaukee area Christians came to the gates of hell... The events of the summer were not only the longest and largest sustained effort against child-killing in any city; they were also entirely local... On August 7, pastors of southeastern Wisconsin called for a solemn assembly; 11,000 Christians gathered to repent and to covenant before God to bring the high places down. The next day 5,000 people went to a local death camp and closed it for the day. This was the largest Christian presence ever to gather outside an abortion mill... Since then, the killing business has never rebounded... Milwaukee can become an abortion-free zone. Already Burlington, a suburb of Milwaukee, has voted to declare itself such a zone – the first in the nation."[4]

That pattern could be duplicated in any city, large or small, at any time of our choosing. Who can deny that this is what an authentic Church should be doing? Who can predict how long it will be before the vision will be embraced and our opportunity becomes a reality?

That opportunity is fading by the minute. Abortion clinics still *are* abortion in the mind of the nation, even though they already represent only a fractional portion of the total baby-killing holocaust. The day is fast approaching, however, when those clinics will resemble ghost towns while the abortion rate remains at epidemic levels, with only the methods of aborting having changed. If the Christian community fails to take a stand for the babies at the abortion clinics while we still have that chance, it is hard to imagine how any form of testimony will be possible once the abortions themselves become as invisible and anonymous as the babies themselves are now.

1 *Acts* 12:5-17.

2 *Luke* 8:4-8.

3 Foreman, xxi.

4 Foreman, 185.

5 See also Jonathan Black, *Radical Lawyers: Their Role in the Movement and in the Courts*, 52-3.

6 Scheidler, 17.

7 Fortas, *Concerning Dissent and Civil Disobedience*, 9.

8 Scheidler, 366.

9 Joan Comay and Ronald Brownrigg, *Who's Who in the Bible,* 421.

10 Whitehead, *The Stealing of America*, 114.

11 *Press*, 4-1-95, A3.

12 Linda Bird Francke, *The Ambivalence of Abortion*, 1978, 249: "At the National Right to Life convention in 1976, detailed minute-by-minute orders on the takeover of a specific abortion clinic were distributed on mimeographed sheets. Participants were advised to meet at the clinic at 8:00 A.M. and to park on side streets so that the staffs of the clinic would not be alerted by an overfull parking lot. *Women participating in the sit-in* were instructed to meet on a street corner next to the clinic, while *husbands and boyfriends who would picket* during the demonstration were to meet in the parking lot next to the toy store across the street... The entrance to the rooms where the abortions are performed were to be blocked by the Right-to-Lifers' bodies... late-comers were instructed to sit outside the elevators to block them." The sophistication of the tactics so early, 1976, is amazing; the instructions included details on how to maximize media coverage and explained the rationale behind what would later be termed *going limp*: "Lay down in a relaxing position with muscles at ease in anticipation of being carried out" by the police!

13 Colson, 250.

SCOPE and FOCUS
I. CONVICTIONS
II. PRETEXTS
III. MANDATE
IV. LEGACY
V. ABORTIVE LINKS
Recreational Sex
Reproductive Technology
Abortion Industry
Problems with abortion
God's law. Bloodguilt
Right to life
Cruelty to the preborn
Inhumane acts
Excuses for inaction
Autonomy of woman
Relativism. Subhuman
Mechanism. Potential
Pragmatism. Tactics
Pleasure. Controversy
Positivism. Legality
Goals of intervention
Stop this abortion
Dissuade women
Fewer locations
Society more pro-life
Government pro-life
Church authentic
Types of intervention
Protest. Witness
Interposition. Rescue
Destruction. Burn
Violence. Killing
Guerilla Warfare
Revolution
Justifications offered
Freedoms: speech...
Civil disobedience
Life vs. property
Deter others
"Execute" the guilty
Necessity. Justifiable
Higher accountability
Governmental Action
Social Climate
Religious Confusion
Personal Decision to Abort
VI. DILEMMA
VII. DESTINY

4. Types of intervention

As we embark on an exploration of the range of possible interventions at the scene of surgical abortions, it must be noted that a catalog of possibilities is not a list of suggestions! [Janet Reno, that was for you.] Pro-life activism *could* range from protest to interposition to destruction of property [tools of the trade or structures]. It could include violence or death to personnel, guerilla warfare against the killer's accomplices including the police, and revolution [civil war] against the government itself.[5]

Joseph Scheidler was a pro-life activist before *Roe v. Wade*. His *Closed: 99 Ways to Stop Abortion* is a pro-life classic. He writes: "No social movement in the history of this country has succeeded without activists taking to the streets. Activism, including demonstrations, pickets, protests, and sit-ins, is necessary not only to save lives, but to garner public attention, bring the media into the struggle, and shake politicians into recognizing the determination of anti-abortion supporters. Anyone who misses this purpose of activism is a poor student of history."[6]

Mid-century Supreme Court Justice Abe Fortas declared: "If I had lived in Germany in Hitler's days, I hope I would have refused to wear an armband, to *Heil Hitler*, to submit to genocide."[7]

Demonstration. Protest. Witnessing

Because Joe Scheidler uses the term guerilla warfare, we must emphasize that he is unequivocally committed to nonviolence. Read carefully: "There is a lot of imagination and creativity still untapped in the pro-life ranks. There are effective means of carrying on the guerilla warfare necessary for victories in the battle against abortion. There are many ideas not mentioned here because we have not thought of them yet."[8]

The absolute minimum standard of Christian witness in-the-face of the abortion industry is the silent protest of standing across the street, praying, quietly singing or reading the Bible. We are the "point men" in spiritual warfare. Saint Paul called Timothy his spiritual son. In the book of Hebrews, the last message "is that Timothy has been set free from some imprisonment... An apocryphal *Acts of Timothy* describes his martyrdom on 22 January in the year 97, when *protesting* at the licentious festivities in honour of [the goddess] Diana of the Ephesians."[9]

John Whitehead asserts, "Picketing should not be a symbolic excursion. Instead, it should be a serious attempt to close the clinic."[10] In 1995 the Associated Press reported: "Taking up a literal front-line position in the battle over abortion, Operation Rescue is moving its headquarters next door to an abortion clinic."[11]

Interposition. Rescue. Love your littlest neighbor

Rescue is tremendously misunderstood, primarily because of the media's systematic efforts to discredit and to demonize Rescuers. In the shadow of the civil rights movement, however, a certain amount of misunderstanding was inevitable. When Chuck Colson wrote *Kingdoms in Conflict* in 1987, even though Operation Rescue had not popularized the concept, Rescue had been a component of the pro-life battle for at least ten years.[12]

His natural mistake was to think of a Rescue as just another "sit-in" and, further, to overlook its primary objective of saving babies from being murdered, and to dismiss it as a publicity gimmick. He wrote: "Joan Andrews is a slight, soft-spoken Roman Catholic who on March 26, 1986, entered an abortion clinic for a Pro-Life sit-in and attempted to damage a suction machine used to perform abortions... In our day, breaking laws to make a dramatic point is the ultimate logic of terrorism, not civil disobedience."[13] Innocent though ignorant comments like this were all too plentiful, and Christians did as much damage in the early months of Operation Rescue as did its enemies.

The Operation Rescue phenomenon

In 1983, four years before Operation Rescue was born, Dave Andrusko wrote a truly prophetic book; even the title was prophetic: *To Rescue the Future: The Pro-Life Movement in the 1980s*. He wrote: "The real issues at stake in the abortion dispute are becoming increasingly evident to more and more thoughtful people. The results may well be a complete transformation of the issue within five years."[1]

Operation Rescue was born at Cherry Hills, New Jersey, in 1987, and the Christian media gave it a big boost. Randall Terry proclaimed, "We had successfully closed down an abortion center for an entire day. No children were killed... Three mothers changed their minds." At the second Rescue, New York City, part of the thrill was that those arrested included "twenty protestant pastors, fifteen Roman Catholic priests, two monsignors, an auxiliary bishop, four nuns, an Orthodox priest, and two rabbis."[2]

On the first day in New York, 503 were arrested. In the four-day period 800 participants logged 1647 arrests.[3] "During one hundred-day period between May 1 and early August, 1988, over 4000 arrests resulted [from Rescues]."[4] "The rescues that captured the most [media] attention were those [during the Siege of Atlanta during the Democratic National Convention in August, 1988]."[5]

After the Siege of Atlanta, two crucial decisions were made: 1) The vast majority of local pastors, at the moment when their joint participation and leadership could likely have mobilized the conservative Christian majority to seize a monumental and decisive victory, instead chose the path of non-controversial security; 2) The secular humanists at the reins of government and the media resolved to stop the Christian "monster" in its tracks. The media began a systematic distortion and demonization campaign and several police departments seemed to have resolved to practice their SWAT-team and anti-terrorism tactics on Operation Rescue.[6]

Joseph Foreman summarizes: "In the summer of 1989, Operation Rescue was peaking... But we still had no strategy beyond creating a climactic event... and the promise of the great groundswell had died."[7]

Several leaders of the Los Angeles Easter Week Rescue were further abused by having to endure a lengthy "conspiracy" trial that summer. Then in September, Randall Terry was tried for his role in the Siege of Atlanta and was sentenced to two years; Atlanta vowed that he would serve the full term.[8]

The last hurrah for Operation Rescue National was when 2,500 of us did the Rescue-thing in the nation's capital in November of 1989, and where "a peculiar national call" was issued: "Now is the time to stand [in solidarity with Randall Terry] in Atlanta... Come and die in Atlanta."[9] Since only 18 responded to that call, it may be concluded that O.R. *did* die in Atlanta.

The O.R. vision has been temporarily resurrected a couple of notable times: 1) The Summer of Mercy in Wichita in 1991, when 2,600 clinic blockaders were arrested in 40 days;[10] and 2) the spectacular 1992 Church-in-the-streets and pro-life revival in Milwaukee [see *Orphans* page 218]. Aside from those two and perhaps a few more exceptions, "Every city knows that we can be bought if they just make the price high enough."[11]

In summary, Brian Clowes says, "Since Operation Rescue hit the pavement in mid-1987, more than 100,000 persons have risked arrest, and more than 70,000 have been arrested. It is estimated that at least 500 lives have been [directly] saved. These numbers mean that the Rescue movement is now ten times larger than the original civil rights movement ever was, in terms of arrests and those who are willing to risk arrest... [Yet] rescuers make up only about one percent of the entire pro-life Movement."[12]

Not to discount in any way the risks and the costs involved in the civil rights movement, but it is important to point out that the vast majority of leaders and participants in the civil rights struggle were members of the oppressed group, fighting for their own rights. By contrast, the hundred-thousand Christians who Rescued had nothing personally to gain by their actions – whatever risks they took were exclusively for the benefit of tiny, nameless and anonymous preborn people, not related to them in any way at all except in the very most important way of all: they are known to be 100% human persons, created in the image of God from the moment of conception, and entitled to any and every right and protection that any and all of us deserve.

SCOPE and FOCUS
I. CONVICTIONS
II. PRETEXTS
III. MANDATE
IV. LEGACY
V. ABORTIVE LINKS
Recreational Sex
Reproductive Technology
Abortion Industry
Problems with abortion
God's law. Bloodguilt
Right to life
Cruelty to the preborn
Inhumane acts
Excuses for inaction
Autonomy of woman
Relativism. Subhuman
Mechanism. Potential
Pragmatism. Tactics
Pleasure. Controversy
Positivism. Legality
Goals of intervention
Stop this abortion
Dissuade women
Fewer locations
Society more pro-life
Government pro-life
Church authentic
Types of intervention
Protest. Witness
Interposition. Rescue
Destruction. Burn
Violence. Killing
Guerilla Warfare
Revolution
Justifications offered
Freedoms: speech...
Civil disobedience
Life vs. property
Deter others
"Execute" the guilty
Necessity. Justifiable
Higher accountability
Governmental Action
Social Climate
Religious Confusion
Personal Decision to Abort
VI. DILEMMA
VII. DESTINY

1 Andrusko, Introduction.

2 Terry, *Operation Rescue*, 25.

3 Terry, *Operation Rescue*, 241-2.

4 Terry, *Operation Rescue*, 244-5.

5 Randy Alcorn, *Is Rescuing Right? Breaking the Law to Save the Unborn*, 166-7.

Destruction. Burn / bomb. Deactivate the killing tools. Sabotage

Michael Bray is perhaps the most articulate of the convicted "abortuary demolitionists." In *A Time to Kill* he offers this view: "It has often been declared that had there been a massive protest and 'nonviolent' intervention in 1973, there would not be legalized abortion in America today. The absence of a faithful response on the part of the masses of Christians has kept abortion a way of life in America. The abortuaries remain 'open by permission of the churches of the neighborhood,' chide activists. All true. But... a remnant band of faithful might also have terminated the legal practice in the land by mounting a substantial campaign of force. What if the first ten abortuaries built had been set ablaze?"[13]

Dates listed in Michael Bray's book reveal that abortion clinic bombs and arsons began as early as 1977. The media tries not to give too much publicity to these events lest they inspire others. The number of incendiary episodes seems to vary from year to year following no identifiable pattern, in the general range of zero [1980] to eight or ten events [1978, '89, '90], but with peak years of twenty-nine fires in 1984, twenty-two in 1985, thirteen in 1986, and fourteen in 1987. With the advent of Operation Rescue, the numbers generally lowered.[14]

Once the government and the media had quashed Operation Rescue, "According to Justice Department statistics, there were at least 15 bombings or arsons at abortion clinics every year from 1993 through 1995," and in recent years up to 39% of abortion clinics surveyed are reporting acts of violence.[15] Bray lists the names of 42 "demolitionists" who had been captured as of 1994, and notes that many remained "at large."[16]

There is no profile of the *typical* abortion clinic bomber. Besides a couple of not-surprising Vietnam veterans, one of them with government training in explosives,[17] the number includes mild-mannered moms like Shelley Shannon [who apparently set fires in 3 states].[18] Before Shelley shot an abortionist, she chose to buy the little gun rather than the big gun because it was less deadly. "Marjorie Reed damaged abortuaries in Ohio and New Jersey. She is also a wife and mother who had been a foster parent, taught migrant workers to read, and as a big Sister, had worked with young people. [She was sent to prison in 1989] under a ten-year prison term."[19]

Despite Attorney General Janet Reno's federal grand jury's best efforts to establish conspiracy charges against any and all pro-life leaders, the peaceful as well as the militant, the government's disappointed conclusion was that "The real extremists – the bombers, the arsonists, the murderers – tend to be 'encapsulated,' planning their most violent acts privately."[20]

Here is Michael Bray's perspective on destruction of abortion buildings [without injury to persons], as compared with Rescue: "The blockades served well the purpose of calling the community to come to the rescue of a neighbor... But the blockade is not necessarily the noblest or highest method of obedience... There is a certain sense of faithfulness that we feel after 'intervening' and blocking access... But might there not be a false sense of faithfulness when the means were available to act to a greater extent on behalf of the innocent? ...If God has said 'Move this mountain' and we use a shovel instead of bulldozers, have we been faithful?"[21]

Violence. Killing the killers

In South Africa, in 1953, Nelson Mandela concluded that "nonviolence was a useless strategy and could never overturn a white minority regime bent on retaining its power at any cost... violence was the only weapon that would destroy apartheid and we must be prepared, in the near future, to use that weapon..."[22]

There was a meeting in Chicago, in 1994, of 60 pro-life "activists." Shooters Michael Griffin and Shelley Shannon were in custody, and future shooter Paul Hill was at the meeting, [not *advocating* future killing but] debating that it was *morally justified* as a defensive action for an abortionist to be killed to prevent him from inflicting death upon the next in his long series of innocent, preborn victims. When Joseph Scheidler realized that "barely half" of those present "specifically repudiated Hill's extremist views," he says, "I thought, 'Wow! The movement has gone through some kind of transition.'"[23]

6 Joseph Foreman, 148: [In Easter week of 1989,] "I stood in a sea of pain watching Assistant Chief Bob Vernon of the Los Angeles Police personally direct the systematic brutalization of 1,000 Christians... torture teams – four to a Rescuer."

7 Foreman, 146.

8 Foreman, 167.

9 Foreman, 143, 183.

10 *Life Advocate*, 5/'94, 15.

11 Foreman, 143.

12 Brian Clowes, *Pro-Life Activist's Encyclopedia*, page 18.1.

13 Michael Bray, *A Time to Kill*, 18.

14 Bray, 135-6.

15 *Press*, 1-17-97, A1, A7.

16 Bray, 135-6.

17 Bray, 138.

18 *Press*, 6-8-95, A5.

19 Bray, 138.

20 *Time*, 8-15-94, 39.

21 Bray, 17-8.

22 Mandela, 136.

23 *Time*, 8-15-94, 39.

We are all members of one body

Respectable pro-life groups go to great pains to distance themselves – *completely* – from all acts of violence and even those deeds that only destroy property. This is, of course, as it must be. The reader is reminded of Nelson Mandela's explanation of the need for totally separate identities, one fervently devoted to one ethic, and the other dedicated to a radically different one.[1]

Mandela explains that there is a silent secret, know by all and acknowledged by none, that "we are all members of one body."[2]

The concept of "justification, not endorsement" is crucial. Perhaps the members of the peaceful African National Congress practiced a little pro-choice terminology. Instead of issuing a press release saying, "We denounce the terrorist tactics of Mandela and his thugs," perhaps they remained silent, and if pressed for a statement, replied, "While we are personally opposed to all acts of violence, we recognize the principle of self defense and the morality of shooting back at those who are shooting you."

In *Time* magazine of all places, Michael Kinsley argues: "The Operation Rescue people are not pacifists. They do not believe in the principle that violence is always wrong, even in response to violence. So why not kill the [abortion] doctors? Paul Hill understands their logic better than they do."[3]

Guerrilla warfare. Terrorism. "Chill" them out

As a purely intellectual exercise ["king's-x" no endorsement] it might be theorized that if simply ten times as many Shelley Shannons and Michael Brays, all at once but without collaboration or conspiracy, simply began torching abortion clinics in a standard sort of way, the result might be seen to have something of the impact that the French Resistance is commended for having had against Hitler. In all of the pro-life arsons we know of, there has been no loss of life or even one significant injury.

Quite different from that would be random acts of violence or destruction of property that was not devoted to the killing industry. Perhaps President Clinton was not far off the mark when he branded John Salvi's shootings "domestic terrorism."[4]

The concept of pro-life guerrilla warfare is not entirely theoretical, it would seem: In 1982 the "Army of God" kidnapped abortionist Hector Zevallos and his wife and held them for eight days before releasing them. At least one perpetrator has been sentenced to 42 years in prison. The conviction for "conspiracy and attempt to interfere with interstate commerce" likely means that the intent was to prevent abortions.[5]

In 1997, the Associated Press reported that members of "an anti-government militia cell with strongly held religious beliefs against banks and abortion, [called] 'Ambassadors from Yahweh' [are being held on] charges related to the bombing of a Planned Parenthood office [and a newspaper office], and the robbery and bombing of a bank... The three were convicted of conspiracy, interstate transportation of stolen vehicles and possession of hand grenades."[6]

While we can find no basis for *either* endorsing *or* justifying such a broad spectrum of criminal activity in the name of pro-life activism, it might yet be remarked that the knowledge that such groups are "out there" might have the effect of chilling abortion activity, and that result, in isolation, is good, not bad.

Revolution.

In *Kingdoms in Conflict*, Charles Colson wrote: "When all recourse to civic obedience has been exhausted and the evil of the state is so entrenched as to be impenetrable, then the Christian may be justified in organizing to overthrow the state."[7]

"Writing last month [July '94] to members of Congress, [David Trosch] warned of a possible civil war marked by 'massive killing' of abortion doctors and their staffs."[8]

Purely to make a conservative point, we believe, Brian Clowes paints this picture: "If only a small percentage of true Christians and Jews – say five percent, or about two hundred thousand – followed the lead of the Communists and repeatedly and simultaneously bombed every abortion clinic, killed all known abortionists, and pronounced the death sentence on any legislator who voted against life or any judge who rendered a pro-abortion decision, legal abortion would stop immediately... [But:] How long would it be before the 'system' and the Neofeminists recovered and struck back with even greater violence?"[9]

With all of this in mind, we would do well to consider at length the words of Winston Churchill: "If you do not fight for what is right when you can easily win without bloodshed, if you do not fight when the victory will be easy and not too costly, the moment may come when you will have to fight with all the odds against you and with only a precarious chance of survival... You may even have to fight when there is no hope of victory, for it is better to perish than to live as slaves."[10]

Obedience unto life

R.C. Sproul declares: "The urgency of the abortion issue requires us to protest to the very limit that our consciences allow."[11]

"Someday there will be a national Rescue somewhere," says Joseph Foreman. "It will begin like Atlanta and Wichita, only instead of shrinking back, the Church will surge forward and experience true revival and it will spread around the country... The only way to succeed is to raise up a generation of people who will lay down their lives."[12]

SCOPE and FOCUS
I. CONVICTIONS
II. PRETEXTS
III. MANDATE
IV. LEGACY
V. ABORTIVE LINKS
Recreational Sex
Reproductive Technology
Abortion Industry
Problems with abortion
God's law. Bloodguilt
Right to life
Cruelty to the preborn
Inhumane acts
Excuses for inaction
Autonomy of woman
Relativism. Subhuman
Mechanism. Potential
Pragmatism. Tactics
Pleasure. Controversy
Positivism. Legality
Goals of intervention
Stop this abortion
Dissuade women
Fewer locations
Society more pro-life
Government pro-life
Church authentic
Types of intervention
Protest. Witness
Interposition. Rescue
Destruction. Burn
Violence. Killing
Guerilla Warfare
Revolution
Justifications offered
Freedoms: speech...
Civil disobedience
Life vs. property
Deter others
"Execute" the guilty
Necessity. Justifiable
Higher accountability
Governmental Action
Social Climate
Religious Confusion
Personal Decision to Abort
VI. DILEMMA
VII. DESTINY

5. Justifications offered

We have come to terms with the fact that several things about abortion are wrong enough to command a response. We examined and dismissed various excuses that tend to dissuade us from conscientious action. We explored several possible goals that might be served by activism in the realm of the abortion business, and the types and degrees of intervention that might be on the pro-life-activism menu. Most importantly we must now seek to understand why a Christian is justified in "intruding on the privacy of the abortion decision" and "imposing her morality on others."

The hierarchy of laws will be central: "Gandhi and his followers were, in fact, scrupulously observing a higher law than the one they were violating, they kept their honor, their openness, their integrity – and the world respected and will not soon forget them."[13]

Justice Abe Fortas detailed the effects of civil rights and youth protest in the '60s, but his description makes clear the differences between those movements and pro-life activism: "The functions of mass demonstrations, in the city or on the campus, are to communicate a point of view; to arouse enthusiasm and group cohesiveness among participants; to attract others to join; and to impress upon the public and the authorities the point advocated by the protesters, the urgency of their demand, and the power behind it."[14]

The paramount distinction that must be made is that while all of these functions may be hoped-for by-products of something like a Rescue, the driving force in this case is a deeply felt, urgent compulsion to defend innocent life from an imminent fatal threat. No such emergency was operative in the agitations of the '60s. For that reason, the judgments of Mr. Fortas, which may have been valid then, are simply not applicable now: "Where the law being violated is not itself the focus or target of the protest... the violation of law merely as a technique of demonstration – constitutes an act of rebellion, not merely of dissent."[15]

The value in exploring the thoughts expressed by Mr. Fortas is that they give us insight into the mental processes that seem to be driving the government's response to pro-life activism. Repeatedly, prosecutors and judges have made their point: "This case is not about abortion, it is about trespassing." Rescuers are not sitting-in to demand the right of non-pregnant people to enter abortion clinics. They are not just breaking trespassing laws to "protest" legalized abortion. They are ignoring the law of trespass as they obey the moral requirement to defend innocent life.

Chuck Colson clarifies: "Breaking laws to make a dramatic point is the ultimate logic of terrorism, not civil disobedience. There may be situations, however, in which one has to respond to a higher law when life itself is at stake."[16]

F. LaGard Smith asks our basic question: "How do we justify being activist in the rescue of wildlife, but adamantly opposed to the rescue of human life?"[17]

Freedoms: speech, assembly and religion

John Whitehead's book *The Right to Picket and the Freedom of Public Discourse* is a great place to begin our study of the justifications for pro-life activism. He says that the right of free speech is so fundamental that "The Supreme Court has upheld the right of such freedom of speech as: burning and cursing the U.S. flag, and the threat of 'revengence' [sic] against the 'President, Congress, and Supreme Court.'"[18]

By the same token, argues Richard Land, "If God's name used in a profanity is [constitutionally-] protected speech, even if offensive to believers, then God's name invoked in a prayer [should be] protected speech, even if offensive to nonbelievers."[19]

1 Mandela, 238.

2 *Ephesians* 4:25, note the whole chapter.

3 *Time*, 8-15-94, 64.

4 Gregory Koukl, *Stand to Reason*, "Abortion Rhetoric," 2.

5 Scheidler, 299-300.

6 Associated Press, in *Press*, 4-3-97, A11.

7 Colson, 249.

8 *Press*, 8-27-94, H3.

9 Clowes, page 19.3.

10 Steven Carr and Franklin Meyer, *Celebrate Life: Hope for a Culture Preoccupied with Death*, 257.

11 Sproul, *Abortion: A Rational Look at an Emotional Issue*, 155-6.

12 Foreman, *Shattering the Darkness: The Crisis of the Cross in the Church Today*, 105.

13 O. Hobart Mowrer, *The Crisis in Psychiatry and Religion*, 145.

14 Fortas, *Concerning Dissent and Civil Disobedience*, 62.

15 Fortas, 63.

16 Charles Colson, *Kingdoms in Conflict*, 250.

17 F. LaGard Smith, *When Choice Becomes God*, 83-4.

18 Whitehead, *The Right to Picket*, 36-7.

19 Land, in William Ball, *In Search of a National Morality: A Manifesto for Evangelicals and Catholics*, 90.

Civil disobedience

As was implied in our introduction to this section on justifications for pro-life activism, all of the reasons that approve of civil disobedience as an avenue of *protest* apply even more strongly to violation of minor laws during acts of rescue in a life-and-death situation.

Francis Schaeffer put civil disobedience in a historical Christian perspective: "The early Christians died because they would not obey the state in a civil matter... They were civil rebels. The Roman State did not care what anybody believed religiously; you could believe anything or you could be an atheist. But you had to pay homage to Caesar as a sign of your loyalty to the state. The Christians said 'No.' That is why they were thrown to the lions."[1]

"Over the course of nearly three centuries," says Randall Terry, "the persecutions saw thousands of Christians put to death by being burned at the stake or beheaded; they were crucified, fed to wild beasts, tortured, and whipped to death for their refusal to 'obey the law.' ...From the Roman government's point of view, these Christians were not being put to death for their faith in Christ. They were killed for their civil disobedience... **If they had simply compromised a little**, believing in Jesus ***and*** burning incense to Caesar, **they could [easily] have saved their lives**... Multitudes of believers confirmed the Higher Laws principle with their blood."[2]

"Civil disobedience is clearly justified," according to Charles Colson, in three situations: "when government attempts to take over the role of the church or allegiance due only to God. Then the Christian has not just the right but the duty to resist. [Colson mentions Shadrach, et. al.] Civil disobedience is also mandated when the state restricts freedom of conscience, as in the case of Peter and John... arrested for disturbing the peace [*Acts* 4:19-20]. Third... when the state flagrantly ignores its divinely mandated responsibilities to preserve life and maintain order and justice."[3]

In *Is Rescuing Right? Breaking the Law to Save the Unborn*, Randy Alcorn enumerates a series of historical situations in which civil disobedience has been exercised by some. He asks his readers, "Would you break civil law in these situations?" In the first century, would you offer sacrifices to Caesar? In the second century, would you "steal" and adopt an infant legally abandoned-to-die by its parents? In an Arab country today, would you illegally share the gospel with your Muslim neighbor? If you were a slave in 1855, would you try to escape? If you were white in 1855, would you hide fleeing slaves? In India, would you rescue a wife from being burned to death on her husband's funeral pyre? During World War II, in Nazi-occupied Europe, would you hide Jews? During World War II, in the United States, would you hide a Japanese family from an American detention camp? As a black in Montgomery, Alabama, would you defy the "back seats of the bus" laws? In Sweden today, would you discipline your child by spanking? In the Netherlands today, would you secretly feed an elderly patient whose chart read, "No food"? In America today, would you kidnap and raise a Down syndrome newborn whose chart read "Do not feed"? In the future, what will you do if the government requires that a permanent mark be placed on everybody's hand or forehead? What would you do to rescue preborn children from abortion?

Nelson Mandela said, "Nonviolent passive resistance is effective as long as your opposition adheres to the same rules as you do. But if peaceful protest is met with violence, its efficacy is at an end... there is no moral goodness in using an ineffective weapon."[4]

Today in America, says Joseph Foreman, "The courts understand civil disobedience as a strategy. To make sure that we keep it a mere strategy, the courts and police will beat us, throw us in jail, or seize our property in lawsuits. The courts want to intimidate us out of protecting children."[5]

Nelson Mandela says: "No people or nation ever freed itself through education alone."[6]

SCOPE and FOCUS
I. CONVICTIONS
II. PRETEXTS
III. MANDATE
IV. LEGACY
V. ABORTIVE LINKS
Recreational Sex
Reproductive Technology
Abortion Industry
Problems with abortion
God's law. Bloodguilt
Right to life
Cruelty to the preborn
Inhumane acts
Excuses for inaction
Autonomy of woman
Relativism. Subhuman
Mechanism. Potential
Pragmatism. Tactics
Pleasure. Controversy
Positivism. Legality
Goals of intervention
Stop this abortion
Dissuade women
Fewer locations
Society more pro-life
Government pro-life
Church authentic
Types of intervention
Protest. Witness
Interposition. Rescue
Destruction. Burn
Violence. Killing
Guerilla Warfare
Revolution
Justifications offered
Freedoms: speech...
Civil disobedience
Life vs. property
Deter others
"Execute" the guilty
Necessity. Justifiable
Higher accountability
Governmental Action
Social Climate
Religious Confusion
Personal Decision to Abort
VI. DILEMMA
VII. DESTINY

Life vs. property

"Rescuers do not believe that the end justifies the means," says Francis Beckwith, "Their view is that the command to save lives is greater than the command not to trespass."[7] Foreman the Rescuer asserts, "The value of human life still precedes mere property in American law. Nevertheless, since the police and courts value property more than life in this matter, they charge us with lawbreaking."[8]

In New Jersey on March 26, 1994, "A four hundred pound cement block with embedded locks was placed to block the front door [of an abortion clinic]; six rescuers locked themselves to it. They were shielded by four [other human] blockers. At the rear door, four people neck and ankle locked themselves together. On the sidewalk were 30 prayer supporters. The local township police arrived shortly and attempted to remove the locks with the Jaws of Life. This did not work and the New Jersey State Police SWAT team, with special equipment, had to be brought in... [but] the electric plugs on the outside of the building were [suspiciously] inoperative and a fire truck had to be brought in to supply power for their cutting tools. The rescuers were cut loose and taken into custody at 11 a.m. ...charged with summary defiant trespass."[9]

What must be learned from the above example? 1) The thirty on the sidewalk are crucial components, not only for prayer support, but as expert witnesses. 2) The fourteen who were willing to submit to certain jail time and fines surely had enough zeal and creativity to have burned the building to the ground had they chosen to. Their obvious restraint probably reflects either that they are reluctant to risk twenty years for arson, *or* that they draw some moral distinction between unilaterally destroying a business building [financially harming the insurance company, not the abortionist] and the act of rescuing babies in such a way that it is the government's option of whether to let the babies live or to expend the resources necessary to produce the timely resumption of child-killing. 3) The two hundred Rescuers who could have closed the clinic for the day with simple trespass were elsewhere doing more important things. 4) One-thousand Christians could probably have conducted a gospel music festival around the building, perhaps curtailing the abortion business without arrests being made, but the choirs were all booked for more righteous gigs. 5) Even though the rescue went like clockwork, the government's current resolve to utterly crush pro-life activism, and to keep the clinics operating despite any cost, resulted in only a few hours' delay in the day's killing schedule. 6) The government will impose consequences [fines and jail time] specifically calculated to deter these and all others from repeating this offense in the future.

Deter others in the future from abortive activity

One possible result of pro-life activism is that it can act as a deterrent to abortionists, clinic staffs, and pregnant women. This attitude risks falling into the end-justifies-the-means trap, and opens the movement to the "domestic terrorism" accusation.

On the other hand, the essential reason that moral justifications are necessary is the very nature of the abortion dilemma: The right to life is the most fundamental of all rights, and yet the Supreme Court of the land has now decreed that one person's autonomous *choice* to deprive an innocent child of her life is also a fundamental, constitutionally guaranteed right. People of conscience are to be appalled by this. Until the lives of the preborn are protected by both the letter of the law and through enforcement by the authorities, then all conscientious acts that deter the practice of abortion should be presumed to be justified *unless* they can be demonstrated to be otherwise!

"This is a war that pro-lifers could win without prevailing in a single court battle," wrote abortion advocate Pamela White, "All they have to do is intimidate physicians into leaving clinics and discourage medical students from entering the [abortion] field in the first place."[10]

The "terrorism" is a fiction according to pro-lifer Sue Finn. She says, "The biased media paints us all as a bunch of crazies. As inaccurate as that is, they're doing a great job of scaring the people in the abortion industry."[11]

"ABC World News Tonight" put it this way: "Neither his gun nor his bullet-proof vest can protect [abortionist] Brian Finkel against the latest weapon in the war over abortion, the malpractice lawsuit."[12]

"The Life Dynamics abortion malpractice program (ABMAL) provides attorneys with the litigation support services they need to be successful in malpractice cases brought against abortionists... We are currently active in almost 100 abortion-injury cases, including 13 which involve the death of the woman who was having the abortion."[13]

In explaining Operation Rescue California's "No Place to Hide Campaign," which – among other tactics – publicly informed residents that their neighbor is an abortionist, *Life Advocate* reported that in California alone "five abortionists have quit in the past two years due to the public exposure of their grisly trade."[14]

1 Schaeffer, in George Grant, *Grand Illusions*, 258.

2 Terry, *Operation Rescue*, 101-2.

3 Colson, *Kingdoms in Conflict*, 247-8.

4 Mandela, *Long Walk to Freedom*, 137.

5 Foreman, *Shattering the Darkness: The Crisis of the Cross in the Church Today*, 10.

6 Mandela, 74.

7 Beckwith, *Politically Correct Death*, 164-5.

8 Joseph Foreman, 29.

9 *Life Advocate*, 5/'94, 16.

10 Pamela White, in Mark Crutcher, *Access: The Key to Pro-Life Victory*, 22.

11 Sue Finn, in *Life Advocate*, 2/'94, 11-12.

12 ABC World News Tonight, March 28, 1995, in Crutcher, *Access*, 25.

13 Crutcher, *Access*, 23-4.

14 *Life Advocate*, 2/'94, 11-2.

Why not just "Execute" the guilty?

At this point we must address not a justification but rather an accusation often leveled at those who have shot abortionists. The shooters are often described as anarchists[1] and terrorists[2] or vigilantes[3] who "set themselves up as judge, jury and executioner.[4] While the charge is no doubt true in some instances of anti-abortion shooting, it is not necessarily always so, as will be seen in the next segment.

We spoke earlier about Gregory Koukl's positivistic view that an abortion is technically not a murder. Here is one way he expressed that: "One final problem relates to my belief that abortion is not murder. If I'm right then Michael Griffin used capital punishment for a non-capital crime."[5] Here, besides holding the abortionist morally innocent of murder on the technicality of [an immoral] human law, Koukl assumes that the proper assessment of Hill's act is as an executioner. To the best of our knowledge, none of those who have declared Paul Hill's act justifiable, nor even Paul Hill himself, holds that he had a right to *execute* an abortionist.

Necessity defense and justifiable homicide

In January, 1995, the Associated Press declared: "In less than two years, two abortion doctors, two clinic receptionists and a volunteer clinic escort have been slain, and two other abortion doctors and five other clinic employees or volunteers have been shot and wounded."[6]

Having a fair understanding of Paul Hill's views,[7] we can assert that even he would declare that most of these shootings were not justifiable. What remains to be determined is whether there is any sound biblical rationale that would justify *any* of these shootings. Greg Koukl [we're back to agreeing with him again] gets us started with the proper ordering or our questions: "Is the unborn child a human being who ought to be protected?" and "Under what conditions is it permissible to take the killer's life?"[8]

With questions like these it would be very wise to consult an attorney who happens to have some biblical expertise. Herbert W. Titus fits that bill and puts us solidly on the right track, although in our opinion he then takes an unfortunate detour: "Did [Paul Hill] have a moral right to kill in order to protect the innocent lives about to be snuffed out by the doctor and his staff? Were his actions biblically defensible? [excellent questions, well stated] To put it simply, no. [Oops. We had better read carefully] The Bible teaches that the 'presumptuous' taking of human life is murder [Ex. 20:13; 21:14; Num. 35:20-21 ('schemes' to kill another). These parameters clearly include abortion]. This rule applies even when the person whose life is taken is guilty of murder and, therefore, deserves death [Gen. 4:8, 13-15 (mark of Cain)]. By definition, a 'presumptuous' killing is one committed without authority... There is only one exception... deadly force in an emergency [an immediate threat] to defend himself or his family [and we are to love our neighbor as ourself]. Such an excuse is not, by definition, available to those who, like the killers of abortionists, have presumed to act as prosecutor, judge and jury."[9]

While we agree, gratefully, with all of the evidence provided, we must question the conclusion drawn by Mr. Titus. Here is what we would add in summarizing and agreeing with most of the above passage: 1) The U.S. government is correct in not arresting abortionists for murder under its current legal code. 2) At some future time it would be appropriate for today's abortionists to be found guilty, as at Nuremberg, of a "crime against humanity" which "shocks the [future] conscience of humanity." 3) Biblically, only the civil government is authorized to arrest, try, and imprison or execute a person for a capital crime. Thus anyone who presumes to usurp that authority and conduct a vigilante execution is guilty of both a civil crime and a biblical sin. However: 4) A verdict of "justifiable homicide" may be properly adjudicated under the "defense of necessity" in all of the courts in America today, and it is consistent with the biblical standard which Mr. Titus paraphrased as, "There is only one exception... deadly force in an emergency to defend himself or his family." This is the moral and legal defense which Paul Hill has claimed, which many others have declared to be appropriate, but which the court in which he was tried disallowed. [Although Mr. Titus might seem to imply that self-defense or the defense of others might be limited to the circle of one's own family, that restriction is not universal, either in the Bible or in American law.]

1 *Press*, 8-27-94, H3. The archbishop who defrocked Rev. David Trosch for calling the killing by Paul Hill "justifiable homicide" said that "no good could come from an evil intent and that anarchy would result if citizens usurped the role of the civil authorities and took the law into their own hands."

2 Bill Clinton, *Press*, 1-17-97, A1, A7.

3 John Whitehead, *The Stealing of America*, 112: "To prevent resistance or civil disobedience from degenerating into taking the law into one's hands, it should be organized and under authority. Vigilantes are not justified under Scripture."

4 Herbert W. Titus, "Paul Hill's Error," Focus on the Family, *Citizen*, 7-17-95, 5.

5 Gregory Koukl, Stand to Reason, "Pulling the Trigger on Abortion," 5.

6 Associated Press, in *Press*, 1-9-95, A1, A8.

7 *Life Advocate*, 4/'94, 13: "Ordained Presbyterian minister Paul Hill has declared that the shooting [of David Gunn] was a 'justifiable homicide.' In a 'Defensive Action' statement [which asserts: '...justifiable provided it was carried out for the purpose of defending the lives of unborn children.' (Ramey, 8)].

8 Gregory Koukl, Stand to Reason, "Pulling the Trigger on Abortion," 5.

9 Herbert W. Titus, "Paul Hill's Error," Focus on the Family, *Citizen*, 7-17-95, 5.

10 Bray, *A Time to Kill*, 175.

11 Cathy Ramey, *In Defense of Others: A Biblical Analysis and Apologetic on the Use of Force to Save Lives*, 9. On page 16, Ramey says, "The concept of defensive action is seen in Scripture in a number of areas: Gen. 14:14-16, Exodus 2:11-12, Heb. 11:24-27, Acts 7:23-25, Judges 4:17-21, I Kings 40:40."

12 *Press*, 11-2-96, B4: "A Temecula [Calif.] man who beat a home intruder to death last week with a baseball bat likely will not face charges [because] 'The presumption is you're using self-defense,' said Deputy District Attorney... Officials gauge whether the force used was reasonable, necessary and justified."

SCOPE and FOCUS
I. CONVICTIONS
II. PRETEXTS
III. MANDATE
IV. LEGACY
V. ABORTIVE LINKS
Recreational Sex
Reproductive Technology
Abortion Industry
Problems with abortion
God's law. Bloodguilt
Right to life
Cruelty to the preborn
Inhumane acts
Excuses for inaction
Autonomy of woman
Relativism. Subhuman
Mechanism. Potential
Pragmatism. Tactics
Pleasure. Controversy
Positivism. Legality
Goals of intervention
Stop this abortion
Dissuade women
Fewer locations
Society more pro-life
Government pro-life
Church authentic
Types of intervention
Protest. Witness
Interposition. Rescue
Destruction. Burn
Violence. Killing
Guerilla Warfare
Revolution
Justifications offered
Freedoms: speech...
Civil disobedience
Life vs. property
Deter others
"Execute" the guilty
Necessity. Justifiable
Higher accountability
Governmental Action
Social Climate
Religious Confusion
Personal Decision to Abort
VI. DILEMMA
VII. DESTINY

Advocates of a forceful response

Here is the way Michael Bray expresses this truth: "The individual, in defending himself or another innocent person, is authorized by God to exercise lethal, defensive force (Ex. 22:2). A distinction must be made between the use of defensive force and retributive force, which is reserved for God and those to whom He delegates it (Rom. 13; Deut. 19:12)."[10]

Cathy Ramey agrees: "It is imperative to understand the defensive nature of the actions taken by Griffin, Shannon, and Hill. A defensive action is one aimed at *preventing* a wrong which is going to be committed rather than punishing for a wrong already done."[11]

David Trosch says: "Short of God's direct intervention, justified homicide, a legal defense in every state of the union,[12] may be the only way to discourage the practice of abortion in the future."[13]

In *Time* magazine, Michael Kinsley was quick to dismiss Paul Hill, but he gave him a compliment nonetheless: "The logic of Paul Hill – that abortion equals baby killing, that there is a 'holocaust' going on and that therefore killing an abortionist is 'justifiable homicide' – may be insane, but it is more consistent than the logic of those who share all of Hill's premises but reject his conclusion."[14]

Michael Bray asks good questions. "How does one: 1) hold a principle of self-defense and the defense of others, 2) affirm the extreme of war as an extension of that principle, 3) affirm that the preborn are innocent people deserving protection, and then 4) deny that these people ought to be afforded even basic forceful defense?"[15]

Paul Hill says: "The key to successfully making abortion illegal is for the people to assert their right to defend life so the government will do so on their behalf."[16]

Higher accountability

In his book about *Operation Rescue*, Randall Terry wrote at length about the supremacy of God's law over man's law. In the foreword to that book, Jerry Falwell referred to that principle in his endorsement of Operation Rescue: "I believe they are right because man's laws permitting abortion are in clear violation of God's higher laws."[17]

Cathy Ramey concludes, "If we wish the right to protect ourselves and other innocent *born* people from the Ted Bundys and Jeffrey Dahmers of this world, we ought not to think that we can deprive the *unborn* of that same standard of protection."[18]

Says Frankie Schaeffer: "We must be willing to risk liberty and, yes, even life in the cause of truth."[19]

THE SANDBOX

A Christian at a fast-food lunch stop, finding no other seat available, sat outside in the children's play area. The Christian vaguely noted happy youngsters scrambling all over the other equipment, but the sandbox was empty.

No sooner had that thought emerged when a harried mom plopped a blinking toddler into the sand and rushed back inside – to buy their lunch, the Christian supposed.

Quite soon came the realization that the child had disappeared – and the parent had, too. Only then did the Christian read the sign overhead:

"Pro-Choice Sandbox..."

The Supreme Court had ruled that prior to "viability," now interpreted as graduation in the top half of one's kindergarten class, one's parent may terminate the non-viable pre-schooler in any convenient manner. ***"...As a public service, this restaurant is proud to offer its patrons this Pro-Choice Quicksand Sandbox."***

When another mother-with-child approaches, the Christian should:

a. Write a letter to Congress
b. Circulate a petition
c. Hold up a picket sign
d. Other: ______________________
e. ALL of the above

13 Trosch, in *Life Advocate*, 5/'94, 32.
14 Michael Kinsley, in *Time*, 8-15-94, 64.
15 Michael Bray, *A Time to Kill*, 78.
16 *Paul Hill Speaks*. Issue No. 1, 6/'97, 2.
17 Falwell, in Terry, *Operation Rescue*, Forword.
18 Ramey, 19-20.
19 Schaeffer, in John Whitehead, *The Right to Picket*, ix.

D. Governmental Action

Many writers have identified key truths that may inform our stance toward the government of the United States of America. "For many people the state has become the church, even God," says Doug Bandow. "Government employs them, houses them, feeds them, regulates them, and even gives them purpose and a reason for being."[1]

"This is the situation that Christians have got to face:" says William Bentley Ball. "The crushing out of religion from modern life by the sheer weight of state-inspired public opinion and by the mass organization of society on a purely secular basis."[2]

"Once our national morality begins moving in a particular direction, it accumulates a prodigious momentum which is virtually impossible to change," according to Brian Clowes, who adds, "Our government is deeply committed to the slaughter of the unborn at all levels."[3]

Writing about the lessons learned from the social movements of the '60s, Henry di Suvero said, "In America, the first Amendment guarantees of freedom of speech, assembly and association were devised as a means through which social change could occur. [As also] in the judicial arena, these 'rules of the game' work well enough when no basic issue of social change is involved but break down completely when such issues are at stake."[4]

From *The War Over the Family*, we learn that "Moral community (and its solidarity) is maintained by an ongoing consensus. Whenever that consensus breaks down, coercion must take its place."[5]

In *Time* magazine, Michael Kinsley has reminded us that "a democratic society cannot fail to protect the exercise of what it has determined to be a fundamental right."[6] A federal court in 1943 expressed this sobering truth: "Those who begin coercive elimination of dissent soon find themselves exterminating dissenters."[7]

Whitehead says, "**As we face the massive machine of government, we are at a very similar position to that of the colonists who congregated to declare their independence from Great Britain in 1776.**"[8]

We here repeat John F. Kennedy's favorite axiom: "Those who make peaceful change impossible make violent change inevitable."[9]

1. Involuntary complicity: Taxes, fines and judgments

It was the view of Henry David Thoreau that "by paying taxes to an unjust government, the citizen condones wrongs committed by the state." His one-man tax revolt protesting that the government was using his tax money to perpetuate slavery and to fight an illegitimate war against Mexico landed him in jail.[10]

Each of us, through our taxes, pays abortionists to kill unborn babies, and some of those babies would otherwise live if their mothers either could not or would not spend their own money for the procedure. Joseph Scheidler asks us to "Consider what the effect might have been on the abortion issue if on January 23, 1973, the day after *Roe v. Wade*, all pro-life church leaders, from the National Council of Catholic Bishops to the anti-abortion heads of pro-life Protestant denominations, speaking in unison, had called for a national tax protest until the abortion ruling was rescinded."[11]

SCOPE and FOCUS
I. CONVICTIONS
II. PRETEXTS
III. MANDATE
IV. LEGACY
V. ABORTIVE LINKS
Recreational Sex
Reproductive Technology
Abortion Industry
Governmental Action
Involuntary Complicity
Supreme Court
Politics
Legislation
Hyde amendment
F.A.C.E.
Blood money
Human life amendment
Partial birth (D & X)
Value of a child
Law Enforcement
Bureaucracy
Police power
Due Process in Court
Injunctions
Crimes charged
"Necessity" defense
"Jury nullification"
Pro-lifer Consequences
Social Climate
Religious Confusion
Personal Decision to Abort
VI. DILEMMA
VII. DESTINY

1 Bandow, *Beyond Good Intentions, a Biblical View of Politics*, 17.
2 Ball, *In Search of a National Morality; A Manifesto for Evangelicals and Catholics*, 208.
3 Clowes, *Pro-Life Activist's Encyclopedia*, pages 1.2 and 5.6.
4 Henry di Suvero, in Jonathan Black, *Radical Lawyers: Their Role in the Movement and in the Courts*, 52.
5 B. & P. Berger, *War Over the Family*, 76.
6 Kinsley, in *Time*, 8-15-94, 64.
7 *West Virginia Board of Education v. Barnetter* [1943], in John Whitehead, *The Right to Picket*, 7.
8 John Whitehead, *The Second American Revolution*, 180.
9 John Kennedy, in Schlesinger, *Bitter Fruit (Guatemala)*, 254-5.
10 Thoreau, in Robert Downs, *Books that Changed the World*, 69.
11 Scheidler, *Closed: 99 Ways to Stop Abortion*, 89.
12 Brian Clowes, *Pro-Life Activist's Encyclopedia*, page 89.6.
13 R.C. Sproul, *Abortion: A Rational Look at an Emotional Issue*, 70.
14 Clowes, page 89.1.
15 Sproul, 70.
16 Sproul, 70.
17 Robert Bork, *Slouching Towards Gomorrah: Modern Liberalism and American Decline*, 109.
18 Bork, 95.
19 Lincoln, in *Life Advocate*, 6/'94, 4.
20 *Prudential Insurance Company v. Cheek*, in Clowes, page 89.9.
21 *Meyer v. Nebraska*, in Clowes, page 89.6.
22 George Grant, *Grand Illusions: The Legacy of Planned Parenthood*, 236.
23 *Skinner v. Oklahoma*, in Clowes, page 89.6. This ruling held that Oklahoma had no right to involuntarily sterilize criminals regardless of their crimes.
24 *Bonbrest v. Kotz*, in Clowes, page 89.6.
25 *Everson v. Board of Education*, in Robert Clouse, *Protest and Politics*, 164.
26 Robert Audi and Nicholas Wolterstorff, *Religion in the Public Square: The Place of Religious Convictions in Political Debate*, 3-4.
27 *Zorach v. Clauson*, in William Bentley Ball, *In Search of a National Morality: A Manifesto for Evangelicals and Catholics*, 88.
28 Robert Bork, 102.
29 *May v. Anderson*, in Clowes, page 89.6.
30 Robert Mnookin, *In the Interest of Children: Advocacy, Law, Reform, and Public Policy*, 7.

2. Supreme Court

The U.S. Supreme Court has overturned more than 184 of its own earlier decisions.[12]

"Our nation has reversed itself on slavery, prohibition, racial discrimination, conscientious objection to wars, capital punishment, and other issues of ethics and justice... Contemporary community standards become the highest court of appeal, the ultimate norm of justice and ethics."[13]

Brian Clowes says, "For more than three decades, the United States Supreme Court has been the vehicle by which sweeping Neoliberal reforms have been forced onto the public. After all, it is much easier to convince nine people of your position than it is to persuade thousands of legislators at the state level... The inevitable progression from artificial contraception to abortion to euthanasia is followed neatly in the Court's opinions."[14]

In the view of R.C. Sproul, "Once a decision has been reached in a nation's highest court, the subsequent influence on shaping public opinion is enormous. We learned this painful fact in the history that followed the Supreme Court's infamous Dred-Scott decision, which perpetuated slavery in the United States."[15]

He continues: "I suspect that the greatest cause of the change of public opinion [in favor of abortion] is the Supreme court decision in *Roe v. Wade*. There is a strong tendency among people of any nation to take their direction for what is ethically right from what the law allows or what the society condones. The unspoken assumption is that if it is legal, it is therefore moral."[16]

"Contrary to the plan of the American government," laments Robert Bork, "the Supreme Court has usurped the powers of the people and their elected representatives. We are no longer free to make our own fundamental moral and cultural decisions."[17]

Bork expands his thought in this way: "It will be extremely difficult to defend traditional values against intellectual class onslaught. Not only do the intellectuals occupy the commanding heights of the culture and the means by which values and ideas are created and transmitted [education and the media], they control the most authoritarian institutions of American government, [and] the federal and state judiciaries, headed by the Supreme Court... the courts have increasingly usurped the power to make our cultural decisions for us, and it is not apparent that we have any means of redress."[18]

As early as 1861, Abraham Lincoln, in his first inaugural address, warned: "If the policy of the government, upon vital questions affecting the whole people, is to be irrevocably fixed by decisions of the Supreme Court... the people will have ceased to be their own rulers."[19]

Here follows an abbreviated overview of significant historical developments at the Supreme Court level:

In 1922 the Supreme Court ruled: "...as we have stated, neither the 14th Amendment nor any other provision of the constitution of the United States... confer[s] any right to privacy upon either persons or corporations."[20]

1923 "The right to conceive and raise one's children has been deemed essential."[21] We must point out that this ruling applied equally to women and men.

1940 The court declared Humanism a religion, subject to all of the rights and protections due other religions.[22]

1942 "...the right to have offspring... [is] ...a right which is basic to the perpetuation of the race."[23]

1946 The Supreme Court defined "child" as "an unborn or recently born human being."[24]

1947 The Court held that "In the words of Jefferson, the clause against establishment of religion by law was intended to erect a 'wall of separation between church and State.'"[25]

By contrast with the ever-expanding "wall of separation" doctrine, Audi and Wolterstorff hold that there are three elements in the "separation clause" of the First Amendment, and none of them implies the slightest restraint on religious practices; to the contrary, all three serve as constraints on the government: "1) the libertarian principle, **tolerance** [all religions are to be tolerated]; 2) the equalitarian principle, **impartiality** [no favoritism is to be shown to any religion]; and 3) the **neutrality** principle, [the government's position is to be neutral, both] among religions [and] between the religious and the non-religious."[26]

1952 "We are a religious people whose institutions presuppose a Supreme Being." [The state] "respects the religious nature of our people and accommodates the public service to their spiritual needs. To hold that it may not would be to find in the Constitution a requirement that the government show a callous indifference to religious groups. That would be preferring those who believe in no religion over those who do believe."[27]

Robert Bork summarizes: "The Court's treatment of religion is of a piece. Under the First Amendment's prohibition of the establishment of religion, the Court has steadily made religion a matter for the private individual by driving it out of the public arena."[28]

1953 The right to bear children is "far more precious than property rights."[29]

1954 Robert Mnookin writes: "Why has the role of the judiciary – particularly the federal courts – expanded? Looking back, there has been no single abrupt departure from the past. Evolution, not revolution, has characterized the change. Nonetheless, the school desegregation cases, beginning with the Supreme Court's 1954 decision in *Brown v. Board of Education*, seem to be a turning point."[30]

Supreme Court developments, continued:

1962 Banned teacher-led prayer in public schools, and

1963 Banned Bible reading in public schools. "Since [these two decisions]," says *Family News from Dr. James Dobson*, "the U.S. Supreme Court has been increasingly hostile to faith and to traditional moral values. Chuck Colson said that America is now ruled by 'a runaway judiciary.'"[1]

According to Thomas Sowell, "The fact that religious conservatives oppose abortion and bans on prayer in school as policies only adds to their frustration with the judicial lawlessness that these Supreme Court decisions represent. Moreover, these decisions are part of a consistent pattern of hostility to religion in the federal judiciary."[2]

1965 The Court discovers that there is a right to privacy after all: "The Constitution does not explicitly mention any right to privacy. In a line of decisions, however, the Court has recognized that a right of personal privacy... does exist under the Constitution."[3]

In the opinion of the writer of *The Pro-Life Activist's Encyclopedia*, ***Griswold*** "is the most important Supreme Court decision ever made (surpassing in significance even *Roe v. Wade)* because it established the 'right of privacy' which would be used later by numerous courts to justify both abortion and euthanasia."[4]

1970 Only three years before *Roe v. Wade*, the Supreme court referred to the unborn as a "person."[5]

1971 Clowes says that in the *Vuitch* case the Court "addressed abortion directly for the first time. The Court upheld the District of Columbia's abortion statute and declared it 'not constitutionally vague.' ...As a result of this ruling, the Supreme Court included 'mental health' for the first time in the overall definition of 'maternal health.' This definition was, in effect, a prescription for abortion on demand."[6]

1972 The court ruled all capital punishment unconstitutional.[7]

Clowes says: "Only one year before *Roe*, the justices made it quite clear that even unwed fathers have parental rights"[8]

"If the right to privacy means anything, it is the right of the individual, married or single, to be free from unwarranted governmental intrusion into matters so fundamentally affecting a person as the decision whether or not to beget a child."[9]

1973 *ROE v. WADE*. Clowes says: "This decision stripped the States of their lawful authority to regulate abortion. It built on *Griswold*'s mythical 'right to privacy' – allegedly based in the United States Constitution – which is also the legal foundation of other anti-life practices such as infanticide and euthanasia."[10]

Roe was based upon four supports: 1) the controversy on when the "fetus" becomes a person; 2) the fiction that the danger-of-abortion [now supposedly remedied by sterile procedures, antibiotics, and new technologies] had been the sole motivation behind the outlawing of abortion in the 1800s; 3) that "privacy" protects the decision in the first two trimesters; 4) that the unborn are not 14th Amendment "persons" [and consequently are not entitled to "due process" or "equal protection under the laws"].[11]

From *The War Over the Family*: "It is safe to say that the judges involved in the 1973 [*Roe v Wade*] decision were unaware of the class dynamics of the issue and did not foresee the furious social conflict that their decision would unleash."[12]

DOE v. BOLTON. Clowes says: "In *Roe v. Wade*, the Supreme Court stated that abortions could be performed in the second and third trimesters for the 'mother's physical or mental health.' In *Doe v. Bolton*, the companion decision to *Roe*, the court expanded this definition so that the abortionist has legal discretion to kill children for virtually any reason whatever throughout the entire nine months of pregnancy."[13]

1975 The Court let stand a lower court's ruling that Utah's law requiring parental consent for a minor's abortion violated the minor's "fundamental right" of "privacy" concerning an abortion.[14]

1976 The Court upheld: Missouri's right to prohibit abortion of viable babies except to save the life of the mother; but ruled unconstitutional: husband's consent requirement, parental consent requirement for minors, and the outlawing [to increase baby's chances of survival or to decrease its suffering] of salt poisoning abortions.[15]

Clowes says that the *Danforth* decision "stripped fathers of any legal right whatever to protect their own preborn children... His relationship to his own child is deemed much less important than his relationship to a piece of property – say a car stereo... The *Danforth* decision enforced 'mandatory fatherhood' for those men who did *not* want a child. In summary, a father has literally no voice whatever in the decision to have or not have a child."[16]

In his dissent to *Danforth*, Justice Byron White stated that "It is truly surprising that the majority finds in the United States Constitution, as it must in order to justify the result it reaches, a rule that the State must assign a greater value to a mother's decision to cut off a potential human life by abortion than to a father's decision to let it mature into a live child."[17]

Death penalty reinstated.[18]

1977 The Court ruled that the death penalty is excessively harsh punishment for the crime of rape.[19]

Wait a minute. Isn't it equally true that abortion is an excessively harsh punishment for the crime of being unwanted by your mother?

1 *Family News from Dr. James Dobson*, 10/'97.
2 Thomas Sowell, in *Press*, 3-20-96, A6.
3 *Griswold v. Connecticut*, in Clowes, page 89.3.
4 Clowes, page 89.8.
5 *Steinberg v. Ohio*, in Moreland and Geisler, *The Life and Death Debate: Moral Issues of Our Time*, 33-4.
6 *United States v. Vuitch*, in Clowes, page 89.9.
7 Name of the case not mentioned; in *Press*, 12-5-96, A7.
8 *Stanley v. Illinois*, in Clowes, page 89.6. "[*Stanley*] struck down a law that automatically took children away from an unwed father if the mother died. The Court said: "The denial to unwed fathers of a hearing on fitness... constitutes a denial of equal protection of the laws."
9 *Eisenstadt v. Baird*, in Clowes, page 89.9.
10 *Roe v. Wade*, in Clowes, page 89.10.
11 Summarized from Jersild and Johnson, *Moral Issues & Christian Response*, 338: *Roe* and *Doe* "marked an important turning point in the abortion debate. In these decisions the Court struck down both the older, more restrictive legislation operative in 30 states and the more lenient legislation of 16 other states."
12 B. & P. Berger, 79-80.
13 *Doe v. Bolton*, in Clowes, page 89.10.
14 *T H v. Jones*, in Clowes, page 89.10.
15 *Planned Parenthood of Central Missouri v. Danforth*, in Clowes, page 89.11.
16 Clowes, page 89.11.
17 Justice White, in Clowes, page 89.11.
18 Name of the case not mentioned; in *Press*, 12-5-96, A7.
19 Amnesty International. "The Death Penalty: Cruel & Inhuman Punishment" pamphlet.

The Court found that a city may refuse to provide publicly financed abortions to indigent women in a public hospital.[20] The Court held that "The Social Security Act does not require the funding of non-therapeutic abortions," and that it is not "preferential treatment" for the state to fund childbirth but not abortion."[21] The Court held that a state could refuse to fund non-therapeutic abortions under Medicaid.[22] The Court found a Constitutional right of minors to have contraceptives.[23]

1979 The Court required that a state's parental consent rule for a minor's abortion must make provision for judicial bypass.[24]

Clowes says about *Coalutti v. Franklin*: "In a particularly terrifying decision, the Court held that any abortionist can decide on his own whim when viability is... As long as the baby is in the womb, it is nonviable *by definition*. This decision actually stated that, should the abortionist become aware that the unborn baby is viable, he is under no obligation to try to save its life or even to decrease its suffering."[25]

1980 In a pair of cases, the Court upheld the Hyde Amendment's federal refusal to fund abortions for women on welfare, and further held that if such federal funds are withdrawn, the states are under no obligation to replace them in whole or in part. [26]

1983 The Court invalidated all of these Ohio statute provisions: requiring of counseling information before providing an abortion, mandating a waiting period, requiring parental notification [after the abortion] if unmarried and under 18, the outlawing of saline [salt] abortions, and requiring a hospital setting for 2nd & 3rd trimester abortions.[27]

Clowes says that *Akron* held it to be unconstitutional for a state to require "that any information be given to women regarding fetal development, alternatives to abortion, and even information on possible abortion complications... [and] stated that the preborn babies who are killed by abortion don't even have the right to be buried. They are nothing but 'biological waste...'"[28]

The *Ashcroft* decision held that the requirement that 2nd trimester abortions be performed in hospitals "unreasonably infringes upon a woman's constitutional right to obtain an abortion." It did, however uphold as permissible: requiring a pathology report for each abortion, the presence of a second physician after viability, and consent from either a parent or the juvenile court for abortion of minors.[29]

In an official report in 1983, the Senate Judiciary Committee stated that it "observes that **no significant legal barrier of any kind whatsoever exists today in the United States for a woman to obtain an abortion for any reason during any stage of her pregnancy**."[30]

1985 Clowes summarizes that the history of Supreme Court decisions "very clearly shows a progression first toward unlimited abortion on demand, and then since about 1985, a reversed and accelerating trend towards protecting the unborn."[31]

1986 The Court declared unconstitutional a Pennsylvania law that required: informed consent, abortion reporting, and the protection of viable unborn children.[32]

Clowes says about the *Bowen* decision: "The Court found a parent's 'right' to refuse treatment [for their handicapped newborn children], based upon the 'right to privacy.' This right to privacy is paramount – even over the [born] child's right to be spared an agonizing death by thirst and starvation."[33]

1988 Clowes says: "In the first 'father's rights' case brought before the Supreme Court, it ruled unanimously by refusing to hear a lower court case that a father has no rights or claim whatsoever to his unborn child."[34]

1989 Moreland and Geisler say that the *Webster* case "placed restrictions on abortion after viability and opened the door for individual States to place more restrictions on obtaining abortions."[35]

To summarize the main provisions of the *Webster* case, the Court upheld these restrictions in a Missouri law: public employees may not assist in abortions; no abortions may be performed in state hospitals or publicly-owned facilities; no public funds may be used to encourage or counsel for abortion except to save the mother's life; viability testing is mandatory after 20 weeks' gestation.[36]

Clowes says about the *Webster* case: "In the most publicized Supreme Court decision of all time, the Justices upheld portions of the Missouri law designed to protect life from conception and place other restrictions upon abortion... Most importantly, Chief Justice William Rehnquist asserted that the 'key elements' of the 'abortion right' – the right to privacy and the 'Constitutional right to abortion' – simply do not exist."[37]

1991 Clowes says about the *Rust* decision: "This decision upheld the constitutionality of the government's decision to cut off Title X family planning funds to those organizations that promote or perform abortions. Planned Parenthood lost tens of millions of annual tax dollars due to this decision because it stated that it would rather give up this money than stop providing the 'complete range of family planning services.'"[38]

1992 Jersild says about the *Casey* decision that it: "upheld *Roe v. Wade* and affirmed the right of a woman to have an abortion, ...[It] also allowed states to pass more restrictive legislation as long as such restrictions did not pose an 'undue burden' on the woman. What constitutes an 'undue burden' should now become a critical legal issue."[39]

20 *Poelker v. Doe*, in Clowes, page 89.12.

21 *Beal v. Doe*, in Clowes, page 89.12.

22 *Maher v. Roe*, in Clowes, page 89.12.

23 *Carey v. Population Services International*, in Clowes, pages 89.11 to 89.12.

24 *Belotti v. Baird II*, and *Hunerwald v. Baird*, in Clowes, page 89.13.

25 *Coalutti v. Franklin*, in Clowes, page 89.13.

26 *McRabe v. Secretary of Health, Education and Welfare* and *Zbarez v. Quern*, in Clowes, page 89.13.

27 *Akron v Akron Center for Reproductive Health*, in Douglas Butler, *Abortion, Medicine and the Law*, 316.

28 Clowes, page 89.15.

29 *Planned Parenthood of Kansas City, Missouri, v. Ashcroft*, in Clowes, page 89.15.

30 Clowes, page 89.3.

31 Clowes, page 89.8.

32 *Thornberg v. American College of Obstetricians and Gynecologists*, in Clowes, page 89.15.

33 *Bowen v. American College of Obstetricians and Gynecologists*, in Clowes, page 89.115.

34 *Conn v. Conn*, in Clowes, page 89.16.

35 *Webster v. Reproductive Health Services*, in Moreland and Geisler, *The Life and Death Debate, Moral Issues of Our Time*, 26.

36 Summarized from Kerby Anderson, *Living Ethically in the '90s*, 208.

37 Clowes, page 89.16.

38 *Rust v. Sullivan*, in Clowes, page 89.16.

39 *Planned Parenthood of Southeastern Pennsylvania v. Casey*, in Jersild, *Moral Issues & Christian Response*, 338-9.

Supreme Court developments, continued:

The Mystery Passage in *Casey*

1992 *Casey*'s Mystery Passage: "At the heart of liberty is the right to define one's own concept of existence, of meaning, of the universe, and of the mystery of human life." A James Dobson publication says this about the *Casey* decision's Mystery Passage: "With those words, the Court discarded its historic reliance on 'a law beyond the law,' or a transcendent standard... The bottom line of the Casey decision is how we define reality. The new definition flows from a 'postmodern' philosophy that acknowledges nothing right nor wrong, nothing moral nor immoral. Truth does not exist and there are no absolutes that transcend time. Everything is relative and subject to individual interpretation. For the U.S. Supreme Court to descend into this abyss of moral relativism is disastrous."[1]

The above was a follow-up to this Dobson piece about *Casey* published a few months earlier: "Pro-lifers always hoped that a subsequent [Court] would overturn [*Roe*]. ... In [*Casey*], however, the majority said that the right to kill babies was guaranteed within the 14th Amendment, rather than simply being implied generally by the principle of 'privacy' in the 14th Amendment. ...According to some constitutional scholars, this was one of the most important rulings in the history of the U.S. Supreme Court... It set the right to abortion in concrete. Therefore, nothing short of a constitutional amendment will protect the unborn child... There IS no other way. According to the Supreme Court, the Constitution now explicitly defends a woman's right to kill an unborn baby, and neither the Congress, state legislatures nor lower courts have the power to override that ruling."[2]

1994 Newspaper report: "The Supreme Court ruled unanimously in 1994 that abortion-rights supporters can sue protesters suspected of violence against clinics under a federal racketeering law [R.I.C.O.]."[3]

[1994] Newspaper report: "With millions of dollars in judgments and a new federal law [F.A.C.E.] barring demonstrators from obstructing access to abortion clinics, it might seem that abortion rights groups have won the decade-long battle over clinic blockades – and been well compensated in the process. [In 1994] the U.S. Supreme Court refused to interfere with the $8.2 million a jury awarded to a Portland, Ore. clinic. And there has been a string of smaller judgments and contempt fines in New York, California, Pennsylvania, Washington D.C., and elsewhere... The amount of judgments is probably more than $10 million."[4]

The court refused to hear the appeal of Alexander Loce, "a man who joined a rescue to save his own unborn child from death in 1990... Loce was attempting to bring the issue of the personhood and humanity of the child to the high court as well as the issue of his parental rights as father of the child."[5]

The Court "ruled that judges can bar protests from getting too close to abortion clinics, and upheld a 36-foot demonstration-free zone ['bubble'] around a Florida clinic."[6]

1995 Newspaper article: "The Supreme Court refused to hear an appeal of arrests under a 300-foot residential buffer zone, and R.I.C.O. judgments for sidewalk counseling, and held that F.A.C.E. does not infringe on anyone's freedom of expression or religion."[7]

1997 Newspaper article: "Citing free speech concerns, the Supreme Court... relaxed a major restriction on abortion protesters by striking down 'floating buffer zones' that separate protesters from clinic patients and workers. Floating buffer zones had required that protesters keep 15 feet away from patients and workers as they approach and leave clinics."[8]

1998 Newspaper article: "By a 6-3 vote [on 3-23-98], the Supreme Court let stand rulings that declared unconstitutional the 1995 Ohio law prohibiting 'partial birth' abortions, saying the law would unduly interfere with a woman's right to abortion... Justices Clarence Thomas, William H. Rehnquist and Antonin Scalia disagreed with the action."[9]

3. Politics

Pro-Life activists are frequently reminded that in a democracy the ballot box is the only legitimate route to political change. The Movement includes scores of educational and political organizations supported by the donations of literally millions of pro-life Christians. They have expended millions of dollars to promote political protection for the unborn. How are we doing at that?

Hal Haffner has said, "If Christians registered and voted every time along pro-life convictions, there would not remain an elected official at any level of government at any time who would be pro-abortion."[10]

Christian Coalition leader Ralph Reed said in 1996: "On election day, the religious conservatives will be the largest single constituency in the electorate." His group, 100,000 volunteers, distributed 45 million voter guides in 125,000 churches and contacted 3 to 5 million voters in person or by telephone.[11]

Nevertheless, the notorious Bill Clinton was re-elected.

Newspapers reported that the Christian Coalition "claims 1.7 million members, but its primary publication, the *Christian American* magazine, was sent to only 310,296 people in September [of 1995, down 12% from the previous year]."[12]

On the other side, what defines the pro-abortion voter base? There is obviously an undefined coalition of secular-humanist groups including Planned Parenthood and other pro-abortion associations, homosexuals and atheists, but the grass roots of that movement is surely the women who have had abortions, and the men who are glad they did.

SCOPE and FOCUS
I. CONVICTIONS
II. PRETEXTS
III. MANDATE
IV. LEGACY
V. ABORTIVE LINKS
Recreational Sex
Reproductive Technology
Abortion Industry
Governmental Action
Involuntary Complicity
Supreme Court
Politics
Legislation
Hyde amendment
F.A.C.E.
Blood money
Human life amendment
Partial birth (D & X)
Value of a child
Law Enforcement
Bureaucracy
Police power
Due Process in Court
Injunctions
Crimes charged
"Necessity" defense
"Jury nullification"
Pro-lifer Consequences
Social Climate
Religious Confusion
Personal Decision to Abort
VI. DILEMMA
VII. DESTINY

The ever-expanding pro-abortion voting block

Mark Crutcher indicates how large that nucleus is: "By the most conservative estimates about 40 percent of all American women of childbearing age have had at least one abortion. Some studies have put the number at more like 60 percent... Moreover, this force grows considerably more powerful every day as another 4,000 abortions are racked up... $64,000 per hour [is] how much money American women take into the abortion industry – every hour of the day, 365 days a year. Obviously, even if only a small percentage of that money eventually reaches the pro-abortion political machine, the dollars could add up fast. Making matters worse, there is no off-setting source of funds for the pro-life political effort. All of our political funds come from direct contributions. This is what creates the great disparity between the amount of campaign money available to the two sides... **As long as** [the pro-abortionists] have $64,000 an hour to draw on, and the potential for 4,000 new pro-abortion voters every day, **the legal status of abortion will never change**. That is simply too much inertia for us to overcome."[13]

Joseph Foreman declares, "We will never transform our culture by politicking for a surface change in the law. Change will only come from the example of Christians who are not afraid to live what they believe – who would rather lose every church [building], house, and job they have than to go down in history as the Christians who presided over the greatest human carnage in the history of the world."[14]

Cal Thomas credits Charles Colson with this thought: "Conservative religious believers are now faced with a clear choice. They can abandon their political interests and **claim resident alien status** in a land that has forgotten their God, no longer concerned, in Colson's words, 'about the fortunes or misfortunes of a flawed republic, no longer considering this land their country.' **Or** they can continue in frustration to **try to restore a moral order from the top down**."[15]

How are we doing on political freedoms? Do you remember that at the Republican National Convention in San Diego in 1996, leaders had to wait in line overnight at the police department for the **chance** to get one of 65 **permits** for a 55-minute window of opportunity for a group **to "protest"** inside a chain-link cage?[16]

Do you suppose that history would have been different if the Boston Tea Partiers had been denied a permit or if Paul Revere had been required to shout "The British are coming!" from inside a particular barn?

But there is still opportunity to have an impact. Woody Jenkins was only 24 when he was first elected to the Louisiana State Legislature in 1971, but by 1990 he was able to lead that state's "highly visible fight to pass the strongest abortion restrictions in the nation following the Supreme Court's *Webster* ruling."[17]

Political party platforms

In 1976, for the first national election following *Roe v. Wade*, both major parties were timid about abortion. The Republican platform ventured that it would support efforts toward a right-to-life amendment, while Democrats mentioned such an amendment as undesirable. By 1980 both platforms were stronger, but "each side left room for its own members to disagree." In 1984 both sides had crystallized: The Democrats were for reproductive freedom as a fundamental human right, and were for "privacy" and abortion funding; the Republicans used the word "sanctity" in expressing the unborn child's fundamental right to life, were for a human life amendment, and stood opposed to federal funds for abortion and abortion groups. In 1988 the Republicans recycled their '84 platform while the Democratic position "hardened considerably, giving virtually no leeway to members who opposed the official party line: 'We believe... the fundamental right of reproductive choice should be guaranteed regardless of ability to pay.'" There was no significant change in party platforms in 1992, but by 1996 with the Democratic platform sounding like it had been written by one of the White House incumbents, Republicans were "waffling big-time" as they say. One newspaper reported in June that pro-lifers "have lost political ground. Sen. Bob Dole, the presumptive Republican presidential nominee, reaffirmed Thursday his opposition to abortion but called for his party's platform to include a 'declaration of tolerance' recognizing differing views."[18]

1 *Family News From Dr. James Dobson*, 10/'97, 2.
2 *Focus on the Family* newsletter, 7/'97, 2.
3 Case not named in news article, *Press*, 6-9-96, A4.
4 New York Times News Service, in *Press*, 6-11-94, A6.
5 *Life Advocate*, 5/'94, 9.
6 Associated Press, in *Press*, 3-19-96, A5.
7 Associated Press, in *Press*, A5.
8 Chicago Tribune, in *Press*, 2-2-97, A8.
9 *Press*, 3-24-98, A3.
10 Haffner, *The High Cost of Free Love*, 174.
11 *Press*, 11-3-96, A18.
12 *Press*, 11-3-96, A18.
13 Crutcher, *Access: The Key to Pro-Life Victory*, 20-2.
14 Foreman, *Shattering the Darkness: The Crisis of the Cross in the Church Today*, 12.
15 Colson, in Cal Thomas, in *Press*, 10-23-96, A10.
16 *Press*, 6-20-96, A5
17 George Grant, *Third Time Around*, 153.
18 *Press*, 6-9-96, A1, A4.

The political process

"Before *Roe v. Wade* the political process was handling the volatile abortion issue successfully," says Phillip Johnson, "granting greater legal freedom without launching anything remotely resembling a culture war. Then the Supreme Court abruptly withdrew the issue from normal politics by declaring abortion to be a 'fundamental right,' and the dominant party no longer had to persuade or negotiate."[1]

Another way of expressing this is that the secular humanists were winning major battles in incremental steps with little notice being taken by the evangelical community until the *Roe v. Wade* wake-up call.

The politician's politician: Bill Clinton

"I am opposed to abortion and to government funding of abortions," wrote Governor Bill Clinton of Arkansas in a September 26, 1986, letter to Arkansas Right to Life.[2]

"Within a day of swearing an oath on the Bible [President Bill Clinton] signed several executive orders designed to increase the number of abortions in the land: [more fetal tissue 'experimentation,' abortions OK'd in military hospitals, 'Title X' money OK'd for Planned Parenthood, and his national 'health' insurance plan called for abortions to be covered]."[3]

"President Clinton vetoed a bill to ban late-term partial-birth abortions Oct. 10 [1997], just as he did last year... even though the American Medical Association declared that it is never medically necessary... The House again passed the ban Oct. 8 by a vote of 296-132, more than enough to override Clinton's veto. But in May the Senate fell three votes short of the two-thirds majority needed to override."[4]

In Oklahoma City on Good Friday, 1996, President Bill Clinton told the gathered crowd, "The miracles of the human spirit in Oklahoma City only reflect the larger miracle of human nature: that there is something eternal within each of us [which] no bomb can blow away, even from the littlest child, that eternity which is within each of us."[5]

The renegade spirit in politics

According to Chuck Colson, the Supreme Court first granted itself the power to declare an act of Congress "unconstitutional" in 1803. "Later, during Andrew Jackson's presidency, the Court did it again. Jackson's response was to ignore the Court's decision; and years later, when the Court handed down the *Dred Scott* decision, President Lincoln followed Jackson's example: He pointedly ignored the Court."[6]

More recently, during our abortion era, as George Grant tells us, "When section 1008 of the Title X appropriations bill for population control went into effect, the bureaucratic minions simply ignored it and did whatever they jolly well pleased. Section 1008 stated that no funds could be issued to 'any program or agency where abortion is utilized as a method of family planning.' Despite that clear injunction, the Department of Health and Human Services has poured millions of dollars into the coffers of Planned Parenthood. Thus, the bureaucracy has illegally provided more than half of the budget for Planned Parenthood's program of death, deception, and perversion, out of *our* tax dollars. Because the bureaucracy is unmonitored and unchecked, it is above the law. Quite literally."[7]

"For years, a federal provision known as the Hyde Amendment... prohibited the use of any federal Medicaid funds for abortions except to save the life of the mother... However, last year [1993] Congress enlarged the abortion provision to provide federal matching funds for Medicaid abortions in cases of rape or incest. In December, officials of the Department of Health and Human Services... ruled that the new language imposes a requirement on the states to provide Medicaid abortions in cases of rape or incest."[8]

SCOPE and FOCUS
I. CONVICTIONS
II. PRETEXTS
III. MANDATE
IV. LEGACY
V. ABORTIVE LINKS
Recreational Sex
Reproductive Technology
Abortion Industry
Governmental Action
Involuntary Complicity
Supreme Court
Politics
Legislation
Hyde amendment
F.A.C.E.
Blood money
Human life amendment
Partial birth (D & X)
Value of a child
Law Enforcement
Bureaucracy
Police power
Due Process in Court
Injunctions
Crimes charged
"Necessity" defense
"Jury nullification"
Pro-lifer Consequences
Social Climate
Religious Confusion
Personal Decision to Abort
VI. DILEMMA
VII. DESTINY

1 Johnson, *Reason in the Balance: The Case Against Naturalism in Science, Law & Education*, 184.

2 *Life Advocate*, 2/'94, 5.

3 Michael Bray, *A Time to Kill*, 150.

4 *Christian Times*, 11/'97, 15.

5 *California Prolife* newsletter, 7/'96.

6 *Christian Times*, 11/'97, 7.

7 Grant, *Grand Illusions: The Legacy of Planned Parenthood*, 255.

8 *Life Advocate*, 5/'94, 8.

9 Joseph Scheidler, *Closed: 99 Ways to Stop Abortion*, 284.

10 Willard Cates, Jr., in Douglas Butler, *Abortion, Medicine, and the Law*, 315-6.

4. Legislation

a. The Hyde Amendment

In July 1976 "the Hyde Amendment had passed for the first time. This amendment to the Department of Health and Human Services and the Labor Department funding bill cut off federal funds for abortion... During subsequent years, the Hyde Amendment has appeared in different forms, but always it has had the effect of stopping some abortions by cutting off federal funding and has set the stage for the cutoff of state and even county funding for abortion."[9]

Willard Cates Jr. says this about the Hyde Amendment: "Approximately 85 percent of the low-income women likely to seek abortion were still covered by state funds. For the nation as a whole, over 90 percent of these women obtained a legal abortion despite the Hyde Amendment... About 7 percent of the low-income women continued their pregnancies to delivery. [Note: there had been 300,000 Medicaid abortions the last year before the first Hyde Amendment went into effect; thus 7% of that number meant that the Amendment was saving 21,000 babies a year!]"[10]

"The new Hyde Amendment as passed in 1993, expands payment for abortion for the first time in over 15 years [and now for the first time] allows payment for the deaths of preborn children conceived by alleged acts of rape or incest [the government pays even if no charges have been brought against the father]."[11]

b. F.A.C.E., the Freedom of Access to Clinic Entrances law

In 1994 Congress passed and President Clinton enthusiastically signed the F.A.C.E. bill, which makes it a federal felony to hinder abortions. Those convicted of non-violent offenses could get up to six months in prison and a fine of up to $10,000 for the first offense, and up to 18 months in prison and a fine up to $25,000 for subsequent offenses, not to mention getting a federal criminal record which would likely terminate basic rights such as voting, serving on a jury, running for political office and holding certain government jobs. F.A.C.E. is worded and interpreted in such a way that 'crime' is in the eye of the beholder. Regardless of what a pro-lifer does or does not *do*, if his/her presence in the vicinity of the clinic makes a staffer or client "feel threatened," then a violation of F.A.C.E. may be alleged to have occurred.[12]

Was it only a coincidence that within the year after F.A.C.E. was passed, Congress was hard at work on a bill that would "require anyone convicted of a federal crime to make restitution to the victim"?[13]

c. Blood money from Congress

Congress gave Planned Parenthood $171,900,000 tax dollars in 1995, 34% of its total income.[14]

In the Spring of 1997, President Clinton asked the House for $193 million for international family planning programs [predominantly to fund abortions and abortifacients]. The representatives of the people didn't even reduce the number or make him a counter-offer; they just voted "yes." What's more, even though "A 1973 Helms Amendment prevents U.S. funds from being used to 'perform' abortions... agencies like International Planned Parenthood Federation use tax dollars to 'set up' their programs, then allocate 'other available funds' to perform and promote abortion... and even to lobby to overturn the [anti-abortion] laws in other countries."[15]

F. LaGard Smith states the seriousness of our situation: "In the absence of any recognized Constitutional protection for the unborn, **we will always and interminably be locked in an impasse**... There is no escaping the dilemma: Pro-choice advocates *will* not relent, and pro-life advocates *cannot*."[16]

Back in 1990, when the abortion struggle began to shift back to the state legislatures, Kerby Anderson offered this appraisal: He saw "22 states moving toward restricting abortions," 12 were expected to remain permissive of abortion, and he predicted that "16 will become fierce battlegrounds."[17]

"We need a paramount Human Life amendment to bring about a national change. That means we must have a political victory... We have obviously been puching the wrong buttons... What politicians fear most is social unrest and upheaval... Ultimately, they desire to give in to the demands of the disgruntled, so that tranquility can be restored to the realm."[18]

–Randall Terry

11 *Life Advocate*, 6/'94, 9.
12 *Press*, 5-13-94, A1.
13 *Press*, 2-9-95, A1, A8.
14 *California ProLife Update*, Spring, 1997, 4.
15 *California ProLife Update*, Spring, 1997, 2.
16 Smith, *When Choice Becomes God*, 252.
17 Kerby Anderson, *Living Ethically in the '90s*, 208.
18 Randall Terry, *Operation Rescue*, 197-8.

d. Human Life Amendment

As we have mentioned in a couple of other contexts, because the Supreme Court has found in the Constitution a *woman's fundamental right* to an abortion any time during a pregnancy and for any reason, there is absolutely nothing short of a constitutional amendment that can prohibit abortion.

It will be remembered that if the President vetoes a bill [such as President Clinton has twice done to partial-birth abortion-ban bills passed by Congress] it can still become law if Congress can muster the required two-thirds majority [Article 1, Section 7, 3] to override the veto. Congress has twice failed to attain the necessary two-thirds vote to pass the partial-birth ban over the President's veto.

Under the Constitution [Article V], there are only two ways a constitutional amendment may be proposed: 1) by a two-thirds vote of both houses of Congress, or 2) by a national convention called by Congress at the request of legislatures of two-thirds of the states [33 of them]. The proposed amendment must then be ratified either by the legislatures of, or by conventions of, three-fourths of the states [38 of them].

What does this mean? It means that a human life amendment will not even be proposed until 2/3 of either Congress or the state legislatures [33 needed] want all abortions to be outlawed, and it will not be ratified until three-fourths of the states [38 of them, either in their legislature or through a convention] want all abortions to be outlawed.

How will we know when we are getting close?

If two-thirds of Congress and 38 states want to totally outlaw abortion today it's a done deal. On the day when those same groups believe that all second and third trimester abortions should be outlawed, then we are in the home stretch. Before that must come a day when those same ratios of decision makers are willing to impose such safeguards as mandatory viability testing and a right to life for viable preborns, a requirement that two anesthesiologists be in attendance at abortions, one for the mother and one for the child, and that all abortion procedures be made to comply with the requirements for humane killing of cats and dogs.

Our present situation is this: We are unable to get two-thirds of Congress to vote to outlaw partial-birth abortions, and only 22 states, far fewer than 38, have been even "moving toward restricting abortions." Obviously, in the long uphill race, we pro-life Christians have not even gotten out of the blocks yet.

e. Partial birth abortion (D & X)

What has been the result of 25 years of political lobbying and pro-life public education? A Wirthlin Poll in May of 1996 found that "only 28% of the public knew what a partial-birth abortion was, only 26% knew that Congress had passed a bill banning the procedure, and 27% knew that President Clinton had vetoed the ban. However, when they learned about the partial-birth abortion procedure, 84% of Americans wanted to stop it."[1]

Jerome Keilman responds to the oft-offered advice that pro-lifers should "Write your congressman." He says, "Oh yeah? Well, this summer there occurred the largest mailing to Congress, ever in history, on one subject. Millions of us asked our senators and representatives to overturn Clinton's veto of the ban on late-term abortions. As you know, the House complied; but not the Senate."[2]

The entire pro-life movement needs to attend a "Poli-Sci 101" course. Consider this: Say that you are a gung-ho freshman member of Congress, and your past educational experience has conditioned you to be such a relativist that you honestly have no moral values of your own to get in the way, and you are determined that in every vote that is taken you will support the wishes of the folks back home who elected you.

The push to override the veto of the partial-birth abortion bill is in progress, so you pile up the evidence from the past 12 months that will tell you the nature and the intensity of your people's convictions on the subject. The first thing you realize is that numerically twice as many of the responses are in the pro-life pile as are in the pro-abortion pile.

Next you examine the nature of the responses to assess the depth of conviction they represent. You note that each pro-lifer has taken the time to prepare a thoughtful hand-written letter and has invested the cost of a postage stamp. When you turn your attention to the pro-abortion side you find that, even though only half as many responded, every one of them has placed her own dead child on the "pro-abortion" pile. ...How then should you vote? The greater intensity of commitment is clearly on the pro-death side!

SCOPE and FOCUS
I. CONVICTIONS
II. PRETEXTS
III. MANDATE
IV. LEGACY
V. ABORTIVE LINKS
Recreational Sex
Reproductive Technology
Abortion Industry
Governmental Action
Involuntary Complicity
Supreme Court
Politics
Legislation
Hyde amendment
F.A.C.E.
Blood money
Human life amendment
Partial birth (D & X)
Value of a child
Law Enforcement
Bureaucracy
Police power
Due Process in Court
Injunctions
Crimes charged
"Necessity" defense
"Jury nullification"
Pro-lifer Consequences
Social Climate
Religious Confusion
Personal Decision to Abort
VI. DILEMMA
VII. DESTINY

1 *California ProLife*, Oct.-Nov./'96, 2.

2 Keilman, in *Press*, 10-7-96, A13.

3 R.C. Sproul, *Abortion: A Rational Look at an Emotional Issue*, 44-5.

4 *Press*, 4-14-97 A1, 4-16-97, A1, 4-19-97, B1.

5 Associated Press, in *Press*, 8-18-96, A18.

6 Joseph Foreman, *Shattering the Darkness: The Crisis of the Cross in the Church Today*, dedication page.

f. The value of a child

It is self-evident that our nation's statutory and judicial record on the value of a child is contradictory. Not only preborn children but born children also are subject to a variety of evaluative factors, including being treated like items of commerce. In a country where one toddler killed in a gang crossfire often gets little more than a footnote in the nightly news, the desperate plight of another child can inexplicably become a national obsession. When a Texas youngster tumbled into a well, "For days Americans monitored the television bulletins for news of the child's fate. No expense was spared, no effort deemed too great to save Jessica's life."[3]

After a ten-year-old boy was kidnapped at knifepoint, his mom made "10 appearances on national news programs and talk shows [to share] her nightmare with the nation." Consequently "Nearly 250 investigators from 23 federal, state and local agencies have assisted in the abduction investigation," and the various rewards total "more than $180,000."[4]

Undoubtedly the media "spin" figures prominently in deciding which child tragedies tug at the heartstrings of the nation. Supply and demand, too. We now live in a country in which simply being unwanted transforms a gift from God into medical waste, yet Birthright can put words to the mixed fate of the preborn child: "If I am unwanted, Why must so many couples wait 5, 8, even 10 years to adopt a baby like me? Some even pay $15,000 for a baby on the black market."

Unwantedness by one, even if it is the mother, does not close the book on a child's value to others. When newspapers worldwide reported that because she thought she could afford one more child but not two, a London woman had made arrangements to have one of her unborn twins killed, cash offers for her to change her mind totaled $77,000. Nonetheless she found a "doctor" who injected poison into one baby's heart.[5]

Some pro-lifers, but not most of us, go to great extremes to show how valuable they think an anonymous, unrelated, preborn child really is: "It was Joan [Andrews Bell]'s uncompromising two-and-a-half years of solitary confinement in prison which forced us all to realize that each child is a real person *worth* any level of sacrifice to protect."[6]

We have shared earlier the fact that even before she is promoted to the status of "fetus" by making her mother pregnant, a person still called an "embryo" has been shown in legal battles to be worth as much as $300,000.[7]

The world's very first "test-tube" baby, Louise Brown, was described in this way by Dr. Robert Edwards: "The last time I saw her, she was just eight cells in a test tube. She was beautiful then, and she's beautiful now [as a born child]."[8]

The legal status of the preborn

Jesus said, "Only in his hometown, among his relatives and in his own house is a prophet without honor."[9] In a similar way: A preborn child has an abundance of respect and protection, unless her mother wants her killed.

In 1968 Russel Shaw, when he put *Abortion on Trial*, wrote: "It is therefore significant that the tendency in law – at least outside the area of abortion – is to recognize the unborn child as a person at all stages before birth... a separate person from the moment of conception."[10] In 1968, Charles Kindregan said the same: "The law has consistently invested fetal life with civil rights in every area of litigation in which the question has arisen."[11] In 1973, Robert Drinan listed the preborn's "right to inherit... right to compensation for prenatal injuries... the right to self-abort [miscarry]."[12]

Michael Hirsh, one-time Operation Rescue leader in Atlanta, is now an attorney. He says that many jurisdictions "recognize the child in his mother's womb as a person for purpose of computing welfare aid [citation] and for other family court services [citation]. Unborn children are persons in traffic court, allowing at least one woman to beat a ticket for driving in the carpool lane. She and her unborn child were counted separately [citation]. In addition, the unborn child is a person within the scope of insurance policies [citation] and can bring an action for wrongful death even though he is not born alive [citation]."[13]

7 Fertility clinic scandal of stolen embryos, and $3 million settlement to ten couples, in *Press*, 2-22-97, A4.

8 Edwards, in Brian Clowes, *Pro-Life Activist's Encyclopedia*, page 72.1.

9 *Mark* 6:4.

10 Shaw, 60.

11 Kindregan, *Abortion, the Law, and Defective Children*, 33.

12 Drinan, in David Walbert, *Abortion, Society, and the Law*, 126-7.

13 Hirsh, in Michael Bray, *A Time to Kill*, 117-8.

Physical protection and medical care for the unborn

In the workplace there are extensive regulations demanding special protection for an unborn child, and when a *wanted* preborn has a medical difficulty she can become a patient with her own medical chart, and be given medicines, therapies and surgeries by the old-fashioned kind of doctor who keeps people alive.[1]

Dr. Ronald Graeser says that "fetal surgery or other in-the-womb procedures may be legally required now that these sophisticated procedures are possible. So far [1994] more than 40 operations have been performed on unborn babies between the ages of 18 and 28 weeks of life just at the University of California, San Francisco."[2]

At Georgetown University, Richard McCormick says of fetal surgery, "Already [1985] I hear the doctors involved in this refer to the fetus as their patient. The fetus now begins to make serious claims for a right to nutrition, to protection, to therapy. How can tolerance of abortion be morally reconciled with those claims?"[3]

The preborn as an heir

In 1970 John Noonan wrote: "An unborn child has been held to be a 'child' or 'other person' allowing him to bring an action for the death of his father where the death occurred prior to the child's birth. The fetus has also been held to be an 'existing person' and a 'surviving child' under various wrongful death statutes."[4]

In 1996 a court ordered that Social Security survivor benefits be paid to a child who was conceived through artificial insemination *after* her father's death![5]

Unborn victims of negligence

In Corpus Christi, Texas, in 1996, "A drunken driver got 16 years in prison Monday for manslaughter in the death of a baby who was delivered prematurely after an auto accident. The case is one of the first in Texas to test whether a person can be held criminally liable for harming an unborn child. Because it touched on the question of when life begins, it was closely watched by both sides in the abortion debate [the baby was seven-and-a-half months along, weighed four pounds, suffered brain damage, and died within two days]."[6]

In 1969 Charles Kindregan reported that court decisions had found that the unborn child is already a "person" under the state constitutions of both Oregon and Ohio.[7]

In 1970 John Noonan wrote that "perhaps the most significant cases for establishing the legal existence of a child prior to birth have been those very modern decisions [regarding stillborn babies in which] the unborn child, to whom live birth never comes, is held to be a 'person' who can be the subject of an action for damages for his death."[8]

Crime in the womb

A man who kills his pregnant wife can be charged with double homicide.[9]

"A man facing two murder charges for killing a pregnant woman... pleaded guilty to first degree murder in [the mother's] death and involuntary manslaughter in the fetus's death. ...The defense attorney [argued for the man's innocence of] a murder charge for the fetus because [the defendant could not tell that the 272 pound victim] was six months pregnant... [The prosecutor] argued that the intent to kill the mother transferred to the fetus."[10]

The viability issue

In 1969, "a California Court of Appeal held that a fetus which has reached the stage of viability is a human being for purposes of the state's homicide statute."[11]

In San Diego in 1993, a California appeals court "concluded that the killing of a fetus at any stage of development is murder when the embryo dies as a result of a crime, such as an armed robbery... But some people are concerned that the unanimous opinion... could be a move toward eroding a woman's right to an abortion. The court, in its published opinion, disagreed with 23 years of court precedent that deemed the killing of an unborn child to be murder only if the fetus was viable."[12]

These words of Dean Prosser were published in 1970: "All writers who have discussed the [tort law] problem have joined in condemning the old rule and in maintaining that the unborn child in the path of an automobile is as much a person in the street as the mother," to which John Noonan added: "We shall see if the unborn child can become less than a person if he stands in the path, not of a negligent motorist, but of a surgeon who would take his life."[13]

SCOPE and FOCUS
I. CONVICTIONS
II. PRETEXTS
III. MANDATE
IV. LEGACY
V. ABORTIVE LINKS
Recreational Sex
Reproductive Technology
Abortion Industry
Governmental Action
Involuntary Complicity
Supreme Court
Politics
Legislation
Hyde amendment
F.A.C.E.
Blood money
Human life amendment
Partial birth (D & X)
Value of a child
Law Enforcement
Bureaucracy
Police power
Due Process in Court
Injunctions
Crimes charged
"Necessity" defense
"Jury nullification"
Pro-lifer Consequences
Social Climate
Religious Confusion
Personal Decision to Abort
VI. DILEMMA
VII. DESTINY

5. Law enforcement

"There is no way to reach these needy [preborn] children," says Foreman, "without crossing to the other side of the iron curtain of American law which has descended protectively around the abortion industry."[14]

Randall Terry instructed Rescuers in 1988: "We can't go down there [to a Rescue at an abortion clinic] hating the police... [because] I submit to you that OUR guilt is far greater than theirs, 'cause we know better, we have the oracles of God [the Bible], and we've taken fifteen years to decide that we are going to do something about this, finally, and then we expect police to not arrest us?"[15]

It was a much wisened Randall Terry who walked out of Fulton County Jail in Atlanta in 1990. In just two years he had gone from a belief that his movement would continue to get respectful, ethical treatment by the authorities to having watched helplessly as L.A.'s Finest [the Los Angeles Police "tangle teams"] systematically tortured the peaceful Christians who had trusted his optimistic predictions. Terry had stood trial in various states, each time having his constitutional rights trashed by prosecutors and judges alike. He and his fellow rescuers had been repeatedly assaulted by pro-abortionists only to have the police who had witnessed the attacks do nothing about them, while the media edited both the film and the stories to portray the Rescuers as the hateful and violent ones.

a. Bureaucratic functioning – "Big Brother" does more than watch

1994 was the year when the Bill Clinton – Janet Reno dynamic duo used the isolated shootings and bombings as their excuse to declare war on all pro-lifers. The FBI launched an "investigation into a suspected violent conspiracy among pro-life activists."[16]

In Sarasota, Fla., "Two men, armed with submachine guns, shotguns, Mace, and semi-automatic pistols, wearing bullet-proof vests, spent several hours photographing and videotaping pro-life protesters at the Sarasota Women's Health Center on March 18 [1994]... All the weapons had rounds in the chambers and most were in the cocked position... [This was all the more incredible because] there has never been a rescue or any incident of vandalism or violence there. [After searching the men and their weapons, the police, mysteriously] released the men with only a trespass warning... The police report indicates that the officer [had become convinced] that the men were in some way connected with the FBI or BATF [Bureau of Alcohol, Tobacco and Firearms]."[17]

At about the same time, a small group of Americans arriving in Norway for the Winter Olympics were intercepted by the authorities upon arrival. Their passports were seized, they were detained in the airport police station, it was decided to eject them from the country, and they were deported to Iceland. It was later revealed that the FBI had contacted the Norwegian government and had even supplied them with the names of the members of the group. The authorities were probably surprised that they were all traveling together and under their true identities. Who were these dangerous characters? Leaders of Operation Rescue.[18]

By Summer, 1998, the FBI had put Eric Robert Rudolph on its ten-most-wanted list as a suspect in the January bombing of a Birmingham, Ala., abortion clinic. The results of the early-morning blast were as ghastly as abortion: the life of an off-duty policeman blown away and a nurse/counselor badly maimed. What the media hides, and the fact which will most likely be barred if there is a trial, is that the "clinic" was not "safe and legal," but was a blatantly illegal business. News sources had spread the clinic's boast that it was "challenging" the new Alabama law prohibiting partial-birth abortion.[19] If the police had shut down the clinic for its admitted lawbreaking, or if the two employees had not chosen to assist in that illegal activity, they would not have died. [We do not justify the timing of the bomb, but we most certainly despise the governmental hypocrisy which aggressively prosecutes pro-life activism even as it not only permits but protects illegal abortion activity.]

1 Robert Orr, *Life and Death Decisions*, 55.
2 Graeser, in *Life Advocate*, 6/'94, 36.
3 McCormick, in Carl Horn, *Whose Values?*, 76.
4 John Noonan, *The Morality of Abortion*, 229.
5 Press, 3-12-96, A7.
6 *Press*, 10-1-96, A5.
7 Charles Kindregan, 34.
8 Noonan, 228.
9 *Life Advocate*, 4/'94, 25.
10 *Press*, 2-26-98, B9.
11 *Keeler v. Superior Court for County of Amador*, in Noonan, 237.
12 *Press*, 5-7-93, A3.
13 Prosser, in Noonan, *The Morality of Abortion*, 230.
14 Joseph Foreman, *Shattering the Darkness*, 152-3.
15 Terry, "If You Believe Abortion is Murder, Act Like It's Murder" cassette.
16 *Time*, 8-15-94, 39.
17 *Life Advocate*, 5/'94, 19.
18 Mark Gronceski, in *Life Advocate*, 4/'94, 18-9.
19 *Press*, 1-30-98, A1, A10.

"Law and Order" justifying the abuse of power

The bombing of the World Trade Center by foreign terrorists gave Bill Clinton the opportunity to unveil his request for additional police powers from Congress without the suspicion that pro-lifers were among the targets of his plans. Here is what the president wanted the green light for: 1) Giving federal investigators authority to tap the telephones of anyone it suspects of participating in terrorist or extremist groups, whether or not there is cause for a court order; 2) Banning fund-raising in the United States for groups the president deems dangerous; 3) Letting federal officials monitor credit card, travel and hotel receipts for people it suspects of being sympathetic to extremist causes, whether or not there is evidence they are planning criminal acts; 4) Spending more money for infiltration of extremist groups and more technologically advanced equipment to tap digital computer lines.[1]

The newspaper coverage of the above information went further, reporting groups that voiced serious concerns about Clinton's ambitions: "The American Civil Liberties Union and others [would have us remember] the abuses by the FBI under J. Edgar Hoover, the shooting of American students at Kent State in Ohio protesting U.S. bombing of Cambodia in 1970 and the Nixon administration's 'enemies list' compiled from FBI information... Clinton waves away objections that constitutional rights might be violated by his proposals by saying that Americans got used to the 'minor inconvenience' of airport metal detectors."[2]

The Associated Press reported in 1996, "An 18-month investigation of violence against abortion clinics found no direct evidence of a nationwide conspiracy. [But despite that,] Attorney General Janet Reno promised to continue pursuing evidence of conspiracy in anti-abortion violence, and to protect clinics 'as vigorously as possible.'"[3]

b. Police practice

Terri and Tim Palmquist were part of a group that was distributing literature to people who were exiting the movie "Schindler's List." The theme of the literature was expressed in the words of Tim Palmquist: "Just as Nazi Germany decreed that Jews were non-persons, and were therefore disposable, so our government has decreed that unborn children are non-persons, and therefore disposable." Even though his pro-life activity consisted of nothing more than politely inviting people to take the free literature, and it was at a movie theater not an abortion clinic, Tim Palmquist was illegally arrested and handcuffed, and finally [only after a news crew arrived] released without charges or an apology.[4]

The Associated Press reported a 1997 court decision which, while it has nothing to do with abortion, has far-reaching ramifications for religious liberty and the freedom of religion: "Authorities' tape-recording of a conversation between an Oregon triple-murder defendant and a priest violated federal law, the Constitution and the historical 'sanctity of the secrets of confession,' a federal appeals court said Monday, [but it nevertheless] rejected a request by the Catholic Church to order destruction of the existing tape."[5]

Police malpractice toward pro-life personnel

Even though this example comes from Canada, it is illustrative of the attitude and of the kind of selective law enforcement that have become all too typical in the United States in the abortion arena: "In Canada, long before abortion was made legal, picketers were arrested for picketing an *illegal* abortion clinic, and a police officer was thrown off the force for refusing to arrest those picketers. We need more than a change of law; we need a change of heart," says Joseph Foreman.[6]

The Rutherford Institute filed a lawsuit on behalf of two rescuers against the Dallas police force, saying that the men "were physically removed from the premises with 'excessive force,' including the unnecessary use of 'pain holds' and the spraying of 'pepper mace' into their faces after they had been handcuffed."[7]

George Grant, whose authentication of sources is beyond question, reports that Pittsburgh police "with brutal efficiency arrested more than one hundred of the peaceful men and women praying on the sidewalk and in the parking lot." One of the women has reported that at the Allegheny County Jail, "It was awful. The prison guards were unbelievably rough. Several of us were grabbed by the fronts of our blouses and bras. Some even had their breasts totally exposed and fondled in full view of the other prisoners."[8]

During the aftermath of that same rescue, "The next day, a number of the protesters were moved again, at the behest of the attorneys advising city and county officials – this time to the Mayview Psychiatric Hospital. 'I couldn't believe it,' Barry related. 'They actually held us in the psych ward for nearly two days. They don't even do that sort of thing in Russia anymore.'"[9]

It is not surprising when Grant reports, "In 1989, sit-ins and rescue operations began to face serious attrition due to the severe treatment of police and the heavy penalties exacted by prosecutors."[10]

SCOPE and FOCUS
I. CONVICTIONS
II. PRETEXTS
III. MANDATE
IV. LEGACY
V. ABORTIVE LINKS
Recreational Sex
Reproductive Technology
Abortion Industry
Governmental Action
Involuntary Complicity
Supreme Court
Politics
Legislation
Hyde amendment
F.A.C.E.
Blood money
Human life amendment
Partial birth (D & X)
Value of a child
Law Enforcement
Bureaucracy
Police power
Due Process in Court
Injunctions
Crimes charged
"Necessity" defense
"Jury nullification"
Pro-lifer Consequences
Social Climate
Religious Confusion
Personal Decision to Abort
VI. DILEMMA
VII. DESTINY

6. "Due process" in court for pro-life activists

Somewhat cynical, street-wise advice from the Sixties is offered by Henry diSuvero: "The liberal notion that the legal system acts as a sieve, separating out the truth and dispensing justice according to neutral norms, is valid enough when the basic issues do not involve the conflict of social forces; however, when such a conflict is involved, legality becomes merely the veneer of repression... The courts must always be viewed by the movement as the territory of the enemy."[11]

This is actually little different from the warning of James Hunter: "Those who define how a contest is to be played out will have the advantage of shaping its final outcome."[12]

Joseph Scheidler never minces his words: "Anti-life bias seems to be a prerequisite for being a judge today."[13]

How about a little confirmation from the other side? Gina Shaw, a spokeswoman for the National Abortion Federation said in 1996: "Courts are now refusing to hear new abortion cases as if they are tired of rehashing the controversy... Now the courts seem most sympathetic to the pro-choice cause."[14]

George Grant was convinced of that fact already in 1988: "The lower courts have proven to be equally hostile to life and liberty. Repeatedly stiff sentences have been handed down to abortion protesters, alternative service providers [CPCs], and pro-life organizers, often on trumped up charges."[15]

Joseph Foreman admits, "Wherever mass Rescues have seriously challenged childkilling, the city quickly finds our price and we go home."[16]

a. Injunctions and restraining orders

Scheidler says that "the rescue phenomenon has mobilized pro-abortion opposition at the clinics and has resulted in unconstitutional injunctions and laws that threaten First Amendment constitutional rights."[17]

"Across the country," *Life Advocate* magazine says, "restraining orders have been issued [and] local ordinances have been passed [targeting pro-life protest, and] the First Amendment rights of Christians have grown noticeably smaller."[18]

b. Prosecution charges

About the time of the launching of Operation Rescue in 1987, a creative pro-abortionist was suggesting that authorities arrest pro-lifers on such charges as "assault, battery, harassment, invasion of privacy, and intentional infliction of emotional harm," but ended with the advice that trespassing "is likely to be the most useful theoretical underpinning since it is the least likely to run afoul of the First Amendment."[19]

The standard rescue tactic of "going limp" has repeatedly been converted into the incomprehensible charge of "resisting arrest."[20]

In Birmingham, Ala., while praying on a public sidewalk, 47 adults and 32 minors were all arrested on the basis of a local ordinance that limited "protests" on a sidewalk to a maximum of six participants.[21]

After Randall Terry "had threatened to present Bill Clinton with an actual aborted baby," someone got a judge to issue a court order forbidding him to do so. He complied. But after other people did the deed, Terry was tried, convicted and sentenced to five months in prison for "contempt" and for "aiding and abetting."[22]

1 *Press*, 4-25-95, A1, A8.
2 *Press*, 4-25-95, A1, A8.
3 Associated Press, in *Press*, 1-26-96, A1, A6.
4 *Life Advocate*, 4/'94, 23.
5 Associated Press, in *Press*, 1-28-97, A7.
6 Joseph Foreman, *Shattering the Darkness*, 120.
7 *Life Advocate*, 5/'94, 9.
8 George Grant, *Third Time Around: A History of the Pro-Life Movement from the First Century to the Present*, 140-1.
9 Grant, *Third Time Around*, 141.
10 Grant, *Third Time Around*, 147.
11 Henry di Suvero, in Jonathan Black, *Radical Lawyers: Their Role in the Movement and in the Courts*, 52.
12 Hunter, *Culture Wars: The Struggle to Define America*, 271.
13 Scheidler, *Closed: 99 Ways to Stop Abortion*, 177.
14 *Press*, 6-9-96, A1, A4.
15 Grant, *Grand Illusions: The Legacy of Planed Parenthood*, 252.
16 Foreman, *Shattering the Darkness*, 102.
17 Joseph Scheidler, *Closed: 99 Ways to Stop Abortion*, 143.
18 *Life Advocate*, 2/'94, 11.
19 Carol Lefcourt, *Women and the Law*, page 10A-13.
20 Life Advocate, 4/'94, 6.
21 *Life Advocate*, 5/'94, 22.
22 *Time*, 6-21-93, page citation lost, sorry.

c. The "necessity" defense

The reader may recall the paragraph from our treatment of Universalism and Relativism [page 18], in which we were discussing the *Casey* decision's Mystery Passage: Dr. Dobson is exactly right, although the mystery passage may have a silver lining. In court, with only the rarest exception, Rescuers have not even been permitted to introduce the "necessity" defense for their action to save a life. The judicial rationale was that in *Roe* the Court declared its inability to determine when human life begins, but it could assert that preborns are not 14th Amendment "persons;" therefore, you can't trespass to save a person if no person is in danger. But now, in *Casey*, the court has declared that every individual – including a Rescuer, we would assume – has "the right to define one's own concept of existence... and of the mystery of human life." From now on, Rescuers on trial do not have to plead insanity to declare that they were convinced that a live human baby was about to be killed!

d. Jury "nullification"

In *Grand Illusions* George Grant gives a clear explanation of the legal principle called jury nullification. He summarizes: "The founding Fathers gave each citizen the jury vote in order to restrain the courts from unjustly applying legitimate laws or from legitimately applying unjust laws."[1] In practice, a judge has little trouble preventing the imposition of jury nullification. Notable exceptions might include the trials of Lorena Bobbitt and O.J. Simpson.

7. "Justice" and consequences of pro-life activism

Paul Hill is under a death sentence and Michael Griffin faces life in prison for killing abortionists. Shelley Shannon expects to spend the rest of her life in prison for wounding an abortionist and for causing an assortment of clinic fires in at least three states.

Of the forty or more convicted of clinic demolitions [and attempts], five, ten or twenty years seems to be the norm. It would appear that the government is relatively confident that the above standard of maximum-sentencing is sufficient to get a handle on the problem of destructive and violent pro-lifeism.

In a sense the civil disobedience of 50,000 American Rescuers was a more frightening dilemma for the government. But the judiciary effectively chilled that style of volunteerism with jail sentences calculated to be long enough to capsize a family's finances and threaten or ruin careers.

The last pro-life law-and-order obstacle seemed to be those fanatical pro-life activists who, while drawing the line short of building-demolition and personal violence, seemed to all have internalized Joe Scheidler's *Closed: 99 Ways to Stop Abortion.* The government's ace in the hole for that group became lawsuits and financial judgments.

The government geared up for this battle in three ways: 1) The Freedom of Access to Clinic Entrances [F.A.C.E.] law in 1994 created new federal felonies, carrying 6 to 18 months in prison and fines from $10,000 to $25,000 for doing precisely the things that peaceful pro-lifers do at abortion clinics. This is not limited to blockers of access. The law is so vaguely written and so broadly applied that restrained sidewalk counseling and even praying at a distance can be F.A.C.E. crimes if abortion staff or clients simply feel threatened by the pro-lifers' presence.[2]

2) Next came test cases under R.I.C.O., the anti-gangster act, and the Supreme Court's ruling in 1994 that indeed, planning an opportunity for folks to sit in front of an abortion business is exactly the same and just as serious as running a national crime organization engaged in illegal gambling, prostitution and gangland executions. The unique thing about R.I.C.O. is that it automatically imposes triple-damage awards.

3) In a certainly-not-unrelated 1995 action, Congress was configuring a law "to require anyone convicted of a federal crime to make restitution to the victim."[3]

As we present the following representative figures, please keep in mind that the most serious harm that any of these pro-life Christians inflicted was a delay of the abortion business by blocking access through their doors for a few hours until the rescuers were hauled away by police.

Sacramento, Calif., $100,000; Jeff White, $800,000 plus others for a total of $1.3 million; Houston, Texas, $1 million; Flip Benham and nine others, $8.6 million; 37 Oregon pro-lifers and Advocates for Life Ministries, $12.5 million specifically for "nuisance and trespass;" There are at least 15 Operation Rescue leaders whose fines are now over $1 million each.

Joseph Scheidler and two others faced their first R.I.C.O. trial in 1986, which resulted in a conviction. The verdict, however, flip-flopped at two appellate levels, and finally was received by the Supreme Court. Those justices revised R.I.C.O. in 1994 so that the person no longer needs to have acted on a personal economic motive to be convicted, and they sent the case back to Chicago. The federal jury there was overwhelmed by the attorneys from NOW [The National Organization for Women] and from four major corporate law firms, convicting Scheidler and the two others [in April 1998, $86,000, automatically tripled] in a "class action" R.I.C.O. lawsuit, which means that any of the nation's other 900 "abortuaries" can bring suit under the auspices of ["joining"] the *NOW v. Scheidler* suit.[4]

SCOPE and FOCUS
I. CONVICTIONS
II. PRETEXTS
III. MANDATE
IV. LEGACY
V. ABORTIVE LINKS
Recreational Sex
Reproductive Technology
Abortion Industry
Governmental Action
Involuntary Complicity
Supreme Court
Politics
Legislation
Hyde amendment
F.A.C.E.
Blood money
Human life amendment
Partial birth (D & X)
Value of a child
Law Enforcement
Bureaucracy
Police power
Due Process in Court
Injunctions
Crimes charged
"Necessity" defense
"Jury nullification"
Pro-lifer Consequences
Social Climate
Education
Media
World view
Power
Bias
re: Christianity
re: Abortion
re: C.P.C.s
re: Rescue
Elite few
Religious Confusion
Personal Decision to Abort
VI. DILEMMA
VII. DESTINY

E. Social Climate

In the '60s Elton Trueblood was telling us: "We cannot be rightly prepared for the fierce straggle of our generation if we do not understand the intensity of the opposition to a committed Christianity."[5]

Our liberal elites, whose "attitude to religion," Christopher Lasch said, "ranges from indifference to active hostility," have succeeded in removing religion from public recognition and debate.[6]

Thomas Gumbleton, while Roman Catholic Bishop in Detroit, said, "Changing hearts and minds is always the most difficult task; it is also the most essential. I would like us to spend a lot more time and effort on it."[7]

1. Education

"The pivotal group in shaping cultural opinion is the middle-ground, pro-'choice' group," says R.C. Sproul. "Here is the most fertile field for finding people who will cross over to the pro-life position. It is always a good strategy to concentrate effort on the most likely prospects... [and here is a very] strategic target: liberal churches and liberals. Though much public protest has taken place around abortion clinics, little or no public protest has occurred around churches where the pastors have stated their pro-choice position. Sadly, the organized church – more than any other institution apart from the Supreme Court – has neglected its duty to inform the public conscience."[8]

2. Media

"The media have given us a town square the size of the world," says Gordon Aeschliman.[9]

Mark Crutcher details the huge resource of abortion industry money for lobbying, and the ever-expanding voting block of women who have had abortions, before concluding that the pro-abortion force in government has "simply too much inertia for us to overcome. Compound that with their absolute stranglehold on the American media, and the idea that we can stop abortion without first lowering the abortion rate is seen for what it really is: utterly laughable."[10]

It is not an overstatement to say that the media defines our reality. "What is presented in the media," says James Hitchcock, "and the way in which it is presented, are for many people the equivalent of what is real. By determining what ideas will be presented in public, the media determines what ideas are to be considered respectable, rational, and true. Those excluded from discussion, or treated only in a negative way, are conversely defined as disreputable, irrational, and false."[11]

NBC's senior analyst, Irving R. Levine, asserts that it is "the reporter who has to determine ultimately what is valid and what is not, whose arguments are the most persuasive and whose are not."[12]

"As the courts keep pushing religion out of sight," declares Robert Bork, "the press either ignores it or treats it as some sort of emotional affliction. It is hardly any wonder that religion slowly loses its grip on the popular mind."[13]

a. World view of the media

Grant tells us: "When writers write, when journalists report, and when broadcasters go on the air, they communicate from the peculiar perspective of their own worldview. From the stories they select, to the way they present them, from the evidence they show, to the time they afford them, newsmen not only slant the news, they *make* the news. They decide what we know. And what we don't know."[14]

In 1961 – if you want a peek at a fundamental shift – an editor of dignified women's magazines was observing: "The younger people on our editorial staff are now in control, and they are insisting that everything we publish, fiction and nonfiction alike, be 'permissive.' Anything that tries to hold up the standards of traditional morality they regard not only as having poor reader appeal but as a kind of evil in its own right."[15]

1 Grant, *Grand Illusions*, 253.

2 *Press*, 5-13-94, A1, and F.A.C.E. itself.

3 *Press*, 2-9-95, A1, A8.

4 *Life Advocate*, Jul.-Aug/'98, 24-6.

5 Trueblood, *The Incendiary Fellowship*, 18.

6 Lasch, in Robert Bork, *Slouching Towards Gomorrah: Modern Liberalism and American Decline*, 274.

7 Gumbleton, in F. LaGard Smith, *When Choice Becomes God*, 264.

8 Sproul, *Abortion: A Rational Look at an Emotional Issue*, 151.

9 Aeschliman, *Global Trends: Ten Changes Affecting Christians Everywhere*, 70-1.

10 Mark Crutcher, *Access: The Key to Pro-Life Victory*, 22.

11 Hitchcock, in George Grant, *Grand Illusions: The Legacy of Planned Parenthood*, 42.

12 Levine, in Grant, *Grand Illusions*, 170.

13 Bork, *Slouching Towards Gomorrah*, 291-2.

14 Grant, *Grand Illusions*, 169.

15 John Drakeford, *The Great Sex Swindle*, 7.

b. The Power of the media

"It has been said that the Vietnam War was not lost on the rice fields and jungles of southeastern Asia, but in the minds and consciences of Americans through the power of the media."[1] *Time* magazine says, "The media help create leaders and then eat them alive – a sort of electronic Aztec sacrifice."[2] An incredibly memorable article appeared in *Christianity Today* in 1968. In it T.W. Harper said:

> At the time of the Reformation, a man with a Bible in his hands was a supremely modern man – a man with the product of the latest technology (the printing press [*Gutenberg Bible*, 1454]) at his service. Today... we still persist largely in a blind devotion to yesterday's methods... In the evening, after Mr. and Mrs. Jones have come home from the office and had dinner, they draw the curtains, pour themselves a drink, and turn on the radio or television set. Hidden away in an anonymous retreat, they put out their antennas and tune in to the communicating world outside. What do they her from us [the Church]? Hardly anything... It will [soon] be possible for America to put Batman, or for the Soviet Union to put Brezhnev, into everybody's living-room world-wide... From its present attitude of disinterest, though, it looks as if there is no danger of the church putting anything in anywhere.[3]

• Half of all Americans, together, watched "Peter Pan" on TV on March 7, 1955. • A 13-year-old boy sent aspirin to Albert Schweitzer at his mission in Africa; after the news made it *news*, the public contributed $400,000 worth of supplies.[4]

October 1960 was an historic turning point in the civil rights movement and in the careers of two politicians: "Martin Luther King, Jr., was jailed in Georgia, refused bail, and was whisked away to a state prison. Many Negroes feared for his life. With the campaign for the Presidency drawing to a climax, the two major candidates were faced with a difficult decision... Nixon said nothing. John F. Kennedy phoned Mrs. King, expressing sympathy and offering assistance... The press reported it [favorably]. Martin Luther King, Jr., was released on bail rather than being held."[5]

Kennedy, of course, won the election.

Newspaper article, October 1996: "Sounding like a crusader, Bob Dole implored his audiences Friday to 'rise up' against the nation's news organizations. ...At a [presidential] campaign rally: When do the American people rise up and say, 'Forget the media in America! We're going to make up our minds! *You're* not going to make up our minds!' ...Don't read that stuff. Don't watch television. This is about saving our country! ...Where is the outrage?"[6]

In 1969 the average American watched television 2 hours a day; now it is seven.

c. Bias of the media

Dr. Bernard Nathanson, now pro-life, tells of his own complicity – as an abortionist – in pro-abortion propagandizing in the '60s and 70's: "We fed the public a line of deceit, dishonesty, a fabrication of statistics and figures. We succeeded in [breaking down the laws limiting abortions] because the time was right and the news media cooperated. We sensationalized the effects of illegal abortions, and fabricated polls which indicated that 85 percent of the public favored unrestricted abortion, when we knew it was only 5 percent. We unashamedly lied, and yet our statements were quoted [by the media] as though they had been written in law."[7]

"This is what is meant by the popular phrase *political correctness*: a position so 'obviously superior,' so 'obviously correct,' and its opposite is so 'obviously out of bounds' that they are beyond serious discussion and debate. Indeed, to hold the 'wrong' opinion, one must be either mentally imbalanced... or, more likely, evil," says Phillip Johnson.[8]

In the words of ace reporter Linda Ellerbee: "We report news, not truth. There is no such thing as objectivity. Any reporter who tells you he's objective is lying to you."[9]

SCOPE and FOCUS
I. CONVICTIONS
II. PRETEXTS
III. MANDATE
IV. LEGACY
V. ABORTIVE LINKS
Recreational Sex
Reproductive Technology
Abortion Industry
Governmental Action
Involuntary Complicity
Supreme Court
Politics
Legislation
Hyde amendment
F.A.C.E.
Blood money
Human life amendment
Partial birth (D & X)
Value of a child
Law Enforcement
Bureaucracy
Police power
Due Process in Court
Injunctions
Crimes charged
"Necessity" defense
"Jury nullification"
Pro-lifer Consequences
Social Climate
Education
Media
World view
Power
Bias
re: Christianity
re: Abortion
re: C.P.C.s
re: Rescue
Elite few
Religious Confusion
Personal Decision to Abort
VI. DILEMMA
VII. DESTINY

1 James Hoffmeier, *Abortion: A Christian Understanding and Response*, 20.

2 *Time*, 12-5-94, 76-7.

3 T.W. Harper, "Give the Winds a Voice," *Christianity Today*, 6-21-68, 48.

4 Clinebell, 278.

5 Charles McCoy, in Robert Lee, *Religion and Social Conflict*, 42.

6 *Press*, 10-26-96, A7.

d. Christianity as portrayed by the media

James Dobson in the summer of 1998 says: "**As conservative Christians continue to lose ground in the great civil war of values, the cultural elites will continue their campaign to marginalize and paralyze us. They want to make it so uncomfortable for Christians to speak up, even within their own denominations, on issues of political correctness and public policy that they will cower in fear. They accomplish this not by dealing with the positions we take, but by name-calling and blatant disrespect. We are referred to as the 'far right,' as 'extremists,' 'right-wing zealots,' 'fundamentalists,' 'fringe groups' and even 'religious nuts.' Note that no one is ever referred to by the press as the 'far left,' 'extreme left' or 'left-wing nuts.' Only Christians can be so marginalized.**"[10]

Robert Bork documents "the hostility or indifference of the national media to religion. Despite the fact that religion is a major feature of American life, it is the subject of only 1 percent of news stories on the four major networks and the national print press, and those are typically hostile."[11]

Elsewhere Bork reports: "A major study of changes in program content over the life of television [finds:] Recreational sex, for example, is pervasive and is presented as acceptable about six times as often as it is rejected. Homosexuals and prostitutes are shown as social victims. Television takes a neutral attitude towards adultery, prostitution, and pornography... The villains in TV's moralist plays are not deviants and libertines but Puritans and prudes. The moral relativism of the Sixties is now television's public morality."[12]

"According to the now famous study of the media," Grant tells us, "the overwhelming majority of newsmen in major media outlets are hostile to biblical values. Only eight percent are regular churchgoers. Eighty percent believe that homosexuality is a perfectly acceptable alternative lifestyle. Eighty-four percent said that they did not have strong aversions to adultery. Ninety-two percent oppose traditional family structures. And a full ninety-seven percent take a clear pro-abortion stand."[13]

e. Abortion as portrayed by the media

"By the mid-1950s press accounts regularly distinguished between abortions conducted by regular physicians and those performed by 'butcher quacks.'"[14]

As we mentioned earlier [page 64] subsequent to the rubella epidemic of 1964-5, *Life* magazine "gave a pat on the back to physicians who performed abortions on these grounds, calling them 'conscientious doctors of highest integrity who acted in defiance of community convention and state law.'"[15]

Grant tells us, "Both *The Post* and *Newsweek* steered fairly clear of the abortion issue throughout the Sixties... But then, with the dawning of the Seventies, they allied themselves unreservedly with Planned Parenthood. They began to laud the heroics of pro-abortion advocates as 'humane and compassionate' and to denigrate prolifers as rabid 'missionaries' and 'crusaders.'"[16]

He goes on to declare, "Planned Parenthood, for all intents and purposes, has the media in its pocket... If we are going to serve our society as prophets and priests, guiding and guarding the land, we are going to have to recapture the media."[17]

In some ways, history is cyclical. Joseph Scheidler says: "During the American Revolution, the colonists were expert in the use of the leaflet; people like Tom Paine and Paul Revere regularly printed articles and handed them out to the people. Since the press at that time was under the sway of England, it was generally hostile to the colonists' ideas. If the colonists wanted to express their views on independence or some other facet of English oppression, they had to resort to the leaflet. We have a similar problem in this country today, with media hostile to the pro-life movement. In fact, it has been estimated that the press is ninety percent against the pro-life position. Consequently, if we want to tell our side of the story we often have to write it and present it to the public ourselves."[18]

f. Crisis pregnancy centers (CPCs) as portrayed by the media

Christians started crisis pregnancy centers as early as 1967 [in Hawaii]. By the mid-Eighties, there were more than three thousand alternative crisis pregnancy centers around the country. Their effectiveness in ministering to women who would otherwise abort was cutting into the abortionists' business. Planned Parenthood launched "a full-scale negative publications campaign to discredit and close [them]."[19]

"The cooperation between the seven major media monopolies and Planned Parenthood was vividly illustrated in a series of coordinated stories during the eighteen months between October, 1985 and March, 1987... labeling the alternative centers as 'bogus' and 'deceptive,' luring clients in by 'masquerading' as abortion clinics and then 'terrorizing' them with 'horror stories,' 'gory photographs,' and 'brainwashing techniques.'"[20]

7 Nathanson, in John Powell, *Abortion: The Silent Holocaust*, 75.

8 Phillip Johnson, *Reason in the Balance: The Case Against Naturalism in Science, Law & Education*, 182-3.

9 Ellerbee, in Grant, *Grand Illusions*, 169.

10 *Family News From Dr. James Dobson*, 7/'98, 5.

11 Bork, 291.

12 Bork, 127.

13 From Robert Lichter, "Media and Business Elites," in Grant, *Grand Illusions*, 170.

14 Marvin Olasky, *Abortion Rites: A Social History of Abortion in America*, 276-7.

15 Russel Shaw, *Abortion on Trial*, 21.

16 George Grant, *Grand Illusions*, 174.

17 George Grant, *Grand Illusions*, 245.

18 Scheidler, *Closed: 99 Ways to Stop Abortion*, 36.

19 George Grant, *Third Time Around: A History of the Pro-Life Movement from the First Century to the Present*, 146.

20 Grant, *Grand Illusions: The Legacy of Planned Parenthood*, 176-7.

g. Rescue as portrayed by the media

After the first big splashes made by Operation Rescue in New Jersey and New York, Randall Terry effused to a group of pastors early in 1988, "We see an *interest* [by the public, in Rescue; we are *news*]. The religious media are saying, 'This is great!' The secular media is acknowledging the heroics of it."[1]

Just one year later everything had changed in the attitudes of both the authorities and the media. Marlin Maddoux, writing *Free Speech or Propaganda?* in 1990, quoted Randall Terry: "This is what is worrying me... The police are beginning to predetermine that they will be brutal. They are putting erroneous felonies on people. But what is most scary to me is that we have the secular media standing right there watching it all happen and then refusing to report it. They are blacking out the police brutality."[2]

Randy Alcorn reported that even "Prior to 1990, the secular media and sometimes the Christian media tended to inaccurately portray rescuers as the cult of Randall Terry."[3] Alcorn also observed, "It is tragic that the average Christian, even the average Christian leader, has formed conclusions about rescuing based on secondhand [media] information."[4]

Randall Terry emphasizes: "During the one hundred day period between May 1 and early August, 1988, over 4,000 arrests resulted from direct action campaigns organized or inspired by Operation Rescue. Not one of these arrests involved verbal or physical violence of any kind on the part of the rescuers."[5]

When *Time* magazine reported on what it called Operation Rescue's "Camp for Crusaders" in Melbourne, Fla., in 1993, it gave Eleanor Smeal, president of the Fund for the Feminist Majority, the chance to smear a 100% peaceful, non-violent and non-destructive movement with the "terrorist" brush. Smeal masterfully reported what did not happen in such a way that her readers were left with the certainty that it did: "Lessons were not given, as far as reporters allowed to witness some of the classroom sessions could determine, in several of [Operation Rescue's] most extreme tactics: torching abortion clinics and suffusing them with noxious chemicals... They've changed their tactics – more harassment, more stalking, more violence."[6]

In reporting the effect of ever-rising court judgments, the Knight-Ridder news wire took the opportunity to feed the extreme fictions that Rescue is violent, sinister and rich: "Operation Rescue starts using guerilla tactics... Financial secrecy draws criticism... Leaders deny wealth. Hit by six-figure fines and penalties from clinic blockades... Operation Rescue leaders have formed an underground network designed to make it impossible for courts and opponents' lawyers to hurt them financially... Operation Rescue has become a forest that keeps outsiders from getting a good look at the trees."[7]

Joseph Foreman summarizes for us: "If you listen to the abortion culture, you can easily get the impression that pro-lifers generally, and Rescuers in particular, are hate-filled, violent, and abusive liars. Much of the Church is emerging from a sixty-year [1932-1992?] cultural sleep to hear all of these accusations willingly portrayed by the press."[8]

SCOPE and FOCUS
I. CONVICTIONS
II. PRETEXTS
III. MANDATE
IV. LEGACY
V. ABORTIVE LINKS
Recreational Sex
Reproductive Technology
Abortion Industry
Governmental Action
Social Climate
Education
Media
World view
Power
Bias
re: Christianity
re: Abortion
re: C.P.C.s
re: Rescue
Elite few
Religious Confusion
Polarization of Believers
Pluralism
Priorities
Theology
Liberalized
Social gospel
Leader crisis
Public Acts of Faith
Religious Right
Self-destructing
Marginalized
Revival time?
Abortion Controversy
"Catholic" view
Image of God
Personhood
Preborn human rights
The exceptions
Choice views
Has Church failed?
Personal Decision to Abort
VI. DILEMMA
VII. DESTINY

1 Randall Terry, "If You Believe Abortion is Murder, Act Like It's Murder" cassette tape.

2 Maddoux, *Free Speech or Propaganda? How the Media Distorts the Truth*, 107.

3 Alcorn, *Is Rescuing Right? Breaking the Law to Save the Unborn*, 167.

4 Alcorn, *Is Rescuing Right?*, 136.

5 Terry, *Operation Rescue*, 244-5.

6 *Time*, 4-19-93, 40.

7 Knight-Ridder, in *Press*, 1-5-92, A1, A10.

8 Foreman, *Shattering the Darkness: The Crisis of the Cross in the Church Today*, 94.

9 Clowes, *Pro-Life Activist's Encyclopedia*, page 15.11.

10 Nathanson, in Grant, *Grand Illusions*, 171.

11 Whitehead, *The Second American Revolution*, 136.

12 Schaeffer, *A Time for Anger: The Myth of Neutrality*, 27; also quoted in Grant, *Grand Illusions*, 175-6.

13 Hunter, *Culture Wars*, 136.

14 The catacombs were elaborate tunnels, rooms and burial chambers [covering an area of 600 acres] carved by the early Christians in the soft tufa rock on the outskirts of Rome in the 200s and 300s. In times of persecution, Christians took refuge in the catacombs because Roman law regarding the sacredness of tombs made them as effective as the Old Testament Cities of Refuge.

h. Elite few who control the media

Ninety-seven percent of the television elite, 96% of the movie elite, and 90% of the press elite describe themselves as pro-abortion, Brian Clowes tells us.[9]

According to Bernard Nathanson, "Almost half of the national news and information outlets are concentrated in the hands of just seven corporate monoliths: CBS, RCA, CapCities, the New York Times, The Washington Post, Gannett, and Time-Life... all seven of these communications monopolies have maintained a consistent pro-abortion editorial policy over the years. Their strict advocacy of Planned Parenthood's agenda has been as much a hallmark of their profile as their slick promotions and high-tech imagery."[10]

John Whitehead warns us, "The massive power of the humanistic media must not be underestimated... The organized media functions much like a nonelected bureaucracy. Presidents come and go, but the controlled press is always present... When this group of highly powerful individuals share the same humanistic consensus, their weight takes on awesome proportions."[11]

In the words of Franky Schaeffer, "Given the concentration of the media's power in relatively few hands, and their shared values, it's nearly impossible to avoid the conclusion that the media represents a monolithic, unelected force in public life: a self-assured, self-perpetuating elite that relishes its power and would have more."[12]

The significance of the stranglehold the media has on our social consciousness is made clear by James Hunter in *Culture Wars: The Struggle to Define America*: "Because each side operates out of a fundamentally different conception of moral authority... because each side employs a markedly different kind of moral logic, neither side will ever be able to persuade the other of the superiority of its own claims... As a consequence, the struggle to gain legitimation requires something besides positive moral persuasion. Inevitably it entails the existence of an enemy to stand against. This is the negative face of moral conflict: the deliberate, systematic effort to discredit the opposition... neutralizing the opposition through a strategy of public ridicule, derision, and insult has become just as important as making credible moral claims."[13]

As a result, we Christians now cower in sanctuaries which function as the catacombs of Rome.[14]

F. Religious Confusion

In a 1968 issue of *Pulpit Digest*, Peter Berger predicted: "By the twenty-first century, religious believers are likely to be found only in small sects, huddled together to resist a world-wide secular culture. I think people will become so bored with what religious groups have to offer that they will look elsewhere."[15]

Tell Mr. Berger that, while church attendance continued to decline, it did level off, and that the boredom is still with us, and he was right-on about the huddling and the resisting a "world-wide secular culture." Tell him that Robert Bork says, "We no longer have a common moral culture and our religion, while pervasive, seems increasingly unable to affect actual behavior."[16]

Oh, and tell him that Brian Clowes wants him to know that "Over 90 percent of all Americans believe in God [but] they simply ignore Him when making moral decisions, [and that] the God they believe in is a nonjudgmental, relativist, wimpy god who would never put anyone in Hell... [also:] Only 10 percent of all Americans said that their faith made a 'discernible difference in their lives.'"[17]

1. Polarization of the faithful

To a degree that perhaps Mr. Berger and his generation of Christian leaders did not realize, a fault line which had been evident for much of the century was to soon create a great schism within the Church. "The liberal churches themselves, including liberal Catholics, are now perhaps the major secularizing forces in the United States," says James Hitchcock, "because their leaders understand one of their principal tasks to be that of 'demythologizing' traditional faith wherever it appears. Many religious liberals regard all forms of 'fundamentalism' (a term they extend to orthodox Catholics now as well as conservative Protestants) as far worse than outright unbelief. They are capable of warmer 'ecumenical' relations with Jews, Buddhists, agnostics, Marxists, and Freudians than they are with many members of their own denominations."[18]

15 Berger, "Bleak Outlook for Religion," *Pulpit Digest*, 9/'68, 54. Not in bibliography.

16 Bork, *Slouching Towards Gomorrah*, 64.

17 Clowes, *Pro-Life Activist's Encyclopedia*, page 42.7.

18 Hitchcock, in William Ball, *In Search of a National Morality: A Manifesto for Evangelicals and Catholics*, 34-5.

a. Religious pluralism

In *Megatrends 2000*, we are told, "In turbulent times, in times of great change, people head for the two extremes: fundamentalism and personal spiritual experience. Millions of Americans have studied yoga, meditation, or other disciplines adopted from the eastern religions. [For others,] fundamentalism offers a return to simpler times, when values were more clear-cut." The author elaborates: "In North America an array of new religions outside the Judeo-Christian framework is taking root... Typically scores of new religious bodies – from denominations to cults – are created each year. But recently their numbers multiplied into the hundreds and then doubled... Four percent of the U.S. population is Moslem, Buddhist, or Hindu... That means there are more Moslems than Episcopalians."[1]

There are more than 405,000 Christian places of worship in the U.S.,[2] yet in any local community, far from seeing themselves as members of one Body, the congregations resemble more than anything else, competing franchises.

Denominationalism's *up*-side / down-side

Denominational tolerance is an American institution dating back to religious Pilgrims who came to these shores to escape religious persecution in Europe. In *The War Over the Family*, the Bergers tell us that "a denomination is a religious body that has given up (in practice if not in theory) its claim to monopoly status. In other words, a denomination is a religious body that recognizes, at least implicitly, that other religious bodies have a right to exist in society as well... Put simply, denominationalism has been a very successful historical experiment." They go on: "Let us just ask the following question: How likely is it that the 'pro-choice' and 'pro-life' camps will become 'moral denominations,' analogous to, say, Episcopalians and Presbyterians?"[3]

Evangelicals should take James Hitchcock's view as a compliment: "The reality of pluralism has been a major reason for the liberalization of Protestantism, which is now about to relativize itself radically with regard to the various non-Christian religions. Only conservative Protestantism, for reasons not altogether clear, has been able to sustain its sense of uncompromising truth in the midst of a dizzyingly varied religious landscape."[4]

On the other hand, Brian Clowes seems to suggest that there is reason to anticipate an ecumenical pro-lifeism: "Pro-abortionists love to employ their deeply ingrained anti-Catholic bigotry to dismiss the opposition as a bunch of Papist puppets, but... opposition to abortion is not just a 'Catholic issue:' it is not even just a *Christian* issue. Buddhists, Hindus, Jainists, Moslems, Jews, Krishnas, and many other non-Christians oppose abortion on both religious and secular grounds."[5]

b. Reshuffled priorities

In the introduction to *Discovering an Evangelical Heritage*, Donald Dayton defines evangelicalism as "a specific wing of the nineteenth-century revivalist tradition that took shape before the emergence of fundamentalism [1910]."[6]

George Grant gives us a broad overview of the ways in which religious priorities shifted in this century: "Righteous indignation and holy zeal became all but endangered species during much of [this] century. Passions were turned inward, as were devotions. Virtues became vices, and the most awful of indulgences became canonized orthodoxies. Risk, jeopardy, and self-sacrifice were replaced by security, certainty, and self-gratification. Thus, the only urgency that drove much of the church during this dark period in history was its own satisfaction."[7]

Donald Dayton devotes fourteen fascinating pages to an analysis of the ways in which evangelicalism shifted – and in some ways reversed itself – during the course of the last 150 years. We will take the liberty of paraphrasing the changes he details: • Fervor always wanes... • Commitment is costly... • Inspiration is not hereditary... • Status breeds selfishness... • Failure to accomplish all that was dreamed leads to disillusionment... • Darwinism attacks creation... • "Biblical criticism" shakes faith... • Rejection of the "social gospel" personalizes faith... • The dream of a Christian America crumbles... • Life gets complicated [urbanized, industrialized, materialistic]... • Decadence corrupts society... • Pre-millennial theology breeds escapism... • Last-days too-lateism increases social distancing... • Controversy polarizes the Church... • Doctrinal purity eclipses social justice... • Elitism replaces egalitarianism... • Rewriting history hacks at the roots. [It must be confessed that such liberty has been taken in paraphrasing that Dayton might have trouble understanding "his own ideas." Sorry.][8]

George Grant has this to add: "It was not assurance in the promises of God that stirred and motivated the bulk of the church in the twentieth century as much as it was the promises of science or experience. As a result... an easy 'instant-everything' mentality developed... thus, abortion became one of many expedients to dispatch unpleasant difficulties."[9]

Martha Ellen Stortz injects yet another view: "As I began to look at the community called church, I saw that an ethos of individualism had eroded the fabric of community within congregational life... Minding one's own business had become an ecclesial ethic."[10]

SCOPE and FOCUS
I. CONVICTIONS
II. PRETEXTS
III. MANDATE
IV. LEGACY
V. ABORTIVE LINKS
Recreational Sex
Reproductive Technology
Abortion Industry
Governmental Action
Social Climate
Religious Confusion
Polarization of Believers
Pluralism
Priorities
Theology
Liberalized
Social gospel
Leader crisis
Public Acts of Faith
Religious Right
Self-destructing
Marginalized
Revival time?
Abortion Controversy
"Catholic" view
Image of God
Personhood
Preborn human rights
The exceptions
Choice views
Has Church failed?
Personal Decision to Abort
VI. DILEMMA
VII. DESTINY

c. Theological shifts

"The theologians of the nineteenth and twentieth centuries mostly went along with naturalism in science because they failed to understand how all-encompassing the ambitions of scientific metaphysicians tend to become," says Phillip Johnson.[11]

William Hutchison says that beginning in 1892, the "editor of the powerful Christian Union, Lyman Abbott, popularized the idea that evolution is compatible with Christianity."[12]

The result of that union, says Hutchison, was to reinterpret "the history of redemption... Looking through the eyes of nineteenth century science and philosophy, [liberal theology] saw the cosmos emerging from an infinitely remote chaos by gradual stages. They saw the slow heave and surge of the process of evolution out of which life, mind, and spirit emerge... [making mankind into] co-workers with God in the task of making the world good."[13]

He says that one effect of Karl Barth's theology was that "God has been made so completely transcendent and far off that it does not make much difference to humanity on earth whether he is there or not... It is a strange paradox that the extreme exaltation of God may have the practical effect of atheism."[14]

James Hitchcock echoes that view of Barth: "When this theology is carried to its extreme the gulf between God and man appears unbridgeable. Robbed of any religious significance, worldly activity simply proceeds by its own rules and its own logic, and the Christian becomes someone whose faith is intensely private, without public manifestation."[15]

Sire tells us that in 1835 when Kierkegaard was faced with deciding what should be his life work, he wrote, "The point is to find the truth for me, to find that idea for which I am ready to live and die. What good would it do me to discover a so-called objective truth?"[16]

Of course, the reverberations of that thought continue to be felt throughout our culture in the relativism of "True for you/true for me."

We are offered an overview of the results of these theological shifts from Ronald Showers, in *What on Earth is God Doing?* "Several principles became characteristic of most liberal Protestantism... [A] spirit of open-mindedness and tolerance toward new modes of thought [Relativism]... Confidence in the scientific method as a means to truth not only in the study of the material world, but also in the realm of Biblical criticism and the history of religion [Naturalism]... A strong feeling against theological dogmatism [Autonomy]... Desire to emphasize similarities rather than differences [Pragmatism]... Theology that would agree with a spark of divinity [but that concludes that man is essentially good, and perfectible – Mechanism]... The denial of hell [denies Accountability]... Denial of a personal God [Accident]."[17]

Franky Schaeffer is not too flattering when he describes those of us who think of ourselves as the descendants of the nineteenth century heroes of the faith: "Evangelicals are a lot like jellyfish. They float with the tides. They do not direct their own course. Sometimes the current of the sea beaches them. Then they melt in the sun on the sand."[18]

1 John Naisbitt, *Megatrends 2000: Ten New Directions for the 1990s*, 276-7.
2 Geoff Tunnicliffe, *One Hundred One Ways to Change Your World*, 82.
3 B. & P. Berger, *The War Over the Family*, 74-5.
4 Hitchcock, in William Ball, 37.
5 Clowes, page 42.11.
6 Dayton, *Discovering an Evangelical Heritage*, xii.
7 Grant, *Third Time Around*, 137.
8 Donald Dayton, *Discovering an Evangelical Heritage*, 121-135.
9 Grant, *Third Time Around*, 137-8.
10 Stortz, in Phyllis Tickle, *Confessing Conscience: Churched Women on Abortion*, 21.
11 Johnson, *Reason in the Balance: The Case Against Naturalism in Science, Law & Education*, 201.
12 Hutchison, *American Protestant Thought in the Liberal Era*, 9.
13 Hutchison, 217-8.
14 Hutchison, 202.
15 Hitchcock, in William Ball, *In Search of a National Morality: A Manifesto for Evangelicals and Catholics*, 33.
16 James Sire, *The Universe Next Door: A Basic Worldview Catalog*, 111.
17 Ronald Showers, 85-6.
18 Schaeffer, in R.C. Sproul, *Abortion: A Rational Look at an Emotional Issue*, 67.

d. Liberalized "mainline" denominations

"From the early nineteenth century," Hitchcock tells us, "liberal Protestantism, as it came to be known, disregarded its traditions and the authority of Scripture and primarily found its bearings in the writings of secular intellectuals, usually university professors."[1]

William Hutchison describes "the liberals' characteristically advanced views on Biblical criticism and their readiness to question religious creeds and institutions, [while] their more fundamental aversion was to 'Bibliolatry,' to strict Biblical literalism."[2]

"During the 1920s and 1930s theological liberals took charge of several mainline American denominations," says Marvin Olasky. "Although an outright shift in policy regarding abortion took another generation, the practical 'pro-choice' application was a natural outgrowth of a liberal faith that opposed God's sovereignty and placed 'reason' above revelation."[3]

Sproul contends that the "Liberal churches have so vigorously supported the women's liberation movement that they have accepted the pro-choice position as part of the package. This has created an almost bizarre liberal contradiction... Traditionally, they have opposed slavery and racial discrimination, and they have been zealous in the cause of human dignity. However, when the crucial issue of the dignity of life pertains to the unborn, the liberal community is strangely absent or on the wrong side of the issue... In their zeal to protect women's rights, liberals have sacrificed the rights of the unborn."[4]

He continues, offering a hopeful note: "The multitudes of honest liberals who have strong convictions about human dignity and fundamental human rights would seem to be a fertile field for reversal of their position on abortion. These people need to be encouraged to look more deeply into the underlying human life issue that is central to the abortion debate."[5]

e. Social gospel

"The social gospel is traditionally viewed," Bandow explains, "as a philosophy that developed in the context of modern, liberal Protestantism. Starting in the late nineteenth century a number of churches began moving away from the spiritual gospel message, emphasizing political reform instead... Advocates of the social gospel held a radically different conception of the role of the state than did members of other more traditional faiths... They were convinced that its chief duty was to promote a just society, and Christians, as believers in justice, were bound to work to advance that end. Most mainline Protestant denominations continue to operate in this tradition."[6]

"By the 1890s," says James Hunter, "an enormous literature advocating the tenets of the 'social gospel' was being published... A significant corollary of the social gospel... was a new spirit of denominational cooperation... [and] the most important reworking of the [theological] traditions involved the deemphasis of the supernatural and miraculous aspects of biblical narrative and an almost exclusive emphasis upon its ethical aspects."[7]

Robert Bork looks at world politics: "The Protestant mainline churches turned to the left; the World Council of Churches identified itself with the Third World as against the West... [Also] liberation theology affected young Catholic priests and nuns who became soldiers in the antiwar, anticapitalist, and anti-American empire movements of the late 1960s and 1970s. ...The Sixties jump-started the leftist politicization of the [mainline] churches, but the process was under way before that."[8]

SCOPE and FOCUS
- I. CONVICTIONS
- II. PRETEXTS
- III. MANDATE
- IV. LEGACY
- V. ABORTIVE LINKS
  - Recreational Sex
  - Reproductive Technology
  - Abortion Industry
  - Governmental Action
  - Social Climate
  - Religious Confusion
    - Polarization of Believers
      - Pluralism
      - Priorities
      - Theology
      - Liberalized
      - Social gospel
      - Leader crisis
    - Public Acts of Faith
      - Religious Right
      - Self-destructing
      - Marginalized
      - Revival time?
    - Abortion Controversy
      - "Catholic" view
      - Image of God
      - Personhood
      - Preborn human rights
      - The exceptions
      - Choice views
      - Has Church failed?
  - Personal Decision to Abort
- VI. DILEMMA
- VII. DESTINY

1 Hitchcock, in William Ball, 34.

2 Hutchison, 2.

3 Olasky, *Abortion Rites: A Social History of Abortion in America*, 261.

4 Sproul, *Abortion: A Rational Look at an Emotional Issue*, 152.

5 Sproul, 152.

6 Doug Bandow, *Beyond Good Intentions, a Biblical View of Politics*, 133.

7 Hunter, *Culture Wars*, 78-9.

8 Robert Bork, *Slouching Towards Gomorrah: Modern Liberalism and American Decline*, 282.

9 Robert Raines, *Reshaping the Christian Life*, 36.

10 Raines, *New Life in the Church*, 15.

11 Terry, in Joseph Foreman, *Shattering the Darkness: The Crisis of the Cross in the Church Today*, 171, 173.

12 Brown, *The Sensate Culture*, 76.

13 James Hunter, *Culture Wars: The Struggle to Define America*, 91.

14 Clowes, *Pro-Life Activist's Encyclopedia*, page 42-4. Examples: United Methodists, only 11 percent of the clergy-delegates believed that the Bible is the 'literal word of God,' while 62 percent of all lay Methodists do; 55 percent of all Presbyterian ministers describe themselves as 'liberal' to 'far left,' while only 13 percent of all Presbyterian lay people do.

15 John Naisbitt, *Megatrends 2000: Ten New Directions for the 1990s*, 274.

16 Bork, *Slouching Towards Gomorrah*, 292-3.

17 Grant, *Third Time Around*, 146.

18 Randall Terry, in Joseph Foreman, *Shattering the Darkness: The Crisis of the Cross in the Church Today*, 167-8.

f. Crises of leadership

Robert Raines was an outspoken critic of the Church's state of health in the 1960s. In *Reshaping the Christian Life* he wrote: "The whole church at every level of its leadership and in every location of its life is in danger of fiercely fighting battles against enemies that have silently slipped away to take us by surprise elsewhere."[9]

In *New Life in the Church*, he expressed the belief that "The church is no longer changing culture, but is being changed by culture. The church is not enabling her people to live with purpose in a world without purpose."[10]

From inside Fulton County Jail in 1989, Randall Terry poured his heart out in a letter "to the Pastoral Community of Atlanta." He wrote: "I believe the moral crisis we face as a nation is a reflection of the crisis within the church – a crisis marked by the lack of courageous, sacrificial leadership... The clergy, with few notable exceptions, have miserably failed to lead the church in Her call to be the 'salt' and 'light' of our culture... Brethren, legalized child-killing simply could not exist in this nation without our continued complicity in this crime."[11]

Harold O.J. Brown wrote in 1996 that Christianity "has within its own ranks hosts of religious officials and teachers who devote themselves to undermining the religion they formally profess."[12]

The reader will recall that James Hunter identifies the opposing sides in the *Culture Wars* as the progressive and the orthodox views, groups we have called the Masters of secular humanism and the Stewards of traditional Christian faith, respectively. Here is a unique polarization he identifies: "In Protestantism the division between progressive and orthodox is seen *within* denominations [in addition to *between* denominations]; Progressive interests are generally pursued by the denominational leadership and the culturally conservative interests are generally promoted by local ministers and the laity. This is particularly true for the mainline Protestant churches."[13]

Brian Clowes puts a slightly different inflection on the same basic thought: "In summary, the mainline Protestant churches are composed of conservative laity listening to Neoliberal preaching."[14]

The mainline churches have lost members in record numbers during the years of the abortion controversy. The views of Hunter and Clowes, above, would go a long way toward explaining a leadership crisis as part of the problem. John Naisbitt offers a more intellectualized rendition: "Mainline churches fare well in stable eras but decline in times of great change... [From 1965 to 1988:] The United Methodist church dropped from a high of 11 million members in 1965 to 9.2 million... The Presbyterian Church, USA, has lost nearly 1 million members (25%)... The Disciples of Christ have lost almost 1 million, with a current membership of 1.1 million (almost 50%). Episcopal Church membership dropped from 3.4 to 2.5 million."[15]

Robert Bork offers another fascinating contrast. "The Protestant mainline denominations are out of touch with the people in the pews because the church's leadership changed, moving well to the left of their membership. That is a different situation than a church [Roman Catholics] that is trying to remain unchanged while the culture changes its members."[16]

During the abortion holocaust there have also been leadership difficulties within the pro-life movement. With so many scores of educational/political action groups, it could be expected that there would arise an occasional problem of competitiveness or stepped-on toes. In addition, Grant tells us that "In 1978, serious infighting erupted between the veteran [pro-life] groups and the various upstarts. Ideological, methodological, and theological differences exploded into full-scale animosity... In 1980, new conflicts arose between Catholic and Protestant groups... [and] In 1982, advocacy of two conflicting pro-life bills on Capitol Hill – the Hatch and the Helms measures – crippled any hope of congressional action and exposed both the disarray and the naivete of the movement."[17]

Additionally, each new development [arson, Operation Rescue, shooting, bombing] has occasioned a new round of choosing up sides to either justify or condemn the various actions. Just as the Church in America is really a wide assortment of denominations, what we have called the pro-life movement is more accurately only an aggregate of diverse organizations and actors with little, really, in common but a hatred of abortion and a love of life.

The stakes are so high in the pro-life/pro-death struggle and in the larger culture war [heaven and hell], that the researcher of *Orphans in Babylon* has deemed it essential to include as broad a range of views as possible, above all else, lest we fail to take seriously the Joel or the Esther of today. With that sense of responsibility one more quotation is offered here. In 1989, in jail for the last time as the founding leader of Operation Rescue, Randall Terry wrote his historic "Letter from Atlanta." He said: "Let me state it plainly. A lot of us in leadership are losing our nerve, wavering in our courage and determination... We have consciously or subconsciously said that the cost is too high, forgetting what terrifying horrors await us and our families right around the corner. I've read and reread Jeremiah lately, and I encourage you to do the same. I have come away seeing a frightening reality that oppression, tyranny, and destruction are stalking the church and the nation. In a short few years, we may find ourselves hiding in the hills to protect our families, or locked up in huge holding facilities. We may find our churches seized, closed or burnt to the ground... do you think it impossible? ...If God didn't spare Israel, why should He spare us?"[18]

2. Public orthodoxy, its rise and fall

In 1964 Charles McCoy was quoted as saying, "A church, precisely because it is inclusive of various social groupings, will tend toward ambiguity on important social issues."[1] In 1969, Harold Patchett wrote, "The church is going to have to be more specific if it is going to be effective. We simply cannot try to be on the fence all the time and have people pay attention."[2]

Also in 1969, Elton Trueblood reflected the degree to which faith had already been marginalized in American culture: "We are tolerated, but not much more than that. We are expected to provide the service of funerals and weddings, and to offer some instruction to children, but the notion that Christians can give a real lead in the intellectual sphere is not even entertained in most circles."[3]

Hunter tells us that after the decade of the '50s, "with the further expansion of pluralism and the collapse of the Judeo-Christian consensus in public culture, the issues that would divide progressive and orthodox forces in the major religious traditions in the decades to follow would become far more extensive... It is still quite possible [however] that these internal tensions would have remained at a fairly low intensity had it not been for two other changes: the waning of denominational loyalty... [and] the proliferation of parachurch organizations."[4]

By 1982, nine years after *Roe v. Wade*, it was time for Franky Schaeffer to write *A Time for Anger: The Myth of Neutrality*. His wake-up call included this: "In the twentieth century, evangelical Christians in America have naively accepted the role assigned us by an anti-religious, anti-Christian consensus in society. We have been relegated to a cultural backwater, where we are meant to paddle around content in the knowledge that we are merely allowed to exist."[5]

Colonel Doner asks and answers the question, "What gave rise to the Christian Right? [It] had been building since the early sixties... Sleepy churches were rudely awakened to a 'new' America, one in which government, media, and the educational elite were no longer practicing a policy of 'benevolent neglect.' ...The 'establishment,' spurred on by a secular humanistic ethic and aggressive antagonists like the American Civil Liberties Union (ACLU), had clearly moved into an adversarial position against the Church."[6]

Kingdoms in Conflict, written by Charles Colson in 1987, fleshes-in the religious factions: "The politization of the church in the sixties was largely the work of liberal mainline denominations whose bureaucracies issued weekly policy papers on social issues... On the other side is privatized faith, which divorces religious and spiritual beliefs from public actions... Fundamentalists separated from the mainstream, leaving the world's concerns behind so they could preach the good news among the faithful. All of this dramatically changed by the late seventies when Jerry Falwell led a fundamentalist stampede back to center stage. Ironically, liberals who had been so socially concerned were now, in reaction perhaps, arguing that faith is a private matter."[7]

Doug Bandow identifies three factors that he says impacted the change. "The most dramatic political phenomenon of the last decade or so [prior to 1988] is probably the entry of evangelicals into the political process. In recent years most theologically conservative Christians had eschewed politics, but a combination of factors – the leftward shift in the mainline churches, the perceived assault by the courts on religious values, and the rise of the televangelists, among others – started bringing more of them to the polls."[8]

SCOPE and FOCUS
I. CONVICTIONS
II. PRETEXTS
III. MANDATE
IV. LEGACY
V. ABORTIVE LINKS
Recreational Sex
Reproductive Technology
Abortion Industry
Governmental Action
Social Climate
Religious Confusion
Polarization of Believers
Pluralism
Priorities
Theology
Liberalized
Social gospel
Leader crisis
Public Acts of Faith
Religious Right
Self-destructing
Marginalized
Revival time?
Abortion Controversy
"Catholic" view
Image of God
Personhood
Preborn human rights
The exceptions
Choice views
Has Church failed?
Personal Decision to Abort
VI. DILEMMA
VII. DESTINY

1 McCoy, in Robert Lee, *Religion and Social Conflict*, 38.

2 Patchett, in *Together* [United Methodist] magazine, 11/'69, 6. Not in bibliography.

3 Elton Trueblood, in *Faith at Work* magazine, Nov.-Dec./'69. Not in bibliography.

4 James Hunter, *Culture Wars: The Struggle to Define America*, 86.

5 Schaeffer, 13.

6 Doner, *The Samaritan Strategy: A New Agenda for Christian Activism*, 13-4.

7 Colson, 221.

8 Bandow, *Beyond Good Intentions, a Biblical View of Politics*, 19.

9 Pierard, in Clouse, 45-9.

10 North, *Backward Christian Soldiers*, 32.

11 Doner, *The Samaritan Strategy: A New Agenda for Christian Activism*, xiii.

12 Doner, 23.

13 Doner, 12.

14 Doner, 11.

15 Paul Simmons, in Edward Batchelor, *Abortion: The Moral Issues*, 176-7.

16 Doner, 17.

17 Atkinson, *Church & State Under God*, 6.

18 Ball, *In Search of a National Morality: A Manifesto for Evangelicals and Catholics*, 114.

19 Richard Pierard, in Robert Clouse, *Protest and Politics*, 49-50.

20 Doner, 12.

a. The Religious Right

We have documentation that the Left was deeply alarmed about the political Right as early as 1968. In that year, in *Protest and Politics*, Robert Clouse quoted this warning from Richard Pierard to his colleagues on the Left: "Methods Utilized by Right Extremists: 1) Forming tightly organized groups with strict vows of obedience; 2) Infiltrating the Republican Party; 3) Need for 'experts' to make facts do what they should; 4) Raising suspicions about a particular group of people; 5) Allege that National Council of Churches is communist; 6) Use high pressure tactics and intimidation."[9]

Here is Gary North's perspective on the end of the '80's: "Many of the leaders of the older, pietistic, 'don't get involved in worldly affairs' version of American fundamentalism made a major switch in their ministries between 1976 and 1980. Jerry Falwell is the most prominent example, but he was not alone. There were several reasons for this: opposition to abortion... humanism in public education... moral decay..."[10]

Colonel Doner provides an insider's view: "In the short span of just eight years [1978-1986] I watched the Christian Right launch itself high into orbit from a platform of enormous success and anticipation only to crash back to earth as a burnt out hulk."[11]

The media giveth and the media taketh away

Doner understates, if anything, the significance of the secular media's role in both the ascendancy and the abrupt decline of political discipleship. "An important factor in the Christian Right's ability to communicate with the nation and even with its own troops was the news media's willingness to make Jerry Falwell the unquestioned spokesman for the Christian Right. In fact, the media soon began referring to the whole Christian Right as the Moral Majority, the name of Falwell's much smaller and less powerful political organization."[12]

Elsewhere the writer relates this insight: "The media coverage was so intense that I remember traveling to a small town in Iowa to speak to a few dozen people and there before me were Japanese and Swedish television network crews filming the event to broadcast 'back home.' It was not unusual for us to have all three networks calling my office on any one day demanding interviews, statements, information, etc."[13]

It sounds a bit like a confession on the part of Colonel Doner, but we all need to ponder the significance of what the writer reveals: "The Christian Right was also 'the big news story' of the early eighties because the media made it big news. Many Christian Right organizations were to some degree a creation of the media. The news media made our organizations look much larger and stronger than we actually were."[14]

Goals of the Religious Right

"Not since the Prohibition era have [Fundamentalists] been so involved politically," declared Paul Simmons. "Thus, New Right religion aims to forge a coalition of nearly 30 million conservative Christians with right-wing politics. Their platform is pro-God, pro-family, and pro-America. They are aggressive, affluent, highly organized, and ambitious, aiming to take control of legislative centers of power by 1985."[15]

Colonel Doner identifies just how radical the political swing was from 1976 to 1980: "Jimmy Carter won the white Baptist vote in 1976 by 56 to 43 percent against Gerald Ford. This time [1980] he lost the white Baptists by a 56 to 34 percent margin. The white followers of the TV Evangelical preachers gave Ronald Reagan two-thirds of his ten-point margin in the election."[16]

Liberal politics, and the liberal media become alarmed

James Atkinson pronounces this truth: "Whenever the state seeks again to become the religious order of society and man, as it seeks to do from time to time, two disastrous consequences appear: either the state decries and destroys the church, or else absorbs it."[17]

William Ball explains this alarmist view: "The religious right is at least as dangerous as the secular left. Religious theonomy (divine law) as the basis for human dignity can be as frightening as secular anarchy. The latter extreme destroys the integrity of law, while the former the liberty of those under the law. Theonomists, or reconstructionists, as they are called, mistakenly superimpose divine law on unbelievers rather than on believers."[18]

As early as 1968, Pierard was raising red flags of warning, using emotionally charged trigger words: "One of the most disturbing aspects of the Radical right is its close relationship with American Protestant Christianity. Nearly every commentator on Right-wing extremism has called attention to the large number of fundamentalists who are associated with the movement... By equating the struggle against communism with a war against sin and atheism, the Rightist appeals to the crusading tendencies of fundamentalists."[19]

"When the media found out that there were forty to sixty million Evangelicals," notes Doner, "they were even more curious, if not down right intimidated... Would we dominate the government *a la* the Ayatolla in Iran?"[20]

A shepherd, to a fault, defends his flock

Colonel Doner's opinion is that "The Christian Right was doomed to failure without the active support of the nation's Evangelical Churches (supposedly home to over forty million 'born again' Christians)... Most Evangelical pastors, including those with admittedly conservative political convictions, opposed 'political involvement.'"[1]

Richard Pierard seemed, himself, to be on a crusade, *against* the Religious Right: "A serious malady presently afflicts a substantial segment of evangelical Christianity, namely, a close identification with the so-called 'Radical Right.' Not only does this tragic situation hinder the effectiveness of the evangelical witness, but also it threatens to negate many of the basic principles of Christianity itself. Because the relationship with the Radical Right is sapping the very lifeblood of the Christian faith, it is imperative that evangelicals become aware of the perils of Right-wing extremism and that they take immediate and forthright steps to combat this plague which has infected the body of Christ."[2]

b. Neutralized from within

On shooting one's self in the foot, wounding multitudes

In *Megatrends 2000*, John Naisbitt catalogs the magnitude of a disaster: "Before falling from grace, Jimmy Swaggart had broadcast in 140 countries weekly and in fifteen different languages. He claimed to reach one third of the planet. Jim and Tammy Bakker's PTL cable TV network reached 12 million households. Jerry Falwell's TV shows reached 610,000 households in 169 markets across the U.S.; his 1987 TV income was $91 million. Robert Schuller is the leading TV evangelist. His Crystal Cathedral claims 10,000 members; many more watch the show on TV."[3]

In *Romanced to Death: The Sexual Seduction of American Culture*, published in 1989, Paul deParrie reveals that "the Swaggart/Bakker soap opera was quietly eclipsed in Virginia where the three top men in the Tony Leyva Evangelistic Association pled guilty to using their sawdust trail as a slave-prostitution transport route for young boys and also guilty to sexually abusing the boys. Dozens of papers in the U.S. report incest and child molestation trials of ministers... Then a collection of ministers appeared on the Geraldo Rivera Show demanding a 'sexual bill of rights' allowing ministers the liberty to be involved in pornography, homosexuality, and other perversions. The church in America reels."[4]

"A 1987 Gallup poll showed 63 percent of Americans called TV evangelicals 'untrustworthy,' while 23 percent voted them 'trustworthy.' Since the PTL, Swaggart, and Oral Roberts scandals, TV evangelists have lost a staggering amount of support. From February 1986 to July 1988 Jimmy Swaggart's viewers in the United States went from 2.3 million to 836,000. ...Jerry Falwell's dropped from 700,000 to 284,000. Even untarnished, upbeat Robert Schuller has taken hits. His audience fell from 2 million to 1.2 million."[5]

c. Faithfulness stigmatized and marginalized

The Religious Right was both torpedoed by the secular media and sabotaged by self-destructing televangelists. Additionally there are those who hold that the movement itself was fatally flawed, making it an easy target. "The Christian right failed in its mission because it was not perceived as Christ-like. The Christian Right, in demanding a society conformed to a Godly moral behavior (righteousness) failed to emphasize an equally important need for social justice and mercy."[6]

"As Evangelical leader John Stott points out, a peculiar interpretation of dispensational pre-millennialism developed that 'portrays the present evil world as beyond improvement or redemption, and predicts instead that it will deteriorate steadily until the coming of Jesus, who will then set up His millennial reign on earth. If the world is getting worse, and if only Jesus at His coming will put it right, there seems no point in trying to reform it meanwhile."[7]

Almost as if listening in on our conversation, Charles Colson writes of the serious danger that many of "those on the political right [may] want to impose Christian values on society by force of law... ignoring Christ's teaching in the parable of the wheat and the tares in which He warns that we live with both good (the wheat) and evil (the tares), and cannot root out the tares. Only "God is able to do that and He will – when the Kingdom comes in its final glory."[8]

"The Christian Right, in its hurry to stop the obvious deterioration of our nation," writes Doner, "failed to devote the time to take stock of root causes. Men of action like to act, not analyze, and most recently the Church's strength has not been in analyzing social trends. Such a failure puts tactics before strategy, short-term goals before long-term objectives, and denies us any way to provide comprehensive answers to the very deep problems facing our generation. The real problems facing us are not abortion, homosexuality, pornography... These are the symptoms of much deeper problems of fear and alienation from God, from government, from each other."

1 Doner, 45.

2 Pierard, in Robert Clouse, 39.

3 Naisbitt, *Megatrends 2000: Ten New Directions for the 1990's*, 279-80.

4 Paul deParrie, *Romanced to Death*, 37-8.

5 John Naisbitt, *Megatrends 2000*, 280.

6 Doner, 3.

7 Doner, 51-2.

8 Colson, *Kingdoms in Conflict*, 117.

9 Doner, 73.

10 Raines, *New Life in the Church*, 17.

11 Roche, *The Bewildered Society*, 325.

12 John Naisbitt, *Megatrends 2000*, 270.

13 Joseph Foreman, *Shattering the Darkness: The Crisis of the Cross in the Church Today*, 180.

14 Mitchell, in Kilner, *Bioethics and the Future of Medicine, A Christian Appraisal*, 130.

d. Revival time? Are Christians also *Orphans in Babylon*?

The Church is surrounded by a godless, pagan culture that clearly plans to obliterate Christian faith. So what's new? That is the story of God's people throughout history. Those who are in the process of being redeemed and who are prayerfully working out their salvation have always been on the endangered species list. The only variable throughout Church history is the degree to which Christians *understand* that they are exiles and aliens in Babylon [or slaves in Egypt], and that their task is to make a desperate escape toward "Zion," taking as many others with them as possible.

SCOPE and FOCUS
I. CONVICTIONS
II. PRETEXTS
III. MANDATE
IV. LEGACY
V. ABORTIVE LINKS
Recreational Sex
Reproductive Technology
Abortion Industry
Governmental Action
Social Climate
Religious Confusion
Polarization of Believers
Pluralism
Priorities
Theology
Liberalized
Social gospel
Leader crisis
Public Acts of Faith
Religious Right
Self-destructing
Marginalized
Revival time?
Abortion Controversy
"Catholic" view
Image of God
Personhood
Preborn human rights
The exceptions
Choice views
Has Church failed?
Personal Decision to Abort
VI. DILEMMA
VII. DESTINY

What would it take to convince us that our "church property," our "sanctuaries" are the ghettos into which we have been herded until plans can be completed for our extermination?

Way back in the Sixties, Robert Raines was warning, "The world believes it has tamed and domesticated the Church and can keep her busily occupied in cultivating her own garden. The world has pulled the teeth of the Church, and no longer listens to her enfeebled message."[10] In 1974, within a year after *Roe v. Wade*, George Roche wrote: "Some sociologists of religion are predicting the end of institutional religion in its present form before the year 2000."[11]

Despite that dire [or revolutionary] prediction, religion seems to have very much retained its "form," but is adjusting to a pensioner's budget. Actually, a significant number of "sheep" have jumped-fold and significant numbers from the liberal denominations are now pastured with evangelicals, and there is even faster growth among charismatics.[12]

It is important to note that, with few exceptions, when you find a congregation that is experiencing numerical growth, most of the influx represents transplanted Christians, not new conversions. Revival and Evangelism are twin sisters, and where one goes the other follows; you may have seen their pictures on milk cartons because no one knows what has become of them.

Rebirth, ignition, blast-off

"Revival, reformation, awakening, reconstruction, renewal – regardless of the vocabulary, it is the reign of Christ shown forth publicly in the lives of His people," says Foreman.[13]

"Grievously," says C. Ben Mitchell, for the most part the church has "neglected the aspects of its 'internal' ministry which best prepare it to engage our culture in general and to address the dilemmas that arise in contemporary bioethics in particular."[14]

Joseph Foreman sees a crucial key to revival: "The day will come when the reality of aborted children burns so deeply into the heart of the Church that tens of thousands will pour out daily into the streets to bring it to an end... But until then, what will bridge the gap, move hearts, and make that outpouring possible? We need to take the next step. We need a bridge... Standing against abortion is a key indicator of revival... because if we will not stand against those next door who rip arms and legs off of little children, God will not give us the strength to stand anywhere. Instead, there will be no revival. He will harden our hearts to further fit us for destruction."[15]

Will and Ariel Durant, representing naturalism the reader will recall, offer this long view of history and our present place in it: "Puritanism and paganism – the repression and the expression of the senses and desires – alternate in mutual reaction in history. Generally religion and puritanism prevail in periods when the laws are feeble and morals must bear the burden of maintaining social order... In our time the strength of the state has united with [the several forces listed just previously in his book] to relax faith and morals, and to allow paganism to resume its natural sway. Probably our excesses will bring another reaction; moral disorder may generate a religious revival."[16]

Colonel Doner says, "The Christian church has an opportunity to lead. But first we must learn some lessons from the failure of those pioneers of the Christian Right who launched the first assault upon the apathy of the church and the multiple tragedies bred by that apathy."[17]

In 1969 Elton Trueblood wrote: "Those who are aware of their minority status realize that they cannot even survive if they are satisfied with anything as tame as three hymns, a sermon, and a benediction. When our backs are to the wall, we realize that our only choices are renewal or death."[18]

15 Foreman, 151.

16 Durant, *The Lessons of History*, 50.

17 Doner, xiv.

18 Elton Trueblood, in *Faith at Work*, magazine, Nov.-Dec./'69, 5. Not in bibliography.

19 Shakespeare, *Julius Caesar*, Act IV, scene 3, in Leroy Augenstein, *Come, Let Us Play God*, 1.

"There is a tide in the affairs of men, Which, taken at the flood, leads on to fortune; Omitted, all the voyage of their life Is bound in shallows and in miseries."[19] –Shakespeare

3. Religious controversy over abortion

The acceptance of religious pluralism in the form of denominationalism, and the generally amicable relations between Catholics and Protestants has been enjoyed by Christians in America, in stark contrast to the sectarian bloodshed which racked Europe [literally] as a result of the Reformation, and which continues today in Northern Ireland. The socio-political events of this century, however, have resulted in complex shifts in affinities and disharmonies between the various branches of Christianity.

We saw in the alcohol battles of the Twenties a distancing of Catholics who favored the concept of moderation from the fundamentalists who demanded nothing less than Prohibition of demon rum. As the mainline liberal denominational identities emerged, the Catholics were in sympathy with the social gospel but were strongly repulsed by the liberal embrace of contraception. With that one exception, Doug Bandow notes a close political affinity between Catholics and Liberal Protestants since about 1948 on such things as "support for civil rights, social welfare spending, and arms control, and opposition to the war in Vietnam and most recently to intervention in Central America."[1]

When abortion became a topic of religious debate, however, Catholics found themselves miles apart from the "pro-choice" mainline Protestants. In the pro-life movement, with the Catholic church taking early possession of the high moral ground, as evangelical Protestants were conscripted by God one by one into that fray, lasting bonds were forged between those two branches of the Church, which had not enjoyed such philosophical unity since the previous anti-abortion movement a hundred years earlier.

a. Universality & the "Catholic" position

Liberal Protestants and their secular cronies labored tirelessly to promote the fiction that Protestants are pro-choice as opposed to the "archaic" stand of the Catholics who, as portrayed by the pro-choice Christian Waldo Beach, "oppose any and all abortions on the grounds of the sanctity of life from the moment of conception."[2] The reader will recall that we challenged the persistent fabrication that "Catholic bishops believe that the baby's right to life is more important than the mother's," on page 81 of *Orphans*.[3]

b. Sanctity & Image of God

Like pro-life Protestants, Catholics believe first of all in the sanctity of the preborn: "Every human life, from the moment of conception until death, is sacred because the human person has been willed for its own sake in the image and likeness of the living and holy God," and "Because it should be treated as a person from conception, the embryo must be defended in its integrity, cared for, and healed like every other human being."[4]

Pope Paul VI declared in his encyclical of July 1968, on human life: "The direct interruption of generation already begun, and especially direct abortion, *except if done for therapeutic reasons*, must be entirely repudiated" [emphasis added].[5]

Here is another example of the effort to marginalize pro-lifeism as the "Catholic" position: Linda Bird Francke wrote, "Attacks on abortion are still highly centered in the Catholic Church. On New Year's Day in 1977, Pope Paul VI not only called abortion a threat to world peace but branded women who have abortions 'killers who freely and consciously murder the fruit of their womb.'"[6]

We earlier discussed abortifacient birth control. Brian Clowes reports that as of November 1988, the "Catholic definition of abortion is not only 'the expulsion of the immature fetus,' but is also 'the killing of the same fetus in any way and at any time from the moment of conception.' This definition of abortion includes: all birth control pills... mini-pills, morning-after pills, and true abortion pills such as RU-486; injectable or insertable abortifacients such as Norplant and Depo-Provera; and the use of all IUDs."[7]

1 Bandow, *Beyond Good Intentions, a Biblical View of Politics*, 133-4.

2 Beach, *Christian Ethics in the Protestant Tradition*, 67.

Additionally, in 1957, Glanville Williams reaffirmed this mistake in *The Sanctity of Life and the Criminal Law*, 192: "**Nearly all Protestants have come to accept therapeutic abortion** [his footnoted reference: 'See Curran in *Therapeutic Abortion*, Harold Rosen, ed. (New York, 19540, pp. 153ff)'] ...**as contrasted with the Catholic position.**"

3 An abundance of writers, Protestant as well as Catholic have demonstrated an understanding of the Catholic doctrine of double-effect: David Brown, *Choices: Ethics and the Christian*, 123; Moreland and Geisler, *The Life and Death Debate: Moral Issues of Our Time*, 38 and 163; Brian Clowes, *Pro-Life Activist's Encyclopedia*, pages 51.6 and 51.7.

4 United States Catholic Conference, *Catechism of the Catholic Church*, 558, §2319 and §2323.

5 Pope Paul VI, in William May, *Human Existence, Medicine and Ethics: Reflections on Human Life*, 91-2.

6 Francke, *The Ambivalence of Abortion*, 249.

7 Clowes, *Pro-Life Activist's Encyclopedia*, page 31.4.

8 Clowes, page 42.8.

9 Jersild, *Moral Issues & Christian Response*, 339.

10 Reeves, in Clouse, *Protest and Politics*, 194.

11 Norman Geisler, *Ethics: Alternatives and Issues*, 219 and 223.

12 *Press*, 8-4-96, A1, A12.

13 Clowes, page 42.9.

14 Beach, 69.

15 Beach, 69.

16 The Commission, in John Klotz, *A Christian View of Abortion*, 47-8.

c. Personhood of the preborn

The liberal denominations that deny the personhood of the preborn by declaring an official "pro-choice" policy may call themselves the "mainline" Protestants, but they are not the main*stream* of religious America. There are only 27 million members in all of these "pro-choice" churches put together: United Methodist, United Presbyterian, Episcopalian, United Church, and the assorted others. By contrast, there are 128 million members in these pro-life churches: Roman Catholic, Mormon, Fundamentalist, Assemblies of God (Pent.), Islam, Southern Baptist, Jehovah's Witnesses, Lutheran (Mo. Synod), and assorted others.[8]

Since there are 250 million Americans, and 128 million members in the various pro-life religions and denominations, it is clear that [contrary to what the media would have you believe] well over half of the citizens of the United States are members of churches that are pro-life.

SCOPE and FOCUS
I. CONVICTIONS
II. PRETEXTS
III. MANDATE
IV. LEGACY
V. ABORTIVE LINKS
Recreational Sex
Reproductive Technology
Abortion Industry
Governmental Action
Social Climate
Religious Confusion
Polarization of Believers
Pluralism
Priorities
Theology
Liberalized
Social gospel
Leader crisis
Public Acts of Faith
Religious Right
Self-destructing
Marginalized
Revival time?
Abortion Controversy
"Catholic" view
Image of God
Personhood
Preborn human rights
The exceptions
Choice views
Has Church failed?
Personal Decision to Abort
Dissuade the mother
Last-ditch miracles
Real pro-life choices
VI. DILEMMA
VII. DESTINY

d. Human rights of the preborn

The right to life of the preborn was slowly eroded away, often with the assistance of conscientious Christians. Jersild tells us: "The argument among Christians is not usually one which questions the reality of life in the womb; it is rather the question whether full legal rights should be given in every instance to that life."[9]

In 1968, Robert Clouse quoted Earl Reeves as recommending that where pro-abortion laws "are designed to provide careful medical and legal controls, such laws may be desirable if they are used only in extreme emergencies."[10]

In the morally turbulent early '70s, when Norman Geisler wrote *Ethics: Alternatives and Issues* [1971], even his title could have the effect of endorsing free "choice." In addition, notice that he uses key concepts like "actual" "potential" and "viable" in regrettably relativising the right to life of unborn children: "Abortion is less serious than murder – murder is a man-initiated activity of taking an actual human life. Artificial abortion is a humanly initiated process which results in the taking of a potential human life... Abortion is not justified after viability... No abortion is justifiable as such after the fetus has become viable, i.e., after birth is possible... To take the life of a viable fetus without higher ethical justification would be murder."[11]

e. Exceptions justifying abortion, & Relativism

Senator Ray Haynes is considered to be pro-life by many, but newspapers report that he "remains convinced that abortion is wrong except in cases of rape, incest or when the mother's life is at risk."[12]

Six percent of all church members belong to the 22 faiths that are pro-life "with exceptions for mother's life and rape/incest."[13]

When pro-choice Christian Waldo Beach, in 1988, wrote a book to tell the world about *Christian Ethics in the Protestant Tradition*, he included this piece of United Methodist relativizing: "When an unacceptable pregnancy occurs, a family, and most of all the pregnant woman is confronted with... a difficult decision [she has a *choice* to make]. We believe that continuation of a pregnancy which endangers the life or health of the mother, or poses other serious problems concerning the life, health, or mental capability of the child-to-be, is not a moral necessity. In such a case, we believe the path of mature Christian judgment may indicate the advisability of abortion."[14]

The same author offers this view from the Presbyterian Church, U.S.A.: "The willful termination of pregnancy by medical means on the considered decision of a pregnant woman may on occasion be morally justifiable. Possible justifying circumstances would include medical indications of physical or mental deformity, conception as a result of rape or incest, conditions under which the physical or mental health of either mother or child would be gravely threatened, or the socio-economic conditions of the family."[15]

In 1970, The Commission on Research and Social Action of the American Lutheran Church drafted a proposal that endorsed all of the "exceptions" alleged, above, to justify abortion, and stated: "All factors considered, an induced abortion may well be preferable to an uninterrupted pregnancy [doesn't it sound a bit like abortion should be the norm, and live birth the alternative that would need to be justified?] issuing in an unwanted child. The probabilities are that a child who feels himself unwanted will live a handicapped, resentful, and hostile life alienated from himself and others."[16]

f. Freedom to choose, & Autonomy

"Pro-choice" and autonomy are the flip sides of the same coin. Paul Jersild says that between strictly pro-life and pro-abortion positions "stand those who are compelled to find a more nuanced point of view. They believe that one cannot give an absolute answer covering every case of contemplated abortion. On the contrary, each case must be considered in light of its own circumstances."[1]

As early as 1968, the American Baptist Convention held that "abortion should be a matter of responsible personal decision."[2] Our pro-choice "expert" on *Christian Ethics in the Protestant Tradition*, Waldo Beach, refers to *Roe v. Wade* as, "This balanced but generally liberal ruling of the Supreme Court..."[3]

"In October of 1977 approximately 200 Protestant and Jewish church leaders, supporting abortion-on-demand, issued a statement entitled, *A Call to Concern*, describing those who opposed abortion-on-demand as "extreme," "blind" and "dangerous," [while] they characterized their own position in support of abortion as "moral," "responsible," "sound" and "rooted in deeply held convictions."[4]

Large numbers of Christians as well as secular citizens depend on the arguments of American Episcopalian Joseph Fletcher for their understanding of the morality of abortion. Few of them realize that Fletcher's own line of reasoning made him "willing to admit the legitimacy of infanticide."[5]

g. Has the Church failed?

George Grant gives us his perspective on the performance of the Church in our era: "For almost a full century, the greatest proportion of the evangelical community had been in a deep cultural hibernation. Thus, despite the largest, most powerful, richest, best organized, and most visible Christian consensus ever, the immoral and unstable humanistic juggernaut was able to gain full control of the cultural apparatus... In the years leading up to the *Roe v. Wade* decision, most Christians... were totally unaware of the abortion issue. When so many evangelical Christian leaders around the world – in lock-step with theological liberals – were guiding their congregations, seminaries, colleges, and denominations toward complete capitulation on the sanctity of life, most of the people in the pews were entirely incognizant of the terms of the debate. They didn't even know there *was* a debate."[6]

Here is one way of viewing our failing: a case of democracy gone amok. "The fact is that the Gallup poll has become more authoritative than the usual sources of Christian ethical understanding. What was said in Sweden in the 1950s now seems to apply in the United States: If a majority of the people hold an act to be moral, it is moral [relativism and positivism]. Even if an airtight Christian policy on abortion were possible, with a theological plug in every hole and biblical verses caulking every seam, it is doubtful most Christians would rally to it."[7]

John Whitehead adds to the indictment. "The American churches and the Christian community have been amply alerted to abortion as the primary issue facing the country today through the books, films, and work of the prolife movement. Still, very little in the way of true resistance to the wanton slaughter of human life is coming from Christianity."[8]

"Can you imagine how different America would be," asks Randall Terry, "if the church had risen up when *Roe v. Wade* became law? What if pastors had said to their congregations, 'Come on, let's go!' and surrounded abortion mills, refusing to allow the wicked to kill children? [see page 218 of *Orphans*.] This holocaust would have ground to a halt almost immediately. But as history reveals, 99% of the church have honored the laws of man above the laws of God."[9]

"Franky Schaeffer has said that if there is an abortion clinic in your neighborhood and it isn't picketed every time abortions are performed there, that community has accepted abortion."[10]

Scheidler says that his book [as his *life*, we'd say] "is about acting on the conviction that every unborn human life is of inestimable value, in itself, to society, and in the eyes of God... It is not enough to believe in the value of that life and condemn abortion... Unless we act on our hatred of abortion we are little better than those who support it."[11]

Joseph Foreman asks a crucial question: "If the Christians, who claim that the people in the womb are their equal, do not treat them as their equal, why should anyone else treat people in the womb with full equality? – especially someone who does *not* think they are equal?"[12]

At the end of the 1980s, clear wake-up calls and battle charges were trumpeted by the Religious Right and by Operation Rescue. In both cases these calls were mostly ignored or discredited at the local level. Because the Church in this century has never developed viable Christian communications links, Church leadership and congregations were like moist clay in the hands of the secular media, and two basic fears paralyzed the majority of local pastors: the fear that controversy would split rather than galvanize their congregations, and the fear that endorsement of Christian witness beyond the perimeter of the "church" property would siphon off funds and energies from their own programs.

Their timorousness when boldness was the order of the day has won the result they dreaded: "The number of people that attended church in America declined from 49 percent in 1991 to 37 percent in 1996."[13]

Beyond the Church, what is the score in the abortion battle? George Grant gets specific: "As a single interest group, the pro-life movement has failed. As a political force, it has proven to be a total disappointment. As an institutional philanthropic enterprise, it has been more than a little impotent. But as an outreach of the historic church, it has had stunning success. The modern pro-life movement has proven that commitment to the sanctity of life is the consequence of the Spirit's work in the authentic sacramental church."[14]

1 Jersild, *Moral Issues & Christian Response*, 337.

2 Harriet Pilpel, *When Should Abortion Be Legal?*, 8.

3 Beach, 69.

4 Jean Garton, *Who Broke the Baby? A Brilliant Disclosure of What the Abortion Slogans Really Mean*, 70.

5 David Brown, *Choices, Ethics and the Christian*, 121.

6 George Grant, *Third Time Around: A History of the Pro-Life Movement from the First Century to the Present*, 142.

7 J. Robert Nelson, in Edward Batchelor, *Abortion: The Moral Issues*, 55.

SCOPE and FOCUS
I. CONVICTIONS
II. PRETEXTS
III. MANDATE
IV. LEGACY
V. ABORTIVE LINKS
Recreational Sex
Reproductive Technology
Abortion Industry
Governmental Action
Social Climate
Religious Confusion
Polarization of Believers
Pluralism
Priorities
Theology
Liberalized
Social gospel
Leader crisis
Public Acts of Faith
Religious Right
Self-destructing
Marginalized
Revival time?
Abortion Controversy
"Catholic" view
Image of God
Personhood
Preborn human rights
The exceptions
Choice views
Has Church failed?
Personal Decision to Abort
Dissuade the mother
Last-ditch miracles
Real pro-life choices
VI. DILEMMA
VII. DESTINY

G. Personal Decision to Abort

"Planned Parenthood claims that sex education is a necessary and effective means of preventing teen pregnancies. But that is an illusion... Instead, it does just the opposite... Planned Parenthood claims that its system of birth control is safe and effective. Not by a long shot. [Its] birth control is nothing but foreplay for abortion. Besides the fact that it is fraught with awful side effects, complications, and medical risks, it is incapable of preventing unwanted pregnancies as well."[15]

"Convenience abortions account for 98 percent of all baby-killing."[16]

1. Dissuade abortion-bound women

The first line of defense against abortion must be to assure that women have resolved firmly, long before they become pregnant, that abortion is not an option. Joe Scheidler says that personal testimonials have a very positive influence, and that excellent ones are provided through organizations like WEBA – Women Exploited by Abortion.[17]

The reader will recall our mention that literally thousands of Milwaukee area Christians descended on abortion clinics in the summer of 1992 [*Orphans*, page 218], with miraculous results. Foreman tells us that a subsequent project there had the goal of delivering 100,000 copies of *The Hard Truth* video into Milwaukee area homes, and to seek "5,000 families willing to open their homes to unwed mothers who have no place to turn."[18]

"Pro-choice" pollster Harrison Hickman admits: "Nothing has been as damaging to our [pro-abortion] cause as the advances in technology which have allowed pictures of the developing fetus, because people now talk about that fetus in much different terms than they did 15 years ago. They talk about it as a human being."[19]

In Chicago, Pro-Life Action League picketers with Joe Scheidler "now carry huge four-by-five foot pictures of the Human Life International photo of the baby head being held in surgical tongs... [and picket literally all day:] an average of 50 show up for the regular pickets, and sidewalk counselors busily contact mothers coming in to the clinic."[20]

Operation Rescue has been conducting pickets at high schools displaying those huge signs and handing out pamphlets warning about the effects of abortions on a woman's health.[21]

2. Last-ditch miracles

"At almost every Rescue one or two mothers will change their minds directly and not kill their children," says Foreman. "Many more will drive by and never return. Even more see the news on TV and decide, before ever getting pregnant, that abortion is not worth it."[22]

Scheidler's book, *Closed: 99 Ways to Stop Abortion*, describes a variety of techniques that attempt to make a life-saving impact on women arriving for an abortion. One such program, called Project Jericho, was a three month span of time when three shifts of picketers assured that a public pro-life testimony was presented all day every day a clinic was open.[23]

Scheidler also describes a "truth team" as a couple, posing as clients for an abortion, "who station themselves in the waiting room area of an abortion clinic in order to discuss a 'proposed' abortion with genuine clients in order to change their decision about having an abortion... One team says in a single morning it has dissuaded six couples from going through with abortions."[24]

A variation on that theme is what Scheidler calls a "Blitz," which is "a brief visit to an abortion clinic... It is done quickly. From four to ten prolifers enter the abortion clinic waiting room as a group, introduce themselves, and talk to the people who are sitting around... they place pro-life literature in the various magazines that are lying about and [replace the clinic's literature] with pro-life literature... The pro-life attitude should be one of peaceful concern."[25]

Note: In the fifteen years since Joseph Scheidler's book was first written, locked doors and a variety of security procedures and personnel at clinics have reduced pro-life access, but also have raised questions in the mind of abortion-bound women, like "What kind of a place *is* this?"

8 Whitehead, *The Stealing of America*, 59.
9 Terry, *Operation Rescue*, 188-9.
10 Joseph Scheidler, *Closed: 99 Ways to Stop Abortion*, 33.
11 Scheidler, 17-8.
12 Foreman, *Shattering the Darkness: The Crisis of the Cross in the Church Today*, 44.
13 Geoff Tunnicliffe, *One Hundred One Ways to Change Your World*, 8.
14 Grant, *Third Time Around: A History of the Pro-Life Movement from the First Century to the Present*, 154-5.
15 George Grant, *Grand Illusions*, 30-2.
16 Brian Clowes, *Pro-Life Activist's Encyclopedia*, page 42.8.
17 Scheidler, *Closed: 99 Ways to Stop Abortion*, 244.
18 Joseph Foreman, *Shattering the Darkness: The Crisis of the Cross in the Church Today*, 185.
19 Hickman, by Frederica Mathewes-Green, in Focus on the Family *Citizen*, 7-28-97, 2.
20 *Life Advocate*, 6/'94, 22.
21 *Press*, 2-13-97, B4.
22 Foreman, 8.
23 Scheidler, 320.
24 Scheidler, 25.
25 Scheidler, 231.

Sidewalk Counseling, an anointed pro-life ministry

Scheidler says, "Sidewalk counseling is a method of saving babies by talking to their parents in front of the abortion clinic. It is probably the single most valuable activity that a pro-life person can engage in. When pro-lifers counsel in front of an abortion clinic, they are coming between the woman and the doctor, between the baby who is scheduled to be killed and the doctor who would do the killing."[1]

This is *Time* magazine's tribute: "Karen Black, whom prolifers describe as one of the nation's most successful 'sidewalk counselors,' [is] good at persuading women not to have an abortion during the 20 seconds or so it takes to walk from a car to a clinic door."[2]

"A particularly effective sidewalk counselor, Lourdes Olivarez, speaks little English but held a picture of an aborted baby and told an abortion-bound mother... 'If you go to the clinic, your baby will look like this.'"[3]

Here is what Joe Scheidler thinks of sidewalk counseling: "Women *can* be turned back. In Chicago, in one thirty-day period, half a dozen sidewalk counselors at only a few clinics were able to stop ninety women from having abortions. Seventeen were stopped in a single morning at a clinic on Michigan Avenue. While a few of these women may have gone back to have their abortions later, more than ninety percent did not return, and they kept in touch with the pro-life counseling center. All because there were sidewalk counselors present."[4]

3. Give women real pro-life choices

"The crux and power of the pro-life movement today," says George Grant, "does not lie in some centralized political bureaucracy lobbying in the corridors of power. Instead, it lies in the deeds of kindness and compassion – performed in thousands of crisis pregnancy centers, unwed mothers' homes, alternative centers, shepherding homes, and mercy ministries all over the country. The power of the pro-life movement today lies in its servanthood orientation."[5]

That view is shared by Margaret Rosenberger: "Support groups [include:] counseling centers, surrogate extended family support, homes for unwed mothers, child development classes, crisis hotlines, day care centers, assistance during maternity leave, financial help for parents of the handicapped."[6]

Scheidler's book reported that "The pro-life movement has four thousand organizations throughout the country dedicated to helping pregnant women carry their pregnancies to term."[7]

These figures are so powerful that they must be repeated even though they are far from current. We can expect that Crisis Pregnancy Centers [CPCs] are even more effective today: "In 1983, about 855,000 women were counseled in the nation's 2,900 crisis pregnancy centers. [Of these women, about 40 percent had first visited pro-abortion 'counseling' centers or abortion mills.] ...About 650,000 decided to keep their babies – a CPC 'success' rate of 76 percent."[8]

There are more than 200 pro-life pregnancy hotlines in the United States.[9]

In Wichita, Kan., "an anonymous $50,000 gift [in 1994] helped a local pro-life group, Serving Women in Crisis Inc. (SWC), to purchase the house beside the abortuary owned by George Tiller for their base of outreach."[10]

1 Scheidler, 19.
2 *Time*, 4-19-93, 40.
3 *Life Advocate*, 6/'94, 22.
4 Scheidler, 19.
5 Grant, *Third Time Around: A History of the Pro-Life Movement from the First Century to the Present*, 155.
6 Margaret Rosenberger, *Issues in Focus: Gaining a Clear Biblical Perspective on the Complex Issues of Our Time*, 109.
7 Scheidler, 149.
8 Brian Clowes, *Pro-Life Activist's Encyclopedia*, page 47.1.
9 Clowes, page 26.3.
10 *Life Advocate*, 5/'94, 15.
11 *Press*, 3-22-96, A22.
12 *Press*, 8-8-96, A6.

What's the real scoop on the abortion rate?

The widely-reported decline in the numbers of surgical abortions is often held up by pro-life groups as a sign of partial victory, and by the abortion industry [in the media and in court] to "prove" that pro-lifer criminality is bankrupting them. In both cases the figures have been used incorrectly. The truth is that the aging of the baby boomers means that we simply have a steady reduction [since 1990] in the number of women in their reproductive years. The Centers for Disease Control and Prevention reported that "the 1993 abortion rate, or the number of abortions per 1,000 women of reproductive age, remained unchanged at 23 and has held steady since the mid-1980s."[11]

If we keep looking, however, a positive shift *is* taking place. The pro-life movement as a whole can surely take credit for the combination of efforts which have resulted in **a reduction of the abortion rate for teenagers**! The facts are: "Abortion rates stayed about the same between 1987 and 1994 among most age groups, but declined significantly among teenagers. For 15- to 17-year-olds, the rate dropped 21 percent. Among 18- and 19-year-olds, it dropped 19 percent."[12]

The younger generation *is* getting the pro-life message that the unborn are tiny human people.

VI. Dilemma: State of the Pro-Life Movement

"The pro-life and pro-abortion forces have been locked in mortal combat for many years now, yet there has been no change in current law. We have obviously failed to convince many Christians of the severity of the problem, and we have not succeeded in significantly reducing the number of abortions [by 1987]" [more correctly now, "the abortion *rate* by 1998"].[1]

George Grant, in the foreword to Foreman's book, reflects: "Questions about methodology or tactics or strategies or personalities have begun to supersede any other consideration – even within the Christian community. As a result, this epic struggle for truth, justice, and mercy has generated far more heat than light."[2]

In Foreman's opinion: "For the most part, the strategy of the abortion culture and its courts has been successful. They discovered that we were only prepared to treat preborn children as equals in theory, but not as equals in real life. Therefore, we drew back... Are the children's lives really worth risking the loss of everything?"[3]

"As I look around today," says Mark Crutcher, "I see a pro-life movement that appears to be giving up. More and more, I see people who are going through the motions of battle, only because they can't bring themselves to just walk away. They may not be shutting off the lights and locking the doors, but they have lost the fire in the belly."[4]

A. Magnitude of the Problem: the Situation *Now*

1. The World Scene

Our world contains 5.3 billion people. "In the last quarter century, the world's abortion addiction has killed one billion unborn children."[5]

In a book published in 1973, John Klotz reported that the world was committing "somewhere between 30 and 35 million abortions, legal and illegal," and revealed, "In Belgium, France, West Germany, and Italy it is believed that the number of illegal abortions each year equals the number of live births"[6]

By 1981 the annual global estimate was 50,000,000 abortions.[7]

In 1997, Geoff Tunnicliffe reports: "For every five births in the world there are two induced abortions."[8]

Closer to home, by 1981, "in cities like New York and Washington, D.C., there [were already] more life-ending abortions than live births."[9]

"Certain countries, including South Africa, have made the injectable abortifacient Depo-Provera mandatory for teenaged schoolgirls, female prisoners, welfare recipients, and the mentally handicapped."[10]

2. The Death toll

By the end of the '90s, F. LaGard Smith tells us, abortion "will have killed 30 times the number of Americans lost in all of our wars from the Revolutionary War down to the heartbreak of Vietnam."[11]

Equally graphically, Brian Clowes says that "We have killed a vast number of children equivalent to the combined populations of 14 states: Montana, Wyoming, North and South Dakota, Colorado, Nebraska, Kansas, Minnesota, Iowa, Missouri, Utah, Nevada, Arizona and New Mexico."[12]

SCOPE and FOCUS
I. CONVICTIONS
II. PRETEXTS
III. MANDATE
IV. LEGACY
V. ABORTIVE LINKS
VI. DILEMMA
Magnitude of Problem
World scene
Death toll
Who Aborts?
Government blunders
Access reduced?
Who cares, how much?
Restrained Outrage
A Century of martyrs
Rhetoric & reality
Worth any cost?
Righteous intolerance
Why this Infighting?
Like children sitting...
Nature of the Problem
Medical fraud
Non-enforcement
Loopholes
Defiance of law
Opportunists
Privatization of death
Undetectability
Definitions of Victory
Close the clinics
Reproductive truth
Pass the Amendment
Reshape society
Pro-life commitments
Personal morality
Religious revival
VII. DESTINY

1 James Hoffmeier, *Abortion: A Christian Understanding and Response*, 20.

2 Grant, in Foreman, *Shattering the Darkness: The Crisis of the Cross in the Church Today*, Foreword.

3 Foreman, 10.

4 Mark Crutcher, *Access: The Key to Pro-Life Victory*, on the cover.

5 Brian Clowes, *Pro-Life Activist's Encyclopedia*, page 57.2.

6 Klotz, *A Christian View of Abortion*, 8.

7 Michael Braun, *The Christian in an Age of Sexual Eclipse*, 12.

8 Tunnicliffe, *One Hundred One Ways to Change Your World*, 67.

9 John Powell, *Abortion: The Silent Holocaust*, 5.

10 Brian Clowes, page 33.2.

11 F. LaGard Smith, *When Choice Becomes God*, 121.

•The National Right to Life Committee's figures, in *Abortion: The Silent Holocaust*, by Powell (page i): 25,324 Americans died in the Revolutionary War; 498,332 in Civil War; 116,516 in WWI; 545,108 in WWII; 54,246 in Korean War; 56,555 in Vietnam War. America's abortion war has killed 36,000,000 since 1973.

12 Clowes, page 48.1.

3. Who aborts?

Thirty-six percent of the women who have abortions are now using abortion as their only form of birth control,[1] and at least 43 percent have had at least one abortion previously.[2] Of women having repeat abortions, this is the second abortion for 70% of them, but 16% have had two previously, and another 14% have had three or more previous abortions.[3]

One study reports that as many as 40% of Catholic women are using the Pill,[4] and David Trosch asserts that at least 50% of all church women have had abortions.[5]

Since studies indicate that 40 – 60% of all American women of childbearing age have had at least one abortion,[6] it would appear that women who are church members might be almost as likely to have an abortion as non-Christians.

In one study women were asked, after having an abortion, if they believed in God. Seventy-two percent said they did not believe in God, but *of those*, 96% said that they regarded abortion as murder.[7]

"Like an animal caught in a trap, trying to gnaw off its own leg, a woman who seeks abortion is trying to escape a desperate situation by an act of violence and self-loss.

Abortion is not a sign that women are free, but a sign that they are desperate."[24] –Frederica Mathewes-Green

---

4. Governmental blunders

The Thomas Malthus theme, overpopulation-disaster, has been oversold in the industrialized nations. The White House Conference on Hunger, in 1969, headed by Planned Parenthood's Dr. Alan Guttmacher, made these recommendations: "1) mandatory abortion for any unmarried girl found to be within the first three months of pregnancy, and 2) mandatory sterilization of any such girl giving birth out of wedlock for a second time."[8]

"Although overpopulation has been touted as the most critical problem in the world, underpopulation in Western countries has become perhaps the most burning issue in recorded history. **A rapid decline in population is something that Western countries cannot deal with. There is no mechanism for enabling the major institutions and the economy to adjust.**"[9]

"In the span of just one generation, the makeup of the American family has changed radically... In 1970, married couples with children made up 40 percent of the U.S. households. By 1995, that number has slipped to 25 percent, according to a U.S. Census Bureau report."[10]

"...The size of families [has been] shrinking over the past 25 years from 3.14 people per household to 2.65... The average number of children born to women [in the U.S.] in 1990 was 'below replacement level [2.0]' at 1.8, compared with 1.9 in 1980."[11]

A law was actually proposed [H.B. 2089] in the Kansas legislature which "identified Norplant, by name, in an act that would provide assistance to female welfare recipients only if they agreed to be implanted."[12]

SCOPE and FOCUS
I. CONVICTIONS
II. PRETEXTS
III. MANDATE
IV. LEGACY
V. ABORTIVE LINKS
VI. DILEMMA
Magnitude of Problem
World scene
Death toll
Who Aborts?
Government blunders
Access reduced?
Who cares, how much?
Restrained Outrage
A Century of martyrs
Rhetoric & reality
Worth any cost?
Righteous intolerance
Why this Infighting?
Like children sitting...
Nature of the Problem
Medical fraud
Non-enforcement
Loopholes
Defiance of law
Opportunists
Privatization of death
Undetectability
Definitions of Victory
Close the clinics
Reproductive truth
Pass the Amendment
Reshape society
Pro-life commitments
Personal morality
Religious revival
VII. DESTINY

1 Clowes, page 42.7.

2 Robert Bork, *Slouching Towards Gomorrah*, 180.

3 David Reardon, *Aborted Women: Silent No More*, 6.

4 Clowes, page 31.4: "The 1988 National Survey of Family Growth (presented as reliable by pro-lifers), conducted by the National Center for Health Statistics, surveyed thousands of married Catholic couples of childbearing age and found..."

5 Trosch, in *Life Advocate*, 5/'94, 31.

6 Mark Crutcher, *Access*, 21.

7 Lurlene McDaniel, in Phyllis Tickle, *Confessing Conscience: Churched Women on Abortion*, 64.

8 Clowes, page 50.10.

9 Philip Ney, in David Mall, *The Psychological Aspects of Abortion*, 34.

10 *Press*, 11-27-96, A1.

11 Ken Bryson, *Press*, 11-27-96, A1, A10.

12 Clowes, page 33.3.

13 *Life Advocate*, 4/'94, 15.

14 Crutcher, *Access*, 5.

15 Crutcher, *Access*, 17.

16 Crutcher, *Access*, 16.

5. About reduced access to surgical abortion

Just how much killing can one abortionist represent? Michael Griffin shot David Gunn just as he "was about to begin a ritual of murder that he had performed some 40,000 times before."[13]

Mark Crutcher really believes in the title of one of his books, *Access: The Key to Pro-Life Victory*. He quotes Rebecca Brooks, spokeswoman for Planned Parenthood of Northern New England, in 1993, as complaining, "We have 28 family planning clinics throughout New England and we provide abortions in only four of them because we don't have enough doctors willing to provide the service."[14]

Crutcher also quotes the United States District Court of the District of Montana, in 1993: "The farther a woman has to travel to obtain an abortion, the less likely she is to obtain one."[15]

In 1997, Vicki Saporta, former director of the National Abortion Federation, said, "Twenty percent of women who want an abortion can't get one because there is not a provider in their area. That is not acceptable. It really impedes women's legal rights."[16]

6. Who cares about the unborn, and how much?

"Most appalling and frightening of all, how can the majority of the American public believe that abortion is the killing of a living human being – yet still want to keep the procedure 'safe and legal'?"[17]

It is clear that Christians know the difference between a congregation where the sanctity of preborn life is defended and those where it is relativized; people still vote with their feet. From 1960 to 1990, membership in the pro-life churches increased 59%, from 80.4 to 128 million; membership in pro-abortion churches decreased 17%, from 32.4 to 26.8 million. Note that there are now five times as many people in the prolife churches as in the "mainline" denominations.[18]

Here is some more good news: "Despite the fact that virtually all of the media, the medical profession, the legal profession, and all of the other elite groups in this country are pro-abortion, the pro-life movement continues to gain ground with the public. Why is this? Simply because the average member of the public knows what is killing and what is not."[19]

James Hunter says that, "without a doubt, public discourse is more polarized than the American public itself."[20]

There really is a "silent majority" in the U.S. While one-fourth of Americans are in favor of making abortions easier to obtain, and one-fourth want to make them harder to get, 50% of our citizens either don't feel strongly that change is needed [42%] or have no opinion at all [8%].[21]

Here are some more responses from the same survey: 62% feel that abortion is OK in the first trimester, while 29% say no; 26% say it is OK in the second trimester, but 56% say no; and 14% feel that abortion is OK in the third trimester, while 64% say no.[22]

To the degree that this survey is an accurate reflection of the convictions of the American public, then here is what we may safely conclude. If the Supreme Court had not ruled that **abortion on demand** is a woman's constitutional right but instead the question had been put to the citizens, then it is obvious that only 14% *at most* [those who think abortion should be permitted during the third trimester] would have voted that way, and it would not have been legalized. On the other hand, no more than 29% would have voted to outlaw all abortions [some or all of those who disapprove of first-trimester abortions – but no more], so a total ban on abortion would not have been possible. But it is obvious that a democratic decision would have sustained a ban not only on third trimester abortions [64%], but also on abortions in the second trimester [54%].

The above conclusions are consistent with James Hunter's assessment:

"Pro-life advocates (correctly) contend that the majority of Americans oppose abortion on demand, while pro-choice advocates (also correctly) contend that roughly 'four out of five Americans reject our opponents' goal of outlawing all abortions."[23]

17 Brian Clowes, page 53.12.

• R.C. Sproul, 117: "In the ongoing debate about abortion, the pro-choice position has become pivotal to public opinion. In a poll conducted in 1989 in the United States, seventy-four percent of those questioned agreed with this statement: 'I personally feel that abortion is morally wrong, but I also feel that whether or not to have an abortion is a decision that has to be made by every woman herself."

18 Clowes, page 42.8.

19 Clowes, page 77.1.

20 James Hunter, *Culture Wars: The Struggle to Define America*, 159.

21 Scripps-McClatchy Western Service survey by Mervin Field, in *Press*, 3-10-97, A3.

22 Press, 3-10-97, A3.

23 Hunter, *Culture Wars: The Struggle to Define America*, 146.

24 Mathewes-Green, in Mark Crutcher, *Access: The Key to Pro-Life Victory*, 21.

B. Paradox of Restrained Outrage

Dr. James Kennedy has said: "Abortion has become *the* issue in this country, for if you lose life, you lose all. If Christians do not win on this issue, we will not win on any issue... The shocking reality is that Christians could stop abortions today if they wanted to... If four million Christians went tomorrow and stood as a visible presence in front of every abortion clinic in the land, no babies would be killed."[1]

James Hunter takes the pulse of the debate: "At present, however, the conflict remains at a level of intensity that is high enough to mobilize resources and to sharpen rhetorical antagonism but not high enough to trigger widespread acts of rage. If this is so, it is in large part because rival activists have in fact agreed to reject overt violence and to pursue their objectives within the boundaries of legitimate political action."[2]

In his 1993 update of his 1985 classic, Joseph Scheidler candidly observed, "Since 1988, a number of different rescue groups have emerged with various philosophies and ideologies. Innovative tactics, such as pro-lifers using kryptonite bicycle locks to attach themselves to blocks of cement or to cars parked in front of clinic doors, have shown the abortionists, the media and the American people the lengths to which pro-lifers will go to save human life."[3]

There are two sides to Scheidler's statement. On one side, Christians who are pro-life in word see pro-life deeds that demonstrate the value of the preborn by the risks and inconvenience rescuers are willing to endure in order to dramatically interrupt the abortion trade. Conversely, the world sees the lengths to which these particular rescuers will *not* go to save human life: 1) they may super-glue a lock to win the delay involved while a locksmith is summoned [and willingly inflict that expense on the abortionist], but they constrain themselves from the fire or acid attacks on the building which would render it incapable of containing death for months; 2) they "lock-down" in front of the doors so that the sidewalk counselor may have 20 minutes rather than 20 seconds to discuss with the prospective abortion client her other options, but they would never kidnap her to gain two days in which to more effectively win her to pro-lifeism; 3) at the abortionist's home, someone may "speedbump" his car – literally lie in the path of the tires – or handcuff himself to the car's frame [risking serious injury or death if the one who has snuffed 50,000 preborns chooses impulsively to hit the accelerator], but they would never inflict injury or death on the abortionist in order ["justifiable homicide"] to prevent him from keeping his appointment to kill the ten to twenty babies whose moms are already waiting at the clinic.

Note well: *Orphans in Babylon* does NOT *advocate* any of the more drastic measures mentioned above. [We have, however, quoted several who have – without *advocating* the use of force, acknowledged the biblical, moral justification for such acts if they are performed non-retributively, without usurping the government's authority to punish, but rather defensively, in protection of a helpless, innocent human being from imminent fatal violence.]

Here is our point in this case. We pro-lifers are demonstrating "restrained outrage." In Vietnam, one of the greatest tragedies was that our government required strict limitations on the amount and types of force our troops could use; we were not waging all-out war to win, but were "fighting with one hand tied behind our back."

In poker, we understand [from those who have played] that once a player has bet $100 on his hand, another player is not permitted to bet just five. Here is the contest we are in as pro-lifers: Our opponent is betting 1,500,000 dismembered babies a year that a preborn is just a *potential* human being, and we are so certain that they are human *persons* from the moment of conception that we're willing to bet 500,000 tax-deductible donations, 50,000 Rescue-arrests, 50 clinic-demolitionists and 5 abortionist-shooters that we are right. The world views our "bet" as insufficient; history will judge us as having been such peaceful and law-abiding citizens that we have tolerated that which is intolerable.

Joseph Scheidler has an excellent grasp of the biblical principle of "many parts, one body."[4] He says, "Pro-life activists must do everything with absolute conviction. Demonstrations, blitzes, sit-ins, removing abortion ads, handing out literature, sidewalk counseling, whatever hurts the abortion business and is not itself immoral. We should support those who carry out these activities even if we cannot do all of them ourselves... **While we do not condone any form of violence, we should not condemn without compassion and understanding those whose strong convictions may lead them to illegal activities... When Christ said to visit the prisoner He did not add, 'But only if he is innocent."**[5]

SCOPE and FOCUS
I. CONVICTIONS
II. PRETEXTS
III. MANDATE
IV. LEGACY
V. ABORTIVE LINKS
VI. DILEMMA
Magnitude of Problem
World scene
Death toll
Who Aborts?
Government blunders
Access reduced?
Who cares, how much?
Restrained Outrage
A Century of martyrs
Rhetoric & reality
Worth any cost?
Righteous intolerance
Why this Infighting?
Like children sitting...
Nature of the Problem
Medical fraud
Non-enforcement
Loopholes
Defiance of law
Opportunists
Privatization of death
Undetectability
Definitions of Victory
Close the clinics
Reproductive truth
Pass the Amendment
Reshape society
Pro-life commitments
Personal morality
Religious revival
VII. DESTINY

1. A Century of martyrs

In *Martyrs of Our Time*, William Purcell writes, "We are called to be Christians in a century of martyrs: Charles de Foucauld, 1916; John and Betty Stam, 1934; Maximilian Kolbe, 1941; Edith Stein, 1942; Alfred Sadd and Vivian Redlich, 1942; Leonard Wilson, 1942; Raoul Wallenburg, 1944; Dietrich Bonhoeffer, 1945; Andrew Kaguru, 1953; Jonathan Daniels, 1965; Martin Luther King, Jr., 1968; Jonani Luwum, 1977; Steve Biko, 1977; Thirteen members of the Elim Pentecostal Church, 1978; Oscar Romero, 1980."[6]

Mr. Purcell is able to give details of the particular courage of a large number of martyrs, but he could not catalogue the heroics of the hundreds, perhaps thousands, who died as rescuers of Jews from the Nazis, or of the anonymous thousands around the world, even today, who are persecuted and killed for simply owning the name of Christ.

Joseph Foreman says:

"This century has seen more Christians murdered by their government than all other centuries put together. It has been illegal in some countries even to state your identification with Jesus Christ. But in others, like America, though it is legal to *profess* your identification with Christ, it has become illegal to *act* as if you belong to Christ... Today in America it is illegal to protect unborn people. When it is illegal to save a child from murder, it is illegal to be a Christian."[7]

2. Rhetoric & Reality

George Grant wrote, "The longer the laws allowing abortion-on-demand remain in effect, the more likely it is that society will be hardened in heart. Continuing the struggle against abortion is not enough. We must accelerate our efforts until no human child is destroyed under the sanction of law... The urgency of the abortion issue requires us to protest to the very limit that our consciences allow."[8]

"Abortion on demand is without question the greatest moral issue facing America today," says Kerby Anderson. He continues:

"No other contemporary moral problem in this country results in the deaths of over a million innocent, unborn children each year. Many Christians today are not sufficiently informed about abortion to form a scripturally based opinion on this issue." [see *Orphans*, pages 79-108][9]

As Randall Terry put it, "Franky Schaeffer has said that any community that has an abortion mill standing unchallenged by Christians should have a sign placed over the door reading, 'This abortion mill owned and operated with the blessing of the Christian community.' Hard words, but true."[10]

Francis Beckwith calls abortion "the most divisive political and religious issue in late twentieth-century America."[11]

1 Kennedy, in Randall Terry, *Operation Rescue*, Forward page.

2 Hunter, *Culture Wars: The Struggle to Define America*, 316.

3 Scheidler, *Closed: 99 Ways to Stop Abortion*, 143.

4 *I Corinthians*, Chapter 12.

5 Scheidler, 328.

6 Purcell, v, viii.

7 Joseph Foreman, *Shattering the Darkness: The Crisis of the Cross in the Church Today*, 153-4.

8 Grant, *Third Time Around: A History of the Pro-Life Movement from the First Century to the Present*, 156.

9 Kerby Anderson, *Living Ethically in the '90s*, 204.

10 Terry, *Operation Rescue*, 208.

11 Beckwith, *Politically Correct Death: Answering the Arguments for Abortion Rights*, 11.

But is it *murder?*

Attorney Mark Belz says, "Abortion is by its nature a premeditated act. Once it is established that the fetus is a human life, the only conclusion can be that abortion is by definition an intentional, premeditated taking of a human life... It is the deliberate killing of a human being."[1]

"Once we have established that human life begins at conception and that the fetus is a human being," say Ankerberg and Weldon, "the question of whether abortion is murder is already answered: The act of abortion is the act of murder."[2] Joseph Scheidler agrees: "Abortion is the premeditated murder of an innocent, unborn human being."[3]

Foreman says, "There will be no lasting solution at law, in alternatives, nor education, until enough people treat the preborn as their human equals. When we begin to treat them as truly equal to ourselves, we will find that there is a tremendous price to be paid. Only by paying that price will we purchase the necessary respect for the preborn to have their inalienable right to life respected by the rest of the world."[4]

In *Idols for Destruction: Christian Faith and Its Confrontation With American Society*, Herbert Schlossberg wrote, "It is crucial for us, as prophets and priests guiding and guarding the land, to do more than point out the dangerous idolatries of Planned Parenthood, we must destroy every idol and we must tear down the high places. Whatever the cost."[5] Lest we infer more than was intended by the author, we must note that Schlossberg wrote the above in 1983, and his words do not necessarily mean that he either prompted or applauds the clinic arsons that began at about that time.

Michael Bray asks, **"Has God been waiting for His People for over two decades to act against the murder of unborn people in the same way that they would respond if the innocent victims were born people?"[6]**

The last several quotes are representative of a huge supply, all of which state that abortion is murder [or the moral equivalent if the technicality of U.S. law is considered], and that Christians must do everything in our power to eliminate abortions. The reality is that with a handful of exceptions, our rhetoric far exceeds our actions.

3. Worth any cost?

As one of the early leaders in Operation Rescue, Joseph Foreman has a right to be self-critical. "Operation Rescue came with a beautifully tailored program: die to yourself on the weekend and still make it to work on Monday (or Tuesday) morning."[7]

He goes on to say, as we quoted earlier, "It is not enough to determine whether or not the *world* permits something. We have to ask whether God allows *us* to permit it... the day may come when we are in danger of being too intolerant of child-killers. Until then, what must be explained is why we are so cooperative with them."[8]

Later the author clarifies, "Revival is not when unbelievers come to Christ, but when believers come to Christ... Pastors and congregations will unite to challenge the killers, saying publicly with a voice that unites all sectors of the church... **'Go ahead and sue us. We would rather lose all our property than go down in history as the Church which bought its peace and prosperity with the blood of innocent children... The murder will stop. So you may as well come after us, because we are coming after you.'"[9]**

SCOPE and FOCUS
I. CONVICTIONS
II. PRETEXTS
III. MANDATE
IV. LEGACY
V. ABORTIVE LINKS
VI. DILEMMA
Magnitude of Problem
World scene
Death toll
Who Aborts?
Government blunders
Access reduced?
Who cares, how much?
Restrained Outrage
A Century of martyrs
Rhetoric & reality
Worth any cost?
Righteous intolerance
Why this Infighting?
Like children sitting...
Nature of the Problem
Medical fraud
Non-enforcement
Loopholes
Defiance of law
Opportunists
Privatization of death
Undetectability
Definitions of Victory
Close the clinics
Reproductive truth
Pass the Amendment
Reshape society
Pro-life commitments
Personal morality
Religious revival
VII. DESTINY

1 John Ankerberg and John Weldon, *When Does Life Begin? And 39 Other Tough Questions about Abortion*, 31.

2 Ankerberg and Weldon, 31.

3 Scheidler, 49.

4 Joseph Foreman, *Shattering the Darkness: The Crisis of the Cross in the Church Today*, 165.

5 Schlossberg, 262.

6 Bray, *A Time to Kill*, 18. Lest the reader be confused by Bray's title, it should be noted that the brand of activism for which he was imprisoned was nighttime clinic fires, not physical violence. But he *is* one of several who are on record as not *endorsing* the killing of abortionists, but finding a biblical *justification* for those who take such defensive action.

7 Foreman, author's introduction, xviii.

8 Foreman, 59.

9 Foreman, 166.

10 Foreman, 28.

11 George Grant, *Third Time Around: A History of the Pro-Life Movement from the First Century to the Present*, 155.

12 David Reardon, *Aborted Women: Silent No More*, 313.

13 Cathy Ramey, *In Defense of Others: A Biblical Analysis and Apologetic on the Use of Force to Save Lives*, 30.

14 Bray, 17-8. [We thought this was good enough to quote two times.]

15 Freeman, 69.

16 Longworth, in *Life Advocate*, 2/'94, 9.

17 Dobson, in Randy Alcorn, *Is Rescuing Right? Breaking the Law to Save the Unborn*, 216.

4. Righteous intolerance

"Laws don't change hearts, hearts change laws," says Foreman. "There must be someone or some group who will show us what this heart change is."[10]

Grant's perspective is this: "More good people have suffered greater extremes of hardship and persecution for the sake of the unborn today than in any other single movement in recent memory. More Christians have sacrificed time, money, energy, reputation, and even physical welfare than anyone could ever hope to quantify... They have done this because the situation is urgent."[11]

"In the nation's largest pro-life group, the National Right to Life Committee," says David Reardon, "there are 7.5 million women working to stop abortion and provide positive alternatives to women with unplanned pregnancies."[12]

Cathy Ramey says that "it is unlikely that we will see more than the occasional man or woman as brave as Michael Griffin, Shelley Shannon, and Paul Hill, who will, at great cost to themselves act to save the life of an innocent *in utero* child. In fact, assuming the morality of defending unborn infants with force, God is under no obligation to raise up other defenders before dealing harshly with all of us, including their detractors, for our neglect of justice on behalf of those who are of the class of persons we refer to as 'unborn'."[13]

"The blockades served well the purpose of calling the community to come to the rescue of a neighbor," says Michael Bray, "but the blockade is not necessarily the noblest or highest method of obedience... There is a certain sense of faithfulness that we feel after 'intervening' and blocking access... But might there not be a false sense of faithfulness when the means were available to act to a greater extent on behalf of the innocent? ...If God has said 'Move this mountain' and we use a shovel instead of bulldozers, have we been faithful?"[14]

Foreman says, "We must do more than make people aware that the unborn are human. We must raise up a generation which will do what it takes personally and corporately to defend the innocent."[15]

Brian Longworth founded "Youth for America." While serving two years in jail for rescuing in spite of a court injunction ["We gave you strict orders not to teach in this name..." *Acts* 5:28], Brian was quoted as saying, **"My life is worth no more than that of the preborn child. If I truly love the baby as myself I will risk my very life merely for a chance to save one baby."**[16]

In *Isaiah* 59:7, 15-6, we read: "They are swift to shed innocent blood... The Lord looked and was displeased that there was no justice. He saw that there was no-one, He was appalled that there was no-one to intervene."

On April 19, 1995, a cruel bomb ended 178 innocent lives; some of them were children's. The President cancelled all other plans and flew to Oklahoma, so great was the sense of grave national loss. What if the bombing was just one in a series sustained by a terrorist group every year on 4/19... or on the 19th of every month... or every Tuesday... for years on end. As we imagine that, we only begin to approach a holocaust of terror like abortion. One hundred seventy-eight preborn people have been violently killed every hour, around the clock, for twenty-five years without stop. We saw our President weep for the 178 in Oklahoma City. Why does the man who "feels our pain" NOT shed a single tear for the innocent victims of abortion? He will be asked that question some day at the throne of God. And he knows it.

James Dobson has said, **"The crux of the entire issue is, do we believe our own rhetoric? Do we believe we're killing babies? ...If 1.5 million children were being slaughtered per year, who are *here*... what would we do about it? Would we stand behind our pulpits and say, 'We don't believe in civil disobedience. If the law says these children must die, then they must die.' No! We wouldn't do that. We'd be in there trying to rescue them any way we could. And if that meant going to jail, we'd go to jail. We don't believe our own rhetoric. That's the problem."**[17]

C. Why all this Infighting?

One of Nelson Mandela's greatest heartaches during his *Long Walk to Freedom* in South Africa was that a rival group [the PAC] actually worked to defeat his ANC's efforts. He says, "to attempt to break a strike by calling upon people to go to work directly serves the interests of the enemy."[1]

Russel Shaw says, "The opponents of abortion seem to have a certain talent for getting tangled in [tactical issues] and often end up wasting their energies in intramural quarrels."[2]

We would observe that even such high-strung types as homosexuals, feminists, and garden-variety humanists, when it comes to being pro-abortion, never have the slightest word of criticism for one another. If they can't say something nice about each other, they don't say anything at all. Would that pro-lifers were so wise. Unity is in short supply in the pro-life movement.

Like Children sitting in the marketplace

One of our Lord's most harsh criticisms was delivered with a wry chuckle, perhaps: "To what, then, can I compare the people of this generation [/movement]? What are they like? They are like children sitting in the marketplace and calling out to each other: 'We played the flute for you, and you did not dance; we sang a dirge, and you did not cry.'"[3]

Foreman asks: "Is this insanity? Welcome to the Church in America; the land where thirty million [1992] children were publicly murdered in sight of at least fifty million people who believe that it is murder. Yet, not only did they do next to nothing to stop it, they attacked anyone who tried to expose it or protect her children."[4]

Time magazine documents the infighting: "A Rescue member allegedly made a bomb threat to a Dallas clinic from a phone in New Jersey. 'These are the tactics of the Mafia,' says [Bill Price, head of Texans United for Life]. Earlier this year, Twin Cities Catholic Archbishop John Roach urged militant antiabortion groups to avoid his area. 'I do not find Operation Rescue to be a positive element in the pro-life movement...'"[5]

Charles Colson's *Kingdoms in Conflict* was published in 1987, just in time for his words to predispose many against Operation Rescue: "Good citizens always avoid breaking just laws to protest unjust laws."[6]

A significant proportion of Church leaders to this day remain confused about the fact that a Rescue is a rescue, not a protest.

In 1982, in *Church & State Under God*, James Atkinson went to great lengths to "prove" that nothing could ever justify lawbreaking by American Christians: "There is a more difficult problem for us to face, and that arises from a fundamental difference between the State as it existed in New Testament times and as it is today, and consequently of the vastly different role a modern Christian has to play in relation to the State from that of the first century Christian. The New Testament knows only an authoritarian state with a compliant population, and therefore speaks of Christians as 'subjects,' whereas the contemporary Christian is a *citizen* rather than a *subject*, and a citizen in a State for which he is in part responsible by democratic procedure and representative government."[7]

Michael Bray's own view is clear as he makes this point: "In an article that appeared in *The Wanderer* (June 27, 1985), Charles Rice, professor of Constitutional law at Notre Dame Law School, responded to the controversy surrounding the bountiful number of abortuary bombings that occurred in that glorious Year of Our Lord 1984. Professor Rice expressed disappointment with the fact that 'some figures in the prolife movement have... denounced these young people as terrorists.' [and beyond that, some 'pro-life' critics] have 'indicated that they are as much opposed to interference with an abortionist's property as they are to the abortionist's termination of the life of his victim.'"[8]

SCOPE and FOCUS
I. CONVICTIONS
II. PRETEXTS
III. MANDATE
IV. LEGACY
V. ABORTIVE LINKS
VI. DILEMMA
Magnitude of Problem
World scene
Death toll
Who Aborts?
Government blunders
Access reduced?
Who cares, how much?
Restrained Outrage
A Century of martyrs
Rhetoric & reality
Worth any cost?
Righteous intolerance
Why this Infighting?
Like children sitting...
Nature of the Problem
Medical fraud
Non-enforcement
Loopholes
Defiance of law
Opportunists
Privatization of death
Undetectability
Definitions of Victory
Close the clinics
Reproductive truth
Pass the Amendment
Reshape society
Pro-life commitments
Personal morality
Religious revival
VII. DESTINY

D. Nature of the Problem: What if "The Amendment" came to be?

Here are two crucial realities that confront a candid pro-life movement today: 1) American women now possess a Supreme Court-manufactured, constitutionally guaranteed **"fundamental right" to abortion**, which nothing short of a constitutional amendment can contravene; 2) A society whose democratic processes are incapable of banning the "partial-birth abortion procedure" are **light-years away from any Human-Life Amendment**.

A third, grim reality, a companion to the two just mentioned, must also be acknowledged: 3) Whenever – and if ever – a right-to-life amendment for preborns *is* passed, far from heralding a glorious era of safety for the unborn, it would only unleash an intensely **quixotic struggle to enforce** such a law. We must now chart the hostile social frontier we would face if abortion were to be re-criminalized in some future U.S.A.

Let us embark on this exploration by revisiting the conclusions which were drawn [*Orphans* pages **148-151**] about the nineteenth-century outlawing of abortion which was accomplished, state by state, predominately from 1860 to 1880: 1) a vigorous and broadly based social movement was enthusiastically pro-woman *and* pro-preborn; 2) the medical, legal and political communities were morally and professionally motivated to outlaw abortion; 3) pastors took a bold public stand against abortion, and congregations followed their crusading leadership; 4) the "media elite" and journalistic community boosted the movement as "news" and sustained it to fulfillment of its goal; 5) democratically, a simple majority in each state legislature could accomplish the political objectives.

A frank comparison of today's scene with yesterday's will evoke a sense of awe at how dramatically less optimistic our current prospects are. In tandem with that realization, the reader is reminded of our last line on page 151: **"The most reliable conclusion is that the imposition of anti-abortion laws nationwide [in the 1800s] reduced the incidence of abortion by no more than fifty percent."[9]**

As we try to project the potential effectiveness of some future outlawing of abortion, knowing the financial health of the pro-life and pro-abortion armies would be helpful. Brian Clowes tells us that "the total combined annual budget of the National Right to Life Committee and all of its hundreds of chapters, Human Life International, American Life League, and all of the other hundreds of national and local pro-life groups in the country is about 22 million dollars. Not a single penny of this comes from the United States government in the form of tax dollars. Compare this to Planned Parenthood, which alone has an annual budget of about 250 million dollars – about 30 percent of which is *your* tax dollars. [Add the $200 million of other anti-life groups... and the total is $450 million vs. $22 million]"[10]

This sociological assertion is secular in origin, but perhaps is relevant to our future plight: "Once a taboo is gone, it's impossible to revive. Once technology is developed, it's impossible to make people forget. Once people have choices, they don't ever give them up. Still, there seems to be a growing realization that a society that values individual fulfillment above all else is a scary place to live."[11]

Dave Andrusko quotes William Brennan: "To be able to kill human beings on a massive scale requires many things, but most of all the ability to dehumanize the victims and to kill them in secrecy... The awesome ability of modern destructive technology to keep the victim's plight concealed goes a long way toward explaining and reinforcing the myth that there is no victim."[12]

"It is unlikely that *Roe v. Wade* will be overturned any time soon. Even if it were, abortion as a major debate and significant practice would continue because it has become so fiercely symbolic and so tied in the public discussion to women's equality and well-being."[13]

1 Mandela, *Long Walk to Freedom*, 235.

2 Shaw, *Abortion on Trial*, 171.

3 *Luke* 7:31-2.

4 Foreman, 96.

5 *Time*, 7-19-93, 29.

6 Colson, 249.

7 Atkinson, 31-2.

8 Bray, *A Time to Kill*, 111.

9 This conclusion is based upon, among others, the text and statistics in Marvin Olasky, *Abortion Rites: A Social History of Abortion in America*, 293.

10 Brian Clowes, *Pro-Life Activist's Encyclopedia*, pages 16.24 and 16.25.

11 *Press*, 11-25-96, A10.

12 Brennan, in Andrusko, *To Rescue the Future: The Pro-Life Movement in the 1980s*, 216.

13 Christine Pohl, in John Kilner, *Bioethics and the Future of Medicine: A Christian Appraisal*, 213.

1. Fraud in the Medical community

Contrary to the propaganda that implied that before *Roe* every abortion was inflicted by a ghoul in a back alley, "Dr. Alfred C. Kinsey showed in 1958 that 84 to 87 percent of all illegal abortions were performed by licensed physicians in good standing."[1]

In 1968 it was reported that Dr. Harold Rosen "takes some of the steaminess out of the horror stories when he remarks matter-of-factly: 'Eighty to ninety per cent of all abortions in the United States are preformed by competent physicians, on referral from other physicians.'"[2]

"Associated Press writers," said Randy Alcorn in 1994, "love to use the term 'back alley' to describe what will happen if abortion is again made illegal... However, the facts are once again to the contrary. Prior to 1973, 90 percent of all illegal abortions were performed in the offices of licensed, reputable physicians, not in 'back alley clinics.'"[3]

Before *Roe*, the Clergy Consultation Service was a group of liberal clerics who envisioned themselves as a sort of underground railroad for desperate young girls, while others of us say that they pimped for abortionists. The "beauty" of their enterprise was that the girls trusted clergymen, and abortionists got a steady stream of screened clients, reducing their fear of detection by the authorities [few of whom cared to investigate the trade, anyway].

The founder of the Clergy Consultation Service, Howard Moody, revealed that when nurses in-training became pregnant all they had to do was present some blood on a pair of panties to verify that a miscarriage had begun and that hospitals would oblige them with "a dilation and emptying of the uterus" which was routinely logged in hospital records as aftercare for a "spontaneous" abortion.[4]

Robert Williams, in a book published in the year of *Roe v. Wade*, 1973, flatly stated: "A physician who has performed an abortion in a licensed hospital has never been convicted of illegal abortion, even though many abortions are performed for reasons beyond those indicated by laws."[5]

Verbal gymnastics to legitimize abortion pre-dated *Roe* by far. Since it was common for state anti-abortion laws to allow exceptions "to save the mother's life," the term "therapeutic abortion" came to mean one that was legally permitted for medical reasons. A pro-abortion pamphlet revealed how far the technicality of "medical necessity" had already been stretched, as of 1969: "Basically, modern-day indications for 'therapeutic abortion' divide into four general categories: (1) medical, (2) fetal, (3) psychiatric, and (4) socio-economic. Theoretically, however, because of present laws in most states, each such abortion is approved because it is 'necessary' to 'preserve the life' of the pregnant woman."[6]

You 'gotta be crazy to have an abortion!

California passed a new law in 1968 permitting abortions on psychiatric grounds, as did various other states at about the same time. This law had an amazingly detrimental effect on the mental stability of California women. It was serious enough that 5,000 were so emotionally unbalanced as to require abortions in the first year, but the epidemic got out of hand; in just three years, by 1971, 100,000 women were certified as requiring therapeutic abortions for psychiatric reasons.[7]

1 Francis Beckwith, *Politically Correct Death: Answering the Arguments for Abortion Rights*, 58.

2 Russel Shaw, *Abortion on Trial*, 35-6.

3 Alcorn, in *Life Advocate*, 5/'94, 10.

4 Brian Clowes, page 18.3.

5 Robert Williams, *To Live and To Die: When, Why, and How*, 82.

6 Harriet Pilpel, *When Should Abortion be Legal?*, 13.

7 Alan Guttmacher, in J. Douglas Butler, *Abortion, Medicine, and the Law*, 234.

SCOPE and FOCUS
I. CONVICTIONS
II. PRETEXTS
III. MANDATE
IV. LEGACY
V. ABORTIVE LINKS
VI. DILEMMA
Magnitude of Problem
World scene
Death toll
Who Aborts?
Government blunders
Access reduced?
Who cares, how much?
Restrained Outrage
A Century of martyrs
Rhetoric & reality
Worth any cost?
Righteous intolerance
Why this Infighting?
Like children sitting...
Nature of the Problem
Medical fraud
Non-enforcement
Loopholes
Defiance of law
Opportunists
Privatization of death
Undetectability
Definitions of Victory
Close the clinics
Reproductive truth
Pass the Amendment
Reshape society
Pro-life commitments
Personal morality
Religious revival
VII. DESTINY

That's not a baby, it's a Transient Situational Disturbance

There was a predominance of particular types of mental illness in California. When an abortion was approved by a psychiatrist, a specific diagnosis was required. In practice, 96% fell into just three categories: roughly 15% of patients suffered from "neuroses" verified by anxiety and depression [normal with pregnancy, we are told]; another 15-16% were shown to have "personality disorders" frequently noted as "passive-aggressive" [they were mad at their babies for making them pregnant, we guess]; but a whopping 65% of the women were diagnosed with "Transient Situational Disturbance." How perfect: a mental illness caused by pregnancy and cured by abortion![8]

Dr. E. James Lieberman declared in 1970: "In recent years, 90 percent of all legal abortions performed in the United States were justified on psychiatric grounds."[9]

While new laws in several states gave the psychiatrists the mixed blessing of becoming the legitimizers of abortion, there were other parallel developments. In 1962 the ALI [American Law Institute] outlined a package of exceptions to allow for abortion, which included "**grave impairment to health**." Between 1967 and 1972 the legislatures of fourteen states adopted that package. The phrase just noted was undoubtedly assumed by most legislators to mean "the pregnancy is threatening the woman's life," but in practice in the medical community we are told, **"'grave impairment to health' included normal conditions of pregnancy."[10]**

A recent newspaper report reveals the kinds of duplicity in the medical community which surround abortion even today. We are told that the State of California, for instance, undercounts the number of tax-paid abortions, omitting "abortions performed by health maintenance organizations [HMOs] that serve Medi-Cal patients." Beyond that, "Some doctors hide abortions as other procedures when they bill Medi-Cal."[11]

In practice, neither the law nor the medical community can constrain a determined abortionist from legitimizing any particular abortion. Candidly, abortionist Lise Fortier says, **"Each and every pregnancy threatens a woman's life. From a strict medical viewpoint, every pregnancy should be aborted."[12]**

In sworn courtroom testimony, abortionist Jane Hodgson declared, "I feel there is a medical indication to abort a pregnancy where it is not wanted. In good faith, I would recommend on a medical basis, you understand, that, and it would be 100%. I think they are all medically necessary. I am concerned with the quality of [the mother's] life, not physical existence."[13]

So our conclusion must be that, both prior to *Roe* and subsequent to it, **the practice of abortion by the medical community has been quite effectively "above the law**."

8 Kristin Luker, *Taking Chances: Abortion and the Decision Not to Contracept*, 172.

9 Lieberman, in Clowes, page 51.2.

10 Robert Mnookin, *In the Interest of Children: Advocacy, Law, Reform, and Public Policy*, 164.

11 *Press*, 8-4-96, A1, A12.

12 Fortier, in Clowes, page 51.3.

13 Hodgson, in Clowes, page 51.1.

2. Non-enforcement

F. LaGard Smith believes, "No one is eager to throw women into jail for having illegal abortions. The idea [behind anti-abortion laws] is to *deter* them from having abortions in the first place. If it should be argued that many women would then seek illegal abortions, the fact is that there is little the state could do in legal terms from that point forward in any case."[1]

Law enforcement officials have great discretion regarding which laws are enforced, and how aggressively. "Before 1970, illegal abortion clinics flourished in most of the larger cities in the United States and were totally ignored by police. Illegal abortionist Ruth Barnett performed more than 40,000 abortions in Portland, Oregon over a 45-year period and was never bothered once by police until an ambitious newspaper reporter made a big fuss over her activities and had her shut down."[2]

In her book, *They Weep on My Doorstep*, Ruth Barnett tells it like it was: "The duly elected officers of the law, members of the medical profession and state medical board knew we were in business, [but] the archaic [anti-abortion] statute had never been considered."[3]

Brian Clowes summarizes: "The police winked at abortion mills before abortion was legalized. They now viciously assault pro-life rescuers and commonly arrest sidewalk counselors engaged in purely legal activities. It makes one speculate as to what the police will do when abortion is criminalized again."[4]

The dilemma was already well understood in 1957 when Glanville Williams wrote: "Although abortion laws exist in all Western countries, there has been a remarkable lack of enforcement. Another reason is the inherent unenforceability of a statute that attempts to prohibit a private practice where all parties concerned desire to avoid the restriction. The result is that the trade of [the] abortionist is conducted with a large measure of impunity."[5]

Susan Landau of the Redding Feminist Women's Health Center has boasted: "The technology is here – you can't take that away. They may make abortion illegal, but they can't control it."[6]

Law professor Laurence Tribe is quite graphic: "State efforts to ferret out prohibited abortions – as defined by the Government – would require not only searches of bedrooms for telltale 'morning-after' pills, but also searches of woman's bodies for intrauterine devices."[7]

3. Loopholes in the law

A motivated pro-abortion movement, or single woman, can easily find technicalities that will enable them to circumvent the law. We earlier mentioned the successful alleging that a spontaneous abortion has begun with no more evidence than a spot of blood. Thomas Hilgers documents that in the first four-and-a-half years after Colorado began permitting abortions in the case of rape [in 1967] 290 women received abortions for "rape induced" pregnancies despite the fact that in all 290 of the cases, "no rapist was even charged with his crime, much less convicted of such."[8]

We will soon consider the entrepreneurial inclination on the part of non-doctors, but under the heading of loopholes in the law it should be noted that some women even now perform abortions but claim that no abortion has occurred, simply on a linguistic technicality: "Women who do menstrual extraction consider it and other home health-care techniques to be completely legal, since an individual woman or a group of women cannot make a medical diagnosis of pregnancy. [Therefore] they would not have the necessary intent required to constitute a criminal act of abortion."[9]

Brian Clowes states what is all too clear:

"In dealing with abortionists, we must remember that any exception whatever – even a 'life of the mother' exception – will eventually be expanded to mean, in practice, abortion on demand."[10]

Following the example of the Supreme Court, judges who do not like the law as it stands sometimes simply revise it. Perhaps the most ridiculous example was provided by Judge Dooling when he overturned the Hyde Amendment. Dooling asserted on page 309 of his opinion that **"Poverty is a medical condition."[11]**

SCOPE and FOCUS
I. CONVICTIONS
II. PRETEXTS
III. MANDATE
IV. LEGACY
V. ABORTIVE LINKS
VI. DILEMMA
Magnitude of Problem
World scene
Death toll
Who Aborts?
Government blunders
Access reduced?
Who cares, how much?
Restrained Outrage
A Century of martyrs
Rhetoric & reality
Worth any cost?
Righteous intolerance
Why this Infighting?
Like children sitting...
Nature of the Problem
Medical fraud
Non-enforcement
Loopholes
Defiance of law
Opportunists
Privatization of death
Undetectability
Definitions of Victory
Close the clinics
Reproductive truth
Pass the Amendment
Reshape society
Pro-life commitments
Personal morality
Religious revival
VII. DESTINY

4. Defiance of the law

An abundance of insiders, and ex-insiders, vividly detail the widespread defiance of the law which exists in the surgical abortion industry. Tommy Tucker's "unlicensed staff were routinely dispensing medications (and filled out drug prescription forms that were pre-signed by Tucker), [and] persons not licensed to administer general anesthesia, including administrative employees, were putting women to sleep even before Tucker would arrive to perform the abortions."[12]

When it was widely rumored that the Supreme Court might overturn *Roe* with its forthcoming *Webster* decision, former NOW president Molly Yard announced, **"We are now declaring a state of emergency for the women of America. We will not go back to illegal abortions. We aren't going to obey the law."**[13]

In 1992, NOW president Jill Ireland boasted: **"We will break the law to make sure women have the right to safe, legal abortions."**[14]

Former Planned Parenthood Federation of America president Faye Wattleton signed a 1984 document called *The Human Right to Family Planning*, which stated that **Planned Parenthood "should not use the absence of law or the existence of an unfavorable law as an excuse for inaction; action outside the law, or even in violation of it, is part of the process of stimulating change."**[15]

In 1983, Wattleton was quoted as saying, **"We will disobey laws requiring notification to parents of minors receiving contraceptive drugs or devices."**[16] In 1982 Planned Parenthood openly provided "suggestions and assistance for bypassing and disobeying various local and national laws restricting abortion."[17] It is well known that, besides illegally providing abortifacient birth control to minors, Planned Parenthood routinely dispenses the Pill for "morning-after" use.

Brian Clowes says that "the Neofeminists are already 'gearing up' for their underground abortion networks by falsifying medical records: [according to the National Women's Health Network] 'Even now, women in this country who are desperate are bringing in doctored sonograms in order to get abortions.'"[18]

As we have mentioned previously, the 1998 bombing in Birmingham, Ala., which regrettably killed a man and maimed a woman, occurred at a location where partial-birth abortions were being performed in proud, public defiance of a recently enacted state law prohibiting the technique.[19]

How does Gloria Steinem justify breaking the law should *Roe* be overturned? **"If the Supreme Court has created disrespect for the law by placing it too far outside public practice and belief, that's their problem."**[20]

1 F. LaGard Smith, *When Choice Becomes God*, 254.

2 Clowes, page 18.5.

3 Barnett, in Clowes, page 18.5.

4 Clowes, page 18.5.

5 Williams, *The Sanctity of Life and the Criminal Law*, 1957, 207.

6 Landau, in Clowes, page 18.4.

7 Tribe, in Clowes, page 54.1.

8 Hilgers, *Abortion and Social Justice*, 49-50.

9 Rebecca Chalker and Carol Downer, in Clowes, page 18.3.

10 Clowes, page 51.2.

11 Dooling, in Clowes, page 51.3.

12 Cathy Ramey, in *Life Advocate*, 6/'94, 11-2.

13 Yard, in Clowes, page 18.3.

14 Ireland, in Clowes, page 18.3.

15 Wattleton, in Clowes, page 18.2.

16 Wattleton, in Clowes, page 18.7.

17 Donal Warwick, in Clowes, page 18.7.

18 Clowes, page 18.4.

19 *Press*, 1-30-98, A1, A10.

20 Steinem, in F. LaGard Smith, 217.

5. Opportunists

"In March of 1994 a university student, Joycelyn White, [filed suit against abortionist Tommy Tucker] claiming that in December of 1992 she was scheduled to have her child killed by Tucker. Instead an unlicensed employee performed the abortion. Her suit claims that abortion was 'unsuccessful.'"[1]

Joy Davis was at one time Tommy Tucker's office manager. "With no medical training, [she states that under Tucker's orders, she] performed abortions herself. On at least ten occasions Tucker was unavailable, 'either out of town or he didn't want to get out of bed,' she claims, [and] on those occasions she was instructed over the phone by Tucker to proceed with an abortion."[2]

We must look within the next statement for an additional truth: "Women's health clinics have frequently been closed by state authorities when abortion procedures were undertaken by anyone other than licensed physicians."[3]

Here is this researcher's double surprise. It is refreshing to be told that authorities have closed down abortion facilities "frequently." Beyond that, if clinics have *frequently* been closed down because abortions by unauthorized staff were discovered, reported, investigated, verified and punished, just imagine what greater number of such abuses occurred but went undetected, unreported, uninvestigated, unverified, and unpunished!

In 1993 "it became legal in Montana for a physician's assistant, supervised by a physician, to perform abortions."[4]

Each reader will need to picture in her/his own mind just how great a distance could exist between the physician and the abortion in progress and have the average abortionist still assert that he was "supervising" the procedure.

Focus on the Family reports that the National Abortion Federation, "along with the American College of Obstetricians and Gynecologists, has stated that 'physician assistants, nurse practitioners and certified nurse midwives offer considerable promise for expanding the pool of qualified abortion providers.' According to AGI [Alan Guttmacher Institute], physician assistants have been performing abortions in Vermont for two decades [since about 1975]."[5]

According to reformed abortionist Dr. Bernard Nathanson, "The practice of abortion was revolutionized at virtually the same moment that the laws were revolutionized, through the widespread introduction of suction curettage in 1970... If abortion is driven underground again, even non-physicians will be able to perform this procedure with remarkable safety."[6]

Note: More than 75% of all current abortions are by suction.[7]

If abortion were to be re-criminalized, Cynthia Pearson asserts, **"Anyone who could get their hands on an electric suction machine would be in business."**[8]

Frances Kissling of Catholics for a Free Choice has a vision: "I would like to see a huge underground of activist women learning how to do menstrual extractions and vacuum aspiration abortions, mothers teaching their daughters..."[9]

"During the period 1969 to 1973, Neofeminists conducted an 'underground railroad' entitled 'Jane' for women who wanted to obtain illegal abortions. During this time, the 'Jane' organizers 'evolved' from merely counseling and referring for abortions to actually performing the abortions themselves... When 'Jane' disbanded in April 1973, its members boasted of having performed 12,000 illegal abortions."[10]

In 1990, F. LaGard Smith quoted an article that revealed the existence of what was termed an "Underground Army." The article stated, "Independently, several [pro-abortion] groups came to the conclusion that they would help women obtain abortions whether or not it was legal and whether or not doctors were willing to perform the procedure."[11]

Here is what we mean by the entrepreneurial spirit: "The Feminist Women's Health Centers began selling $79.95 '**home suction aspiration kits**' in mid-1989, immediately after the Supreme Court's *Webster* decision. These kits consisted of **aquarium tubing, Mason jars, and syringes, and the materials cost about 10 dollars.** Therefore, the FWHCs were making about 800 percent profit on what they called 'menstrual extraction kits.'"[12]

SCOPE and FOCUS
I. CONVICTIONS
II. PRETEXTS
III. MANDATE
IV. LEGACY
V. ABORTIVE LINKS
VI. DILEMMA
Magnitude of Problem
World scene
Death toll
Who Aborts?
Government blunders
Access reduced?
Who cares, how much?
Restrained Outrage
A Century of martyrs
Rhetoric & reality
Worth any cost?
Righteous intolerance
Why this Infighting?
Like children sitting...
Nature of the Problem
Medical fraud
Non-enforcement
Loopholes
Defiance of law
Opportunists
Privatization of death
Undetectability
Definitions of Victory
Close the clinics
Reproductive truth
Pass the Amendment
Reshape society
Pro-life commitments
Personal morality
Religious revival
VII. DESTINY

6. Privatization

As we consider the increasing privatization of abortion, we return to Russel Shaw's prophetic words in 1968:

"It may very well be, as Paul Ramsey says, that the controversy over abortion and the law will become irrelevant once the abortion pills now being developed become generally available. Abortion then will be an issue in a private sphere which law cannot reach."[13]

Michael Bray observes that "it's going to be very difficult to picket a woman's medicine cabinet."[14]

F. LaGard Smith refers to "over-the-counter death" and says, "If some people have their way, we will see the day when abortions come packaged in plastic bottles with brand names like 'Oops!' and 'Second Chance.' Abortion-by-vending-machine will make abortion-on-demand look absolutely antiquated! For many people any future abortion pill will be the ultimate guarantor of the selfish 'good life.'"[15]

Randy Alcorn puts the privatization of abortion in stark focus for us: "Trends indicate that in years to come there will be fewer surgical abortions, because of the popularity and 'ease' of chemical abortions. If the church herself is committing chemical abortions as a way of life [the Pill], then we are woefully unprepared to fight the abortion battle at any level, let alone this one."[16]

7. Undetectability

"As far back as 1966, Garrett Hardin and other population theorists were dreaming and hoping that the major 'contraceptive' of the future would be an abortifacient pill... The best part (from the anti-lifer's view) is that **she would never actually know whether or not she had aborted, and so her conscience could remain clear."[17]**

Lawrence Roberge points out two major problems with the new trend toward chemical death: "Mobilizing protestors for all the physicians distributing abortifacient vaccines would be next to impossible... [Also] with the destruction of life occurring so early after conception, **the sense of personal responsibility for the destruction of unborn life is further diminished. In a sense, if there is no body, then there exists no crime."[18]**

1 Cathy Ramey, in *Life Advocate*, 6/'94, 12.

2 Cathy Ramey, in *Life Advocate*, 6/'94, 11.

3 Carol Lefcourt, *Women and the Law*, page 8.2.

4 *Life Advocate*, 6/'94, 7.

5 Focus on the Family, *Citizen*, 7-17-95, 4.

6 Nathanson, in Francis Beckwith, *Politically Correct Death: Answering the Arguments for Abortion Rights*, 59.

7 Right to Life Crusade, Inc., Tulsa. Not in bibliography.

8 Pearson, in Clowes, page 18.4.

9 Kissling, in Clowes, page 18.4.

10 Clowes, page 18.3.

11 Article by Japenga and Venant, in Smith, *When Choice Becomes God*, 216.

12 Clowes, page 18.4.

13 Shaw, *Abortion on Trial*, 169.

14 Bray, *A Time to Kill*, 205.

15 Smith, *When Choice Becomes God*, 1990, 254 and 256.

16 Alcorn, in *Life Advocate*, Sept.-Oct./'97, 30.

17 Clowes, page 31.1.

18 Roberge, in John Kilner, *Bioethics and the Future of Medicine, A Christian Appraisal*. 184.

1 Pope John Paul II, in *Life Advocate*, 2/'94, 5: "Woe to you if you do not succeed in defending life."

• Terry, cassette in 1988: "When you get into the fray, and you just see the power of God, and you see the unity, and you realize that *we can win this war*, we can change the course of history."

2 Our seven "links" are: recreational sex, reproductive technology, abortion industry, governmental action, social climate, religious confusion, and personal decision to abort. [*Orphans* pages 187-260].

• Sproul, 151-6, "Strategic targets: pro-choice adherents... liberal churches and liberals... the medical community... politicians and public officials... parents and the family... rescuing at clinics..."

• Judie Brown, in Foreman, 99: "...the entire pro-life movement: compassionate counseling... offering alternatives... creating the basis for a legal challenge to *Roe*... making a political statement... giving politicians a platform on which to take action... personally involving a cross-section of the community... reviving churches... physically save a baby's life..."

3 Sproul, 15, "Can such a web of interwoven and conflicting issues be untangled?"

4 Foreman, 39: "There are no cheap or simple solutions to abortion, certainly no purely political and educational solutions." 117: "We must support legal, intellectual, moral, and physical intolerance of murder... to protect your neighbor, to honor God, to be like Jesus..."

5 Foreman, 135: "Why do we all feel as though we have not done enough no matter how much we do? ...It is inherent in the shock of realizing that we have permitted even one legal abortion. How much more should we expect to be weighed down by the 1.5 million legal murders each year!"

6 Crutcher, *Access*, 2: "The future of abortion in America is in serious jeopardy simply because access to abortion is evaporating."

7 Foreman, 103-4: "Rescuers in Milwaukee prove that it is worth rescuing every day to protect children."

• Foreman, 163-6: "I do not believe that we will see an end to child-killing until enough people do for the children what Christ did for us – make it a personal matter of life or death to protect them, [willing to say,] 'Quit killing or we die.'"

• Crutcher, *Access*, 23: "On the day we win the access battle, the possibility of an all-inclusive Human Life Amendment is a reality."

8 Crutcher, *Access*, 22: "This is a war pro-lifers could win without prevailing in a single court battle. All they have to do is intimidate physicians into leaving their clinics and discourage medical students from entering the field in the first place."

9 F.L. Smith, 254: "Unlike pre-*Roe v. Wade* abortion statutes, future legislation will have to reach beyond illegal abortionists to deal with new technology which promises to revolutionize the manner in which pregnancies are terminated."

10 "The Surgeon General strongly warns you that one effect of this product is to prevent implantation in the womb of a child if one happens to be conceived."

11 *Newsweek*, 3-13-95, 61: "Nowhere are the battles more fierce than with RU-486... U.S. firms refused to touch it, frightened by controversy and threatened boycotts by abortion opponents... The pharmaceutical industry has washed its hands of birth control."

12 Sproul, 134: "The national issue is abortion-on-demand. Even if it were decided in extreme cases that abortion is an ethical option, the extreme cases should not dictate the general law."

• F.L. Smith, 254: "Cut off the availability of legal abortions, and for the most part abortions will cease."

• *Focus on the Family* newsletter, 7/'97, 2: "Nothing short of a constitutional amendment will protect the unborn child... There IS no other way."

13 Ralph Reed, in *Press*, 11-3-96, A18: "On election day, the religious conservatives will be the largest single constituency in the electorate."

• Carl Landwehr, in Andrusko, 19: "An organized, motivated pro-life voting constituency – the product of an all-out, massive voter identification process – represents the only way to out-maneuver the pro-abortion elitists."

14 Crutcher, *Access*, 2: "The only way around [the current Supreme Court] is either the appointment and confirmation of a new Supreme Court dominated by pro-lifers or the passage of a Human Life Amendment."

15 Foreman, 44: "The Constitution, after all, can protect only those whom the people have a will to protect."

• John Leo, in F.L. Smith, 263: "As Aquinas says, where there is no consensus, there is no law."

• Foreman, 151-2: "There will be no secular solutions to abortion. This is because abortion is itself the best secular solution to the problem of unwanted pregnancy."

• Bork, 339: "Hollywood, the network evening news, universities, church bureaucracies... Institutions that are overwhelmingly left-liberal... will continue to misinform the public and distort public discourse."

• Sproul, 156: "The longer laws allowing abortion-on-demand remain in effect, the more likely it is that society will be hardened in heart."

• Foreman, xxii: "If our goal is not to transform society, but just tinker with it, then we will fail."

• Sproul, 151: "Sadly, the organized church – more than any other institution apart from the Supreme Court – has neglected its duty to inform the public conscience."

• Foreman, 185: Milwaukee can become an abortion-free zone. Already Burlington, a suburb of Milwaukee, has voted to declare itself such a zone – the first in the nation."

SCOPE and FOCUS

I. CONVICTIONS

II. PRETEXTS

III. MANDATE

IV. LEGACY

V. ABORTIVE LINKS

VI. DILEMMA

Magnitude of Problem
- World scene
- Death toll
- Who Aborts?
- Government blunders
- Access reduced?
- Who cares, how much?

Restrained Outrage
- A Century of martyrs
- Rhetoric & reality
- Worth any cost?
- Righteous intolerance

Why this Infighting?
- Like children sitting...

Nature of the Problem
- Medical fraud
- Non-enforcement
- Loopholes
- Defiance of law
- Opportunists
- Privatization of death
- Undetectability

Definitions of Victory
- Close the clinics
- Reproductive truth
- Pass the Amendment
- Reshape society
- Pro-life commitments
- Personal morality
- Religious revival

VII. DESTINY

16 Foreman, xxii: **"If we want to take back the power bases of our society, we must first learn to lay down our lives in service."**

[*Notes continue on page 278*]

E. Victory as Defined by Various Pro-lifers

Literally hundreds of thousands of pro-life Christians are regularly devoting their time, effort and money toward projects that have as their objective killing the abortion monster.[1]

Earlier we introduced seven battlefields[2] we described as links in a chain.[3] In some of those arenas,[4] even a total victory would not eliminate abortion in America [the surgical abortion industry, reproductive technology, Human Life Amendment]. In others, however, a complete solution to that one problem could, theoretically at least, rescue every baby conceived in the U.S.[5] from suffering an unnatural death [pro-life society, personal pro-life commitments, personal moral virtue]. The seventh and most essential link of all is revival in the Church. That is the key to even the slightest progress in any of the other arenas. Based upon all that we have presented, *Orphans in Babylon* now reshuffles the "Seven Links in the Abortive Chain" and suggests 23 crucial goals for the focus of our prayers and energies:

1. Close Down the Abortion Clinics.[6]

GOAL A **Access denied. Abort the surgical abortion business.[7]**

GOAL B **Hippocrates resurrected. Doctors don't kill; they just heal.[8]**

GOAL C **Death with Dignity. Only humane procedures.**

GOAL D **Viability matters. Emancipate the "unwanted."**

2. Reform Reproductive Technology.[9]

GOAL E **Birth control Labeling. Abortifacient warnings.[10]**

GOAL F **Pro-life Contraception. A Pill that won't kill.[11]**

3. Pass Pro-life Laws and a Human Life Amendment.[12]

GOAL G **Pro-life options. Build a pro-life, pro-family political party.[13]**

GOAL H **Pro-life States. Elect pro-life, pro-family legislators.**

GOAL I **Pro-life Nation. Elect pro-life, pro-family reps to Congress.**

GOAL J **Pro-life Chief. Elect only pro-life, pro-family presidents.[14]**

4. Reshape a Pro-life Society.[15]

GOAL K **Academic takeover. Pro-life professors and teachers.[16]**

GOAL L **Media metamorphosis. Pro-life journalists and directors.[17]**

5. Promote Personal Pro-life Commitments.[18]

GOAL M **Empower front-liners. Support sidewalk counselors and CPCs.[19]**

GOAL N **Frontier pro-lifeism. Educate the ignorant and deluded.[20]**

GOAL O **Embrace life. Get commitments to abortion-rejection.[21]**

6. Upgrade Personal Morality.[22]

GOAL P **Mention sin. Celebrate virtue in pulpit and pew.[23]**

GOAL Q **Promote chastity. Aggressive programs in church and school.[24]**

7. Ignite Religious Revival.[25]

GOAL R **Promote salvation. All parishes become evangelism-centered.[26]**

GOAL S **Congregation identification. This branch of the Vine is pro-life.[27]**

GOAL T **Public witness. This Christian is pro-life.[28]**

GOAL U **Political responsibility. This voter is pro-life.**

GOAL V **Home missions. Support and uplift pro-life missionaries.[29]**

GOAL W **Witness for life. Keep a prayer vigil over every abortion.[30]**

Notes from page 277

17 Terry, cassette: "The secular media [in 1988, *before* the radical change] is acknowledging the heroics of [Rescue]. They're saying [temporarily], 'It's peaceful.' They're not painting us as terrorists [yet]. We have the ship off the ground... The only thing that can stop us now is either division or we run out of fuel."

• Sproul, 69-70: "I think it is safe to assume that prior to *Roe v. Wade* public opinion ran overwhelmingly against abortion. Yet in less than twenty years, societal attitudes have shifted to a much more tolerant position."

• Grant, *Grand*, 245: "If we are going to serve our society as prophets and priests, guiding and guarding the land, we are going to have to recapture the media."

18 William Bennett, in Olasky, *Abortion Rites*, xii: "The most pertinent question now... is not how to pass laws against all abortions, but rather how best to *reduce the number* of abortions."

19 Franky Schaeffer, in Scheidler, 15: "We may not be able to save every baby, but we can save many."

20 Sproul, 151: "The pivotal group in shaping cultural opinion is the middle-ground, pro-choice group. Here is the most fertile field for finding people who will cross over to the pro-life position. It is always a good strategy to concentrate effort on the most likely prospects."

• Sproul, 151: "A strategic target: liberal churches and liberals. Though much public protest has taken place around abortion clinics, little or no public protest has occurred around churches where the pastors have stated their pro-choice position."

• Larry Frieders, in Bray, 195: "It's not that the knowledge isn't there, but rather that there's something keeping that knowledge from descending from one's intellect, down into the area of your heart where you can recognize the awesome tragedies that are happening."

• Bray, 99: "There is a delusion in our time which has lured many into denial of the humanity of preborn people... the Pax Americana has seduced many into a love for peace which exceeds a love for righteousness. After the delusion is dispelled those who were prosecuted as criminals will suddenly become heroes. So it has been; so it will be."

21 Foreman, 117: "All pro-lifers have the same goal: End choice in the realm of child murder."

• Thomas Klasen, in Bandow, 169: "If we make abortion illegal, without doing much more than that, it won't solve anything, since we will not be addressing the reasons that abortion was a desirable option in the first place."

• Crutcher, *Access*, 22: "[Because of the abortion industry's] absolute stranglehold on the American media, the idea that we can stop abortion without first lowering the abortion rate is seen for what it really is... utterly laughable."

22 Terry, cassette: "God could again turn America back to moral sanity, and to some semblance of social godliness. 'Cause what we're talking about is turning the whole course of this nation."

• Foreman, 103: "Sooner or later, [society] will flock to moral integrity, because only moral integrity will prepare people to pay the price of bringing lasting change."

• Roche, 322: "Our present difficulties are so great and so basic as to demand nothing short of revolution, not so much political revolution or economic revolution as moral revolution."

• Foreman, 264-5: "What is needed in the long run is a reasoned response to pro-choice that captures America's moral imagination."

23 Scheidler, 367: "People often say that we cannot impose our morality on others... It is true that we cannot force others to be moral, but we can certainly show them what morality is."

• Terry, in Foreman, 173: "I fear we will be remembered with scorn and contempt – a disgrace to church history – because in an hour when we could have turned the tide in America, we chose not to... I'm talking about God judging America, the way that He has judged every civilization in history that turned its back on Him."

• Terry, cassette: "If we are going to see this country restored it's going to be because the church led the way in repentance. And the repentance that we need is going down to these death camps, saying, 'God, we are sorry.' Not in a hateful, vengeful attitude, but going down and saying, 'Lord WE are guilty...'"

24 Thomas Gumbleton, in F.L. Smith, 264: "We need above all to change the hearts and minds of people. This is really the root of the whole problem. To some extent we have put so much effort into getting laws on the books that we have failed to persuade people of the basis for our moral stance."

25 Foreman, 55: "I do not have any plans for success apart from God's changing hearts of stone to hearts of flesh. It does not matter that it is Christians who need a heart transplant. The most famous evangelistic text, from *Revelation* 3:20, 'Behold I stand at the door and knock,' was not written to unbelievers, but to the Church."

26 Whitehead, *Second*, 180: "It is now time for another revolution, a revolution in the reformative sense... a revolution in the minds and the souls of human beings – a revolution promulgated to be a total assault on the humanistic culture. A Second American Revolution founded upon the Bible in its totality. In this, and only this, is there hope for the future."

• Foreman, 156: "In the arena of childkilling, I believe it is time to turn the Church back to its own historical and Biblical roots: Gospel missions."

27 Foreman, 28: [Long-range strategy, to reach the day when we can say,] "We fifty million Christians in America would rather rot in jail and see our houses and churches seized for the next 100 years than possess them at the expense of cooperating in any way with child-killing."

28 Foreman, 166: "Revival is not when unbelievers come to Christ, but when believers come to Christ... [to make abortion] impossible... unthinkable, [and] illegal by default."

29 Foreman, 180: "Your missionary in jail is not in need of help because he is stuck there. Getting out is easy enough, all he needs to do is cooperate with child-killers the way everyone else does. He is in jail because the rest of our society is willing to work together to keep Christians from protecting the preborn."

30 Foreman, xviii-xix: "The 1991 Summer of Mercy in Wichita showed that it is easy to make child-killing physically impossible and unpopular. Any city large enough to sport a child-killing doctor has more than enough Christians to make him stop killing and to keep the legal system from persecuting the Christians who stop the killing."

• Foreman, 185: "From June through August [1992], on the average each week, 3,000 to 5,000 Milwaukee area Christians came to the gates of hell [abortion clinics]. The killing business has never rebounded."

• Foreman, xvi: "If Wichita's 1991 Summer of Mercy is a foretaste, next time there will be tens of thousands in the streets."

• Terry, *Operation Rescue*, 212: "Satan will not give up this stronghold without a fight to the very end. Anyone who enters this conflict must be prepared for the spiritual battle of his or her life."

• Clowes, page v: "Many of these new activists have been very unpleasantly surprised to find that the pro/anti-life battle has really just begun. Christians now face an escalated continuation of a bitter and protracted struggle that will inevitably last until the end of time."

VII. Our Destiny: Future Course of Action

A. We must answer the "Hell Objection"

Referring back to Part I of *Orphans in Babylon*, it is essential that every Christian understands that the foundation of a defensible pro-life commitment is a bedrock belief in creation, design, commandments, justice, virtue, universalism and accountability, which is summed up in a phrase like: "...fully human from the moment of conception because of the sanctity inherent in having been created in the image of God."

Despite our best efforts, however, the pro-life view is subject to a strong attack stemming from our belief in heaven and hell. The pro-abortionist's assertion, "Babies will go to heaven anyway!" was addressed by Randy Alcorn in *Is Rescuing Right?* He even says that "One church's statement against rescuing reassures us that '...the death of the children will not alter the sovereign plan of God. The testimony of David was that he would see his dead infant son (2 Sam. 12:16-23) and Jesus spoke of children taking part in His Kingdom (Mt. 19:13-14).' ...I have actually been told, 'Don't you believe babies go to heaven when they die? That means they're better off anyway. In fact, if you *rescue* them, they may grow up to be non-Christians who go to hell. Dying now is probably the best thing for them.'"[1]

We will lean on Catholic theology for illumination here, for two reasons: Orthodox theology *exists* in Catholicism in a way that is impossible for the menagerie called Protestantism, and much of the best Protestant theology is derived from Catholic theology anyway. Catholic Catechism states, first of all, "The teaching of the Church affirms the existence of hell and its eternity. Immediately after death the souls of those who die in a state of mortal sin descend into hell... The chief punishment of hell is eternal separation from God."[2]

It may be assumed that all persons, Christian and pagan alike, recoil from the thought of a loving and merciful God condemning the soul of an innocent baby to hell. Our first rationale for rejecting that notion is the very grace of God: the fundamental Christian doctrine that salvation is an unmerited gift from God. Brian Clowes expresses this view, that the unborn, just as "persons who have never heard of Christ may be worthy of Heaven if they live a benign lifestyle that generally adheres to the precepts of Christianity" should be presumed to be granted a place in heaven by the grace of God.[3]

Underscoring our belief in God's heavenly grace toward aborted children is the fact that "priests generally do not administer Extreme Unction to very young children [under 7] because they have no intentional sins to remit,"[4] and the truth that the Church does conduct funeral rites for children who have died without Baptism,[5] and also provides instructions for the burial of stillborns and fetuses in a Catholic cemetery.[6]

Direct theological support for the belief that aborted preborns go to heaven comes from the early Church fathers. "Clement of Alexandria (ca 150 – ca 215), in his *Prophetic Eclogues*, a commentary on earlier Christian writing, quotes the *Apocalypse of Peter* with approval, noting again that both exposed and aborted children will be delivered to safety by a care-taking angel (but that the parents will suffer punishment because of their sins)."[7]

Bernard Dickens reveals that it was the belief of Thomas Aquinas [13th century] that infants who die before birth may be assumed to be with God, not the devil.[8]

Another pertinent doctrine of the Church is called the Baptism of Desire. This belief holds that salvation is granted by God to "such persons who would have desired Baptism explicitly if they had known its necessity,"[9] which belief is easily extended to include the unborn.

Catholic pro-life groups, Clowes tells us, "commonly pray the Rosary for the dying and the dead outside abortuaries... to request the baptism of desire for the unborn babies being slaughtered there that day."[10]

SCOPE and FOCUS
I. CONVICTIONS
II. PRETEXTS
III. MANDATE
IV. LEGACY
V. ABORTIVE LINKS
VI. DILEMMA
VII. DESTINY
The Hell Objection
Repentance, Dedication
Witness & Activism
Proclamation
Banner
Declaration of Dependence
Final Word

1 Alcorn, *Is Rescuing Right? Breaking the Law to Save the Unborn*, 189.
2 U.S. Catholic *Catechism*, 270, §1035.
3 Clowes, *Pro-Life Activist's Encyclopedia*, page 43.13.
4 Clowes, page 43.13.
5 U.S. Catholic *Catechism*, 321, §1261.
6 John Huels, *The Pastoral Companion: A Canon Law Handbook for Catholic Ministry*, 286.
7 Michael Gorman, *Abortion & the Early Church: Christian, Jewish & Pagan Attitudes in the Greco-Roman World*, 51-2.
8 Bernard Dickens, *Abortion and the Law*, 17.
9 U.S. Catholic *Catechism*, 321, §1060.
10 Clowes, page 42.13.

He's God; He can do whatever He wants

Clowes also informs us that some theologians believe that "God gives aborted and miscarried babies full knowledge and does so that they may make their own decision about eternity, just as they would have done on earth."[1]

I don't want any pipsqueeks in *my* heaven!

R.F.R. Gardner says, "Protestant theology denies the existence of a limbo, but affirms that the souls of the innocent are received into heaven," and then he goes on to reveal his own earthbound view that "If all these early miscarried fetuses [up to half of all conceptions] possess souls, the majority of 'humans' in heaven will have never even reached the stage of being organized into fetal human shape... In my view the idea would debase the doctrine of Man."[2]

A special place for tiny martyrs

Brian Clowes also addresses the belief in The Baptism of Blood. "Many religions share the belief that those who die for God are martyrs who gain Heaven. Catholicism is no exception. Many believe that the little preborn babies who die of abortion are sacrificed for convenience (of necessity, in rare cases), and are therefore true martyrs, as were the Holy Innocents, the babies who died at Herod's hands in place of Jesus."[3]

The basic Catholic belief in heaven includes the following: "Those who die in God's grace and friendship and are perfectly purified, live for ever with Christ. They are like God for ever, for they see Him as He is, 'face to face.'"[4]

This belief is consistent with *Matthew* 18:10, which many hold as sufficient verification, in the words of Jesus, that aborted babies go to heaven: "See that you do not look down on one of these little ones. For I tell you that their angels in heaven always see the face of my Father in heaven."

Ankerberg and Weldon give scriptural comfort to women who grieve over the children they have aborted: "The good news is not only that if we believe in Christ, our sins are forgiven here, but it is also that, in heaven, you will be with your [aborted] child. Scripture gives us good reason to believe your baby is alive in heaven and that you will one day see him or her (2 Samuel 12:23; Job 3:16-17, 19; cf. Mark 10:13-16)."[5]

How is it a problem if aborted babies go to heaven?

So, there is abundant evidence to support the belief that aborted children go to heaven, not hell. There is also truth, then, in the allegation that being aborted with a sure ticket to heaven is a better fate than the uncertainty of being born unwanted, born against your mother's wish to abort you, and facing the possibility of a lifetime of rejecting God, and being doomed to hell upon death.

As pro-lifers we have no rebuttal to the worldly logic of this argument. If we are wise we will acknowledge *that*, whenever the argument is presented. However, that is not the end of the discussion. Because it is never considered a favor to kill a born person – even one confident of an eternal reward – in order to "send them to heaven," the same holds true for the unborn: they have a God-given right to life, and nothing on earth justifies killing the innocent.

Shortcuts to heaven are not in God's basic plan

To "save the baby from hell" is never a pro-life argument against abortion. Babies should be saved in order that they might live the life that they were intended by God to live, on this earth.

SCOPE and FOCUS
I. CONVICTIONS
II. PRETEXTS
III. MANDATE
IV. LEGACY
V. ABORTIVE LINKS
VI. DILEMMA
VII. DESTINY
The Hell Objection
Repentance, Dedication
Witness & Activism
Proclamation
Banner
Declaration of Dependence
Final Word

1 Clowes, page 43.13.
2 Gardner, *Abortion: The Personal Dilemma, A Christian Gynaecologist Examines the Medical, Social and Spiritual Issues*, 123-4.
3 Clowes, page 43.13.
4 U.S. Catholic *Catechism*, 267, §1023.
5 John Ankerberg and John Weldon, *When Does Life Begin? And 39 Other Tough Questions About Abortion*, xvi.
6 Durant, 49.
7 Alcorn, *Is Rescuing Right?* 215.
8 Hunter, 297.
9 Barclay, in Clowes, page 42.11.
10 Schaeffer, in Scheidler, 14.
11 Clowes, page 27.1.
12 Silverman, 256.
13 Roche, 324.
14 Herwaldt, in Kilner, *Bioethics and the Future of Medicine, A Christian Appraisal*, 31.
15 Smith, *When Choice Becomes God*, 267.
16 Bonhoeffer, in Purcell, *Martyrs of Our Time*, 81.
17 Kerby Anderson, *Living Ethically in the '90s*, 103-4.
18 Santayana, *Winds of Doctrine*, 56.
19 Roche, 324.
20 Terry, *Operation Rescue*, 174.

B. Repentance & Dedication: One Body, Many Parts

The dilemma of the Church today

Here is another of the *Lessons of History* provided by the Durants: "If another great war should devastate Western civilization, the resultant destruction of cities, the dissemination of poverty, and the disgrace of science may leave the Church, as in A.D. 476 [Fall of the Roman Empire to the 'barbarians'], the sole hope and guide of those who survive the cataclysm. One lesson of history is that religion has many lives, and a habit of resurrection."[6]

Here is a truth we might prefer not to face. Randy Alcorn says that, like it or not, "We must realize that there has never been a movement of God – whether the Protestant Reformation, the Underground Railroad, the Christian resistance in [Nazi] Germany or any other – that has not been strongly opposed by respected Christian leaders."[7]

In 1991, James Hunter in writing *Culture Wars: The Struggle to Define America*, pronounced this maxim: "The truth is that the two sides of the cultural divide peacefully coexist only so long as neither side gains actual or symbolic advantage over the other."[8]

In our giant cultural *Monopoly* game, there can be no doubt that the secular humanist side has bought up every square on the board, including "Go to jail..." Our culture war has progressed to phase-B, when the Masters tighten the noose around the neck of the Stewards of God.

William Barclay has said, "There is nothing that the world would like so much as a silent Church."[9] The thought is expanded by Franky Schaeffer: "To remain silent in the midst of evil is to side with that evil."[10] It has been observed that in Dante's *Divine Comedy*, "The hottest spot in Hell is reserved for those who, in time of crisis, preserve their neutrality."[11] In *Religion for Skeptics*, Silverman noted that "The real slavery of the children of Israel in Egypt was that they learned to endure it."[12]

The Bewildered Society was written in 1974 by George Roche. His words are more true today than they were in the year after *Roe v. Wade*: "The world, hurtling on toward political, economic, psychic catastrophe, is not going to be saved, if it is saved at all, by the Church if the Church remains an uncommitted host of politely respectable people, willing to be led by (worldly) professional ecclesiastics."[13]

A crucial experience of life-changing revelation is shared by Dr. Loreen Herwaldt: "I realized that my job was not to ensure my survival – that was God's job. Instead my job was to obey God and to stop usurping his role in my life. As long as I valued survival above obedience, I was in danger of prostituting myself to the gods of this world..."[14]

F. LaGard Smith reveals, "The victory will be achieved only when, as a chorus of one people joined together in pained conscience, America cries out in anguish at our greatest national sin [abortion]. When that day comes, there will be no more need of laws... Not until then will the battle over abortion have ended."[15]

Hear the words of Dietrich Bonhoeffer: "There is only one hope for our age, which is so powerless, so feeble, so wretched, disliked and pitiable, and with all this so forlorn: a return to the Church, to the place where one man bears up another in love, where one man shares a life of another."[16]

Kerby Anderson reminds us, "The prophets of Israel spoke to the social issues that troubled Israelite society both in matters of religious orthodoxy and social justice." Anderson says that then, as now, it was made clear that two things were required of God's people: "1) to repent of their evil and turn back to God; 2) to exercise justice, righteousness, and loyalty."[17]

"In a frank supernaturalism," wrote George Santayana, "not in a pleasant secularization, lies the sole hope of the Church. Its sole dignity also lies there. It will not convert the world; it never did and it never could. It will remain a voice crying in the wilderness; but it will believe what it cries, and there will be some to listen to it in the future, as there have been many in the past."[18]

We must contemplate the view of George Roche: **"Traditionally, the role of the Church was to confront a failing world with God. Today the struggle of a remnant within the various denominations is to confront a failing church with God."**[19]

"The Church has no chance of defeating abortion, no chance of restoring our quickly disappearing liberties, no chance of bringing America back to moral sanity" said Randall Terry, "unless we repent of our idolatry and compromise. But **if we repent, God can and will do wonders – even through a remnant of his people."**[20]

C. Witness & Activism

1. Proclamation

"The Church has failed because, though it has realized the necessity of distinction from the world," said Elton Trueblood, "it has fastened upon distinctions which are essentially trivial."[1]

"The church cannot be timid in the face of crises," writes John Whitehead. "One strong local church can demand respect from the entire community. The world is looking for someone or something that will take a stand. Moreover, the bolder the church becomes, the stronger Christians in general become."[2]

"So how active should our intolerance to child-killing be?" asks Foreman. "Surely we need a symbolic form of intolerance: it must include a philosophical and theological dimension in addition to visible demonstrations, protests, and lobbying. We should be providing positive intolerance in our alternatives to murder – crisis pregnancy centers, mom's houses, shepherding homes, chastity-based sex education..."[3] The writer adds: "Each Christian should find where God is calling him to give his life, and lay it down there."[4]

As Saint Benedict said, "After the Lord has ended His exhortation, He waits every day for us to respond to His sacred counsels."[5]

George Grant shares with us the words of Hilaire Belloc: "A man who knows that the earth is round but lives among men who believe it to be flat ought to hammer in his doctrine of the earth's roundness up to the point of arrest, imprisonment, or even death. Reality will confirm him, and he is not so much testifying to the world as it is – which is worth nothing – as to Him who made the world and Who is worth more than all things."[6]

We must implement a truth-in-labeling policy for local congregations. Being boldly pro-life is the litmus test of a congregation that is taking seriously its commission to be salt and light in its community. The very first piece of paper we hand a newcomer, and the words spoken from the pulpit every Sunday must leave no room for doubt about the stand we take for the right-to-life of the preborn, and of our accountability to God in how we participate in the culture war. Until your congregation writes its own, we offer this Proclamation for your consideration:

Pro-Life Proclamation

**We, as a part of the Body of Christ,
uphold and defend the sanctity of human life
from the moment of conception until natural death,
and bear witness against all who offend their Creator
by inflicting death upon innocent, eternal beings
whom He has made in His own image.**

SCOPE and FOCUS
I. CONVICTIONS
II. PRETEXTS
III. MANDATE
IV. LEGACY
V. ABORTIVE LINKS
VI. DILEMMA
VII. DESTINY
The Hell Objection
Repentance, Dedication
Witness & Activism
Proclamation
Banner
Declaration of Dependence
Final Word

1 Trueblood, *The Incendiary Fellowship*, 31.

2 Whitehead, *The Second American Revolution*, 179.

3 Foreman, 98.

4 Foreman, 132.

5 Benedict, *The Rule of St. Benedict*, 45.

6 Belloc, in Grant, *Third Time Around*, 139.

7 Bandow, *Beyond Good Intentions: A Biblical View of Politics*, 222.

8 *Press*, 2-20-97, A1.

9 Scheidler, 100.

• "Precious Feet"™ the International Pro-Life Symbol. These feet are the exact size and shape of an unborn baby's feet at ten weeks after conception. © 1979 V. Evers. Heritage House '76, Inc., 919 S. Main St. Snowflake, AZ 85937. $2.50 per pin, includes tax and shipping; specify goldtone or silvertone. Phone for quantity discounts: 1-800-858-3040.

10 Jacques Semelin, *Unarmed Against Hitler: Civilian Resistance in Europe, 1939-1943*, 36.

2. Banner

Doug Bandow asks, "If there are really forty-eight million evangelical Christians, a commonly-cited figure, then why is the moral fiber of the nation so badly torn? A group representing more than one-fifth of the entire population is a large amount of salt. That much seasoning, used properly, should flavor every part of society. In combating declining moral values, Christians need to first look to their personal interaction with those around them."[7]

One individual can have a monumental impact; remember the tenacity and courage of the lone, unarmed student who stood his ground in defiance of the tanks in Tiananmen Square in 1989.[8]

Joseph Scheidler believes, "It is important for us to use every means at our disposal to bring the issue of abortion to public attention." He says "The use of buttons, pins, and the Precious Feet can be excellent devices for creating interest. People sometimes wonder what the feet represent. You explain that this is the size 'your feet' were when you were ten weeks old in the womb."[9]

While Hitler was forcing Jews to wear identifications such as the Star of David, it became a practice among non-Jewish citizens in various places to wear signs that identified them as opposing the Nazis. "These signs of dissidence were expressed publicly through codes of signs and symbols... The Dutch wore white carnations in their buttonholes as a sign of their attachment to the Crown. Norwegians wore staples inside their jackets as a sign of resistance. Beyond national differences, the letter 'V' for victory appeared all over Europe... Different cultural signs thus progressively made up a language of distinctions, a way of saying 'no' to the values of the occupier and his collaborators and of maintaining a certain loyalty toward themselves."[10]

A few years ago, before bumper stickers became embarrassing [or whatever caused them to effectively disappear], our automobiles were projecting a better pro-life witness than we were in our face-to-face dealings with others. Here is the hard truth: the government has taken decisive steps to eliminate from the public culture 98% of the possible acknowledgment of God or opportunity for Christian witnessing, but we have *given away* the last two percent!

If you are wearing the Precious Feet, and talking about them regularly, then keep doing so. If you have a dramatically pro-life button, piece of jewelry or tattoo [just kidding!] that is working, keep using it. But if you do not, we have a pro-life emblem to propose.

If you look up "flag" in the *World Book* encyclopedia, you will be reminded that the inverted American flag is a sign of emergency, a call for help in a situation of grave peril. When viewed through a telescope at sea, the inverted flag would summon the viewer to assist in fighting pirates or to rescue people from a sinking ship.

Several years ago we fashioned a black armband that displayed an inverted U.S. flag with "ABORTION" embroidered diagonally across the front of the flag. After a few weeks the armband was set aside in favor of removable stickers, the same upside-down flag with "ABORTION" across the front, worn on the chest, shoulder-high, or on the front of a baseball cap. The flag symbol was clearly a statement about abortion, and when others asked for clarification or displayed a puzzled look, we took the opportunity to express a quick pro-life testimony, usually explaining the "grave peril" message of the upside-down flag. It would be exciting to shop in a community where one-tenth [or half!] of the people we encountered were wearing an "ABORTION (grave danger to America)" pin!

In 1997 we commissioned the creation of a metal pin with a tie tack fitting, which has proven to be effective, memorable and durable. It is our intent to surrender any copyright/trademark claims to this *symbol* so that it can become immediately a part of the public domain, for any and all to use, but "owned" or "regulated" by none. [See the page opposite the title page for information on ordering this pin or copies of *Orphans in Babylon* from Turnstyle Ministries.]

Our goal is not to become a marketer of pins but rather to encourage every pro-life Christian to become a walking, visible testimony to the sanctity of human life. If your new inspiration/innovation works for you, please tell us about it!

3. Declaration of Dependence Upon God

It is the opinion of John Whitehead that, "As we face the massive machine of government, we are at a very similar position to that of the colonists who congregated to declare their independence from Great Britain in 1776."[1]

We are convinced that our situation is even more desperate than theirs was, although we would think it premature to begin discussing revolution. But a **Declaration** is an absolute necessity. Because we so strongly agree with Whitehead, *Orphans in Babylon* offers a form which, with simple modification, can become your personalized "**Declaration of Dependence Upon God**." It is intended to be sent to every pro-life Christian's elected representatives and to the people who shape policy and opinions in her/his community. Until we have informed the persons in positions of responsibility – in a direct and concise manner – the exact nature of our convictions, we have no right to complain about any actions to the contrary.

You will notice that the two-sided form provided is designed to be photocopied, folded twice, stamped and mailed to the people listed. **Revise the list** for the equivalent people according to where you live, and be sure to mask out the **signature** and **return address**, replacing those with your own, to totally personalize the document **before** making multiple copies.

Before even discussing the potential impact these documents might have on the recipients, it must be noted that the first benefit to be derived is certain and automatic: the sender instantly becomes an on-record combatant in the culture war, on God's side! How we view ourselves, as *authentic* for instance, is at least as significant as how others perceive us. If you want to rephrase the "Declaration" itself, we encourage you to do so. The essential thing is that receiving such a document puts people in responsible positions on notice that you take your faith and your citizenship seriously, and that they should too.

C. Final Word

"Do you see what I see?" from the great Christmas song, expresses the prayer of the researcher of *Orphans in Babylon*. During my five months in Atlanta's finest jail in 1990, God illuminated 500 Scripture passages which became the spiritual basis of this work [*see pages 302-311*]. The nucleus of the research was contained in coursework taken pursuant to master's degrees earned at Simon Greenleaf University [now Trinity Law School] and at Trinity Graduate School.

The majority of the research was made possible by the extensive and unique holdings of the Human Rights Library and the Masters [Christian Apologetics] Library at Simon Greenleaf. "Turnstyle" is a tentmaking ministry; my day job is as a missionary to seventh grade History/English students in a Southern California public school.

My prayer is that you will do four things:

1. Join a congregation, or build a congregation that boldly identifies itself as a bunch of pro-life, pro-family culture-war fanatics [see page 282].
2. Make a distinctive pro-life/pro-family/pro-God badge or emblem the most basic component of your wardrobe... and talk about it like you pray: without ceasing [see the page opposite the title page].
3. Paper your world with copies of your personalized "Declaration of Dependence Upon God" [see pages 285-6].
4. Undertake, without reservation or doubt, whatever ministry God places in your heart, doing all to His glory.

Martin Luther said:

If I profess with the loudest voice and clearest exposition every portion of the truth of God except precisely that little point which the world and the devil are at that moment attacking, I am not confessing Christ, no matter how loudly I may be professing Christ. Where the battle rages, there the loyalty of the soldier is proved, and to be steady on all the battlefields besides is mere flight and disgrace if he flinches at that point."[2]

F. LaGard Smith gets the last word [before God takes over *big time*]: "No longer do you and I have the luxury of avoiding the conflict. Our culture is being ravaged by a secularist philosophy of choice that threatens to destroy, not only the babies in the womb, but our dignity as human beings. Without overstating the case in the least, moral choice is at risk. The very survival of our nation is at stake... For each of us, the moment has come. It's time to decide."[3]

SCOPE and FOCUS
I. CONVICTIONS
II. PRETEXTS
III. MANDATE
IV. LEGACY
V. ABORTIVE LINKS
VI. DILEMMA
VII. DESTINY
The Hell Objection
Repentance, Dedication
Witness & Activism
Proclamation
Banner
Declaration of Dependence
Final Word

1 Whitehead, *The Second American Revolution*, 180.

2 Martin Luther, in Alcorn, *Is Rescuing Right?*, 234.

3 F. LaGard Smith, *When Choice Becomes God*, 271.

Declaration of Dependence

upon

GOD's RULES

Here I Take My Stand:

- ❑ LIFE and the universe were CREATED by God.
- ❑ ABORTION is murder of a human child.
- ❑ Government-FUNDED abortions make me an accomplice.
- ❑ HOMOSEXUALITY is an addiction, like alcoholism;
  it needs correction, not protection.
- ❑ The Constitution guards RELIGIOUS EXPRESSION
  from government interference;
  it does not exclude religion from public places,
  nor politics from the pulpit.
- ❑ VIRGINITY & CHASTITY are commendable.
- ❑ FIDELITY should be expected of husbands and wives.
- ❑ VIOLENCE is not entertaining.

____

Signature

TURNSTYLE MINISTRIES
Post Office Box 207
Sun City, CA 92586

THE SANDBOX

A Christian at a fast food lunch stop, finding no other seat available, sat outside in the children's play area. The Christian vaguely noted happy youngsters scrambling all over the other equipment, but the sandbox was empty.

No sooner had that thought emerged when a harried mom plopped a blinking toddler into the sand and rushed back inside.... to buy their lunch, the Christian supposed.

Quite soon came the realization that the child had disappeared... and the parent had, too. Only then did the Christian read the sign overhead: ***"Pro-Choice Sandbox..."***

The Supreme Court had ruled that prior to "viability," now interpreted as graduation in the top half of one's kindergarten class, one's parent may terminate the non-viable pre-schooler in any convenient manner. ***"...As a public service, this restaurant is proud to offer its patrons this Pro-Choice Quicksand Sandbox."***

When another mother-with-child approaches, the Christian should:

a. Write a letter to Congress
b. Circulate a petition
c. Hold up a picket sign
d. Other: ________________
e. ALL of the above

SUGGESTIONS FOR YOUR PRAYERFUL CONSIDERATION

1) REPLACE the signature and return address with your own.
2) Write in current names and addresses for YOUR government officials, etc.
3) PAY to PHOTOCOPY 100 or more, two-sided (recipients *will* do this too!).
4) Hand-address and MAIL one to each of the names listed.
5) PERSONALLY DELIVER copies to your pastor, family members, friends, co-workers and neighbors.

AUG.'98, for: Sun City , CA 92586 ***and/or*** **Menifee, CA 92584**

President Bill (Hillary too) Clinton, 1600 Pennsylvania Ave.,Wash.D.C. 20500

U.S.Supreme Court, 1 First St. N.E., Wash. D.C. 20543.
Chief Justice William H. Rehnquist; Justices David Souter, Clarence Thomas, Ruth Bader-Ginsburg, Stephen G. Breyer, John Paul Stevens, Anthony Kennedy, Sandra Day O'Connor, Antonian Scalia

Senators Barbara Boxer **and** Diane Feinstein, Hart Ofc. Bldg. Wash.D.C. 20510
Congresswoman Mary Bono, 1600 W. Florida Avenue #306, Hemet, CA 92544

ABC-TV, 7 Lincoln Square, New York, NY, 10023
CBS-TV, 524 West 57th Street, New York, NY 10019
NBC-TV, 30 Rockefeller Plaza, New York, NY 10020
TBS-TV, 1050 Techwood Drive NW, Atlanta, GA 30318

Governor Pete Wilson, State Capitol, Sacramento, CA 95814
State Senator Raymond Haynes, 6840 Indiana Ave #275, Riverside, CA 92506
Assemblyman Bruce Thompson, 27555 Ynez Rd. #205, Temecula, CA 92591

County Supervisor Jim Venable, P.O. Box 1486, Riverside, CA 92502-1486

Mayor (N/A)
City Council (N/A)

Perris Union **H.S.District**, 1151 N. A St., Perris, CA 92570-1909
Superintendent Dennis D. Murray; Board President Nan E. Sanders; Bd.Mbrs. Joe Daugherty, John Denver, Robert Cooley, DeWitt Ruth

Menifee Union **School Dist.**,30205 Menifee Rd., Menifee, CA 92584
Superintendent Dr. Gary Cringan; Board Chmn. Robert O'Donnell; Board Members Victor Giardinelli, Patricia Hanson, Chester Morrison, Elaine Rowen

School principal and teachers...

L.A. *Times* **Editor**, Times-Mirror Square, Los Angeles, CA 90053
Press-Enterprise Editor, P.O.Box 792, Riverside, CA 92502
Sun City & Menifee Valley *News*, 27070 Sun City Blvd., Sun City, CA 92586
The *Californian* Editor, 27450 Ynez Road, Temecula, CA 92591
Rancho *News* Editor, 27645 Jefferson Ave., Temecula, CA 92590

WORKS CITED

A

Abel, Reuben. Man is the Measure: A Cordial Invitation to the Central Problems of Philosophy. New York: The Free Press, 1976.

Ackad, Louise. Declaring the Human Rights of the Preborn Child, a master's thesis, 1997. Alliance for Life International, Box 7375, Laguna Niguel, CA 92607.

Aeschliman, Gordon. Global Trends: Ten Changes Affecting Christians Everywhere. Downers Grove, Ill.: InterVarsity, 1990.

Alcorn, Randy C. Does the Birth Control Pill Cause Abortions? Eternal Perspective Ministries, 2229 East Burnside #23, Gresham, OR 97080. (503) 663-6481. 1997. E-mail: ralcorn@epm.org Web site: http:/www.epm.org/~ralcorn

---. Is Rescuing Right? Breaking the Law to Save the Unborn. Downers Grove, Ill.: InterVarsity Press, 1990.

---. Pro-life Answers to ProChoice Arguments. Sisters, Ore.: Multnomah Press, 1992.

Alexander, Shana. Women's Legal Rights, State-by-State Guide to. Los Angeles: Wollstonecraft, 1975.

Alston, Philip. "The Unborn Child and Abortion Under the Draft Convention on the Rights of the Child." Human Rights Quarterly 12 [1990]: 156-178.

Altherr, Thomas L. Precreation or Pleasure?: Sexual Attitudes in American History. Malabar, Fla.: Robert E. Krieger, 1983.

Amnesty International. "The Death Penalty: Cruel & Inhuman Punishment" pamphlet. 322 Eighth Ave., New York, NY 10001.

Anderson, J. Kerby, ed. Living Ethically in the '90s. Wheaton, Ill.: Victor Books, 1990.

Anderson, Norman. Issues of Life & Death: Abortion, Birth Control, Capital Punishment, Euthanasia. Downers Grove, Ill.: InterVarsity Press, 1976.

Andrusko, Dave, ed. To Rescue the Future: The Pro-Life Movement in the 1980s. Harrison, N.Y.: Life Cycle Books, 1983.

Ankerberg, John and John Weldon. When Does Life Begin? And 39 Other Tough Questions about Abortion. Brentwood, Tenn.: Wolgemuth & Hyatt, 1989.

Atkinson, James. Church & State Under God. Oxford: Latimer House, 1982.

Audi, Robert, and Nicholas Wolterstorff. Religion in the Public Square: The Place of Religious Convictions in Political Debate. Lanham, Md.: Rowman & Littlefield, 1997.

Augenstein, Leroy. Come, Let Us Play God. New York: Harper & Row, 1969.

Augustine, Saint. The Confessions of St. Augustine, trans. by John K. Ryan. New York: Doubleday, [354-430 A.D.] 1960.

B

Bahm, Archie J. Why Be Moral? Albuquerque, N.M.: World Books, 1992.

Ball, William Bentley, ed. In Search of a National Morality: A Manifesto for Evangelicals and Catholics. Grand Rapids, Mich.: Baker Book House, 1992.

Bandow, Doug. Beyond Good Intentions: A Biblical View of Politics. Westchester, Ill.: Crossway Books, 1988.

Barclay, William. Ethics in a Permissive Society. New York: Harper & Row, 1971.

Batchelor, Edward, Jr. Abortion: The Moral Issues. New York: Pilgrim, 1982.

Beach, Waldo. Christian Ethics in the Protestant Tradition. Atlanta: John Knox, 1988. Author is clearly a "pro-choice Christian."

Beckwith, Francis J. Politically Correct Death: Answering the Arguments for Abortion Rights. Grand Rapids, Mich.: Baker Books, 1993.

---, ed. Do the Right Thing: A Philosophical Dialogue on the Moral and Social Issues of Our Time. Boston: Jones and Bartlett, 1996.

Benedict, Saint. The Rule of St. Benedict, trans. by Anthony C. Meisel and M.L. del Mastro. New York: Doubleday, 1975.

Berger, Brigitte and Peter L. Berger. The War Over the Family: Capturing the Middle Ground. Garden City, N.Y.: Anchor Press, 1983.

Betsworth, Roger G. Social Ethics: An Examination of American Moral Traditions. Louisville, Ky.: Westminster/John Knox Press, 1990.

Bienenfeld, F.R. Rediscovery of Justice. London: George Allen & Unwin, 1947.

Black, Jonathan, ed. Radical Lawyers: Their Role in the Movement and in the Courts. New York: Avon, 1971.

Black Heritage Library Collection. The Dred Scott Case: Three Volumes in One. Plainview, N.Y.: Books for Libraries Press, 1973.

Bonhoeffer, Dietrich. Ethics, ed. by Eberhard Bethge. New York: Macmillan, 1955.

Bopp, James, Jr., ed. Restoring the Right to Life: The Human Life Amendment. Provo, Utah: Brigham Young UP, 1984.

Bork, Robert H. Slouching Towards Gomorrah: Modern Liberalism and American Decline. New York: HarperCollins, 1996.

Braidfoot, Larry. The Bible and America. Nashville, Tenn.: Broadman Press, 1983.

Braine, David. Medical Ethics and Human Life. Old Aberdeen, Great Britain: Palladio Press, 1982.

Braun, Michael and George Alan Rekers. The Christian in an Age of Sexual Eclipse. Wheaton, Ill.: Tyndale House, 1981.

Bray, Michael. A Time to Kill. Portland, Ore.: Advocates for Life Publications, 1994.

Brown, David. Choices: Ethics and the Christian. Oxford: Basil Blackwell, 1983.

Brown, Harold O.J. The Sensate Culture. Dallas: Word, 1996.

Brunner, Emil. The Divine Imperative: A Study in Christian Ethics, trans. by Olive Wyon. London: Lutterworth, 1937.

Buergenthal, Thomas. International Human Rights, In a Nutshell. Second Edition. St. Paul, Minn.: West, 1995.

Butler, J. Douglas and David F. Walbert, eds. Abortion, Medicine, and the Law. Third Edition. New York: Facts on File Publications, 1986.

C

California ProLife. California ProLife Council, 2306 J St., Suite 200, Sacramento, CA 95816.

Carr, Steven A. and Franklin A. Meyer. Celebrate Life: Hope for a Culture Preoccupied with Death. Brentwood, Tenn.: Wolgemuth & Hyatt, 1990.

Chesterton, Gilbert K. What's Wrong with the World. New York: Dodd, Mead, 1910.

Christian Center for Bio-Ethics. "Keeping The Promise to Protect Your Family: Would You Gamble with the Life of Your Child?" pamphlet. Christian Center for Bio-Ethics, Portland, OR 97213-13656.

Christian Times newspaper, Southern California, Orange Co./LA Co. edition. P.O. Box 2606, El Cajon, CA 92021.

Citizen. Focus on the Family, P.O. Box 35500, Colorado Springs, CO 80935-3550.

Clinebell, Howard. Mental Health Through Christian Community. 1960s. Out of print.

Clouse, Robert G., et. al., eds. Protest and Politics: Christianity and Contemporary Affairs. Greenwood, S.C.: Attic Press, 1968.

Clowes, Brian. Pro-Life Activist's Encyclopedia. Stafford, Va.: American Life League, 1993.

Colson, Charles, with Ellen Santilli Vaughn. Kingdoms in Conflict. New York: William Morrow, 1987.

Comay, Joan, and Ronald Brownrigg. Who's Who in the Bible: Two Volumes in One. New York: Wings Books, 1971.

Cotham, Perry C., ed. Christian Social Ethics. Grand Rapids, Mich.: Baker Book House, 1979.

Cottrell, Jack. Tough Questions - Biblical Answers. Joplin, Mo.: College Press, 1985.

Couple to Couple League. P.O. Box 111184, Cincinnati, OH 45211-1184, E-mail: 73311.256@Compuserve.com Web site: http://206.185.7.88/ccl/index.html

Crutcher, Mark. Access: The Key to Pro-Life Victory. Denton, Texas: Life Dynamics, 1998.

---. Lime 5: Exploited by Choice. Denton, Texas: Life Dynamics, 1996.

D

Davis, John Jefferson. Abortion and the Christian: What Every Believer Should Know. Phillipsburg, N.J.: Presbyterian and Reformed Publishing Company, 1984.

Dayton, Donald W. Discovering an Evangelical Heritage. Peabody, Mass.: Hendrickson, 1976.

deParrie, Paul. The Rescuers: The Gripping Stories of Ordinary People Who Risked their Reputations and Freedom to Save Babies from Abortion. Brentwood, Tenn.: Wolgemuth & Hyatt, 1989.

---. Romanced to Death: The Sexual Seduction of American Culture. Brentwood, Tenn.: Wolgemuth & Hyatt, 1989.

Dickens, Bernard M. Abortion and the Law. Bristol, England: Macgibbon & Kee, 1966.

Dobson, James. Family Under Fire. Kansas City, Mo.: Beacon Hill Press, 1976.

Doner, Colonel V. The Samaritan Strategy: A New Agenda for Christian Activism. Brentwood, Tenn.: Wolgemuth & Hyatt, 1988.

Downs, Robert B. Books that Changed the World. New York: New American, 1956.

Drakeford, John W. The Great Sex Swindle. Nashville, Tenn.: Broadman Press, 1966.

Draper, James T. and Forrest E. Watson. If the Foundations be Destroyed. Nashville, Tenn.: Thomas Nelson, 1984.

DuBois, W.E.B. The Suppression of the African Slave Trade to the United States of America, 1638-1870. New York: Dover, 1970.

Durant, Will and Ariel. The Lessons of History. New York: Simon and Schuster, 1968.

Duster, Troy. The Legislation of Morality: Law, Drugs, and Moral Judgment. New York: The Free Press, 1970.

E

Eidsmoe, John. God and Caesar: Biblical Faith and Political Action. Westchester, Ill.: Crossway Books, 1984.

Evans, Debra. Without Moral Limits: Women, Reproduction, and the New Medical Technology. Westchester, Ill.: Crossway Books, 1989.

Everett, Carol with Jack Shaw. The Scarlet Lady: Confessions of a Successful Abortionist. Brentwood, Tenn.: Wolgemuth & Hyatt, 1991.

F

Falwell, Jerry. Listen, America! Garden City, N.Y.: Doubleday, 1980.

Family News From Dr. James Dobson, newsletter. Focus on the Family, Colorado Springs, CO 80995.

Fletcher, Joseph. Situation Ethics: The New Morality. Philadelphia: Westminster Press, 1966.

Floyd, Mary K. Abortion Bibliography for 1972. Troy, N.Y.: Whitston Publishing, 1973. Lists over 1150 articles on abortion in U.S. periodicals in 1972.

Focus on the Family. Citizen. Colorado Springs, CO 80935.

Foreman, Joseph Lapsley. Shattering the Darkness: The Crisis of the Cross in the Church Today. Montreat, N.C.: The Cooling Spring Press, 1992.

Fortas, Abe. Concerning Dissent and Civil Disobedience. New York: Signet Books, 1968.

Fowler, Richard A. and H. Wayne House. The Christian Confronts His Culture. Chicago: Moody, 1983.

Francke, Linda Bird. The Ambivalence of Abortion. New York: Random House, 1978.

G

Gardner, R.F.R. Abortion: The Personal Dilemma. A Christian Gynaecologist Examines the Medical, Social and Spiritual Issues. Grand Rapids, Mich.: Eerdmans, 1972.

Garton, Jean Staker. Who Broke the Baby? A Brilliant Disclosure of What the Abortion Slogans Really Mean. Minneapolis, Minn.: Bethany, 1979.

Geisler, Norman L. Christian Ethics. Grand Rapids, Mich.: Baker Book House, 1989.

---. Ethics: Alternatives and Issues. Grand Rapids, Mich.: Zondervan, 1971.

---. Is Man the Measure: An Evaluation of Contemporary Humanism. Grand Rapids, Mich.: Baker Book House, 1983.

---, et. al. Worlds Apart: A Handbook on World Views. Grand Rapids, Mich.: Baker Book House, 1989.

GoodNews newsletter. American Life League, P.O. Box 1350, Stafford, VA 22555.

Gordon, Cyrus H. and Gary A. Rendsburg. The Bible and the Ancient Near East. Fourth Edition. New York: W.W. Norton, 1997.

Gorman, Michael J. Abortion & the Early Church: Christian, Jewish & Pagan Attitudes in the Greco-Roman World. Downers Grove, Ill.: InterVarsity, 1982.

Grant, George. Grand Illusions: The Legacy of Planned Parenthood. Brentwood, Tenn.: Wolgemuth, 1988.

---. Third Time Around: A History of the Pro-Life Movement from the First Century to the Present. Brentwood, Tenn.: Wolgemuth & Hyatt, 1991.

Green, Harvey. The Uncertainty of Everyday Life, 1915-1945. New York: HarperCollins Publishers, 1992.

Gutman, Israel, ed. Encyclopedia of the Holocaust. New York: Macmillan, 1990.

H

Haffner, Al. The High Cost of Free Love. San Bernardino, CA: Here's Life Publishers, 1989.

Harper, T.W. "Give the Winds a Voice," Christianity Today, 6-21-68, 48.

Hart, Michael H. The 100: A Ranking of the Most Influential Persons in History. New York: A&W Publishers, 1978.

Hatcher, Robert A., et. al. Emergency Contraception: The Nation's Best-Kept Secret. Atlanta: Bridging the Gap Communications, 1995.

Hauerwas, Stanley. God, Medicine, and Suffering. Grand Rapids, Mich.: Eerdmans, 1990.

---. Resident Aliens: Life in the Christian Colony. Nashville: Abingdon, 1989.

"Help From the Unborn." Time magazine. 1-12-87, 62.

Hilgers, Thomas W., et. al. Abortion and Social Justice. New York: Sheed & Ward, 1972.

---, et. al., eds. New Perspectives on Human Abortion. Frederick, Md.: University Publications of America, 1981.

Hoffmeier, James K., ed. Abortion: A Christian Understanding and Response. Grand Rapids, Mich.: Baker Book House, 1987.

Horan, Dennis J., et. al. Abortion and the Constitution: Reversing Roe v. Wade Through the Courts. Washington, D.C.: Georgetown University Press, 1987.

---. Infanticide and the Handicapped Newborn. Provo, Utah: Brigham Young University Press, 1982.

Horn, Carl, ed. Whose Values? The Battle for Morality in Pluralistic America. Ann Arbor, Mich.: Servant Books, 1985.

Howard-Johnston, Xenia, and Michael Bourdeaux. Aida of Leningrad: The Story of Aida Skripnikova. Reading, Berkshire, England: Gateway Outreach, 1972.

Huels, John M. The Pastoral Companion: A Canon Law Handbook for Catholic Ministry. Chicago: The Franciscan Herald Press, 1986.

Hunt, Robert, and John Arras. Ethical Issues in Modern Medicine. Palo Alto, Calif.: Mayfield Publishing, 1977.

Hunter, James Davison. Culture Wars: The Struggle to Define America. New York: HarperCollins, 1991.

Huse, Scott M. The Collapse of Evolution. Grand Rapids, Mich.: Baker Book House, 1983.

Hutchison, William R. American Protestant Thought in the Liberal Era. Lanham, Md.: University Press of America, 1968.

Hyde, Henry J. For Every Idle Silence. Ann Arbor, Mich.: Servant Books, 1985.

J

Jackson, Robert H. The Case Against the Nazi War Criminals. New York: Alfred A. Knopf, 1946.

Jacobs, Thomas A., ed. Legal Directory of Children's Rights. Volume 1 [Federal Statutes]. Frederick, Maryland: University Publications of America, 1985.

Jameson, J. Franklin. The American Revolution Considered as a Social Movement. Princeton: Princeton University Press, 1926, reprinted 1967.

Jersild, Paul T. and Dale A. Johnson, eds. Moral Issues & Christian Response. Fort Worth, Texas: Harcourt Brace College Publishers, 1993.

Johnson, Phillip E. Reason in the Balance: The Case Against Naturalism in Science, Law & Education. Downers Grove, Ill.: InterVarsity Press, 1995.

Jonas, Hans, et. al. Ethical Aspects of Experimentation with Human Subjects. Issued as Vol. 98, No. 2, of the Procedings of the American Academy of Arts and Sciences, Spring 1969.

Jones, D. Gareth. Brave New People: Ethical Issues at the Commencement of Life. Downers Grove, Ill.: InterVarsity Press, 1984.

Jorgenson, Dale A. Christianity and Humanism. Joplin, Mo.: College Press Publishing, 1983.

"Journey of August King." Video movie by Miramax Films. Portrays clash over Fugitive Slave laws.

K

Kamm, F.M. Creation and Abortion: A Study in Moral and Legal Philosophy. New York: Oxford University Press, 1992.

Kilner, John F. Life on the Line: Ethics, Aging, Ending Patients' Lives, and Allocating Vital Resources. Grand Rapids, Mich.: Eerdmans, 1992.

--- and Nigel M. de S. Cameron and David L. Schiedermayer, eds. Bioethics and the Future of Medicine: A Christian Appraisal. Grand Rapids, Mich.: Eerdmans, 1995.

Kindregan, Charles P. Abortion, the Law, and Defective Children. Washington/Cleveland: Corpus Books, 1969.

King, Donald B. Legal Aspects of the Civil Rights Movement. Detroit: Wayne State University Press, 1965.

Klotz, John W. A Christian View of Abortion. St.Louis: Concordia, 1973.

Kohl, Marvin. Infanticide and the Value of Life. Buffalo, N.Y.: Prometheus, 1978.

Koop, C. Everett. The Right to Live; the Right to Die. Wheaton, Ill.: Tyndale House, 1976.

Koukl, Gregory. Stand to Reason radio broadcast transcripts. 2420 Pacific Coast Highway, Hermosa Beach, CA 90254. 1-800-2-REASON.

L

Lee, Robert and Martin E. Marty, eds. Religion and Social Conflict. New York: Oxford UP, 1964.

Lefcourt, Carol H. Women and the Law. New York: Clark Boardman, 1987.

Life Advocate magazine. Box 13656, Portland, OR 97213. Advocates for Life. * Web site: http://www.spiritone.com/~lifeadvo

**Note separate listing for:* Alcorn, Randy C. Does the Birth Control Pill Cause Abortions?

Lotz, David, et. al. Altered Landscapes: Christianity in America, 1935-1985. Grand Rapids, Mich.: Eerdmans, 1989.

Luker, Kristin. Taking Chances: Abortion and the Decision Not to Contracept. Berkeley, Calif.: University of California Press, 1975.

Lutzer, Erwin W. The Morality Gap: An Evangelical Response to Situation Ethics. Chicago: Moody, 1972.

M

Maddoux, Marlin. Free Speech or Propaganda? How the Media Distorts the Truth. Nashville: Thomas Nelson, 1990.

Mains, David R. The Rise of the Religion of Anti-Christ-ism. Grand Rapids, Mich.: Zondervan, 1985.

Mall, David. In Good Conscience: Abortion and Moral Necessity. Libertyville, Ill.: Kairos Books, 1982.

---, and Walter F. Watts. The Psychological Aspects of Abortion. Washington, D.C.: University Publications of America, 1979.

Mandela, Nelson. Long Walk to Freedom: The Autobiography of Nelson Mandela. Boston: Little, Brown, 1994.

Marshall, Robert and Charles Donovan. Blessed are the Barren: The Social Policy of Planned Parenthood. San Francisco: Ignatius Press, 1991.

May, William E. Human Existence, Medicine and Ethics: Reflections on Human Life. Chicago: Franciscan Herald Press, 1977.

Mellon, Matthew T. Early American Views on Negro Slavery: From the Letters and Papers of the Founders of the Republic. New York: Bergman, 1934 and 1969.

Miller, Keith. A Taste of New Wine. 1960s. Out of print.

Mnookin, Robert H. In the Interest of Children: Advocacy, Law, Reform, and Public Policy. New York: W.H. Freeman, 1985.

Mohr, James C. Abortion in America: The Origins and Evolution of National Policy, 1800-1900. New York: Oxford University Press, 1978.

Montgomery, John Warwick. "The Rights of the Unborn Children." The Simon Greenleaf Law Review. Vol. 5 [1985-1986], 65-67. Anaheim, Calif.: The Simon Greenleaf School of Law.

Moreland, J.P. and Norman L. Geisler. The Life and Death Debate: Moral Issues of Our Time. New York: Greenwood Press, 1990.

Mowrer, O. Hobart,. Crisis in Psychiatry and Religion. 1960s. Out of print.

N

Naisbitt, John. Megatrends: Ten New Directions Transforming Our Lives. New York: Warner Books, 1982.

---. Megatrends 2000: Ten New Directions for the 1990s. New York: Avon Books, 1990.

Nathanson, Bernard with Richard N. Ostling. Aborting America. Garden City, N.Y.: Doubleday, 1979.

National Geographic Society. The Incredible Machine, Washington D.C.: National Geographic Society, 1986.

Newsweek. 251 West 57th Street, New York, NY 10019-1894.

Newsweek Extra. "Two Thousand, A New Millennium: The Power of Invention." Winter 1997-98.

Noonan, John T., Jr., ed. The Morality of Abortion. Cambridge, Mass.: Harvard UP, 1970.

North, Gary. Backward, Christian Soldiers? An Action Manual for Christian Reconstruction. Tyler, Texas: Institute for Christian Economics, 1984.

O

Olasky, Marvin. Abortion Rites: A Social History of Abortion in America. Wheaton, Ill.: Crossway Books, 1992.

Olasky, Susan and Marvin Olasky. More Than Kindness: A Compassionate Approach to Crisis Childbearing. Wheaton, Ill.: Crossway Books, 1990.

Orr, Robert D., et. al. Life & Death Decisions: Help in Making Tough Choices About Bioethical Issues. Colorado Springs, Colo.: NavPress, 1990.

Osborne, Kenan B. The Christian Sacraments of Initiation: Baptism, Confirmation, Eucharist. New York: Paulist Press, 1987.

P

Patterson, David and Richard D. Ryder, eds. Animals' Rights - A Symposium. London: Centaur Press, 1979.

Paul Hill Speaks. Issue No. 1, June 1997. Reformation Press, 2927 Tarragon Lane, Bowie, MD 20715.

Pelt, John. The Soul, the Pill and the Fetus. Philadelphia: Dorrance, 1973.

Perrett, Geoffrey. America in the Twenties: A History. New York: Simon and Schuster, 1982.

Perry, Michael J. The Constitution, the Courts, and Human Rights: An Inquiry into the Legitimacy of Constitutional Policymaking by the Judiciary. New Haven, Connecticut: Yale University Press, 1982.

Pilpel, Harriet F. and Kenneth P. Norwick. "When Should Abortion be Legal?" pamphlet. New York: Public Affairs, 1969.

Powell, John, S.J. Abortion: the Silent Holocaust. Allen, Texas: Argus Communications, 1981.

Press-Enterprise newspaper. 3512 Fourteenth Street, Riverside, CA 92501.

Prisoners of Christ, [monthly listing of pro-life prisoners in jail for attempting to protect the unborn] Prisoners of Christ, Box 583, Skyforest, CA 92385-0583.

Purcell, William. Martyrs of Our Time. St. Louis, Mo.: CBP Press, 1985.

Q

Quinn, Daniel. Ishmael: an Adventure of the Mind and Spirit. New York: Bantam/Turner, 1992.

R

Raines, Robert. New Life in the Church. 1960s. Out of print.

---. Reshaping the Christian Life. 1960s. Out of print.

---. The Secular Congregation. 1960s. Out of print.

Ramey, Cathy. In Defense of Others: A Biblical Analysis and Apologetic on the Use of Force to Save Lives. Portland, Ore.: Advocates for Life, 1995.

Ramsey, Paul. Ethics at the Edges of Life: Medical and Legal Intersections. New Haven: Yale University Press, 1978.

---. The Ethics of Fetal Research. New Haven: Yale University Press, 1975.

Reagan, Ronald. Abortion and the Conscience of the Nation. Nashville: Thomas Nelson, 1984.

Reardon, David C. Aborted Women: Silent No More. Westchester, Ill.: Crossway Books, 1987.

Reiser, Stanley Joel, et.al. Ethics in Medicine: Historical Perspectives and Contemporary Concerns. Cambridge: Massachusetts Institute of Technology Press, 1977.

"Rescue of Danish Jewry 1943-1993" display. Simon Wiesenthal Center, Los Angeles, Calif.

Roberts, Alexander, et. al., ed. The Ante-Nicene Fathers, vol. I, Justin Martyr's Apology; vol. III, Tertullian's Apology; vol. IV, Origen's De Principiis. Grand Rapids, Mich.: Eerdmans, 1989.

Roche, George Charles, III. The Bewildered Society. Hillsdale, Mich.: Hillsdale College, 1974.

Rosen, Harold, ed. Abortion in America: Medical, Psychiatric, Legal, Anthropological, and Religious Considerations. Boston: Beacon Press, 1954 & 1967.

Rosenberger, Margaret, compiled by. Issues in Focus: Gaining a Clear Biblical Perspective on the Complex Issues of Our Time. Ventura, Calif.: Regal Books, 1989.

S

Salisbury, Harrison E., ed. Vietnam Reconsidered: Lessons from a War. New York: Harper Torchbooks, 1984.

Santayana, George. Winds of Doctrine. 1960s. Out of print.

Schaeffer, Franky. A Time for Anger: The Myth of Neutrality. Westchester, Ill.: Crossway Books, 1982.

Scheidler, Joseph M. Closed: 99 Ways to Stop Abortion. Westchester, Ill.: Crossway Books, 1985.

Schlafly, Phyllis. The Power of the Positive Woman. New Rochelle, N.Y.: Arlington House, 1977.

Schlesinger, Stephen, and Stephen Kinzer. Bitter Fruit: The Untold Story of the American Coup in Guatemala. New York: Anchor Press, 1982.

Schlossberg, Herbert. Idols for Destruction: Christian Faith and Its Confrontation with American Society. Nashville: Thomas Nelson, 1983.

Scudder, C.W., ed. Crises in Morality. Nashville: Broadman Press, 1964.

Semelin, Jacques. Unarmed Against Hitler: Civilian Resistance in Europe, 1939-1943, trans. by Suzan Husserl-Kapit. Westport, Ct.: Praeger, 1993.

Shaw, Russel. Abortion on Trial. London: Robert Hale, 1968.

Sherlock, Richard. Preserving Life: Public Policy and the Life Not Worth Living. Chicago: Loyola UP, 1987.

"Should Medicine Use the Unborn?" Newsweek, 9-14-87, 63.

Showers, Renald E. What on Earth is God Doing? Satan's Conflict with God. Neptune, N.J.: Loizeaux Brothers, 1973.

Silverman. Religion for Skeptics. 1960s. Out of print.

Sire, James W. The Universe Next Door: A Basic Worldview Catalog. Third Edition. Downers Grove, Ill.. InterVarsity, 1997.

Smith, David T., ed. Abortion and the Law. Cleveland: The Press of Case Western Reserve University, 1967.

Smith, F. LaGard. When Choice Becomes God. Eugene, Ore.: Harvest House, 1990.

Sorokin, Pitirim A. The American Sex Revolution. Boston: Porter Sargent, 1956.

Sproul, R.C. Abortion: A Rational Look at an Emotional Issue. Colorado Springs, Colo.: NavPress, 1990.

St. John-Stevas, Norman. Life, Death and the Law: A Study of the Relationship Between Law and Christian Morals in the English and American Legal Systems. London: Eyre & Spottiswoode, 1961.

"Steps Toward a Brave New World." Time, 7-13-87, 57.

Stone, Christopher D. Should Trees Have Standing? Toward Legal Rights for Natural Objects. Los Altos, Calif.: William Kaufmann, 1972.

Strauss, Leo. Natural Right and History. Chicago: University of Chicago Press, 1953.

Stringfellow, William. Dissenter in a Great Society: A Christian View of America in Crisis. New York: Holt, Rinehart, & Winston, 1966.

Swomley, John M. "Human Beings: In God's Image," Pages 340-345 in Moral Issues and Christian Response, ed by Paul T. Jersild and Dale A. Johnson. Fort Worth, Texas: Harcourt Brace, 1993.

T

Tec, Nechama. When Light Pierced the Darkness: Christian Rescue of Jews in Nazi-Occupied Poland. New York: Oxford University Press, 1986.

Temkin, Owsei, William K. Frankena, and Sanford H. Kadish. Respect for Life in Medicine, Philosophy, and the Law. Baltimore, Md.: Johns Hopkins UP, 1977.

Terkelsen, Helen E. Counseling the Unwed Mother. Englewood Cliffs, N.J.: Prentice-Hall, 1964.

Terry, Randall A. Accessory to Murder: The Enemies, Allies, and Accomplices to the Death of Our Culture. Brentwood, Tenn.: Wolgemuth & Hyatt, 1990.

---. "If You Believe Abortion is Murder, Act Like It's Murder," cassette tape of a 1988 [before July] speech to pastors. Anaheim, Calif.: Operation Rescue, 1989.

---. Operation Rescue. Springdale, Pa.: Whitaker House, 1988.

Thielicke, Helmut. The Doctor as Judge of Who Shall Live and Who Shall Die. Philadelphia: Fortress Press, 1970.

Thomas, Cal. The Death of Ethics in America. Waco, Texas: Word Books, 1988.

Tickle, Phyllis, ed. Confessing Conscience: Churched Women on Abortion. Nashville: Abingdon Press, 1990.

Time. New York: Time-Life Bldg., Rockefeller Center, NY 10020-1393.

Trueblood, Elton. The Incendiary Fellowship. 1960s. Out of print.

---. New Man for Our Time. 1960s. Out of print.

Tunnicliffe, Geoff. One Hundred One Ways to Change Your World. Colorado Springs, Colo.: Chariot Victor, 1997.

U

United Nations. Abortion Policies: A Global Review. Vol. I Afghanistan to France. New York: United Nations, 1992.

---. Abortion Policies: A Global Review. Vol. II Gabon to Norway. New York: United Nations, 1993.

---. Abortion Policies: A Global Review. Vol. III Oman to Zimbabwe. New York: United Nations, 1995.

---. Human Rights: A Compilation of International Instruments. Volume I [First Part] Universal Instruments. New York and Geneva: United Nations, 1994.

---. Human Rights: A Compilation of International Instruments. Volume I [Second Part] Universal Instruments. New York and Geneva: United Nations, 1994.

United States Catholic Conference, Inc. Catechism of the Catholic Church. English Translation for the United States of America. Liguori, Mo.: Liguori Publications, 1994.

U.S. News and World Report. 1290 Avenue of the Americas, Suite 600, New York, NY 10104.

V

Verduin, Leonard. The Anatomy of a Hybrid: A Study in Church-State Relationships. Grand Rapids, Mich.: William B. Eerdmans, 1976.

Vigeveno, H.S. Jesus the Revolutionary. 1960s. Out of print.

W

Walbert, David F., and J. Douglas Butler. Abortion, Society, and the Law. Cleveland: Case Western Reserve University, 1973.

Westen, Peter. "The Empty Idea of Equality." Harvard LR 95 [1982]: 537-96.

Western Center for Law and Religious Freedom. Defending Pro-Life Activists in Court. Whittier, Calif.: Western Center for Law and Religious Freedom, 1990.

Whitehead, John W., ed. Arresting Abortion: Practical Ways to Save Unborn Children. Westchester, Ill.: Crossway Books, 1985.

---. The Right to Picket and the Freedom of Public Discourse. Westchester, Ill.: Crossway Books, 1984.

---. The Second American Revolution. Elgin, Ill.: David C. Cook Publishing, 1982 and 1985.

---. The Stealing of America. Westchester, Ill.: Crossway Books, 1983.

Williams, Glanville. The Sanctity of Life and the Criminal Law. New York: Alfred A. Knopf, 1957.

Williams, Robert H. To Live and To Die: When, Why, and How. New York: Springer-Verlag, 1973.

Willke, J.C. Handbook on Abortion. Cincinnati, Ohio: Hayes Publishing, 1971.

World Almanac and Book of Facts, 1991. New York: Pharos Books.

TIMELINE

Note: Citations are omitted for the sake of brevity, but the majority of these facts are also presented within the text of *Orphans in Babylon*, with citations.

1215

Gov't. *Magna Charta*: civil & political rights for some.

1500s

Relig. **Protestant Reformation** promotes spiritual individuality.

1600s

Relig. Religion privatized to restore peace in England.

SocClim. Spinoza says "miracles" are natural events misunderstood.

Tech. Microbes are identified & described. Condom is invented in Britain.

1635

Zeal Roger Williams is banished from Massachusetts Bay Colony for preaching repentance for English claims to own native Americans' land.

1677

Tech. Sperm are identified & described.

1743

Relig. John Wesley's "General Rules" prohibits buying or selling slaves. He writes that slave-*buyers* "are the spring" that puts "frauds, robberies, and murders" into motion.

1776

Gov't. *Declaration of Independence*, and American's Revolutionary War.

1781

SocClim. Thomas Jefferson writes of the paradox of men fighting a Revolutionary War of Independence for a nation of slaveholders.

1783

Legisltv. Jefferson's proposal that slavery be prohibited in new states is defeated by only one vote [Hart, 269].

1784

Relig. Founding documents of [American] Methodist Episcopal Church call for expulsion of a member who buys or sells slaves.

1787

Legisltv. The *U.S. Constitution* validates slavery by declaring that a slave equals three fifths of a person.

1789

Int'l. French *Declaration of the Rights of Man.*

1791

Legisltv. Bill of Rights: First ten Amendments...

First Amendment to the *U.S. Constitution*: Freedoms of religion, speech, and the press; rights of assembly and petition.

Fifth Amendment to the *U.S. Constitution*: "No person shall... be deprived of life, liberty, or property, without due process of law;..."

Sixth Amendment to the *U.S. Constitution*: "In all criminal prosecutions, the accused shall enjoy the right to a speedy and public trial, by an impartial jury... [and has a right to a] compulsory process for obtaining witnesses in his favor; and to have the assistance of counsel for his defense."

Eighth Amendment to the *U.S. Constitution*: "Excessive bail shall not be required, nor excessive fines imposed, nor cruel and unusual punishments inflicted."

1791, continued:

Legisltv. *Ninth Amendment* to the *U.S. Constitution*: "The enumeration in the Constitution, of certain rights, shall not be construed to deny or disparage others retained by the people.

Tenth Amendment to the *U.S. Constitution*: "The powers not delegated to the United States by the Constitution, nor prohibited by it to the states, are reserved to the states respectively, or to the people."

1793

Legisltv. First "Fugitive Slave law" requires the return of escaped slaves to their "owner."

1795

Int'l. Book published by the Marquis de Sade attacks church restrictions on abortion and extolls the values of abortion.

1798

SocClim. Thomas Malthus's *Essay on Population* begins fears of inevitable cycles of "famine, pestilence and war" as the only natural remedies to the population explosion he foretells.

1800

Judicial Under British common law, which appplies in the U.S., the prohibition of execution of a pregnant woman is a fundamental recognition of the preborn's right to life. Intentional expulsion and destruction of a preborn without due cause is considered a crime, but only after quickening.

1800 – 1870

SocClim. Surgical abortion is an open, legal, business.

1800 – 1900

Gov't. U.S. grows from 16 states to 45, grows from 0.9 million sq. miles to nearly 4 million, and from a population of 5 million to 76 million.

Legisltv. In 1800 not one state has statutes against abortion, but by 1900 all states will forbid abortion and most will make it criminal.

SocClim. This century sees a marked weaking of moral standards, particularly sexual ones, a subsequent awakening to the nature and magnitude of the abortion problem, followed by a successful grass-roots, broad-based, anti-abortion movement.

1803

Int'l. English Parliament outlaws all poison-induced abortions, not just after quickening.

SocClim. Second edition of Malthus's *Essay on Population* reaffirms population bomb predictions: recommends sexual abstinence but disapproves of other means to limit population.

1807

Int'l. England abolishes the slave trade; the credit is given to Wilberforce for his unflagging zeal.

Legisltv. U.S. abolishes the slave trade [importation of new slaves].

1812

Judicial *Commonwealth v. Bangs.* Massachusetts Supreme Court sets precedent of abortion-by-poison convictions only after quickening.

1817

SocClim. American Colonization Society organized to promote expatriative solution to the nation's black "dilemma."

1820s – 30s

Relig. Methodist position accommodates slavery in order to promote church growth and prosperity.

1821

Legisltv. Connecticut is the first state to outlaw chemical abortions, and it creates the "life of the mother" exception. Over the next 20 years nine other states will follow this example.

SocClim. At her death in 1821, Elizabeth Ann Seton's crusade against abortion has already seen success in legislation and enforcement, and the pro-life community she nurtured will carry her vision into the 1990s.

1827

Tech. Human egg is first discovered. Prior to this, the woman was seen as a receptacle for the "man's seed."

1828

Legisltv. By 1828, Southern States have made printing, circulating or posessing anti-slavery literature criminal, with punishments ranging from fines, the lash and prison, to death.

Judicial *Antelope* decision declares that blacks are not 5th Amendment "persons."

1829

SocClim. *Appeal to the Colored Citizens of the World*, a pamphlet by freed slave David Walker, raises national sensitivity to selective denials of free speech [regarding slavery].

1830s

Tech. **Abortion pills by mail-order** are widely advertised through the newest communication innovation, the "penny press," although the actual word *abortion* is not used.

1830

Relig. The Great Revival begins. Apparently with no human architect, the revival movement becomes an ad hoc anti-slavery society whose influence eventually sways Congress.

Slavery is becoming very controversial, and most churches – local and national – tend to sin by silence or by professing neutrality.

1830s – 40s

Legisltv. Increasingly tough "Fugitive Slave" laws, but...

Relig. The Christian community at Oberlin, Ohio, cites "higher law" for its civil disobedience.

1830 – 1880

Relig. Surgical abortion business flourishes – even where "illegal" – with no unified Christian opposition.

1831

Event Nat Turner's foiled slave uprising strikes terror in the South and increases controversy in the North.

SocClim. Alexis de Tocqueville observes that Americans love equality more than freedom.

1833

Int'l. Wilberforce gets his dying wish: England emancipates its slaves.

SocClim. William Lloyd Garrison's *Liberator* newspaper, Evangelist Theodore Weld's efforts, and Tappan borthers' finances create American Anti-Slavery Society.

1834

SocClim. Colleges – including "Christian" ones – have purged staffs of abolitionists; Oberlin College opens as abolitionist, and the first to welcome women, and blacks – 300 students pour in.

1836

Relig. Methodist General Conference votes [120 – 14] to oppose abolitionism; the attitude is that Christians should not impose their morality upon the privacy of master and slave.

SocClim. American Anti-Slavery Society sends out "The Seventy" to spread abolitionism.

1837

Event Abolitionist pastor and editor Elijah P. Lovejoy is murdered for his efforts and effectiveness. [Mobs destroyed his presses four times and the **authorities refused to protect him**].

SocClim. **Many Christians are chilled by accusations that their abolitionist rhetoric incites violence.**

1840s

CivDis. The Christian community at Oberlin, Ohio, forcibly re-liberates escaped slaves who were in the hands of the legal authorities.

Legisltv. John Quincy Adams hires evangelist Theodore Weld to do research for his antislavery struggle in Congress.

Politics **The antislavery Liberty Party is formed.**

Relig. Methodism's vote [1836] and Lovejoy's murder prompt Orange Scott and Luther Lee to found abolitionist Wesleyan Methodism.

SocClim. The sensational *National Police Gazette* is the only newspaper to regularly attack surgical abortion.

The media spotlights major changes: The incidence of abortion is rising at an alarming rate, particularly among married, protestant, "respectable" women.

Tech. Union of sperm and ovum is demonstrated.

1844-46

CivDis. Henry David Thoreau is arrested for a one-man tax protest of the immorality of forced complicity in slavery and the Mexican war. His essay *On the Duty of Civil Disobedience* will later inspire both Gandhi and Dr. Martin Luther King Jr. and countless others.

Outside an abortionist's mansion, Leslie Printice leads a rally that becomes "physical and fierce." Her life is threatened repeatedly by paid gangsters, but she goes on to testify at the abortionist's trial, bringing with her several children she's saved.

Legisltv. Massachusetts abandons "quickening" and criminalizes any abortion attempt at any stage of pregnancy.

Relig. Both the Baptist and Methodist denominations split North and South over slavery.

SocClim. A Cincinnati Abolition Society debate on the sinfulness of slavery is published as a 500-page book, going through several editions.

1847

CivDis. Pastor Luther Lee's sermons have changed; 10 years ago he was defending abolitionist views against the attack that they incited violence, now he is part of the underground railroad, and preaches civil disobedience based on the principle of "higher law."

Event American Medical Association **[AMA]** is founded. It soon plays a decisive role in the Physician's Crusade Against Abortion [1857-1880].

1848

Relig. Wheaton College – founded by the Wesleyan Methodists – and Oberlin College may be the only two abolitionist campuses in the U.S.

1850

Legisltv. *The* Fugitive Slave Law of 1850.

CivDis. Charles Finney of Oberlin writes: "We are bound in all cases to disobey when human legislation contravenes moral law."

1852

Relig. Methodism is debating the morality of pew-renting, instead of addressing slavery.

SocClim. *Uncle Tom's Cabin* by Harriet B. Stowe

1853

Relig. Luther Lee ordains history's first female Christian minister, Antoinette Brown.

1854

Tech. Dr. Hugh Hodge, esteemed embryologist, concludes that life begins at conception and that abortion is murder. He impresses his convictions on his pre-med students and on the AMA.

1855

SocClim. Prominent Boston Ob/Gyn H.R. Storer begins writing anti-abortion books. The AMA will soon tap him to launch the first national right-to-life organization.

1856

Event When a local girl nearly dies from mail-order abortion pills, pharmacist Samuel Taylor begins a crusade to influence pharmacists, doctors and legislators. He drafts anti-chemical-abortifacient legislation that is adopted in 16 states.

Int'l. *Treaty of Paris* prohibits the slave trade worldwide.

1857-1880

SocClim. Physician's Crusade Against Abortion.

1857

Judicial *Dred Scott* decision affirms that since blacks aren't 5th Amendment "persons," even free blacks can't become citizens.

1858

CivDis. Several hundred members of the Christian community of Oberlin, Ohio, storm a hotel and re-liberate an escaped slave from the four armed men who had legally captured him.

Judicial 21 Christians on trial for the "Oberlin-Wellington Rescue [above], base their defense on "higher law," stating, "We must obey God always, and human law, social and civil, when we can." They refuse to post bail to dramatize the fact that they are in jail for their convictions.

1859

Event John Brown is executed at Harper's Ferry.

SocClim. Charles Darwin's *Origin of Species* is published. John Stuart Mill's *On Liberty* asserts the right of individual autonomy – limited only by the requirement not to harm others.

1860

Relig. Because Methodism has rescinded its prohibition of pew-renting instead of addressing slavery, the Free Methodist Church is founded, for free pews and free slaves.

1860, continued:

SocClim. Abortion carries high maternal mortality rates due to unsanitary methods and absence of antibiotics; two-thirds of the clients are prostitutes [having 1.8 abortions per year], surgical abortion in 1860 is big business.

Tech. The contraceptive cervical cap is developed.

1860-90

SocClim. A few major newspapers wage a protracted battle of exposing the realities about abortions and abortionists, impacting the number of providers and clients.

Legisltv. After 1860, state legislatures drop "quickening" from abortion statutes, protecting the preborn from conception onward, and abandon common-law immunity from prosecution for abortive women.

1861-65

Event Civil War: 3 million Americans [11%] take up arms against one another; 620,000 die [2.3% of population]. To be comparable, a civil war over abortion in the year 2000 would see 29 million Americans killing 6.1 million.

1861

Judicial Courts begin ruling that government should be "indifferent" to the church.

Relig. Presbyterians don't split over abolition until the beginning of the Civil War, 1861.

1863

Gov't. Lincoln's war-time *Emancipation Proclamation* orders federal troops to free all slaves.

1864

Int'l. *Geneva Convention of 1864*: nations agree to humanitarian rules for conducting war.

1865

Legisltv. 13th Amendment abolishes slavery.

Tech. Joseph Lister develops Antiseptic surgery; [ten years earlier would have *greatly* reduced the fatality rate in the Civil War].

1866-1868

Legisltv. Federal Assimilative Crimes Statute adopts strong anti-abortion laws nation wide.

Note: Just two years later, the **14th Amendment** guarantees due process ***and*** equal protection of law.

Within a two year period, Congress protects America's preborn children from abortion and guarantees due process and equal protection to all persons. How could the *Roe* court conclude that the 14th Amendment does not consider preborns to be "persons"?

Relig. Congregationalist churches denounce abortion.

1869

Event Berea College in Kentucky opens as a bi-racial school.

Relig. The "Old School" Presbyterian Church declares abortion "a crime against God and nature..."

Pope Pius IX invokes excommunication for abortion at any time after conception, and urges local parishes to take pro-life action.

Widely-circulated booklets of pro-life sermons provide biblical evidence that life begins at conception and that abortion is murder.

1870s

Legisltv. Many states outlaw contraceptives.

1870

Relig. *New York Times* is owned and edited by committed Christians.

SocClim. *New York Times* writer Augustus St.Clair initiates a moral crusade against abortion. His effort is joined by newspapers nationwide, even though as much as 25% of advertising revenue has previously been from abortionists.

Legisltv. The tough news-reporting will continue until every state has outlawed abortion, and numerous abortionists have been prosecuted.

15th Amendment to the *U.S. Constitution*: Blacks are given the right to vote. [Women wait 50 more years.]

Gov't. *Times* editor Louis Jennings shows that legislation alone is hollow; he wins anti-abortion support from the legal and medical communities and provokes public outrage, all of which together assure enforcement.

1871

SocClim. Special Committee [of New York doctors] on Criminal Abortions spreads alarm that New York has become an abortion mecca.

1872 – 1880

Judicial U.S. Post Office special prosecutor Anthony Comstock oversees the arrest and conviction of 55 abortionists on the East Coast.

1875

Tech. Doctors prove that human sperm and egg unite at conception.

1876

Legisltv. Georgia law makes the abortion of "any woman pregnant with child... an assault with intent to murder."

1878

Int'l. *Treaty of Berlin* protects Christian minorities in the Ottoman [Turkish] Empire.

1880

Legisltv. Every state has enacted laws prohibiting abortion except to save the mother's life.

1880 – 1900

Legisltv. Pennsylvania, among others, reflects public sentiment by renewing the "quickening" distinction, assigning lesser penalties for abortions before quickening. Many states give the mothers immunity from prosecution, or make that a possibility in exchange for testimony against the abortionist.

SocClim. Distain for anti-abortion laws is reflected in the average of nine, eight-line abortion ads running in the *San Francisco Examiner*, daily. Across the country, enforcement is erratic, so that laws function more as educational tools, and are a deterrent only for some. Prostitutes persist in their trade and in their aborting. An abortionist can still build a mansion on Fifth Avenue.

Full criminalization of abortion has succeeded in reducing the abortion rate by 50% to 60% at best. [Olasky, *Rites*, 293]

1880 – 1930

SocClim. Demographics: female labor force jumps from 2.6 million to 10.8 million. Unmarried women move away from relatives to live alone in cities. Sexual restraints drop; abortion climbs.

1882

Tech. Contraceptive diaphragm is popularized.

1884

Judicial *Dietrich v. Northampton* holds that an injured preborn was not a separate human being but, rather, a part of the mother's body.

1889

Relig. Frances Cabrini arrives in America and for the next 28 years conducts multiple ministries, including anti-abortion education and two maternity homes. By 1895, Chicago has 12 homes for the unmarried pregnant.

By 1900, Christians are providing "hundreds of crisis pregnancy centers and shepherding homes for unwed mothers, some with room for more than 1,000 to live at one time" [Clowes, 47].

1895

Tech. X-rays are discovered.

1900-1930

Relig. Modernist vs. Fundamentalist controversy. Modernism in theology takes the mainline denominations down the liberal path to the social gospel. In reaction, Fundamentalists withdraw from a perishing world into isolationist spirituality and *right doctrine*, abandoning all centers of influence to the Modernist Christians and naturalists.

SocClim. In 1900, "Josef Stalin was a twenty-one-year-old seminary student... Benito Mussolini was a seventeen-year-old student teacher... Adolf Hitler was an eleven-year-old aspiring art student... and Margaret Sanger was a twenty-year-old shy and out-of-sorts nurse probationer... Who could have guessed..." [Grant, *Grand Illusions*, 42].

Medical societies continue to be anti-abortion in word and deed.

1900

Tech. One standard abortion pill used by prostitutes is taken for three days along with hot baths.

1909

Tech. I.U.D. The intrauterine device is invented.

1910

Relig. Fundamentalism is launched with publication of the 12-volume *The Fundamentals*, in which major doctrines of orthodox Christian faith are defended in more than ninety articles.

1914

SocClim. Sanger's *The Woman Rebel* promotes the idea that contraception is an alternative to abortion.

1914-1918

Int'l. World War I

1915-1935

Tech. Intrauterine device sales begin. By the mid 1930s multiple companies are exploiting the lucrative I.U.D. market.

1916

Relig. Methodists are the first denomination to open a Washington, D.C., office [*promoting* temperance].

Tech. Margaret Sanger's first [contraceptive] clinic.

1918

SocClim. *Medical World* calls for a repeal of birth control bans, but reaffirms that abortion "should not be performed except, if ever, as a last resort to save the life of the mother."

1919-1920

Int'l. A series of treaties at Versailles protects minorities from discrimination, affirming their right to schools, language and religion.

The League of Nations is formed.

The Soviet Union legalizes abortion.

Legisltv. *18th Amendment* to the *U.S. Constitution*: Prohibition of the manufacture, transportation or sale of alcoholic beverages.

19th Amendment to the *U.S. Constitution*: **Women** are given the right to **vote**.

1920-1929

Event The Submachine gun is invented.

Legisltv. To combat Darwinism, 37 anti-evolution bills are submitted to 20 state legislatures.

Relig. Many Fundamentalists hold that the Bible forbids all forms of birth control.

SocClim. Birth control advocates shrewdly promote the economic plight of large families.

Dr. W.C. Bowers: "Pressure is brought to bear on every physician from the day he opens his office till the end of his life, to have him commit abortion."

1922

Judicial *Prudential Insurance Company v. Cheek* "...neither the 14th Amendment nor any other provision of the Constitution of the United States... confer[s] any right of privacy upon either persons or corporations."

1923

Judicial *Meyer v. Nebraska:* "The right to conceive and raise one's children has been deemed essential."

1924

Legisltv. U.S. citizenship given to native Americans

1925

Event Hitler publishes *Mein Kampf*.

Tech. Radio broadcasts the Scopes trial progress and its verdict nationwide [First "media event"?].

1926

Event Talking movies begin.

Relig. The Bible Crusaders of America is formed to "combat Modernism, Evolution, Agnosticism and Atheism."

1927

SocClim. Sinclair Lewis's *Elmer Gantry* stereotypes the fundamentalist as a hypocrite, swindler, charlatan and bigot.

President of Science League of America: "...today there exist, side by side, two opposing cultures, one or the other of which must eventually dominate our public institutions... progress and enlightenment [vs.] traditionalism... diametrically opposed armies" [Hunter, 137].

1929

Tech Penicillin is developed. It will dramatically reduce the danger of infection and death in all surgeries, including abortions.

Progesterone is discovered to do two things: sustain pregnancy and stop ovulation.

1930s-1960s

Relig. Conservatives taking a hard line against birth control alienate those moderates who see no biblical prohibition of contraceptives for married couples. Prohibition and Contraception controversies yield two generations of ambivalent Christians who believe that "I shouldn't impose my views on others."

1930

Relig. The Anglican church endorses contraception for just the "hard cases."

SocClim. Dr. Frederick Taussig's book *Abortion* presents an estimate of 681,600 illegal abortions annually, and a wildly fictitious "8000" maternal abortion deaths, and is boosted when a full-page review in *Time* magazine calls the book "authoritative."

1931

Relig. The liberalized Council of Churches caves in to Margaret Sanger's staff's lobbying blitz and agrees that contraception should be a matter of personal choice for "married people." Many denominations echo the view: Quakers, Northern Presbyterians, the Congregational church, the Methodist-Episcopal church, and several Baptist groups.

This shift sabotages any possible united moral stand by Protestants and Catholics on any issue, including abortion.

1933

Int'l. Hitler comes to power in Germany, and his "Law for the Prevention of Progeny of Hereditary Disease" is enacted. He legalizes abortion.

Legisltv. *21st Amendment* to the *U.S. Constitution*: Repeals Prohibition, etching into the nation's psyche, "You can't legislate morality."

Relig. Humanist Manifesto signed by 34 intellectuals including education guru John Dewey.

1935-1938

Int'l. Sweden becomes the first democratic, Christian nation to legalize abortion in the 1900s.

Tech. *Facts and Frauds in Women's Hygiene* reports that 50% of birth control clinic clients who rely on condoms are becoming pregnant.

The trade magazine *Manufacturing Chemist* reveals that 9% of condoms fail to contracept. Such information is successfully denied public exposure.

1939-1945

Int'l. World War II

1940s

Tech. A very effective morning-after pill is introduced, high-dose estrogen, called DES. Not until the 1970s is its use stopped when research uncovers serious long-term dangers to mothers and their children [Hatcher, 6].

1940-1941

Int'l. The Atlantic Charter reaffirms human dignity.

Judicial The Supreme Court declares that Humanism is a "religion."

Politics "Four Freedoms" speech by President Franklin D. Roosevelt names these essential human freedoms: freedom of speech and expression, freedom of religion and freedom from want and from fear.

1942

Event Japanese bomb Pearl Harbor, Hawaii.

Gov't. Thousands of Japanese Americans are "relocated" to camps in the interior.

Judicial In *Skinner v. Oklahoma,* the Supreme Court first recognizes reproductive autonomy as a basic civil right, "the right to have offspring," on equal protection grounds, regarding involuntary sterilization of certain convicted felons.

SocClim. New York Medical Academy has become strongly pro-abortion. It presents **themes designed to win public support for legalization**: not-yet-human, too many mouths to feed, abortion laws violate church-state separation and are unenforcable, and lack compassion for the plight of the woman.

1946

Judicial In *Bombrest v. Katz* a federal district court sets a new precedent, abandoning *Dietrich*'s 1884 "mother's body" ruling in favor of the individuality of a viable preborn who was injured. The federal court defines "child" as "an unborn or recently born human being."

1948

Int'l. United Nations is formed. Its General Assembly adopts the *Universal Declaration of Human Rights.*

Faced with South Africa's increasingly repressive Apartheid, the African National Congress ends 36 years of working within the system and embarks on campaigns of passive civil disobedience.

1949

Judicial In *Williams v. Marion Rapid Transit,* the Supreme Court of Ohio declares that an unborn child is a person within the meaning of the Ohio Constitution.

1950

Relig. Despite protracted schisms over contraception, every major Christian and non-Christian church denomination in the U.S. remains "vigorously and unashamedly" anti-abortion [Clowes, 42].

Tech. Synthetic progesterone is created.

First successful transplanting of a cow-to-cow embryo.

1952

Judicial In *Zorach v. Clauson,* Justice Douglas writes, "We are a religious people whose institutions presuppose a Supreme Being." If the government should show "a callous indifference to religious groups... that would be preferring those who believe in no religion over those who do believe."

Relig. The Methodist General Conference reaffirms the social gospel, stating that its duty is to "bring Christ to the individual," and "bring" society "more nearly in conformity with the teachings of Christ..."

Tech. Amniocentesis is developed.

First sex-change operation.

1953

Judicial *Kelly v. Gregory* is a New York tort case which holds that viability is no longer necessary, and a preborn injured during the third month of his mother's pregnancy was a separate human being entitled to damages.

In *May v. Anderson*, the Supreme Court rules that the right to bear and raise children is "far more precious than property rights."

1954

Int'l. Planned Parenthood holds an international conference calling for "reform" of abortion-restricting laws, worldwide.

Judicial *Brown v. Board of Education*, the Supreme Court's first school desegregation case, perhaps marks the end of the Court's role as guardian of the Constitution, and the beginning of its rogue era as architects of social engineering.

Legisltv. Congress adds the words, "under God," to the Pledge of Allegiance.

Tech. Oral contraceptive Pill is invented and tested.

1955

Event The Civil Rights Movement is launched when Rosa Parks refuses, illegally, to relinquish her seat to a white passenger on a bus in Montgomery, Ala., and is arrested. Pastors, led by M.L. King, Jr., call for bus boycott 4 days later.

Judicial In *Mallison v. Pomeroy,* the Supreme Court of Oregon affirms that the state has recognized "the separate entity of an unborn child by protecting him in his property rights and against criminal conduct..." and concludes that an unborn child is a person within the meaning of the state constitution.

SocClim. Planned Parenthood Federation of America sponsors a three-day conference in order to win support for legalization of abortion from leaders in medicine, psychiatry, law, sociology and other fields.

PPF's conference proceedings emerge as a book, which *Time* publicizes, and *Coronet* magazine touts as "the most comprehensive and authoritative book of information ever compiled on the vital subject of abortion."

1956

Event Bomb destroys M. L. King Jr.'s front porch. His picture is on the cover of *Time* magazine.

Int'l. Fourteen nations of Europe have now legalized abortion, eleven of them since 1949.

Judicial Montgomery Bus Boycott leaders indicted for conspiracy to hinder and prevent the operation of business. Four months later U.S. District Court rules racial segregation on city bus lines unconstitutional, and U.S. Supreme Court agrees.

1957-1975

Int'l. Americans are fighting and dying in Vietnam.

1958

Tech. Ultrasound examination of the preborn begins.

1959

SocClim. American Law Institute publically proposes abortion be legalized in cases where two physicians certify its requirement for the "physical or mental health" of the mother.

1960s

SocClim. The oral birth control Pill is so masterfully marketed as a "contraceptive" that few voices are raised to suggest its abortifacient effect, and those questions are smothered by non stop propaganda heralding a new age of sexual freedom and equality for women. Nearly forty years – and countless anonymous lives – will pass before the blissfully-ignorant begin to hear the stark truths.

Among the four basic principles that will guide secular medical ethics 30 years from now – beneficence, non-maleficence, justice and autonomy – the newcomer, autonomy, will grow to reign over all, elevated by the unstoppable fixation on individual rights which begins its ascent in the Fifties and Sixties.

Secular humanism, which has held sway at the universities for roughly thirty years, is – in the generation of the Sixties – going to seize first communication, then public education, and finally the political machine.

1960

Event Black college students "sit in" at lunch counters in Nashville, and Greensboro [N.C.]. MLK is arrested for trespassing at a lunch counter in Atlanta.

Legisltv. The American Law Institute's Model Penal Code sections on liberalized abortion laws will soon be implemented by the legislatures of California, New Hampshire, New York, Illinois and Kansas.

Politics John F. Kennedy, our first Catholic president, proves – for good or for ill – that the moral tenets of one's religion should not always be assumed to influence either his public or his private life. Church and state *can* be kept separate.

Tech. Birth control PILL first marketed.

1961

Event Ku Klux Klan violence in Alabama prompts Congress of Racial Equality [CORE] leadership to abandon the Freedom Rides. The Freedom Rides continue, led by black college students, who go on to press voter registration in the deep South.

Int'l. U.S.A. loses face by botching the Bay of Pigs effort to impose its politics on Cuba.

Judicial In *Torcaso v. Watkins,* The Supreme Court expressly notes that "Among religions in this country... would generally be considered a belief in..., Secular Humanism, and others." The Court's view is that all faiths should be "leveled" by the state. [see also 1940-41].

1962-1965

Judicial The Supreme Court, in *Abington v. Schempp* and *Engel v. Vitale,* bans teacher-led prayer and Bible reading in public schools.

Legisltv. Civil Rights Act of 1964 and Voting Rights Act of 1965.

SocClim. Anguish and empathy, nationally and internationally, are focused on the mothers' "nightmare" of birthing deformed babies following the recent American rubella epidemic [20,000], and the thalidomide tragedy in Europe [5,000-7,000]. Abortion proponents are cranking up the "hard cases" rhetoric.

1962-65, continued:

SocClim. The American Law Institute and the American Bar Association seem to be in a contest to see which can most effectively reshape public opinion and move legislatures to liberalize abortion statutes.

The Gallup poll, for the first time, mentions abortion. Asked whether Sherri Finkbine [an American who had taken the European tranquilizer thalidomide] did right or wrong "in having this abortion operation" [in Sweden], 52% say "right," 32% say "wrong," and 16% have no opinion.

1962-1968

SocClim. SDS [Students for a Democratic Society] issues its *Port Huron Statement* to promote the idea of human perfectability. SDS membership grows from 600 to more than 100,000.

1963

Event President John F. Kennedy is assassinated.

1964

CivDis. *Life* magazine gives public praise to physicians who perform illegal abortions on women who have contracted rubella while pregnant, calling them "conscientious doctors of highest integrity who acted in defiance of community convention and state law."

Event MLK is awarded Nobel Peace Prize.

Judicial South Carolina's Supreme Court upholds a judgment for a wrongful death tort for a preborn child [Bray, 117].

Legisltv. Congress passes the *Civil Rights Act*.

Relig. Christian pro-lifers Dr. Jack and Barbara Willke publish their first book on abortion.

1965

CivDis. The Clergy Consultation Service, led by Methodists and nominal Catholics, is formed to refer refer women to illegal abortionists, like an Underground Railroad.

Judicial In *Griswold v. Connecticut,* the Supreme Court mandates that state law may not restrict access of married persons to contraceptives. In dissenting, Justice Potter Stewart says, "I can find no such general right of privacy in the Bill of Rights, in any other part of the Constitution, or in any case ever before decided by this Court... it is not the function of this Court to decide cases on the basis of community standards." Clowes [89-90] says that *Griswold*'s "privacy" makes it a more important case than *Roe*.

SocClim. "The liberalization proposals [for abortion] ...deal with extreme cases: rape, deformity... [but] nothing less than absolute freedom of abortion for everyone in every situation will satisfy them" [Shaw, 40].

Opinion polls successfully relativize the abortion dabate. The percentage of Americans who approve of abortion for: mother's health seriously endangered, 71%; rape, 56%; likelihood of serious defect, 55%; very low income, 21%; unmarried and doesn't want to marry, 18%; married but wants no more children, 15% [Shaw, 39].

An internal bias may be detected in which "side" of an issue is stressed; subliminally there is a tendency to view that side as the "right answer" to a question. The 18% "approval" of abortion statistic above would more accurately be stated as "82% say that being unmarried and not wanting to marry *does not* justify abortion."

1966

SocClim. National Organization for Women [N.O.W.] is established with the liberalization of abortion laws as a major goal.

1967

Judicial In *Gleitman v Cosgrove,* a wrongful-birth suit, the Supreme Court of New Jersey states: "**The right to life is inalienable in our society.** A court cannot say what defect should prevent an embryo from being allowed life... The sanctity of the single human life is the decisive factor in this suit in tort... We firmly believe the right of their child to live is greater than and precludes their right not to endure emotional and financial injury."

Legisltv. California is the first of 14 states [by 1972] to adopt the [1962] American Law Institute-recommended guidelines for exceptions permitting abortion. California doctors quickly demonstrate that pregnancy itself can be defined as a "grave impairment to health" to justify *any* abortion.

Colorado is the first of many states to follow the pro-abortion suggestions of the American Bar Association – "regulations" so vague as to permit abortion on demand.

Relig. Religious polarization goes public. Eight New York bishops issue a pro-life statement. In response, the Protestant Council of the City of New York and various Jewish groups issue a 1000 word public criticism of the Catholic church's "harsh and unbending posture" opposing abortion [Shaw, 29-30].

Hawaii's first CPC [Crisis Pregnancy Center].

SocClim. Dr. Robert Hall: "In the United States every year there are about 4 million births, 1 million spontaneous abortions, and 1 million induced abortions" [Shaw, 32-33].

The American Medical Association [AMA], abandons 100 years of being pro-life, and calls for decriminalization of abortion.

1968

CivDis. When Russel Shaw puts *Abortion on Trial*, he reveals the prevalent view that "...if more than a million women are violating the existing laws each year, the laws are clearly unacceptable in the contemporary American social climate and should be changed..." [34].

Shaw continues, "80 to 90% of all abortions in the United States are performed by competent physicians, on referral from other physicians" [35-36].

Event Both Dr. Martin Luther King Jr. and Robert F. Kennedy are murdered.

Int'l. The United Kingdom legalizes abortion. *The Proclamation of Teheran*, an International Conference on Human Rights, "solemnly proclaims" the paradox in article 16, that children have a right to be protected, *and* that parents have the right-to-choose [abortion].

1968, continued:

Relig. Pope Paul VI, in his *Humanae Vitae* encyclical, reaffirms the sanctity of life. In the public arena, for lack of Protestant voices, opposition to abortion is successfully dubbed the "Catholic" position.

Historians Will and Ariel Durant predict that America's Catholic minority may some day win out over both the Protestant Reformation and the French Enlightenment because of superior "fidelity and fertility" [24].

53% of Catholic couples now use some form of birth control other than the approved rhythm method, according to a Ryder-Westoff survey [Clouse, 189].

The American Baptist Convention endorses abortion on demand in the first trimester.

When *Christianity Today* gathers prominent evangelical leaders; their consensus report [11-8-68 article] sounds very liberalized and relativized: "...the Christian physician will advise induced abortion only to safeguard greater values sanctioned by Scripture. These values should include individual health, family welfare, and social responsibility."

The United Methodist Church is nicknamed "the 'abortion church' for its vigorous efforts to legalize abortion..." [Clowes, 42-47].

SocClim. Madalyn Murray O'Hair begins radio broadcasts on the "Atheist Point of View."

Nationally and internationally there is a strong movement... toward legalized abortion focusing the debate on the exceptions, the hard cases: life of the mother and rape.

Alan Guttmacher, president of Planned Parenthood declares, "The fetus... is merely a group of specialized cells that do not differ materally from other cells" [Mnookin, 164].

Planned Parenthood, like Zero Population Growth, now promotes abortion on demand.

Tech. A Christian missionary doctor has already defined the abortifacient function of both the popular IUD, and the experimental "morning after pill," calling both, "microscopic murder" [Clouse, 191; *also* Shaw, 169].

These concerns are quashed by many who should be on God's side; Earl J. Reeves says, "Even the question of the possibility of destroying life by destroying a fertilized egg through an IUD or a pill seems likely to be dismissed by most evangelicals as a highly theoretical and legalistic controversy" [Clouse, 193].

1969

CivDis. In parts of America where only "therapeutic" abortions are legal, doctors are willing to certify that 8,000 to 10,000 abortions were necessary to save the life of the mother.

Event USA accomplishes first moon landing.

Legisltv. Forty of the 50 United States still hold abortion a crime, except to save the mother's life.

Relig. National Council of Churches approves abortion to preserve mother's life *or health*.

1969, continued:

SocClim. Both Planned Parenthood and the American Public Health Association promote total decriminalization of abortion.

The fictitious "statistics" are now routinely repeated: one million illegal abortions causing 8,000 maternal deaths per year.

Dr. Bernard Nathanson helps found National Association for the Repeal of Abortion Laws [NARAL], later to be renamed National Abortion Rights Action League. The doctor will later become pro-life.

Tech. In vitro fertilization is successful; the morning after pill is still experimental.

1970

Judicial In *Keeler v. Superior Court,* the California Supreme Court rules that the unborn are not human beings as pertains to murder.

Legisltv. Four more states legalize abortion on demand.

Relig. The United Methodist Church calls for abortion to be removed from the criminal code and placed under medical regulation.

SocClim. The Value of Life Committee is founded by black doctor Mildred Faye Jefferson.

Tech. The "**vacuum**" method, later to be called **suction curettage**, is instantly very popular. At least one entrepreneur makes day time use of one wing of a motel, rolling a suction machine from room to room.

1971

Judicial In *United States v. Vuitch,* the Supreme Court extends the definition of "maternal health" to include "**mental health**," opening the floodgates of abortion on demand.

Legisltv. Nearly a half-million *legal* abortions are performed this year.

Relig. Paul Marx has been preaching against abortion for 10 years; this year he writes *The Death Peddlers: War on the Unborn*, soon followed by *The Mercy Killers*; next year he will start the Human Life Center at St. John's University.

1972

Judicial In *Eisenstadt v. Baird,* the Supreme Court extends reproductive privacy to the unwed: access to contraceptives equal to that previously guaranteed only to married couples.

In *Stanley v. Illinois,* the Supreme Court recognizes that fathers have [some] parental rights. Even if they do not marry the mother, they may not be denied custody [after the mother's death] without due process.

U.S. v. Dougherty reaffirms jury nullification.

Legisltv. Thirty of the 50 United States still hold abortion a crime, except to save the mother's life.

1973

Judicial In ***Roe v. Wade***, the Supreme Court rules that the "right to privacy" makes abortion on demand a constitutional right, voids the pro-life statutes of 30 states, and prohibits legislative protection of preborn life.

In ***Doe v. Bolton***, the Supreme Court gives a green light to abortion *clinics* and expands "maternal health" to include "general maternal well-being," justifying abortion throughout nine months of pregnancy.

1973, continued:

Relig. Immediately after the *Roe* decision, the National Conference of Catholic Bishops proclaims "...no Court opinion can change the law of God prohibiting the taking of innocent human life" [Clowes, 43].

SocClim. Nobel laureate James Watson asserts that the the only "rational, compassionate" policy would be to give parents a 3-day grace period after a child's birth, during which they may exercise a lethal choice, euthanasia.

James McFaddon launches the Ad Hoc Committee in the Defense of Life on Capitol Hill.

The *Humanist Manifesto II* is signed by 114 leading humanists 40 years after the original, then joined by thousands.

Tech. Prostin F2-Alpha, a synthetic hormonal drug developed by Upjohn, is designed to induce violent early labor, causing miscarriage.

1975

Judicial *Bigelow v. Virginia* strikes down abortion clinic advertising restrictions.

The District Court of Utah, in *T H v. Jones,* holds that "privacy" includes a minor's fundamental right to abortion. The Supreme Court lets it stand.

Relig. Evangelical leaders including Billy Graham launch the Christian Action Council, a pro-life education and advocacy organization.

1976

CivDis. The tactics that will be popularized by Operation Rescue 12 years from now are already being implemented at the national Right to Life convention [Francke, 249. See *Orphans*, 218, note 12].

Int'l. Two United Nations Covenants – one recognizing civil and political rights and the other affirming economic, social and cultural rights – enter into force. Both covenants bar discrimination based on "...race, color, sex, language, religion, political or other opinion, national or social origin, property or birth" [Buergenthal, 38-39].

Judicial In *Planned Parenthood v. Danforth*, the Supreme Court invalidates spousal or parental consent requirements for abortion [hence men have no reproductive rights], and holds that states may not require abortionists to attempt to sustain viable abortees, and may not prohibit salt-solution abortions in order to decrease a preborn's suffering.

In *Singleton v. Wulff,* the Supreme Court gives abortionists the right to challenge government abortion funding restrictions "on behalf of their patients."

Legisltv. The Hyde Amendment to the Health and Labor bill limits abortion funding.

Politics Party platforms are cautious about a right to life amendment: Republicans support it, and Democrats call it "undesirable."

SocClim. Polls show that barely 1% of the public considers abortion a national election issue.

Dr. Joycelyn Elders [later to become Clinton's Surgeon General] says, "Abortion has had an important and positive public health effect... the number of Down's syndrome infants in Washington state in 1976 was 64% lower than it would have been without legal abortion" [*Life Advocate*, 2/'94, 33].

1977

Judicial In *Poelker v. Doe*, in *Maher v. Roe* and in *Beal v. Doe*, the Supreme Court ***rejects*** the argument that for government to fund childbirth but not abortion constitutes preferential treatment and discriminates against a "class of women seeking abortions."

In *Carey v. Population Services International*, the Supreme Court finds a constitutional right of minors to have contraceptives.

Legisltv. There are 36 bills before Congress to amend the Constitution, either by a right to life for the unborn, or by returning abortion decisions to the states.

Politics 35,000 join the annual Right to Life march in Washington, D.C., on *Roe*'s anniversary.

Relig. "Pope Paul VI not only calls abortion a threat to world peace but brands women who have abortions 'killers' who 'freely and consciously murder the fruit of their womb'" [Francke, 249].

Pro-choice Christian Waldo Beach [70] agrees that, "Considering the best medical advice, the best moral insight, and a concern for the total quality of the whole life cycle of the born and the unborn, we believe that abortion may in some instances be the most loving act possible."

Pro-life rallies and picketing at abortion clinics happen frequently, with some success.

SocClim. The National Committee for a Human-Life Amendment raises more than $900,000 in fourteen months [Francke, 248].

Tech. The National Right to Life Committee is boycotting the March of Dimes [which endorses amniocentesis, and thereby possible abortion of handicapped or damaged preborns].

1978

Legisltv. Pro-abortionist: "The anti-abortion camp is very adept at practicing legislative harassment, sometimes taking it to the level of the absurd... death certificates... the aborted fetus be buried... clinic's obligation to show the woman pictures of the stages of fetal development" [Francke, 247].

SocClim. Judie Brown forms the American Life League, and her husband launches the Life Amendment Political Action Committee.

Some secular abortion clinic staffs – for a *very* brief time – express a desire to support a client's right to choose life, proposing to offer services very much like a CPC. Such views abruptly cease [Francke, 251-52].

Tech. First test-tube-baby.

Depo-Provera is available.

1979

Judicial In *Coalutti v. Franklin*, the Supreme Court holds that viability is whatever an abortionist says it is; he is under no obligation to save a viable baby's life or even to decrease her suffering.

With *Bellotti v. Baird* and *Hunerwald v. Baird*, the Court invalidates parental consent laws unless they permit judicial bypass.

Relig. Francis Schaeffer's book and film series: *Whatever Happened to the Human Race?*

1980

Event Ronald Reagan is elected by a landslide.

Judicial In *McRabe v. Secretary of Health, Education and Welfare and Zbarez v. Quern*, the Court honors the Hyde Amendment's refusal to fund welfare abortions, and says that states are not obligated to fund them, either.

Politics Platforms of both parties have gotten stronger regarding abortion, but both parties leave room for internal disagreement.

Relig. *Moody Monthly* chastizes evangelicals: "Do we need time to think abortion through? Isn't seven years enough? The Catholics have called abortion the Silent Holocaust. The deeper horror is the silence of the Evangelical" [Grant, *Third Time...*, 145].

SocClim. Americans United for Separation of Church and State: "The emergence of the Evangelical Christian political movement was the most significant Church-state development of 1980 – groups like Moral Majority and Christian Voice."

1981

Int'l. Human Life International begins. In 10 years it will have chapters in 22 nations.

Judicial In *H.L. v. Matheson*, the Supreme Court *seems* to uphold a state's parental consent requirement, but after stating that parents of a minor must be notified by the abortionist a week in advance, the words "if possible" are added, making the "rule" totally worthless.

Relig. Francis Schaeffer's *A Christian Manifesto* will quickly galvanize pro-life forces.

SocClim. A life insurance survey identifies "a cohesive and powerful group of Americans, approximately 45 million strong, ...intensely religious ...that could change the face of America" [Doner, 8-9].

1982

Event The bodies of 16,500 aborted children are discovered in a steel storage container. It will require 3 years in court to get permission to bury them in a Los Angeles cemetery.

Zeal Don B. Anderson helps firebomb two abortion facilities in Florida, bombs one in Virginia, and "kidnaps a husband-and-wife abortion team for a day in an attempt to persuade them to take leave of baby killing." He is sentenced to 42 years in federal prison.

1983

Event Two Pensacola, Fla., abortion clinics are burned.

Judicial In *Akron v. Akron Center for Reproductive Health*, the Supreme Court asserts that a state may not prohibit saline abortions, nor "restrict a woman's right to abort" with required counseling information, waiting periods, or required notification of parents of girls under 18. *Akron* and *Planned Parenthood of Kansas City v. Ashcroft* declare second trimester abortions are safe enough to be permitted in outpatient clinics. *Ashcroft*, however *does* uphold these requirements: parental consent with a judicial bypass option, requiring a second MD after viability, and a pathology report for all abortions.

1983, continued:

Relig. In 1983, about 855,000 women are counseled in the nation's 2,900 crisis pregnancy centers. About 650,000 of them decide to keep their babies – a CPC success rate of 76%.

Tech. First human embryo transfer.

Zeal Joan and Miriam Andrews are widely recognized, having been repeatedly arrested, jailed, and suffering broken bones, while blocking access to abortion clinics. Joan Andrews serves 2½ years, two years of it in solitary confinement as a consequence of remaining limp and speechless as an act of solidarity with the helpless unborn.

Curt Beseda sets four abortion clinic fires. Later sentenced to 20 years, he says that a sit-in "is a nice thing to do for puppies... also a fine thing to do to gain the right to eat at lunch counters... But is it a sufficient response to childslaughter?" [Bray, 16].

Joseph Grace is sentenced to 20 years in jail for starting a $250,000 clinic fire.

1984

Judicial South Carolina Supreme Court speaks in defense of a preborn child killed by a criminal act: "It would be grossly inconsistent for us to construe a viable fetus as a 'person' for the purposes of imposing civil liability [if we refused] to give it a similar classification in the criminal context" [Bray, 117].

Politics Party platforms have crystalized regarding abortion. Democrats are for privacy, and funding of a fundamental human right to abort; Republicans are for the sanctity of the preborn, and a human-life amendment.

The Christian Right's TV preachers figure heavily in President Reagan's reelection.

Rocked by Republican victories, Democrats sound the alarm about the Religious Right.

Relig. Six hundred attend the first national pro-life activists' convention to form a national action-plan.

Tech. First fetal surgery.

Zeal Curt A. Beseda gets 20 years for arson.

Michael Bray burns seven abortion clinics.

1985

Int'l. Clowes estimates 55 million surgical abortions annually and "at least twice as many more ...by abortifacient 'contraceptives'" [2-21].

Relig. Joe Scheidler writes *Closed: 99 Ways to Stop Abortion*. The founder of the Pro-Life Action League was a pro-life activist before *Roe*.

SocClim. Norman Stone is walking across America with the bodies of seven slain [late term, saline] babies in little caskets, displaying them at gatherings of concerned citizens along the way. [Bray, 138-39].

The Silent Scream film, hosted by ex-abortionist Bernard Nathanson, jolts all who see it.

"The cooperaton between the seven major media monopolies and Planned Parenthood was vividly illustrated" in an unrelenting 18-month propaganda blitz to discredit CPCs. [Grant, *Grand Illusions*, 176-77].

1985, continued:

Zeal Thomas E. Spinks, 15 years for arson. John Brockhoeft, "a Vietnam veteran, returned home to a land which decided to legalize killing American babies." He burns Planned Parenthood's Margaret Sanger [abortion] Center to the ground [Bray, 138]. He will be convicted in 1988, sentenced to 10 years.

Joan Andrews does a non-violent, peaceful rescue in Pittsburgh.

1986

CivDis. "More property damage was caused [but it was not prosecuted] in the 1986 [U.S.A.] campus demonstrations against apartheid than in all abortion clinic bombings put together [from 1973 to 1992]," says Foreman [94].

Event 106 people block access to an abortion clinic in St. Louis.

Int'l. The Dutch Reformed Church in South Africa admits that its support of apartheid has been an error.

Judicial "[Joan Andrews entered an abortion clinic for a Pro-Life sit-in and attempted to damage a suction machine... The prosecution asked for a one-year sentence.] The judge gives her five... The same day, two men convicted as accessories to murder are sentenced by the same judge to four years," says Colson [250]. Joan Andrews will serve 2½ years, two years of it in solitary confinement as a consequence of her passive and nonviolent non co-operation – an act of solidarity with the helpless unborn.

In *Bowen v. American College of Obstetricians and Gynecologists*, the Supreme Court "found a parent's 'right' to refuse treatment [for their handicapped, new-BORN children], based upon the 'right to privacy.' This right to privacy is paramount – even over the [BORN] child's right to be spared an agonizing death by thirst and starvation," says Clowes [page 89.15].

In *Thornburgh v. American College of Obstetricians and Gynecologists*, the Supreme Court rules that states, effectively, may not regulate the abortion industry: no informed consent or information reporting requirements, and no obligations to viable abortees.

Beckwith says that the effect of *Roe, Bolton* and *Thornburg* is that there can be no legal or legislative challenge to sex-selection abortions [*Correct*, 31].

1987

CivDis. First Operation Rescue. A Cherry Hill, N.J., clinic is closed all day; 300 are arrested and later released. Three mothers change their minds.

Event Jim Bakker causes the PTL scandal.

SocClim. Pro-abortionists, in analyzing pro-life activism "from demonstrations... to firebombings," say, "It is the conduct in the middle of the spectrum – efforts to interfere physically with access to abortion short of violence – that presents difficult problems for providers and practitioners" [Lefcourt, 10A-11].

Although the Media has clearly resolved to discredit, stigmatize and marginalize the Religious Right, News is still News: Media reporting of Cherry Hill Rescue is very positive, launching Operation Rescue.

1987, continued:

SocClim. The Republican Party is embarrased by scandals in the electronic church. By mid-1987 Cal Thomas, former vice-president of the Moral Majority, pronounces the Christian Right "dead."

1988

CivDis. Randall Terry says at a rally: "We have reduced the murder of a million-and-a-half children a year to the level of whether or not we want a stop sign up some place, so we write a letter to the editor... We call abortion murder, and yet we don't act like it's murder... We have failed to produce the necessary social tension that affects political change."

Event In New York, in four days in May, there are 1647 Operation Rescue arrests.

Atlanta – and the Democratic National Convention – are greatly embarrassed by Operation Rescue. One thousand two hundred Christians are arrested for blocking access to abortion clinics.

Gov't. There are more than 4000 Operation Rescue arrests during the four months beginning May 1. Treatment by police and courts generally follows the indulgent pattern employed during the civil rights and campus demonstrations of the '60s and '70s.

President Reagan reads a historic Presidential Proclamation of "the unalienable personhood of every American from the moment of conception until natural death."

Int'l. Major changes, 1988 to 1995: End of the Soviet Union and the Cold War; Apartheid is abolished; a new Europe; democratically-elected governments in Latin America.

Judicial In *Conn v. Conn*, its first "father's rights" case, the Supreme Court upholds by [refusing to hear] a lower court case ruling that a father has no rights or claim whatsoever to his unborn child.

The Court greatly expands the racketeering laws, holding that RICO may be invoked if a single illegal scheme is advanced by more than one criminal act – Operation Rescue leaders will soon be charged with this federal felony for giving a speech at a rally the night before rescuers are arrested for misdemeanor trespassing. [Los Angeles, 1989].

The Court holds that "The government may seize a suspect's assets [whatever happened to 'innocent until proven guilty'?] even if such confiscations leave the suspects unable to hire the lawyers of their choice." [*Press*, 7-9-89, A5; The Associated Press].

Politics The Republican Party platform regarding abortion is identical to four years ago, but the Democrats now avow: "...the fundamental right of reproductive choice should be guaranteed regardless of ability to pay."

Relig. The United Methodist Church, the '60s "abortion church," now says it is opposed to abortions for birth control or for sex-selection.

SocClim. The Media generally gives Operation Rescue broad and favorable coverage. Pro-abortion [anti-God] factions become united in their **frustration and fury over Operation Rescue's successes and positive press.**

By year's end the media is painting Rescuers with a broad brush as hate-filled, wacked-out fanatical Christian anarchists.

1988, continued:

Tech. Seven genetically identical bull calves are produced from laboratory-altered embryos. Forced twinning in animals by breaking a single embryo into pieces can produce as many as 20 identical [calves] from a single "good-blood-line" mating.

RU-486, "the abortion pill," is invented.

Zeal John Brockhoeft gets 10 years for a 1985 arson.

1989

CivDis. When the *Webster decision* is rendered [see below], "Although this ruling would directly affect only about one percent of all abortions [those performed in publicly-funded facilities], the uproar was deafening. The pro-aborts promised extensive civil disobedience and illegal activity," says Clowes [page 89.16].

This year will see Rescues in 220 cities, with an average of 615 Christians every week [32,000 total] arrested for trying to non-violently intervene to stop abortions.

Event Across the nation, district attorneys, judges and police have decided that Operation Rescue is not at all the leading edge of social change like civil rights and campus activism. It is anachronistic religious bigotry bent on anarchy. It must be crushed at any cost.

By Easter week, "Assistant Chief Bob Vernon of the Los Angeles Police personally [directs] the systematic brutalization of 1,000 Christians [Operation Rescue], by torture teams – four to a Rescuer," says Foreman, [148].

Gov't. Atlanta "throws the book" at Randall Terry: a two-year term for misdemeanor trespassing. From jail, he writes "Winning the war for America's soul will not come easily, cheaply, nor quickly... we're going to have to suffer. Some of us may get lengthy jail sentences... lose our jobs... our 'respectable' ministries... or homes..." The D.C. [Rescue] Project a month later echoes the call – to stand in solidarity with Terry – to 2,500 Rescuers from around the country: "Now is the time to stand in Atlanta." In December, Atlanta's headlines scream, "THEY'RE COMING BACK!" on the day 18 of us show up to answer that call. Operation Rescue as a mass movement has been aborted – government has found the price it won't pay.

Judicial *Webster v. Reproductive Health Services, Inc.* The Supreme Court has been invalidating state efforts to protect viable preborns, but this year it turns, upholding a Missouri requirement that doctors must test for fetal viability if at least 20 weeks old, and prohibiting abortion if the baby is found to be viable. "Additionally, state funds, employees, and hospitals may not be used to provide or counsel for abortions" [Clowes, 89.16]. **Chief Justice William Rehnquist asserts that the "key elements" of the 'abortion right' – the right to privacy and the "Constitutional right to abortion" – simply do not exist.**

Zeal Marjorie Reed causes fire damage to abortion clinics in Ohio and N.J..

1990

Event 500,000 rally at the Washington monument with National Right to Life. The media treats it as a non-event.

American Life League links up multiple rallies by satellite.

Int'l. The UN *Convention on the Rights of the Child* enters into force. The extensive catalogue of rights recognized for children must be accorded "irrespective of race, color, sex [several others, and] birth, or other status" [Art.2 (1)]. Although the current international consensus is that "birth" means, "whether illegitimately or legitmately born," future generations might easily understand it to mean "born or preborn."

South Africa "unbans" the African National Congress, releases Nelson Mandela from his 27 years in prison, and sets forth on the road to free elections.

Judicial A court in Greenville, S.C., convicts 40 Rescuers on RICO charges, ordering $120,000 in damages to be paid to an abortion clinic. It will take seven years to win an appeal in Federal Circuit Court, in 1997.

Legisltv. Pro-life state legislator Woody Jenkins leads Louisiana to pass the strongest abortion restrictions in the nation after *Webster*.

Tech. The FDA approves Norplant, calling it a "contraceptive."

Zeal Marjorie Reed, 10 years in federal prison for arson.

Alexander Loce is convicted of blocking access to an abortion clinic to save the life of his own preborn child.

16 who Rescue in Atlanta to stand in solidarity with Randall Terry include Karen Black, Linda Simpson and Joe Stauder. These are sentenced to 2 years each: Rev. Jesse Lee, Joe Washburn, Joe & Kim Wright, Chris & Gaylen Keyes, Johnny Mercier, Richard Benson, Michael Frazer, Dan Betts, RuthAnn Tedman, David Nuzum and Roger Domingo.

Pastor Matt Trewhella in Milwaukee leads 15 others to form *Missionaries to the Preborn*. Following the historic sacrificial tone of Father Norman Weslin and his *Lambs of Christ*, the missionaries vow to non-violently prevent abortions from being committed, "every day they are out of jail," *but* will reveal their identities, etc., in order to win early release so that they can Rescue again.

1991

CivDis. Wichita's Summer of Mercy sees 2,600 Rescue arrests in 40 days.

Event In Visalia, Calif., Judge Howard Broadman orders a woman to have an abortifacient implanted. A man named Bodine fires a bullet that narrowly misses the judge's head. Bodine cites the just war theory, and remarks that Justice Blackmun's life is "not worth 27 million babies" [Bray, 144].

In Springfield, Mo., an unidentified man in a ski mask enters a clinic with a 14-gauge shotgun and asks for the abortionist. The clinic's owner and manager are wounded in a scuffle [Bray, 144].

Int'l. Breakup of the U.S.S.R.

Judicial In *Rust v. Sullivan*, the Supreme Court upholds the constitutionality of the government's cutting off Title X family planning funds from organizations that promote or perform abortions. Planned Parenthood alone loses tens of millions of tax dollars.

1991, continued:

Judicial The Court refuses to hear an appeal of a $12.5 million civil judgment against Oregon pro-lifers accused of "nuisance and trespass" by the owner of an abortion clinic.

Zeal Leland J. Smart, 20 years for destruction of an abortion clinic with a weapon.

Roy Streicher gets 3-15 years for vandalism and burglary.

Bill Cotter, 2½ years, "criminal contempt" for committing trespass.

1992

Event Pastors of southeastern Wisconsin draw 11,000 Christians to a solemn assembly. The next day 5,000 gather prayerfully in the vicinity of an abortion clinic – it is closed for the day.

From June through August, an average of 3,000 to 5,000 Christians per week pray in front of the abortion clinics of Milwaukee.

Int'l. The U.S. signs UN Covenants, on *Civil and Political Rights*, and on *Economic, Social and Cultural Rights*. Both covenants prohibit discrimination based on race, color, sex [several others, and] birth, or other status." As with the children's convention [1990], international consensus is that "birth" means, "whether illegitimately or legitmately born," not "whether born or preborn."

Judicial In *Planned Parenthood v. Casey*, the majority opinion of the Supreme Court is that not only the "right of privacy" inferred from the 14th Amendment, but the Amendment itself, guarantees an abortion right.

In *Casey*, the Court says that a state may not require that a husband be notified of his wife's abortion. It does, however, uphold Pennsylvania's requirements of informed consent, 24-hour waiting period, required reporting of abortion data, and parental consent with judicial bypass.

...While upholding various kinds of state regulation, it stresses that states may not infringe on the abortion right. *Casey* includes Justice O'Connor's "undue burden" criteria which holds that a state may not create "absolute obstacles or severe limitations on the abortion decision."

In *Casey,* Justices O'Connor, Kennedy and Souter reaffirm *Roe*'s mandate that a woman has a right to abortion prior to viability. Four justices, however – Rehnquist, White, Scalia and Thomas – vote to overturn *Roe* outright.

Legisltv. Burlington, a suburb of Milwaukee, votes to become an abortion-free zone.

Tech. FDA approves Depo-Provera, after 25 years of scrutiny.

Zeal [**Rev. John Funk was trying to keep his wife from aborting their child**. In an argument, he broke the abortionist's little finger.] **The sentence for "aggravated assault" is 41 months.**

John Brockhoeft, 10 years, arson.

Michael A. Fix, 10 years for arson and "assault."

Dennis Malvasi sentenced to a year for arson and parole violation.

Dan Gibson, gets 37 months for "conspiracy to defraud the government." Dan is a Rescuer. His "crime" is teaching pro-life Christians how to defend themselves in court.

1992, continued:

Zeal Judges see fit to elevate trespass to an act of criminal contempt. Rev. Joseph Foreman and James Soderna receive this treatment in Milwaukee, as do Jeff White, Rev. Joe Slovenec, and four others in Buffalo.

A judge in Allentown, Pa., imposes one-year sentences for trespassing to seven rescuers: Kathleen Doherty, Gretchen Nelson, Nancy McNulty, Mark Nelson, Fr. John Osterhout, Joseph McCormick and Joseph O'Hara.

1993

CivDis. A "Defensive Action Statement," which justifies of the use of force in stopping abortion, is signed by 30 pro-life leaders and clergy, including Andrew Burnett, Rev. Michael Bray, Father David Trosch, Roy McMillan, and Paul Hill.

Gov't. The Department of Health and Human Services rules that the new language of the Hyde Amendment not only permits but requires states to provide Medicaid abortions in cases of rape or incest.

Int'l. Apartheid ends.

Legisltv. This year the Hyde Amendment permits more tax-funding of abortions than before: alleged rape or incest [even if no criminal charges are filed], and pregnancies that "threaten" the life of the mother.

Relig. Father David Trosch is immediately defrocked for publicly defending the shooting of abortionists as "justifiable homicide."

300,000 families are supporting the American Life League.

Tech. Female condom invented.

Zeal Michael Griffin kills abortionist David Gunn [3/10]. He will be sentenced to life for homicide.

Rachelle Shannon wounds Wichita third-trimester abortionist George Tiller [8/19]. Sentences for attempted murder and a variety of arsons will total 31 years.

Michael H. Ross, 10 years for felony intimidation. He wrote letters to an abortionist suggesting that what she does to the babies, or that what happened to Dr. Gunn, might happen to her.

Joshua David Graff is sentenced to 37 months for arson.

Danny Bramwell, 3 years for trespass.

Arrested for violation of injunctions, given two-year sentences: Cathy Wommack, Bryan Longworth, John Casserly, Sean Brogan.

Jane Doe "C" [Lambs of Christ name "Petra"], indefinite sentence, contempt of court and trespass.

When standard Rescue non-cooperation is elevated to resisting an officer, rescuers Jim Lucero and Chuck LaCroix are sentenced to 18 months.

1994

Event Eight citizens, including a Missouri State Representative, Richard Chrismer, a nursing mother and a grandmother, attempt a citizens arrest of an **illegally** operating abortionist. The abortionist subsequently loses his medical license and the clinic is closed down. Nevertheless, the eight are arrested and tried for trespass, and sentenced to 90 days each [*Prisoners of Christ*, 1-10-95].

1994, continued:

Judicial The Supreme Court refuses to hear the appeal of Alexander Loce, who was convicted of blocking access to an abortion clinic to save the life of his own preborn child.

A court injunction has been issued to prevent Randall Terry from acting on the idea of presenting an aborted baby to candidate Clinton. When Joseph Foreman and Harley Belew do the deed, Terry is jailed for 5 months for "aiding and abetting."

Legisltv. [FACE] ***Freedom of Access to Clinic Entrances*** elevates the crime of simple trespass to a federal felony if it is committed at an abortion facility. Congress is persuaded that anyone who participates in non-violent civil disobedience at an abortion clinic is automatically to be put in the class of those disqualified from voting or holding public office, and who are unfit to pursue many occupations in this country.

F.A.C.E. defines the targeted crimes so loosely that such activities as picketing and sidewalk counseling, without impeding access, can be criminal acts if a clinic patron feels fearful of those persons.

Tech. San Francisco doctors begin testing RU-486 as a "morning-after" pill – it was designed for use after a woman knows she is pregnant.

RU-486 is to be produced in the U.S. under a agreement signed between a New York abortion-rights group and the patent holders.

Zeal The Pro-Life Action Network, Operation Rescue-National and Rescue America-National get together in Little Rock, Ark., to test F.A.C.E.

Paul Hill kills an abortionist and his armed escort [7/29]. Sentenced to death in Florida.

John Salvi kills two and wounds three at abortion clinics. His death in jail is ruled suicide.

Richard Czekaj, one year for trespass.

Linda Gibbons, a grandmother in Ontario, Canada, serves repeated six-month terms in jail for violating an injuction against sidewalk counseling on public property. Each time she is released, she does it again within three days. She will spend the majority of the next four years in jail.

Arrested under federal F.A.C.E. charges: Ronald Brock, Jim Soderna, Dan Balint, Jim Ketchum, John Stambaugh, Rev. George Wilson, Colin Hudson, Rev. Mike Skott.

Arrested for violation of injunctions: Anne Franczek, John Stambaugh, Rev. Matt Trewhella, Ronald Brock, James Chinavare, Drew Heiss, Dale Pultz, Bryan Longworth.

1995

Event Oklahoma City bombing kills 178 innocent people. President Clinton sets all appointments aside for three days to show support, in person, for the families of victims. [Note: for those who view death of a preborn by surgical abortion as equivalent to blowing up children in a day-care center, Clinton himself is an accomplice to a holocaust that equals the destruction of an Oklahoma City bombing, EVERY hour, every day, every month, for 25 years! 178 x 24 x 365 x 25= 38,982,000 babies killed by freedom of "choice"].

1995, continued:

Judicial [James and Pennie Hudson rescued in Los Angeles, were sentenced to do community service, and they completed that order.] A judge disputes the nature of the community service and sentences them to jail: 6 months for James and 1 year for Pennie.

John Brockhoeft, imprisoned since 1985, is subjected to mandatory release, house arrest, electronic monitoring, "mental health aftercare," and a mandate that he have zero contact with anyone involved in pro-life activity of any kind.

Zeal John Arena, age 74, gets 41 months on a federal extortion charge. [In 1997 the government will threaten to seize John's and his wife's Social Security checks. After serving the 41 months, he immediately will be ordered to serve 10 more months for having sent non-threatening, abortion-picture postcards to abortionists.]

David A. Lane, 18 years for vandalism at two abortion clinics.

Arrested under federal F.A.C.E. charges: Michael Suhy, Chuck La Croix, Jim Lucero, Frank L. Bird Jr.

Arrested for violation of injunctions: Rev, Mike Skott.

1996

Politics Bob Dole wants the Republican platform to include a "declaration of tolerance" of non pro-life views.

Zeal On the day after a federal judge rules that minors do not need permission from anyone, not their parents nor a judge, to get an abortion, Brian Clayton Charles is arrested for smashing computers and walls in an Arizona abortion clinic with a club.

Brian Clayton Charles is sentenced to $7^1/_2$ years for "burglary."

Ted Cadwalader is given a sentence of 15 months for trespass.

1997

Event More than 125,000 pro-lifers gather in Washington, D.C., for Nellie Gray's March for Life.

Judicial In *Boerne v. Flores*, the Supreme Court declares unconstitutional the Religious Freedom Restoration Act, which had passed almost unanimously in both houses of Congress.

For the first time a Federal Appeals Court overturns a RICO conviction: 40 South Carolina Rescuers had been ordered to pay $120,000 in damages to an abortion clinic in 1990.

Tech. First cloning of an adult mammal [a sheep].

Zeal Robert Alleva, age 15, is sentenced to three years for arson.

Peter Andrew Howard drives a truck loaded with gasoline and propane cylinders into a Fresno, Calif., clinic; nothing ignites; 9-17 years for arson.

James Anthony Mitchell, 10 years, arson.

John Yankowski, arson.

Jennifer Sperle, 30 months for conspiracy to commit an arson which caused $500 damage. She is the nursing mother of a 10-month old baby.

Clark Ryan Martin, 7 months for conspiracy with Jennifer Sperle.

Angela Shannon, sentenced to 46 months for dropping a letter into a mailbox for her mother, Shelley Shannon. The letter to an abortionist was considered threatening.

Michelle Wentworth, 37 months for conspiracy with John Arena for felony intimidation. Court testimony indicated that Michelle's "crime" was hosting a meeting in her home, because during that meeting a "stink attack" on an abortion clinic was planned.

1791, continued:

Zeal Dale Pultz, 13 months for "slander of title" for filing a lien against a pro-abortion judge's property.

David C. Kanz, two years for "forgery and slander" for filing a lien against a pro-abortion judge's property.

Curt Beseda completes his 1985 sentence for arson and is released. His probation officer demands he take a prescription tranquilizer even though two of three doctors who see him say it isn't needed. He is returned to jail "indefinitely."

Arrested under federal F.A.C.E. charges: Rev. George Wilson, Colin Hudson [two years & $3000 fine], Daniel Lamantain, Dwight Monagan, Arnold Matheson and Father Norman Weslin.

In Hackensack, N.J., 15 Rescue America "J. Does" are being held indefinitely for not divulging their names after arrest for Rescue. Among the "jail names" are: Corazon, Scout, Lifer, Hound Dog, Lifeboat, Indiana Jones and Angel.

1998

Event An estimated 80,000 to 100,000 pro-lifers participate in this year's March for Life in Washington, D.C., on the 25th anniversary of *Roe*.

Bomb blast kills an off-duty police officer and critically injures a clinic counselor in Birmingham, Ala. Media portrays this as an act of terrorism, implying that the victims are innocents engaged in a legal activity. Little notice is given to the fact that this abortion clinic is criminal – it has announced that it is continuing to perform "a certain type of late-term abortions" in defiance of "new state laws." Thus the "counselor" and the moonlighting policeman are accomplices in the illegal killing of legally-protected preborn children [Facts from *Press*, 1-30-98, A1, A10].

Judicial Flip Benham leads 250 pro-lifers in a "Show the Truth" event at a Lynchburg, Va., high school, displaying 6-foot-high graphic photos of aborted babies and handing out gospel tracts. Even though 47 police officers are on the scene, no tickets are issued and no one is arrested because no crimes have been committed. A Grand Jury, after the fact, finds cause to jail flip Benham "for one year," beginning 2-18-98.

The Delaware teens who threw their newborn child into a motel dumpster are sentenced to two, and to $2^1/_2$ years in prison.

Zeal Joan AndrewsBell is jailed for "up to 23 months" for "probation violation."

Robert Braun and John Stambaugh, sentenced to one year for a 1994 "car rescue."

Richard T. Andrews, 7 years for arson.

Eric Robert Rudolph's truck is spotted near the New Woman All Women Clinic in Birmingham [Ala.] on Jan. 29, the morning an explosion kills an off-duty policeman working as a security guard and critically injures a nurse. Most of the media fails to mention that the clinic had announced that it would operate illegally in defiance of a new state ban on partial-birth abortions.

For updates on incarcerated pro-lifers: *Prisoners of Christ*, a ministry of Missionaries to the Preborn, Box 583, Skyforest, CA 92385-0583; (607) 655-4247; Fax: (607) 655-4242; E-mail: poclist@aol.com Web site: http://integracom.net/mttu/poc

If the TRUMPET does not sound a clear call, who will get ready for battle?
1 Corinthians 14:8

INTRODUCTION

The spiritual foundation of *Orphans in Babylon* emerged during a providential "forty-days-and-forty-nights" in 1990 when the researcher prayerfully examined every verse in the Bible, asking, "Lord, what does this say about my sin, abortion, discipleship, and the Church in America today?"

The five hundred biblical verses which were illuminated during that study eventually arranged themselves into twenty-one themes. A representative sample of the Bible verses is offered below, along with the twenty-one foundational themes.

THEME 1
GOD'S PEOPLE ARE ALIENS ON EARTH

The Bible requires that every Christian's life be regularly re-aligned with God's eternal priorities.

Many live as enemies of the cross of Christ. Their destiny is destruction, their god is their appetite, and their fame is their shame. Their mind is on earthly things. But our CITIZENSHIP is in heaven.
Philippians 3:18-20

Blessed are those whose strength is in You, who have set their hearts on PILGRIMAGE. As they pass through the Valley of Tears, they make it a place of springs... They go from strength to strength, till each appears before God in Zion.
Psalm 84:5-7

Each man's life is but a breath. Man is a mere PHANTOM as he goes to and fro: he bustles about, but only in vain; he heaps up wealth, not knowing who will get it...
I dwell with you as an alien, a stranger, as all my fathers were.
Psalm 39:5-6,12

By the rivers of Babylon we sat and wept when we remembered Zion. There on the poplars we hung our HARPS, for there our captors asked us for songs, our tormentors demanded songs of joy... How can we sing the songs of the Lord while in a foreign land?
Psalm 137:1-4

If you belonged to the world, it would love you as its own. As it is, you do not belong to the world, but I have CHOSEN you out of the world. That is why the world hates you.
John 15:19

Do not be YOKED together with unbelievers... We are the temple of the living God. As God has said, "I will live with them and walk among them... Therefore come out from them and be separate."
2 Corinthians 6:14, 16-17

...though we live in the world we do not wage war as the world does. The weapons we fight with are not the weapons of the world. On the contrary, they have divine power to DEMOLISH strongholds.
2 Corinthians 10:3-4

Am I trying to PLEASE men? If I were still trying to please men, I would not be a servant of Christ.
Galatians 1:10

Anyone who chooses to be a friend of the WORLD becomes an enemy of God.
James 4:4

Dear friends, I urge you, as ALIENS and strangers in the world, to abstain from sinful desires, which war against your soul.
1 Peter 2:11

Do not love the world or anything in the world... For everything in the world.. CRAVINGS.. lust.. boasting.. comes not from the Father but from the world.
1 John 2:15-16

THEME 2
GOD'S WORD FLOWS THROUGH US

We are to immerse ourselves in the Bible every day, not so that we can conduct ourselves biblically, but so that God can take charge and use us to His glory.

I am ridiculed all day long; everyone mocks me... The word of the Lord has brought me insult and reproach all day long. But if I say, "I will not mention Him, or speak any more in His name," His word is in my heart like a fire, a FIRE shut up in my bones. I am weary of holding it in; indeed, I cannot.
Jeremiah 20:7-9

King Balak said to BALAAM, "What have you done to me? I brought you to curse my enemies, but you bless them?" Balaam answered, "Must I not speak what the Lord puts in my mouth?"
Numbers 23:11-12

These commandments that I give you today are to be upon your hearts.. Talk about them when you sit.. walk.. lie down.. get up. Tie... bind them on your FOREHEADS. Write them on the doorframes...
Deuteronomy 6:6-9

Take to heart all the words I have solemnly declared to you this day, so that you may command your children to obey carefully all the words of this law. They are not just idle words for you – they are your LIFE.
Deuteronomy 32:46-47

Do not let this book of the law depart from your mouth; MEDITATE on it day and night, so that you may be careful to do everything written in it.
Joshua 1:8

David said, "Here I am, living in a PALACE of cedar, while the ark of the covenant of the Lord is under a tent." Nathan said, "Whatever you have in mind, do it, for God is with you." That night the word of God came to Nathan, [tell David] "You are NOT the one to build me a house to dwell in."
1 Chronicles 17:1-4

I have not departed from the commands of His lips; I have TREASURED the words of His mouth more than my daily bread.
Job 23:12

The law of the Lord is perfect, reviving the soul.. making wise.. giving joy.. giving light.. enduring forever.. more precious than gold.. sweeter than honey.. by them is your servant warned; in keeping them there is great REWARD.
Psalm 19:7-11

...Teach me your decrees.. I rejoice in following your statutes as one rejoices in great riches.. Open my eyes that I may see wonderful things in your law.. Though rulers sit together and slander me, your servant will meditate on your decrees. Your statutes are my delight; they are my COUNSELORS.
Psalm 119:12-24

Wisdom is supreme.. Though it cost all you have, get understanding. Esteem her, and she will exalt you; embrace her, and she will honor you.. The PATH of the righteous is like the first gleam of dawn, shining ever brighter till the full light of day.
Proverbs 4:7-8, 18

A discerning man keeps wisdom in VIEW, but a fool's eyes wander to the ends of the earth.
Proverbs 17:24

Then the Lord reached out his hand and touched my mouth and said to me, "Now, I have put My words in your mouth. See, today I appoint you over nations and kingdoms to UPROOT, and tear down, to destroy and overthrow, to build and to plant."
Jeremiah 1:9-10

Let the prophet who has a dream tell his dream, but let the one who has My Word speak it faithfully. For what has straw to do with grain? Is not my Word like fire, ..and like a HAMMER that breaks rock in pieces?
Jeremiah 23:28-29

I will put My law in their minds and write it on their hearts.. No longer will a man teach his neighbor, or a man his brother, saying, "Know the Lord," because they will ALL know Me, from the least of them to the greatest.
Jeremiah 31:33-34

What I tell you in the dark, speak in the daylight; what is whispered in your ear, proclaim from the ROOFTOPS.
Matthew 10:27

Jesus answered [the devil], *"It is WRITTEN: 'Man does not live by bread alone..' 'Worship the Lord your God and serve Him only..' 'Do not put the Lord your God to the test.'"*
Luke 4:4, 8, 12

The good man brings good things out of the good STORED UP in his heart.
Luke 6:45

When they saw the courage of Peter and John and realized that they were UNSCHOOLED, ordinary men, they were astonished and took note that these men had been with Jesus.
Acts 4:13

I myself [Paul] *am convinced, my brothers, that you yourselves are full of goodness, complete in knowledge, and COMPETENT to instruct one another.*
Romans 15:14

..you shine like the STARS in the universe as you hold out the word of life.
Philippians 2:15-16

Let the word of Christ dwell in you richly as you teach and ADMONISH one another with all wisdom...
Colossians 3:16

All scripture is God-breathed and is useful for teaching, rebuking, correcting and training in righteousness, so that the man of God may be thoroughly EQUIPPED for every good work.
2 Timothy 3:16-17

The word of God is living and ACTIVE, sharper than any double-edged sword, it penetrates even to dividing soul and spirit, joints and marrow.. Let us hold firmly to the faith we profess.. Let us then approach the throne of grace with confidence.
Hebrews 4:12, 14, 16

Like newborn babies, CRAVE pure spiritual milk, so that by it you may grow up in your salvation, now that you have tasted that the Lord is good.
1 Peter 2:2-3

THEME 3
PRAYER IS LISTENING TO GOD

We must repent of the prayers that treat God as our servant, and learn to listen to the voice of the Holy Spirit.

The PATH of the righteous is like the first gleam of dawn, shining ever brighter till the full light of day.

Proverbs 4:18

At Marah.. bitter water.. people grumbled. The Lord showed Moses a piece of wood.. He threw it into the water, and the water became sweet. There the Lord made a decree, a law.. He tested them.. He said, "LISTEN carefully to the voice of the Lord."

Exodus 15:23-26

Joshua said to the Lord.. "O sun, stand still over Gibeon." ..The SUN stopped in the middle of the sky and delayed going down about a full day. There has never been a day like it before or since when the Lord listened to a man.

Joshua 10:12-14

The Israelites said to Gideon, "Rule over us.. because you have saved us.." But Gideon told them, "I will not rule over you, nor will my son rule over you. The Lord will RULE over you."

Judges 8:22-23

..There was a famine for three successive years; so David sought the face of the Lord. The Lord said, "It is on account of Saul and his BLOOD-STAINED house.. because he put the Gibeonites to death.." [After seven of Saul's descendants were killed, then] *God answered prayer in behalf of the land.*

2 Samuel 21:1, 6, 14

[Elijah:] *"I am the only one left."* [Cave: wind, earthquake, fire; gentle WHISPER = God:] *"What are you doing here? ..Go back.. anoint Elisha to succeed you as prophet.* [By the way:] *I reserve 7,000 in Israel – all whose knees have not bowed down to Baal."*

1 Kings 19:10-18

[Isaiah:] *"This is what the Lord says: 'Put your house in order, because you are going to die; you will not recover.'" Hezekiah turned his face to the wall and prayed.. Before Isaiah had left the middle court, the word of the Lord came to him: "GO BACK and tell Hezekiah.. 'I will heal you.'"* [+ 15 yrs.]

2 Kings 20:1-6

The pillars of the heavens quake, aghast at His rebuke. By His power He churned up the sea; by His wisdom He cut Egypt to pieces.. and these are but the outer fringe of His works; how faint the whisper we hear of Him! Who then can understand the THUNDER of His power?

Job 26:11-14

The Lord CONFIDES in those who fear Him..

Psalm 25:14

O Lord God almighty, how long will Your anger SMOLDER against the prayers of Your people.. ? Our enemies mock us.

Psalm 80:4, 6

Does the CLAY say to the potter, "What are you making?" ..Concerning things to come, do you question Me.. or give Me orders about the work of My hands? ..I will raise up Cyrus in My righteousness.. He will rebuild My city and set My exiles free, but not for a price or reward.

Isaiah 45:9, 11,13

The king asked Daniel, "Are you able to tell me what I saw *in my dream and interpret it?" Daniel replied, "No wise man, enchanter, magician or diviner can explain to the king the mystery he has asked about,* but *there is a God in heaven who reveals MYSTERIES.."*

Daniel 2:26-28

[Daniel:] *"I turned to the Lord God and PLEADED with Him in prayer and petition, in fasting, and in sackcloth and ashes.."* [485-word opening to his prayer! Gabriel interrupts:] *"Daniel, I have now come to give you insight and understanding. As soon as you* began *to pray, an answer was given.."*

Daniel 9:3-23

[Jesus:] *"When you pray, go into your room, close the door and pray to your Father, who is unseen. Then your Father, who sees what is done in SECRET, will reward you.. Your Father knows what you need before you ask Him."*

Matthew 6:6, 8

I was the craftsman at His side, I was filled with delight day after day, REJOICING always in His presence, rejoicing in His whole world and delighting in mankind.

Proverbs 8:30-31

[Jesus:] *"My Father, if it is possible, may this cup be taken from me, yet not as I will, but as You WILL."*

Matthew 26:39

[Jesus:] *"The Son can do nothing by Himself; He can do only what He sees the Father doing.. By Myself I can do nothing; I judge only as I HEAR."*

John 5:19, 30

[Jesus:] *"The Counselor, the Holy Spirit, ..will teach you all things and will REMIND you of everything I have said to you."*

John 14:26

We do not know what we ought to pray for, but the Spirit Himself intercedes for us with GROANS that words cannot express.

Romans 8:26

Devote yourselves to prayer, being WATCHFUL and thankful.

Colossians 4:2

You do not have because you do not ASK God. When you ask, you do not receive, because you ask with wrong motives, that you may spend what you get on your pleasures.

James 4:2-3

THEME 4
ABORTION KILLS CHILDREN

The law of our land now makes it a federal felony to interfere with the business of killing human children. God's law still says, "Thou shalt not kill" [Exodus 20:13 and Leviticus 24:17].

Why are you silent while the wicked swallow up those more righteous than themselves? You have made men like fish in the sea.. The wicked foe pulls all of them up by HOOKS.. By his net he lives in luxury and enjoys the choicest food. Is he to keep on emptying his net, destroying nations without mercy?

Habakkuk 1:13-17

[If fighting men hit a pregnant woman,] *..if there is serious injury, you are to take life for life, eye for eye, TOOTH for tooth, hand for hand, foot for foot, burn for burn, wound for wound, bruise for bruise.*

Exodus 21:22-25

Do not give any of your CHILDREN to be sacrificed to Molech, for you must not profane the name of your God.

Leviticus 18:21

If the people of the community CLOSE their EYES when that man gives one of his children to Molech and they fail to put him to death, I will set My face against that man.. and all who follow him..

Leviticus 20:4-5

Ahaz.. walked in the ways of the kings of Israel and even sacrificed his son in the fire, following the DETESTABLE ways of the nations the Lord had driven out before the Israelites.

2 Kings 16:2-3

[Great revival] *Josiah desecrated Topeth.. so no one could use it to sacrifice his son or daughter in the fire to Molech.. He also desecrated the high places that were east of Jerusalem.. and SLAUGHTERED all the priests of those high places on the altars.*

2 Kings 23:10, 13, 20

What right have you to recite My laws or take My covenant on your lips? You hate My instruction and cast My words behind you.. These thing you have done and I kept silent.. CONSIDER this, you who forget God, or I will tear you to pieces, with none to rescue.

Psalm 50:16-22

He will deliver the needy who cry out, the afflicted who have no one to help. He will take pity on the weak.. and save the needy from death. He will rescue them from oppression and violence, for PRECIOUS is their blood in His sight.

Psalm 72:12-14

Let this be written for a future generation, that a people not yet created may praise the Lord: "The Lord looked down from His sanctuary on high.. to hear the groans of the prisoners and RELEASE those condemned to death."

Psalm 102:18-20

They MINGLED with the nations and adopted their customs. They worshiped their idols, which became a snare to them. They sacrificed their sons and their daughters to demons. They shed innocent blood, the blood of their sons and daughters.. and the land was desecrated by their blood.

Psalm 106:35-38

RESCUE those being led away to death; hold back those staggering toward slaughter.

Proverbs 24:11

This city has so aroused My anger and WRATH that I must remove it from My sight.. They built high places for Baal.. to sacrifice their sons and daughters to Molech.

Jeremiah 32:31, 35

The children rebelled against Me: they did not follow My decrees, they were not careful to keep My laws.. I also gave them over to STATUTES that were not good and laws they could not live by; I let them become defiled through their gifts – the sacrifice of every firstborn – that I might fill them with horror so they would know that I am the Lord.

Ezekiel 20:21, 25-26

I will give you over to bloodshed and it will pursue you. Since you did not hate bloodshed, BLOODSHED will pursue you.

Ezekiel 35:6

The DRAGON stood in front of the woman who was about to give birth, so that he might devour her child the moment it was born.

Revelation 12:4

THEME 5
WE CHRISTIANS KEEP ON SINNING

Because of our silence in public, the government, the media, society, and our own children have rightly concluded that the church doesn't think abortion is such a big deal.

[Paul:] *Christ Jesus came into the world to save sinners, of whom I AM the worst.*
1 Timothy 1:15

David had done what was right in the eyes of the Lord and had not failed to keep any of the Lord's commands all the days of his life – except in the case of URIAH the Hittite.
1 Kings 15:5

They [converts to the faith] *would not listen, but PERSISTED in their former practices. Even while these people were worshiping the Lord, they were serving their idols. To this day their children and grandchildren continue to do as their fathers did.*
2 Kings 17:40-41

[Solomon's prayer:] *WHEN they sin.. if they have a change of heart.. repent.. plead with You.. If they turn back to You with all their heart and soul.. then.. hear their prayer and their pleas, and uphold their cause. And forgive Your people who have sinned against You.*
2 Chronicles 6:36-39

This only have I found: God made mankind upright, but men have gone in search of many SCHEMES.
Ecclesiastes 7:29

Has a nation ever changed its gods? But My people have exchanged their glory for worthless idols. Be appalled at this.. My people have committed two sins: they have forsaken Me, the spring of living water, and have dug their own CISTERNS, broken cisterns that can not hold water.
Jeremiah 2:11-13

Peter followed Him at a DISTANCE, right into the courtyard of the high priest. There he sat with the guards and warmed himself at the fire.
Mark 14:54

..No one will be declared righteous in His sight by observing the law; rather, through the law we become conscious of sin.. Righteousness comes through faith in Jesus Christ.. There is no difference, for all have sinned and FALL SHORT of the glory of God.
Romans 3:20-23

In my inner being I delight in God's law; but I see another law at work in the members of my body, waging war.. making me a prisoner of the law of sin.. What a WRETCHED man I am! Who will rescue me from this body of death?..God, through Jesus Christ our Lord!
Romans 7:22-25

Everything that does not come from FAITH is sin.
Romans 14:23

Whoever keeps the whole law and yet STUMBLES at just one point is guilty of breaking all of it.
James 2:10

Anyone, then who knows the good he OUGHT to do and doesn't do it, sins.
James 4:17

You have HOARDED wealth in the last days.. You have lived on earth in luxury and self-indulgence. You have fattened yourselves in the day of slaughter.
James 5:3, 5

THEME 6
WHAT WE SOW WE SHALL REAP

Defiled by the innocent blood of the aborted one-third of an entire generation, our land is now convulsed by greed, decadence and violence.

Do not judge, and you will not be judged; do not condemn, and you will not be condemned. Forgive, and you will be forgiven. Give, and it will be given to you.. For with the MEASURE you use, it will be measured to you.
Luke 6:37-38

[God, to Adam:] *"Cursed is the ground because of you.. It will produce thorns and thistles for you.. By the SWEAT of your brow you will eat your food."*
Genesis 3:17-19

..this [by sexual sins and child sacrifice] *is how the nations that I am going to drive out before you became defiled.. and if you defile the land, it will VOMIT you out as it vomited out the nations that were before you.*
Leviticus 18:24-25, 28

If you follow My decrees: peace.. If you reject: I will punish you.. I will break down your stubborn pride. You will eat, but not be satisfied.. The land of your enemies will DEVOUR you.
Leviticus 26:3-6, 15, 18-19, 26, 38

Your children will be shepherds here, suffering for your unfaithfulness.. for 40 YEARS – one for each of the 40 days you explored the land.
Numbers 14:33-34

Saul died because he was unfaithful to the Lord; he did not keep the word of the Lord and even consulted a medium for guidance, and he did not INQUIRE of the Lord. So the Lord put him to death and turned the kingdom over to David son of Jesse.
1 Chronicles 10:13-14

[Nathan to David, for God, about Uriah:] *"Therefore the sword will never depart from your house, because you despised Me and took the wife of Uriah.. the Lord says, 'Out of your own household I am going to bring calamity* [see 2 Samuel 16:22] *upon you.. You did it in secret, but I will do this thing in broad DAYLIGHT before all Israel.'"*
2 Samuel 12:9-12

[The Lord, to Rehoboam, through Shemaiah:] *"Since they have humbled themselves, ..My wrath will not be poured out on Jerusalem through Shishak* [king of Egypt]. *They will, however, become SUBJECT to him, so that they may learn the difference between serving Me and serving the kings of other lands."*
2 Chronicles 12:7-8

[Levites' prayer during a great revival under Ezra:] *"In all that has happened to us, You have been just; You have acted faithfully, while we did wrong.. See, we are SLAVES today, slaves in the land you gave our forefathers.. Because of our sins, its abundant harvest goes to the kings you have placed over us. They rule over our bodies.. as they please."*
Nehemiah 9:33-37

..so they hanged Haman on the GALLOWS he had prepared for Mordecai..
Esther 7:10

[About the godless:] *Though evil is sweet in his mouth.. yet his food will turn sour in his stomach; it will become the VENOM of serpents within him. He will spit out the riches he swallowed.. Surely he will have no respite from his craving.. In the midst of his plenty distress will overtake him.*
Job 20:12-22

He who is pregnant with evil and conceives trouble gives birth to DISILLUSIONMENT... [He] *falls into the pit he has made.. His violence comes down on his own head.*
Psalm 7:14-16

You were to Israel a forgiving God, though you punished their MISDEEDS.
Psalm 99:8

The wicked man will see and be vexed, he will GNASH his teeth and waste away; the longings of the wicked will come to nothing.
Psalm 112:10

..ruthless men gain only wealth.. The wicked man earns DECEPTIVE wages, but he who sows righteousness reaps a sure reward. The truly righteous man attains life.
Proverbs 11:16, 18-19

Food gained by fraud tastes sweet to a man, but he ends up with a mouth full of GRAVEL.
Proverbs 20:17

If a man digs a PIT, he will fall into it; if a man rolls a stone, it will roll back on him.
Proverbs 26:27

Cut down the trees and build SIEGE ramps against Jerusalem. This city must be punished; it is filled with oppression. As a well pours out its water, so she pours out her wickedness. Violence and destruction resound in her; her sickness and wounds are ever before Me.
Jeremiah 6:6-7

Their silver and gold will not be able to save them.. I will turn My face away and robbers will enter and desecrate My treasured place.. Because the land is full of bloodshed and the city is full of violence.. teaching of the law by the priest will be lost.. By their own STANDARDS I will judge them.
Ezekiel 7:19-27

[Repeated from #4] *I will give you over to bloodshed and it will pursue you. Since you did not hate BLOODSHED, bloodshed will pursue you.*
Ezekiel 35:6

[Jesus:] *"Do not judge, and you will not be judged; do not condemn, and you will not be condemned. Forgive, and you will be forgiven, give, and it will be given to you.. For with the MEASURE you use, it will be measured to you."*
Luke 6:37-38

Why do you judge your brother? Or why do you look down on your brother? For we will all stand before God's judgment seat.. "Every knee will bow.. every tongue will confess.." Each of us will give an ACCOUNT of himself to God.
Romans 14:10-12

Whoever SOWS sparingly will also reap sparingly, and whoever sows generously will also reap generously.. God loves a cheerful giver.
2 Corinthians 9:6-7

Do not be deceived: God cannot be mocked. A man reaps what he sows.. Let us not become weary in doing good, for at the proper time we will reap a HARVEST if we do not give up.
Galatians 6:7-9

..He who began a good work in you will carry it on to COMPLETION until the day of Christ Jesus..
Philippians 1:6

THEME 7
JUDGMENT BEGINS WITH THE CHURCH

We Christians have "despised our birthright" [Genesis 25:34] as proclaimers of God's holy law regarding civil rights, legislated godlessness, the sexual revolution, abortion, violent entertainment, and gay "rights." Every time we surrender with a whimper instead of a fight, the devil is empowered and God's Bride is enfeebled.

Peter followed Him at a DISTANCE, right into the courtyard of the high priest. There he sat with the guards and warmed himself at the fire.

Mark 14:54

King Josiah said, "..repair the temple of the Lord.." Hilkiah the high priest said to Shaphan the secretary, "I have FOUND the book of the law!"

2 Kings 22:3-8

..If My people who are called by My name will HUMBLE themselves and pray and seek My face and turn from their wicked ways, then I will hear from heaven and will forgive their sin and will heal their land.

2 Chronicles 7:14

This is what Sennacherib king of Assyria says: "On what are you basing your CONFIDENCE, that you remain in Jerusalem under siege?"

2 Chronicles 32:10

You [God] *have shaken the land and torn it open.. You have shown Your people desperate times.. But for those who fear You, You have raised a BANNER to be unfurled against the bow.. God has spoken from His sanctuary: "Who will bring Me to the fortified city?"*

Psalm 60:2-4, 6, 9

[The Babylonians] *said in their hearts, "We will crush them completely!" They BURNED every place where God was worshiped in the land. We are given no miraculous signs; no prophets are left, and none of us knows how long this will be. How long will the enemy mock You, O God?*

Psalm 74:8-10

I am the Lord your God, who brought you up out of Egypt, [saying:] *"Open wide your MOUTH and I will fill it." But My people would not listen.. would not submit.. so I gave them over to their stubborn hearts to follow their own devices.*

Psalm 81:10-12

These are rebellious people.. unwilling to listen.. They say to the prophets, "Give us no more visions of what is right. Tell us pleasant things, prophesy illusions.. Get off this path and stop CONFRONTING us."

Isaiah 30:9-11

Let him who walks in the dark, who has no light, trust in the name of the Lord.. But now, all you who light fires and provide yourselves with flaming TORCHES, go, walk in the light of your fires and of the torches you have set ablaze.. You will lie down in torment.

Isaiah 50:10-11

Raise your voice like a trumpet. Declare to my people their REBELLION.. For day after day they seek Me out; they seem eager to know My ways, as if they were a nation that does what is right and has not forsaken the commands of its God.

Isaiah 58:1-2

..Prophets and priests alike, all practice deceit. They dress the WOUND of My people as though it were not serious. "Peace, peace," they say, when there is no peace.

Jeremiah 6:13-14

The Lord says, "Stand at the CROSSROADS and look; ask for the ancient paths, ask where the good way is, and walk in it, and you will find rest for your souls.." But you said, "We will not walk in it."

Jeremiah 6:16

I [God] *said, "Listen to the sound of the trumpet." but you said, "We will not listen." Therefore* [God says] *"I am bringing disaster on this people, the fruit of their schemes, because they have not listened to My words and have REJECTED My law."*

Jeremiah 6:17-19

Though they blow the trumpet and get everything ready, no one will go into battle.. Outside is the sword, inside are plague and famine.. Every hand will go LIMP, and every knee will become as weak as water.. because the land is full of bloodshed and the city is full of violence.. I will deal with them according to their conduct..

Ezekiel 7:14-17, 23, 27

[God to His messenger:] *"..put a mark on the foreheads of those who grieve and lament over all the detestable things.."* [to the guards of the city:] *"Follow him through the city and kill* [all others]. *Begin at My SANCTUARY.. The land is full of bloodshed and the city is full of injustice.. I will bring down on their own heads what they have done."*

Ezekiel 9:4-6, 9-10

[Repeated from #5] *You have HOARDED wealth in the last days.. You have lived on earth in luxury and self-indulgence. You have fattened yourselves in the day of slaughter.*

James 5:3, 5

So, because you are LUKEWARM – neither hot nor cold – I am getting ready to spit you out of My mouth.

Revelation 3:16

It is time for judgment to begin with the FAMILY of God.

1 Peter 4:17

THEME 8
WE MUST NOT FAIL GOD'S TESTING

The nature of Godly warfare is non-violent confrontation. Goliaths strut until Davids step forth.

God tested Abraham.. "Take your son, your only son, Isaac, whom you love.. SACRIFICE him.. on one of the mountains I will tell you about."

Genesis 22:1-2

[The Lord to Abram] *"They will be enslaved and mistreated four hundred years.. In the fourth generation your descendants will come back here, for the sin of the Amorites has not yet reached its FULL MEASURE."*

Genesis 15:13, 16

Moses said to the Lord, "..I am SLOW of speech and tongue.. O Lord, please send someone else to do it."

Exodus 4:10, 13

When you eat and are satisfied, be careful that you do not FORGET the Lord who brought you out of Egypt.

Deuteronomy 6:11-12

Because you did not serve the Lord your God joyfully and gladly in the time of PROSPERITY, therefore in hunger and thirst, in nakedness and dire poverty, you will serve the enemies the Lord sends against you.

Deuteronomy 28:47-48

[The Lord through Moses:] *This day I call heaven and earth as a witness against you that I have set before you life and death, blessings and curses. Now CHOOSE life, so that you and your children may live and that you may love the Lord your God, listen to His voice, and hold fast to Him.*

Deuteronomy 30:19-20

Elijah went before the people and said, "How long will you WAVER between two opinions? If the Lord is God, follow him; but if Baal is god, follow him."

1 Kings 18:21

[Four Hebrew lepers, plundering the deserted Aramean camp...] *Then they said to each other, "We're not doing right. This is a day of GOOD NEWS and we are keeping it to ourselves." ..The gatekeeper shouted the news, and it was reported within the palace.*

2 Kings 7:9, 11

In his time of trouble king Ahaz became even more unfaithful to the Lord. He offered sacrifices to the gods of Damascus, who had defeated him; for he thought, "Since the gods of the king of Aram have helped them, I will sacrifice to them so they will help me." But they were his DOWNFALL.

2 Chronicles 28:22-23

Hezekiah had very great riches and honor.. He succeeded in everything he undertook. But when envoys were sent by the rulers of Babylon.. GOD LEFT him to test him and to know everything that was in his heart.

2 Chronicles 32:27, 30-31

Do not hand over the life of your dove to wild beasts.. because HAUNTS of violence fill the dark places of the land.

Psalm 74:19-20

The men of Ephraim, though armed with bows, TURNED BACK on the day of battle; they did not keep God's covenant and refused to live by His law. They forgot what He had done, the wonders He had shown them.

Psalm 78:9-11

Who will rise up for Me against the wicked? Who will take a stand for Me against evildoers? ..Can a corrupt THRONE be allied with you – one that brings on misery by its decrees? They band together against the righteous and condemn the innocent to death.

Psalm 94:16, 20-21

TERROR and pit and snare await you, O people of the earth. Whoever flees at the sound of terror will fall into a pit. Whoever climbs out of the pit will be caught in a snare..

Isaiah 24:17-18

Before I formed you in the womb I knew you [Jeremiah].. *set you apart.. appointed you as a prophet to the nations. "Ah, sovereign Lord," I said, "I do not know how to speak; I am ONLY a child."*

Jeremiah 1:5-6

If you have raced with men on foot and they have worn you out, how can you compete with horses? If you stumble in safe country, how will you manage in the THICKETS by the Jordan? [see Joshua 3:15, crossing at flood stage to take the promised land.]

Jeremiah 12:5

Endure hardship as DISCIPLINE.. If you are not disciplined.. then you are illegitimate children and not true sons.

Hebrews 12:7-8

Consider it pure joy, my brothers, whenever you face trials of many kinds, because you know that the testing of your faith develops PERSEVERANCE.

James 1:2-3

THEME 9
WE ARE CALLED TO DISCIPLESHIP

Jesus said, "Here are my mother and my brothers" [Matthew 12:49], not about those who came to Him for sermons and potluck suppers, but to those who signed on to walk and serve and die-to-self for Him.

Prepare for war! Rouse the warriors! ..Beat your PLOWSHARES into swords and your pruning hooks into spears. Let the weakling say, "I am strong!" ..Multitudes, multitudes in the valley of decision!
Joel 3:9-10, 14

Gideon asked [God]*: "How can I save Israel? My CLAN is the weakest.. and I am the least."* [God's message:] *"Go in the strength you have...I will be with you.." The Spirit of the Lord came upon Gideon, and he blew a trumpet.*
Judges 6:14-15, 34

[Elijah threw his CLOAK around Elisha] *Elisha took his yoke of oxen and slaughtered them. He burned the plowing equipment to cook the meat and gave it to the people.. then he set out to follow Elijah, and became his attendant.*
1 Kings 19:19-21

Elijah went up to heaven in a whirlwind.. Elisha picked up the cloak that had fallen from Elijah and went back and stood on the bank of the Jordan.. When he struck the water it divided to the right and to the left, and he CROSSED over.
2 Kings 2:11-14

In God I trust; I will not be afraid. What can man do to me? I am under VOWS to you, O God.. You have delivered me from death.. that I may walk before God in the light of life.
Psalm 56:11-13

[Repeated from #7] *You* [God] *have shaken the land and torn it open.. You have shown your people desperate times.. But for those who fear You, You have raised a BANNER to be unfurled against the bow.. God has spoken from His sanctuary: "Who will bring Me to the fortified city?"*
Psalm 60:2-4, 6, 9

Speak up for those who cannot speak for themselves, for the rights of all who are destitute. SPEAK UP and judge fairly; defend the rights of the poor and needy.
Proverbs 31:8-9

Is not this the kind of FASTING I have chosen: to loose the chains of injustice and untie the cords of the yoke, to set the oppressed free and break every yoke? Is it not to share your food with the hungry, and to provide the poor wanderer with shelter, when you see the naked, to clothe him..
Isaiah 58:6-7

If the WATCHMAN sees the sword coming and does not blow the trumpet to warn the people.. I will hold the watchman accountable.. I have made you a watchman.. So hear the word I speak and give them warning from Me.
Ezekiel 33:6-7

Not everyone who says to Me, "LORD, LORD," will enter the Kingdom of Heaven, but only he who does the will of My Father who is in Heaven.
Matthew 7:21

Love the Lord your God with all your heart and with all your soul and with all your mind.. LOVE your neighbor as yourself.
Matthew 22:37, 39

I was hungry.. thirsty.. a stranger.. in need of clothes.. sick.. in prison.. Whatever you did for ONE of the least of these brothers of Mine, you did for Me.
Matthew 25:35-36, 40

It was He who gave some to be apostles.. prophets.. evangelists.. pastors.. teachers.. to PREPARE God's people for works of service.
Ephesians 4:11-12

Continue to work out your salvation with fear and TREMBLING, for it is God who works in you to will and to act according to His good purpose.
Philippians 2:12-13

..Let us leave the elementary teachings about Christ and go on to MATURITY.. Enlightened.. we have tasted the heavenly gift, have shared in the Holy Spirit, and have tasted the goodness of the word of God, and the powers of the coming age.
Hebrews 6:1-5

Do not merely listen to the word, and so deceive yourselves, DO what it says.
James 1:22

Whoever claims to live in Him must WALK as Jesus did.
1 John 2:6

THEME 10
STANDING WITH JESUS MEANS STANDING APART

Predictions of family friction were Jesus' way of telling us that although the soldier's calling is only different [not higher], dissension – judgment of each "side" by the other – is a reality we must struggle to avoid.

They took offense at Him. Jesus said to them, "Only in his hometown, among his relatives and in his own house, is a prophet without honor." He COULD NOT do any miracles there, except lay His hands on a few sick people and heal them.
Mark 6:3-5

[Joshua:] *"Choose for yourselves this day whom you will serve.. but as for ME and MY household, we will serve the Lord."*
Joshua 24:15

The princes of Issachar were with Deborah.. In the districts of Reuben there was much SEARCHING of heart.. Gilead stayed.. Dan lingered.. Asher remained.. [but] *the people of Zebulun risked their very lives; so did Naphtali on the heights of the field.*
Judges 5:15-18

These were the men who came to David at Ziklag, while he was banished from the presence of Saul.. They were KINSMEN of Saul from the tribe of Benjamin.
1 Chronicles 12:1-2

[Amaziah, king of Judah, had 300,000 troops; he hired 100,000 more from Israel] *The man of God said, "O king, these troops from Israel must not march with you, for the Lord is not with Israel. ..Even if you go and fight courageously in battle, God will OVERTHROW you before the enemy."*
2 Chronicles 25:5-8

[Hezekiah's invitation to Jerusalem for the Passover:] *"If you return to the Lord, then your brothers and your children will be shown compassion by their captors.." Couriers went from town to town.. The people SCORNED and ridiculed them. Nevertheless, some men humbled themselves and went to Jerusalem. ..a very large crowd.*
2 Chronicles 30:9-13

If an enemy were insulting me, I could endure it.. But it is you, a man like myself, my COMPANION, my close friend, with whom I once enjoyed sweet fellowship as we walked with the throng at the house of God.
Psalm 55:12-14

[His own people said:] *"Come, let's make PLANS against Jeremiah, so the teaching of the law by the priests will not be lost.. So come, let's attack him with our tongues and pay no attention to anything he says."*
Jeremiah 18:18

They will be mine in the day when I make up my treasured possession. I will spare them.. and you will again see the DISTINCTION between the righteous and the wicked, between those who serve God and those who do not.
Malachi 3:17-18

No one can serve two MASTERS. Either he will hate the one and love the other, or he will be devoted to one and despise the other. You cannot serve both God and money.
Matthew 6:24

Do not suppose that I have come to bring peace to earth. I did not come to bring peace, but a SWORD. For I have come to turn [man: father, daughter: mother..] *A man's enemies will be the members of his own household.*
Matthew 10:34-36

[Jesus:] *"Who is my MOTHER, and who are my brothers?" Pointing to his disciples, He said, "Here are my mother and my brothers. For whoever does the will of my Father in heaven is my brother and sister and mother."*
Matthew 12:48-50

Again a crowd gathered, so that He and His disciples were not even able to eat. When His family heard about this, they went to TAKE CHARGE of Him, for they said, "He is out of His mind."
Mark 3:20-21

[Jesus:] *"The child is not dead but asleep." But they laughed Him to SCORN. After He put them all out, He took the child's father and mother and the disciples who were with Him, and went in where the child was..*
Mark 5:39-40

All men will HATE you because of me, but he who stands firm to the end will be saved.
Mark 13:13

I have come to bring fire on the earth, and how I wish it were already kindled! ..Do you think I came to bring peace on earth? No, I tell you, but DIVISION.
Luke 12:49,51

If anyone comes to Me and does not hate his father and mother, his wife and children, his brothers and sisters – yes, even his own life – he cannot be My disciple. And anyone who does not carry his CROSS and follow Me can not be My disciple.
Luke 14:25-27

Jesus' brothers said, "..Leave here and go to Judea.. No one who wants to be a public figure acts in secret.. Show your [miracles] *to the world." For even His own BROTHERS did not believe in Him.*
John 7:3-5

Am I trying to PLEASE men? If I were still trying to please men, I would not be a servant of Christ.
Galatians 1:10

Guard what has been entrusted to your care.. TURN AWAY from godless chatter and the opposing ideas of what is falsely called knowledge, which some have professed and in so doing have wandered from the faith.
1 Timothy 6:20-21

Warn a DIVISIVE person once, then warn him a second time. After that, have nothing to do with him.
Titus 3:10

Anyone who chooses to be a friend of the WORLD becomes an enemy of God.
James 4:4

THEME 11
WE MUST EXPECT AND ACCEPT PERSECUTION

To take a stand for God against the powers of this world is to be caught in a crossfire – to be attacked by God's enemies, and to be misunderstood and misjudged by His flock.

There will be TERRIBLE times in the last days. People will be lovers of themselves, lovers of money.. unholy, without love.. without self-control.. lovers of pleasure rather than lovers of God – having the form of godliness but denying its power. Have nothing to do with them.. Everyone who wants to live a godly life in Christ Jesus will be persecuted.

2 Timothy 3:1-5, 12

VINDICATE me, O God, and plead my cause against an ungodly nation; rescue me from deceitful and wicked men.

Psalm 43:1

The officials said to the king, "This man should be put to death. He is discouraging the soldiers.." So they took Jeremiah and put him into the cistern.. in the courtyard of the guard.. It had no water in it, only mud, and Jeremiah sank down into the MUD.

Jeremiah 38:4, 6

As [a heavenly voice] *spoke, the Spirit came into me.. He said.. "Whether they listen or fail to listen.. They will know that a prophet has been among them.. Do not be afraid, though briers and thorns are all around you and you live among SCORPIONS."*

Ezekiel 2:2, 5-6

[Shadrach, Meshach and Abednego:] *"..We will not serve your gods or worship the image of gold you have set up." Then Nebuchadnezzar was furious with* [them] *and his attitude toward them changed. He ordered the FURNACE heated seven times hotter than usual.*

Daniel 3:18-19

[Daniel's vision:] *As I watched, this horn was waging war against the saints and defeating them.. Another king will arise.. He will speak against the Most High and oppress His saints and try to change the set times and the laws. The saints will be HANDED OVER to him for a time...*

Daniel 7:21, 24-25

[Jesus:] *I am sending you prophets and wise men and teachers. Some of them you will kill and crucify; others you will FLOG in your synagogues* [churches] *and pursue from town to town.*

Matthew 23:34

No one who has left home [or family] *or fields for Me and the gospel will fail to receive a HUNDRED times as much in this present age.. and with them, persecutions...*

Mark 10:29-30

WHENEVER you are arrested and brought to trial, do not worry beforehand about what to say. Just say whatever is given you at the time, for it is not you speaking but the Holy Spirit.

Mark 13:11

All men will HATE you because of Me, but he who stands firm to the end will be saved.

Mark 13:13

I have CHOSEN you out of the world. That is why the world hates you.

John 15:19

A time is coming when anyone who kills you will think he is offering a SERVICE to God.

John 16:2

While they were trying to kill [Paul], *news reached the commander.. When the rioters saw the commander and his soldiers they stopped beating Paul. The commander came up and ARRESTED him.*

Acts 21:31-33

We are not trying to please men but God, who tests our hearts.. We sent Timothy.. so that no one would be unsettled by these trials.. We were DESTINED for them.. In fact.. we kept telling you that we would be persecuted.

1 Thessalonians 2:4; 3:2-4

Dear friends, do not be surprised at the painful trial you are suffering, as though something strange were happening to you. But rejoice that you PARTICIPATE in the sufferings of Christ.

1 Peter 4:12-13

THEME 12
GOD'S LAW SUPERSEDES MAN'S LAWS

Although they counsel that we should generally submit to worldly authority and accept the civil consequences of our obedience to God, the Apostles' own "rap sheets" include frequent defiance of court orders, resisting arrest ["lowered in a basket"] and a couple of jailbreaks.

They called the apostles in and had them flogged. Then they ORDERED them not to speak in the name of Jesus.. Day after day, in the temple courts and from house to house, they never stopped teaching and proclaiming the good news.

Acts 5:40-42

The king of Egypt said to the Hebrew midwives, "..If it is a boy, kill him." The MIDWIVES, however, feared God and did not do what the king of Egypt had told them to do, they let the boys live.

Exodus 1:15-17

Pharaoh gave this order: "Every boy that is born you must throw into the NILE." ...She became pregnant and gave birth to a son [Moses]. *..When she saw that he was a fine child, she hid him for three months.*

Exodus 1:22; 2:1-2

This is what you are to do to them [godless nations]*: break down their altars, SMASH their sacred stones, cut down their Asherah poles and burn their idols in the fire.*

Deuteronomy 7:5

Ahab summoned Obadiah, who was in charge of his palace. Obadiah was a devout believer in the Lord. While Jezebel was killing off the Lord's prophets, Obadiah had taken 100 prophets and hidden them in two CAVES.. and had supplied them with food and water.

1 Kings 18:3-4

When Athaliah saw that her son was dead, she proceeded to destroy the whole royal family. But Jehosheba.. took JOASH and stole him away from among the royal princes who were about to be murdered. She put him and his nurse in a bedroom to hide him.. [and then] *at the temple of the Lord for six years while Athaliah ruled...*

2 Kings 11:1-3

All the royal officials knelt down and paid honor to Haman, for the king had commanded this.. But Mordecai would not KNEEL down or pay him honor.. Day after day they spoke to him, but he refused to comply.

Esther 3:2-4

[Mordecai to Esther:] *"Who knows but that you have come to royal position for SUCH a TIME as this?"* [Esther's reply:] *"I will go to the king, even though it is against the law. And if I perish, I perish."*

Esther 4:14-16

When a land falls into the hands of the wicked, he BLINDFOLDS its judges.

Job 9:24

[Lord, to Jeremiah:] *"Today I appoint you over nations and kingdoms to UPROOT and tear down, to destroy and overthrow, to build and to plant."*

Jeremiah 1:10

[Daniel's friends:] *"If we are thrown into the blazing furnace, the God we serve is ABLE to save us from it.. But even if He does not, we want you to know, O king, that we will not serve your gods or worship the image of gold you have set up."*

Daniel 3:16-18

King Darius put the decree in writing [lion's den for those who pray]. *Now when Daniel learned that the decree had been PUBLISHED, he went home to his upstairs room where the windows opened toward Jerusalem. Three times a day he got down on his knees and prayed, giving thanks to his God, just as he had done before.*

Daniel 6:5, 7-10

Jesus went out and saw a tax collector by the name of Levi sitting at his tax booth. "Follow Me," Jesus said to him, and Levi got up, left EVERYTHING and followed him.

Luke 5:27-28

Peter and John replied, "JUDGE for yourselves whether it is right in God's sight to obey you rather than God, for we cannot help speaking about what we have seen and heard."

Acts 4:19-20

[High priest:] *"We gave you strict orders not to teach in this name, yet you have filled Jerusalem with your teaching.." Peter and the other apostles replied: "We must obey God RATHER than men!"*

Acts 5:28-29

Then some Jews came from Antioch and Iconium and won the crowd over. They STONED Paul and dragged him outside the city, thinking he was dead. But after the disciples had gathered around him, he got up and went back into the city.

Acts 14:19-20

The SPIRITUAL man makes judgments about all things, but he himself is not subject to any man's judgment.

1 Corinthians 2:15

I [Paul] *care very little if I am judged by you or by any human court.. My CONSCIENCE is clear, but that does not make me innocent. It is the Lord who judges me.. Wait till the Lord comes. He will bring to light what is hidden in darkness, and will expose the motives of men's hearts.*

1 Corinthians 4:3-5

In Damascus the governor.. had the city guarded in order to arrest me. But I was lowered in a BASKET from a window in the wall and slipped through his hands.

2 Corinthians 11:32-33

THEME 13
WE ARE CALLED NOT TO SUCCESS BUT TO FAITHFUL OBEDIENCE

Walt Disney-ed Christians who think that the good guys must always win will be rudely shaken up during the '90s, and beyond. We are to fight tooth-and-nail to the End, knowing that we are on the Side that can lose every battle and ultimately win the war!

Go and make disciples of all nations, baptizing them in the name of the Father and of the Son and of the Holy Spirit, and teaching them to OBEY everything I have commanded you.

Matthew 28:19-20

[Moses said:] *"Stand firm.. The Lord will fight for you; you need only be still." Then the Lord said to Moses, "Why are you crying out to me? Tell the Israelites to MOVE ON."*

Exodus 14:13-15

[David – fleeing Jerusalem, from his son Absalom – to Zadok:] *"Take the ARK of God back into the city. If I find favor in the Lord's eyes, He will bring me back and let me see it and His dwelling place again.. Let Him do to me whatever seems good to Him."*

2 Samuel 15:25-26

[Elisha summoned a prophet to anoint Jehu king of Israel – to destroy Ahab's survivors:] *"Take the flask and pour the oil on his head and declare, 'This is what the Lord says: I anoint you king over Israel.' Then don't DELAY; open the door and run!"*

2 Kings 9:1-3

[Jehoshaphat:] *"Do not be afraid or discouraged because of this vast army. For the battle is not yours, but God's.. You will not have to fight this battle. Take up your positions; STAND FIRM and see the deliverance the Lord will give you.."* [When they] *looked toward the vast army, they saw only dead bodies..*

2 Chronicles 20:15-17, 24

Search me O God, and know my heart; test me and know my anxious thoughts. See if there is any offensive way in me and LEAD me in the way everlasting.

Psalm 139:23-24

There is no wisdom, no insight, no plan that can succeed against the Lord. The HORSE is made ready for the day of battle, but victory rests with the Lord.

Proverbs 21:30-31

[God to Jeremiah:] *"Do not say, 'I am only a child.' You must go to everyone I send you to and say whatever I command you. Do not be afraid of them for I am with you.. Get yourself ready! Stand up and say to them whatever I command you.. Today I have made you a fortified city, an IRON PILLAR and a bronze wall to stand against the whole land."*

Jeremiah 1:7, 17-18

[God to Ezekiel:] *"I will make your forehead like the hardest stone.. Go now to your countrymen in exile and speak to them.."* [So] *I sat among them for seven days - OVERWHELMED..* [God:] *"I have made you a watchman.. I will hold you accountable..* [if you do not warn them], *but if you do warn the wicked man and he does not turn.. you will have saved yourself."*

Ezekiel 3:9, 11, 15-19

King Nebuchadnezzar leaped to his feet in amazement and asked his advisers, "Weren't there three men that we tied up and threw into the fire? ..I see four men walking around in the fire, unbound and UNHARMED, and the fourth looks like a son of the gods."

Daniel 3:24-25

[Amos:] *"I was neither a prophet nor a prophet's son.. but the Lord took me from TENDING the flock and said to me, 'Go, prophecy to my people..'"*

Amos 7:14-15

I will wait patiently for the day of CALAMITY to come on the nation invading us. Though the fig tree does not bud and there are no grapes on the vines, though the olive crop fails and the fields produce no food.. yet I will rejoice in the Lord, I will be joyful...

Habakkuk 3:16-18

"Not by might or by power, but BY MY SPIRIT" says the Lord almighty.

Zechariah 4:6

[Jesus:] *"So do not worry, saying, 'What shall we eat?' or 'What shall we drink?' or 'What shall we wear?' For.. your heavenly Father knows that you need them. But SEEK FIRST His kingdom and His righteousness, and all of these things will be given to you as well."*

Matthew 6:31-33

By dying to what once bound us, we have been RELEASED from the law so that we serve in the new way of the Spirit, and not in the old way of the written code.

Romans 7:6

Offer your bodies as living sacrifices.. Do not conform any longer to the pattern of this world, but be TRANSFORMED by the renewing of your mind. Then you will be able to test and approve what God's will is – His good, pleasing and perfect will.

Romans 12:1-2

As servants of God.. in great endurance.. in troubles.. hardships.. distresses.. beatings.. imprisonments.. riots.. hard work.. sleepless nights.. hunger.. With WEAPONS of righteousness in the right hand and the left.

2 Corinthians 6:4-5, 7

Are you so FOOLISH? After beginning with the Spirit, are you now trying to attain your goal by human effort?

Galatians 3:3

The only thing that counts is faith expressing itself through love.. Since we live by the Spirit, let us keep IN STEP with the Spirit.

Galatians 5:6, 25

THEME 14
GOD IS RAISING A DISCIPLINED ARMY

We must confront, challenge, convict and convert God's foes if possible, but above all else, we must love them.

Love your enemies, do good to those who hate you, BLESS those who curse you, pray for those who mistreat you. If someone strikes you on one cheek, turn to him the other also.

Luke 6:27-29

Jehoshaphat had great wealth and honor and he allied himself with Ahab by marriage.. [To Ahab:] *"I am as you are and my people as your people; we will join you in the war; but FIRST SEEK the counsel of the Lord."*

2 Chronicles 18:1-4

[Upon return under Cyrus's decree] *the people assembled as one man in Jerusalem.. DESPITE their fear of the peoples around them, they built the altar on its foundation and sacrificed.. to the Lord.*

Ezra 3:1-3

[Sanballat's ridicule of the wall-rebuilding:] *"Can they bring the stones back to life? ..If even a FOX climbed up on it, he would break down their wall of stones."* [So] *those who carried materials did their work with one hand and held a weapon in the other, and each of the builders wore his sword at his side.*

Nehemiah 4:1-18

All who separated themselves from the neighboring peoples for the sake of the law of God.. all these now join their brothers the nobles, and BIND themselves with a curse and an oath to follow the law of God..

Nehemiah 10:28-29

He who goes out weeping, carrying SEED to sow, will return with songs of joy carrying sheaves with him.

Psalm 126:6

All a man's ways seem innocent to him, but motives are weighed by the Lord. Commit to the Lord whatever you do, and your plans will succeed. The Lord works out everything for His own ends.. In his heart a man plans his course, but the Lord determines his STEPS.

Proverbs 16:2-4, 9

He will be a spirit of justice to him that sits in judgment, a source of strength to those who turn back the battle at the GATE.

Isaiah 28:6

I will send against Jerusalem my four dreadful judgments: sword, famine, wild beasts and plague.. Yet there will be some survivors – sons and daughters.. They will come to you and when you see their conduct and their actions, you will be CONSOLED...

Ezekiel 14:21-23

I saw a great many bones on the floor of the valley, BONES that were very dry.. He said to me, "Prophecy to these bones.." So I prophesied as He commanded me, and breath entered them, they came to life and stood up on their feet – a vast army.

Ezekiel 37:2-10

As a shepherd saves from the LION'S MOUTH only two leg bones or a piece of an ear, so will the Israelites be saved.

Amos 3:12

Hate evil, love good; maintain justice in the courts.. Why do you long for the DAY of the Lord? That day will be darkness, not light. It will be as though a man fled from a lion, only to meet a bear, as though he entered his house and rested his hand on the wall only to have a snake bite him.

Amos 5:15, 18-19

..Now you must leave the city to CAMP in the open field.. You will go to Babylon; there you will be rescued. There the Lord will redeem you out of the hand of your enemies.

Micah 4:10

Although they [Nineveh] *have allies and are numerous, they will be cut off and pass away. Now I will break their yoke from your neck and tear your SHACKLES away.*

Nahum 1:12-13

Everyone who competes in the games goes into strict TRAINING.. Therefore I do not run like a man running aimlessly; I do not fight like a man beating the air. No, I beat my body and make it my slave, so that after I have preached to others, I myself will not be disqualified for the prize.

1 Corinthians 9:25-27

THEME 15
GOD WEIGHS CHARACTER: HEARTS AND REINS

We must be willing to be judged wrong – by both the world and by the church – for doing right, confident that God, who guides our steps and judges the heart, knows all.

...GENUINE yet regarded as impostors; known, yet regarded as unknown; dying, yet not killed; sorrowful, yet always rejoicing; poor, yet making many rich; having nothing, and yet possessing everything.

2 Corinthians 6:8-10

Caleb said "[Moses sent me] *to explore the land. And I brought him back a report according to my CONVICTIONS, but my brothers who went up with me made the hearts of the people melt with fear. I, however, followed the Lord my God wholeheartedly."*

Joshua 14:6-8

[Samuel, viewing Jesse's sons:] *"..the Lord does not look at the things man looks at. Man looks at the outward APPEARANCE, but the Lord looks at the heart."*

1 Samuel 16:7

[David's charge to Solomon:] *"Acknowledge God and serve Him with wholehearted devotion and with a willing mind, for the Lord searches every heart and understands every motive behind the thoughts. If you seek Him, He will be found by you.. Be strong and DO THE WORK."*

1 Chronicles 28:9-10

Create in me a PURE heart, O God, and renew a steadfast spirit within me. Do not cast me from Your presence or take Your Holy Spirit from me. Restore to me the joy of Your salvation, and grant a willing spirit, to sustain me.

Psalm 51:10-12

Search me O God, and know my heart; test me and know my anxious thoughts; see if there is any offensive way in me, and LEAD me in the way everlasting.

Psalm 139:23-24

Above all else, guard your heart for it is the WELLSPRING of life.

Proverbs 4:23

What the wicked dreads will overtake him; what the righteous desire will be granted. When the STORM has swept by, the wicked are gone, but the righteous stand firm forever.

Proverbs 10:24-25

All a man's ways seem right to him, but the Lord WEIGHS the heart.

Proverbs 21:2

The wicked man flees though no one pursues, but the righteous are as BOLD as a lion.. He who conceals his sins does not prosper.. He who hardens his heart falls into trouble.

Proverbs 28:1, 13-14

I will give them an UNDIVIDED heart and put a new spirit in them; I will remove from them their heart of stone and give them a heart of flesh. Then they will follow My decrees and be careful to keep My laws. They will be My people and I will be their God.

Ezekiel 11:19-20

I have learned the secret of being CONTENT in any and every situation, whether feasting or fasting, whether living in abundance or doing without. I can do everything through Him..

Philippians 4:12-13

THEME 16
CHRIST RESURRECTS SURRENDERED BODIES

We must trust Christ's promise that He will speak and heal and love through us.

I have been CRUCIFIED with Christ and I no longer live, but Christ lives in me. The life I live in the body, I live by faith in the Son of God who loved me and gave Himself for me.

Galatians 2:20

The Israelites camped opposite them like two small flocks of GOATS while the Arameans covered the countryside.. The Israelites inflicted 100,000 casualties in one day. The rest of them escaped to the city of Aphek, where the wall collapsed on 27,000 of them.

1 Kings 20:27-30

[Ezra:] *"I was ASHAMED to ask the king for soldiers and horsemen to protect us from enemies on the road, because we had told the king, 'The gracious hand of our God is on everyone who looks to Him' ..So we fasted and petitioned our God about this, and He answered our prayer."*

Ezra 8:22-23

Each of the [wall] *BUILDERS wore his sword at his side as he worked..* [Nehemiah said:] *"We are widely separated from each other along the wall. Wherever you hear the sound of the trumpet, join us there. Our God will fight for us."*

Nehemiah 4:17-20

Blessed are those who have learned to acclaim You, who walk in the LIGHT of Your presence, O Lord.

Psalm 89:15

I have chosen the way of truth; I have set my heart on Your laws. I hold fast to Your statutes.. I RUN in the path of Your commands, for You have set my heart free.

Psalm 119:30-32

My heart is not proud, O Lord, my eyes are not haughty; I do not concern myself with great matters or things too wonderful for me. But I have stilled and quieted my soul; like a WEANED child with its mother, like a weaned child is my soul within me.

Psalm 131:1-2

I was the craftsman at His side. I was filled with delight day after day, REJOICING always in His presence, rejoicing in His whole world and delighting in mankind.

Proverbs 8:30-31

Even youths grow tired and weary, and young men stumble and fall; but those who hope in the Lord will RENEW their strength. They will soar on wings like eagles; they will run and not grow weary, they will walk and not be faint.

Isaiah 40:30-31

I will help you. Do not be afraid, O WORM Jacob, O little Israel.. I will make you into a threshing sledge, new and sharp, with many teeth. You will thresh the mountains and crush them, and reduce the hills to chaff..

Isaiah 41:14-15

I will POUR out My Spirit on all people. Your sons and daughters will prophecy, your old men will dream dreams, your young men will see visions.

Joel 2:28

Let your light so *SHINE before men, that they may see your good deeds and praise your Father in heaven.*

Matthew 5:16

Immediately Jesus KNEW in His spirit that this was what they were thinking in their hearts.

Mark 2:8

..unless a KERNEL of wheat falls to the ground and dies, it remains only a single seed. But if it dies it produces many seeds.

John 12:24

To each one the MANIFESTATION of the Spirit is given for the common good: wisdom.. knowledge.. faith.. healing.. miraculous powers.. prophecy.. distinguishing between spirits.. tongues.. interpretation of tongues.. He gives them to each one, just as He determines.

1 Corinthians 12:7-11

In the CHURCH God has appointed first of all apostles.. prophets.. teachers.. workers of miracles.. healing.. help.. administration.. tongues.. But eagerly desire the greater gifts.

1 Corinthians 12:28-31

We have this treasure in JARS of clay to show that this all-surpassing power is from God and not from us.. We always carry around in our body the death of Jesus, so that the life of Jesus may also be revealed in our body.

2 Corinthians 4:7-10

We who are alive are always being given over to death for Jesus' sake, so that His life may be revealed in our mortal body.. Therefore we do not lose heart. Though outwardly we are wasting away, yet INWARDLY we are being renewed day by day.

2 Corinthians 4:11, 16

We demolish arguments and every pretension that sets itself up against the knowledge of God, and we take CAPTIVE every thought to make it obedient to Christ.

2 Corinthians 10:5

[God:] *"My power is made perfect in weakness."* [Paul:] *"Therefore I will boast all the more gladly about my weaknesses, so that Christ's power may rest on me.. for when I am WEAK, then I am strong."*

2 Corinthians 12:9-10

Are you so FOOLISH? After beginning with the Spirit, are you now trying to attain your goal by human effort?

Galatians 3:3

The FRUIT of the Spirit is love, joy, peace, patience, kindness, goodness, faithfulness, gentleness and self-control.

Galatians 5:22-23

It is God who WORKS in you to will and to act according to His good purpose.

Philippians 2:13

FAN into flame the gift of God which is in you.. For God did not give us a spirit of timidity, but a spirit of power, of love, and of self-discipline.

2 Timothy 1:6-7

Let us throw off everything that HINDERS and the sin that so easily entangles, and let us run with perseverance the race marked out for us.

Hebrews 12:1

Prophecy never had its origin in the will of man, but men spoke from God as they were CARRIED along by the Holy Spirit.

2 Peter 1:21

The One who is in you is GREATER than the one who is in the world.

1 John 4:4

Those whom I love I rebuke and discipline. So be earnest, and repent. Here I am! I stand at the door and KNOCK. If anyone hears My voice and opens the door, I will come in and eat with him, and he with Me.

Revelation 3:19-20

THEME 17
WE ACT BECAUSE THE END IS NEAR, BUT NOT YET HERE

Although others seem to be trying to coast to the Finish Line, we are filled with a tranquil sense of urgency, that we may be found ready when He returns.

I press on to take hold of that for which Christ Jesus took hold of me.. Forgetting what is behind and straining toward what is ahead, I press on toward the GOAL.. God has called me heavenward.
Philippians 3:12-14

Though hail flattens the forest and the city is leveled completely, how blessed you will be, sowing your seed by every STREAM, and letting your cattle and donkeys range free.
Isaiah 32:19-20

[1948, Israel?] *Can a country be born in a day or a nation be brought forth in a moment? Yet no sooner is Zion in labor than she gives birth to her children. Do I bring to the moment of birth and not give DELIVERY?*
Isaiah 66:8-9

The Lord said to me [Hosea], *"Go, show your love to your wife again, though she is loved by another and is an adulteress. Love her as the Lord loves the Israelites, though they TURN to other gods..." They will come trembling to the Lord and to his blessings in the last days.*
Hosea 3:1, 5

On that day His feet will stand on the Mount of Olives, east of Jerusalem.. [then the Mount will split] *..Then God will come.. On that day there will be no light, no cold or frost. It will be a UNIQUE day, without daytime or nighttime.. When evening comes, there will be light.*
Zechariah 14:4-7

[Daniel's vision] *As I looked, THRONES were set in place, and the Ancient of Days took His seat.. Ten thousand times ten thousand stood before Him. The court was seated and the books were opened.*
Daniel 7:9-10

No one knows about that day or hour, not even the angels in heaven, nor the Son, but only the Father.. Keep watch because you do not know.. So you also must be READY, because the Son of Man will come at an hour when you do not expect Him.
Matthew 24:36, 42, 44

When you see the ABOMINATION that causes desolation standing where it does not belong.. flee to the mountains.. [Don't] *enter the house to take anything out.. Days of distress unequaled.. days shortened.. false christs and false prophets.. So be on your guard.*
Mark 13:14-23

..When you see these things happening, you will know that it is near, right at the door.. This GENERATION will certainly not pass away until all these things have happened.
Mark 13:29-30

Don't let anyone deceive you in any way, for that day will not come until the REBELLION occurs and the man of lawlessness is revealed, the man doomed to destruction. He will oppose and will exalt himself over everything that is called God or is worshiped, so that he sets himself up in God's temple, proclaiming himself to be God.
2 Thessalonians 2:3-4

..even now many ANTICHRISTS have come.
1 John 2:18

THEME 18
WE HAVE CONFIDENCE, FOR OUR GOD REIGNS

We know that our job is to stand firm and to witness, leaving the results up to others ...and to God.

A better hope is introduced, by which we draw near to God.. the power of an INDESTRUCTIBLE life.
Hebrews 7:19 + 16

[Joseph to his brothers:] *"God sent me ahead of you to preserve for you a remnant on earth and to save your lives by a great deliverance. So then, it was not you who SENT me here, but God."*
Genesis 45:7-8

[Balaam to Balak:] *"God is not a man, that He should lie.. I have received a command to bless; He has blessed, and I cannot CHANGE it."*
Numbers 23:19-20

They will come at you from one DIRECTION but flee from you in seven.. On everything you put your hand to, the Lord your God will bless you in the land He is giving you.. as His holy people.
Deuteronomy 28:7-9

The Philistines.. carried the Ark into Dagon's temple and set it beside Dagon. When the people of Ashdod rose early the next day, there was Dagon, FALLEN on his face on the ground before the Ark of the Lord.
1 Samuel 5:1-3

Absalom [David's traitorous son] *and all the men of Israel said, "The advice of Hushai the Arkite is better than that of Ahithophel." For the Lord had determined to FRUSTRATE the good advice of Ahithophel in order to bring disaster on Absalom.*
2 Samuel 17:14

[Ahab was DISGUISED in battle, Jehoshaphat in royal robes.] *But someone drew his bow at random and hit* [Ahab] *between the sections of his armor.* [All day long he was propped up in a chariot, bleeding]; *that evening he died.*
1 Kings 22:29-35

[Lord to Sennacherib, through Isaiah:] *"I ORDAINED it.. I have brought it to pass that you have turned fortified cities into piles of stone.. But.. because you rage against Me and your insolence has reached My ears, I will put My hook in your nose and My bit in your mouth.."* [An angel killed 185,000 soldiers; his two sons killed him.]
2 Kings 19:25, 27-28, 35-37

[Solomon:] *"The temple I am going to build will be great, because our God is greater than all other gods. But who is able to build a temple for Him, since the heavens, even the highest heavens, cannot CONTAIN Him? Who then am I to build a temple for Him, except as a place to burn sacrifices before Him?"*
2 Chronicles 2:5-6

[Hezekiah to troops:] *"Be strong and courageous. Do not be afraid or discouraged because of the king of Assyria and the VAST army with him, for there is a greater Power with us than with him. With him is only the arm of flesh, but with us is the Lord.."*
2 Chronicles 32:7-8

In the first year [Cyrus was king].. *the Lord moved the heart of Cyrus king of Persia to make a proclamation: "The Lord, the God of heaven.. has APPOINTED me to build a temple for Him at Jerusalem in Judah."*
2 Chronicles 36:22-23

[Darius to governor of Trans-Euphrates:] *"Stay away.. Do not interfere with this temple of God.. Moreover.. the expenses are to be fully paid* [from the Trans-Euphrates treasury].. *If anyone changes this edict, a beam is to be pulled from his house and he is to be lifted up and IMPALED on it.. His house is to be made a pile of rubble."*
Ezra 6:6-11

Some trust in CHARIOTS and some in horses, but we trust in the name of the Lord our God. They are brought to their knees and fall, but we rise up and stand firm.
Psalm 20:7-8

The Lord will FULFILL His purpose for me.
Psalm 138:8

Many are the plans in a man's heart, but it is the Lord's purpose that prevails.. A man's steps are directed by the Lord, how can anyone UNDERSTAND his own way?
Proverbs 19:21; 20:24

Give me neither poverty nor riches, but give me only my daily bread.. Many seek an audience with a ruler, but it is from the Lord that a man gets JUSTICE.
Proverbs 30:8; 29:26

[God to Jeremiah:] *Tell the king of Judah.. "Even if you were to defeat the entire Babylonian army that is attacking you and only WOUNDED men were left in their tents, they would come out and burn this city down."*
Jeremiah 37:6-7, 10

[Daniel:] *"The great God has shown the king what will take place in the future. The dream is true and the interpretation is trustworthy." Then king Nebuchadnezzar fell PROSTRATE before Daniel and paid him honor.. "Surely your God is the God of gods and the Lord of kings.."*
Daniel 2:45-47

[Daniel:] *"My God sent his angel, and he shut the mouths of the lions.." The king was overjoyed and gave orders to lift Daniel out of the DEN. And when Daniel was lifted from the den, no wound was found on him, because he had trusted in his God.*
Daniel 6:22-23

When a trumpet sounds in a city, do not the people tremble? ..Surely the sovereign Lord does nothing without REVEALING His plan to His servants the prophets. The lion has roared – who will not fear? The sovereign Lord has spoken – who can but prophecy?
Amos 3:6-8

[Gamaliel:] *"Let them go! For if their purpose or activity is of human ORIGIN, it will fail. But if it is of God, you will not be able to stop these men; you will only find yourselves fighting against God."*
Acts 5:38-39

[Jews became abusive..] *Paul left the synagogue and went NEXT DOOR to the house.. The Lord spoke to Paul in a vision: "Do not be afraid; keep on speaking, do not be silent, for I am with you."*
Acts 18:6-10

We know that in all things GOD WORKS for the good of all who love Him, who have been called according to His purpose.
Romans 8:28

God's gifts and His call are IRREVOCABLE.
Romans 11:29

No eye has seen, no ear has heard, no mind has conceived what God has PREPARED for those who love Him.
1 Corinthians 2:9

..He who began a good work in you will carry it on to COMPLETION..
Philippians 1:6

THEME 19
WE ARE THE "POINT MEN" IN SPIRITUAL WARFARE

Remembering that we are [spiritually] indestructible, we count our earthly lives as expendable, essential pawns in the eternal struggle.

"Don't be afraid," Elisha answered. "Those who are with us are more than those who are with them.." The Lord opened the servant's eyes, and he looked and saw the HILLS full of horses and chariots of fire all around Elisha.

2 Kings 6:16-17

Sin is CROUCHING at your door; it desires to have you, but you must master it.

Genesis 4:7

When [Balaam's] *DONKEY saw the angel of the Lord standing in the road with a drawn sword in his hand she turned off the road into a field. Balaam beat her to get her back on the road.*

Numbers 22:23

Now the Spirit of the Lord had departed from Saul, and an evil spirit from the Lord TORMENTED him.

1 Samuel 16:14

[Losing the battle, the king of Moab] *took his first-born son, who was to succeed him as king, and offered him as a sacrifice on the city wall. The FURY against Israel was great; they withdrew and returned to their own land.*

2 Kings 3:26-27

[Lord through Isaiah, about Sennacherib's attack on Jerusalem:] *"He will not enter this city or shoot an ARROW here. He will not come before it with shield or build a siege ramp against it.." That night the angel of the Lord went out and put to death 185,000 men in the Assyrian camp.. Sennacherib returned to Nineveh and stayed there.* [His two sons killed him.]

2 Kings 19:32-37

Satan rose up against Israel and incited David to take a CENSUS of Israel..

1 Chronicles 21:1

[David's choice after census: famine/enemies/plague. He chose plague. 70,000 died. An angel was sent to destroy Jerusalem] *David looked up and saw the angel of the Lord standing between heaven and earth, with a DRAWN SWORD in his hand extended over Jerusalem. Then David and the elders, in sackcloth, fell facedown..*

1 Chronicles 21:11-16

The angel of the Lord ENCAMPS around those who fear Him, and He delivers them.. May those who plot my ruin.. be like chaff before the wind with the angel of the Lord driving them away; may their path be dark and slippery, with the angel of the Lord pursuing them.

Psalm 34:7; 35:4-6

Confuse the wicked, O Lord, confound their speech, for I see violence and strife in the city. Day and night they PROWL about on its walls; malice and abuse are within it. Destructive forces are at work in the city; threats and lies never leave its streets.

Psalm 55:9-11

[God] *unleashed against* [Egypt] *His hot anger, His wrath, indignation and hostility – A BAND of destroying angels.. struck down all the firstborn of Egypt.*

Psalm 78:49-51

If you make the Most High your dwelling.. He will command His angels concerning you to guard you in all your ways; they will lift you up in their hands, so that you will not strike your foot against a stone. You will tread upon the lion and COBRA; you will trample the great lion and the serpent.

Psalm 91:9-13

[Jesus to Peter:] *"Satan has asked to SIFT you like wheat. But I have prayed for you, Simon, that your faith may not fail. And when you have turned back, strengthen your brothers."*

Luke 22:31-32

[Paul and group] *having been KEPT by the Holy Spirit from preaching the word in Asia, ..they tried to enter Bithynia, but the Spirit of Jesus would not allow them to.*

Acts 16:6-7

Satan himself MASQUERADES as an angel of light. It is not surprising, then, if his servants masquerade as servants of righteousness.

2 Corinthians 11:14-15

Our struggle is not against flesh and blood, but against the rulers, against the authorities, against the POWERS of this dark world and against the spiritual forces of evil in the heavenly realms.

Ephesians 6:12

Are not all angels MINISTERING spirits sent to serve those who will inherit salvation?

Hebrews 1:14

THEME 20
SALVATION IS UNDESERVED AND UNEARNED

There are no merit badges in God's club. All that we can ever do for God is always less than the least that He does for us.

He reached down from on high and took hold of me; He drew me out of deep waters.. He rescued me because He delighted in me.. according to the cleanness of my hands in His SIGHT.. You stoop down to make me great.

Psalm 18:16, 19, 24, 35

..chosen by lot as the SCAPEGOAT.. presented alive before the Lord to be used for making atonement by sending it into the desert.

Leviticus 16:10

[Ezra's prayer:] *"I am too ashamed and disgraced to lift up my face.. because our sins are higher than our heads.. Because of our sins, we.. have been subjected to the sword and captivity, to PILLAGE and humiliation.. What more can we say, for we have disregarded the commands You gave.."*

Ezra 9:6-11

What is man that You are mindful of him, the son of man that You care for him? You have made him a little lower than the heavenly beings.. You made him RULER over the works of Your hands.

Psalm 8:4-6

For as HIGH as the heavens are above the earth, so great is His love for those who fear Him; as far as the east is from the west, so far has He removed our transgressions from us.

Psalm 103:11-12

With joy you will draw water from the WELLS of salvation.

Isaiah 12:3

For even the Son of Man did not come to be served, but to serve, and to give His life as a RANSOM for many.

Mark 10:45

For God so loved the world that He gave His one and only Son, that whoever believes in Him shall not PERISH but have eternal life.

John 3:16

Whoever hears My word and believes Him who sent Me has eternal life and will not be CONDEMNED; he has crossed over from death to life.

John 5:24

[Peter:] *"Repent, then, and turn to God, so that your sins may be wiped out, that times of REFRESHING may come from the Lord.*

Acts 3:19

No one will be declared righteous in His sight by observing the law; rather, through the law we become conscious of sin.. righteousness comes through faith in Jesus Christ.. There is no difference, for all have sinned and FALL SHORT of the glory of God.

Romans 3:20-23

..justified through faith we have PEACE with God.. At just the right time, while we were still powerless, Christ died for the ungodly.. While we were still sinners, Christ died for us.

Romans 5:1, 5-8

For the WAGES of sin is death, but the gift of God is eternal life in Christ Jesus our Lord.

Romans 6:23

THEME 21
REVIVAL IS NOT FOR *OUR* BENEFIT

We do what is right because we must, ...but never in expectation of "blessings," success, acclaim or reward.

[Josiah renewed the covenant, removed from the temple all articles made for Baal/Ashera, desecrated the high places, broke down shrines at the gates, slaughtered all the priests of the high places on the altars.. turned to the Lord with all his heart... soul... strength..] *NEVERTHELESS the Lord did not turn away from the heat of His fierce anger.*

2 Kings 22; 23:1-26

Jacob said, "Get rid of the foreign gods.. PURIFY yourselves and change your clothes.. And the terror of God fell upon the towns all around them so that no one pursued them.

Genesis 35:2-5

Hezekiah did what was RIGHT.. He removed the high places, smashed the sacred stones and cut down the Asherah poles. He broke into pieces the bronze snake.. Hezekiah trusted in the Lord.. held fast to the Lord.. He kept the commands the Lord had given Moses.

2 Kings 18:1-6

"The Lord is with you when you are with Him.." When [the king of Judah,] *Asa heard these words.. he removed the detestable idols.. repaired the altar.. assembled the people..* [All who would not seek the Lord were to be put to death] *They took an oath.. rejoiced.. because they had sworn it WHOLEHEARTEDLY. They sought God eagerly, and He was found by them.*

2 Chronicles 15:2, 8-15

[Josiah] *CALLED together.. all the people from the least to the greatest. He read all the words of the book of the covenant.. He removed all the detestable idols.. and he had all who were present in Israel serve the Lord.. as long as he lived..*

2 Chronicles 34:29-33

OUTLINE for Quick Reference

ORPHANED by CHOICE 1
I. CONVICTIONS.................2
Polarizing Certainties 5
Creation vs. Accident 6
Design vs. Mechanism 7
Commandments vs. Positivism 9
Justice vs. Pragmatism 12
Virtue vs. Pleasure 14
Universalism vs. Relativism 16
Accountability vs. Autonomy 18
World View Confusion 21
Human Condition & Life 31
Stewards vs. Masters 36
II. PRETEXTS.....................39
Autonomy **41**
Fundamental Right 41
Privacy 43
Equality 44
Tolerance 46
Cost-Free Right 49
Relativism **50**
Personhood Denied 51
Humanity Challenged 53
Mechanism **57**
When Life Begins?
Implantation 58
Heartbeat
Looking Like a Child
Brain Functioning
Pain Response 59
Quickening
Viability 60
Birth Only, Nothing Less
Pleasure **63**
Personal Tragedy
Burden-Bearing
Anonymous & Different
Accident **66**
(Justifies Abortive "Remedy")
Birth Control Failed
Incapacitated Mom
Pragmatism **66**
Self-Defense
Political Expediency
Social Benefits
Positivism **77**
Political Arguments
Futility of Criminalizing
III. MANDATE................... **79**
Biblical Authority 79
Pro-Abortion View
Pro-Life View 82
Roles of a Disciple 93
Alien & Pilgrim within God's Creation 93
Theologian, revealing Divine Design 94
Priest, proclaiming God's Commandments 95
Prophet, crying out for Godly Justice 98
Loving Neighbor, displaying Virtue 100
Zealot, fighting for Universal Truths 102
Evangelist, witnessing to our Accountability 107
IV. LEGACY......................**109**
Christian Tradition
Early Church
Reformation Era
World Precedents 114
Holocaust 115
Nuremberg 123
Geneva 124
United Nations and Int'l Human Rights 124
Unborn Child's Rights 125
Global Abortion Norms 126
Apartheid 128
United States History 135
Independence 135
Liberty & Rights 137
Abolition of Slavery 138
Women's Passage Rites 147
Seeds of Destruction 158
Nietzsche 158
Malthus 159
Darwin 160
Marx 160
Freud 160
Between World Wars 161
Pivotal Developments 166
Public Education 166
Great Depression 169
Post-War Materialism 169
Synthetic Heroes 170
Post-War Paranoia 171
Kinsey-Elvis-Madonna 171
Clinton Generation 172
Civil Rights 174
Parental Responsibility 177
Humaneness 178
Animal Rights 179
Endangered Species 181
Environmentalism 182
Aliens Welcomed 183
Criminal Rights 183
Children's Rights 184
V. ABORTIVE LINKS........**187**
Recreational Sex 188
Reproductive Technology 189
Abortion Industry 206
Problems with Abortion 206
Goals of Intervention 212
Types of Intervention 219
Justifications Offered 223
Governmental Action 229
Involuntary Complicity 228
Supreme Court 229
Politics 232
Legislation 235
Hyde Amendment
F.A.C.E.
Human Life Amendment
Partial-Birth (D&X)
Law Enforcement 239
Due Process in Court 241
Pro-Lifer Consequences 242
Social Climate 243
Education 243
Media 243
Religious Confusion 247
Polarization of Believers 247
Pluralism
Priorities
Theology
Liberalized
Social Gospel
Leader Crisis
Public Acts of Faith 252
Religious Right
Self-Destructing
Marginalized
Revival Time?
Abortion Controversy 256
"Catholic" View
Image of God
Personhood
Preborn Human Rights
The Exceptions
Choice Views
Personal Decision to Abort 259
Dissuade the Mother
Last-Ditch Miracles
Real Pro-Life Choices
VI. DILEMMA.................. **261**
Magnitude of the Problem 261
Restrained Outrage 264
Why this Infighting? 268
Nature of the Problem 269
Definitions of Victory 277
VII. DESTINY.....................**279**
The Hell Objection 279
Repentance, Dedication 281
Witness & Activism 282
Proclamation 282
Banner 283
Declaration of Dependence 284
• BIBLIOGRAPHY.............**287**
• TIMELINE........................ **292**
• BIBLE THEMES.............. **302**
THIS OUTLINE................. **312**